Sales Encyclopedia

The most comprehensive "how-to" guide on selling.

Robert J. Chapin
John J. Chapin
Kyle Andrews
Bill Hall
Keith Mooradian
Jean Marie Reheuser

www.completeselling.com   Eagle View Publishing

Eagle View Publishing

Publisher's Cataloging-in-Publication *(Provided by Quality Books, Inc.)*

Sales encyclopedia : the most comprehensive "how-to" guide
  on selling / Robert J. Chapin ... [et al].
    p. cm.
    Includes bibliographical references and index.
    LCCN 2008903393
    ISBN-13: 978-0-9719684-1-7
    ISBN-10: 0-9719684-1-1

  1. Selling--Encyclopedias.   I. Chapin, Robert J.

  HF5438.25.S35 2008   658.8'003
                              QBI08-855

The editor for this book was Arlene Prunkle of Pen Ultimate Editorial Services –
Vancouver, BC
Cover design and formatting done by Accurance Co.
– Bloomington, IN
Printed and bound by BookMasters, Inc. – Ashland, OH

www.completeselling.com
www.pretiumpartners.com

What You'll Get out of This Book

If you study this book, master its principles, and apply what you've learned, you will find yourself at the very top of the selling profession and you'll possess the benefits of that position; namely, lots of money, time, job security, and options.

Top salespeople are some of the highest-paid people on the planet. Top salespeople never have to worry about finding or keeping a job regardless of the economy or how bad everyone else thinks things are. Top salespeople cut through red tape, get around obstacles, and get to the sale faster, thus reaching their goals, objectives, and dreams more rapidly than most. And top salespeople have options; they can work where they want and create the most lucrative conditions for themselves.

This book contains the key information that can make you a top salesperson, and if you're already there, this book can make you even better.

But first, let's face one thing: our profession of selling is only half the equation. The truth is that everyone needs to be a salesperson to have a successful life. Roughly 85 percent of the happiness or despair you will have in your life will be directly dependent upon your relationships with other people. Those relationships will rely largely on your ability to communicate your ideas effectively and persuasively. Whether you're a parent trying to influence your child, a concerned citizen trying to influence your community, or you're trying to persuade your significant other, we all sell—or we try to. Ultimately, you will either sell people on your ideas, or they will sell you on theirs.

In this book, you will learn to sell your ideas and your vision at work, at home, and in other social situations. In short, if you learn, own, and employ the ideas in this book, people will pay more attention to your needs, desires, and the causes that are important to you. You will develop the ability to lead a happier life and enjoy a better standard of living professionally, socially, and financially.

Real Sales Knowledge from Real Top Salespeople

When you want to learn to do something to the best of your ability, who do you want to learn from? Of course, you want to learn from individuals who are highly skilled and experienced in that area. Well, you're about to do just that.

The book you hold in your hands is the most comprehensive guide ever written on the subject of selling. The authors of this book have a combined total of over 141 years of real-world, highly successful selling experience.

Most sales books either discuss only one aspect of selling, such as presentations or cold calling, or they speak generally on each area of selling and lack depth. Many of these training resources are by people with only a few years of selling experience, or by people with experience in only one industry. These books are filled with the same advice and worn-out closes that salespeople have been using for fifty years or more. Some of the newer books focus solely on "relationship" or "solution" selling, and while relationships and solutions are very important, they miss the other important aspects of selling.

This book is different. The authors of this book have been at the very top of each industry in which they have sold. They have vast selling experience in both face-to-face and telemarketing sales. They have sold both products and services. They have sold to large corporations as well as to individuals, in good economic times and in bad. They have sold tangibles such as ATM machines, cars, and dental equipment, and they have sold intangibles such as stocks and bonds, insurance, and other services. They have made twenty-five-cent sales and multi-million-dollar sales. They've excelled in fiercely competitive markets, and have sold locally, nationally, and internationally. They have worked for small companies and large.

In some jobs sales was their only responsibility, and in other jobs they had to wear many hats. They have trained many salespeople from some of the largest companies around the world. They have been mentors to new salespeople, they've done one-on-one, individualized training, and they've done group sales training. They are very well read on the subject of selling, having studied hundreds of books, tapes, CDs, DVDs, and other training materials on selling, communication, psychology, and other subjects relating to human relations and motivation. In short, the authors of this book know how to sell with the highest degree of success in the real world in *any* situation.

Whether you have been selling professionally for a long time, or you're just beginning your selling career, you will find new gems of information in this book.

No matter where you've been in selling, the authors of this book have probably been there and can relate.

In this fast-paced world, two of the most important ingredients are information and education. This book has ideas, advice, insight, and specific examples that can be adapted to any selling environment, under any conditions. It covers all aspects of selling, from the obvious items such as presentations, handling objections, and closing, to the not so obvious such as wearing the right clothes, driving the right vehicle, where to park in a customer's parking lot, and other subtleties that aren't covered in any other sales books.

This book will give you new ideas, reinforce or challenge some current ones, and perhaps remind you of some great ideas you've forgotten. This book is designed to be a complete reference tool. If you need to brush up in a certain area or need some quick ideas, this book will provide them. In a nutshell, this book will provide you with all the tools necessary to excel at selling in your industry, no matter what that industry might be.

Acknowledgments

A special thanks goes out to the people who helped make this book possible.

Among them are Bill Corcoran, Dawn Ertel, and Bill Earle of Accurance Company for their wonderful work on cover and book design.

Arlene Prunkle of Pen Ultimate Editorial Services.

Rita Schiano for her editing help.

Brenda Culler and Chris Parkison at BookMasters.

Bo Bennett and Ryan Levesque of iGroops for their great customer service, expert advice, and help setting up our website and for being our website provider.

Simon Shendelman for his photography and design work.

Fran McConville for his help and guidance.

Gail Cassesse for her sales insight and expertise.

Dan Poynter for his outstanding ideas on publishing, John Kremer and Jeffrey Lant for all their great ideas on book marketing. Also thanks to Jeff Herring, The Article Guy, for all his wonderful ideas on writing.

Brian Tracy for his great sales ideas.

Lee Ann Price for pointing us in the right direction.

Michelle Nichols of Savvy Selling for giving us advice along the way.

Finally, Bob Chapin would like to thank Paul Taylor, his manager for 27 of his 40+ years in sales. Paul taught Bob many ideas that helped make him a major sales success story. Those ideas are among the many shared in this book.

Table of Contents

What You'll Get out of This Book...iii
Real Sales Knowledge from Real Top Salespeople v
Acknowledgments vii
How to Use This Book xxvii

SECTION I – BUILDING THE FOUNDATION 1

Chapter 1 – The Difference between Success and Failure in Selling....................3
    The Twelve Success Factors...3

Chapter 2 – The Foundation for Top Achievement 10
    The Six Ingredients Needed to Build Your Foundation 10

Chapter 3 - How to Become *Great* at Selling 13
    Eleven Steps to Greatness 13
    Rules of Top Salespeople..26
    A Day in the Life of the Successful Salesperson 27

Chapter 4 – More Detail on Important Items...29
    Taking Responsibility 29
    Going the Extra Mile 31
    Creativity and Persistence...31
    Other Ways to Set Yourself Apart 33

Chapter 5 – Mental Notes 36
    Get Yourself to Do What You *Must* Do 36
    Ideas for Maintaining a Positive Attitude 40

Chapter 6 – Your Best Foot Forward 44
    Dressing for Success..44
    Physical Grooming..45
    A Final Thought on Grooming 46

Other Things That Can Affect Your Appearance 46
    Your Handshake..46
    Eye Contact..47
General Business Etiquette 48
How to Act in Social Situations..49
Items You Present to the Prospect or Customer 49
The Pen You Use 51
The Car You Drive...51
Your Actions at the Customer's Facility 52

A Summary of Ideas on Building the Foundation **53**

SECTION II – COLD CALLING 55

Chapter 7 – Getting Ready to Cold Call..**57**
Getting Mentally Prepared to Cold Call 57
Gather Information on Your Prospects 59
Your Sales Tool Kit 60
Sales Materials to Carry into a Cold Call 61
Your Goals and Objectives 61
Planning the Logistics of Your Day..63
Whom Are You Calling On? 64
Name Pronunciation...65
How to to Discover the Name of the Person You Need to Cold Call.................66
What If You Don't Know the Name or Title of the Person with Whom You
    Should Talk? 68
Sources of Names and Calling Lists 69
How to Obtain Association Directories 73
Your Cold Call Script 74

Chapter 8 – Showing Up **80**
"No Soliciting" Signs...80
Finding Out Who the Decision-maker Is 80
Getting to the Decision-maker 82
What If the Person You're Cold Calling Isn't There? 85
What If the Receptionist Won't Let You Through? 86

Other Notes Regarding Showing Up 87

Chapter 9 – Talking to the Prospect **89**
How to Address the Prospect...89
The Opening of the Cold Call...89
Qualify the Prospect..90
What Does the Prospect Value Most? 94
Building Rapport with the Prospect...94
Other Components on Which You Will Be Judged.......................................96
    Mirroring..96
    Speech Factors That Alienate You from the Prospect 98
    Topics of Discussion to Avoid..101
    Using Humor..102
    Your Business Materials 103
What is the Prospect *Really* Interested In? 103
Name-dropping 106
Asking Questions and Listening to the Prospect 107
Body Language 112
Identifying the Prospect's Personality Type 113
    The Driver...114
    The Thinker...114
    The "Yes" Person...115
    The Partier...115
Things to Look for and How to Deal with Different Personality Types 115
    The Driver...115
    The Thinker...117
    The "Yes" Person...119
    The Partier...120
    Rules for Dealing with *All* Personality Types....................................121
I See, I Feel, I Hear 123
How Age Affects Your Prospect's Focus...123
How Gender Affects Your Prospect's Focus..124

Chapter 10 – Other Thoughts Regarding the Cold Call......................**126**
Keep Track of Your Calls 126

How Much Time Should You Spend on a Call?....................................126
Don't Make Your Mistakes on the Big Guys 127
Objections during the Cold Call 127
What Are You Calling to Sell Me?..128
Getting in Touch with the Hard-to-Reach "Hot" Prospect 129
Creative Ideas to Crack That Big Account When All Else Fails..........129
Become Involved in Businesses to Which You'd Like to Sell 131
You Need to Think Quickly on the Cold Call 131
The Show Must Go On 132
There's No Such Thing as a "Good Lead" 132
Put Your Prospect's Customers First..133
Have Conversations 133
Put Yourself in the Other Person's Shoes on *All* Calls.....................134

Chapter 11 – The Cold Call—Putting It All Together.....................**135**

Chapter 12 – Your Opening Statement **139**

Chapter 13 – Writing Sales Letters..**143**
Sample Business Letter...147

A Summary of Ideas on Cold Calling **148**

SECTION III – PRESENTATIONS **149**

Chapter 14 – Putting Your Presentation Together **151**
The Importance of a Powerful Presentation.......................................151
The Elements of a Powerful Presentation 152
The Three Parts of Your Presentation..153
Why People Buy 154
What You're *Really* Selling..154
The Carrot and the Stick 156
Use Emotion *and* Logic in Your Presentation 157
Enthusiasm Sells!...159
Emotion is Unique to Each Individual..160

Add Emotion by Bringing Family into the Presentation 160
Let's Talk "Logical" Numbers...162
    The Cost of *Not* Owning Your Product or Service 162
    Return on Investment (ROI) Models 166
Involve as Many of the Senses as Possible in Your Presentation.......................167
Paint Pictures and Tell Stories while Selling...167
    Some Quick Illustrations and Stories..169
    Create Your Own Stories and Paint Your Own Pictures 170
Present Colorful Pictures, Drawings, and Charts...171
Use Technology 172
Have a Contingency Plan Should Your Technology Fail....................................172
A Note on *All* Visual Aids 173
Watch What You Use as a Screen Saver 173
Different Presentations for Different Audiences 173
Talk about What Your Target Audience Is Interested In....................................175
Expand Your Horizons 176
The Steps to Creating Your Presentation...176
Other Quick Ideas 178

Chapter 15 – Preparing to Deliver Your Presentation 180
Have a Presentation Script...180
Make Sure Your Presentation Materials and Equipment Are Fully Prepared.....180
Make Sure *You* Are Fully Prepared 181
Have the Right Mental Attitude...181
Overcoming the Fear of Presenting 181
Practice Your Presentation...182
Make Sure Everyone Knows Their Parts..183
Presentation Tools...183
Exhibit A: Testimonial...188
Exhibit B: Endorsement Page 189
Building a Reference List 190
Reference Rules 190
Exhibit C: Reference List...192
Building a User List 193
Exhibit D: User List...194
A Final Point on Testimonials, References, and User Lists 195

Chapter 16 – Delivering Your Presentation..**196**

Deliver Your Presentation with Energy and Enthusiasm 196

Getting and Keeping the Prospect's Full Attention during the Presentation.......196

Make More "Hit 'Em between the Eyes" Statements at Various Points in the
   Presentation...197

The Prospect Has Her Own Agenda 197

Competing for the Prospect's Attention 199

Find Out Where You're at during the Presentation 200

Look for Other Indicators 200

Sell the Relationship in Addition to the Product or Service 200

Name-dropping in Your Presentation 201

Where to Sit When Presenting..201

Where to Look during Your Presentation 202

Get by with a Little Help from Your Friends 202

Point Out Weaknesses..202

Give the Prospect Enough but Not Too Much Information..................................203

Talk in Terms the Prospect Can Understand 204

Words and Phrases in your Presentation...205

Mistakes People Make during Presentations 210

Some Notes on Group Presentations...212

Chapter 17 – A Sample Presentation **214**

Chapter 18 – More Presentations Points to Consider **227**

Appointments that Cancel or Are Absent when You Arrive 227

How to Introduce Tough Subjects 228

How Location Affects Your Presentation..229

A Summary of Ideas on Presentations...**232**

SECTION IV – COMPETITION **235**

Introduction...**237**

Chapter 19 – Gathering Competitive Intelligence................................**239**
Where to Get Competitive Intelligence 239
Exactly Where Is the Competition on Price?.....................................245
Where the Competition Stands on Everything Else............................246
Get Competitive Information When You Win Too 246

Chapter 20 – The Competitive Comparison **248**
Figure 1: Competitive Matrix 249
The Competitive Comparison: Supporting Information 250
Figure 2: Support Information on Competition 250
So That's Your Competitive Comparison..255
Critique the Above Competitive Comparison.....................................255
Critique Your Product or Service 258

Chapter 21 – More Elements of Competition **260**
Price and Value..260
Areas to Look at When Building Value...261
Proving Your Point 265
Positioning You and Your Company against the Competition............265
Some Final Thoughts on Comparison with the Competition 275

Chapter 22 – Competitive Accounts **277**
Be Number One 277
Be Number Two...278
Providing a Competitive Account with a "Token" Quote 279
Following up after a Meeting with a Competitive Account 282
Sample Thank-you for Meeting Letter 283

Chapter 23 – Interacting with the Competition..............................**284**
Never Bad-mouth the Competition 284
Talking to the Competition versus Not Talking to the Competition ...285
Rules to Follow When Talking to the Competition 286
When Not to Talk to the Competition...287
A Final Word on Interacting with the Competition............................288

Chapter 24 – Other Ideas Related to the Competition..................................**289**

Make Sure the Competition Does What They Say They Will Do......................289

Have the Competition Put Misrepresentations in Writing.................................290

The Other Side of the Coin: Watch What *You* Say..291

The Domino Effect: The Importance of Beating the Competition 292

Chapter 25 – Other Ideas Related to Competing **294**

Do You Sound Just Like the Competition? 294

How to Differentiate Yourself When Selling the Same Product as the
    Competition..294

Phantom Competition and Misrepresenting the Competition............................296

Chapter 26 – Other "Competitive" Items in This Book..........................**297**

Name-dropping in Competitive Situations 297

The Competitive Advantage Close 297

Objections Created by the Competition 297

Going Over Someone's Head 297

A Summary of Ideas on Competing **298**

**SECTION V – SELLING TO EXECUTIVES AND BUILDING
         A BUSINESS CASE** **299**

Chapter 27 – Selling to Executives..**301**

What Executives Value in Salespeople..302

What Prevents Salespeople from Calling High?...303

Why Use Value Assessment? 304

A Summary of Ideas on Selling to Executives **307**

Chapter 28 – Building a Business Case **308**

The Major Elements of the Written Business Case 308

Value Assessment Methodology..313

The Five Phases of Value Assessment 315

A Detailed Look at the Value Assessment Methodology 317
Value Assessment Phase One: Profiling..317
Value Assessment Phase Two: Executive Introduction...................................319
Value Assessment Phase Three: Discovery 333
Value Assessment Phase Four: Executive Feedback Session...........................343
Value Assessment Phase Five: Business Case Presentation............................348
Value Assessment Summary..349

A Summary of Ideas on Building a Business Case **350**

SECTION VI – OBJECTIONS **351**

Chapter 29 – Preparing for Objections **353**
Ten Reasons You Get Objections...353
Becoming Great at Answering Objections 355
Rules for Handling *All* Objections...358
When to Deal with Objections...361

Chapter 30 – The Price Objection...**363**
Preventing the Price Objection during the Qualifying Stage..............................363
Handling the Price Objection during Your Presentation 367
Some Answers to the Price Objection 368
Other Answers to Specific Money Objections..372
I Have No Money..373
I'm Waiting until after April 15...373
Your Price Is Too High...374
Ignoring the Price Objection...374
How to Determine if Price *Really* Is the Sole Reason the Prospect Is Not
      Moving Ahead 375
How to Deal with the "Price" Shopper 376
My Cost to You? One Cent...377
Are You *Cheap*? 378
Will the *Real* Cheapo Please Stand Up?..378
Other Things to Consider in the Price War..379
The Psychology of the Purchase Agent 379

Are You the Lowest Price in the Market, the Highest Price, or Somewhere in Between?...379
Build Value and Avoid Cutting Price 380

Chapter 31 - More Objections **381**
I Want to Think about It...381
Leave Me Some Information 382
I Want to Check Other Places First...384
I Want to Watch It..386
I Need to Talk to Someone Else 387
I Need to Talk to My Wife/Husband/Significant Other....................................388
I Need Approval from My Boss/Accounting Department/Purchasing/Etc.........390
I Need to Talk to My Accountant/Attorney...391
Annual Budget Spent/Not in Budget 393
I'm Happy with My Current Vendor 395
I'm Waiting to See What Happens with the Election 398
I'm Waiting until Next Year 399
Another Answer for *All* "Wait and See" Objections 399
Call Me Back at Some Point in the Future 400
I'm Waiting Until the New Models Come Out...401
I Do It Myself/I Use the Internet...401
I Just Lost My Job/My Cat Just Died/My House Just Burned Down.................403
I Only Deal Locally 404
I Only Buy Stocks/Real Estate/Etc. 405
I Don't Like You...405
I Had a Bad Experience with…or I Don't Like Your Company or Product 405
Comebacks to *Any* Objection...407
As a Last Resort If You Are Unable to Find the Objection...............................408
Objections during the Cold Call 408
Objections Created by the Competition..408
Do You Work on Commission?..410
What If You Keep Getting the Same Objection?...411
The Best Way to Avoid and Defuse *All* Objections 412

A Summary of Ideas on Objections...**413**

SECTION VII - CLOSING 415

Introduction 417

Chapter 32 - Preparing to Close 419
Closing Rules 419
The Right Attitude 420
Get in Front of the Prospect to Influence a Decision in Your Favor 421
Create the Right Closing Environment 422

Chapter 33 - Closing the Prospect 423
Adapt to the Personality of the Person You're Closing 423
Speak the Same Language as the Person You're Closing 424
Timing is Important When Closing 424
Look for Indicators That It's Time to Close 425
Specific Answers to the Closing Indicators Above 430
Paint Pictures When Closing 434
Bring the Other Senses into the Close 434
Bring the Prospect's Family Members and Dreams into the Close 435
Hard Sell Versus Soft Sell 435
Be Prepared to Hear "No" a Few Times 436
How Many Times Should You Hear "No" Before You Give Up? 438
What If a Prospect Asks You a Question More Than Once? 439
Don't Let *Not* Having an Answer to a Question Stop the Close 440
Don't Let the Wrong Answer to the Prospect's Question Stop You 443
The Words You Use When Closing 444
How Far Can You Go? 445
Presenting the Contract 445

Chapter 34 – Various Closes 449
The Puppy Dog Close 449
The Assumptive Close 450
The Alternative Choice Close 450
The Take Away Close 451
The Feel, Felt, Found Close 453
The Similar Situation Close 453

The Follow-up Close..454
The Summary Close...457
The Shortened Summary Close 459
The Largest Amount Possible Close...459
The Smallest Amount Possible Close 461
The Price Is Going Up Close 462
The You Get What You Pay For Close..463
The They're Exactly the Same Close..463
The Advantage, Disadvantage Close 464
The He Said, She Said Close 465
The Can You Do Me a Favor Close..466
The Guinea Pig Close 467
The Best Solution for the Prospect Close 468
The Something to Live up To Close...470
The Price Sheet Close 472
The Competitive Advantage Close 474
The Contrarian View Close 475
The Doorknob Close..476
The Why or Why Not Close..477
The What Would You Tell Your Salespeople to Do in This Situation Close 478
The Friend, Family Member, Neighbor, Colleague, Significant Other Close.....479
The See How Great My Product Is Close..480
The Prospect Close 481
The K.I.S.S. Close...482

Chapter 35 – Other Thoughts Regarding Closing.................................483
Offer Incentives to Make the Sale *Now* 483
An Important Ingredient behind Your Incentives.............................485
Other Ways to Consummate the Sale *Now!*...................................487
Some Great Times to Close 488
What If You Are Leery about Your Prospect? 489
Each Sale Must Be Win-Win..489
Keep Track of Your Closing Percentage 490

A Summary of Ideas on Closing 491

SECTION VIII – AFTER THE CLOSE 493

Chapter 36 – What If You Don't Get the Business? 495
In Person versus Over the Phone 499
You're Never Completely Down and Out 499
Go Over the Prospect's Head...............500
Go Under the Prospect's Head...............505
Why Bother Going Over and Under? 508

Chapter 37 – What If You *Do* Get the Business? 509
Closing Is Not the End of the Road 509
Sample Thank-you for Your Business Note: 512

Chapter 38 – Referrals...............516
When and How to Ask for Referrals...............516
Potential Roadblocks to Getting Referrals...............521
Creative Ways to Get Referrals 522
Calling the Referral...............523

Chapter 39 – Servicing Your Customers...............525
How Often Should You Contact Customers? 525
Information You Want to Have on Each Customer...............526
What to Do with All That Customer Information...............530
Give Your Customers Such Great Service That They Sell for You 534
Show Great Appreciation for Gifts Received from Customers 535
Take Anything a Prospect or Customer Hands to You...............535
Respond to Mailings and Other Information You Receive from Customers and Prospects 535
Be Your Customer's Customer...............536
Give out Your Home Phone Number...............536
Your Business Voice Mail and Related Information...............538

Chapter 40 – Account Management 541
Maximize the Business You Do with Customers 541
Establish Relationships throughout the Organization...............543

Introducing the Rest of the Sales Team 545
Sample Letter 548
The Correct Way to Pass a Customer to Someone Else in Your Company 550
How to Handle Difficulty in Getting Two People Together...............................547

Chapter 41 – Customer Challenges **551**
Set a Positive Tone for Challenging Customer Meetings................................551
Dealing with Unhappy Customers 553
Don't Add Fuel to a Customer's Fire 554
Taking Attitude from Customers 556
How to Handle Problem Accounts 556
Firing a Customer 557
How to Annoy or Anger Customers 559
Two More Ways to Annoy Customers 560
What If You Truly Anger a Customer? 561
Stop Customer Complaints before They Begin 561
Preventing Problems with Detailed Customer Notes...563
Another Potential Hot Potato—Employee Turnover 564
Another Place to Be Careful 567
One More Landmine 568

A Summary of Ideas for after the Close **570**

SECTION IX – TELEPHONE SELLING..**571**

Introduction...**573**

Chapter 42 – Preparing to Get on the Phone...**575**
Do as the Top Telephone Salespeople Do 575
Mental Preparation...576
Phone Attire 577
Your Surroundings..577
Phone Etiquette 577
Phone Physiology 578
Make Your Phone Work Easier 579
Other Ways to Be at Your Best on the Phone..581

When to Make Phone Calls..584
Take Advantage of Different Time Zones 585
What to Do When You're Unsure of How a Name Is Pronounced....................586

Chapter 43 – Calling Prospects 587
Getting through the Receptionist 587
Always Start at the Top...594
Ask for the Prospect Using His First Name When Calling Residences 594
Ask for the Prospect Using His First and Last Name When Calling Businesses 595
Leaving Effective Messages on Cold Calls 596
Always Get the Receptionist's Name at the End of the First Unsuccessful Call 601
Calling the Prospect the Second Time 601

Chapter 44 – Talking to the Prospect 603
Your Cold Call..603
A Note on Qualifying over the Phone..604
Building Rapport with the Prospect...604
Find Similarities between You and the Prospect 605
A Quick Note on Questions 606
Personality Types..607
The Conclusion of the Cold Call 607
Your Cold Call in a Nutshell 608
What If You Cold Call Someone Who Already Has an Account with Your
    Company? 609
Make Sure They're with You on the Cold Call 609
The Tough Prospect 610
Your Cold Call Follow-up Letter and Information.......................................611
Sample Follow-up Letter 612

Chapter 45 – The Second Call...613
Second Call Opening Lines 613
Two Questions to Ask about Your Second Call Opening 614
Second Call Opening Lines *Don'ts*..615
Second Call Objections...615
The Presentation..616
The Three Parts of Your Presentation..616

Objections 619
What If You Simply Can't Get around the
    "Send Me Some Information" Objection?.....................................622
What Do You Say When You Call the Person Back after You've Sent the
    Information?...624
Another Way to Answer Telemarketing Objections.............................624
Other Things to Remember about Objections 626
Questions during the Presentation 626
How Much Time Should You Spend with One Prospect? 627
Follow up after an Enthusiastic Telephone Sale.................................627

Chapter 46 – Other Thoughts on Telephone Selling..........................**630**
How Long Should Your Calls Last?..630
Keep Track of Calls and Results..631
Meeting Someone in Person 636
Keeping the Listener's Attention 639
Keeping Control of the Conversation 640
Improve Your Voice with a Recording Device 642
    Record Yourself When You're in a Slump...................................643
    Even Veterans Should Record Calls Occasionally 644
    Keep Some Recordings of Successful Calls 644
Up, Down, and In-between Notes..644
Using Humor on the Phone..645
Left Ear versus Right Ear..646
An Advanced Technique: Using More Than One Phone 646
Using the Speakerphone 647
Automatic Calling Machines 648
Have an Assistant..648
Ask for Referrals...648
Have Conversations 648
Put Yourself in the Other Person's Shoes on All Calls 648

A Summary of Ideas on Telephone Sales...**650**

SECTION X – SELLING WITHIN YOUR COMPANY 651

Introduction..653

Chapter 47 – Getting Along with Others at Work 655
Rules for Getting Along...655
Keep Your Manager Happy 655
Take Your Manager on Sales Calls 658
Watch Whom You Get Caught Up With 660
Rules for Effective Communication 660
Document Inter-company Projects and Communications 665

A Summary of Ideas on Selling within Your Company 667

Conclusion 668
Keys to Remember...668
The Rest Is up to You—You Control Your Destiny! 669

Contact Us...670

Author Bios...671

Index 676

Free info. – Why the new sales gimmicks don't work…Join us on line 679

How to Use This Book

If you read this book and follow through on what it teaches you, you will get better at selling, guaranteed. *You control your destiny.*

All the information in this book can be overwhelming, especially if you are new to selling. Some salespeople will sit down, read the entire book, take lots of notes, set up a plan to implement every strategy possible, and shortly thereafter, they'll be overwhelmed, frustrated, and go right back to the same ineffective practices they'd been previously using. *Do not* make that mistake. Follow the steps below and implement *only a few* strategies at a time. Once you own the new strategies and they become commonplace, go back to the book and add a few more. Rome wasn't built in a day and neither are great sales careers.

Some ideas in this book are highly advanced. Some will require a good amount of selling experience before they can be fully grasped. Be enthusiastic, energetic, positive, and patient. You will get to the top of the mountain if you choose to—just remember, getting there is a process.

If you are just starting out in professional selling, you'll want to strictly follow steps 1 through 5 listed below. If you have been in selling for quite some time, we would also highly recommend following steps 1 through 5. However, you may wish to simply reference some areas you need to strengthen or areas where you feel you need to brush up a little.

With the help of this tremendous resource, you can become a top sales professional. If you're already a top sales professional, you can become even better. In both cases, you must be 100 percent committed. You will learn most effectively from this book if you adhere to the following guidelines:

1) **Read this book from cover to cover, underlining, highlighting, and taking notes.** This may seem like a major undertaking at first, yet if you make a goal of reading just ten to twenty pages a day, you'll find yourself making very good progress in no time.

   As you go through your selling day, look for opportunities to apply what you have read. The quickest way to learn anything is to use it. The techniques discussed may feel awkward at first. That's normal; they are brand new. Once you've tried a new technique a few times, you will become comfortable with it and it will become second nature to you. You will own it; it will be a part of you.

2) **Read this book again, focusing on the areas that pertain most closely to the type of selling you're currently doing.** Once again, apply *some* of the information you're learning to your everyday selling.

3) **As you go through the book again, study your underlined and/or highlighted areas and review your notes.**

4) **After you have thoroughly read and reread the book, keep it with you at all times as a reference tool.** Difficult or new situations will arise from time to time, and you will need some guidance on how to handle them. This book will serve you greatly in that regard.

5) **Finally, review this book thoroughly at least once a year.** In addition to the underlined and highlighted sections, it is a good idea to reread sections that have not been underlined or highlighted. We have found that many times, although we thought we had read something completely the first or second time through, there were things we had completely missed. Also, as your selling experience changes, your focus will tend to shift, and items that you previously thought were unimportant may now be very important. So review this book completely from time to time and reference it often. Always look for ways to build upon and apply what you've learned and to improve every aspect of your selling—every day.

SECTION I

BUILDING THE FOUNDATION

Chapter 1

The Difference between Success and Failure in Selling

The Twelve Success Factors

Several important factors separate those who succeed in selling from those who fail. Although some of the following items are arguably more important than others, they are all critical to a salesperson's success.

When we talk about top salespeople, we're referring to people who are not only great at the profession of selling, they are also great human beings. Anyone who has been in sales for a while may know some seemingly successful salespeople with enormous egos. They are good at pushing product but have little regard for customers. This kind of success doesn't last; moreover, the other areas of their lives are often plagued by neglect and mismanagement. It is our hope that you will use the tools in this book to get what you're after, at the same time as helping those around you get what they're after. That being said, let's take a look at some of the common denominators that set the top salespeople apart from mediocre and poor salespeople.

1) Positive attitude – enthusiasm, drive, competitiveness, and confidence.

Top salespeople have a positive, can-do, winning attitude. Specifically, it calls for enthusiasm, drive, competitiveness, and confidence—the four most critical aspects of a top salesperson's personality. Top salespeople have dynamic energy. They are highly motivated to succeed. And it shows. You can see it in their eyes. A top salesperson is easy to spot the second they walk into a room. Their posture, their clothing, the way they walk, their overall demeanor—everything about them exudes an air of confidence. This belief in themselves is borderline cocky, yet doesn't cross the line into arrogance. They are not just pumped up when everyone else is. They see selling as a competition, and they *love* competition.

Top salespeople do whatever it takes to win—ethically, of course—and they do not quit. They are extremely persistent, yet they are not pests. They are always moving ahead, changing, growing, and pushing through the bad times until they make it. They never give up on themselves and their dream of success, *ever*.

Top salespeople have a win-win attitude. They believe that both they and the person getting involved in their product or service win as a result of the transaction. They are genuine and they truly like and care about other people.

Top salespeople have a healthy attitude about change. They realize that change is natural and is always occurring. They embrace change and realize that one of the greatest attributes an individual can have is the ability to adapt to change. They see the advantages and the positive side of change.

Top salespeople see themselves as professionals and take their jobs very seriously. They thoroughly enjoy selling. They know who they are and why they are where they are. They are confident in themselves and every aspect of their being.

Top salespeople view victories and defeats in proper context. They don't allow a victory to make them comfortable or a defeat to ruin their day. They have an expectant attitude that something good *will* happen every day, and they will work hard for it.

2) Being action oriented.

Top salespeople are people of purposeful, focused, well-thought-out action. They are not frozen by fear or paralyzed by indecision. Like others, they may occasionally feel fear, yet they act in spite of it.

Top salespeople are clear about what they are doing and why they are doing it. They don't procrastinate. They are protective of their time and use it wisely. Top salespeople have a plan and they work their plan every day. They know what actions lead to their success and that's where they spend their time. They follow the 80/20 rule, realizing that 80 percent of their results should come from 20 percent of their effort. They do not waste time on menial tasks. They effectively delegate these tasks and focus their efforts on the crucial 20 percent.

3) Preparation.

Top salespeople are prepared for anything and they over-prepare for everything. They never wing it. They have prepared scripts, presentations, answers to objections, and proposals. They practice, drill, and rehearse. They never rest on their laurels and are always looking for ways to improve.

They are familiar with *all* the paperwork and other, more detailed aspects of their job. They make sure they have all the tools of their trade with them, and they know how to use each one. They are ready for anything and expect the best, yet they have a plan if the worst or anything else in between shows up.

4) Being businesslike and business-savvy.

Today's consumers are smarter, competition has increased, and consumer focus has shifted to acquiring goods and services for the least cost possible. There has also been a change in corporate culture. Companies now focus on a well-thought-out business plan to make sure they're getting the most for their money. Their objective is to run more efficiently and be more cost effective than the competition. Consequently, top salespeople partner with customers and build a compelling business case based upon what's best for the customer. They know their customers' business and problems intimately. They ask intelligent questions that both set them apart from other salespeople and, more important, let the customer know they thoroughly understand the business.

Top salespeople embrace technology, know where to use it, and how much of it to use. They utilize e-mail, faxes, and computer technology but not to the point where they distance customers and/or remove the human element. They also know how to use technology within their own organizations, which, in most cases these days, requires the salespeople to do much more with much less.

5) Ability to stand out from the crowd.

Top salespeople have the ability to differentiate themselves from other salespeople. They don't sound or act like other salespeople. They don't say the same things that other salespeople say—they are original.

A top salesperson doesn't come across as someone trying to sell; he or she comes across as an interested and informed party—someone there to help.

Top salespeople have an aura of respect around them. The way they walk and talk demonstrates to others that they are professionals and in turn, they are treated professionally. Top salespeople are real, human, and down to earth, and people like them for this reason. Their caring, sincerity, and helpful dispositions stand out. They are memorable.

6) Likeability, trustworthiness, and the ability to build relationships.

Now, more than ever in this fast-paced world, selling is about doing everything necessary to build solid, loyal, long-term relationships. This is true even in businesses such as real estate and car sales, where the frequency of sales can be years apart. Top salespeople develop and nurture customer relationships and consider most of their customers to be friends. They get many referrals and do business with their customers' friends, family, and associates.

One of the most critical keys to selling and building relationships is the ability to get others to like and trust you. Top salespeople possess that trait along with the ability to and build strong, long-term relationships. If people like and trust you they will usually buy from you, even if your product is not the best. Conversely, if people don't like or trust you, many times they won't buy a product from you, no matter how good it is. In fact, they may *not* buy just to spite you. You may have the best price and exactly what someone wants, but if they don't like or trust like you, most of the time they will still walk away.

Top salespeople have the ability to put people at ease and win others to their side. They are able to establish a connection and build rapport quickly and effectively. They build trust and credibility. Top salespeople can walk into a room and emerge fifteen minutes later having made a new friend. They come across to others as kind, caring, and most important, as someone who can be trusted.

Top salespeople have the ability to "win friends and influence people" (Dale Carnegie, 1936). They are genuine, open, and honest. They make other people feel important. They convey a sincere interest in other people, what makes them tick, and what interests them. Top salespeople become personally involved with their clients, and their clients feel their sincerity. Top salespeople truly like to serve people.

7) Effective communication.

Top salespeople are great communicators, knowing what to say and when to say it. They actively listen to people and are able to hear them well and read between the lines. They ask many questions, *listen well* to the answers, and take notes.

Top salespeople don't confuse people by giving them more information than they need; yet they give them enough information to make a well-thought-out buying decision. Top salespeople are clear and concise in the information they convey.

Top salespeople have frank, direct conversations with people and talk to them the way they want to be talked to.

Top salespeople also get the information they need such as finding out who the decision-maker is and making sure the prospect is qualified.

8) Empathy.

Top salespeople have empathy for their customers and prospects. They are able to put themselves in other people's shoes and become emotionally involved. Top salespeople genuinely like people; in return, people feel their understanding and compassion. Top salespeople enjoy helping people and they believe, with every fiber of their being, that buying and owning their product or service will help people.

9) Professionalism, integrity, and work ethic.

Top salespeople are complete professionals with complete integrity. In addition, they have a great work ethic. Their mannerisms, language, tone of voice, and all other aspects of their demeanor are nothing but professional.

Top salespeople do not burn bridges. They do not talk negatively about the competition. They are *always* on their best behavior because they're aware that they never know who is watching them and who is taking inventory of them.

Top salespeople are honest. If they don't know an answer, they admit it, and then proceed to find the answer and follow up promptly. Top salespeople don't encourage others to become involved with their product if it isn't right for them. They are straightforward with people.

Top salespeople work both hard and smart. In addition to following the 80/20 rule, they prioritize customers and prospects. Top salespeople recognize their bread-and-butter clientele and focus closely on nurturing those "productive" relationships and finding more people like them. They are willing to work as hard as possible in order to get the job done, while at the same time realizing that working smart is the ultimate goal. They don't rest on their laurels or relax when things are going well.

Top salespeople go the extra mile. They always deliver more than they promise and never leave anything to chance.

Top salespeople always follow up, doing what they say they will do, when they say they will do it. They return phone calls and reply to correspondence promptly. They follow up on unfinished business.

Top salespeople take 100 percent responsibility for everything they do, both in their professional and personal lives. By being responsible, they are empowered to take control of any situation.

10) Team player and leader.

Top salespeople are team players. They look for ways to contribute to the team. They share information such as success stories that may help the other salespeople in their company. They pull for their peers and colleagues. They use a big sale by another person in the office to motivate them. They are focused on becoming better as individuals and believe that by doing so, they help the people around them improve and make their company stronger.

Top salespeople work well with other departments. They develop strong professional relationships with co-workers. They get along with everyone, including the person no one else can relate to. They let the people they work with know they are appreciated.

Top salespeople are leaders. They expect to be at the top and they are comfortable there. They do not look down on or see others as inferior. Top salespeople realize that others do certain, non-sales-related things better than them, yet in the world of selling, they always see themselves at the top of the mountain. They help other salespeople to be successful. They lead by example.

Top salespeople lead prospects and customers to the right decisions. They skillfully set the ground rules for the buying process and they are not at the mercy of the buyer or the buying decision.

11) Continuing education and training.

Top salespeople are committed to being the best they can possibly be. They are always getting better at selling. They read sales books, listen to sales information at home and in their car, watch videos, and talk to other successful salespeople. Top salespeople constantly look for ways to improve, add to, and build upon every tool in their selling arsenal. They know selling and they know their business, yet they also know there is *always* more to learn. Top salespeople are teachable.

They study their competition inside and out. Often they know more about the competition's product than the competition does.

Top salespeople stay up-to-date on all new developments in their industry—particularly new product developments—everything that could affect business. They are constantly looking through trade publications and magazines. They study daily newspapers for any news on their industry or the customers they serve.

12) Company product and support.

Top salespeople cannot remain at the top without reliable products and support. They pick companies and products in which they can believe 100 percent, and they continue to look for reasons their product is better than any other. If the company or product does change to the point where they no longer have a product or the support necessary to satisfy their customers at the highest level, they work together with colleagues to make necessary improvements. If for some reason things don't work out, they move on—they find another company and product they can believe in. Top salespeople know that without a great product and great support, they cannot achieve long-term success.

So there you have it—the twelve factors necessary to become a top salesperson. While twelve factors may seem like a great deal, being a top salesperson really comes down to having a great attitude, a sincere interest in helping other people, and a burning desire to succeed. With those elements in place, everything else will follow.

Now that we've reviewed the twelve key characteristics of a top salesperson, let's look at what it takes to put those pieces in place.

Chapter 2

The Foundation for Top Achievement

The Six Ingredients Needed to Build Your Foundation

As the saying goes, "A house is only as strong as its foundation." It takes a strong foundation to support the twelve traits we've just discussed. Following are the six high-achievement ingredients necessary to build that strong foundation.

Ingredient 1 for high achievement: Be in sales for the right reasons.

Why are you in sales? If money is the primary reason you got into sales, that's good. Provided your desire for money is strong enough, it will motivate you to work hard and do all that's necessary to have at least *temporary* success in sales. In order to have long-term success and become a top achiever, however, genuine caring and a desire to serve your customers must back your motivation for money.

Ingredient 2 for high achievement: The right attitude and beliefs.

What is your daily attitude like? Do you *always* see solutions when you face problems? Do you stay positive in the face of all challenges?

Looking for the positive side of a situation is a habit, and, like most good habits, this one will take time and effort to develop if you don't already have it. Obviously, we're all human and some things will occasionally stress us out. At the same time, if you become aware of what is going on around you and begin to develop the habit of looking on the positive side, you will be far better off in work and in life. We're not saying you need to have a smile on your face twenty-four hours a day and naïvely believe problems or issues never arise in life. What we are saying is: Don't allow yourself to go to the other extreme of complete negativity and get overwhelmed to the point where you can't act. When you see a tough situation, recognize it, try to find some positives, keep a good attitude, and ultimately resolve the situation as quickly as possible.

What is your motivation level? You need to be highly motivated and ready to work as hard as you have to in order to reach the top and remain there.

How self-confident are you? To get to the top in selling requires high self-confidence and high self-esteem.

Are you a self-starter or do you need someone to give you a push? To get to the top in sales, you must be a self-starter. You must be motivated from within rather than needing someone to keep pushing you or keep you driven to succeed.

How much money do you believe you can make? In sales, the sky really is the limit. If you grew up in a household with a maximum annual income of $25,000, you may have trouble believing you can make $250,000 or more a year in sales. You must challenge any such limiting beliefs if you are going to become a top salesperson.

Do you consider yourself to be a professional with integrity? To get to the top, you must be a consummate professional and every ounce of your being must exude integrity—at *all* times.

Finally, do you see yourself as a person who is completely responsible for your life and what happens in it? This kind of responsibility is the cornerstone needed for great achievement.

Ingredient 3 for high achievement: A willingness to pay the price for success.

How far are you willing to go in order to be successful? There is a price for success and top salespeople have chosen to pay it. Are you willing to do whatever it takes, *ethically*, to get to and stay at the top?

Ingredient 4 for high achievement: "Hanging out" with the right people.

Who do you hang around with and where are they going? You must hang around with successful people who are growing personally and professionally and who support your goals and dreams. Birds of a feather *do* flock together, and the wrong group of people can drag you down quickly. This doesn't mean you need to immediately discard your friends and family if they aren't completely supportive of you. However, as you progress toward your goals, you may find yourself gathering a new, different group of friends and hanging out with certain negative people less often. Let friends and family know the track you're on and ask them to help or even to join you in the adventure.

Ingredient 5 for high achievement: Good health.

How is your health? It isn't possible to operate at your highest levels both mentally and physically if your health isn't good. If you are tired, run down, or frequently ill, you will not be motivated and you will not perform well. It seems obvious, but it is worth noting that you need to get plenty of sleep, eat properly, and exercise on a regular basis in order to be a consistently top salesperson.

Good health also includes your overall mental condition. While sleeping, exercising, and eating right will help your mental state, you must also develop the ability to handle stress, unexpected problems, and other similarly negative things that may affect your emotions.

Ingredient 6 for high achievement: A life with balance and growth.

For short periods, you can devote an inordinate amount of time to one area of your life and neglect the others. However, if you do that for too long, your attitude will suffer tremendously. To be truly happy in the long run, you must find a way to balance work, family, recreation, personal time, and other important areas of your life.

Usually when there is imbalance, it's caused by too much focus on work. The striving to get ahead, make more money, get that next promotion, and be noticed can whip some of us into such a frenzy that many times it's all too easy to get completely caught up in this injurious routine. We begin to take the important people in our lives for granted, and we justify this by claiming that we're simply trying to give our spouses and family members a better life with the extra income and status we'll soon enjoy. However, the long-term results of this imbalance are almost always negative.

You must spend time with family and friends, spend time with yourself, as well as spend time at work. You must also spend time working on your physical health, mental health, and spiritual health. You may not get to each area every day, but in the course of a week, be sure each area of your life is getting its share of attention.

Finally, you must be passionate about what you are doing, and you must always be growing personally and professionally.

The six ingredients above are necessary for consistent, long-term top performance. If you have these ingredients in place, many of the other characteristics of top salespeople will fall into place. If you don't have these six essential ingredients in place, you will face some daunting challenges. The good news is that all of these ingredients can be learned. Granted, few of them are mastered easily if you haven't already developed them. However, if you are truly committed to becoming a top salesperson, you *can* develop them. There is *always* hope.

Next, we'll discuss the quickest way to become great at selling.

Chapter 3

How to Become *Great* at Selling

Eleven Steps to Greatness

Here's what to do to become great at selling.

1) Do what the top salespeople do.

This is arguably the most obvious, most basic, and most important step to becoming a top salesperson. The premise here is simple: If you take the same actions as the top salespeople, you will eventually also be a top salesperson. If you do the same things as a mediocre salesperson, you will be a mediocre salesperson.

Find the top salespeople in your company and pick their brains. In addition to top salespeople in your company, get advice from top salespeople in other industries. Start by approaching each of the top producers in your company and asking them if you can have some of their time to find out what makes them successful. Most will be happy to share information with you. Have a recording device with you so you can record their answers to the following questions:

- What has made you successful as a salesperson?
- What has made you successful with your customers?
- What books, tape programs, and other training resources have you found helpful and/or do you recommend I read, listen to, or reference?
- What are your answers to the following objections? (Have a list prepared of all the objections you'll encounter in your business.) Can you think of any objections I may have left out?
- What are your best closes?
- How do you handle competition?
- What is your best technique for cold calling?
- What sales tools do you use? This could include anything from questionnaires and Return-on-Investment models to brochures, specification sheets, scale rules and measuring tapes, sample parts,

software programs, boiler-plate presentations, and the like—any tools that you should carry with you or have close at hand at all times. **Note:** If they do have questionnaires, Return-on-Investment models, and other items they carry with them, ask if you may have copies of these.

- What motivates you?
- What other advice do you have for me?
- Is there anything you can think of that I've missed?
- May I have a copy of your cold call, or may I record it?
- May I make a copy of your presentation or record it?

Then, after you've turned off your recorder, ask:

- If I run into a situation in the future that I need some advice on, may I ask you for advice?

Later, after you've asked these questions and recorded the answers, type them into a document and print it out.

Next, assemble a binder that contains the cold call, presentation, answers to all objections, closes, and other items you need to convey—written out and organized. Over the years, there has been some controversy over this point. Some people believe that having a written-out cold call, presentation, and other information is too unnatural and you may sound rehearsed. The best way—really the only way—to avoid this is by practicing, drilling, and rehearsing to the point where you know the information verbatim and thus can concentrate on *how* you're saying something rather than *what* you are saying.

There are several advantages to having everything written out:

- You won't forget to mention anything.
- You can work on *how* to say something instead of trying to think about *what* to say.
- You won't be thrown off track if you are interrupted in the middle of a cold call or presentation.
- Knowing what you're going to say will help you stay focused, and help ensure that you are prepared to handle any situation that arises.
- The alternative is being unprepared and "winging it," and that's *not* how you want to present yourself.

In our experience, the quickest way to get to the top is to have all your material written out and eventually memorized.

Following are some steps for putting your binder together:

a) Start with a three-ring binder that holds 8" x 11" sheets of paper.
b) Buy dividers with tabs. Label one of the tabs *Cold Call*, then label tabs for each presentation you have. Make a tab for each objection and another tab labeled *Closes*.
c) Finally, take the pages you typed up with all the information you recorded from the top salespeople, punch the pages with a three-hole punch, and insert them into your binder under the appropriate tabs.

Behind your *Cold Call* tab, have some responses to questions, comments, or objections you might encounter during the call, and get them memorized. For example, suppose you sell office supplies and the prospect responds with, "I'm not interested," strike at the objection quickly with, "Bob, if I could save you 40 percent on your office supplies, would you be interested?" He may decline but at least you took a shot at it.

It's possible that you may have more than one cold call for different products or circumstances. If so, have a tab for each cold call and label each tab so you can quickly tell them apart.

Next is the *Presentation* section. Some businesses will require you to have several different sales presentations, depending upon the product and/or the prospect. For example, if you are an investment advisor you may have presentations for several different stocks, bonds, annuities, REITs, etc. Each presentation should have its own tab and supporting information.

Note: If you have an array of products, it may be easier to have separate binders for each product you sell. If the objections and closes vary widely from product to product, it would be advisable to have several binders.

Your *Objections* tabs, which follow your presentation, will include tabs such as:

- must talk to spouse first
- I have to think about it

- I want to check around
- it costs too much

and all other objections you may encounter. Behind each tab, have a page with several answers to that objection along with an appropriate close to use after answering each objection.

The next tab in your binder will be *Closes*. These will be additional closes that were not used in your *Objections* section above. Following your *Closes* tab, have several pages with many different closes that can be used in almost any situation.

Note: In addition to the above, you may have other items you need to convey. For example, you may want to have your guarantee written out if it is something that arises with frequency. In this case, take another divider, make up a tab with the word "Guarantee," type out your answer and put this information toward the back of your binder.

Preparing a binder in the way we've described may seem like a lot of work. However, the very process of assembling the binder will assist you with the memorization of its contents. Following are some guidelines for using your binder:

a) Know your binder inside and out; know all the information in it by heart. While you obviously can't have the binder in front of you if you're in face-to-face selling, having your material memorized will serve the same purpose—that is, to be using proven material that works. In telephone sales, you will have your binder in front of you.

b) Update your binder from time to time. As you come across more, better, or different responses, get them into your binder.

Note 1: In the beginning, it's important to say *exactly* what the top salespeople say. One of the biggest mistakes new salespeople make is learning valuable skills from the top salespeople and then putting those lessons into their own words and style. In the process, they lose the very effectiveness they are trying to achieve. Only after you have proven yourself with consistent solid numbers should you consider tweaking the experts' approaches to make it better.

Note 2: Watch out for the mediocre or poor salespeople who may be anxious to help you. Many times these people are more than willing to help. The only problem is, if you do what they do, you'll end up with the same results they have—precisely, mediocre or poor.

Note 3: Most of the top salespeople will be very helpful, although some may not. Be persistent, but considerate of their time. Above all, don't bother someone during prime calling time.

2) Learn everything you possibly can about the subject of selling.

Read, listen to programs, watch videos, and study everything you can get your hands on that relates to selling. If you are new in sales, there will be a huge amount of information to absorb. Even if you've been in sales for a while, there are always new ideas coming out on handling objections, cold calling, and all other aspects of selling. Be a sponge and absorb as much information as you can. Be open and curious and realize that no matter how much you know, there's always more to learn.

3) Learn everything you can about your industry and your prospects.

Read industry publications, newsletters, magazines, and the like. Pay attention to "local" sources such as newspapers, Chamber of Commerce letters, and other news bulletins that are printed in the geographic proximity of the companies you're interested in. Look for breaking news, new products, new laws, regulations, or changes in legislation, interesting articles, stories on people making an impact in the industry, and other pertinent information.

Stay on top of the latest innovations and technology within your industry.

Study the companies and individuals to whom you're selling. Obtain annual reports, look in *Who's Who*, and tap the Internet and company websites for information.

Get creative by sitting down and brainstorming by yourself and with others to come up with ideas to sell more effectively. Share best practices and competitive information.

Information is power. The more information you have on selling, on the industry you're in, and on the people to whom you're selling, the more confident and successful you'll be.

4) Work on yourself.

To be a top salesperson, you must constantly improve personally as well as professionally. Following are some ideas for both personal and professional development:

a) Make it a habit to think positive and stay motivated. Pick up some books and audio and video programs on psychology, motivation, and staying positive. People like to be around and do business with positive people. Put as much positive information into your brain as you can and keep negatives out.

b) In order to stay motivated in the long term, you need to be growing. To sustain a positive attitude, you must focus on becoming a better, more accomplished person. You must be working toward something that is meaningful to *you*.

c) Your highest values and ideals must be reflected in your daily life. Your job and personal life must be in line with your highest values and ideals.

d) Ask yourself what is most important to you in each area of your life. List your values such as honesty, integrity, loyalty, trustworthiness, etc., and place them in order of importance. Decide which values are most important from a standpoint of family, money, career, health, and so on. Are you living those values in each area of your life?

e) Discover what you ultimately want to do with your life and what you have a passion for. If you love your present job, great; if you don't, can you use your present job as a stepping stone to develop the skills you need to get to the place you ultimately want to be? Discover where you want to be and develop a plan to get there.

5) Set goals.

Goals are important because they give you direction. Your goals can be as simple as doing 120 percent of quota and making the annual awards trip, or as complex as a list of daily, weekly, monthly, and annual goals in all the major areas of your life. Some people find a complete list of complex goals overwhelming. If this is the case, simply set one or two major goals at a time.

Here are some guidelines for your goals:

- Make sure your goals inspire and motivate you.
- Your goals must be clear, measurable, and believable. "More cold calls" isn't measurable. "Ten percent more cold calls" is.

- Break each goal down into small pieces. Break a goal down into monthly, weekly, and daily goals.
- Don't just list the goal, list its ultimate benefits to you. Who will you become and how will your life change?
- The most important factor is *why* you are striving to achieve a goal. Come up with many strong reasons *why* this goal must happen.
- Take some action on your major goal(s) every day.
- Have a timeline and deadline for your goals.
- Envision yourself already there. Act as though you are already there, or "fake it until you make it," and imagine yourself as the person who has already achieved your goal.
- Keep your goals in front of you. Put reminders on the bathroom mirror, bedroom mirror, refrigerator door, and other places where you will see them every day.
- Be flexible. Things won't always go exactly as you plan. Be flexible in your approach, and manage roadblocks and other obstacles with optimism and an open mind. Make it a habit to turn problems into solutions.
- Reward yourself. You can reward yourself not only for reaching your goal but also for reaching milestones on the way to your goal.

Here are some good questions to ask regarding goals:

- What do you want for all areas of your life five years from now? Ten years?
- What do you want for your family?

And the most important question:

- What kind of person do you want to be?

Note 1: While it's nice to have material goals, it is more important to have goals in which you *become something*. "Becoming" goals such as becoming more self-confident, creative, or knowledgeable in a certain field do much more for your happiness, self-confidence, and self-esteem. Yes, becoming more self-confident will *give* you even more self-confidence. These qualities build upon themselves.

Note 2: It is important to own a knowledge library. You should have a collection of sales and motivational books, audio and video programs, and other related information at your home.

Note 3: Find a mentor, hire a personal coach, or do both. If you have someone with whom you have to check in regularly, you're more likely to work harder and achieve more.

Note 4: Ask customers, peers, and even family to evaluate you. Ask only those who truly care about you and ask them to be *completely* honest with you. As well, your manager should be evaluating you at least once a year.

The point to remember from all we've just discussed is that you need to keep growing as a person and continually work on yourself and your attitude. Once you have a strong foundation in place, you'll notice your sales ability will increase tremendously. This is a positive Catch 22: As your attitude about yourself improves, your sales ability will increase; and as you get better at selling, your attitude about yourself will improve.

6) Record new ideas quickly and develop new information.

Always have a recorder and/or pen and paper handy. Have them in your car, by your bed, at your desk, and everywhere you go so you can record good ideas as soon as they hit you.

A recorder is also great if you hear someone say something that you'd like to use. You can either have them repeat it or record it yourself. Use your recorder in the car when you're listening to sales tapes or compact discs and you come across ideas you like.

Take notes on information you read, see, or listen to. This helps to further reinforce the idea so you'll remember it more easily.

Once you've captured some good ideas, develop them further and review your notes regularly.

7) Practice, drill, rehearse, and apply new ideas.

Take sayings, closes, and other information you like and make them your own. Practice them on other salespeople, family members, friends, and practice them on yourself. Most important, once you've mastered them privately, look for places to use these new ideas in real-world selling situations.

8) Review motivational and educational information often.

Actively listening to tape and CD programs while taking notes is the optimal way to learn. However, this is not always possible, and when it's not, passive listening in the car or elsewhere will also work well. To absorb tape and CD programs through passive listening, listen to them ten to fifteen times.

With books and other written material, read them, take notes, highlight sections, flag pages, and then review your notes and highlighted sections ten to fifteen times. With videos, watch them, take notes, and then review.

Again, you also want to be looking for ways to apply the new information you're learning.

Continually look for new material on selling and motivation.

Occasionally you will want to review resources you've already studied. As you need help in particular areas, you can return to several resources and get different ideas.

9) Work hard *and* smart.

Obviously if you're given a choice, it's much better to work smarter than harder. At the same time, when you are just starting out and don't know anything about the business, you simply must work hard until you figure things out. But even in the beginning, there are some basic rules you can follow that will ensure you get the most out of your hard work and understand things as quickly as possible. They are:

a) Do what the top salespeople do, as we've already discussed.

b) Make more calls and work longer than anyone else. There are no shortcuts here. This is an area in which you simply must work hard.

c) Be persistent. Persistence is most important when you are just starting out because you must remain driven and motivated through the trial-and-error period. You will run into most of your challenges, both real and imagined, in this beginning stage.

Persistence takes the form of hard work, hard thinking, and hard planning while staying positively motivated and keeping your emotions in check.

Persistence is necessary in order to stay disciplined. You must remain disciplined in your work ethic, in learning, in chasing the top producers down to find out what they're doing right, and in every other aspect of your job. Without persistence and discipline, you simply will not last long in a sales career.

d) Use your time effectively. An entire book could be written on this subject alone, but we won't go into a lot of detail here. Just remember a few important items:

- Use travel time to get things done.
- Do non-time-sensitive tasks during off hours, not during prime selling time.
- Try to eliminate "fire drills." These are usually tasks that could have been handled long ago and weren't.
- Have a plan for each day.
- Use the 80/20 rule. Spend as much time as possible on the most important 20 percent of your tasks that will produce 80 percent of your results; delegate the other 80 percent—those that produce only 20 percent of your results.
- Use e-mail to save time and money and have information documented.
- Use the fax machine to expedite items and update customers.
- Take vacations and spend quality time with family, friends, and loved ones.
- Organize your schedule so it makes sense logistically. Divide your territory and make multiple calls in a particular area.
- Carry work with you just in case you get "stuck" somewhere.
- Hire a personal assistant to run your errands for you.
- Hire a sales assistant whom you can train to do virtually everything you do and who can run the business when you are away or tied up doing something else.
- Take a course, read books, and listen to tapes or CDs on managing your time most effectively.

Following are some key questions to ask about your daily tasks:

- Is this the best use of my time right now?
- Is this something I can delegate or even eliminate?

- Is there a quicker, easier, or more efficient way to get this activity done?

One of the most important items we talked about above was delegating tasks. Ultimately, you are trying to achieve two goals by delegating.

- The first goal of delegating is to allow you to spend your time on *only the most important* tasks.
- The second goal of effective delegating is to be in a position where the business can run smoothly even when you are not around.

e) Stay organized. Here are some ideas to help keep you organized:

- Have a weekly call sheet listing whom you will call on during the week.
- Have a monthly calendar handy so you can keep track of appointments you've already scheduled. You can buy computer software that specializes in scheduling and contact management.
- Set up a contact schedule to stay in touch with customers and prospects.
- You may use a Daytimer along with a calendar, some sort of filing system, a computer, Blackberry, or similar system that will keep you on track with all your contact informationand follow-up items.
- Set up a reminder system to follow up on important tasks.
- If you have projects, each consisting of the same tasks, make a checklist of items that are required for each project.
- Manage information properly.
- Keep your work area organized.
- Take a few minutes at the end of the day to organize your work area and prepare for the next day.
- Keep proposals, customer files, and other records in one location in alphabetical order.
- Have daily and weekly goals for the number of calls, prospects, and sales you want to generate.
- Take good, clear notes, and keep them in one location.

- Keep backup copies of important records at a separate location.
- Take a course, read books, and listen to tapes and CDs on getting organized.

f) Come up with "smart" ideas and alternatives. One particular day, we found ourselves in a real jam. We were preparing to demonstrate some technical equipment when we had a problem. We tried to reach the technician who had set the equipment up, but to no avail. We tried to get to several other people who could help and still no luck. We had customers coming in less than an hour and our equipment was dead. Just then, one of us had an idea. We called an engineer who had been laid off about a month earlier due to budget constraints. Although you'd think that a person in that position would not be willing to help, guess what? He helped us. It took him about five minutes and we were ready to go.

Bottom line: in order to work smart, you need to think smart. You need to be creative when solving problems. The best way to build your creativity is to develop your brain. Read, play games that challenge your brain, and work on your problem-solving skills. Also, make sure to get enough sleep, eat right, and exercise. Finally, obtain books and other information on developing the brain. Your brain is like a muscle; the more you use and develop it, the stronger it will become.

Hopefully, the above ideas will help you to work smarter as you go through your day. But while it is definitely better to work smart instead of hard, there are some areas in which there is no substitute for hard work. All of us have to work hard to acquire the knowledge and experience necessary to become top salespeople. There is simply no substitute for experience, and the only way to get experience is through hard work and making many calls.

Your overall objective is to work smarter and harder than anyone else. You will achieve this by copying the successful habits of the top salespeople, making the best possible use of your time, making more calls than everyone else, putting in more hours, and going the extra mile. If you combine brains with hard work, you'll soon get to where you want to go.

10) Pick the right product and company.

As we discussed earlier, in order to be successful it takes a good product and good support. If you don't have a good product, or you can't service that product effectively, any success you have will be short-lived. Pick a reliable product you can believe in and a company with people and support that will back you up. Obviously, it's important to be able to get along with your manager and other people you work with. It's also important to represent a product or service that works well, provides value to your customers, and makes you and your company look great.

Try to get some objective opinions of the company you are considering working for. Find out as many details as you can through annual reports, the Internet, and other information sources. Talk to customers, employees, and former employees if possible. Find out who your manager will be and who you'll be working with most closely, and determine your compatibility with those people. Discover the company's values, beliefs, mission statement, and objectives, and see if they match your own. After some research, you'll develop a gut feeling as to whether you and the company are a good fit.

11) Follow the principles discussed in chapter 1 and review this book often.

The list of twelve principles in chapter 1 *is* long; however, all elements are necessary to become a top salesperson. Review the list often and keep close track of where you are in the process. Focus on strengthening each principle.

Refer to this book often and try to reread it in its entirety at least once a year. It is our hope and our belief that this book will become your favorite and ultimate resource. At the same time, in today's dynamic world, new information and new ideas are constantly being created, so you want to stay on the lookout for new sources of information on selling and business. Always keep looking and keep learning.

Becoming great at selling involves working hard to gain knowledge and experience. It also involves working hard to make lots of calls and working smart to be most effective at every aspect of your job. Ensure your success by staying positive, being persistent, working hard, working smart, and refusing to give up.

Rules of Top Salespeople

These are the habits or "rules" to which top salespeople adhere:

- Be customer centered with a sincere interest in helping the customer—make this your number one priority.
- Be motivated, enthusiastic, and positive.
- Show up to all appointments early.
- Be honest and straightforward.
- Be empathetic.
- Find out what people need and how you can fill their needs.
- Sell *benefits.*
- Follow up.
- Ask thought-provoking questions and *listen* well to the answers.
- Return all calls and other correspondence promptly.
- Sell to others as *they* would like to be sold to.
- Have goals.
- Work hard and smart.
- Believe in yourself and what you are selling.
- Continue learning and getting better.
- Listen to educational and motivational tapes and CDs in the car.
- Try new ideas as soon as possible.
- Don't argue or be defensive.
- Don't make up answers or pretend to know answers you don't know.
- Be a team player and work well with others.
- Anticipate and be proactive.
- Take good notes and read them back to make sure you're on target.
- Be persistent, yet not obnoxious.
- Develop relationships and continue to build upon them.
- Ask for the order, then say absolutely nothing until the prospect responds.
- Know your product, your competition, and your industry.
- Expect things to go your way but realize things won't always go as planned.

- Be prepared by having a plan and backup plan, and being ready for anything.
- Keep good records.
- Act with confidence, speak with confidence.
- Have meaningful conversations.
- Send thank-you notes, newspaper clippings, and other items of interest to customers.
- Give them something to remember you by.
- Know your customer—interests, children, etc.
- Keep your name in front of the customer.
- Personalize customer relationships.
- Deliver more than expected, earlier than expected.
- Demand more from yourself than your customer could ever expect.
- Go the extra mile.
- Take responsibility for your life and your business.
- Be balanced in your life and work.

A Day in the Life of the Successful Salesperson

What follows is a typical daily schedule for a successful salesperson:

6:00 a.m. – Get up, make sure the attitude is in check and look forward to the day ahead. Read, listen to, or watch either something positive, something about the industry, or something sales related. Often it will be a combination. Also, review your major goals and brainstorm solutions to your biggest roadblocks.

7:00 a.m. – Review the day ahead and mentally rehearse and picture a positive outcome to all upcoming calls and meetings. Use positive affirmations while showering and dressing to further increase enthusiasm to tackle the upcoming day. Eat a well-balanced breakfast—not too heavy—and drink some water.

7:30 to 8:00 a.m. – Off to work, prepare materials, review daily goals, set up for the first calls of the day, and check for any early morning messages.

8:00 a.m. – The selling day begins. It is time to be in front of the customer or prospect, or on the phone with them. If there are any "unpleasant" tasks to be handled, such as breaking bad news to a client, handle these first and get them out of the way. From 8:00 until about 11:45, spend time on time-critical, client-related tasks, such as prospecting, presenting, and closing.

11:45 a.m. – Check for messages, return any calls, e-mails, or other communications that need to be taken care of.

Noon – A light lunch with some protein and a glass of fruit juice or water.

12:30 p.m. – Back to prospect/client time-critical tasks.

4:45 p.m. – Check for messages, return calls, e-mails, or other communications that need to be taken care of. General wrap-up of the client-related, time-sensitive tasks of the day and a positive and objective review of the day's events.

5:30 p.m. into evening – Exercise, a good dinner, relaxation with the family.

An hour or so before bed, work on non-time-critical tasks such as paperwork and follow up on e-mails, communications, proposals, etc. Read motivational or sales-related material, do some mental exercises such as positive affirmations, plan the following day, and check messages one more time.

Use the above example to design your successful day. Keys to designing your day are:

- Planning
- Organizing
- Time management
- Balance throughout the day

To summarize this chapter, stay positive, work hard and smart, and refuse to give up if things get difficult. You can and will succeed in sales if you pay the price for success and decide that nothing will stop you.

Chapter 4

More Detail on Important Items

Taking Responsibility

To become and remain a top salesperson, you must take 100 percent responsibility for your life and your business. Mediocre and poor salespeople try to shift blame to everyone but themselves. Top salespeople take complete responsibility and control of the situation and work to solve the problem. Taking responsibility means *owning the problem*. Once you own the problem, you will be motivated to solve it.

When blame is placed on your company, you need to shift that blame to yourself. Your primary goal is to keep company market share, not your individual market share. Once your competitors get a foothold in an area, they can spread like wildfire.

If a customer blames a salesperson and that salesperson falls out of favor, a different salesperson can take over that account. However, if a customer blames a company and that company gets a bad name, the company as a whole is out. Often, if you have a good relationship with the customer, she will be willing to forgive you. After a mistake, tell the customer that you value her highly as a client, but if she is unhappy with you, you would be pleased to bring in a different sales representative. The bottom line: take the personal blame; take responsibility.

Taking responsibility also means resolutely dealing with the problem. For example, if you've sold a product and you're informed during the installation that something has gone awry, you have to get on the phone, get in touch with your people, figure out what's going on, get back to the customer with an update, and then jump in your car and get out there. Stay there until the installation has been completed; at the same time, call the customer every so often with updates. If you cannot reasonably get to the site in person, you need to stay on top of the situation every step of the way, preferably by phone, and hang on to the situation with the tenacity of a pit bull.

One of your first steps should be to inform management of the situation by letting them know precisely what is going on and how things are being resolved. You want to keep management involved for several reasons. First, they may have some ideas that can help you, or they may go to bat for you immediately; second, if you do eventually need their help, you won't catch them completely off guard; and third, if the proverbial doo-doo does hit the fan, they aren't going to wonder why you didn't make them aware of the situation earlier.

You also want to make sure the people tackling the problem have all the resources they need. Inform the person directly above the people working on the problem about it. Occasionally, you will have to escalate an issue up the chain of command and go over people's heads.

Also, pass messages from customers on to other people involved, including management. You do this for some of the same reasons listed above. In addition, messages from the customer keep everyone apprised of how the customer views the situation and offer insight into the customer's state of mind.

Remember that one of your objectives in staying on top of the situation is to support your people and help them do their job. Bring food, coffee, and other items to take care of the people working at the site and to let them know you appreciate their efforts. You want them to regard you as moral support. Similarly, don't be afraid to get your hands dirty. Ask your people what you can do to help them and what they need to get the job done. As a salesperson, you may not have their technical knowledge, but they may simply need an extra pair of hands or need you to be an intermediary.

Occasionally, you'll run into someone who does not want to escalate an issue up the chain of command even though he needs help. In this situation, it is your job to recognize it and either have him escalate the situation or do it yourself. Be diplomatic—there may be some egos in play here. But never forget: your most important priority is to get the situation resolved for your customer. Start by simply making a suggestion, and if that doesn't work, take action.

For example, if you know that a particular individual is adept at solving the issue facing you, you might say to your person, "I'm very confident that you'll figure this out. I also know that Steve Smith faced the same problem about a month ago. I'm going to try to get him on the phone and see if he has any suggestions." And then make the call. If you can't think of anyone who can help, try this: "If you could have anyone here to help right now, who would it be?" Once you get a name, start tracking him or her down.

Take responsibility, own the problem, and then resolutely deal with it. Solve the problem or otherwise make sure the customer is satisfied with the end solution.

Going the Extra Mile

With the speed of business accelerating every day and with competition getting much tougher, it is extremely important to go the extra mile and do things that set you apart from your competition. Here is an example:

We once had an installation that, due to unforeseen problems, caused our installers to be on site all day Sunday to ensure the bank was ready to open on Monday. The installation was completed just after 11:30 on Sunday night and we, the salespeople, had been there the entire day on Sunday, roughly fifteen hours. This situation could be used as an example of taking responsibility or, as we suggest here, going the extra mile. However you categorize it, this is an example of what you must be willing to do to be at the very top of the selling profession. When you bring that kind of dedication to your sales job, you will rarely, if ever, have to worry about job security or *not* being at the top of your profession.

When we were in the automatic teller machine (ATM) industry we used to look for "out of service" ATMs while we were traveling. If we saw a machine that was down, we'd make a written note. If it was one of our machines, we'd make sure that the service department was aware of the problem. Sometimes service calls can get lost in the shuffle. Once we'd alerted them to the problem, they could jump on it quickly.

If it was a competitor's machine, we'd keep tabs on how long it was down for. If the machine was down for an extended period of time, we knew it would be a good account for our sales representative to call on.

That is just a small example of keeping on top of what's going on in your business, while simultaneously taking an extra step to make sure the customer is being taken care of. Demonstrate to customers and prospects that you are committed and willing to go the extra mile, serving them in ways beyond what they might reasonably expect.

Creativity and Persistence

Top salespeople are creative and persistent. Here are two examples:

1) Persistence pays off.

A salesperson stopped in to see the owner of a company where he really wanted to work. The first day, he arrived at about 10 a.m. and waited until 6 p.m. to see him.

When the owner wouldn't see him, he showed up the next day at 6 a.m. and waited until 6 p.m. On day three, he showed up again at 6 a.m. The owner finally decided to see him at about 10:30 a.m. and he hired that persistent salesperson shortly thereafter.

2) I'll give you $1,000 for fifteen minutes of your time.

A salesperson called a prospect with whom he had been trying to get an appointment with for about four months. The prospect's secretary, mistaking the salesperson for one of the prospect's friends, said, "Sorry Rich, he's out shopping for a new Cadillac Escalade." The salesperson replied, "Actually this isn't Rich, it's Steve Henry. Do you know when he'll be back?" The receptionist laughed at her mistake, apologized and then said, "Yes, he should be back in about an hour."

The salesperson, Steve, happened to have a friend who was a sales manager at one of the local Cadillac dealerships. Steve called his friend, said he had a hot prospect he'd been trying to get in to see for a while, and this prospect was looking for a Cadillac Escalade. He then asked if his friend could do anything to help. His friend replied, "I'll tell you what. If he comes down here to see me I'll save him $1,000 on the best price he can find on a Cadillac Escalade."

Steve called the prospect back a little over an hour later, and when he got the receptionist on the phone he said, "Hello, it's Steve Henry again. Please tell Mr. Sampson that if he'll give me fifteen minutes of his time, I will save him $1,000 on the best price he can find anywhere on a Cadillac Escalade." The receptionist put the call through.

Steve said, "Mr. Sampson, Steve Henry with ABC Company. If you'll give me fifteen minutes to show you what I have, I'll save you $1,000 on the best price you can find on a Cadillac Escalade."

Of course, Mr. Sampson was full of questions. Why had this call from a stranger been allowed through to him? How did this stranger know of his desire for a Cadillac? Steve explained that the secretary had simply made an honest mistake, but asked that Mr. Sampson trust him on the $1,000 deal for the fifteen minutes.

He agreed to see Steve, signed a medium-sized order, and bought the Cadillac from Steve's friend. Since that initial meeting, Mr. Sampson has become a good customer.

The point is that you must go above and beyond, you need to be willing to do what other salespeople are not doing, and you need to be creative.

What can *you* do to show extraordinary commitment? Are there other money- or time-saving items not related to your product or service that you could use to get in the door? The bottom line is: What creative ideas can you use to get in the door and set yourself apart from other salespeople?

Other Ways to Set Yourself Apart

1) Everyone has to eat, right?

Dropping off breakfast, lunch, or other treats at a prospect's or customer's office is a great way to stand out from other salespeople. You can even call ahead and take everyone's order. You can also bring special items at festive times of the year. For example, you might bring in some Halloween candy late in October, some Easter candy in April, or chocolates during the Christmas season.

We know of several individuals who dress up for Halloween and put in a full day of sales calls. Walking into a prospect's or customer's office in a Halloween costume will definitely set you apart from the crowd, not to mention the fact that you'll definitely introduce a little humor into the sales call. Of course, your costume should never be too risqué or politically sensitive.

2) Happy Cinco de Mayo!

Find excuses to stay in touch with your customers. Think of reasons to send a card to your customers every month of the year. Valentine's Day, St. Patrick's Day, Cinco de Mayo, the Fourth of July, you name it. For more information on staying in touch with customers, please refer to pages 513 through 515.

3) Go out of your way for your customer's customers.

Once, when we were cold calling on a competitive account, we approached the receptionist, who was busy helping some customers. While we were waiting, one of us noticed an older woman seated, her walker in front of her. My associate caught her eye, said hello, and began a conversation about the weather, housing, and the local economy. It was soon evident that she didn't get an opportunity to talk to many people during her day.

They continued talking for a few minutes until the receptionist was free. My associate didn't rush away; he continued to talk with the woman a little longer before saying goodbye. The receptionist, observing this, apparently thought he was a great guy and grinned widely as she asked how she could help us.

My associate asked for the contact person and mentioned that although he was not familiar with us, he would probably recognize the name of our company. He also mentioned we simply needed a moment of his time.

With a big smile on her face, the receptionist said, "Oh don't worry. I'll get you in to see him." She was on our side at that point because one of us had taken the time to brighten one of her customer's days.

4) Work Fridays.

Yes, this may sound self-evident, but it's amazing how many salespeople leave early on Friday or simply do a bunch of "busy" work yet get nothing accomplished. Most people are in great moods on Friday, and that's precisely when you want to catch them. You will also impress people by calling on them on Fridays because they don't see many salespeople on Friday. The same goes for the day before a holiday. Take advantage of these times when people are in good moods and most other salespeople aren't working.

5) Get involved in installation and implementation.

Installation and/or implementation of your product or service are areas in which you can stand out from other salespeople. Most salespeople just sell, and then let the installation and implementation departments do their work. Finally, the salespeople return, after the fact, if they ever come back into the picture at all. There are very few salespeople hanging around the customer's office when the installation and implementation are taking place. You should be different. Customers will be very impressed if you're there for installation and implementation. You don't have to go to every single one, but you should be there for a customer's first install and occasionally on future installs. This also keeps your installers on their toes, as they will not know when you will be showing up. At the same time, the primary point of stopping in isn't to catch someone doing something wrong, but to impress the customer with your diligence. You will also learn a little more about your product, which is a nice side benefit.

6) Find creative ways to make customer problems go away.

What problems do customers call you with? Billing problems, service problems, installation problems? Make notes on all of these, particularly the most frequent ones. Be proactive. Try to correct any recurring problems at the front end to prevent them from happening in the first place. Also, brainstorm more effective ways of handling problems.

7) Exceed customer expectations.

Exceeding customer expectations means delivering more, better, or faster. Over-promising is the surest way *not* to meet customer expectations. If typical turnaround time is three weeks, tell your customer, "Typical turnaround is about four to five weeks." When you call a couple of weeks later and say you can deliver sooner, you'll look like a hero. If you make it a habit to deliver more than is expected, you will have happy customers.

The bottom line of the above seven points is that you need to be unique and stand out from the crowd. Let the people you deal with know you are a nice person, someone they can trust, and someone with whom they want to do business. Stand out by looking for ways to make life easier for your customer. Also, always be cognizant of the image you are projecting. Work on your "great person" image everywhere you go. Make sure the foot you put forward is one that says you are professional, positive, energetic, trustworthy, friendly, helpful, and different—in a good way—from all the other salespeople.

Chapter 5

Mental Notes

Get Yourself to Do What You *Must* Do

Successful salespeople don't like to do the same things that unsuccessful salespeople don't like to do. The difference is that successful salespeople motivate themselves to do these things while unsuccessful salespeople do not.

If you ask one hundred salespeople how many of them like to cold call, ninety-eight will say they don't and the other two are either lying or crazy. While at times it helps to be crazy in the world of selling, we doubt that any salespeople truly love cold calling. So what can we do to a) get ourselves to do it, b) make it bearable, and c) get ourselves to do it effectively?

To get yourself to do an unpleasant but necessary task it is helpful to use the carrot-and-stick approach (pleasure and pain). The more carrots and sticks you involve, the more effective you will be at altering your behavior in the long term.

Here are some examples of effective "stick" or painful questions you can focus on to help drive you to cold call:

- What will happen to my business if I don't cold call?
- How will that affect my income and my lifestyle?
- What will that do to my self-esteem and my view of myself as a person?
- Can I reach my goals and dreams if I don't cold call?
- What is my manager going to say to me when she realizes I'm not making the cold calls and, in effect, not doing my job?
- If I don't do what I know I need to do in this area, what other obstacles will I face down the road that I will also let stop me?

Here are some examples of "carrot" or pleasure thoughts to change your behavior:

- If I were to increase my cold calls by 20 percent, what would 20 percent more sales and referrals do to my business and my income?

- If I got good at this, it would have a very positive impact on my self-esteem and confidence, and that would flow into other areas of sales and my life.
- I will reward myself with (something that would really motivate you) if I increase my cold calls by 20 percent over the next thirty days.
- Imagine the mental edge I'll have when cold calling is no longer a problem.
- Imagine how much more energy and time I'll have when I stop fighting with myself and procrastinating over cold calling.

These are just a few examples. Take some time to come up with other motivators you can put in the form of statements or questions that will work most effectively for you.

One of the best ways to achieve behavior change is to "step into" the experience and imagine what you will lose and what you may gain. Take an area that you need to improve upon—let's suppose, again, that you really need to do more cold calling. Picture your goals and dreams. Think of those around you who are positively or negatively affected by your success—or lack of success—at work. Now imagine the negative effect that *not* cold calling will have on your business.

- Visualize your business shrinking.
- See yourself going from prosperity and happiness to debt, worry, and despair.
- Imagine your goals and dreams washing away.
- Think about how that will affect those you love.
- Think about what you will be depriving them of—the better lifestyle, better schools, happiness, and prosperity.

Allow yourself to see, feel, smell, taste, and hear exactly what this will be like. The more senses you involve and the more "real" you can make these thoughts, the more effective they will be.

Now do the opposite. Feel the positive effects of cold calling and doing it effectively.

- How will your business improve?
- What will that do for your goals and dreams?

- What will that do for your self-esteem, self-confidence, your feelings about yourself, and your ability to tackle other tasks effectively?

Again, "step into" these feelings as much as possible, involving as many of the senses as you can.

Once you've completed this exercise, realize that simply motivating yourself to cold call and to do it more effectively can help steer you away from the overwhelming pain of failure and drive you toward the tremendous pleasure and rewards of success.

Next, focus on this area for at least the next four weeks until it becomes a habit. During this time, you will get yourself to do more cold calling, get better at doing it, and find ways to make it more enjoyable. In order to achieve this, you'll want to take the following steps:

- Set an achievable goal for the number of cold calls you would like to make daily and weekly.
- Study cold calling. Read books, listen to tapes, talk to other salespeople, and discover as much as you can about cold calling more effectively.
- Every morning, and at times during the day when you need some motivation, repeat the negative and positive "stepping into" process.
- Use affirmations such as, "I am making more cold calls and am getting better at them each day." Say the affirmations with as much feeling and conviction as you can. Say them in the morning upon awakening and in the evening just before bed, and try to say them several times during the day.
- Keep track of how many cold calls you're making daily and weekly.
- Record how many cold calls turn into appointments and how many appointments turn into sales.
- Figure out how much each cold call puts in your pocket. If one sale gives you five hundred dollars and it takes you five presentations to get a sale and ten cold calls to get a lead to present to, then each cold call, whether they say yes or no, is worth $10.00 to you. If you increase cold calls by 20 percent and sales by 20 percent, what will that do to your income?
- Report to someone. In sales, it's good to report to someone with authority such as a sales manager. Let him know what you're trying to accomplish,

and tell that person you will be reporting your numbers to him. In most cases, this person will encourage you and give you more ideas on how you can improve.

- Turn cold calling into a game. How many different ways can you find to have fun with the process? Find another salesperson with whom you have a good relationship and have a contest to see who can make the most calls, get the most leads, etc. You can also partner up with another salesperson and go on cold calls together if you're in face-to-face sales, or block out certain hours of the day when you both cold call.

Once you have worked on a particular area, pick another area and work on it for four weeks. After those four weeks, pick another area. By the end of a year, you will have *significantly strengthened thirteen selling areas*; moreover, you'll see marked improvement in your business, your image, and your overall sales career.

In addition to the steps above, here are three more ideas to ensure your overall success:

- Stay as positive as you can by having positive conversations with yourself. Surround yourself with positive sayings, quotes, and other motivational items. At times when a quick inspirational quote won't do, have a point–counterpoint discussion with yourself. If you find that small, negative voice rising up and it won't be stilled, engage it in conversation. Let it know that you realize things may not be going well at the moment, but you are committed, you have a plan, you believe in yourself, and you *will* succeed!

- Work on your self-image. We all have certain beliefs about ourselves that either limit or empower us. Those beliefs are not always correct, yet we act as though they are. The beliefs that limit you need to be challenged if you are going to make any progress.

    For example, if you have a belief that you do not make good first impressions, cold calling will be a challenge for you, to say the least. Start by questioning that belief. Where did it come from? Obviously, there have been times when you *have* made a good first impression. What did you do at those times, and is it not possible for you to duplicate that behavior more often? After questioning the erroneous belief, decide what you can do to weaken it and replace it with the belief that you can and do make a good first impression. Join a speaking group, ask friends and family for help, and study the subject by reading and listening to information on it.

- Give yourself small rewards for following through and achieving your goals. Whether it's partaking in a favorite activity, or going out to a favorite restaurant, reward yourself for hitting your weekly goals. Also reward yourself with larger items, such as a vacation, for reaching quarterly and annual goals.

Ideas for Maintaining a Positive Attitude

Everyone in life has problems. *Everyone.* The people in life who perform at the highest levels are those who can put their problems aside and do what must be done. Doctors, pilots, news reporters, athletes, and anyone else who has to be "on" at all times in their profession must become experts at putting their problems aside and getting the job done.

Salespeople also fall into this group. You can't be focused on the flat tire you got earlier in the day or the significant other who broke up with you last night. You must be able to put these away for the moment and do your job.

In a successful sales career, you must have a thick mental skin. Not only do you have to handle your personal problems, but you also must deal with many professional problems. A lost sale, an angry customer, a bad installation, or a botched service call on your best customer's equipment—all of these can challenge your attitude. While no one is entirely immune to the effects of negative events, there are a few things you can do to build up your mental immune system. Here they are:

1) **Stay healthy.**

Eat, sleep, and exercise as we've already discussed.

2) **Find ways to keep yourself mentally pumped up.**

Everyone is different, thus different things work for different people. Get some motivational books, tapes, and CDs. Look for stories, movies, and music that inspire you. Make a list of all the tremendous events in your life, all the good things you're thankful for, and all the times you want to remember, and then focus on those good things as much as you can. Relive them in the morning and at night before you go to bed. Really get into living each one. See what you saw, hear what you heard, feel what you felt, smell what you smelled, and taste what you tasted.

Use affirmations such as "I can do it," "I am the best," and "I feel healthy, I feel happy, I feel terrific." Say them with as much enthusiasm and energy as you can muster when you first get up in the morning and whenever you need some enthusiasm during the day.

Keep in mind that you control what happens to you. Remember, Rome was not built in a day and neither was an outstanding life. It is what you strive to become in your life and the difficulty of the obstacles you've had to overcome that will determine how you feel about yourself and what kind of life you'll have. Look for challenges, conquer them, learn from them, and grow. Life is not always a smoothly paved road.

Take time out on occasion to focus on the big picture. Even though most of the time you will need to have short-term vision, remember to take some time to look at the big picture and what you *really* want from life. Also—it can't be said enough— strive to achieve balance in your life.

3) Assign the proper meaning to events.

Probably the best way to make yourself immune to the negatives of life and develop an extremely strong psyche is to adopt beliefs that empower you. See problems as challenges to overcome. What can you learn from each situation? How can you best handle each situation? How might you look at the situation differently? Is it just your negative attitude or is there a *real* problem? If there is a real problem, face it head on and tackle it immediately.

4) Maintain your perspective.

Very few things are matters of life and death. One large sale made or lost will not make or break you. If you lose a big sale, you might have to work harder to recover; however, there are more sales to be made. If you make a big sale, enjoy it but don't rest on your laurels. And *don't take things personally*. A rejection of your offer is not a rejection of you.

5) Be positive yet stay grounded in the real world.

Be cheerful and optimistic, expect the best, but have a plan for when the worst happens—because occasionally it will.

6) **Watch your mental diet and stay away from negatives.**

Your mental diet is just as important as your physical diet—both can have a significant effect on your health and your overall quality of life. You have to watch what goes *into* your brain. The saying for computers, "Garbage in, garbage out," holds true for your brain as well. Let's take a look at what goes into your brain during the day.

- How much television are you watching?
- How much of the local news do you watch?
- Do you read the newspaper every day? If so, how much and which sections?
- What do you listen to when you're in the car?
- Who do you hang out with during the day and what is their general outlook on life? This includes family, friends, and colleagues.
- What kind of environments do you live in? Is your work environment positive or negative? How about your home life and social life? To some degree, your environment is related to the above category, because it's largely the people in each environment who determine its character. It also relates to whether you are growing or stagnant in each area.
- What do your daily thoughts look like? Are your thoughts mostly positive, mostly negative, or somewhere in between?

Here are some suggestions for counteracting the negatives in your life and focusing only on the positives (we mentioned some of these earlier):

- Avoid television except for inspirational stories or movies, sports, and other "good" television. Avoid negative movies, stories, and music.
- Instead of watching the local news, watch the national news or CNN.
- Skip the local newspaper except for the business, weather, and sports sections. To stay abreast of current events, scan the front page. *USA Today* and/or *The Wall Street Journal* are good sources of information.
- Instead of listening to music on the radio, listen to motivational, inspirational, or educational tapes or CDs. Occasionally music is a good break or even a good motivator.

- Be very selective about whom you hang out with—they will have a *major* impact on you. As we mentioned earlier, hang out with positive people. Negative people can prevent any progress.
- Work at a job in which you are growing, or where there is potential for you to grow. Being in a job where you are sitting still or moving backward can have a negative impact on your psyche and your self-image.
- Your thoughts are the one thing over which you have complete control. If you don't like them, change them. Now, we know that is probably much easier said than done, but you'll find that if you work at it, little by little you can develop the habit of having only positive thoughts.

  ➤ Start by focusing on what's good about your life instead of what's bad. If you find yourself dwelling on a bad memory, simply remember a good memory and live that moment instead. Take an inventory of your strengths and what you have going for you.
  ➤ Next, develop and write down your goals if you haven't already.
  ➤ Third, make developing a positive attitude a goal. Absorb anything you can on staying positive from books to tapes and CDs. Shift from negative beliefs and realize that each negative thought takes you further away from your goals while each positive one brings you closer.

- Avoid negative environments. A smoky bar in the bad section of town is probably not the most productive place to be. Use your best judgment.
- Avoid any situation that tends to bring out negative emotions. You will have to attend a wake or funeral from time to time or visit someone in the hospital, and you should. Don't break accepted social rules; just don't torture yourself with situations or places that continually bring you down.
- Watch what and whom you allow into your mind. Do everything you can to let in as much good stuff as possible and do everything you can to keep all negative ideas, people, and thoughts out.

Your attitude and your state of mind are extremely important to your long-term sales success. You will still have good days and bad, but ultimately you control your attitude. Put lots of good things into your mind and surround yourself with the right people. *If you do what you need to do each day with a positive frame of mind, and never give up on your goals and beliefs, you will be successful.*

Chapter 6

Your Best Foot Forward

Before you make any sales calls, you must realize that people will judge you on how you look, your mannerisms and general demeanor, what you present, and what comes out of your mouth. They will also judge you by the car you drive, the clothes you wear, and anything else the senses can pick up. While selling over the phone will save you from being judged on many of these, keep in mind that while it may not be fair, you will be judged on every superficial and non-superficial characteristic imaginable. We don't tell you this to scare you; we tell you this so you can reasonably prepare and put yourself in the best position to sell. The bottom line is that you want to project an image that fits what you are selling. Let's start with the clothes you wear.

Dressing for Success

Often clothes are the first thing people will notice about you. Observe what customers and other salespeople in your industry are wearing and mirror them. You always want to err on the side of overdressing. Your goal should be to be the best dressed but not at a completely different level.

Watch for wrinkles, spots, dirt, tears, etc. in clothing. Also, take care of your clothing. If it says dry clean only, then dry clean only. Hang up suits and other clothes as soon as you take them off at the end of the day. Have four or five different business suits or outfits so you can wear roughly one per day, each day of the week. You will significantly increase the life of your clothing by alternating it. At the absolute least, you'll need two or three.

Keep your shoes polished and well cared for. If you're a woman, you usually have a few different pairs of shoes to match different outfits. Like clothing, try not to wear one pair too often. Men should make it a point to have at least two pairs of shoes that they alternate—one pair one day, the other pair the next.

Have shoes and clothing you can wear when it is raining or snowing or you're in other kinds of inclement weather. You should have a "bad weather" business outfit. Keep in mind when you're shopping that your bad weather business outfit should be the same outfit you would wear on a good day, just a slight step down in quality. In your car, keep a good pair of boots, gloves, a hat, and other protective clothing such as a raincoat, heavy winter coat, and anything else that will protect you from the elements should your car break down or you find yourself stuck somewhere in bad weather. Obviously some of these items will vary based upon the climate in your particular area of the country.

Wear different "uniforms" when doing different parts of your job. For example, if you sell office equipment your standard outfit may be a suit and tie or business suit, but if you go to a construction site to meet with a general contractor you may want to wear Dockers and a golf shirt if you're a man, or slacks and a sweater if you're a woman. Not only is a construction site tough on business clothes, but you'll also find that most contractors will relate to you better if you're dressed down a little.

Finally, dress in appropriate colors and refrain from gaudy jewelry. If you wear other clothing accessories such as cufflinks, be sure they are tasteful and subtle. Use your best judgment.

The objective with clothing is the same as your physical appearance: look clean, crisp, fresh, and professional.

Physical Grooming

With regard to physical grooming, deodorant, cologne, or perfume (although not too much), bathing regularly, and taking care of yourself properly should do the trick. Clean clothing will also help to defer any unwanted odors. If you work out at lunch, a shower and good cleaning will work. Make sure hair is neat and clean. Men, if you have any facial hair, keep it properly maintained.

Breath is probably one of the most overlooked areas. Proper dental hygiene and using mouthwash or breath mints after you eat should take care of most breath issues.

If you can, brush your teeth and use mouthwash after each meal. If you can't, strong breath mints, or the like, are the next best thing. You should make it a point *always* to have some good breath mints with you. If you can't brush and don't have breath mints, simply don't get too close to anyone. If you're comfortable with your associates or customers, you might tell them you just ate so you don't want to kill them with your breath. This will sometimes suffice in a pinch, and usually get a bit of a chuckle.

Another way to attack bad breath is by preventing it to begin with. Coffee, alcohol, dairy products, garlic, and several other foods create a thriving atmosphere for bad breath. Garlic is probably the worst culprit, as it tends to stick around for more than one day. Try to avoid anything with garlic during the workweek.

A Final Thought on Grooming

When it comes to physical grooming, err on the side of caution. If you've just come from the gym and aren't sure whether to take a shower or skip it, take one. If you think your breath is okay, but there's some question, pop a breath mint. You don't need to be a fanatic but you do want to know you aren't going to offend anyone. Even a little mistake in this area will usually be unpleasantly remembered.

Finally, try to get a look in the mirror every few hours during the day to make sure everything is still in place and you're still looking clean and crisp.

Other Things That Can Affect Your "Appearance"

Your Handshake

Your handshake gives people a definite impression of you. A firm handshake will make you appear confident and self-assured, while a weak handshake can undermine any confidence you may have. A weak handshake may leave people with the impression that your character is weak and ineffectual, causing people to hesitate to do business with you. While a firm handshake is the objective, you don't want it to be bone-crushing. It should be firm but not overwhelming.

Your hand should be warm and dry. In cold weather, wear gloves and keep your right hand in your pocket to keep it as warm as possible. If you have sweaty hands, hold the palm side of your hand on your clothing before shaking someone's hand. This is much more subtle than wiping your hand on your clothing.

When you approach to shake hands, look at the other person's hand briefly. Aim the crux of your thumb and index finger—the bottom area where both fingers come together—at the same spot on the other person's hand. No one likes having the ends of their fingers grabbed, as you've likely had happen in the past. Once the crux of your fingers hits theirs, grab hold and shake firmly. Look the person in the eye and smile while shaking hands.

You may have heard of some gimmicks to use while shaking someone's hand. Probably the most popular in recent years is turning the person's hand so that your hand is on top. The theory suggests that the person whose hand is on top is in control.

First, if the person doesn't like you to begin with, it doesn't matter whose hand is on top. Second, if you come across someone who is conscious of what they're doing, you'll either make a bad impression instantly, or the two of you will start arm wrestling. Leave the gimmicks to the unprofessional salespeople.

The last rules regarding handshaking concern physically challenged individuals. If you come across someone who is unable to shake hands with their right hand for any reason, shaking the left hand is fine. If he or she is unable to shake hands at all, touching on the arm is appropriate. If for some reason you cannot touch the person's arms, then a touch on the shoulder is also appropriate.

Eye Contact

Eye contact builds trust and credibility and a lack of it will destroy the chances for either. The best way to convey strong points, such as closing questions, is to look the prospect directly in the eye while making your statement. Don't glance away at all, and minimize blinking.

The general rule is to look the other person in the eye as much as possible. At the very least, look the other person in the eye the entire time he is talking. If you look elsewhere at any time in the conversation, do it while you are talking. Even then, keep straying eyes to a minimum. The only time you want to break eye contact is when the other person draws your attention to something else, or vice versa. As much direct eye contact as possible during a conversation will help build all the positive feelings you're looking for.

Focus on only the left eye when talking to people. Most people look back and forth from one eye to the other and this tendency can give people the impression you are "shifty-eyed." As a result, you want to look in only one eye. Looking into the left eye seems to get the best results. Why? Have you ever had an instantaneous connection with a person you just met? That connection occurred in the in the right side of the brain, which is the creative and emotional side of the brain. The left eye is controlled by the right brain. Will you always have instantaneous connections by looking in the left eye? No, however, you will have more of them and you will completely eliminate the "shifty-eyed" feeling some people will leave with after having a conversation with you. And no, no one will be able to tell you're looking only in their left eye.

Eye Contact in Other Specific Situations

If you're talking to someone with a "lazy" eye and are having difficulty discerning which eye is focusing properly, look at the bridge of the person's nose. It will appear to him as if you are looking him in the eye.

When someone is signing a contract, *don't* look directly at him. Shift your focus somewhere else so the person does not feel as if he is under a microscope. Some people get nervous when they know someone is watching them sign a contract. Your best bet is to glance through your appointment book or some other paperwork while the signing is taking place.

When you are an observer in a conversation in which three or more people, including yourself, are present, your primary focus should be on the person who is speaking and your secondary focus on the person or people to whom he is talking.

Finally, the eyes are the most important body language indicator. To find out exactly where you're at in the selling process, look to the eyes for an indication.

General Business Etiquette

Most business etiquette is common sense. The following are simply some finer points:

- Don't sit down until the customer or prospect is seated.
- Never assume anything, and always give the customer or prospect a chance to save face.
- Always be polite and take the high road. If someone tells you that you didn't get the business, smile, find out why, thank the person for his or her time, make sure the door is open for the next opportunity, and exit courteously.
- Extend common courtesy to everyone you encounter. This includes all people at the company you're calling on, not just the person you're there to see. In addition, be polite to the competition, people you pass on the street, and even the in-laws you don't particularly like. You don't have to ask for the person's life story or go overboard—just be pleasant and professional.
- Always allow the customer or prospect to decide where you're going to eat unless she is visiting your home turf and asks you to choose. At that

- If you have someone else from your company with you, always let the customer or prospect sit in the front seat of the car, unless he begs you to sit in back.
- *Always* pick up the check.
- Know the rules of any game you're going to play with a customer or prospect. Walking across someone's putting line in golf can really tick some people off.
- Don't be overly competitive and allow the customer to win if possible.
- Make sure you're at least of average skill before you try bonding over any kind of game.
- Never argue with the customer or prospect.

How to Act in Social Situations

Here are some general rules for how to act in social situations:

- Don't drink too much.
- Be selective about whom you hang out with.
- Watch what you do and how you act.
- Watch what you say. Don't say anything you don't want someone to hear. For the most part, you want to avoid any topics related to sex, religion, and politics unless you know your customer *extremely* well. Read more about this in Chapter 9's section: Topics of Discussion to Avoid.
- Be sociable.
- If you're unsure of what to wear, it's always better to overdress. You can always remove your suit jacket, tie, scarf, or other "dressy" item.

Items You Present to the Prospect or Customer

Brochures, proposals, business cards, gifts, and other items you present to your prospects and customers speak volumes about you, your company, and your product. These materials may not make or break the sale, but they can dramatically affect your image.

Here is a checklist to follow in preparing materials to present to your prospects:

- Brochure pictures and the brochure itself should be in color and professionally printed.
- Make sure all spelling and grammar is correct.
- Make sure you have the prospect's name and title correct.
- Proposals should be thorough but not overwhelming. If you are answering a request for proposal (RFP), follow the instructions completely.
- Make sure all gift items are clean, brochures and proposals are not wrinkled or soiled, and written information is clear, concise, and professional.

Don't skimp on business cards. Here are some quick rules:

- Get your cards printed by a professional, not on your home computer.
- Use raised print.
- Use color.
- Add your picture to your business card.
- Add distinguished honors, club memberships, etc., to your business card.
- If you are a member of the 100 Percent Club, the Inner Circle, or any other specially recognized group within your industry, have these printed on your card.
- If you would like to present an image that's out of the ordinary and a "cut above," try:
  - ➢ A card that is twice as thick as a standard business card.
  - ➢ A larger card than usual.
  - ➢ A shape other than rectangular.
  - ➢ A magnetic business card.
  - ➢ A folded card with details inside.

Use good judgment with your business card design. If you're selling to conservative bankers, you don't want hot pink business cards. At the same time, if you're in the flower business, a scented and colorful card might be just the ticket.

The Pen You Use

Have a high-quality pen and make sure it works. Also, have a backup pen. By high quality, we mean a Cross pen or something similar.

Note 1: Many businesses give out company pens. If you have a good-quality pen from the company you're calling upon, bring the pen with you and use it while you're on the call.

Note 2: All the pens you use should have black or blue ink unless you have a great reason related to your business that dictates another color.

The Car You Drive

If you have a company car, you can disregard this part, but it's still a dynamic that's nice to be aware of.

The car you drive will project a certain image. You can really impress people with a car, you can turn people off with a car, and you can make people jealous with a car. Some potential customers will decide you make too much money or perhaps not enough money based solely upon what kind of vehicle you drive.

When selecting a car, your objective is to drive a business car that is appropriate for what you are selling and one that puts you in a position where you are least likely to be judged negatively. A fire-engine red 700 Series BMW may not be the best car for calling on conservative banks, yet it would be appropriate for calling on dentists, doctors, or lawyers. A Ford Taurus may not be the best car to drive if you're selling yachts or Lear jets, but it is fine if you're selling office products. If you sell Cadillacs, you'd better be driving one.

Look at what your customers and other salespeople in your industry drive. Also, think of the demands you will be putting on a vehicle.

Keep your car as clean as possible, inside and out. Fuzzy dice and other idiosyncrasies may help you stand out, but the odds of making a bad impression are too great. There aren't too many bumper stickers we'd recommend either, especially political or religious ones.

Keep the car smelling good. You don't need to hang an air freshener from your mirror; typically a spray of cologne, perfume, or air freshener in a spray bottle works fine.

Use your best judgment and err on the conservative side if you add any little trinkets, unless, of course, you're selling fuzzy dice or car air fresheners.

One more note: out-of-state license plates can be a potential red flag. While a New Hampshire license plate in Massachusetts isn't bad, a Georgia plate may be. Make sure the out-of-state plates are appropriate or that you have an appropriate answer for why you have them.

Your Actions at the Customer's Facility

All the World's a Stage

Your approach to a sales call begins in the prospect's parking lot, sometimes even before. We know of one person who was cut off in traffic and gave the other driver a "not so nice" gesture. The driver proceeded to follow him into the parking lot of the company he was calling on. The salesperson was horrified to discover it was the CEO's secretary. Not good.

When you get out of your car, you never know who can see you from which window or who is in the parking lot with you. You must act as if you have a TV camera and open microphone focused on you at all times. We all know of situations where people have said something inappropriate, not realizing that others were listening. Watch what you say about the competition and other people anytime you are in public. It is indeed a small world—as many of us have learned the hard way.

Where You Park Your Car

Do not park up front in the prime parking spots. These are reserved for customers and sometimes upper-level management. Heaven forbid you should park in the President's parking spot. And don't laugh—it happened to someone we know. Again, not good. You should park in spots at the back of the lot or spots that are the farthest from the facility.

Watch What You Bring into a Customer's Facility

Never walk into a customer's facility with a competitive product that is sold on the premises. If your customer happens to be a furniture store that also has a shop where they sell coffee, soda, and snacks, don't walk in with your own coffee, soda, or snacks—buy them there. This may require some research.

A Summary of Ideas on Building the Foundation

- Selling is a tremendous industry in which your earning potential is virtually unlimited. You control your destiny.

- Top salespeople have a great attitude, a sincere interest in other people, and a burning desire to succeed. They truly enjoy being of service to other people. Their primary focus is on what is right for the prospect or customer. They are up front and honest about how they can or perhaps can't help.

- Emulate the words, techniques, thoughts, feelings, and actions of top salespeople, and you will become a top salesperson.

- One of the most critical keys to selling is having the prospect or client like and trust you.

- Learn as much as you can about selling, your industry, and the people you sell to.

- Stay healthy mentally, physically, and spiritually, and keep your life balanced in all areas.

- Work to improve yourself daily.

- Work smart *and* hard. In the beginning of your sales career, you must work hard until you figure things out. Make a decision to work harder than anyone else.

- Surround yourself with the right people.

- Always have a plan and a contingency plan.

- Take complete responsibility for your life and your selling career.

- Under-promise and over-deliver. Go the extra mile for customers.

- Be the best you can be, and be different. Set yourself apart from other salespeople.

- Work on keeping your attitude positive. Watch what you put into your brain. Maximize the amount of good, positive information going in, and minimize the amount of negative information.

- Make sure your clothes, appearance, grooming, car, and everything else about you projects the proper professional image.

- Always put the customer first.

- Always watch how you act and what you say in social situations.

- Finally, be persistent and never stop believing in yourself. If selling were easy, everyone would be doing it and making great amounts of money. If you remain positive, continue to learn, and refuse to be beaten, *you will be successful.*

SECTION II

COLD CALLING

Chapter 7

Getting Ready to Cold Call

Two words—*cold call*—make most salespeople shudder. Cold calling is one of the most time-consuming and difficult tasks in selling. It requires the most mental energy and can be psychologically draining. Cold calling is the one area in sales where you are guaranteed to encounter rejection.

Take comfort in knowing you are not alone. The top salespeople in your business started out at ground zero. There may have been a few exceptions, but they were just that—exceptions. When they started, the majority had nothing more than you did, and so they simply did what had to be done—they cold called prospects.

Note: In this chapter most references will be to face-to-face cold calling. We will be discussing the intricacies of telephone cold calling in the section on telemarketing.

Getting Mentally Prepared to Cold Call

Here are some ideas for getting ready to cold call:

1) Be prepared.

Know your cold call, have all materials with you, and be ready for anything to happen. The more prepared you are, the more confident you will be.

2) Accept the nerves.

Being nervous is normal. Accept it as part of being human and as part of the cold-calling landscape.

3) Don't take the rejection personally.

People aren't rejecting you; they're rejecting your offer. If someone does not want what you are selling, the reason has to do with that person, not with you. For all you know, the person's pet dog may have just died, and he is in no mood to talk to anyone at the moment.

4) What's the worst that can happen?

No one ever died from making sales calls. Who cares if someone says no, is rude to you for five seconds, or otherwise rejects your offer? The worst thing that can happen is that you'll have to call on someone else.

5) Rejection is part of the cold-calling territory.

If you're cold calling, you will run into rejection from time to time no matter how good you and your product are.

6) One lead, or lack thereof, will not make or break you.

There are plenty of people to call on and there will be plenty of opportunities to present your product and get many yes's.

7) Before the call you're at Ground Zero.

You started with nothing, so if you end up with nothing, you're no worse off than you were before the call.

8) Each call you make brings you closer to a sale.

Every call you make, even if you get a negative response, is worth something—the law of averages brings you that much closer to a sale. Figure out how much each call is worth by calculating roughly how many calls you have to make in order to get a sale and then divide the dollar amount of the sale by the number of calls.

If it takes ten calls to get a lead and ten leads to get a sale, it then takes a hundred calls to get a sale. If each sale is worth $1,000 to you, then each call is worth $10 even if the person says no. If you can see that "no" as a stepping-stone to a sale, it will take on a much different aspect than seeing it as rejection.

9) Each call brings you closer to your goals and dreams.

This is related to the above point. Think of the things that really inspire you—perhaps time with family and friends, or material things such as cars, boats, planes, trips, real estate—and realize that each call gets you closer to enjoying them.

10) View cold calling as a character- and strength-builder.

View yourself as someone strong and capable of doing what most salespeople won't. View cold calling as a game. Again, it's not life or death; it is simply a game you are partaking in. How many calls can you make? Can you beat what you did yesterday? Can you get one more lead, one more yes, before you knock off for the day?

11) The more cold calling you do, the easier it will become.

Do the thing you fear enough, and the death of fear is certain. Just like anything else, after a while you'll get used to it.

Top salespeople make as much or more money than the best lawyers, doctors, and top executives. If selling were always easy, everyone would be doing it. Pay your dues. Keep getting up and pushing forward, even when you think you can't. Very few worthwhile things in life come without a great deal of hard work and an equal measure of intestinal fortitude.

Gather Information on Your Prospects

If you have a limited number of prospects to call on, you simply *must* make the cold call count. In this case, it is a good idea to gather some information on your prospects so you know precisely whom you're calling upon before you arrive.

Here are some ideas on information gathering:

- Go to the prospect's company website. Read their mission statement, learn about their goals and objectives, ascertain their financial situation, and look for areas where they could benefit from your product or service.

- Read their annual report and absorb as much information as you can.

- Search newspapers for articles, advertising, and other information.

- Do a search via the Internet for articles and other items related to the company. Also, if you type a company's name into a Google search, followed by the word "scam," you can often discover if a company has been involved in any recent scandals. (Just don't put quotation marks around the phrase.)

- Ask people with whom you are already doing business in that industry what they know about the company, or if they know any important individuals within that organization. Ask them to refer you to those people.

- Ask around. Find any colleagues or other business partners who have had any contact with the company.

Following are some ideas regarding gathering information on individuals:

- Do a Google search on the Internet using the person's name.

- Check out the *Who's Who* directory in their area and see if the person is listed.

- Research school directories. If you know where the person went to school or college, you may be able to get a yearbook at the school or local library.

- Do a search on the local newspaper's website. Again, use the person's name.

- Ask other people at companies you are doing business with if they know the prospect personally, or know anything about him or her. Ask if you may you drop their name.

The more information you have and the more homework you do, the better position you'll be in to make a positive impression on the cold call. Once you've tracked down some good information, it's important to drop pieces of it—let the person you're cold calling know you've done your homework. Use phrases such as: "As I noticed in your annual report...," "I was reading in (whatever the name of the newspaper was) that you are...," and so on.

Most salespeople don't do this groundwork ahead of time. If you do, it will set you apart from the rest of the sales crowd and give you a far greater advantage.

Your Sales Tool Kit

Every business has certain tools of the trade. For example, to service the banking industry we needed literature about our equipment, maps of our territory, a to-scale ruler to measure architectural drawings, a tape measure, and lithographs of all our equipment.

In addition to the tools of your particular trade, you also need the tools of a salesperson, such as plenty of contracts and other paperwork, an extra pen that works, your computer, a calculator, and other items needed to present your ideas and execute contracts. If you're on the road, you also need a map or GPS, some money, credit cards, AAA, and a cell phone.

Make a list of the items you need to do business, and check it before you start your day. The key is to be prepared for *anything*.

In addition to having everything you need for your cold calls, you also need to be able to react to the hot prospect who is ready for the presentation and the sale *now*. If the prospect asks to see what you have, a comeback such as, "Well, actually, I was only planning to drop off some information today" will kill you. Or, just as bad, "Well, I'd like to do my presentation, but I don't have my material and contracts with me." You have to be able to shift gears quickly if a cold call turns into a presentation. If you're in sales long enough, it *will* eventually happen.

Have price sheets, contracts, computer demos, and other presentation support materials in your car in case you need them. Finally, make sure you look your best and have your best lines ready.

To summarize, have *everything* you could possibly need for *any* selling situation. If your presentations require equipment that you don't typically carry with you, set up a follow-up presentation appointment for the earliest available time, even later that day, if possible.

Sales Materials to Carry into a Cold Call

When making a cold call, the best approach is to carry your company's annual report, customer testimonials, and literature outlining your unique products and your unique advantages in the marketplace. On your cold call, you don't want to have anything that goes into too much depth. You want basic information that will pique the prospects' interest and leave them wanting more.

You can carry this information either in an unassuming 8 ½ x 11-inch brown envelope or a leather carrying case.

Your Goals and Objectives

You need to determine your goals and objectives regarding cold calling. Namely, how many calls do you plan to make, how many leads do you want to get, and what are you trying to accomplish with your call?

First, how many calls do you want to make? How many calls you will make depends upon the logistics of your sales territory. For example, if you are selling office products door to door and you have many companies in a small geographic area, your goal may be twenty, thirty, or even more cold calls per day. If you are selling a product only to manufacturing plants that are twenty to forty miles from one another, you may be able to fit in only three to five calls a day.

When setting a goal for the number of cold calls, err on the high side. You will need to do some research to get an idea of what is typical for your industry, and then add to that number. For example, if ten cold calls a day is a decent number based upon demographics, geography, and what the typical salesperson is capable of, make your goal twelve. If the typical number is three, make your goal four.

If you are a new salesperson at a new company, most of your "call" time will probably be devoted to cold calling. As a result, you should be making far more cold calls than the average sales rep who is busy with all other aspects of the business. Again, your goal should be to make more calls than anyone else.

Next, how many leads are you looking to get? Are you looking for five leads out of every ten people you talk with? Two out of ten? One out of ten? Again, your goal will depend upon what you are selling and what the industry averages are for your product or service.

Find out the average number of leads the top salespeople are getting and work to achieve that number. Eventually your goal will be to surpass it, but set your initial "leads" goal at the average of the top producers. If you hear numbers between two and three out of ten, set your goal at three.

If the top producers no longer cold call, discover what numbers they were at just before they stopped cold calling. In addition, find out what they do now to bring in new business, and see if there are any ideas you can work into your own search for new prospects.

Now that you have set your goals, what about the objective of your cold call? Is your objective to set up an appointment, and then return at another time and do a full-blown presentation? Is it simply to drop off information and get the name of the key decision-maker, or is it just to find out if there is any interest at all? And, if there is interest, are you prepared to go for a sale right then and there?

Planning the Logistics of Your Day

Whom you're going to call on and where you're going to call are two more items that relate to your goals and objectives. When deciding where you are going to make your calls, you want to do some planning ahead to make things as easy on yourself as possible.

Make the most of your time. Group your calls together based upon geographic location and minimize criss-crossing your territory. For example, if you are calling on four prospects in the western part of your territory and you come in from the east, on your way you can call on two in the east, then call on the four in the west, and finally catch another two in the east on your way home. Also, if you have an appointment in the east on Tuesday, and another account in the east calls to set up an appointment with you, ask if she can meet you on Tuesday as you'll already be out that way. You can also make some cold calls in the east.

As you set up your day, keep grouping in mind; it will save you much time, effort, and energy—not to mention gas.

If you have a large territory and you have to travel a great distance to make a cold call, it is a good idea to phone first and try to schedule an appointment. That's better than arriving unannounced, only to discover the prospect is not there.

The time of day you make your cold calls can also be important. What is the best time of day for your industry?   For example, if you are calling on retail establishments, you can bet they won't be too busy late Monday mornings or early Monday afternoons. On the other hand, Friday afternoons (usually a good time to cold call other types of businesses) or Saturdays will likely be very busy times when cold calling should be avoided.

Note: Be careful about assumptions you make when you cold call. For example, if you get to a location at 12:05 p.m., don't just assume the person will be at lunch. Also, remember that if you are just starting out and primarily making cold calls, your objective is to get as many cold calls in as possible, regardless of when it's "best" to catch people. Simply keep the logistics of "timing" in the back of your mind when planning your day.

Whom Are You Calling On?

Now that you have your day planned, it's a good idea to know whom you'll be calling on at each company. Obviously, this will depend upon your product or service. In servicing the banking industry, we typically wanted to talk to the President and/or the Chief Operations Officer of a bank or credit union. We had a directory that listed all the financial institutions in our territory, along with the names of the executives. Consequently, we knew who to ask for when we walked in. And we always made sure to have two names—if the President wasn't available, we could ask for the Chief Operations Officer. This leads to three important points:

1) You're in a better position when you have at least two people you can ask for.

Obviously your "hit" rate will be better, and it's unlikely that both key decision-makers will be gone at the same time.

2) Always start at the top.

When you cold call any organization, you're always better off starting at the top of the executive level and working your way down to the right person, rather than doing it the other way around. Clearly, in smaller companies it's easier to gain access to the top person than it is in larger companies; still, you should initially aim as high as possible.

If you start with the President and he tells you to talk to the Chief Operations Officer, you can use that on your call to the Chief Operations Officer. For example, when calling on the COO, you would open your call with something like: "Hello, this is Bob Chapin. I was just speaking with Mr. (President's last name) and he told me to give you a call."

That's a wonderful opening, one that will undoubtedly get you the COO's attention. And if you have to go over this person's head in the future, you will have already made contact with the person higher up the ladder.

3) Make sure the person(s) you're calling on still works there.

Even when you have a current directory, you want to check the names you'll be cold calling before you show up.

Here's the scenario: You're getting ready to do some cold calling. You pull out your directory—maybe it's current, or maybe it's a year or so old. You look up the names of the CEO and the top operations person at several locations you want to hit and you head out to do some cold calling. You get to the first stop, greet the receptionist, ask for the person you had listed as CEO, and then you hear, "Oh, I'm sorry, he hasn't been here for a year and a half."

How can you avoid this embarrassment? Pick up the phone, call the main number, and when the receptionist answers the phone, say, "Hello. I'm sending a letter to Mr. (whatever the name is) and I was wondering…is his official title CEO, or President and CEO?"

If the person is no longer there you'll find out now, not when you show up. If they say he's no longer there, you simply say, "Really? Wow, I guess it's been a while since I've been down there. Who took his place?"

They'll usually tell you. If they ask who this is and why you're calling, tell them. Say, "This is Bob Chapin with ABC Company and I just wanted to send some very pertinent industry information."

If they still won't give you the information, use one of the other techniques on the next page, where we discuss how to find out the name of the person you need to cold call.

Name Pronunciation

Occasionally, as you are reviewing the names of the people you want to cold call, you will come across a name or two that you don't know how to pronounce. In this case, call the company and get the proper pronunciation before you arrive. The best approach is to call the company's main number and say, "Hello. I have a message here and I'm having trouble reading the handwriting. The name on the message looks like (you then begin to spell the name you're having trouble with) Mr. P-E-R-F something or other."

Invariably, the receptionist will say the person's full name. Repeat it back, and then say, "And how do you spell that?" (Even though you have it right in front of you.) Once they spell it, you can ask them to pronounce it again if you still don't have it completely down.

If you now believe you've caught the pronunciation correctly, say the name back again just to make sure you have it correct. Next, make your own phonetic spelling of the name so you know how to pronounce it when you cold call. If they ask if you would like to be connected but your intention is to stop by and cold call in person, you can say, "No, I'm just sending out some information, but wanted to be sure I was sending it to the right person."

Note: Do not show up and attempt a name you're unsure of because nine times out of ten, you'll get it wrong.

How to Discover the Name of the Person You Need to Cold Call

Let's say your product or service requires you to call on the Chief Information Officer of each company, but you don't know any of their names. Do not just show up on a cold call and ask to speak with the Chief Information Officer, but rather call ahead and get the person's name. Here are a few approaches:

1) The "note" approach.

This is the best way to get someone's name, and similar to the name pronunciation technique. With this approach, call and say, "Hello. This is (your name) at (your company's name) and I have a note here to send some information to the CIO. Frankly, though, I'm a little embarrassed because I can't read the handwriting here. Um, what is your CIO's name?"

Once the person gives you the name, say, "Oh, okay, now it makes sense. Could you spell that for me?"

Once you get the person's name and the correct spelling, say, "Okay, thank you very much for your help. Have a nice day."

This approach will work most of the time. The person answering the phone may ask for your name or company. If this happens, that's fine—give him or her your name and company's name. At this point, some sales books will tell you to answer the question, and then ask for the name again—something to the effect of, "Yes, this is Bob Chapin. And how do I spell that name again?"

We *don't* recommend that approach. We recommend that you give *only* the information asked for and then be quiet. You want to tread softly and give the person on the other end of the phone the impression that you are absolutely no threat. When you start answering questions with more questions, it becomes a game that the person on the other end of the phone is often more than happy to play.

If you're asked more than one question, you can follow your second answer with a question but, again, don't do this after the first question. Here is an example:

Receptionist: And who is this?
You: Oh, this is (your name).
Receptionist: And who are you with?
You: I'm with (the name of your company). So how do I spell the name?

It's important to watch your tone when answering questions and giving answers. You don't want to sound as if you're getting frustrated or annoyed, even though you may be. Your side of the conversation should be as pleasant as possible.

2) The "send a letter" approach.

The second-best way to get someone's name is with the "send a letter" approach. With this approach, call and say, "Hello. This is (your name) at (your company's name), and I'm sending a letter over to your (whatever position, in this case the CIO). Could you spell that person's name for me?"

Again, once you have the name, thank the person for his or her time and hang up.

3) The direct approach.

With the direct approach, simply call and ask to speak with the person in the position you're looking for. For example, in this case you would say, "Hello. This is (your name) with (your company's name). Could I speak with your (the position you're looking for, in this case the CIO) please?"

If the person on the other end of the phone says, "Sure," jump in quickly before you're transferred and say, "Oh, and could you give me that person's name, please?"

It should be obvious that this approach will result in a low contact rate in almost all cases. This is about the equivalent of someone cold calling you at home and saying, "Hello. Could I speak with the homeowner, please?" It's an immediate tip-off that you have had no previous contact with this person and that you are calling to sell something. That combination will squash you 95 percent of the time or more.

4) The research approach.

A fourth approach is to look up the names of the people you want to call. This could include looking through annual reports or gathering company information at the library or online. This is unquestionably a time-consuming approach. However, you could look up this information during off-hours in the evenings or on weekends.

Alternatively, you could hire someone to do it for you. You need to evaluate this idea by how much time is involved and what the ultimate payoff will be.

Note: With this approach, you also need to call the companies to make sure the names you have are current. And if you plan to hire someone to look up names, you could also have that person make the phone calls to verify that the names are still good.

What If You Don't Know the Name or Title of the Person with Whom You Should Talk?

If you sell computer software solutions, you're clearly looking for the person in the organization who purchases computer software, even though you may not know the title of that person. In this case, following are various telephone approaches you can use before you hit the road.

1) The "letter" approach.

In this approach, simply call and say you are sending a letter to the person who makes decisions on whatever you sell, and you are wondering who should receive the letter. You then visit later in the day and ask for the person by name. The initial call would go something like this: "Hello. This is (your name) at (your company) and I'm planning to send out some information on (whatever you sell). Whom should I send that to?" Once the receptionist gives you a name, get the person's title. Next, ask if that person is the one who makes the purchasing decisions on the product or service you are selling.

2) Ask for the sales department.

The sales department can be a very helpful place. Salespeople tend to be a little more sympathetic toward other salespeople than receptionists are. Simply call the company and ask for someone in sales. When you've been connected, say, "Hello. This is (your name) with (your company) and I have information I'm sending out on (whatever you sell). Could you tell me who at your company makes purchasing decisions on (whatever you sell)?"

If there is no sales department, or if the sales department is unable to help you, you can ask for any other department. Purchasing would be a good one, but you can also talk to accounting, accounts receivable, or again, any other department. The mailroom is another place to try at large companies.

3) The direct approach.

This is the same as approach #3 where you didn't know the name of the person. Call and ask who makes purchasing decisions on what you sell and then ask to speak with him or her on the same call. Say, "Hello. This is (your name) with (your company). May I speak with the person who makes purchasing decisions on (whatever your product is), please?"

If the person on the other end of the phone says "Sure," jump in quickly before you're transferred and say, "Oh, and could you give me that person's name, please?"

Again, the success rate with this approach isn't great.

4) Look up the information.

If you have a general idea of whom you should be talking with at the company, you can look the information up. For example, let's suppose you usually talk to someone in the Controller's position, but you don't know if the company you're calling has a Controller. Find company listings either at the library, online, or somewhere else, and look for the name of the Controller, or someone in a similar position. Remember that once you get the names, verify them by phone before you stop by. Again, the downside to this approach is that it can be time consuming.

Sources of Names and Calling Lists

If you are not assigned to specific accounts or are not targeting a specific group such as all bank Chief Operations Officers in Massachusetts, you're going to need some lists of names and numbers of people to call. But what lists are out there and how can you get them?

There are many different sources for lists. As a general rule, the easier a list is to get, the more people will be calling it. You can run down to the library and get the latest *Contacts Influential*, which lists businesses, names of the owners, and contact numbers. However, chances are everyone and their brothers and sisters are already calling this list. The best approach is to have unique lists that no one else has access to. The question is: How do you get unique lists, or at least lists that everyone else isn't using? The answer? You have to do some work and use your imagination.

Here are a few sources:

1) Referrals.

You should *always* be asking for referrals. Referrals will be your best list because they come from trusted friends and family members who are using your product or service, and many times they come pre-qualified. We will talk about getting referrals and how to deal with them in Chapter 38 in the section titled After the Close.

Note: Once you have customers and you are looking for new ones, it is helpful to look at the characteristics of your best customers and find other prospects like them. Where do they work? Where do they live? What groups do they belong to? Can you join these groups? Can you give a seminar where they work? Can you call on other people in their neighborhood who might be looking for your product or service? Birds of a feather *do* flock together. Your best customers are probably flocking with your future best customers.

2) School directories.

These include alumni directories from your high school or college. Don't be afraid to use directories from the high schools and colleges of friends and family members. You can target people by geographic area or by profession, whichever suits your needs. If using your high school or college directory, don't hesitate to mention that to build some rapport. If you are using the directories of friends and family, you can still use that piece of information to your advantage even though you did not personally attend the school.

3) Associations, clubs, and other group directories.

These are a great source of people to call. Do you belong to any groups or associations? How about a car club? What groups could you join? Sometimes you don't even need to have any particular association with the club in order to join. Join the club and then obtain the membership directory. What associations or groups contain the people whom you are trying to target? Do your friends or family members belong to any clubs or groups?

4) Street directories.

The *Hill Donnelly Directory* and the *Cole Directory* both rank streets from most affluent to least affluent and are your best residential lists. You can usually find these directories at the local library, or you can invest in them yourself or ask your company to purchase them. If you are an investment advisor, you probably want to call the most affluent neighborhoods. If your product has more mass appeal, you can call the other areas. Again, it will depend upon your product and target market. If the affluence of the person you're calling doesn't matter, use the phone book instead.

5) Houses and neighborhoods.

If income levels do matter in the potential purchase of your product or service, you can drive through town in search of the best prospects. Check out the houses in the various neighborhoods. Once you find the streets with the most promising prospects, you can refer to the street directories we mentioned above. Do a mailing to the addresses without phone numbers.

6) Company directories.

Company directories can be great lists for cold calling because very few salespeople can get their hands on them; thus, very few salespeople will be calling them. Do you know anyone who works at a particular company? Can he or she get you a directory?

7) List brokers.

List brokers can be a decent source of names and numbers to call; however, you need to get a good broker. There are several reputable firms. Go on the Internet and do a search under "list brokers."

How do you know you've found a good list broker? Check with the Better Business Bureau and the Attorney General's office, and ask for references. These sources will weed out the *really* bad ones. To find the good brokers out of the ones remaining, you'll need to put them to the test. Pick out a few that seem reliable and order a minimal amount of names and numbers to see how things work out. How many leads do you get and how good are they?

Occasionally list brokers will feed you a good "first" list to entice you to buy more. The best way to deal with list brokers is to tell them you want to test them out with a small list. If the first list does well and you'd like to buy more, buy once again in small numbers. Continue telling them that as long as they continue to provide good lists, you'll be back for more. Many will try to get you to buy in a very large quantity by offering discounts and other incentives. You can slightly increase your orders, but don't buy excessively after one or two sample lists that have worked out well. You want to keep the list brokers honest by buying a little at a time. If you develop a long-term, solid relationship with a list broker and he or she treats you right, you can eventually step up and buy some larger quantities. Buy small and build slowly. Judge the broker only according to the most recent list you receive.

8) The Yellow Pages.

The *Yellow Pages* is a source of names and numbers, but not a unique one.

9) Business cards.

Business cards are another good source of leads. Ask upscale restaurants if you can place a fishbowl for business cards at the check-in area and give away a free dinner. Place a sign on the fishbowl that reads: "Drop in your card to win a free dinner." Then pick up the cards at the end of the month. Draw a card and give away a free dinner each time you pick cards up.

10) Here are some other sources for lists:

- Court records
- Other public records
- Magazines
- Books
- The Internet
- Guest directories
- The local newspaper. Who bought a house recently? Who just won the lottery? Who just won a court case? Which companies are adding personnel?

11) Finally, use your imagination.

There is an endless supply of lists and people to call. The key is to dream up your perfect list and then work on tracking it down. If you could have any list, what would it be? Who would be on it? What other information would you want included on the list? Start surfing the Internet. Search for groups and organizations and then use the instructions below on acquiring directories.

How to Obtain Association Directories

The following is an example of how to acquire association directories. You can adapt these steps to get other lists as well.

Visit the library and find the *Encyclopedia of Associations.* There are usually several volumes. Start with the first volume and thumb through it, looking for associations whose member directories you would like to own. When you find one, simply write down the name of the association and the telephone number. Search through all the directories and select all the associations with members who you believe would be a good target for your product or service.

Once you have all the names and phone numbers, it's time to get the directories. You can go about this a few different ways. One way is to simply call and ask if you can get a copy of the membership directory. Quite a few associations sell their directories. The downside is that some won't sell you the directory, and the ones that do can be prohibitively expensive. A way around this is to ask if they have last year's directory available for sale at a lower cost. The downside here is that some of the listings will be outdated; however, most will probably still be valid.

Another approach that works well is to call the association and say the following: "Hello. This is (your name) and I was looking for a listing of names and numbers of people in the (whatever association you're calling) industry to talk to. Could you help me with that?"

Keep in mind that your objective is to obtain the membership directory. The person who answers the phone may respond with, "Well, gee, we really don't have anyone here." Or, "Well, I might be able to come up with a couple of names for you." Or, "Well, how many names do you need?" In those cases, respond with, "I figured maybe you had a membership directory or something like that."

She will now tell you either a) she isn't allowed to give it to you or b) it costs X amount of money. If she says she can't give it to you, ask if there is any way you can get some names and numbers of people in the industry you can talk to? If she gives you a price, unless it's very cheap ($5–$10), act overwhelmed by the high cost and ask if she might have some old directories she can give to you.

A more effective way to get association lists is to hire a college student part-time to come in and call the associations for you. The student will call, tell the person at the association he is a student doing some research work in the particular industry, and ask for a listing of names and numbers of people in the industry whom he can contact. The conversation usually goes something like this:

Student: Hi, my name is (student's name) and I'm a student at (student's college). I'm doing some work in the (whatever association he's calling) industry and I'm looking for a list of names and numbers of people in the industry I can talk to. Could you help me with that?

Receptionist: Well, we really don't have a list of names and numbers we can give out.

Student: I had heard that some associations have membership directories or something similar to that.

Receptionist: Well, we do have a membership directory, but it costs $200.00.

Student: Wow, I'm just a student. I could eat for about eight weeks on that. Um, is there any way I could get it for less than that?

Receptionist: No. I'm sorry, but we have to charge that much for it.

Student: Do you have an older directory that I might be able to get for less?

Receptionist: Well, I could probably send you out one of last year's directories.

Student: That would probably work.

Note: Whether it is you calling or you have a student calling, it's important that the caller doesn't sound like a silver-tongued, well-practiced phone expert. Be soft-spoken, low key, and monotone, with some "ahs" and "ums" thrown in.

Your Cold Call Script

Now that you know your goals and objectives and you know *whom* you're going to be calling upon, you need to concentrate on *what* you're going to say.

As stated in Section I, in order to get to the top the fastest, you must have a cold call script that is well thought out, well prepared, written down, committed to memory, and most important, one that is proven to work.

If you have thoroughly memorized your cold call and you're interrupted in the middle by a prospect's question or comment, you'll be able to deal with it and then go right back to where you were in the cold call. You can also focus of *how* you're saying something rather than *what* you're saying.

Granted, in face-to-face selling you can't have your written-out cold call in front of you. But writing it out and committing it to memory ahead of time will ensure that you have a consistent call and get consistent results.

Note: If you are in face-to-face sales but do have phone work to do, have your written call in front of you. This will give you something to fall back on if you get off track.

When creating your cold call script, make it interesting and to the point. Your words need to catch and keep the prospect's attention and interest, qualify the prospect (making sure he needs your product, can afford it, and meets other necessary requirements) build rapport, and finally—assuming the prospect is qualified—close on the next step in the selling process, whether it's to set up an appointment or get a sale.

Start your call with your name, your company's name, and a powerful statement or a thought-provoking question. Here is an example: "Hello, Mr. Prospect. Bob Chapin with ABC Company. Very nice to meet you. We have been saving companies in your industry an average of 36 percent on office supplies."

It's important to open strong. To make powerful statements, simply take the benefits of your product or service and turn them into statements. Here are some examples:

- "We have been saving customers (a certain percentage or amount of money) on (your product or service)."
- "We have been reducing customers' monthly payments by (a certain percentage or amount of money) on (your product or service)."
- "We have been providing customers with the same amount of (your product—life insurance, for example) coverage for less money."
- "I can show you how to get more (your product) coverage for the same price you're paying now."
- "We have been helping customers pay (your product) off an average of five years earlier."
- "We have been helping customers get the same (results of your product or service—for example, X-ray development) in half the time."

You can also turn your benefits into opening questions such as:

- "If I could show you how to save (a certain percentage, or amount of money) on (your product or service) would you be interested?"
- "If I could reduce your monthly payments on (your product or service) by (a certain percentage or amount of money) would you be interested?"
- "If I could show you how to get the same amount of coverage on (your product or service) for less money would you be interested?"

Statements work better than questions, as some prospects will feel that the type of "no-brainer" questions above insult their intelligence. However, we included both because some people feel the questions suit their style better.

In addition to starting your cold call with your name, company name, and a thought-provoking statement or question, you can also begin your cold call with your name and what you do worded in such a way that it immediately piques the prospect's interest. For example, if you are an investment advisor, you might say, "Hello. I'm (your first and last name). I'm a money return specialist."

If you're an insurance agent, you might say, "I protect your most valuable assets."

After this introduction, pause and wait for the prospect to say, "What's a money return specialist?" or "What do you do?" At that point, explain what you do and then go into your cold call script.

Other attention-getting openings involve mentioning an organization that is familiar to the prospect and that endorses you or your product. You can also mention other companies that use you or your product. Just be sure this meets with the approval of the current customer(s) you're mentioning. Here are some openings using this type of information.

- "Hi Joe. This is Bob Chapin with ABC Company. We've been working with XYZ Corporation and have helped them cut costs on office supplies by over 35 percent during the past year."
- "Hi Joe. Bob Chapin with ABC Company. We've been endorsed by the National Association of Credit Unions and have been doing work for most of the credit unions in your area."

Again, the key to your opening is to catch the prospect's attention and build some interest quickly.

After your opening, explain *why* you are calling, followed by a commitment question. Here is an example: "All I'd like to do today is set up a time when I could spend about fifteen minutes with you to determine if and how much we could help you. Could we take a look at your schedule right now?"

From that point, you will bridge into the rest of your cold call.

Your entire cold call should take the following format:

- Your name.
- Your company name.
- A greeting such as, "Very nice to meet you."
- Your product or service's primary benefit.
- Why you're calling followed by a commitment question.
- Some discussion to determine interest.
- Qualifying (do they meet all necessary criteria—affordability, need, health requirements, etc.)
- Rapport building.
- Closing on the next step.
- A strong final statement.

The following is a sample cold call (we're only showing the salesperson's side of the conversation):

Hi, Joe. Bob Chapin with ABC Company. Very nice to meet you, Joe. We've been saving companies such as yours an average of 34 percent on information storage and backup. All I'd like to do today is set up a time when I could spend about fifteen minutes with you to determine if and how much we could help you. Could we take a look at your schedule right now?"

"Joe, let me ask you, what system are you using currently for information storage and backup?"

"How's that been working out for you?"

Now ask more qualifying questions such as:

- "And how are you storing those currently?"
- "How long have you been doing it that way?"
- "Joe, if you could change anything about the present system, what would it be?"

- "What do you like best about your current system?"
- "And Joe, what is your annual budget for information storage?"
- "So, you're open to some good ideas that could potentially save you money and improve your overall system?"
- "Great. Joe, in addition to you, who makes the decisions on information storage?"

Next, ask some rapport-building questions. These questions will obviously vary based upon which state or town you're making your calls in and your personal history or background. Here are some questions:

- "Joe, do you have any relatives in Wisconsin, by any chance?"
- "I grew up in Wisconsin and a few friends of mine were named Harvey."
- "Are you from this area originally?"
- "Oh, where did you go to school?"
- "Did you play any sports for them?"

Finally, close with a brief statement summarizing your next meeting: "Okay, great, Joe. I look forward to seeing you next Tuesday the 14th at 10 a.m. and discussing some ways we may be able to save you some time, effort, and money. Have a nice day."

That's it—short and to the point. Your cold call should be brief, spark some interest, determine how ready, willing, and able the prospect is to purchase your product or service, and be a bridge to the next step in the selling process.

Note: In face-to-face selling, you want to send a note out after the call. The note will simply thank the prospect for his or her time, remind them of when you are meeting or what the next step will be, and provide your name and contact information. If you have neat handwriting, handwrite it; otherwise, do it on a computer and sign it in blue ink.

In telemarketing sales, you will send the note described above if you made the call to set up an in-person visit. If you will be following up with another phone call, you will send out some basic information along with a cover letter. This will be covered in the section on telephone selling.

We will deal much more extensively with qualifying, building rapport, and other aspects of interacting with the prospect in Chapter 9. Please refer to that Chapter for more details on creating your cold call.

Now that you are mentally prepared to cold call, have all the logistics down, have your goals and objectives in mind, know whom you're calling on, and have your cold call scripted, it's time to begin cold calling.

Chapter 8

Showing Up

As we've mentioned, all sales calls begin in the parking lot and some even begin before that. People may be watching and listening to you when you least expect it. *Always be on your best behavior* and speak as if you are being recorded at all times. People can look out the window and see you in the parking lot well before you approach the receptionist's desk. And remember, you don't want to take up prime parking spots in the customer's parking lot. Those are for your prospect's customers, not you. That being said, let's move from the car to the receptionist's desk.

"No Soliciting" Signs

If you run into a No Soliciting sign between your car and the receptionist's desk, ignore it. Occasionally, someone you call on will refer to the sign, but for the most part you'll find that people won't bring it up. If they do, simply acknowledge what was said, and then state the purpose of your call. For example, you could smile and say, "Oh, I'm sorry. My name is (your name) with (your company), I was just hoping to catch (prospect's name) for a moment."

If they persist, say, "I'm not selling anything. I was simply hoping to introduce myself to (the prospect)." If they continue to stick to their guns, say thank you and leave. You can call on the phone later and try to set up an appointment or call before or after the receptionist is in.

Finding Out Who the Decision-maker Is

When you reach the receptionist's desk, your objective is to find out who the decision-maker is, or try to gain access to the decision-maker directly. Your approach and what you say will be different depending upon your objective.

In the case where you are making live cold calls and don't know the name of the person you need to call on, the best approach is to go in with some information you can drop off for the decision-maker.

As you approach the receptionist, you must present a pleasant demeanor. Everything about you should state that you are professional and a nice person. You want to be dressed impeccably and have a slight smile. Walk at a normal pace and walk tall with good posture. You don't want to charge in too briskly like a bull in a china shop. You also don't want to walk in as though you own the place; you want to be confident and professional, but humble as well.

Once you make eye contact with the receptionist, say, "Hi, how are you?"

Most likely her response will be, "I'm fine, thanks. Can I help you with something?"

Continue with, "Yes, I have some information that I just wanted to drop off about (whatever you sell) and I was wondering whom I should leave it for." She will either give you a name or she'll say, "Oh, I'll take that and get it to the right person."

If the receptionist gives you the name, ask, "Is (he or she) the person who makes the buying decisions on (whatever you sell)?"

If she answers yes to this question, say, "Great. I'll also leave my business card. I'll follow up with (him or her) by phone in a day or two." Then smile and wait for her to respond to that comment.

You then want to thank her for her help and get her name before you go. You might say, "Thank you very much for your help. Oh, and what's your name?"

During your conversation, you want to be looking for nameplates. Often the receptionist will have a nameplate on her desk. If this is the case, say, "Thank you very much for your help (looking at the nameplate), Mary, right?"

You want to know her name because when you call back, you will use her name. For example, you might say, "Hi Mary. This is (your first and last name) with (your company). I was trying to get to (the name of the decision-maker)."

Again, be pleasant and professional on the phone and have a smile on your face—people will "hear" your smile over the phone.

If the receptionist does *not* give you a name when you ask who you should leave the information for, probe a little to get it; after all, that is the primary reason you're there. Again, let's assume she says, "Oh, I'll take that and get it to the right person." At this point, say, "Great. Thank you. I'll also leave a business card and I'll follow up on the information in a day or two. Whom should I ask for when I call to follow up?"

If she still won't give you the name, use a little humor. For example, you might say, "Hmm. No way you're giving me that name, huh?" And give her a smile and a little laugh. Then say, "I'll tell you what. When I call back I'll ask for you, okay?" Again, make sure you get her name before you leave.

Whether she receives that pleasantly or completely shoots you down, there are several other approaches you can use to find out the decision-maker's name. If the receptionist is pleasant and agrees to your comment about calling back and talking to her, take advantage of this friendliness. Try one more time to get the name of the decision-maker when you call back in a couple of days. Say, "Hi Mary. This is (your name) with (your company). I was there two days ago with the information on (whatever you sell)."

Pause for a moment and get her response. Follow with, "I was really hoping to get to that person who makes decisions on (your product or service). Could you help me with that?"

If this doesn't work, use one of the backup methods for getting the decision-maker's name which we will discuss shortly.

Getting to the Decision-maker

Now let's assume you have the name of the decision-maker, and the objective of your cold call is to reach that person directly. Approach the receptionist in your pleasant, professional manner, make eye contact, smile, and say, "Hi. I'm here to see (decision-maker's name)." Then pull out your business card, present it to her, and repeat, "(Your name) with (your company)."

The receptionist's typical response will be, "And may I ask what this is regarding?" To which you will reply, "Yes, I'm the new sales rep for the area and I'd simply like to take a moment to say hello and introduce myself."

Another response you might get from her is, "Is he expecting you?" To which you would say, "No, he isn't. I'm the new sales rep for the area and I'd simply like to take a moment to say hello and introduce myself."

Note: If you have any leverage, use it. For example, if you work for a company that is a household name, use that to your advantage. In this case, if the receptionist asks if the prospect knows you or is expecting you, simply say, "He's familiar with my company. I just happened to be in the area and figured I'd try to catch him for a minute."

If you are *not* a new sales rep and have been there enough times in the past that the prospect will probably recognize your name, simply say, "He's familiar with me, although he's not expecting me. I just happened to be in the area and figured I'd try to catch him for a moment."

Another approach is to drop the name of another company with which you are doing business in the area. You might say, "No, he's not expecting me. We've been doing quite a bit of work with (the names of the companies) down the street, and I just wanted to catch him for a minute while I was in the area." Of course, if you are doing business with many companies in the area, hopefully one will give you a referral to this prospect.

Based upon what we outlined above, following are some additional responses to the receptionist's questions:

1) "And can I ask what this is concerning?"
    a) "Sure. He's familiar with my company. I'm the new sales rep for the area and I simply want to take a moment and say hello."
    b) "Sure. He's not expecting me, but he knows me. I was just dropping in to say hello."
    c) "Sure. We've been doing quite a bit of work for ABC Company down the street and I just wanted to drop in and catch him for a moment."

2) "And is he expecting you?"
    a) "No, but he's familiar with my company. I'm the new sales rep for the area and I simply want to take a moment to say hello."
    b) "No, I just happened to be in the area and thought I'd try to catch him for a moment if I could."

The receptionist may say, "I'm sorry, but he doesn't see anyone without an appointment." If she does, respond with, "Okay, I'd be happy to set up an appointment." Pull out your schedule and ask, "What times does he have available?"

Note: You want to be firm with the receptionist, but *not* confrontational. If you get a question from the receptionist, *don't* ask a question after answering her question. Here is an example of what most salespeople do:

Salesperson: Hi. I'm looking for Mr. Jim Smith. Bob Chapin with ABC Company.
Receptionist: Is he expecting you?

Salesperson: No, he isn't. I'm the new sales rep for the area and I simply want to take a moment to say hello and introduce myself. Can I speak with him, please?

This approach is not only confrontational, but it will usually annoy the receptionist. Your overall objective is to get past the receptionist. The best way to accomplish this is by being pleasant and professional. If you're not confrontational and don't sound like the typical salesperson, most of the time you won't be treated like one.

When you get a question such as those above, simply answer it.

If the receptionist gives you any sort of brush-off such as: "I'm sure he's not interested," "He already has someone who takes care of that," "We're all set with that service," "He doesn't talk to salespeople," or anything else for that matter, respond with, "I can definitely understand that. And if he'd extend me the courtesy of a moment of his time, I'd really appreciate it." That phrase, said in a non-confrontational, pleasant, and professional manner, works wonders.

If you still can't get through and you have a number of other places you can call on, and if this account isn't a major one, there may be better places to spend your time. Of course, it's always better to hear: "I'm really, completely, and totally *not interested*!" from the decision-maker instead of the receptionist!

So what should you do if you can't get the name of the decision-maker from the receptionist?

If she won't give you the name of the decision-maker, you can either look up the information in an annual report, on the company website, at the library, or you can use the phone and chase down the name.

If you're going to use the phone, avoid the receptionist by either calling when she isn't there or by asking to speak with another department.

Most receptionists start at 8 or 9 a.m. and work until 5 p.m. Thus, if you call before or after those hours, you will avoid the receptionist. Often, someone else may answer the phone instead. If so, say the following: "Hello. This is (your name) with (your company), and I was looking to send out information on (your product or service). Could you please tell me to whom I should send it?"

When the person gives you the name, follow with, "Is (he or she) the person who makes the purchasing decisions on this?"

When you call at these times you may get the owner or a high-level executive on the phone, as they are typically the ones who work before and after regular working hours. Be prepared if the person on the phone says something like, "I'm the one who makes decisions on that" or "Actually, that's my department. What have you got?" If this happens, give them your cold call script and set up an appointment.

You can also call during regular office hours and ask to speak with another department. As we mentioned earlier, the sales department is a good bet because they are most likely to help other salespeople. When the receptionist answers, simply ask to speak to someone in sales. Once you are connected, say exactly what you would say to someone answering the phone during off-hours: "Hello. This is (your name) with (your company) and I was looking to send out information on (your product or service). Could you please tell me to whom I should send it?"

If this person cannot help you, ask if there is someone else who can. Alternatively, you could call back and ask for another department such as accounts receivable.

Yet another approach is to ask one of the companies with which you're currently doing business for a name at the company you're trying to get into. You should be asking for referrals anyway, but even in cases where a customer may not feel comfortable referring you to another company directly, he or she may still know the name of the person you need to talk to.

If these approaches fail, you can leave information with the receptionist and put together some creative notes and other eye-catching items to encourage the decision-maker to return your call. We will talk about some of these creative ideas beginning on page 129.

Note: *Don't misrepresent yourself to get in the door.* This should go without saying. Don't pretend to be an old college buddy, someone calling from an organization you do not represent, or use any other "tricks" to get through to the prospect. Not only will the prospect be upset upon realizing he or she has been deceived, but they will also immediately feel that you cannot be trusted.

What If the Person You're Cold Calling Isn't There?

If you don't catch the person you're seeking, ask if he or she will be around later. Follow up by driving back later if that works with your schedule, stop by at another time, or call on the phone to set up the appointment. Either way, leave a business card and say, "I'll leave this as evidence that I was here. If you could just get that to him, I'd really appreciate it."

What If the Receptionist Won't Let You Through?

If you know the name of the person you need to contact but the receptionist won't let you through, there are a couple of approaches you can use.

1) Call during off hours and set up an appointment.

Again, call before or after normal business hours in an attempt to avoid the receptionist. If you do get the receptionist, ask to speak with the prospect. Many higher-level executives have their own receptionist. If you get their receptionist, simply say you are calling to set up an appointment with the prospect and ask when might be a good time. Be prepared for questions such as, "Can I ask what this is regarding?" or brush-offs such as, "He's not interested."

Note: If you showed up in person, weren't able to get through the receptionist, and decide to call back later to set up an appointment by phone, make your phone call within twenty-four to forty-eight hours of your in-person visit. Mentioning you stopped in earlier and left your card is a good opening and people will feel more obligated to give you a moment or two if they know you've been working to reach them.

When you do reach the prospect, say the same thing over the phone that you would say in person. Arrange an appointment to meet with the prospect. Don't give out too much information over the phone. You simply want to build enough interest to get you physically in the door. Once you get in, you can use your heavy artillery and all your good stuff.

2) Show up when the receptionist isn't there.

In addition to calling on the phone when the receptionist isn't there, you can also show up in person either before or after normal business hours. This technique is one you should consider when trying to get to business owners and high-level executives.

3) Send or leave creative information and follow up with a phone call.

For some creative ideas when all else fails, refer to page 129, "Creative Ideas to Crack That Big Account When All Else Fails" in Chapter 10.

4) Catch the prospect out of the office at his favorite lunch spot, the club where he works out, or the golf or tennis club he belongs to.

If there is a popular restaurant in the area where most people congregate, or if the person you're trying to contact belongs to a local country club, you could catch up with him or her there.

Remember that pleasant persistence pays off! You don't want to be a pest and you don't want to get the nickname "The Eyesore." But if you stop by occasionally and are pleasant and professional, often that will be enough to eventually get you in the door.

Other Notes Regarding Showing Up

1) Be nice to *everyone* at the facility.

Outside of the fact that you should be treating all people with dignity and respect all the time, you never know who has influence and you never know who will be making decisions at some point in the future.

We remember one security officer at a bank who climbed the corporate ladder and became the person in charge of all purchasing decisions on bank equipment. Years before, the salesperson who'd had our territory used to snub this person. You can imagine that when this former security officer became the decision-maker, it was "payback" time. Even though that salesperson was long gone, our company still paid the price.

2) Say hello and goodbye to everyone.

Make it a point to say goodbye to receptionists and/or the person with whom you spoke when you arrived. A quick wave and "Thank you. Have a nice day" goes a long way. In addition to the receptionist, you also want to greet any employees whom you encounter when entering or leaving.

3) No matter how your cold call goes, you need to remain courteous and professional.

Even if the receptionist is rude, simply smile and say, "Have a nice day" and leave. The problem is hers, and you don't want to become part of it. On the other hand, if your cold call goes extremely well, you don't want to be bouncing off the walls on the way out. Keep your professional composure.

4) Using humor on the receptionist can get you to the prospect.

One of the contributors to this book had a humor technique he used on almost every receptionist, and it worked 99 percent of the time. He was calling on small to medium-sized, owner-operated businesses. At almost every business, he noticed that the owner had an impressive car or truck, as well as a special parking place directly in front of the business.

The salesperson would walk in and say to the receptionist, "Wow, I love your Mercedes!" or whatever vehicle it was. Most of the time the receptionist would laugh and say, "Oh, that's not mine, that's the owner's." To which he would respond, "Yeah? Well, I bet you wish it was yours." Then he'd follow with, "Well, I wish it was mine too." From this point, he would then give his name and company name and ask who made their printing decisions. He almost always got the answer.

Find places to interject humor into your calls. You can also say, "Hi! My name is (your name) with (your company), and I'm here with the joke of the day." Yes, it's unconventional and it takes some guts, but it will set you apart from other salespeople. And if you can get a laugh, your odds of getting through the receptionist will be much greater. Incidentally, you want to make sure you have a joke you can tell. Get a clean joke book or sign up for a joke of the day online.

Chapter 9

Talking to the Prospect

How to Address the Prospect

When you first meet the prospect, address him or her using both first and last names. Also, don't guess what the prospect prefers to be called. For example, don't assume Robert Smith goes by Bob Smith. The only time you can make that assumption is when you hear someone refer to the person that way, or you're using the phone to make mass cold calls to residences. We'll discuss that at greater length in the *Telemarketing* section.

The Opening of the Cold Call

When you developed your cold call script, you started with the basics: your name, company name, and an opening line to create interest. You can also start with your name and what you do worded in such a way that it piques the prospect's interest.

For example, if you are an investment advisor, you might say, "Hello. This is (your first and last name) and I'm a money return specialist." After this introduction, pause and wait for the prospect to ask, "What's a money return specialist?" Answer the question, proceed with your cold call and move toward the next step in the process, such as setting up an appointment or getting the prospect to agree to receive your call in the future when you have an investment that warrants his or her attention.

As we discussed when we spoke about your cold call script beginning on page 74, use a powerful opening statement and use any leverage you have such as companies you currently do business with.

We gave examples of openings in that section, but here's another one using this kind of information:

- "Hi Joe. Bob Chapin with ABC Company. We've been working with the Reilly Corporation next door and have helped them cut their information storage cost by over 22 percent during the past year."

The key is to build credibility and interest quickly. You want to capture the prospect's attention and keep it.

Note: Make sure any statement you make is grounded in fact and can be backed up with solid proof. Your next step is to build credibility in the statement, your product, you, and your company.

After you've told the prospect who you are and piqued some interest, tell the prospect why you're calling and ask for a meeting. For example:

- "All I'd like to do is spend fifteen minutes with you to determine if and how much we might help you. Would you have some time right now, or could we take a look at your schedule and set up a more convenient time?"

Depending upon your business and your product, here's another opening you can use:

- "Hi Joe. Bob Chapin with ABC Company. We've been endorsed by the National Association of Credit Unions and have been doing work for most of the credit unions in your area. Today I simply wanted to stop by, introduce myself, and see if any projects you're working on might benefit from our help."

With this opening, you don't have to ask a question at the end—simply make your statement and then be completely quiet and wait for the prospect to respond.

Qualify the Prospect

Do You Have the Decision-maker?

After your opening, you need to qualify the prospect to learn whether he has the power to make a decision. Your question should simply be: "Are you the one who makes the buying decisions for (whatever it is you're selling)?" Once you get an affirmative reply, you need to find out if anyone else is involved. Instead of asking if he is the sole decision-maker, ask, "And is anyone else involved in the decision-making process?" This question is more subtle and effective than a question such as, "And are you the only decision-maker?"

People higher on the ladder, or those with sole decision-making authority, are generally not offended by a question regarding decision-making authority. The people you need to watch out for are those lower on the ladder who may tell you they have complete authority but in reality, they do not. When you ask, "Who else?" you are suggesting, "Look, I understand there are others involved besides yourself. Who are they?" With the "Who else?" question you will usually get the correct answer and you won't upset anyone in the process.

You also need to find out how decisions are made. For example, are any committees or boards involved in the decision-making process? To uncover this information, come right out and ask directly, "And will any committees or boards be reviewing this?"

Of course, if the person says she is *not* the decision-maker, you must ask who is and ask to speak to that person.

Is the Prospect Right for Your Product or Service?

Now that you know your interested prospect has the authority to make a decision, you need to further qualify the prospect to make sure she is right for your product or service and make sure she can afford it. In addition, you are looking for ways in which you can best help the prospect. You want to learn what is most important to the prospect, least important, any hot buttons, and keywords or phrases. In general, you want to find out how to tailor your product or service to the prospect. Your ultimate goal is to present the prospect with exactly what he needs and make a sale.

Examples of qualifying questions:

- "Joe, let me ask you: What system are you using currently for information storage and backup?" You could also ask, "How are you currently handling the need for (your product)?"
- "Who is your current vendor?"
- "How's that been working out for you?"
- "How long have you been doing it that way?"
- "What do you like best about your current situation (or vendor)?"
- "I have a few ideas for you. But first, in what areas do *you* think I might be able to help you?"

- "What is your current time frame for making changes?"
- "And Joe, what is your annual budget for (your product)?"
- "So, you're open to some good ideas that could potentially save you money and improve your overall system?"
- "What price range are you looking at?"
- "How many kids do you have? How old are they?" (This would usually be a rapport-building question, but could also be used by a realtor to find the right house for the prospect.)
- "Great. Joe, in addition to you, who else makes decisions on (your product)?"

Examples of questions that a typical investment advisor might ask:

- "What investments do you currently own? Stocks, bonds, mutual funds?"
- "Do you consider yourself more of an aggressive or a conservative investor?"
- "Do you look for more growth stocks, more income stocks, or a combination?"
- "What do you look for in a stock before you invest?"
- "What would you say has been your best investment?"
- "What did you like about that investment?"
- "What would you say was your worst investment? Why?"
- "How much money would you have liquid and available if the right stock investment were to present itself today?"

These are some questions we asked in the banking industry:

- "What kind of functionality are you looking for from your ATMs?"
- "When are you looking to replace these ten ATMs?"
- "What's more important to you—price, or the highest quality and best service?"

Note: We sold the most expensive product, but we also had the highest-quality product and the best service. We asked the last question in such a way as to get the answer we were looking for. If you are selling the lowest-priced product in your industry, you might ask, "Are you resigned to buying the most expensive product out there, or are you looking to control cost and get the best value for your money?"

You will need to qualify individuals and corporations differently. When qualifying an individual, if the right opportunity presents itself, ask if the money is "liquid and available now." Alternatively, you may ask what price range the prospect is considering. For example, a typical investment advisor might ask the following qualifying questions:

- "Mr. Prospect, when you see an investment opportunity you like, how much money do you typically invest?" (Wait for an answer.)
- "And if you did see that kind of opportunity in the near future, is that kind of money liquid and available to you now?"

A real estate agent might ask:

- "Ms. Prospect, what dollar range are you looking in?" (Wait for an answer.)
- "And do you plan to mortgage most or all of the investment?" (Wait for an answer.)
- "Do you already have a bank you're working with that has pre-approved you for a certain amount?"

With corporations, you want to ask how much money is budgeted for a particular project and if it is available now. To extract this information, ask questions such as:

- "What is your current time frame for making changes?" (Meaning: "What budget year will you be making changes?")
- "What is the scope of this project?" (Meaning: "Are you completely changing the network across the entire company or are you simply changing a couple of offices?")

These "time frame" questions give you a good idea of what kind of urgency there is, if any. You may get an answer such as: "We need to make a decision by the end of the week." Or "We're just starting the process. This is something we want to do a year from now."

In a nutshell, your objective in the qualifying stage is to make sure the prospect is ready, willing, and able to purchase your product or service.

What Does the Prospect Value Most?

You also want to ask questions during the qualifying stage that will give you insight into the prospect's beliefs and values.

For example, if you are selling cars and the prospect doesn't have a specific car in mind, ask questions such as, "What is most important to you in a new car? Safety? Appearance? How well it retains its value? Gas mileage? How 'green' it is?"

The answer to these questions will inform you of what it will take to sell the prospect. Also, the prospect has probably never been asked these questions before so it will set you apart.

Another similar question that can apply to almost any product or service is, "What's most important to you—price, bells and whistles, options, or opportunities to upgrade?" A question such as this will give you a good idea as to what you have to discuss to make the sale.

Following are further good questions that will help you determine what is most important to the prospect and what he or she is looking for:

- "Do you have any suggestions as to the best way for me to help you?"
- "What most concerns you about this type of product (or service)?"
- "What do you hope to achieve by evaluating how this is currently being handled?"

Building Rapport with the Prospect

Building rapport with the prospect is one of your key objectives during the cold call. You build rapport by demonstrating to the prospect how you are like him, how you can help him, that you can be trusted, and that you have his best interests in mind.

When we first meet someone, most of us try to find some common ground. After taking a visual inventory of the other person, we ask questions to find similarities in our backgrounds and interests. We ask questions about where the person is from, where they attended school, what they do for work, and what they enjoy doing for fun.

We also evaluate how someone talks, their mannerisms, and their habits. From this information, we begin to form an opinion of the person and decide on what level we would like to know the person in the future. Are they someone we will probably never talk to again? Will they perhaps become a friend? A good friend? Or more than that? We may not have immediate answers to all these questions. Yet from the moment we meet someone new, we begin this evaluation process.

In the business world, prospects and customers also go through this kind of evaluation process, although the initial questions are different. Prospects ask themselves whether they can trust you and whether you and your company can do the job satisfactorily for them. At the same time, they are asking themselves whether they like you as a person. Are you like them? Are you someone they can have a successful business relationship with? Do you instill confidence in them? And they may ask questions similar to those we ask when we meet someone in a non-business setting.

As a salesperson calling on prospects and customers, you want to put yourself in the best possible position to be liked, accepted, and trusted. They don't have to fall in love with you; at the same time, you don't want them on the other end of the spectrum. So what can you do to give yourself the best chance of making a good first impression?

Details on Your Appearance

We have already discussed some of the following items on pages 44 through 49. Please refer to those pages for other important information.

Building rapport on the cold call and making a good impression begins with your appearance. The key with regard to your appearance is to look professional; in doing so, you will make a positive impression right off the bat. Here are some guidelines:

1) **Dress for success.** Please refer to pages 44 through 45 for more on this.

2) **Your hair should be properly groomed.** If you're a man, unless you're selling an item such as surfboards, where longer hair is okay, your hair should be short and cut above your collar. If you're a woman, shoulder length or shorter is best, yet a little longer than shoulder length is fine. When selling traditional products and services, hair too short or too long

for a woman is generally not good. A man's hair can be as short as he wants or non-existent, but anything past the collar is not good.

3) **Men—always wear socks. Women—always wear socks or hose.**

4) **Do your best to keep any visible skin and your teeth and nails clean and presentable.**

5) **Watch tattoos and piercing.** Piercing is a little easier to cover up than a tattoo. If you must have a tattoo, get it in a spot that's easy to cover with clothing.

6) **Men, facial hair is debatable.** The safest facial hair is a mustache. Goatees are becoming more acceptable but are still viewed by many as unprofessional. Ensure any facial hair you do have is clean and properly groomed. Also, it's *not* okay to go on face-to-face calls without shaving in the morning.

Physical Grooming

Please refer to Chapter 6, "Your Best Foot Forward," beginning on page 44 for more information on this subject.

Your Handshake and Eye Contact

Your handshake and eye contact are two more important items which we also touched on in the Chapter 6. Please refer to pages 46 and 47 for more information.

Other Components on Which You Will Be Judged

On the cold call, you will also be judged on body language, how you speak, what you say, and the materials you present to the prospect.

Mirroring

Mirroring is a useful tool when you are trying to connect with people. It is a process whereby you copy or mirror the other person's movements, speech, and other mannerisms. Theoretically, if you talk and move as the other person does, they will subconsciously connect with you and feel that the two of you are similar. It is well known that the more someone believes you are like them, the more they will tend to like you. This is a powerful technique when used properly, but it must be done with skill and subtlety.

Mirroring Speech

There are three areas of speech you want to match during your conversations. They are: speed and rhythm, volume of speech, and the words the prospect uses.

You want to do your best to come as close as possible to the speed and rhythm of the person to whom you're talking. You don't have to match the speed and rhythm perfectly, but try to come close. Here's an extreme example to make a point.

Imagine for a moment that a salesperson from New York City is speaking to a prospect from Alabama. It's safe to say that two typical people from these locations will not have the same speed and rhythm of speech. If the typical New Yorker calls the typical person from Alabama and proceeds with typical New York speech, speed, and rhythm, he'll alienate that prospect in a "New York minute." In order to be understood on any kind of an emotional level by the person in Alabama, the salesperson from New York *must* slow down. The reverse is also true. The typical Alabama salesperson must speed up his speech when selling to the typical New Yorker.

Try to consciously match the speed and rhythm of every person you talk to both over the phone and in person, and in both business and personal settings, until matching speed and rhythm becomes a habit for you.

Next, match the prospect's volume. If the prospect is talking softly, you should talk softly; if the prospect is speaking loudly, you should speak loudly. You don't have to go to extremes with this, either. Just make it similar.

Finally, use similar words and phrases as your prospect uses. We all have certain words and phrases we like to use. We tend to like people who "speak the same language" as we do. For example, if your prospect says he liked a particular investment because it gave him a lot of "bang for his buck," make a note of this phrase and feed it back to him when you call him back with a recommendation. You might say, "Joe, we believe this stock will give you a lot of 'bang for your buck.' That's what you're looking for, right?"

Make a note of words, phrases, and sayings that a prospect uses often; then look for ways to use those words, phrases, and sayings in your presentation and close.

You want to particularly note what people say when describing what they like best or what they liked least about a product or service. These will tend to be emotional words for them.

Note 1: You don't want to overdo keywords, phrases, and sayings. Usually using a few of them once in a presentation is enough. If you use them too many times, people will notice what you're doing and wonder if you're sincere or making fun of them.

Note 2: The one area of speech you *do not* want to mirror is profanity. Even if the other person is swearing like it's going out of style, refrain from lowering yourself. It instantly puts you in the category of unprofessional.

The bottom line is that you want to be speaking the same language as your prospect. When you talk as she does and use the same words she uses, you'll find it much easier to understand each other and make a connection.

Speech Factors That Alienate You from the Prospect

While we're on the subject of speech, let's talk about several speech factors that can alienate you from your prospect. They are accents and speech extremes, or abnormalities.

Obviously, if you've spent your entire life in one part of the country, it's more than likely that you have developed an accent. If you have a different accent from the person you're talking to, it can become a negative differentiator. If you believe a heavy accent may be holding you back, you can work on it yourself or with a speech therapist.

In certain cases, an accent can be a benefit. People seem to be intrigued with certain foreign accents. French, British, or Australian accents always seem to catch people's attention—in a positive way. If you have a foreign accent and it seems to be of benefit—wonderful! Use it. Just be sure people can understand you. Also, be cautious when using any slang terms that "foreigners" may not understand.

Other speech factors that can alienate you from prospects involve extremes and speech impediments. Two examples of extremes are very high voices and very low voices. Speech impediments include stuttering or talking with a lisp. Whatever speech issues you have, they can usually be improved or eliminated altogether either through self-help, by recording and listening to your voice and practicing corrections, or with the assistance of a speech therapist.

To recap, the most important "speech" aspects of selling are to:

- Make sure people can understand you.
- Mirror your prospect's speed and rhythm.
- Talk without any speech impediments.
- Talk without an accent that differs from that of the prospect.

Note: Your words may alienate you from the prospect. If you're talking to a brain surgeon and he starts speaking his lingo, you won't understand a thing unless you've done a great deal of research on brain surgery.

Similarly, stay away from sales industry acronyms and other industry lingo that the prospect may not understand. You may think you sound intelligent and cool, but all the other person will be hearing is "Blah, blah, blah."

Other Areas to Mirror

You also want to mirror posture and movement. Think of this as any physical movement or positioning that you observe. For example, if the other person is tilting her head slightly to the right with legs crossed and hands folded out in front of her, your head should be tilted slightly left as she's tilted right and you're her mirror image. Your legs will also be crossed and hands folded. As she shifts and changes position, after a few moments, you also shift and change position. If she gestures with her hands, gesture with your own hands.

Again, the point is to be as much like the prospect or customer as possible so that the prospect's subconscious mind is positively reinforcing that "this person is like me."

Breathing is another area to mirror, although this can be difficult and takes some practice. Matching someone's breathing can have a strong subconscious effect. You want to be breathing out when the prospect is breathing out and breathing in when he is breathing in. Of course, if he just ran up the stairs and he's huffing and puffing, you don't need to mirror this. Just try to get in sync with the rising and falling of the prospect's chest. Interestingly, often when you are in ultimate rapport with someone you'll notice that, without even trying, you are both breathing at exactly the same pace.

Note: Some aspects of mirroring require you to act slowly and subtly. Posture and movement are two of them. If you make all your moves a millisecond after your prospect has made his, he's going to notice. When you're sitting and he crosses his legs, wait a minute or two before crossing yours. Do the same with any other similar movements.

The only movements you want to copy as soon as possible are sitting, standing, and walking. As far as repetitive motions such as reaching for a drink, as a general rule, you can mirror those movements once or twice, but no more than that.

Speech and breathing are other areas you can mirror immediately as they are generally much more subtle.

The technique of mirroring has three advantages. They are:

1) **To give the prospect or customer the subconscious feeling that you are like them,** thus making them comfortable with you. You want to put the other person at ease and establish a subconscious connection with him or her.

2) **To gain a better understanding of how the customer or prospect is feeling.** Researchers have studied what happens when two people are brought together and coached until they are an exact mirror image of each other in every aspect. They are then instructed to turn to each other and ask what the other person is thinking. Many times, one person's answer to what the other is thinking is correct. This is because our physiology *very accurately* reflects what is going on inside of us.

If you were asked to describe the physiology of someone who was depressed, you would probably be able to give a fairly good description of what that person looked like: shoulders slumped, eyes and head down, shallow breathing, etc. If you were asked to copy the physiology of someone who was depressed, you would suddenly find that you were feeling a bit down. The mind follows the body and the body follows the mind.

Thus, if you can duplicate someone's physiology, you can often also get an indication of whether they are "with you" or whether you're losing them. If you realize you're losing them, you can then take action to draw them back into the conversation.

3) **Mirroring will enable you to lead the other person.** Once you're in sync with the other person, if you've mirrored correctly, you will find that you can begin to lead them. This is a powerful tool—if your prospect has taken on a closed stance or posture, you can gradually bring her around to a more open demeanor.

For example, suppose the prospect has her arms folded, with a skeptical "what are you trying to pull" look on her face. As you mirror this posture, speak at the same pace and tone, and mirror other aspects, you should notice a connection start to happen. Now begin to lead. You can unfold your arms, relax your face, and present a more open demeanor.

Be sure to make these moves gradually and one at a time. When you are leading, you make one move at a time and wait for the other person to follow. In the above situation, for example, you would first unfold your arms. Once the prospect has followed you, you would then relax your face, and once they follow that, you would then extend your hands.

Note: Some people believe that mirroring is a form of "manipulation." If you're one of those people, try to think of it like this: Your ultimate goal is to have a pleasant exchange while getting along with and helping this person.

Your best way of accomplishing this is to play by your prospect's rules for a while and live in their world. As someone we know once described, "It's kind of like walking into a room where everyone is talking sports and even though you're not a sports enthusiast, you also talk sports in order to mingle with the crowd." Or, as the saying goes, "When in Rome, do as the Romans do." When you meet a potential new friend, what do you do first? As we've suggested, you ask questions and look for things you have in common. You already use many of these techniques with friends and family without even being aware of it. When you are really in sync with people, many of these "mirrors" occur naturally. Also, mirroring helps you to "get in someone's world" and better understand her, thus, you will better understand how to help her.

Topics of Discussion to Avoid

On your cold call, and other calls for that matter, you want to avoid subjects where feelings and emotions can run high, namely topics such as religion, sex, and politics. As soon as you profess your atheism to a devout Catholic or sing the praises of the welfare state to an extreme right-wing conservative, you're likely to have a problem.

If your prospect gets on his soapbox about a particular issue and you happen to feel the same way, by all means, have at it and let your views be known. If you *don't* agree with the opinion being expressed, simply listen to what the person has to say and keep quiet. You can say something from time to time such as, "Hmm, that's a very good point." Never debate the other person unless you don't want his business.

Using Humor

We mentioned humor earlier when we talked about showing up for your cold call. Humor can also be a very effective tool once you're talking to the prospect. Light humor helps to relax the atmosphere and pave the road for a smooth discussion. Humor can also alleviate a tense situation.

Have you noticed that laughter is contagious? Laughter lets people know you are down to earth, relaxed, and fun to be around. Of course, you need to be able to be serious as well. Overall, one of your objectives should be to have fun and add some humor, but make certain you're ultimately seen as a business professional with a sense of humor, and not a clown trying to do business.

When using humor it is helpful to know a little about whom you are talking to. Some people you will call on simply will not appreciate humor, no matter how good it is.

So where can you find some good jokes or become a comedian overnight? To start with, you can visit Darren LaCroix's website at www.humor411.com. LaCroix is the 2001 World Champion of Public Speaking and a professional comedian. You can also visit a bookstore or go online and pick up a few joke books, buy a calendar with a joke of the day, or subscribe to online services that e-mail a joke of the day.

Remember to keep the jokes clean. We all know people who tell off-color jokes from time to time. Just make sure you know your audience *extremely* well if you're going to cross that line.

Telling jokes takes some practice—you need to be relaxed and your timing needs to be on. Don't be too hard on yourself if at first you tell a couple jokes that flop. Keep trying and you'll have it down in a relatively short time.

Try to find jokes that are related to your business. Perhaps you have a funny story or two you can tell. Have you made any mistakes that you can turn into funny stories? Admit your mistakes, look for humor in them, and make fun of them and yourself where you can—self-deprecating humor can be highly effective.

Your Business Materials

You will also be judged by the materials you carry with you and what you present to the prospect. Examples are business cards, brochures, flyers, and anything else you carry such as a briefcase or leather carrying case.

Make sure anything you carry with you is clean and in good shape. You don't want carrying cases bursting at the seams. Also, organize the contents. You don't want to open your carrying case and start shuffling through papers.

As we discussed at length on pages 49 and 50 of Chapter 6, you want business cards, brochures, and other information you present to the prospect to be professional. Make sure written materials are printed on good paper stock, all names, spelling, and grammar are correct, and that all other details such as font type and size, print size, and wording are accurate, consistent, and appropriate.

What is the Prospect *Really* Interested In?

During the cold call, discreetly examine the prospect's office for pictures, awards, and various other items that identify the prospect's hobbies, interests, alma mater, and other similar facts.

In addition to seeking visual clues, ask some questions to gather information that will help you build rapport with the prospect. Here are some sample questions and statements you can use when building rapport:

- "Are you from this area originally?"
- "How did you get here?" (If the prospect is from another area of the country.)
- "I see you went to the University of Wisconsin—I went there too. When were you there?"
- "Did you play any sports or were you involved in any activities there?"
- "I noticed all the birdhouses outside. Is that something you've been interested in for a while?" (If you're visiting the prospect at her home.)

- "Wow, that's a neat sculpture." (Or picture, or whatever it is. Just make the comment and let the prospect react to it.)
- "How did you two meet?" (To a couple you are meeting with.)
- "How did you get the golf trophy?"
- "I used to drive a Cadillac a few years ago. Is that a picture of yours?"
- "Is that a picture of your children?" (You then want to follow with, how old, do they play any sports, other extra curricular activities?)
- "What business are you in?" (If the prospect is an individual at home.)
- "What did you do for work?" (If the prospect is retired.)
- "How did you get into that business?"
- "What are your favorite activities outside of work?"
- "What are your personal goals at this point?"
- "How do you like the United States?" (If the prospect is from another country.)

Obviously, the most useful topics for discussion are ones in which you share an interest or in which you can share your own stories.

Share your personal information as well, but *do not* dominate the conversation. Let the prospect have the spotlight. You don't want to talk too much or end up speaking for twice as long as your prospect. The focus should be on them.

You also don't want to "one-up" your prospect. For example, if the prospect tells you he has three Harley-Davidson motorcycles, don't tell him about your friend who has four. You can tell him your friend has some too, but don't bring up the larger number. You want to contribute something to the conversation, but don't retort with something that says: "You think that one's good? I've got a better story."

Be cautious about showing the prospect how knowledgeable you are in any area outside of your business and industry. If you start talking about facts she may be unfamiliar with in one of her areas of interest, she may start to feel that you are undermining her knowledge. Start with some basic questions or comments, and see how she reacts. If it becomes evident that she is very knowledgeable, you can then pursue a detailed conversation.

If, on the other hand, it becomes evident that she is a novice on the subject, back off and simply listen closely. Finally—and we're sure we don't even need to say this—you *never* want to correct any information the prospect is giving you unless it's a matter of life or death.

Whatever information you do obtain, add it to the prospect's profile. Continue to gather more personal information on future calls. Your overall long-term objective is to get lots of information and turn your customers into friends. Armed with this information, you can learn more about her interests and hobbies through sources such as the Internet, books, tapes, magazines, and the like. You can then send copies of articles or new books you find on the subject. This is a great way to build rapport and set you apart from all the other salespeople. A list of the information you should have on each customer is located on pages 526 through 527 in section VIII titled *After the Close*.

The more "pleasant" personal information you acquire, the better are your chances of building rapport, having a good conversation, and creating a positive selling experience.

At this stage, you need to gauge to the prospect's openness in talking about his or her personal life. If he is dominating the conversation, that's great! Let him talk. It's a marvelous way to gather personal information. On the other hand, if he is quiet or reticent, simply bridge back to the cold call.

In addition to the examples above, you can ask how long the prospect has been with his company and what other companies he has worked for. You may have some connections with the previous companies, if not the current one.

What about the person's name? Do you know anyone with the same last name? Even if the person you know is from another part of the country, you can ask if the prospect has relatives there. Also, listen for accents that may give you an idea of the prospect's origins.

Ask about local sports teams and local events. It truly is a small world. Begin probing with the above questions and see what turns up. When you do finally hit a common area of interest, the rapport will begin to build quickly. And that is your key objective at this stage.

Note: While you're visiting your prospect's office, you want to keep your eyes open for signs of the competition. In fact, you want to be looking *everywhere* for signs of the competition. Some examples of where to look are "sign-in" books, equipment, proposals or binders, letters, and gadgets in the prospect's office.

Name-dropping

Name-dropping is great way to add credibility to you, your company, and your product. We touched on this briefly when we referred to using leverage in the opening of your cold call. If you're talking to a person whom you don't know at all, dropping a common name or two of a person or a company with which you currently do business can quickly build credibility.

For example, do you do business with some well-known companies in the industry, or perhaps some companies in the area? In these cases, introduce this information in the cold call. That's assuming these companies approve of you doing so, and they won't become offended that you're now dealing with a potential competitor. You might say something like: "We've been doing business with most of the (whatever industry you're in) companies in the area. For example, in your area we deal with ABC Company, DEF Company and GHI Company and we're saving them an average of 28 percent on office supplies."

You can also drop the name of a well-recognized "outside" source that endorses your company. That might sound something like: "We're endorsed by the Better Business Bureau."

You may also want to introduce some of the big names in the industry. For example, if XYZ is the largest company in your territory and you're doing business with them, don't hesitate to mention this fact. You might say: "XYZ Bank, the largest bank in my territory, just installed three of the machines you're considering."

Clearly, if you're doing business with the largest competitor, you must be doing something right.

Finally, you may wish to mention the names of some individuals with whom you do business. If one of your current customers personally knows the prospect(s) you're calling upon, it would of course be a good idea to get a referral from your customer. There are times, however, where individuals are known throughout the community, although they might not personally know the people you're calling on. If your customer is a well-known political figure, entertainer, or business leader, you can build some credibility by casually dropping that person's name.

Note 1: Make sure it's all right to use a customer's name. As well, be aware of any situations in which a current or potential customer may be competing. You can use this to your advantage, but it can also annoy or anger some people.

Note 2: Some smaller companies may feel unimportant if you're doing business with all the big guys. Sometimes the competition will even use that against you. In these situations you need to reassure the "small guy" that he will be treated just like a VIP. You could say: "One of the things my customers appreciate is that even though we deal with some major companies, they still get very personalized attention and are treated as a very important customer. You will have my office number, cell number (also include your home number if possible), and I promise to respond to you quickly."

Asking Questions and Listening to the Prospect

Asking Questions

Question asking is one of the most overlooked aspects of selling and is most important during the cold call. Most salespeople are so eager to sell something that many never even bother to find out what, if anything, the prospect is looking for. Rather than ask questions to determine how to best help the prospect, they spend most of their time trying to talk the prospect into buying their product. If you spend some time asking *the right questions* in the beginning of the selling process, you will find closing is much easier and happens more often.

When you are speaking with a prospect, ask mostly open-ended questions, questions that require *more* than a yes, no, or other one-word answer. Open-ended questions allow for more detail and more specifics. As well, open-ended questions generally tend to be higher-quality questions, and higher-quality questions will give you credibility and set you apart from other salespeople. Occasionally, questions with yes-or-no answers are appropriate, but open-ended ones are almost always better.

Sometimes during a cold call, you want to ask a ridiculous yes-or-no question to get the prospect's attention and find out if you're wasting your time. The following is an example:

- "Joe, if I could guarantee you the stock would go up, would you be interested?"

These are also questions that lead the prospect in the direction you want her to go. Ask questions that the prospect must answer in the way you want her to answer. Here are some examples:

- "Mary, if I could show you a way to increase the return on your investments by 30 percent, would you be interested?"
- "Mary, if I could show you a way to increase your machine uptime and efficiency by 35 percent, would you be interested?"

If she answers no, you simply say, "Thanks, Mary. Have a nice day." If, on the other hand, she says something like, "Well, yes, of course. But there's no way you can guarantee that, at least not legally." Then you have an opening. At that point, with regard to the first question, you might say something like: "Look, Mary, we know there are no guarantees except death and taxes. At the same time, let me ask you a question. If you make your first investment with me and it goes up, we'll probably do more business, right? (Wait for an affirmative answer.) If you invest and it goes down, what are the odds you'll send me a bunch of money and referrals? Not very good, right?"

Again, wait for an affirmative answer. Then say, "Mary, do you see why it's imperative that I do well for you on the first trade? I promise to call you only when I have something that merits your attention. Is that fair enough?"

Without asking questions, you will be operating on assumptions. Many salespeople are so convinced their product is the best they assume people will want it more than other products on the market. They also assume that the features they find most admirable will also be most admirable in others' views. The same is true of the lesser features.

Assumptions are the reason most salespeople fear certain objections and find they encounter them repeatedly. They believe that *everyone* will reach the same conclusion. The point is that people vary dramatically in how they view the world and thus how they view you, your company, and your product or service. In order to figure out what that view is, you need to ask pertinent questions to find out what is *really* going on in the prospect's mind.

For example, a salesperson's product may have a cutting-edge 17-inch plasma color screen that he thinks is the greatest feature to hit the market in years. It may be inconceivable to the salesperson that someone would *not* want this feature. As a result, he assumes the prospect will want it and adds it to the pricing. Later, the salesperson discovers that the prospect bought the product for $3,000.00 less from a competitor because they opted not to buy the 17-inch plasma screen. Instead, they bought the 12-inch monochrome screen.

The salesperson had made a big assumption that ultimately cost him the sale. On the other hand, instead of assuming, the next salesperson asked the question, "17-inch plasma or 12-inch monochrome?"

When asking questions, realize that every person that you encounter is a unique person, has a unique life experience, a unique intelligence level, and unique needs and desires. It's amazing how many salespeople lump everyone into one category.

So your objective is to ask questions that get the information you need to make the sale and at the same time set you apart from all other salespeople.

We've already discussed the issue of questions on pages 90 to 94. Following are some additional questions that an investment advisor might ask:

- "What are your investment goals?" (These may be early retirement, paying for a college education, caring for parents, or just building as big a nest egg as possible.)
- "Do you have certain companies or industries in which you'd prefer to avoid investing for ethical or other reasons?"
- "Are there certain countries in which you want to avoid investing?"
- "Are there any industries, companies, or countries that you think may be good investments?"
- "Do you have any ideas on how you'd like to achieve your financial goals?"
- "Have you considered setting up a trust fund, scholarship fund, or investing in a college savings program?" (If they have children.)
- "How did you get to where you are today?" (Did he or she inherit money, start penniless and become a multi-millionaire? This will tell you whether they are risk-takers, conservative, or otherwise.)
- "Do you follow any rules when you invest?"
- "Why are you looking outside of your current advisor for advice at this point?" (You might use the word vendor instead of advisor depending upon your business)
- "How much investment knowledge do you have?"
- "How did you acquire your knowledge?"

Treat the meeting with your prospect as a job interview. Find out what he or she is seeking and how you can help.

The point of all these questions is to learn about your prospect's beliefs, values, likes, dislikes, and fears. Questions such as these help you discover what makes each person unique. You will learn about people's history, which, in turn, will give you an idea of where they may be going.

Did the prospect work for a union for years or does he detest unions for some reason? Is there an area of the world he dislikes due to some negative past experiences? Was he fired from IBM?

All of these pieces of information are important because, for example, if he was fired from IBM, you don't want to tell him how IBM looks like a great investment and suggest he load up on it.

What if you were to recommend a fund that invests in Asian Pacific Rim countries, only to discover the prospect has a negative view of that part of the world? Not only would you not get the sale, but you might also create a rift in the relationship. And if you don't ask questions, it will appear to the prospect that you are interested only in making a sale.

We tend to judge a book by its cover and make assumptions based solely upon what we see. For example, as an investment advisor you might assume that a prospect in his seventies is looking for some conservative investments. Before you group him with your other clients in the same age range, ask questions. He may be a typical investor in his seventies, but before you assume so and allow conservative recommendations to fly out of your mouth, ask some questions and be sure you're not wrong.

Asking the right questions during the cold call conveys an image of professionalism and caring. These are two of the most important factors in building rapport with a prospect.

Effective Listening

The other side of asking questions is listening effectively. If you ask the right questions, you're halfway there. By asking the right questions, you open the possibility of receiving the right answers. But in addition to asking the right questions, you must also listen correctly. Following are several good listening tips:

- Pay very close attention. Be interested in what your prospect is saying and don't allow your mind to wander, thinking about what you want to say next.
- Write key information down but make sure you're not missing information while writing.
- Don't interrupt. Be sure your prospect is finished talking.
- Make sure you body language matches your active listening.
- Ask follow-up questions. Be sure you understand what the person is saying.
- Read between the lines and hear what is *really* being said.

The more listening you do, the more effective you will become with people. People like to talk about themselves, and they like people who listen to them. On the other hand, people—particularly potential clients—do not gravitate to those who talk about themselves too much.

At the beginning of the cold call, you will be the person talking to let your prospect know who you are and why you're there. You will also be talking to build rapport and to discuss ideas that lead to the next step in the selling process. Outside of that, all the talking you do should be in the form of questions. You should spend the majority of the cold call listening. The more you listen, the more the prospect will be willing to listen to you.

Here are some guidelines to follow regarding the notes you take during your cold call:

- Take comprehensive notes when listening. You want to capture all relevant information.
- Write down the prospect's answers to your questions. They don't need to be verbatim, but they should capture the essence of what was said.
- Your notes need to be legible. You don't want to be struggling when you try to read them later.
- Write down keywords and phrases the prospect uses so you can use those during the presentation and close. This is a kind of mirroring.
- Organize and expand your notes immediately after the call while everything is still fresh in your mind.

Ultimately, the formula for asking questions and listening is simple: Ask a good question, then be quiet and actively listen to the answer!

We love pertinent sayings. As this one goes: "People don't care how much you know until they know how much you care." By asking smart questions and actively listening, you will convey a professional message, and people will open up to you and want to do business with you.

Great questioning and listening skills will pay enormous dividends. If you're good at these, keep working on this strength. If your questioning and listening skills could use some work, do everything you can to improve both.

Body Language

You want to be alert to what your prospect may be telling you with his or her body language. As a rule, a person's eyes are the best indicator as to how he or she feels.

While most books on body language will tell you that crossed arms suggest someone is closed to your communication, that's not necessarily true. These books will also tell you to watch the prospect's hand position, shoulders, and other body parts for clues as to how the person feels. But if you want to know what the person is really thinking, watch their eyes—they are the most telling.

- Is your prospect looking around?
- Are his eyes glazed over?
- Is he fighting to stay awake?
- Does he have a look of confusion?
- Is he looking at his watch or otherwise looking away from you?
- Does he have an intense look?
- Is he focused on and absorbed with what you're presenting?
- Is he looking at you from time to time?

The eyes are mirrors of what's going on internally. Other bodily gestures and mannerisms enter into the equation only when extremes are involved. If your prospect is completely reclined and relaxed when she should be on the edge of her chair, you have a problem. If she is leaning back with her arms folded, and she really looks as though she couldn't care less—once again, you have a problem. These are extreme reactions and not difficult to notice. But subtleties in body language are very rarely indicators of exactly how someone feels.

In addition to watching the prospect's body language or eye movements, pay attention to your own body language and eye movements. While the body language of your prospect may not be a big indicator of her reaction to you, you still want to ensure your body language sends all the right messages.

Keep your posture "open"—keep your arms uncrossed, your hands open with palms mostly upward, a relaxed facial expression, and *look your prospect in the eye as often as possible.* As we've noted, when you're looking at a person, look directly into her left eye. We realize you will be looking at things other than the prospect from time to time, such as information you may be discussing. But you want to be focused directly on the prospect's left eye as much as possible. *Always* be looking at the prospect when she is speaking. The only time you may look away is either when you are talking, looking at your written material, or when the prospect draws your attention to something else.

Be on guard for body language gimmicks. We used an example of a body language gimmick earlier when we discussed shaking hands. While it may be true that the person whose hand is uppermost during the handshake is in control of the conversation, the car salesperson who grabbed one of our hands and deliberately turned them so his was on top immediately lost control of the conversation.

While people you encounter may be familiar with mirroring, looking into the left eye, and other subtle body language, these techniques are generally accepted as a way to connect with and understand another person. On the other hand, gimmicks like the handshake technique tend to tell people, "I'm in control and my objective is to dominate you and the conversation." That's *not* a good message to send.

Identifying the Prospect's Personality Type

Make a note of the personality type of your prospect. Identifying personality type will help during the presentation and closing portions of the selling process. Your discussions should flow differently from one personality type to another. For example, with one personality type, you will spend a good deal of time building personal rapport. With another type, you will spend very little time with personal rapport and get to business quickly.

Although everyone is different and there are as many different buyer types as there are people in the world, psychologists and psychiatrists break people down into four buying types. We will call them the Driver, the Thinker, the "Yes" Person, and the Partier. In the following paragraphs, you will learn who they are, how to spot them, and how to deal with them.

While most of us are a combination of these four types, and we can be any one depending upon the situation, we all have a tendency toward one or another. After watching and listening to someone for a very short period, you can usually tell which category he or she generally falls under. Here are some basic definitions of the four personality types.

The Driver

The label pretty much says it all. The Driver drives decisions. The Driver makes things happen. Most leaders are Drivers. Owners of companies, Presidents, CEOs, and other corporate hierarchy are usually Drivers. They tend to be early risers and hard workers. They are usually short, quick, and to the point. Drivers are very possessive of their time. Drivers like to make decisions and they like to make them quickly. They are direct and tend not to show a lot of emotion.

You want to be talking to Drivers, as they are your avenue to the quickest buying decision. Typically, the Driver will be able to make the decision himself, and if he can't, he is usually effective at getting others to follow once you've won him over.

The Thinker

The Thinker likes to see vast quantities of information. Once they see your initial offerings—verification on paper—they want to see more. Thinkers have a difficult time making decisions because they always feel as though there is some minute detail they have overlooked that could possibly change the whole picture. They are very detail-oriented and go over information repeatedly. They want to become an expert themselves. Thinkers have trouble taking someone else's word on something—they need to see, touch, smell, hear, and feel for themselves.

Of the four personality types, you will have the most trouble getting the Thinker to trust you. You can sell the Thinker, but it's going to take a while—no cold call closes here. You need testimonials, references, and *proof* that your product or service is the best for them. You need to demonstrate to the Thinker in detail that your product or service will do exactly what you say it will.

The "Yes" Person

"Yes" people want to get along with everyone and do not like conflict. They start nodding their head "yes" before you get the first word out of your mouth, and they continue nodding their heads five minutes after the conversation is over. They will agree with you on everything except when it comes to signing the contract.

The "Yes" Person is probably the toughest of the personality types to sell. It is simply not in their nature to make a decision, and to get them to make a decision on their own is virtually impossible.

The Partier

The Partier has lots of energy and displays lots of emotion. The Partier gets along well with others and can make decisions. These personality types actually thrive in a dynamic environment and get bored very quickly with routine, mundane tasks. The Partier is the life of the party and the most likely to be disciplined after the office holiday party. These people are creative and full of life.

The Partier is more difficult to sell than the Driver, but is much easier to sell than both the "Yes" Person and the Thinker. But Partiers need more proof than Drivers and they need time to think about the decision. Their decisions are not lightning-quick, but they are not slow like the Thinker or impossible like the "Yes" Person.

Things to Look for and How to Deal with Different Personality Types

You identify someone's personality type the same way you identify anything else: by observing. What do you see and hear?

The Driver

The Driver's office, clothes, and car:

The Driver's office has flashy awards, trophies, and other "king of the hill" and prestigious mementos. The head of the 12-point buck he shot on his Canadian hunting trip, the die-cast model of his Harley, or the award he won at the car show for his 1972 Chevelle SS. The speaker's award from the Women's Business Forum, her business degree from Yale, and her golf trophies.

The business male (office executive) Driver wears dark suits (black, brown, gray, or navy blue) with either conservative or bright ties. The worker male (working executive) Driver wears the highest quality work clothes—maybe sneakers, but probably boots, gloves, and quality outerwear.

The business female Driver wears dark (black, brown, gray, or navy blue) or bright (red, green, blue) business suits. The worker woman Driver wears the highest quality work clothes—probably sneakers, maybe boots, sweaters, gloves, and quality outerwear.

The Driver drives either a luxury automobile, something big, or both. Luxury: Cadillac, Mercedes, 740 BMW, Porsche, Ferrari. Or something big: Ford Expedition, Chevy Suburban, Hummer, or Cadillac Escalade.

The Driver's body position:

The Driver will not show a great deal of emotion, although some can show a lot of energy. She may appear impatient if not interested or if you go into too much detail. She may have a somewhat intense look on her face with her eyes slightly squinted and brows slightly furrowed when taking in information, but she'll sit up slightly and move closer when she sees something that catches her attention.

Other Driver characteristics:

While some Drivers can be high energy and flamboyant, most tend to be monotone, use little hand movement, and have controlled facial expressions and a rigid posture. All Drivers like to get right down to business. Drivers are active and direct, formal and self-sufficient.

Signs that the Driver is not interested:
- Directly states his or her objection.
- Will try to end the conversation.
- Appears to be impatient, looking at his watch, using phrases such as: "Okay, I understand that. What's the bottom line?" or "Look, all I really want to know is…"

Driver do's:
- Get down to business.
- Be straightforward and to the point.
- Keep points short and succinct.

- Stroke their egos.
- Let them believe they are in control of the meeting.
- Name-drop your biggest and most impressive customers.
- Speak directly and honestly.

Driver don'ts:
- Don't use wishy-washy, feel-good language.
- Don't go off on tangents or talk about unrelated issues.
- Don't spend too much time on anything unless they want to.
- Don't get technical or give a lot of detail.

The Thinker

The Thinker's office, clothes, and car:

The Thinker's office is filled with gadgets, parts, and technical manuals. For the most part, the office is a mess. There are probably enough new and used parts to build a Space Shuttle from scratch. They have group photographs from classes they've taken. They may also have maps or technical posters on the walls.

Thinkers like jeans and short sleeves, sneakers, or boots. They are not particular about their clothing or appearance. If they must dress up, they look out of place—a red tie with a blue short-sleeved shirt. They also wear the latest gadgets. They have the latest wireless earpiece to answer their phone. They have a wireless computer and can send e-mails, drink coffee, and drive all at the same time. The Thinker can often take a computer apart and put it back together—blindfolded.

The Thinker drives a car that makes sense from all aspects, good in all kinds of weather, reliable, good gas mileage, big enough to carry people and parts. The Thinker drives a Ford Taurus, Chevy Impala, or a typical company car.

The Thinker's body position:

The Thinker will sit back, shut up, and listen to what you have to say without showing much emotion. The Thinker tends to have a somewhat intense look on his face with eyes slightly squinted and brows furrowed. His arms may be folded. He may not be looking at you, but he is absorbing and analyzing what you are telling him.

Other Thinker characteristics:

Thinkers tend to make less direct eye contact, don't say much, have relaxed hand movements, and are interested in facts and data. The Thinker uses logic as opposed to emotion. The Thinker is also quite reserved.

Signs that the Thinker is not interested:
- Will try to stump you or get you off track with a bunch of highly technical questions that he hopes you can't answer.
- Will sit back, arms folded, eyebrows furrowed with a negative facial expression.
- Will begin making excuses as to why you must conclude the presentation.

Thinker do's:
- Use a slow pace.
- Provide lots of backup information and proof.
- Use detail.
- Focus on the logical reasons to move ahead.
- Be prepared. We're not saying you shouldn't be prepared for other buyer types, but Thinkers can pick you to pieces on details. With a Thinker, you need to be able to answer every conceivable question.
- Use technical language, but be sure they understand what you are saying, and you understand what they are saying.
- Be specific with numbers and facts and ensure they are correct.
- Compliment the Thinker's knowledge level. Talk to them as though they know more than you do.

Note: When you are meeting with a Thinker, you may want to bring one of your technical people along. Just make sure he or she is prepared to answer any questions you can't.

Thinker don'ts:
- Don't give generalizations or ballpark numbers.
- Don't overstate or exaggerate. Thinkers like exact data; they don't like "gray areas."

The "Yes" Person

The "Yes" Person's office, clothes, and car:

The "Yes" Person's office is clean, neat, and organized, with an inbox and outbox. A calendar with a scenic or animal motif typically hangs on the wall, and there are photographs of loved ones on her desk. She may also have figurines on her desk—the M&M guys, and the like. There may even be a small stuffed animal or two.

The "Yes" Person is a clean, neat dresser. If there is a dress code at work, she defines it. She is always well groomed and her clothes are well taken care of.

The "Yes" Person likely drives a small car or mini-van.

The "Yes" Person's body position:

The "Yes" Person is on the edge of his chair and attentive. His eyes are wide open and he is nodding his head "yes" and giving you a verbal "uh huh, uh huh" as you speak. He will typically show *only* positive emotions. His arms are open with hands resting on his knees when sitting and by his side when standing.

Other "Yes" Person characteristics:

The "Yes" Person likes to talk about the weather and people-related subjects. Facial expressions tend to be animated, and the "Yes" Person makes direct eye contact. "Yes" People support others and are interested in others' feelings.

Signs that the "Yes" Person is not interested:
- Will tell you he has to talk it over with someone else.
- Will tell you he has to think about it or come up with another reason why he can't make a decision right now.
- Will express negativity through questions.

"Yes" Person do's:
- Use emotion, humor, and be sure to smile.
- Spend time building personal rapport. Talk about families and community activities.
- Show some excitement and energy.
- Once the conversation gets to business, keep it there *most* of the time. Many "Yes" People will get off track and start talking about other things.

You need to spend some time there, but bring the conversation back to business quickly.
- Keep the business conversation clear and to the point.
- Use "together" words like "our" and "we" and stress your commitment to them.

"Yes" Person don'ts:
- Don't use a stern business tone. Keep it warm and friendly.
- Don't push while closing. You do want to be firm, however.
- Don't dictate or be too forward, but stand your ground.

The Partier

The Partier's office, clothes, and car:

The Partier's office is a mess. The mess does not include the same things as the Thinker's mess, but it is still a mess. There are papers everywhere. Most times the calendar is on the wrong month.

The Partier is a flashy dresser. Men wear flashy ties, women wear colorful outfits. They can occasionally have a slightly disheveled appearance, but for the most part are fairly well groomed for meetings.

The Partier drives a nice car but, in most cases, not as nice as the Driver's. She may drive a 3 or 5 Series BMW, a sporty car, an Infinity, or a company car.

The Partier's body position:

The Partier is on the edge of her chair if interested and sitting back if not interested. The Partier will show emotion and let you know in which direction she is swaying. If not interested, she will take on much the same posture as the Thinker, arms crossed, brows furrowed, with a negative look on her face. If interested, the Partier will take on almost the same posture as the "Yes" Person—open, interested, and positive.

Other Partier characteristics:

Partiers are faster paced, show emotion, use lots of hand movement, have a louder voice than the other types, lean forward, and make direct eye contact. Partiers, as their title indicates, are the life of the party. Partiers are dynamic communicators and express their opinions openly.

Signs that the Partier is not interested:

- Will make direct negative statements or jokes about your product or company.
- Will tell you what she doesn't like about you, your product, or your company.
- Will tell you directly and bluntly that she does not have time to listen to you or has to end the conversation immediately.

Partier do's:

- Make it fun and convey yourself as a fun person.
- Be businesslike, but also open and friendly.
- Be direct, but soften your approach a little.
- Build rapport by talking about social activities, fun vacation spots, or extreme sports.
- Give lively, fun presentations, and incorporate computer graphics.

Partier don'ts:

- Don't get overly technical or bogged down in detail.
- Don't get sidetracked talking about social events. Partiers love to talk about what they did last weekend or on their last vacation. While it's fine to talk about these things and build rapport, don't spend too much time here. You want to keep the conversation mostly on business.

Rules for Dealing with *All* Personality Types

Here are rules for dealing with *all* people:

- Be professional.
- Don't argue or tell people they're wrong.
- Don't talk negatively about the competition.
- Be prepared.
- Be presentable.
- Don't tell off-color jokes or make off-color remarks.
- Be honest and straightforward.
- Put yourself in the other person's shoes.
- Align with the other person and try to make a friend.

Your objective is to notice your prospect's characteristics, and then mirror him. If your prospect gets down to business, you get down to business. If he talks about the weather, then you talk about the weather—at least initially before you shift the conversation to business. If he talks fast, you talk fast; slow, you talk slow. If she's on the edge of her chair, get on the edge of your chair.

Remember: You also have a personality type. As a salesperson, you are probably either a Driver or a Partier, but you could be any of the four. Let's take a look at some examples of salespeople and their interactions with different personality types.

The salesperson with a soft style: Tom is open, friendly, and begins his sales call by trying to build personal rapport. He uses a soft-sell approach that is indirect and unassuming.

Tom's first sales call of the day is Jill. Jill is quiet, laid back, and is also interested in personal relationships. From a personality standpoint, this call should go well.

Tom's second call of the day is Sam. Sam is a direct, hard-nosed, and get-down-to-business individual. From a personality standpoint, unless Tom changes his approach, this will be a train wreck.

Now let's look at Susan:

Susan is a real go-getter, a very enterprising salesperson. She has a Type A personality, and she cuts through all the subtleties and gets right to business. Suppose her first call of the day is with Sam, above. In this case, she probably won't have a problem; their personality types match.

Now, suppose her second call is with Jill, above. Unless Susan slows down, warms up slightly, and takes a personal interest in Jill, she will have a problem making a sale.

As a salesperson, you'll find it helps to know your own personality type and tendencies, and then adapt it to your prospects'.

I See, I Feel, I Hear

In addition to determining your prospect's personality type, it will also be helpful to know whether the prospect is visual, auditory, or kinesthetic. In other words, through which sense(s) does she tend to perceive the world? Through the eyes, the ears, or through touch and feel?

Visual people tend to speak quickly and use phrases like, "It looks good to me" or "I see what you mean." They think in pictures and their brains move rapidly through thoughts. They need to see and read things.

Auditory people process ideas somewhat more slowly and use phrases like, "I hear what you're saying" or "That sounds good to me." They experience the world through sound.

Kinesthetic people process things even more slowly than auditory people, and they tend to speak slowly. They use phrases like, "This feels right" or "I'm trying to grasp that idea." They experience the world through feelings.

About 70 percent of all people are visual. To a degree, as with personality types, we can be a combination of two or all three of these even though we all favor one over the others. In sales, the important thing to keep in mind is that while you want to involve as many of the senses as possible in your presentation and close, try to emphasize the sense that your prospect prefers.

After your cold call, make a note of which personality type you believe the prospect is and which sense you believe is dominant. From there, use that information to tailor your presentation and closes appropriately.

How Age Affects Your Prospect's Focus

Depending upon your business, it may be helpful to look at the various life stages people go through. This will be particularly helpful in the insurance and securities fields. Keep in mind there will be exceptions to these generalizations, but they will apply to approximately 95 percent of the population.

Although the following are good guides, you still need to do your homework to discover the unique characteristics of each individual.

Young Adults	**Middle Age**	**Mature Adult 60+**

General Life Situation:

Very materialistic	Family/less materialistic	Family focused
Focused only on the present	Present and future	Leaving a legacy
Little savings	Building wealth	Largest nest egg
Little money knowledge	Some knowledge/beliefs	Solid money beliefs

Focus and Perception:

Small picture – details	Less detail; more big picture	Focus on big picture
More focus on logic	Logic and emotion	Focus on gut feeling
More focus on price	Can be convinced of value	Focused on value
Technology focused	Learning technology	Prefer hard copy
Faster is better	Pace depends on situation	More methodical pace
More fickle – change easily	Open minded	Set in their ways
No concrete life view	Fairly firm beliefs	Set values and beliefs

Use these tendencies in your approach and in the entire selling process. Mirroring someone in his sixties versus someone in his thirties will usually vary greatly.

How Gender Affects Your Prospect's Focus

Gender is another factor that will affect buying decisions. Following are some generalizations that will give you a good idea of gender-specific tendencies.

Women	**Men**
More relationship focused	More focused on the business deal
More family focused	More business focused
Team focused	Focused on competition
Big-picture focus	Tunnel vision
Softer, indirect approach	More direct
More creative and descriptive	More concise

As a salesperson, you need to adjust your language to your prospect's gender. Also, women tend to want a closer relationship and to hear from the salesperson more often than men do. To most men, interactions with salespeople are simply business transactions. Women view the transactions more on a personal level.

Important Note: Factors relating to personality type, the senses, age, and gender can get confusing, especially if you're new to selling. If that is the case, don't be too concerned or allow yourself to feel overwhelmed. These are some of the subtleties you'll become more aware of as your career advances.

Chapter 10

Other Thoughts Regarding the Cold Call

Keep Track of Your Calls

Keep track of the number of calls you make and what happens on each call. For example, if you made ten calls, perhaps two weren't there, two you didn't get in to see, two weren't qualified, two weren't interested, and you got two leads.

You also want to get some reasons behind the numbers. *When* will the two people be there? *Why* didn't you get in to see the two prospects? *Why* didn't the two qualify? *Why* weren't the two interested? *Why* were the two leads you did get interested?

From this information, you will start to recognize patterns and areas that need work. For example, are you calling at the right time of day? Are you effectively handling the gatekeeper? Are you calling a qualified list? Are you building sufficient interest? What are you doing right on the leads you do get?

Keep track of this information on a sheet of paper, recording the information after each call. Take the results to your manager and the top salespeople in your company, get their feedback, and then work on your weak areas. Save this information to review, and look for trends.

How Much Time Should You Spend on a Call?

Keep an eye on the amount of time you spend on each call. Spending too much time on each call can cut into your total number of calls and/or keep you from other potentially more productive calls. Not spending enough time on each call can lead to less qualified leads, less rapport, and less business.

Generally, your cold calls should last about five to twelve minutes. This should be enough time to create some interest, build rapport, and ensure the prospect is qualified and open to doing business with you.

In addition to the time you spend speaking, watch other aspects of your calls. For example, how much time do you spend waiting for prospects? This may be unavoidable in your industry. Talk to the top salespeople and your manager and find out what is standard and how they deal with this. What other tasks do you spend time on during the day?

Don't Make Your Mistakes on the Big Guys

When you start working for a new company, or you are just beginning your selling career, it doesn't matter how good a salesperson you think you are, *don't* make your first sales call on the biggest account(s).

Many salespeople have enormous egos and are lured into selling by the promise of big paychecks. Others, particularly veteran salespeople who have just started with a new company, have visions of becoming a hero by landing that *big* account during their first week. While this can be tempting, whatever you do, don't attempt it when you're new.

Great salespeople aren't born, they're developed. You need to go through the learning process before you go after the biggest accounts. Learn your product, learn your presentation, learn the answers to the questions you'll most likely be asked, learn the responses to objections, and then start practicing on the little guys. Even though you think you know all the sales tricks, with a new company, product, or service, you're going to make lots of mistakes with the little guys. And that's fine. That's the place to make your mistakes and get them out of the way. Only after you've learned the ropes and have become seasoned can you then get in your boat and chase Moby Dick.

Objections During the Cold Call

If a prospect gives you objection after objection during the cold call, there may be better places you can spend your time. When you get an objection during the cold call, take a quick swing or two at it, and then move on. You may get, "I'm not interested" or "We're all set" or "I've already got that covered." One of the best comebacks to any objection on the cold call is: "Joe, if I can show you (your major benefit), would you be the slightest bit interested?"

If you get a no, move on. If you get a yes, a maybe, or a question such as "How would you do that?" then you have a potential prospect.

For example, let's say you are selling office supplies and the prospect tells you: "I'm all set." Follow with, "Joe, if I could guarantee you a 25 percent savings on supplies, would you be at all interested?" If he says no, let him go. If he says anything other than no, keep going.

If he says, "How could you guarantee that type of savings?" Say, "Joe, there are no guarantees but death and taxes, yet we've been averaging 25 to 35 percent savings for our customers. Would you agree to simply let me compare prices on some of the more popular items you're using?" Then just keep the conversation going.

The key is to test that first cold call objection with a "hit 'em between the eyes" statement just to see how serious he is. If he slams the door, move on. If he begins to close the door but stops and peaks out, keep asking questions.

If you respond with your strongest benefit and don't get anywhere, take one more crack at the objection with the following: "While I can appreciate you have a good relationship with (the competition), occasionally people will get outside quotes just to keep their current vendors honest. That makes sense, doesn't it?" While you may not be successful, you at least want to take a shot at this objection.

In general, the more time you have invested in the prospect, the more effort you want to put into countering the objection before moving on. Even though you haven't invested much time in the cold call stage, you still want to test the objection, but only briefly. On a follow-up call, you can spend a little more time on the objection. And if you are in the middle or at the end of your presentation when you get the objection, give it the most time and the best shot you can.

What Are You Calling to Sell Me?

This isn't an objection; however, it's a close relative. This question is a prospect's defense mechanism used to extract information from you quickly, just to make sure he or she isn't missing anything. After you get your first sentence or two out you'll usually hear, "Look, just get to the point. What do you want to sell me?"

When you get this question on a cold call, answer it like this: "Mr. Prospect, I don't want to sell you anything today—in fact, I'm not even sure my product or service is right for you. We have been (give one of your major benefits here such as, 'saving companies in your area an average of 36 percent on printing'). All I'd like to do is spend ten minutes with you (or however much time you need) and see how much, if any, money we could save you. Do you have some time now or would next Tuesday be better for you?"

When the prospect asks this question, it's important to stay calm, cool, and collected. State emphatically that you're *not* trying to sell anything right now, give a major benefit, and then ask for the appointment. You may still get, "I'm not interested," but at least you took a shot at it.

Getting in Touch with the Hard-to-Reach "Hot" Prospect

Here's the scenario: You've got a hot prospect who said to give him a phone call next Tuesday because he's going to make his decision then. You call on Tuesday and get his voice mail. You leave a message stating that you're calling to follow up and ask that he get back to you. You hear nothing. On Wednesday, you call again. Again, nothing. Here's what to do next.

On Thursday, telephone every hour starting at eight in the morning. *Do not* leave any messages. Call in the hopes of getting the person *on the phone*.

Use this technique any time you need to get in touch with someone on a critical issue and you think she may be ducking you. With this technique, you are being persistent without being obnoxious. If you were to call every hour and leave a message, you'd severely annoy the prospect. Obviously, you want to avoid aggravating her.

Note 1: It is very possible the prospect will have caller I.D., especially at a residence, and know that you called every hour and didn't leave a message. If this is the case, block your call or make sure you're calling from a number that is blocked. In the worst-case scenario, even if the person did know you were calling, you're starting from zero anyway. You have nothing, so if you end up with nothing, you're no worse off.

Note 2: In a case such as this you can and should also show up in person. In the above scenario, make it Wednesday. You can say you happened to be in the area.

Creative Ideas to Crack That "Big" Account When All Else Fails

Okay, you've cold called, you've left voice-mail and e-mail messages, you've sent letters, you've tried everything you know, and nothing is working. Now what?

The first thing you can do is give up. Let's face it—there may be better places you can spend your time than chasing a prospect who simply is not responding. On the other hand, this may be one of those large accounts that could propel your numbers through the roof. If you decide to chase the account despite rejection, you're going to have to get creative, and you're going to have to be both patient and persistent. You need to stand out and catch the prospect's attention—without being a pest.

We know one sales rep who would visit a Halloween store and buy plastic skeletons for tough prospects. She'd put the skeleton in a large manila envelope and attach her business card to it with a note. The note read, "This is me waiting for you to call me."

The same sales rep would also buy fake arms at the Halloween store. They were actually fake forearms with a hand and part of a white shirtsleeve attached. She would secure the arm to the top of a metal container that was filled with her company's cookies. They had one special large-sized cookie that she would secure in the hand of the fake arm. When the prospect opened the cookie container, a note popped out that read, "I'd give my left arm to be your sole cookie supplier."

Another sales rep we know used cheap baby shoes. She would glue a shoe in the middle of a metal platter and place samples of her product all around the shoe. She would put her business card in the shoe with a note on the back that read, "Just trying to get my foot in the door."

Someone else we know used a helium balloon in a box to land a job interview. She simply attached her résumé to a helium balloon so that when the interviewer opened the box, the balloon floated out with her résumé attached.

These are just a few of the thousands of creative ideas you can use to catch a prospect's attention. We can guarantee that people will not be able to ignore you for long with ideas such as these. Eventually, you will get prospects to talk with you if you use creative ways to catch their attention. And often, you'll also get the prospect's business.

Besides the novel ideas above, what other things can you do to crack that big account?

- Can you obtain an introduction through someone else, perhaps a current customer or friend?
- What groups, organizations, or health clubs does the prospect belong to? You can join or attend events.
- What school did he or she attend? Do you know someone who also attended that school?
- Does he own a luxury car such as a BMW? If so, is he a member of the BMW Club? Does the prospect own a motorcycle, or an exclusive vehicle like a Hummer? Do you own a similar vehicle or have a friend or relative who does? You can bring this up or you or your friend or relative can join the club.

You need to look at all the angles, then *use* them. You can send articles and other tidbits that relate to the prospect's interests. Again, you can join the same health club, automobile club, or country club. You can use your friends and family members who belong to those organizations to get you in the door.

You can send flowers or balloons on the person's birthday. Get creative. There are unlimited opportunities for you to get your foot in the door. Just make sure that once you do get that foot in, you make it count.

Become Involved in Businesses to Which You'd Like to Sell

Becoming a customer of the businesses you'd like to sell to is another creative way to get in the door. Of course, you have to watch out for rules and regulations that prohibit conflict of interest. In the banking industry, vendors occasionally invest in the banks in their territory, and then use that investment as leverage in order to bid on projects for the bank.

Another angle in the banking business is to open a savings or checking account or buy a certificate of deposit or other product from the bank. When you become a customer and ask for their business in return, you want to be polite and do it properly. The following example is an approach you can use.

One of the banks in our area had the lowest loan rate around for mortgages. Because we were trying to land the account, we took out a mortgage and then let our contact know about it. We simply said, "By the way, you have some great people in your loan department. I recently took out a mortgage and everyone was very nice and helpful and made the entire process a pleasure."

Once your contact knows you are doing business there, he or she may feel an obligation to let you quote on jobs, and some will even find a way to give you business.

You Need to Think Quickly on the Cold Call

As we've mentioned before, you need to be ready for *anything* and you need to be able to think and react quickly.

Here's an example: A salesperson had a receptionist from a prospect's office hand him back his business card—ripped in half. The salesperson thought for a moment, then asked if he could borrow some tape. He proceeded to tape the card back together and also put tape all around the edges. He handed the taped card back to the receptionist and asked if she would please present it once again to the prospect.

This time she returned with the card—cut into three pieces. The sales rep proceeded to tape the card back together and also tape paper clips all around the edges, using about half the roll of tape to make sure they were secure. He then handed the card back to the receptionist. She smiled as she took it and left again, now apparently enjoying the game herself. This time the prospect came out laughing, and said, "Okay, come on in."

If you have the ability to think quickly in situations such as the one above, you will absolutely set yourself apart and you'll get through to see more prospects.

The Show Must Go On

If you have a tough cold call or two, you have to pick yourself up and move on. The prospect may tell you you're not only the worst salesperson he's met, but you're the worst person in the world. Despite this, you need to march to the next appointment with your head held as high as you can hold it. You can't take it personally. You'll never know what may have happened before your call or what kind of day the person has been having.

In sales, you need to have skin thicker than a rhinoceros's. The most successful salespeople keep going no matter what. Don't get us wrong—you'll have bad days, you'll have bad calls, and you'll probably have a bad attitude sometimes, but you need to learn how to handle rejection and use it as a fire beneath you to spur you on. Tell yourself, "Okay, I got that one out of the way and now I'm that much closer to my next sale!"

There's No Such Thing as a "Good Lead"

Almost all of us have been there. We get that great lead that we just know is going to buy. If we had to bet our life on it, we would. The conversation seemed to flow perfectly. The prospect said, "I can't believe you called! I was just looking into purchasing (whatever you sell)."

Great! You're on the same page as the prospect and she was enthusiastic while talking to you. You're already counting the appointment not as a lead, but as a sale.

You show up for the appointment and the receptionist informs you that the prospect is not there. You're a little thrown off, but you still feel pretty good about the prospect. You ask when she will be back so you can follow up. The receptionist tells you, "She should be back by two, but I would call first just to make sure."

You call a little after two, but she's not in. You call back at four—nothing. You call the next day and leave a message on voice mail for her to return your call.

Finally, you catch her the following week and she says, "Oh, hi. Yes, I've been quite busy. I know you've tried to reach me several times. Um, actually I bought (whatever you're selling) and I'm all set. I appreciate you following up, though."

You've either already had at least one experience like this or if you stay in sales long enough, you will. The point is that until you have a signed order, you have nothing. One signed order is worth ten good leads, maybe more. Even if you do have a good lead and someone who is ready to sign, you may run into other unforeseeable roadblocks.

One of us had an experience where the prospect was just about to sign an order when the phone rang. The prospect answered, then hung up the phone, said he needed to leave immediately, and in a rather abrupt manner ran out of the room. That order never got signed.

By no means are we telling you to be negative or to start looking for reasons why a deal isn't going to go through. We are simply saying you should maintain a level emotional state until the deal is actually done and it is truly time to celebrate. Stay focused and "in the game." Too many sports teams have started the celebration with one minute remaining, only to see the "impossible" happen, and next thing they know the other team is celebrating a victory.

Sales managers hate to hear about good leads, but they love to hear about good sales. Stay positive, stay focused, and count your chickens *when* they actually hatch.

Put Your Prospect's Customers First

Show respect for the people and businesses you are calling on. If you are walking into the facility at the same time as a customer, hold the door and allow that person to enter before you. Also, give up your chair in the waiting area and again, don't take up prime parking spots. These are for the prospect's customers.

Have Conversations

You want your sales calls to be sales conversations. Whether the objective of your sales call is to get an appointment, sell something, simply make a service call, or anything else, view the sales call as a conversation you are having with a close friend. In other words, keep it smooth, natural, and easy. If you keep your sales calls conversational, you'll find the other person will be much more relaxed and open with you.

Put Yourself in the Other Person's Shoes on *All* Calls

How do you like to be treated? How do you respond to certain salespeople or telephone marketing tactics? Chances are most people feel much the same way as you do. Think of the various salespeople you've encountered or telemarketers who have called you over the years. Were there any whom you liked? What did you like about them? They probably came across as friendly, honest, and straightforward. There were probably others you did not like. Why not? Were they pushy, obnoxious, or rude? Put yourself in the shoes of the person to whom you are talking and treat him or her the way you would like to be treated.

Chapter 11

The Cold Call—Putting It All Together

Now that we've covered cold calling extensively, let's summarize with an example of a successful cold call.

Before you begin cold calling, keep these keys in mind:

- You have to believe that what you are selling is the best, whether it is the best quality or the best value for the money.
- You must also believe that people are better off with your product than without it, and that they truly need your product.
- You have to look the part.

Let's focus on that last point first. *You must look professional.* By this we mean both your physical appearance and any actions you take as you prepare to make the cold call.

Your cold call starts in the parking lot, so realize you are on stage from that point forward. Make sure that your vehicle looks decent and clean and isn't filled with junk. Park in an appropriate spot. You don't want to be in someone else's spot and you also don't want to be towed or get any parking tickets.

Before you leave your vehicle, check your outfit and your appearance—your tie, coat, hair, teeth, etc. Make sure any materials you are carrying also look professional. No ugly bag, oversized hardware, and such. Eat a breath mint and use some eye drops, if necessary.

Have a basic brown business envelope or leather case containing a recent company annual report and literature on an item that may be of interest to your prospect.

Your main objective on the cold call is to introduce yourself to a prospective customer in a professional manner designed to pique their interest in doing business with you and your company. First impressions last forever, so make sure yours is *impeccable!*

Points to remember: If you are not sure you have the proper name of the contact person, call the company ahead of time. Tell them that you are directing a letter to Mr. or Ms. Prospect and want to confirm that you have the proper name and title. You also want to verify how the name is pronounced. If you have more than one person to contact, check the other names at the same time.

When you enter the business, walk into the reception area with a professional, businesslike demeanor and a sincere, confident expression. Approach the receptionist and say, "Hello. I was hoping to see Mr./Ms. (prospect's last name) for a moment."

Now that she knows what you want, present your card. Don't present the card first! If you do, she will be asking herself, "What's this character here for?" Her mind will be buzzing as she wonders how she's going to handle you—with a good, bad, or indifferent attitude. In most cases, her attitude will be bad or indifferent.

Note 1: Some offices don't have an official receptionist. If this is the case, move to a person who sits back a little farther from those near the front of the office. Often this will be a person with higher status in the company than the others.

When you approach the receptionist professionally and ask for a top person in the business by name, you will usually be treated well. As you present your card, say: "I've recently taken responsibility for this territory and simply want to introduce myself to Mr./Ms. Prospect. I won't be more than a few minutes."

If the highest-ranking person is not available, ask for one of the other contacts you have. The second contact should be close to the level of the first person you asked for. You don't want to ask for someone at too low a level. If an upper-level person is not available, leave your card with the receptionist with the assurance that she will present it to the person you asked for. Say something like: "Okay, I'll leave my card as evidence that I was here. Could you make sure Mr./Ms. Prospect gets it?"

Once she answers in the affirmative, say, "Great! I'll give Mr./Ms. Prospect a call to set up a meeting when it is convenient for him/her. Thanks for your help."

Note 2: It is important to get the receptionist's name as well. When you call on the phone, you want to be able to call this person by name first, and then ask to speak to the prospect.

Even if you don't get to the top person, you have still introduced yourself at some level in the account. Impressing the receptionist or an assistant while not seeing "the boss" is important. They are the ones who will allow or prevent your access to the boss.

When you reach the prospect, begin your call with something like: "Mr. Prospect, I'm (your name) with (your company). I'm simply here to introduce myself so if I can be of service to you at some point, you'll know whom to contact."

Note 3: You may also name drop or use a "hit 'em between the eyes" statement depending upon your call objective and other circumstances.

Open the discussion with a comment such as: "I'd like to tell you about our plans for the future, but frankly, I'm more interested in what your future plans are."

Generally speaking, the higher the level of person to whom you are talking, the more enthusiastic they will be when talking about their company's future. Your good listening skills will have a great deal to do with how much you learn here and what impression this person forms of you. Listen well and take notes.

Points to remember: As the prospect is talking, maintain good eye contact, lean slightly forward, and wear an expression on your face that says you are listening intently and are interested. You can comment from time to time, but only to demonstrate that what the prospect is saying is important. Keep your comments short because you want to keep the prospect talking.

The prospect will tell you more if she senses you appreciate and are interested in the information she's sharing. An expression of empathy will also help you greatly toward gaining respect, which is an important objective of the cold call. A nod of the head or a very short comment in which you show agreement can be important in keeping the prospect's conversation going.

Do not interrupt while the prospect tells you of the company's plans for the future, and be sure she is finished before you start to talk about you or your company. If you have something to say that you feel is important, perhaps triggered by a comment the prospect has made, hold it whenever possible until she has completely told her story. To be certain she is finished, pause five seconds before you speak.

After the prospect has completely finished, you can then introduce any ideas you have regarding what you heard. You might say something like: "As you were talking about (whatever triggered an idea) it crossed my mind that…" and then state what you thought. What you say should be relevant to what you heard. Your comment should be one that demonstrates your understanding and appreciation of the importance of what the prospect mentioned.

Be open-minded and pay close attention to ensure the prospect is comfortable as she talks to you. The keyword here is *empathy*, or your ability to understand and appreciate the prospect's concerns about where she and her business are headed.

Two Key Aspects of the Successful Cold Call

Number One: By the end of your cold call, the executive or key person in the company knows and respects you.

Number Two: By the end of your cold call, you understand what this company's goals are—both short term and long. This is a key to knowing where your product or service fits into their plan.

Express your appreciation for "getting the story" with a comment such as, "I certainly appreciate your time, Mr./Ms. Prospect." Make a positive comment on the story. You might say something like "You have some solid work ahead of you and it sounds like your plan will be very successful."

At this point, you will be in a good position to talk about yourself, your company, and the solutions you can bring to the prospect. Refer to points the prospect mentioned and tie in what you and your company could bring to the table. For example, "In the area of (whatever the prospect mentioned), we could definitely help you with (whatever you have)."

Another comment might be "We helped out ABC Company with (whatever issue the prospect raised) recently, and we also helped XYZ Company last year." This is a good place to name-drop and build credibility.

Continue your cold call with an attempt to set up a presentation. "I'd like to outline our solution for you, along with any other appropriate person, at some time that's convenient for you. There are a few other ideas that have worked for others that I could quickly introduce. What day of the week would work for you?"

If trying to set up a presentation does not work, you at least want to ensure the door is still open for future calls. "Well, you have my card. I'll send you our basic literature with a short cover letter detailing (whatever item you discussed with the prospect). Thanks very much for your time today. I'll be in touch from time to time. And please don't hesitate to give me a call anytime. I look forward to being of service to you and your company. Thanks again."

Even if the call did not go well, be professional. "I'm new in the territory and was eager to introduce myself to you. While your interest may be limited right now, I do appreciate your time. Again, please call if I can be of any help. Thanks, and have a nice day."

The more successful cold calls you make, the more self-confidence and self-esteem you'll have. Each call will go a long way toward building your positive self-image as a true sales professional.

Chapter 12

Your Opening Statement

An opening statement isn't a cold call, but it is similar in nature to the cold call so we're including it in this section. You will use your opening statement anytime you need to catch someone's attention quickly and/or reach as many people as possible as quickly as possible. You will use it primarily at trade shows, networking events, business meetings, and similar venues.

Your opening statement should hit hard and fast with basic information and key benefit(s) for the prospect. We'll give you an example of one that we used at a book fair to create some interest for this book. Once we found the right person, our opening statement went like this:

"Hi. I'm Bob Chapin. We're currently working on the most comprehensive how-to guide ever written on the subject of selling. The authors have over 141 combined years of highly successful selling, sales training, and marketing experience, and have the resources and connections to ensure substantial book sales. We're here seeking a publisher for the book, and you're one of the companies we'd like to give that opportunity to."

Let's take a closer look at the elements found in the example from the book show.

1) Your name, and most times your company name as well.

"Hi. I'm Bob Chapin." Only the person's name was stated because the company name was not one that would have been recognized and would have added nothing to the statement. Often, however, the company name is important so you will want to include it. If your company is recognized in its industry and/or carries a lot of weight, you want to mention the name.

2) What you have to offer.

"We're currently working on the most comprehensive how-to guide ever written on the subject of selling." The product or "offering" is "the most comprehensive how-to guide ever written on the subject of selling." To the offering, "a how-to guide on the subject of selling," a key differentiating feature was added: "the most comprehensive guide ever written."

3) Your strongest feature(s) and benefit(s), stated as concisely as possible.

"The authors have over 141 years of highly successful selling, sales training, and marketing experience, and have the resources and connections to ensure substantial book sales." We present three strong features: experience, resources, and connections, related to the result or benefit that the publisher is *most* interested in, namely, substantial book sales.

4) Your closing question or statement.

"We're here looking for a publisher for the book, and you're one of the companies we'd like to give that opportunity to." This type of closing statement is not used often, yet in the right situation it is highly effective. What you are implying is that you are not selling, you're buying—you're shopping for a publisher. *They should be selling you.* You are telling them you have a unique product that will have substantial sales, and subtly but clearly suggesting they are up against all their major competitors.

Note: Your closing question or statement doesn't have to knock prospects out of their chairs. It simply needs to pique interest to get the conversation going in the right direction. From there you will qualify the prospect.

Now it's time to design your own opening statement. As in the example above, your opening statement should contain the following:

- Your name and company name.
- What you have to offer stated creatively and concisely.
- Your strongest feature(s) and benefit(s), stated as concisely as possible.
- A closing statement or question.

When designing your opening statement, keep the following points in mind:

a) Make it short and sweet.

The above statement took about twenty seconds to deliver. Attention spans are often short at events such as these, so keep your statement short and sweeten it with strong features and benefits that have emotional appeal.

b) Get to the point.

Your statement should contain only the "meat," the most important information stated as briefly and succinctly as possible. No extra words or fluff.

c) Get attention with your strongest features and benefits.

Hit prospects with your best points and give them your most powerful benefits.

d) Be different.

You want to stand out from the crowd. You want people to remember you—and not group you with all the other salespeople. That is the point of having an attention-grabbing opening statement. Following are some other examples:

- "Hi. I'm Bob Chapin with ABC Company. We secure banks against all forms of internal and external theft and maximize their profits at the ATMs and teller lines. How many ATMs do you currently own?"

- "Hello. Keith Mooradian with Universal Business Forms. We present you to the world on paper as a highly professional company that everyone should be doing business with. Who does your printing for you?"

- "Hi. I'm Bob Smith with XYZ Company. We save companies in your industry an average of 32 percent on office supplies. Are you currently getting your supplies online, through a catalog, or at an office superstore?"

After you've designed your opening statement, you practice, drill, and rehearse it to the point where, if someone were to awaken you at 3 a.m., you could rattle it off flawlessly. In other words, once you have it, you need to own it and be prepared to deliver it. You also need to be prepared for the next steps after you've established some initial interest with your statement. These steps include qualifying the prospect and closing on the next step in the process.

After your opening statement, ask some qualifying questions to learn how ready, willing, and able the prospect is to buy your product or service.

Note: When someone asks you what you do for a living, use part of your opening statement as the answer. For example, if you are a travel agent and someone asks what you do, you might say, "I design great memories that last a lifetime." That's a little more exciting than, "I'm a travel agent," and it piques peoples' interest.

You don't have to be too flamboyant with your answer—just try not to give the same "run of the mill" answer everyone else is giving. For example, if you're an investment advisor say, "I help people get rich." Instead of being an insurance salesperson, you "Help people protect their most valuable assets." That answer will get peoples' attention and they'll ask you to elaborate. From there, you can give them your opening statement. Of course, if you're in a social situation having a drink after work, you'll approach it differently than if you're attending a business function.

Your response should be something fairly short and simple. The keys are to differentiate yourself, be memorable, and if possible, appeal to the emotions.

Chapter 13

Writing Sales Letters

Occasionally, salespeople will send letters to "open the door" before cold calling a prospect in person or over the phone. The objective of a sales letter is to catch someone's attention, create interest, educate, and get him or her to take a particular action. In short, you're looking for impact and interest, followed by action. Here are some ideas to consider when writing sales letters:

1) **Who is getting your sales letter and what drives them?**

    You must determine who your future readers will be and what their needs, desires, and concerns will be.

2) **Speak their language.**

    A letter to someone in the IT department will be much more technical. It will address different needs, desires, and concerns from those people in upper-level management or the purchasing department.

3) **What are the demographics of your reader?**

    If you are sending sales letters to individual consumers at their homes, you need to know details of their age, sex, financial situation, marital status, family situation, occupation, and so on. This will give you an idea of what is important to them.

The Opening

The objective of your opening is to catch the prospect's attention *immediately* and spark interest that causes them to read on. Your sales letters should have two parts to the opening. The first part of your opening will be a quotation, testimonial, statement, or question that hits the prospect right between the eyes. For example: "Ruggiero Inc. saved over $76,000 on machine parts over the last six months by using ABC Company." The opening line should be concise, powerful, and to the point!

This opening line should be in bold print, italicized, in color, or a combination of any two of these; you need to make it stand out. If it is a quotation, be sure to include an attribution to its author right after the quote.

The Opening Paragraph

The opening paragraph should bridge into the body of the letter. From the above opening sentence, your opening paragraph might look something like this: "This is but one example of the savings that ABC Company customers are enjoying. Here are some other benefits of using ABC Company to replace used machine parts." From there, you would list several benefits as bullet points, then bridge into the body of the letter.

The Body of Your Letter

The body of your letter will simply contain more benefits of your product. It is very important to mention benefits and *not* features.

List your strongest benefit first, your second strongest benefit last, your third strongest number two, fourth number three, and so on. List a minimum of three and a maximum of five benefits. The body of your letter might look like this:

- Customers are saving an average of 56 percent on the cost of machine parts.
- Parts can be customized to meet your specific needs.
- Repaired parts last an average of 67 percent longer than brand-new parts due to a more wear-resistant alloy used in our refurbishing process.

It's important that you can back each of these claims up with solid proof. Also, it should go without saying that you should never exaggerate a claim. Your credibility will go straight to zero if your misrepresentation is discovered.

Use benefits that are specific as opposed to subjective. In the example above, the first and third statements are very specific: "56 percent on the cost" and "67 percent longer than new parts." The second example is less specific and would require further clarification based upon the prospect's situation. Finally, if you say "studies show" in your letter, include a footnote following it with a reference to the study at the bottom of the page.

Closing Your Letter

The closing portion of your letter will be a quick wrap up along with some follow-up details or a request for action. The action may be to send a card in for more information, to call an 800 number, or to respond in some other way.

Follow-up details may include a time when you will be calling or stopping by along with contact information so the prospect can reach you in the meantime.

The closing of your letter with follow-up details might look like this:

- "Can we save you 56 percent of the money you're currently investing in new machine parts and make them last 67 percent longer? We will need to sit down and get some details to answer that question accurately. At the same time, we are confident you will have greater peace of mind knowing either way. We will follow up with you within the next week to discuss this opportunity for you. In the meantime, if you have questions or comments, please give us a call right now at (123) 456-7890."

Packaging Your Letter

1) Your mailing should consist of one 8 ½" x 11" piece of paper in a standard envelope. No other company information should be included, but you should attach a business card, paper-clipped to the top corner of the letter.

2) Your letter should be printed on quality company letterhead and placed in a quality *plain* envelope. Don't use a company envelope. Do, however, be sure your contact information is included in the letter.

3) Use stamps as opposed to metered mail.

4) For the return address, put your name first, company name under your name, and your business address beneath that.

The above items will help to differentiate your mail from most of the "junk" mail that gets thrown away. If your letter looks like a mass mailing and screams, "I'm trying to sell you something," no one will open it.

To summarize: Harness your prospects' attention with your opening line and hold on to it with interesting benefits throughout. Make your letter conversational, easy to read, and short, and spell out what action you wish the prospect to take or the follow-up action you will be taking. Package your letter in such a way that it doesn't get labeled, "sales material" and thrown in the trash.

The following is an example of a well-written sales letter:

Complete Selling, Inc.
27 Curtis Street
Auburn, MA 01501

Mr. Michael N. Lussier   October 10, 2008
President/CEO
Webster Machine Company
110 N. Main St.
Webster, MA 01570

Dear Mr. Lussier:

Ruggiero Inc. saved over $76,000 on machine parts over the last six months by using ABC Company.

This is but one example of the savings that ABC Company customers are enjoying. Here are some other benefits of using ABC Company to replace your used machine parts:

- **Customers are saving an average of 56 percent on the cost of machine parts.**
- **Parts can be customized to meet your specific needs.**
- **Repaired parts last an average of 67 percent longer then brand-new parts due to an improved wear-resistant alloy used in our refurbishing process.**

Can we save you 56 percent of the money you're currently investing in new machine parts and make them last 67 percent longer? In order to accurately answer that question, we will need to sit down with you and get some details. At the same time, we are confident you will have greater peace of mind knowing either way. We will follow up with you within the next week to discuss this opportunity for you. In the meantime, if you have any questions or comments, please give us a call at (508) 555-7890.

Sincerely,

(Signature goes here)

Robert J. Chapin

A Summary of Ideas on Cold Calling

- The objective of the cold call is to find someone who has a need for your product and the means and authority to purchase it.

- Don't overwhelm the prospect. Simply give enough information on the cold call to pique the prospect's interest.

- When you're cold calling you're on the clock, so make it quick and make it powerful.

- Remember that great salespeople have a genuine, sincere interest in the people they are helping. Focus on what's best for the prospect and how you can help.

- Ask meaningful questions and then actively listen and take notes.

- Thank the prospect for his or her time.

- Be memorable on the cold call. Be the best you can be and be different.

- Build rapport by showing your prospects you have their best interests in mind, that you can be trusted, and that your product will solve their problems or fulfill their needs and desires.

- Be professional, straightforward, and courteous. If you go into your cold calls with a belief that you have a great product that people truly need and you genuinely want to help them, your sincerity will come across and the prospect will open up to you.

- After you've made a good impression with cold calling, make sure you follow up and do what you say you're going to do.

- Cold calling is a numbers game. Every call brings you closer to a sale.

SECTION III

PRESENTATIONS

Chapter 14

Putting Your Presentation Together

Note: Use this section on presentations along with Section IV on competition. Both focus on strengths, weaknesses, and compelling reasons why someone should get excited about owning your product or service. You'll also want to look at Section V if you need to call on executives and build a strong business case for your solution.

* * *

So you have a qualified prospect. In other words, you have someone with an interest in what you have to offer, the authority to make a decision, and the means with which to own your product or service. The prospect is "all ears." The only thing remaining to do is present your product or service and close the sale.

The Importance of a Powerful Presentation

In sports, the best defense is a good offense. In sales, the best close is a great presentation. If you have a great presentation that successfully addresses all the prospect's concerns, builds need and desire for your product or service, and completely covers all the bases, the close is simply a foregone conclusion.

Here's another way to look at a powerful presentation. Let's assume you're at a singles' dance. You meet someone who appears perfect—looks, personality, brains, loving, compassionate—or whatever qualities you, and probably everyone else, just happen to be looking for in the perfect date. The close is inevitable—all they have to do is ask for the order (or the date). In fact, this person will probably be closed before they themselves close. Their presentation is simply so strong that the sale is already made.

If you show your product or service as the "perfect date," people will be breaking down your door to get it. You'll have prospects saying, "I'll take it!" before you even have a chance to close. All you need to do is get out there and educate people on what you have to offer.

Obviously the "perfect date" is an exceptional example. However, the point is this: Keep working on your presentation, keep honing it, and keep improving it until you have it as close to the "perfect date" as possible.

The Elements of a Powerful Presentation

Several elements are crucial to a powerful presentation. A powerful presentation should:

- **Be interactive and keep the prospect interested and involved.** Your presentation should keep the prospect on the edge of her seat. Make it interactive. Ask the prospect questions and involve her in ways that make her an active member in the proposed solution.
- **Be delivered with lots of energy, enthusiasm, and emotional logic.** This ties in directly with the above item. With some prospects, you will be more laid back; with others you'll be bouncing around. In any case, you need to have lots of life, energy, and enthusiasm in your voice, and your presentation should make logical sense, stemming from enthusiasm.
- **Be delivered in a clear, concise, and articulate manner.** Your presentation should be easy to understand, to the point, and it should be delivered in terms that the prospect will understand, based on her personality type. As we discussed in the cold calling section, you need to be speaking the same language as the prospect.
- **Address the needs, desires, and concerns of the prospect, and speak to her hot buttons.** If you've done your work properly during the cold call, you thoroughly *understand* what the prospect is looking for and you've uncovered some hot buttons. You will now educate the prospect on how your product or service fills her needs and desires. Show caring, understanding, and empathy for the prospect, and show that you are seriously interested in helping her out.
- **Lead naturally to the close.** Your presentation should be designed in such a way that it walks the prospect smoothly through the presentation, addressing all needs and concerns, and flows right into the close.

The Three Parts of Your Presentation

Your presentation will consist of three parts: a) the opening, b) the main part or body of the presentation, and c) the close.

The time you spend on each section will vary based upon your product or service. In an ideal world, you will spend the least amount of time on your introduction, the most time on the body of your presentation, and the close will be somewhere between the two. But of course we don't live in a perfect world, thus the time spent in each area will vary depending upon the type and number of objections and questions that arise.

1) The Opening.

After you exchange greetings and build some rapport with your prospect, you will transition the conversation to business. You do this by capturing her attention, setting an agenda for the meeting, clarifying an objective, and getting agreement from the prospect on both the agenda and objective. The *primary* objective of your opening is to create some initial interest and urgency, and pave the way for the main portion of your presentation.

2) The Body of the Presentation.

The body of your presentation will focus on the three or four most compelling reasons to buy (the benefits) depending upon your prospect's needs, wants, and desires (as identified when you qualified the prospect). You must create compelling reasons for the prospect to change the way she is currently doing business, or give her reasons to add your product or service to her business. Your *primary* objective in this part of the presentation is to demonstrate to the prospect that a) there is a need to change, b) the need to change is immediate, and c) *you* have the best solution for that change.

3) The Close.

In the closing section, you will tie everything together by summarizing how your product or service meets or exceeds all her needs and desires. Finally, you will ask for the order.

Why People Buy

When developing your presentation, it's important to keep in mind *why* people buy. Three factors go into any buying decision:

- Relationship with the salesperson and/or the salesperson's company.
- Perceived value and quality (benefits) of the product or service. How does your product or service make your prospect or her company look or feel? How well does it serve or protect them?
- Price.

Some of these areas will require a different focus based upon where you fit in the marketplace. For example, if you are the lowest-priced vendor, and thus have a price advantage, your presentation will focus more on the selling price. If you are the higher-priced product or service, and thus don't have a price advantage, you will focus more on quality and the other advantages that you, your product, and your company bring to the table.

In your presentation, you need to focus on all three areas. Build rapport and be personable, show the benefits of the product, and make a case equal to or better than the price you are asking.

Note: Please refer to the *Competition* section (IV) for tips and ideas. In that section, we look at cost and value compared with the competition, and we cover many other areas that you can build into your presentation.

We talked about building rapport and gaining the prospect's trust, confidence, and friendship in the *Cold Call* section. The keys are to be professional, friendly, and genuinely interested in helping the other person.

Let's take a closer look at value, quality, benefits, and price.

What You're *Really* Selling

When the prospect buys your product or service, she is buying the *feelings* and *emotions* that she believes the *benefits* of your product or service will give her. She is *not* buying the *features*. People don't want pieces of paper with deceased notables—otherwise known as money—they want freedom and power. People don't want just the new boat, Corvette, or Harley—they want excitement, status, a feeling that they belong. Perhaps they even want to be "cool." A woman buys a stunning new outfit because of how it will make her feel when others see her in it.

If you're selling cars, you're not just selling steel, glass, and rubber. You're selling safety, security, exhilaration, excitement, and a plethora of emotions depending upon what kind of car it is and what your prospect is looking for. While it's sometimes important to mention the features, you will tie them directly to the benefits. For example, "This car has front and side air bags; thus, your family will be twice as safe in the event of a crash."

Now, you may be thinking that your business is different. Perhaps you sell copiers and you're thinking, "How can copiers create feelings or emotions?" We're here to tell you that copiers evoke emotions too. When someone buys a copier, some of the benefits—or feelings and emotions—she might be buying are image, luxury, peace of mind, security, and a raft of other emotions. Seem far-fetched? Let's take a closer look.

Suppose she selects a copier that works only 60 percent of the time and has constant problems. What do you think that will do to her image in the eyes of her boss and co-workers? Do you think her boss will trust her with larger decisions? How do you think this will affect her peace of mind and self-image? She'll cringe and feel about two inches tall every time she walks by that faulty copier.

On the other hand, if the copier does work well, she'll have the luxury of using a machine that makes her job easier. Now, assuming this copier really stands out and she negotiated a good price, she knows that only good things can happen to her image. Her boss and colleagues will be impressed, may trust her with bigger decisions, and she may eventually get a promotion. All these possibilities lead to peace of mind, security, and many other positive emotions and feelings.

It's also important to note that most of the mental pictures your prospect makes about your product or service are *future* pictures. The prospect sees himself driving down the road in his new car, the envy of his neighbors. The prospect sees herself in Paris standing in front of the Eiffel Tower, looking up with awe. Whether it will happen in fifteen minutes, two months, or two years—it will be future enjoyment. And it is those mental pictures, those future dreams, that make the sale happen. As we will discuss, you want to help the prospect paint such pictures with as much emotion and as many of the senses as possible.

Here are some of the most common feelings and perceived benefits the prospect is buying:

- Peace of mind.
- A feeling of safety or security. In addition to physical security, this feeling is also about job security.
- Status or a feeling of being important.
- A better standard of living.
- The feelings of being young and energetic.
- The feeling of looking good or being more attractive.
- Longevity or longer life.
- Something that will be around after the buyer is gone; leaving a legacy.
- Fun, excitement, adventure, or thrills.
- Feeling better about themselves.
- Attention diversion.

Keep these feelings in mind when developing your presentation. Which of the above benefits does your product or service provide? Be creative. The more you come up with the better. Through proper questioning, both in the cold call and in your presentation, you will know which are the most important to your prospect and where you can help.

During your presentation, sell the benefits, sell the future, sell the dream, the *big picture*, and sell what the product or service will do for the prospect. *Do not* spend all your time talking about the features.

The Carrot and the Stick

In Chapter 5 we looked at how the carrot-and-stick approach can help you motivate yourself when selling. Buyers, too, are motivated in a similar fashion. Most people are driven by the carrot-and-stick analogy; that is, by pleasure and pain. The benefits of your product or service will help the prospect either to avoid pain or to gain pleasure. Usually it is a combination of the two. Your objective is to show the prospect how he or she will minimize pain and maximize pleasure by using your product or service.

People buy home insurance to avoid the pain of the replacement cost should their house burn down. People buy the newest sports car for the pleasure it brings them. They may buy a Volvo for pleasure, because they like the car, as well as to avoid the potential pain of being injured in an auto accident.

Typically, people will do more to prevent pain than they will to gain pleasure. Think about it—would you do more to earn $100,000 or more to prevent someone from taking $100,000 away from you?

What is the primary objective of your product or service? Does it protect something? Does it enhance something? Come up with as many "carrots" and "sticks" as you can. Having both the carrot (the reward) and the stick (the pain caused by *not* buying your product) in your presentation is important. To be completely effective, you need to include both sides of the equation. You have to talk about both the heaven the prospect will experience as a result of owning your product and the hell he'll go through without your product.

Try to think of as many benefits or "carrots" and as much pain or "sticks" as you can. We will use these when we talk about putting together your presentation.

Use Emotion *and* Logic in Your Presentation

Your presentation should focus on a strong logical argument backed up with strong emotional appeal. These two factors, more than anything, will keep the prospect listening and interested while you pave the way to closing the sale.

Too many salespeople focus primarily on the facts, figures, and statistics of their product and thus fail to get the prospect emotionally involved. People unequivocally *do not* buy on logic alone. People may look at all the logical reasons to buy and even build a logical case to buy, but ultimately they buy emotionally, using logic to justify their buying decision. In other words, *people always buy on emotional logic.* One of the best places to spot this dynamic is in personal relationships.

Have you ever known someone who was involved in a relationship that made absolutely no sense to you or anyone else? A relationship that seemed like such a mismatch it completely astounded you? This happens because the two people involved view the relationship emotionally, whereas everyone else views it logically. The people in the relationship feel, taste, smell, hear, and see their relationship. They experience their relationship entirely internally—they are inside it. The people outside the relationship are unattached, unemotional, "logical" observers; they experience it externally. We all see things much differently from an emotional viewpoint than from a logical one. Thus, a relationship that makes no logical sense to the outside observer may make complete emotional sense to the people involved.

The same dynamics are also at work in the business world. Becoming emotionally involved in business might be the equivalent of becoming infatuated with a product's bells and whistles (features). Once you get the emotional purchase home, logic will begin to enter the equation. Do the bells and whistles work properly? How effective are they at helping you do what you want to do? And when you do have a problem, how quickly can you get it resolved? If it turns out that the bells and whistles work only 50 percent of the time, and when you need service you have to wait much longer than expected, these "logical" problems will ultimately make the "emotional" purchase of this item a poor decision.

In the short term, emotion sells. In the long term, logic will show whether the decision was a good one. If you start dating someone because he or she is drop-dead gorgeous and makes you laugh, you are buying emotionally. Once the infatuation wears off, you will now be focusing on logical factors such as, does this person support you? Is he or she there for you at important times? Can you have meaningful discussions? Can you work out finances equitably? What about shared interests? What about distance? If these logical areas are a problem, the relationship probably will not last.

If someone sells you emotionally, but there is no logic to back up that emotion, you will not buy from that person again. If you get sold emotionally on prime rib and it turns out logically to be a tough cut, you won't be back. On the other hand, if you get emotionally sold on prime rib and it turns out logically to be the best prime rib you've ever had, you'll be back again and again.

Once a decision is made, service after the sale, performance of the product, efficiency and profitability, or lack thereof, will give solid, logical proof as to whether the decision was a good or bad one.

Keep in mind some of the dynamics that are at work with your prospect. At the corporate level, decision-makers are concerned with how the buying decision will move them up the corporate ladder, earn the company more money, make them look good to peers and/or superiors, and overall, how the decision will give them more power within the organization.

On the other side of the coin, they are afraid of making a mistake that could do the opposite and decrease their power within the organization. Ultimately, the buyer will weigh the two sides and make an emotional decision based upon a preponderance of evidence, and then use the evidence to logically justify the decision to others.

Most people, when they're buying for business, desire to look good to others so that they can experience more positive emotions. Will they be seen as intelligent, frugal, tough, and a great negotiator? Or will they be seen as someone who paid too much and got taken advantage of? Remember this when putting together your presentation.

A Potential Emotional and Logical Pitfall

Many salespeople with a superior product focus solely on the logical reasons to buy, believing that details, statistics, and hard facts will be enough to sell a high-quality product. While logic might be enough to initially arouse interest in a superior product, the salesperson needs to add emotion to ensure the prospect will pay higher dollars for a higher-quality product.

On the flip side, salespeople with a weaker product or service will often use an emotional selling approach exclusively while disregarding logic. The salesperson may feel that unless they throw an excess of enthusiasm and emotion at the prospect, they will not have a shot. In this case, the salesperson tends to oversell the emotion.

The bottom line is that as a salesperson, you need to know your product's strengths and weaknesses, and then sell the strengths with logical enthusiasm. Stir up strong emotions and justify those emotions with logical reasoning. Sell the steak (logic) and the sizzle (emotion). Sell the logic of prime rib, but paint "juicy" emotional pictures along with it. Conversely, you can sell the tough cut emotionally, but also sell the logic of the great price or "deal" the prospect is getting.

All products and services have strengths and weaknesses. A lower-quality product or service, or one with fewer options and less flexibility, usually has low price as a strength. On the other hand, a product with a high price as a weakness usually has options, flexibility, superior performance, or other strong features as strengths.

Whether you have the highest-priced, highest-quality product or the lowest-priced, lesser-quality product, you can emotionally sell the logical benefits of whatever you're selling.

Enthusiasm Sells!

Enthusiasm is another important aspect of emotion. Often new salespeople are able to sell purely on enthusiasm. Typically, they have little product knowledge and know very little about the industry. Enthusiasm and excitement are all they have to offer.

We had a situation in the investment business in which a young stockbroker became overwhelmed with emotion and excitement when a company stock he was buying for clients made a surprise announcement regarding a major new contract.

The young broker hit the phone like a maniac and opened three accounts in two hours. Considering he had only opened two accounts in the previous two months, it was obvious that the difference in his ability to open accounts came down to his enthusiasm and conviction. By the way, when we called to verify these accounts, we received many questions such as, "What was the name of that broker?" and "What is the name of the stock?" They had become so caught up in the emotion of the broker that they bought completely on enthusiasm!

Bear in mind that logic, or how the stock eventually performs based on historical and projected data, will determine whether the buying decision was good in the long term. At the same time, high emotion alone made three sales in two hours, while logic alone made two sales in two months.

Emotion is Unique to Each Individual

Focus on the person you are facing and his or her unique situation. Many salespeople focus on general information that applies to everyone and lose sight of the individual. When the presentation is focused on information that applies to everyone, as opposed to the individual prospect, the prospect becomes detached and has no emotional involvement in the process.

On the other hand, when we focus on the personal history of individuals and speak to their unique issues, they become emotionally involved in the presentation. One way to do this is to bring the prospect's family into the presentation.

Add Emotion by Bringing Family into the Presentation

Think about the following for a moment: A child's future, a parent being cared for in their later years, the death of a loved one. All of these are events that most of us will deal with in our lifetimes. These subjects create very strong emotional responses in most of us. Some of these, such as a college education, can be positive events; others, such as the death of a loved one or nursing home care, have negative overtones. Most people don't like to face the negative subjects. You may have that challenge if you sell products such as life insurance or long-term care insurance. We'll talk about "How to Introduce Tough Subjects" such as these on page 228.

What potential "family" benefits does your product or service address? If you sell a product such as life insurance, the "family" impact is immense. Here is an example of bringing family into your presentation: "Mr. Prospect, as you know, the objective of this life insurance is to financially protect your family should something happen to you unexpectedly. Obviously, the grief is bad enough without having to worry about finances. Imagine your children going to college, your wife making the house payments, and weddings paid for all because you had the courage and foresight to protect your and your family's dreams with the right life insurance policy."

Adding a statement like the one above will personalize the presentation and definitely add some emotion. At the same time, before you use a similar example, you need to know something about your prospect's family.

Following is another example of "family" emotion. Although this emotional picture was drawn with regard to an objection, it is a good example of bringing family into the presentation.

One of us used to sell long-term care insurance for future use for nursing homes. A common objection was: "If I become sick, my son (or daughter, granddaughter, neighbor, etc.) will take care of me so I don't have to go into a nursing home."

This objection was easily handled by asking a few questions and allowing the prospect to draw his or her own conclusions. The first question was: "So if you require twenty-four-hours-a day, seven-days-a-week care, your son is going to care for you?"

At this point, the prospect's facial expression would start to change. The follow-up question was: "Let me ask you, with all due respect, do you think it would be fair to your son to ask him to do that?"

Believe us, it created some emotion *quickly!* All at once, the prospect visualized the burden this would be on his offspring.

In reality, people often do not picture the implications of long-term care. They don't see it as something that might involve their relatives twenty-four hours a day, seven days a week. They imagine it might involve the relative helping them out of a chair from time to time or fixing a meal or two. They rarely see the real commitment this type of intensive care usually requires.

Having been asked the right questions, the prospect began to realize the true implications of long-term care, namely, that the caregiver may need to give up his or her life and focus completely on care giving. Once that "emotional" picture hit home, the presentation and the sale became much easier. This is an example of educating the prospect, which is one of your jobs as a salesperson.

Weddings, college, a new home, not to mention family—all have plenty of emotion attached to them. Paint the picture of your product or service helping make dreams a reality. If you are an effective painter, the pictures and the sale will follow.

Let's Talk "Logical" Numbers

As we said, you need to back up your emotion with logic. And it's best to deliver your logic *with* some emotion.

Some numbers are emotional in and of themselves. Extreme numbers can be emotional. For example, an insurance company has an advertisement stating that although they didn't have any cute animals as mascots, they did have over six hundred billion dollars in assets. Six hundred billion is a number that catches people's attention.

In another example, a precision welding company talked about the welding wire they used with a diameter of three-thousandths of an inch, or the diameter of a human hair. In the welding field, that number opens peoples' eyes. Of course, after you've captured the prospect's attention with the numbers, you need to give the benefit— why the numbers are important to him or her.

You also have to present your numbers the right way. You want the prospect to have a clear picture of the bottom line. For example, as an investment advisor, instead of telling the prospect she will receive 7 percent on her investment, let her know that with this investment she will receive a quarterly check for $647, or whatever the number happens to be. When you mention a percentage, the prospect has to make all the calculations to get to the bottom line. In the second example, you are giving the prospect the bottom line directly. She doesn't have to go through any confusing calculations in her head to figure out what 7 percent ultimately means to her.

The bottom line: *Make it easy to understand!* Deliver the numbers in a way that they will have impact, and deliver them with energy and enthusiasm.

The Cost of *Not* Owning Your Product or Service

First let's start with a basic presentation premise: During your presentation, your objective is to show the prospect that he or she will be better off with your product or service and worse off without it. You want to use both the carrot and the stick, as discussed. If you have a prospect who sees a need for what you're selling, you're halfway there. If, on the other hand, the prospect does not necessarily see a need for what you're selling, you have to change his or her perspective.

For example, if the prospect believes your product costs too much, you need to change her perspective to the point where she understands that it is costing more *not* to have your product. If she is spending $1.00 a day for something because she doesn't have your product and your product costs $100, then after one hundred days she's making money with your product. You need to shift her thinking from up-front cost to long-term cost.

How about lifestyle? Does your product provide a better way of life? If so, what is it costing mentally and emotionally *not* to have your product? Once you build value to the point where it outweighs cost, you've got a sale (assuming the prospect is qualified to buy).

Here is another way to look at this: Once you shift the cost from the prospect's "hang on to my money" side of the ledger to the "buy your product and save money" side, the sale is made.

In addition to comparing long-term and short-term costs, what other cost factors can you use in your presentation?

1) **Cost of labor**. How many working hours, and thus dollars, are saved—daily, weekly, monthly, annually—by having your product or service?

2) **Cost of maintenance and materials**. If the business has an old copier, how much more expensive is the service contract? How many hours is the machine costing in lost production when it's down? How many more hours do office personnel spend fixing the current machine? How about the number of ink cartridges and their cost compared with the newer, longer-lasting ones?

3) **Longevity**. How long does your machine last compared with the competition's? If the competition's machine lasts ten years and yours lasts fifteen, the prospect will have to buy three machines for every two of yours. Point this out. Give the prospect a "per year" price as opposed to a total price, and have numbers ready to support your claim of the lifespan of your machines versus the competition's.

Your challenge is to find as many cost factors associated with your product as possible and to show them in a favorable light. Show your prospect what it is costing him or her *not* to own your product or service and make the evidence so overwhelming that the prospect is compelled to buy. Some of these factors are easier to put into numbers.

Let's look at a few examples in which we take some otherwise intangible items and make them tangible.

Let's suppose your prospect has an old, outdated piece of equipment. From experience you know that an old machine will require company personnel to spend time repairing, using another machine, waiting for another machine, or working on various other activities as a result of problems with the current machine. The prospect may realize this or he may not, so your first step is to discover whether he is aware of this, and then encourage him to take ownership of these "costs."

Your side of the conversation might go as follows: "Mr. Prospect, obviously your old equipment is costing you man hours as your employees spend time repairing it, using another machine, waiting for another machine, or doing various other activities because of problems with the current machine. Am I correct in that assumption?"

Once your prospect agrees, present him with the number of manpower hours the old equipment is most likely costing him (based on your experience). Next, have the prospect himself figure out the number of manpower hours the failing equipment is costing him. Say something like following: "Mr. Prospect, in my experience the old equipment is probably costing you about ten man hours per week. But from your end, if you had to guess how many hours it's actually costing you, what would you guess?" If the prospect gives you a number, whatever number it is, use that number in your calculations.

If the prospect says no, he has no idea how many hours, say, "I'll tell you what. My experience says it's probably about ten hours. To be conservative, let's use half that, or five hours. Will you agree that between repairs, waiting, and other activities, it's taking at least five hours per week?"

Using whatever number he gave you or, based upon the five hours, do your calculations and put a "cost" on the old machine.

Note: It's important for your prospect to give you a number—that way he can't argue with it later. You'll also need to get the salary in dollars per hour of the employee who is wasting her time. Your prospect may not want to reveal it, but you've got to question until you get a ballpark figure that he's comfortable giving out.

Now, do the math. Five hours a week at the hourly rate of the person wasting his or her time. Say, "So five hours at $15 an hour is $75 per week, or $750 for ten weeks, or roughly $3,750 per year. Is my math right? So, in personnel hours alone you're losing $3,750 per year by not having our new machine. In addition, you're losing the added productivity of that energy, or 250 working hours a year that could be put into doing more profitable work elsewhere—isn't that correct? But that would be a little difficult to calculate, so we'll leave it out for now. Just realize that there is some 'real' added cost there, okay?"

Next, jump to the price of a service contract. "Joe, you're currently paying $800 per year for a service contract on your present equipment—correct? The service contract on a new machine is only $550. That equals another $250 per year, so now we're up to $4,000 per year that the old machine is costing you. Correct?"

Now, jump to other maintenance and supply issues such as toner cartridges. Continue to build the "cost" in each area until you have overwhelmingly shown that it is less expensive to buy the new machine than it is to keep the old one. Your ultimate goal it to show that it is *much* less expensive, but if you can at least show it is less expensive by any amount, and the prospect trusts all your numbers, you'll be in a good position to close the sale.

Note: Again, you want to be using the prospect's numbers. If you help him come up with the numbers, make sure he "owns" them. If you use your numbers, they are open for debate. If you use the prospect's numbers, they are law.

How about more difficult intangibles such as: quality of life, sick days, safety issues, longer life, less stress, and getting more enjoyment and happiness out of life? These are more difficult factors to put dollar amounts on, but you want to use them where possible.

Some companies, including many insurance companies, *do* put dollar values on these more difficult intangibles. They have numbers on obscure things such as how much one extra year of life is worth or how much an arm or a leg is worth. You may find it helpful to refer to some of their statistics as "evidence" when making your case.

In legal disputes, dollar amounts must to be assigned to almost everything, including intangibles. You can gather numbers from court judgments, insurance claims, and so on, or you can build a psychological case and ask the prospect how much factors are *really* worth. An example:

"Mr. Prospect, studies have shown that this therapy can add years to your life. Suppose it only added one year, or six months, or even only one month. Would you agree with me that one month would be a conservative number?

"Mr. Prospect, the insurance companies and other industries can actually put a dollar amount on one extra month of life. But let me ask you, what is one more month of sunsets, one more month with the ones you love, one more month of enjoying life really worth?

"If someone told you that you had to leave this world today, and let that sit with you for a while, and returned ten minutes later saying, 'Okay, I'm giving you one more month,' what would that extra month be worth then?"

Let the prospect come up with the "priceless" psychological value. In a case such as this, the prospect doesn't have to put a specific dollar number on it. The psychological number will always be higher.

Ultimately, you need to build as much real and psychological cost as you can of *not* owning your product or service. At the same time, this will build your product's value.

Note: In competitive situations, you want to show how it will cost the prospect more money to own the competition's product than yours. Equate the intangible— headaches, lack of peace of mind—and the tangible issues, such as the documented life of your machines versus the competition's and the "real" cost involved. We will look at this in depth in the Competition Section.

Return on Investment (ROI) Models

In the last section, we looked at the cost–benefit analysis of owning versus not owning your product, and we mentioned using something that costs $1.00 a day. The alternative was to purchase your product for $100.00. For this example, let's assume the prospect's buying bottled water at $1.00 a day versus buying a water filtration system for $100.00. You could put this into a simple return on investment model as follows:

	Initial Cost Day 1	After 100 Days	After 365 Days
Water @ $1.00 per day	$1.00	$100.00	$365.00
Filtration system	$100.00	$100.00	$100.00

Conclusion: By buying the water filtration system, the return on the initial investment of $100.00 is a $265.00 savings after one year.

Of course, this model is basic and shows only one parameter. You can increase the complexity by introducing several other factors such as the cost of replacement filters. The point is that ROI models are an effective way to drive numbers home with impact.

Note 1: You'll find an example of an ROI model in our sample presentation in graph form on page 220 and in numerical form on page 221.

Note 2: For an extensive look at detailed ROI models and a supporting business case, please refer to Chapter 28, Building a Business Case, which begins on page 308.

Involve as Many of the Senses as Possible in Your Presentation

During your presentation you want to get the prospect's mind involved. You do this by invoking the senses. While people tend to be primarily visual, auditory, or kinesthetic, we are all a combination of these along with the other two senses, taste and smell. Simply put, the more senses you stimulate, the more the prospect's brain will be involved in your presentation. While it's a good idea to gear your language toward your prospect's preferred sense, cover as many of the senses as you can in the presentation. Here are some ways to do that:

Paint Pictures and Tell Stories while Selling

Painting pictures and telling stories are great ways to involve all the senses and to add emotion to your presentation. Everyone loves a good story. Good stories are entertaining. Good stories grab our attention and pull us to the edge of our seats. Good stories and analogies are also a great way to teach. Stories will make your presentations more interesting and intriguing, and that's what you want. If you can entertain the people you're talking to, your sales will increase dramatically.

If you listen to the most effective communicators and leaders, you'll find they are very good at telling stories, painting pictures, and creating a vision. They do not talk in terms of numbers and show a bunch of statistics. Instead, they paint a picture of prosperity, of all children having the opportunity to attend college, of jobs being created, of great health care, and of a strong nation in which tremendous opportunities abound, a nation in which everyone's wildest dreams are possible. This "vision" has much more psychological and emotional impact than a chart with a bunch of numbers showing how money moved from one sector to another will cut taxes and increase benefits.

As a salesperson, you want to sell the vision. You want your prospects to *visualize* themselves using your product or service and living a better life because of it. You want the prospect to *see, feel,* and *hear* themselves living a happier, more productive life because they are using your product. And you need to be able to back up the vision with sound logic.

Make sure you concentrate on the vision you are creating and look for ways to interject emotional logic into your story. Even the politician who paints the picture of a Utopia with low taxes and maximum services and benefits must have some logic to back up that claim. And remember that people want to believe in the Utopia. If you have a great story and you have a way to deliver the promise, tell your story, then back it up with sound, solid emotional logic.

Here's a small example of using logic versus painting an emotional picture:

Logic: "Joe, we have a 99 percent uptime guarantee and we also promise to fix the machine right the first time so you don't have to continually call us back to the location. This will also maximize your uptime and profitability."

Emotional picture: "Joe, let's look for a moment at the big picture and what we're really trying to do here. Imagine for a moment that all your machinery is running at maximum efficiency and with maximum uptime. Picture the effect that would have on your customers, your employees, and you.

"Imagine your customers' peace of mind knowing they could always rely on you and your equipment to meet their needs, no matter what time of the day or night. Picture how this would lead to positive word-of-mouth advertising to their friends and families. It would pave the road for lots of referrals.

"Imagine how relaxed your employees would be, free from customer complaints and hostility. Picture what all this would do for employee morale. Imagine how much more productive they would be, how much more they might look forward to coming to work, and even, perhaps, how many sick days you'd cut down on. You would be able to enjoy your weekends, holidays, and days off knowing that you would not receive a call that your machine is down. This is turn would make *you* happier and more productive.

"Imagine, too, the peace of mind in knowing that when the machine does need service it will be done promptly and correctly the first time. You won't have to call several times and you won't have to deal with customer and employee frustration.

"That's the big picture, Joe. That's what we've created elsewhere and we'd like to create here: happier, more productive employees and customers, and at the same time, a happier you. Does that sound like a worthy objective for us?"

This is an example of helping the prospect paint the emotional benefits instead of just hearing them and processing them in a logical fashion.

Granted, it took longer to tell the emotional story, but you're sure to garner much more interest. And because you aren't throwing out specific numbers, you are not giving the prospect something he can argue or contend with.

For example, a prospect can argue with 99 percent uptime. He might think, "Hmm, that number seems awfully high. I think Charley at X Company told me he's only getting about 98 percent uptime." On the other hand, a prospect will have much more trouble arguing with "maximum uptime."

Now bear in mind that you have to be able to back up your story with hard, logical facts and evidence. If you are talking about maximum uptime and efficiency, you have to be able to prove that on paper.

Also, depending upon the buyer's personality type, you will receive different responses to your story. For example, a Thinker will probably interrupt you in the middle of your story looking for documentation and other forms of "proof." Be prepared.

Some Quick Illustrations and Stories

An investment advisor could use a chart that shows the performance of stocks versus other investments from 1900 to the present day. Such a chart clearly and unequivocally shows that, over the long term, stocks have far outperformed bonds, money markets, savings accounts, and all other related investment vehicles. In this case a picture truly is worth a thousand words.

Instead of trying to logically persuade your client that the stock market is the best place to be in the long term, you simply show the chart and explain how the stock market has performed compared with other investments.

Be sure your chart shows a beginning investment of, say, $100 back in 1900, and then shows what has happened to that $100 over the past one hundred-plus years in each of the following areas: the S&P 500, the average savings account, treasury bills, corporate bonds, government bonds, and inflation. For someone who is not convinced that the stock market is the best place to be over the long term, this chart will be a real eye-opener. For many people, it will simply put an exclamation mark on what they already know deep down inside.

As convincing as this chart is for long-term investing in stocks, not all your clients will be candidates for the stock market. For example, you may have a client who needs the money within a year for the purchase of a house or other major financial outlay. In this case, you will have another chart prepared that illustrates the best safe investments that help preserve capital while giving the best short-term return. This chart may be the same one you use to convince investors that stocks are best for the long term. In this case, however, you will point out the line that doesn't decline at all. Granted, the client won't realize much of a return from this, but she will get what she does need—protection of capital while earning some return.

How about an analogy to help someone understand why mutual funds are a safer investment than one single stock? In this case, you could relate investing in one company versus many to gambling.

You might ask, "Joe, have you ever gambled before?" Many people will smile at this and say, "Well, sure." You continue, "When you gamble, what do you play?"

Let's say he plays roulette. "Okay, what if you take $500 with you to gamble. Does it make more sense to take that entire $500 and place it on one number on one spin of the roulette wheel, or does it make more sense to spread your risk out and bet maybe $25 at a time on various numbers?"

His answer will be the latter. You follow with, "That's exactly why you should be investing in mutual funds. With a mutual fund, your money is spread out over many companies instead of putting it on one single company and completely sinking or swimming with just that one. Does that make sense to you?"

Now, if the client said he'd risk his entire $500 on one bet, you can still try the analogy, but you may want to simply help him pick the best company if that's what he truly wants.

Create Your Own Stories and Paint Your Own Pictures

Right now, some people reading this are thinking, "Are you kidding me? There's not a creative bone in my entire body." Let us ask you a question. Can you picture yourself enjoying the benefits of your product or service? If you sell cars, can you picture yourself driving down the road as the envy of the neighborhood? Visualize what it would be like to live the benefits, and then paint pictures for your prospect as we did earlier with our 99 percent uptime example.

Brainstorm with other salespeople. Work daily on becoming more creative. Find some books on the subject and do the things we suggested earlier to exercise your brain and improve your mental agility. Word association games and games where you need to invent word definitions are some of the best for developing creative stories.

What experiences in your life could you draw from? How about a story for risk tolerance? What kind of driver are you? Do you like roller coasters? Have you ever jumped out of an airplane? How about bungee jumping? All these can be tied to risk, excitement, adventure, safety, and many other emotional benefits found in your product or service. The more you work on it, the better you will become and the more effective your stories will be.

Here's another idea for painting pictures. Suppose you sell boats. Keep in mind that your prospect paints future pictures when he imagines owning a boat. With that in mind, you might say the following: "Mr. Prospect, would you be using this boat just for recreation or do you have any special events coming up this summer that you'll be using it for?"

If the prospect mentions a family reunion and his brother coming out from Illinois, you might continue with, "A family reunion—that's great. When I think of summer I imagine the taste of watermelon (or whatever your favorite summer food is), the smell of sunscreen, a barbecue, and the warmth of the sun. And I picture and hear everyone having a great time."

In this example, we've covered all the senses: taste, smell, feel, sight, and sound. Later in the section on closing, we'll talk about bringing this picture into your close. Remember, use your imagination and you'll be able to come up with endless great examples for your presentations.

Present Colorful Pictures, Drawings, and Charts

In addition to helping prospects paint mental pictures, real pictures, illustrations, colorful charts, and other similar items also arouse the senses.

Have some charts and pictures prepared, but also illustrate scenarios while you are presenting. Use colorful markers and keep the items neat. Be sure the drawings are simple and legible. You don't want to confuse the prospect with pictures that are too busy.

Use Technology

Using technology is a great way to add visuals, color, and sound to your presentation. Have computer animation with lots of color and some sound here and there. Make your presentation come alive with great visual and auditory effects. You can also include some funny clips as part of your humor in the beginning and throughout the presentation. Don't overdo the humor. Use your best judgment and sprinkle some lightly here and there.

PowerPoint is a valuable tool for presentations. The software program is fairly user-friendly if you can feel your way around a computer. If not, there are several good books on the subject and courses you can take. Don't rely too much on technology, however. You must stay in control and not allow the technology to steal the show. Some of the best technology in the world can put prospects to sleep unless you, the human element, bring it alive with your voice, your choice of words, and your overall presentation.

It's a good idea to use a projector to display your presentation on the wall. Be sure you project onto a solid white background.

Remember, technology can be your friend, so *use it!* But be certain to strike a happy medium. Be high tech, but don't be so far out there that you alienate your audience. The objective is to show the prospect, in a way that's creative and grabs her attention, precisely how your product or service fits her needs.

Have a Contingency Plan Should Your Technology Fail

Always have a backup plan when you are using technology in your presentation. Know your equipment inside and out. This includes setting up the equipment and on-the-spot repairs. If you're using a projector, have a backup bulb and know how to replace it, or better yet, have a backup projector. It's also a good idea to have a backup computer.

Get to the location early so you can set up your equipment and do a test run through your presentation before the meeting begins.

As a final note, make sure you have your presentation in hard copy just in case your equipment completely fails. Also, ensure the hard copy is professional and presentable. Use color wherever possible.

A Note on *All* Visual Aids

- Be sure your PowerPoint slides, graphs, charts, and other visual aids are clear, easy to read, and easy to understand.
- Visual aids should not be too involved or confusing.
- Make sure that your older clients and prospects can read them. Don't use microscopic print.
- Avoid handouts before you go over something as people will tend to read the handouts and they won't focus on you.

Watch What You Use as a Screen Saver

If you use a computer to give your presentation, it's important that your screen saver is in good taste. Obviously, it's not a good idea to have scantily clad women (or men) as your screen saver. Company logos and the like are fine. Family pictures and/or pictures of your kids can be good conversation starters. Overall, use your best judgment and realize that customers and prospects may see your screen saver. You don't want anything on there that will embarrass you or offend them.

Different Presentations for Different Audiences

Your presentation will vary based on the status of your audience. By status we mean:

- Are you presenting to an established customer or a new prospect?
- Is this a competitive account or a friendly account?
- Is the audience familiar with you and your company, or not at all?

The answers to these questions will dictate how involved your presentation should be and the areas you should cover.

Established customers will typically need a shorter presentation than new prospects and competitive accounts. At the same time, you don't want to get so lax that you miss or fail to mention important points. Don't assume that your best customers know everything there is to know about you and your company. You want to end each presentation with a reminder of the other things your company can provide, things they currently may not be getting from you.

With established customers, it is unlikely that you'll spend much time, if any, selling yourself or your company. However, you want to give them updates regarding new developments. For the most part, if the company has been doing business with you for a number of years and you are treating them right, they are most likely already sold on you, your product or service, and your company.

On the other hand, new prospects and competitive accounts need a full-blown presentation that includes selling yourself and your company in addition to your product or service.

With competitive accounts, you want to cover the competitive comparison and related items which we will discuss in Section IV on competition. Please refer to that section (Chapter 20 in particular) when preparing a presentation for a competitive account.

In general, here is what your presentations should cover in each of the different accounts:

1) **The existing, extremely loyal account.**
   - A brief introduction with some humor.
   - A presentation on the product or service and how it will fill your client's needs and desires.
   - Close.
   - New developments or other ways you may be able to help them.

2) **The new prospect.**
   - A brief introduction with some humor.
   - A brief history of you and your company.
   - A review of the prospect's needs, desires, goals, and objectives.
   - A presentation on your product or service showing how it fills their needs and desires.
   - Close.

- Intense follow-up upon returning to your office after the presentation, whether you close or not.

3) The competitive account.

- A brief introduction with some humor.
- A brief history of you and your company.
- A review of the prospect's needs, desires, goals, and objectives.
- A presentation on your product or service showing how it fills their needs and desires, along with your competitive comparison and related items.
- Close.
- Intense follow-up after the presentation whether you close or not.

Note: By intense, we mean pleasant persistence and doing what you say you will do when you say you will do it. We also mean sending thank-you notes and keeping the lines of communication active. Please refer to Section VIII (After the Close) for more detail.

Talk about What Your Target Audience Is Interested In

Gear your presentation to the interests of your audience. For example, if you are presenting to a bunch of high-tech people ("techies"), you need to be talking in terms that are important to them, namely, technology lingo. If you don't "talk tech," make sure you have people there who do, otherwise you'll be at a great disadvantage.

If you are speaking to upper-level management for a publicly traded company, your language had better be in their terms. Outline what your product or service will ultimately do for the bottom line and the shareholders, the price of the stock, and how they, the leaders of the company, will be looked upon favorably by the shareholders as a result of having chosen your product or service.

With private corporations, talk about returns to the owners and employees and how your product or service will make their lives easier.

You will need a different script when you talk to an individual. You need to talk in terms of the value she will get for her money and what your product or service will do to improve her life.

In a nutshell, you need to know the focus of each group and revolve your presentation around that focus. When presenting to owners or upper-level management, you might start with stock price, profits, and the like, but also show how your product will make the employees' and customers' lives easier, and how your product is the most technologically advanced.

Other groups such as the "techies" may not care at all about profits and pricing. Their concerns may focus solely on how their network, bandwidth, or other internal operations may be affected.

In any case, even in situations where you cover several areas, you want to put the most emphasis on the area *most important* to the audience you are speaking to. Each group will have one particular area that has overriding importance to them and their business.

Expand Your Horizons

When building the case for your product or service, focus on all aspects of your customer's business. Instead of focusing on just one department within the company, focus on all of them and how they will each benefit from your product or service. Give your prospects the information it takes to convince them that your product is the best for the entire company.

The Steps to Creating Your Presentation

If you can "borrow" a presentation from one of the top sales producers in your industry, you'll be one step ahead of the game. It's always better to use something that has been proven to work instead of reinventing the wheel. If that's not possible and you need to come up with your own presentation, the format that follows will give you some guidelines.

1) Brainstorm for the basic ideas of your presentation and what you want to say.

Keeping in mind the ideas we've discussed, jot down some quick notes on what you'd like to say. Let your thoughts flow freely. Don't worry about grammar, spelling, punctuation, the order of what you're saying, or anything else. Just get all your ideas down.

What do you want to get across about your product? Why is it the best? Start with your key benefits and expand upon them. How can you position yourself in the best possible light versus the competition? Examine your weaknesses. Examine the competition's weaknesses (study Section IV on competition). Can you think of any articles, trade publications, etc., that you should take a look at to solidify your facts? Brainstorm and come up with some creative ideas.

2) Put your presentation away and return to it the next day.

You want your subconscious to have some time to work on your presentation while you get a full night's rest. Take a fresh look at your presentation ideas the next morning, add any new ideas, and remove any extraneous ones.

3) Edit your presentation.

Go back and put the ideas in order. Try to keep your ideas short and to the point. Cut out any fluff or unnecessary wording. Give your presentation a little more structure. Look for places where you can use more powerful words. Look at ways you can strengthen your features, benefits, and competitive analysis. Are there some other ways to put your weaknesses in a better light? (Refer to Section IV for more about competitive analysis.)

4) Prepare a final edition of your presentation.

Get a little more detailed. Check your presentation for proper grammar and write down the exact words you want to say.

5) Have others critique your presentation.

Turn your presentation over to others. Have them read it first for content. Ask top salespeople and management you trust and respect how the presentation looks and sounds to them. Ask them what they would add. Have you missed anything? Is there anything they would remove? Practice it on friends and family. Don't be sensitive or defensive about any criticism—remember that it's all constructive and in your best interest.

6) Review and make necessary corrections.

Think about the feedback you've received, make some final notes, and then put your presentation away for a day or two. Return to it and make any final changes.

7) Make sure you have all the necessary ingredients of a good presentation.

Ask yourself the following questions about your presentation:

- Does it grab your audience's attention immediately with a strong opening line?
- Does it continue to hold them by getting them involved, giving them powerful statements, and using humor and stories?
- Do the words have enough energy, power, and overall impact?
- Are there questions or comments that you can make more powerful? You want something that touches, moves, and inspires individuals to want to own your product or service.
- Does it address all the prospect's needs and concerns?
- Does it flow well? Is it easy to understand?
- Does it lead naturally to the close or the next step in the selling process?

8) Practice, drill, and rehearse your presentation, then get out there and try it.

Know your presentation thoroughly—to the point that if someone were to wake you in the middle of the night, you could recite it without a problem.

Note: Don't worry about your presentation being perfect, because it won't be. If you wait until you have a perfect presentation, you'll never get out there. With your best effort, put something solid together, prepare by memorizing and rehearsing, and then hit the streets.

Other Quick Ideas

A Play on Words

Would you rather sip a martini with blue food coloring, or an Electric Lemonade? Would you rather have a problem or an opportunity? Would you rather be a housewife or a domestic engineer?

How you word things and the spin you put on them can have an impact on how they are perceived. When creating your presentation, be sure to dress your product or service in its best "verbal" clothes.

Have a Catch Phrase

A catch phrase, especially a humorous one, is a great way to make your presentation stand out and be remembered in a positive way.

For example, a local sub shop ran a special on Wednesdays: If you simply ask, they will make your six-inch sub a twelve-inch sub. They called it "Give 'em six extra inches for free on Wednesday."

One of the salespeople we know in an unrelated business added it to his presentation. He had a special promotion for new customers whereby they could get twice the product for their money on their first order. When he was getting to the end of his presentation, he brought up a slide that read, "Get six inches for free." He then explained the special at the sub shop and how he had adapted the "twice as much for the same price" idea.

Note: Obviously, you want to be careful with your catch phrases—you don't want to offend anyone. The slogan above is good, but it may be too risqué for some audiences. Humorous, risqué, or borderline items work best with Driver and Partier personality types, and generally not as well with "Yes" People and Thinkers.

Chapter 15

Preparing to Deliver Your Presentation

Have a Presentation Script

Everything related to your presentation should be written out. As we discussed in the introduction and Chapters on cold calling, some people believe that having a written presentation is too unnatural—you may sound as though you are reading (if on the phone), or canned (if in person). The way to avoid this is by practicing, drilling, and rehearsing your presentation to the point where you know it verbatim. If someone were to wake you up at 3 a.m., you should be able to fire off your presentation word for word.

Also, have all your responses to objections, your closes, and your answers to frequently asked questions written out and committed to memory. These should be in a binder, which we discussed in detail on pages 14, 15, and 16.

If you have your presentation, objection answers, and closes all memorized, you will have much more freedom, flexibility, and control during your presentation and will be able to concentrate on *how* you are saying things as opposed to *what* you are saying.

Make Sure Your Presentation Materials and Equipment Are Fully Prepared

Make sure your proposals, sales literature, pens, and all other presentation and sales materials are crisp, clean, organized, professional, and otherwise presentable. Be sure all your equipment works, and know where everything is. You don't want to be fumbling around during your presentation. Be organized and arrive early at your presentation location if you need to set up equipment.

Make your handouts as personal and professional as possible. Present them on quality materials and in business colors. Make sure all spelling and grammar is correct.

Have a backup plan for your technology as we discussed in Chapter 14.

Have supporting information with you such as testimonials, user lists, guarantees, your concept book, articles, and other "proof" that you may need to make a point or back up your information. (We will discuss these items very soon, in this Chapter under the heading Presentation Tools which begins on page 183.)

Make Sure *You* Are Fully Prepared

In addition to your materials, make sure *you* are also crisp, clean, neat, professional, and otherwise presentable. Know your material well; be well rested, confident, energetic, and completely prepared.

Make sure you've done your homework on the company and that you know the individuals who will be at the meeting.

Eat properly beforehand and in accordance with your system. You don't want to be excusing yourself to "check the plumbing", otherwise known as the men's or ladies room. And be sure to clean your teeth and freshen your breath after eating.

Finally, be prepared to talk about anything.

Have the Right Mental Attitude

You can't go into a presentation feeling superior or inferior to the people to whom you're presenting. You need to be at their level, as their partner. It's all right to be confident in your ability and believe that they will be impressed with your presentation. At the same time, don't have an attitude of cockiness or superiority. Be confident and professional, but also be humble.

Overcoming the Fear of Presenting

We discussed overcoming the fear of cold calling. If you have a fear of presenting, the same dynamics are at work, so we'll reiterate a few ideas here. First, realize that this one presentation is not going to make or break your sales career. The absolute worst that can happen is that you don't get a sale and you will be no worse off than when you walked in the door. In fact, you'll be better off because you've gained that much more experience. And don't take it personally. Remember that you won't make every sale. It's a numbers game.

Keep in mind that most people are pulling for you when you are presenting. To some degree or other, the majority of people have a tremendous fear of standing in front of others and talking. It's a psychological fact that these same people put themselves in your shoes. From their mental standpoint, if you make it, they make it. If you get up there, relaxed and composed, and immediately make a humorous point or two, you'll find most people will relax and open up quickly. Most people want to see you do well.

There are many good programs and organizations to help you overcome the fear of public speaking. Toastmasters is a wonderful venue in which to gain confidence in your public speaking ability. They can be found at www.toastmasters.org. The more you get up in front of people and speak, the easier it will become.

Preparation is another great way to build your confidence before a presentation. Know your material well before you present.

If you find the above suggestions don't work for you, you can seek professional help by way of a psychologist, hypnotist, or someone who specializes in helping people overcome fears. Many books are also available on the subject.

Conquering the fear of speaking in public will do amazing things for your confidence in other areas of life as well. Those who have had this fear and overcame it say it is the most liberating experience they've ever been through.

Practice Your Presentation

To prepare for your presentation, practice in front of an audience. Some people practice their presentation in their head, others practice out loud, and some practice in front of the mirror. If no one else is around, that's fine. In fact, the mirror method is recommended. However, *nothing* beats an audience, even if it's just one other person. Another salesperson, your husband, your wife—anyone will do. You will get a lot more feedback with an audience and it will prepare you to speak in front of people.

Whether you practice in front of another person or simply by yourself, get plenty of practice before you present. Make sure that one of your practice runs is the night before your presentation, right before you get plenty of sleep.

Note: Don't practice immediately before your presentation. At that point you either know it or you don't. It is better to get your mind off the presentation and to focus instead on relaxing.

Make Sure Everyone Knows Their Parts

If there will be other people from your company involved in your presentation, go over their parts with them before the prospect arrives. Make sure each person knows what they are expected to do and say, and when they are expected to do or say it.

For example, let's say you'll have your manager with you at the presentation. At some point he should be prepared to say something to the prospect about the commitment of your company and how important the prospect's business is to the company. You simply want to get a general idea—in advance—of when he will be speaking and what he will be saying. Also, often a manager may want to jump in and expand on an idea or add to something you've said. Speak with him ahead of time and get an idea of what role he will play in the presentation.

If you have other team members involved, you want them to know when they will be speaking and how you will transition to them.

The bottom line: Know which parts your team members are playing and when they will participate. Make sure everyone is familiar with the game plan and the objective. And ensure they each have the necessary background information on the prospect.

Each member of the team is important. You need to recognize the strengths and weaknesses of each team player, and draw on that person's strengths in areas where he or she will be most effective.

One final note: If you have any members of the team who don't get along, keep them separated. Keep them out of view of each other, if possible. Don't seat them directly across from each other, where they will have eye contact. Seat them on the same side of the table and place someone in between them, if possible.

Presentation Tools

The Concept Book

You should have a binder with you at all times that includes all your "evidence." We refer to that binder as a concept book.

Note: This binder is different from the one we discussed earlier that contains your cold call, presentations, closes, and other sales information.

Your concept book should include testimonials, your user list, reference letters, endorsements, articles, guarantees, and all documentation that supports any claims you make during your calls. It should contain examples of situations in which your product or service was applied with successful results. Some of these may be specialized applications. For example, did a customer have a special need in which your product or service was adapted to fit their particular situation?

One of the objectives of your concept book is to show the prospect "proof" of other situations, similar to their own, in which your product or service was applied with successful results. Another objective is to give examples of the possibilities that are available to the prospect with your product or service.

Finally, your concept book will be there to support any claims and add credibility to you, your company, and your product. If a prospect asks for references, you've got them. If a prospect asks how well your product will work in a particular situation, you have examples.

Note: Use your concept book as backup and support. You don't want to go through the entire book on each call. Simply use it to support information you may be discussing with the prospect.

Testimonials

The concept book is a good tool to use for name-dropping. In addition to dropping names, you should have written testimonials from your good customers. Written testimonials will add another layer of credibility to you and your product. It's one thing for you to say you have many happy customers; it's another to have this verified in writing. Testimonials should be an integral part of your business. Here are some guidelines to follow on obtaining and putting together testimonials.

1) Turn a customer compliment into a testimonial.

At the end of a sales call, a follow-up service call, a courtesy call, or at any other time, ask your customer how happy he is with your product or service. As soon as a customer gives you thanks or praises your product or service, seize the opportunity *immediately* by asking for a testimonial.

If the customer agrees to give a testimonial, ask him if it would be possible for you to create one for him based on his compliments. Assure him that you will write it up and get his approval on the text. We'll discuss this in greater detail under #4 beginning on the next page (186).

Often, customers will prefer this method—it saves them the time and trouble of doing it themselves. So what should you do? Get some specifics. Ask the following question: "Joe, what feature or features of our product do you like the most?"

Once you get an answer, probe a little deeper: "Joe, has that saved you time, money, or employee turnover?" Whatever answer he gives you, you want to have him elaborate on it. For example, if he tells you it's saved him money, ask, "If you had to guess, percentage-wise or dollar-wise, how much money would you say you've saved?"

Next, probe for more information and detail. "Is our product easier to use than your previous supplier's? How about our service?" Once you get two or three good tidbits, tell him you'll put something together and get it to him for his approval.

2) Another good way to get a testimonial is to create one yourself and present it to the customer.

In order to do this, you need to calculate how much time, money, or other valuable resources you've saved the customer. Let's say you are in the business of refurbishing parts for companies. In a situation such as this, look at the total number of parts you've refurbished for him, the cost difference between new parts and the refurbished parts, and calculate the total they've saved. Here is an example:

A welding company repaired worn metal parts, machining them back to original specifications. The refurbished parts were lasting just as long as new parts and all this was being done for one-third of the cost of a new part. So the sales department reviewed their records as to how many parts they received from a particular company.

For simplicity's sake, let's say it was one hundred parts. They looked at the cost of a new part ($300) and the cost of the refurbished part ($100), and figured the company had saved $200.00. Multiply this by one hundred parts for a total savings of $20,000 in six months. They called the key contact at the company, informed him of their findings, and asked if it would all right to put a testimonial together for his approval. It was, and the contact approved it. After running the numbers for nine other companies, they put together a powerful endorsement page (discussed below) that impressed many new prospects in the ensuing years.

Note: When using numbers, if the sheer numbers themselves have impact, use the numbers. If not, use percentages.

For example, one company had saved over $50,000, which, relatively speaking, was a huge number in terms of the cost of parts. Another much smaller company had saved only about $4,000, but that represented a 70 percent savings for that company. In the first example, use the number; in the second example, use the percentage. Obviously everything is relative. You know which numbers are big in your industry and which are small. Use your best judgment.

Keep in mind that the calculations can be more complex than this, with several elements to be factored in. For instance, if the refurbished parts were lasting only half as long as the new, you'd need to figure this into the equation. If two refurbished parts will last as long as one new one, you would compare the cost of a new part ($300), to the cost of two refurbished parts ($200), for a savings of $100 per each new part they would normally have to buy.

3) Your testimonials should be concise and have plenty of punch.

Your testimonials should be all meat and no fluff. Each word and sentence in the testimonial should be there for a reason. They should contain *benefits*, which are measurable and eye-catching. For example: "Our business increased by 34 percent in the three months following the seminar by ABC Company."

Testimonials should also compare you favorably to the competition. An example would be, "The sales training course presented by Pretium Partners was by far the most extensive, comprehensive, and most informative sales training course I've ever attended." In this example, Pretium Partners is not being compared to anyone in particular, but more generally to the industry as a whole. (See this testimonial on page 188.)

Note: Do not mention the competition's name in a testimonial. You don't want to give your competitors any free advertising.

4) Write the testimonial yourself.

It is best to write the testimonial for your customer and have him approve it. By writing the testimonial yourself, you can add lots of punch and say what you want it to say. When a customer is asked to put something in writing it becomes extra work for him to do, and often he'll procrastinate. If he does write it, it probably won't be the glowing review you'd like, and it can be awkward asking for revisions.

Obviously, what you write needs to be very close to what the customer actually said. You will simply dress it up a little with more powerful wording. You will also make sure all the grammar and spelling is correct. Put something together and then fax, e-mail, or otherwise get it to the customer for approval. Once you get approval, ask if he can do you a favor and copy it onto his company letterhead. Finally, have him sign it, fax it, and send the original to you.

File the original of the testimonial in a safe place. You can then make copies when needed. All copies should be made from the original, as they will be the best quality.

5) Create a page of powerful endorsements from your best testimonials.

In addition to using full testimonials, select powerful one-line excerpts from ten testimonials and put them on one page. This will be your page of "best endorsements." The objective is to impress prospects without making them read through lengthy testimonials.

List the most powerful excerpt first, the second strongest last, the third strongest second, the fourth strongest third, and so on until the weakest ends up at number nine. (See an example of an endorsement page on page 189.)

6) Keep clean, crisp color *copies* of your testimonials in plastic sheets in your concept book.

Keep the concept book handy as a tool that can be used on *all* sales calls. Use it on cold calls and during your first meeting with a prospect. You can also use it to overcome objections during presentations. You can show a prospect a testimonial from a customer who was in the same position and explain how the customer used your product or service to solve the problem.

Exhibit A: Testimonial

Complete Selling, Inc.
Auburn, MA 01501

Since taking the Pretium Partners "Selling Solutions" Training Course two years ago, I can equate roughly $625,000 of revenue income directly to the techniques learned through the course. Considering my annual quota of $2 million, that's substantial.

The Pretium Training Program provided me with the ideas and methods to open many doors that had previously been closed to me.

After taking the course, I targeted one particularly large competitive account. I reviewed their annual report and did some other research. Based upon the training I received through Pretium, I selected one area that I felt might be of particular interest to the bank's management. I then sent a mailing to upper-level management at this bank and expressed my product's ability to increase teller efficiency by 25 to 50 percent. I compared that to bottom line dollars based upon industry averages.

Once in the door, I asked questions I learned in the Pretium course that were based upon my previous findings. I then presented ideas based upon the ROI model, which we worked with while in the Pretium class. Through the techniques learned, I was able to visit several branches, observe teller transactions, and apply specific numbers to cost savings, increased teller efficiency, etc. I was then able to bring in other members of the team, tell my company's story, and show how we were best qualified to meet their customers' needs. All these were techniques I learned in the Pretium course.

That particular account has produced roughly $225,000 worth of revenue over the past two years and is now a solid Chapin Enterprises account.

The Pretium Partners Training Course is well thought out, thorough, and a refreshing alternative to many other sales courses, which too often offer more than they deliver. I highly recommend the Pretium course to anyone who needs to increase sales, increase sales efficiency, and spend less time getting better results. For someone who's been in sales almost forty-five years, I can attest that this is the best sales course I've been involved with.

Robert J. Chapin
Chapin Enterprises

Exhibit B: Endorsement Page

Endorsements for ABC Company

"We've saved over $76,000 on machine parts over the last six months by using ABC Company."
~~ Chris Ruggiero, Ruggiero Inc.

"The repaired parts we receive from ABC Company are lasting almost twice as long as brand-new parts!"
~~ Lisa Chipps, Dyer Industries

"On average, the parts we receive from ABC Company are one-third the cost and last just as long and many times longer than original parts."
~~ James Campanello, California Manufacturing Co., Inc.

"We are saving 62 percent on new needle plates that ABC Company is manufacturing for us."
~~ Mike Cavender, Atlanta Manufacturing Company

"ABC Company was able to customize parts for us, which led to a 43 percent increase in production line efficiency."
~~ Jim Graham, Fieldcrest Company

"We had eight machines that were out of production because we could no longer get parts for them. Thanks to ABC Company, all those machines are back on the assembly line."
~~ Joseph P. Smith, Fabrication Technology Inc.

"We've cut our annual cost of machine parts by an average of 56 percent each of the past three years by using ABC Company."
~~ Nick McCarthy, Auburn Industries, Inc.

The testimonial in Exhibit A on page 188 is a very long testimonial. Not all your testimonials will be this long, nor do they need to be. Ultimately, you want something that covers the basics and packs as much punch as possible.

Notice how the opening line in this testimonial catches the reader's attention with a specific number: $625,000. The customer then gives a comparison so the reader has something to relate it to: "my annual quota of $2 million." This is important because without the comparison, the $625,000 number might seem like a lot, or it might seem like a little. When it is compared with the annual quota of $2 million, it becomes a large number.

The customer then gives another benefit of the course, stating that it "open[ed] many doors that had previously been closed to me." This was followed with a specific example of applying techniques learned in the course.

Finally, in the last paragraph, the customer gives a ringing endorsement and compares Pretium very favorably to the competition.

Building a Reference List

Once a customer gives you a testimonial, take it a bit further. Ask the customer if you can also use her as a reference. Many will be happy to do this. With this step, you are getting the customer's okay to receive phone calls from prospects you're working on. Ultimately, you want to have about ten solid references for each product you have.

Reference Rules

These are five important rules regarding references:

1) Make sure a reference is not inundated with phone calls.

Remember, these people are important and they're busy. If you have twenty people call them in a week, not only will they call you and say, "Take me off your reference list!" but they'll be angry too. On average, one call per month per reference is the maximum number you want to be at.

When a prospect asks for references, ask if three will suffice. Most will say yes. If he wants more, ask how many he is looking for. Very few will come back with a number even close to ten. Pick the references that you feel will be the best for that particular prospect. By having to use only three at a time, you can rotate your references quite nicely so that none get bothered with excessive frequency.

2) Inform your references of when your prospect may be calling, make sure they're willing to take the call, and let them know the exact nature of the call.

If Joe Schmoe from ABC Bank calls your reference and he is not expecting the call and/or doesn't know the prospect at all, he may not take the call. If he does take it, he won't be as prepared as he might have been and likely won't provide as good a reference.

Simply give your reference a quick call and ask if it is okay to have Joe Schmoe from ABC Bank call. Once the reference agrees, inform him of what Joe is looking to purchase and what the reference may want to focus on.

3) Reward your active references.

Give your active references some sort of perk, such as tickets to a baseball game, a gift certificate to their favorite restaurant, or something similar. Be sure to let them know what the gift is for.

If you have a reference who goes above and beyond, you need to go above and beyond in thanking that person. Perhaps your customer has invited the prospect to visit his place of business, or does some training with the prospect, or otherwise goes way out of his way to truly assist your prospect rather than simply giving you a glowing review. In this case, you should give him an expensive gift certificate or something else that says "thank you very much" instead of just "thank you." And you need to do it immediately after the favor.

4) If you have several different types of products, have references for all of them.

If you sell software, hardware, alarms, and video surveillance, try to have ten references for each.

5) Have your reference lists with you on all sales calls.

Being prepared with references will help you build credibility with prospects. For a sample reference list, see Exhibit C on the following page.

Exhibit C: Reference List

References for Complete Selling, Inc.

1. Ms. Tami Germain, President, Auburn Credit Union – (508) 555-3725

2. Mr. Joel Keller, COO, Winchendon Savings Bank – (508) 555-1433

3. Mr. David R. Eid, Owner, Ball Park, Inc. – (207) 555-6968

4. Ms. Kathy Reno, CFO, Crowley Savings Bank – (617) 555-5500

5. Mr. Paul Taylor, President, Colony Bank – (978) 555-0171

6. Mr. Chris Ruggiero, Owner, Ruggiero Enterprises – (617) 555-6600

7. Ms. Thea Simolari, CEO, California Manufacturing Co. – (213) 555-5200

8. Mr. Peter Page, CFO, Dyer Industries – (248) 555-5835

9. Mr. Jim Keenan, President, Waters Savings Bank – (617) 555-9200

10. Ms. Terri Zwicker, CEO, Rothschild, Inc. – (202) 555-1846

Building a User List

After your customer has agreed to be a reference, get the customer's approval to be put on a user list. This will be the most basic of your lists—one page listing the people, companies, or organizations that use your product.

You do not need any phone numbers or even physical locations on this list. You will simply list ABC Company, DEF Company, GHI Company, etc. The objective of this list is to show the prospect that you are doing business with many companies, and hopefully some significant ones. Obviously, the more prominent companies you can add to the list, the better.

List the largest company first, then the second largest, and so on down the line. Have a large user list that includes all your active customers, and if you have a large number of customers, have a small or partial user list that includes only your key customers.

The most common place for the user list is in proposals. However, as with your testimonials and your references, you want to have this list with you on all sales calls just in case you need it to build some credibility.

For a sample user list, see Exhibit D on the following page.

Exhibit D: User List

Chapin Enterprises
27 Curtis Street Auburn, MA 01501

This is a partial user list. All Chapin Enterprises equipment is manufactured, installed, and serviced by Chapin Enterprises.

This means you will have all the experience you will ever need at your disposal to maximize your business's efficiency and profits.

Partial User List

Autoworkers Bank
Smithville Bank
Jamestown Savings Bank
Waters Savings Bank
Massachusetts National Bank
Bay County Savings Bank
Crowley Savings Bank
Charles River Company
Colony Bank
Curtis Savings and Loan
Dominion National Bank
Northeast Bank and Trust Company
Forest Bank
Harvard Bank
Harvey Federal Credit Union
Leadership Bank
Lancaster Bank
Lincoln Five Cent Savings Bank
Middletown Savings Bank
Stone Bank
North West Savings Bank
Worcester Bank
Steel Workers Bank
Wellington First Federal Credit Union
Xavier Bank

A Final Point on Testimonials, References, and User Lists

Make sure your testimonials, references, and user lists are politically correct. What does politically correct mean? Here are two examples.

Example One:

In the financial industry, banks and credit unions are two separate and distinct groups. For the most part, they mix about as well as oil and water. Consequently, when we use testimonials, a reference list, or a user list in this industry, the list contains either banks or credit unions—not both, but whichever we are talking to.

Occasionally our lists contain both. Just be aware of any sensitive dynamics that might exist in your particular industry and be prepared to deal with them appropriately.

Example Two:

Another issue you want to keep an eye on is who competes with whom. This can be a double-edged sword. If you're doing business with the prospect's major competition and sworn enemy, this can be used as leverage in a "keeping up with the Joneses" type of way. However, occasionally you may have a prospect who says, "If you're doing business with them, we don't want to do business with you."

In this case, it's best to remember that "business is business." The bottom line: You're in business to sell a product or service and make money. Use your best judgment here. If you have plenty of other testimonials, references, and users, you may want to leave the major competition off the list.

Of course, you don't want to be sneaky. If you are asked if you do business with the major competition, and you do, look the prospect straight in the eye and simply say, "Yes, we do." If the prospect objects, say, "Mr. Prospect, I appreciate and understand what you're saying. Let me ask you a question. If you were in my shoes, and had a superior product that you knew would highly benefit those who used it, would it make sense to you that you should go out and try to do business with as many companies as you possibly could?"

You won't get a *no* to this question but, if for some crazy reason you do, move on as you probably don't want this person as a customer.

Chapter 16

Delivering Your Presentation

Deliver Your Presentation with Energy and Enthusiasm

We've already touched on this, but it's important. A key aspect of delivering your presentation is *how* you deliver it. You want to infuse your presentation with lots of life and passion. In other words, deliver your presentation with plenty of energy and enthusiasm.

If you deliver the most inspiring speech ever written in a monotone, uninspiring way, you'll put people to sleep. If you deliver a less than perfect speech with lots of enthusiasm, energy, and voice fluctuation, you'll capture people's attention.

You need to deliver the message properly in order to keep people interested. If you use weak, unemotional words to deliver your message, people will turn off quickly. On the other hand, if you use words with lots of juice and power, people will pay attention.

Getting and Keeping the Prospect's Full Attention during the Presentation

Open strong. The most critical first step of any sales presentation is to get the prospect's full and complete attention. The second most important step is to keep the prospect's attention. This is the same dynamic that applies to the cold call.

In order to get the audience's attention at the beginning of your presentation, make an irresistible statement that hits them right in between the eyes. How? Give them a very strong benefit of your product or service.

For example, at the beginning of a presentation on helping people cut taxes, the presenter might say, "In the next thirty minutes I will show you how to cut your taxes by 35 percent." Obviously, that will perk up some ears and grab people's attention immediately. After all, who doesn't want to save 35 percent on taxes?

A presentation for some type of investment vehicle might begin with, "Here's a safe way to make 10 percent a year on your money—tax free." Some people might be skeptical, but we can guarantee you that opening will get their attention.

Note: Make sure any statement you make is grounded in fact and can be backed up with solid proof. Your next step will be to build credibility in the statement, your product, you, and your company.

Make More "Hit 'Em between the Eyes" Statements at Various Points in the Presentation

Just as you did at the beginning of your presentation, you want to hit people between the eyes again at certain points throughout the presentation just to make sure they are still with you.

The average person's attention span is short. If your presentation is monotone or otherwise uninspiring, you'll soon have your target audience thinking about their vacation two weeks from now, walking out, or changing the channel mentally. One "hit 'em between the eyes" statement at the beginning won't hold them forever, no matter how good it is. You have to sprinkle a few throughout the presentation.

Start with the benefits of your product or service then build them into short statements and questions with lots of punch. Questions are very important to keep your audience involved. In the example above, after the initial benefit of saving customers up to 35 percent on taxes, the next strongest benefit might be helping them to audit-proof their tax returns. Put this in question form: "Now, how many people would like me to show them how to almost completely audit-proof their taxes?" This is a very strong question that everyone will be interested in and that will perk people up again and get them involved. You'll need several of these "wake-up" statements and questions throughout the presentation to bring people back into the room and away from thinking about what they're going to do this weekend.

The Prospect Has Her Own Agenda

Occasionally someone will try to throw you off the path. The prospect may not care how you want the presentation to go—she has her own agenda. As a result, some prospects will try to control the conversation by asking you questions in an attempt to steer the conversation in the direction they want it to go.

Some people are impatient and will try to get you to cut to the chase. They will tell you they have only a few short minutes and ask you to get to the bottom line. Or they will tell you they've already looked into the matter extensively and have learned everything there is to know, and now they would just like to know your price.

Obviously keeping control of the conversation is important in selling. Maintain control of the conversation by being prepared and by asking questions.

1) Preparation

One of the most effective ways to control the conversation is through preparation. You must practice, drill, and rehearse your presentation, your closes, and your answers to objections. As we've mentioned before, write all this information out, memorize it, and know it thoroughly.

The prospect, on the other hand, will not be as well prepared as you are. If the prospect tries to throw you off track with a question or comment, simply acknowledge it, respond to it, and then return to where you were in the presentation.

2) Questions

Questions are another highly effective way to control the conversation. Questions can steer the conversation in the direction you want. Questions allow you to keep the conversation going on the same subject or take it in a completely different direction. Let's look at a typical conversation:

Person A: "Hi, how are you?"
Person B: "Good. And you?"
Person A: "Good. Hey, can you believe that game last night?"
Person B: "That was unbelievable. How about that run back on the kick?"
Person A: "I know, and how about that fumble in the fourth quarter?"
Person B: "Yeah, unreal. Hey, did you look at those numbers from the meeting the other day?"

Notice how the questions in this example dictate exactly where the conversation is going. Each question either keeps the conversation on the same subject or shifts it to a completely different subject.

If the prospect goes on a tangent, acknowledge what has been said, respond to it with an answer or comment, and then take the reins of the conversation and steer it back to where you want it.

When someone asks for the bottom line, ask the questions you need answered in order to work out a price or take an order. For example, you might ask what features and functions are most important to them. You can then write these on an order form and continue with all the questions you need answered to fill out the form.

If they push with, "Look, I just want the bottom line." Say, "I understand. I simply need to get this information so I know what exactly to include in the price I give you."

Competing for the Prospect's Attention

In addition to personal agendas, prospects also have their minds on other things. We all have things going on in our lives that are important. If your presentation is boring or you talk over people's heads, they will tune out very quickly. Their brains literally stop hearing you and they jump to the most emotionally charged item on its agenda. It may be an upcoming vacation, the boss's demands, or another project the prospect is working on. You may also be catching someone who is in the middle of a bad day, or worse, some other highly emotional situation such as a divorce. If this is the case, you will often find yourself in a tug-of-war for the person's attention.

Let's look at one "worst-case" scenario: the prospect is in the middle of a bitter divorce. In this case, a majority of his waking hours will be spent focused on the divorce. Let's say that on the emotion scale, the divorce rates an 8.5 on a scale of one to ten. When you arrive for your appointment, you will most likely have the prospect's attention initially. The trick is to keep his attention during your meeting.

In order to do that, you will need to keep your discussion on a level higher than an 8.5. Now this may not be possible for the entire presentation, and it is likely that the prospect will think about his divorce occasionally, even if you are over 8.5. However, if your presentation is consistently below an 8.5, you will get to the end and the prospect will have heard *very little* of what you said.

Granted, competing with an issue at an emotional level of 8.5 is not easy no matter how good a salesperson you are. It is also a situation you're unlikely to encounter with any regularity. Still, you want to get your presentation as close to an emotional and logical ten as possible. If you are able to get your presentations close to that level, assuming you are talking to a qualified decision-maker, you will more than likely make the sale.

Find Out Where You're at during the Presentation

Ask questions. During your presentation, ask questions and get feedback to make sure you are headed in the right direction. These questions will also keep the prospect involved and make sure he is paying attention. In a sense you will be using trial closing questions. However, these questions are not quite as direct as those in your close. You want to embed these questions into your presentation in various places.

Too many of these questions can irritate the prospect, so keep them to a minimum. As a general rule, you should ask one question about every five minutes. Here are some examples of questions to ask:

- "How does this solution sound so far?"
- "Are we heading in the right direction with this solution, Mr. Prospect?"
- "Do you feel that feature would be beneficial to you?"

With these questions, you are taking the prospect's temperature. Is he hot, cold, or somewhere in the middle? If he's hot, you want to be closing *now* or very soon. If he's cold, you need to find some hot buttons and areas of interest or otherwise figure out what the problem is. If he's somewhere in the middle, you need to find more hot buttons and areas of interest before you attempt to close him.

Look for Other Indicators

In addition to asking questions, be aware of other indicators such as body language, nervous habits, and facial expressions that indicate how the prospect is reacting to your presentation. This will tell you which points are hitting home, which are not, and they'll even tell you what the prospect's hot buttons are. The key point to remember is that you need to be able to read between the lines and "hear" and "see" what people are not telling you with their words.

Sell the Relationship in Addition to the Product or Service

When you are presenting, emphasize the importance of the long-term relationship, and show the prospect that you understand the importance of service after the sale as well as the long-term quality and value of your product. To achieve this end, say,

"Mr. Prospect, the most important thing is the relationship five, ten, twenty years down the road. Now obviously, today price is important. At the same time, the long-term relationship we develop with you depends on the quality and longevity of the product we supply, as well as the service we provide to you. We grow our business by making you happy today and for years to come. Does that make sense?"

Name-dropping in Your Presentation

Your presentation is a great place to name-drop. Name-dropping builds credibility. If some of the high-profile companies in the industry use you, let it be known! If some other companies in the same area as your prospect use you, you might want to consider dropping their names too. You can also mention the names of some individuals with whom you do business.

One way to name-drop in a presentation is to put up a slide that lists some or all of the companies you do business with. You can also use your concept book—using your testimonials, reference lists, and user lists to simply show some examples of where and how your product or service worked for other companies and drop names at the same time. Here are two reminders with regard to name-dropping:

Note 1: Be sure to obtain permission to mention those you are doing business with. Also, be careful about who competes with whom and how you use that information.

Note 2: Some smaller companies may feel unimportant if you're doing business with all the big guys. Sometimes the competition will even use that against you. In these situations you need to reassure the "small guy" that he will be treated like a VIP.

Where to Sit When Presenting

Try to position yourself on the same side of the table as the prospect(s) during your presentation. When you sit on the same side of the table, people usually feel more comfortable than when you are across the table from them.

The chair at the head of the table, farthest from the door, is typically where the "leader" sits. If the President of the company will be attending your meeting, he or she will probably sit in that spot. If, instead of the President, you are meeting with the purchasing agent and a Vice President, you might want to take the head chair since most people in the company are used to saying "yes" to the person who sits in that chair—namely, the President.

This is called a power anchor. By power anchor we mean that people typically equate power to that chair and that position at the table. Before you sit in that chair, ask indirectly if it's permissible. Simply ask, "Will anyone be sitting here?"

Where to Look during Your Presentation

Look directly at the customer or prospect during your presentation. *Do not* look at the other people from your company who might be present. You are not selling them, you're selling the prospect. The only time you want to be looking at someone from your company is if he or she is talking or you want to signal someone to jump in or help you out.

Get by with a Little Help from Your Friends

If you are presenting to a large audience, you will typically find some interested faces as well as some uninterested ones. Focus on the friendly faces in the audience and try to avoid looking at the unfriendly ones. You need to stay positive and upbeat while you are speaking. Friendly faces will lift you up while unfriendly faces can drag you down.

Point Out Weaknesses

Don't try to hide weaknesses from the prospect. Point them out and then show the advantages. For example, if you are in the retail industry or car business, you may have some inventory that you need to sell before you can bring in the new models. You might say, "Mr. Prospect, we need to move these in order to make room for the new model. As a result, I can give you a *great* price on this model, and this product is virtually the same as the new one will be."

A house may be a bargain because it's located near some railroad tracks, airport, or some other undesirable item. If that's the case, don't avoid the railroad tracks, point them out and then state the advantage, which is price.

Give the Prospect Enough but Not Too Much Information

Your overall objective in your presentation is to give your prospect enough information to make an informed decision, but not so much that you overwhelm or confuse her.

People will keep track of a only few key points. After three or four major points are made, the information starts to become overwhelming and your prospect may mentally shut you off and stop listening. Above all, you want to keep things simple.

You may have heard the saying, "The less you tell, the more you sell." Too much information can lead to objections or stalling measures such as "Leave me some information" or "I need to think about it." It is usually better to give too little information rather than too much. With too little information you have the best chance of remaining within the prospect's attention span and realm of understanding. Keep the information to three or four major points and leave the others for objections, additional closes, or as an opening when you follow up on a second or third closing call.

There are two times when it's better to over-explain. First, in some cases there are legal ramifications to not giving the full story. In cases such as these, you need to ensure the prospect has all the required information. Second, if you are going over a difficult subject such as an investment, it is important to make sure the person fully understands what you are talking about.

For example, if you are a financial advisor discussing a company's P/E ratio, you can say something to the effect of, "As I'm sure you know, the P/E ratio is the company's price-to-earnings ratio. Meaning, if the stock trades at $100 and the company has earnings of $10 per share, the price-to-earnings ratio would be ten—the price of the stock divided by the earnings per share. Does that make sense?"

Starting with, "As I'm sure you know" tells the prospect, "I know you're intelligent so you probably already know this, but I'll explain it anyway." If you simply launch into the explanation and the person already knows what a P/E ratio is, she might think, "Does this guy think I am an idiot?" If the person does know what a P/E ratio is, she will let you know when you begin your explanation.

Finally, remember, when explaining, to be careful not to talk down to the person or use a patronizing or condescending tone.

Talk in Terms the Prospect Can Understand

Give the prospect information in the simplest of terms. By this we mean you should keep it concise and talk in layman's terms unless you are speaking with someone who is very familiar with your industry's language. Some salespeople automatically assume everyone knows all the same terms and phraseology that they do. As a result, often in an effort to impress, they throw out all sorts of acronyms and industry jargon. But this can backfire. Here is an example from one of our experiences:

We had an appointment with a customer to discuss some new industry regulations. For training purposes, we'd brought along one of our new sales representatives. After some small talk, we started to ask a few questions to gauge how familiar the customer was with the new regulations. He stated that he was not familiar at all with them and was also not very technologically-minded. And then he asked us to "explain it to me like I was a third-grader."

We gave some background, spelling things out carefully, when the new sales representative chimed in. He asked the customer how familiar he was with another obscure regulation that would have no impact on this company whatsoever.

Immediately, the expression on the customer's face changed from one of understanding to sheer confusion. The experienced sales rep turned the conversation back to the regulations we were there to discuss. The conversation was back on track—until the new sales rep prodded the customer to get on the Internet and find the information on our website. Considering the fact that the customer had commented that he was "not technologically-minded," our new rep should have assumed the client was not too adept with a computer. As things turned out, watching the client struggle with the Internet was like watching a two-year-old try to juggle.

This scenario makes a few points. First, you need to get a feel for the prospect's level of expertise. Do this by asking how much he knows and by observing his reaction to the information you are giving. Some people will be afraid to tell you they know nothing on a subject; thus, it's always important to pay close attention to the prospect's reaction to your presentation. You need to know if he's with you or if you're losing him.

How do you know if you're losing him? He'll either start asking a lot of questions or he'll clam up completely, nodding and mumbling, "Uh huh, okay," even though he may be completely baffled by what you're saying. You'll also observe a look of confusion on his face.

The second point from the above example is that you need to stick to your objective and keep it simple and straightforward. Don't get off course with unrelated items.

Third, you need to be familiar with the customer's situation, and discuss only those areas that are relative to him.

When answering questions, listen to what the prospect is asking for, give only the information necessary and then clarify that the prospect understood your answer.

Words and Phrases to Avoid in Your Presentation

1) To be honest with you.

Synonyms for this are *honestly*, *frankly*, and *to tell you the truth*. Even worse: "Well, I wasn't going to say this, but…" or "I shouldn't be saying this, but…" Ugh! Those are real killers. All these phrases give people the impression that you haven't been completely up front or you have something to hide.

2) I think/I believe.

Both of these phrases give the impression that you're not sure of what you're saying. If you're not sure, say so and make a commitment to follow up with the answer.

3) Listen (followed by the person's name).

The word "listen" along with a person's name is confrontational. You can almost hear someone automatically responding with, "No, you listen!" Subconsciously, it comes across as a command and sounds more like, "Hey! Pay attention, will you?"

4) What do you think?

Thinking is work. Instead, you always want to ask someone how something sounds, looks, or feels. You want to get the senses involved in the buying process. When you ask someone what she thinks, she immediately goes into analysis or point-counterpoint mode. Thinking is much more involved than simply using our senses to evaluate something.

5) Buy and Sell.

Change buy or sell to invest. For example: Instead of saying, "If you were to buy this gadget today" say, "If you were to invest in this gadget today…"

6) But.

Generally speaking, the word *but* can be confrontational. Occasionally, it's appropriate when you want to contrast two ideas, yet often *but* is used unnecessarily. The word *but* is sometimes interpreted as, "Okay, forget everything I just said. Now I'm going to tell you how I really feel."

When you can, try to replace the word *but* with *and.* Read the following two sentences and listen for which one sounds better:

a) "Jim, you've really done some great work on this article, *but* I think we should make sure we have all the facts correct here."

b) "Jim, you've really done some great work on this article, *and* I think we should make sure we have all the facts correct here."

The first sentence sounds like you're telling Jim that you're not sure all his facts are correct. The second sentence sounds like you're telling Jim that he's done some great work and once you both verify that all the facts are correct, you'll have a truly great article. While there may not be a major difference, simply changing the word *but* to *and* definitely makes the sentence less confrontational and more agreeable.

There will be times when you deliberately want to use the word *but* for emphasis. For example, if you are writing a factual account of something, *but* serves as a good separator between two opposing thoughts. However, sometimes eliminating *but* from your vocabulary and replacing it with *and* will make the tone of your conversation more positive.

7) No.

No is the ultimate in negative words. Avoid answering questions with a direct *no* and avoid asking questions which elicit a *no* from the prospect. Try to formulate questions that bring out a positive response—*yes.* For example, instead of asking: "Obviously, you don't want higher premiums, do you Joe?" ask a question such as, "Joe, if I could substantially lower your premiums, would you be interested?"

There will be times when you need to say the equivalent of *no* when responding to a prospect or customer. Just try to limit them and try to answer in a way that has a little less edge than a flat-out *no*.

8) Nice to meet you.

This one may seem a bit confusing, so here's an explanation. We've all had a situation in which we've met someone before and that person remembers, but we don't. We've also been on the other end.

Fortunately, there's an easy remedy to this. Instead of saying "Nice to meet you," say, "Nice to see you." Whether you are meeting the person for the first time, second time, or one-hundredth time, "Nice to see you" is always appropriate.

Words to Use in Your Presentation

When you present your ideas to others, use positive words and words that spur agreement. Here are some examples:

1) A person's name.

People like to hear their names. Don't overdo it, but try to use the person's name at the beginning of the conversation, at the end, and a few times in the middle.

2) Two of the most powerful words you can use are *me too*.

The words *me too* imply, "I'm just like you"; they also say, "I hear and understand you."

3) Use *you*, *your*, and *yours* as much as possible.

Keep *I*, *me*, and *my* to a minimum in your conversations. People like the focus to be on them and what they are interested in. *You* and *your* refer to the person with whom you are talking. Go through all your presentations, closes, answers to objections, and even letters and advertising, and look for places to use *you* or *your* instead of *I*, *me*, or *my*. Change words and phrases so the focus shifts from you to the prospect. Change statements such as the following:

- Change "I have found…" to "you will find…"

- Change "Based upon the research, I believe…" to "The research indicates that you will find…"
- Change "I wanted to give you a call with this latest information" to "There is some new information you're likely to be very interested in."

Some phrases will simply need a word change from *I* to *you* while other phrases will need to be completely reworded. Some phrases will even go from a statement to a question. Shifting from "I" to "you" changes the focus. You always want the focus on the prospect.

4) Positive words and phrases/action words.

Add words to your presentation that create excitement and positive feelings. You want to keep your overall message positive. Review all your copy and change negative words to positive ones. Think of this in terms of a political campaign. The positive message is usually better received than the one loaded with mud slinging. At the same time, don't use million-dollar words that people have to look up in the dictionary. Liven and enlighten, don't daze and confuse.

Note: It's all right to use some negative words when trying to describe a painful situation or outcome, or when trying to show the prospect what could happen if he continues on his current course of action. Overall, however, you want to keep the message upbeat and show the positive impact your product will have on the prospect's life.

Words That Capture People's Attention

1) Free

Obviously, everyone likes something for free. The word *free* is a great attention getter.

2) Guarantee

People like a guarantee because it limits their risk. If you have a 100 percent, no questions asked, money-back guarantee, people are less likely to be afraid to part with their money. Of course, there must be a reputable person and company behind the guarantee.

3) Risk free

This is another statement that limits the buyer's risk. If there is no risk in trying, why not try it?

4) New, latest technology, cutting edge

Everyone wants the latest and greatest or something that is better than anything else out there.

5) Secret

Everyone likes to be special and wants to have something no one else has.

Look for areas in your presentation where you can add some of the above words and phrases.

Make Sure *What* You Say and *How* You Say It Is Consistent

The elements of effective communication are:

- What you say
- How you say it
- Your body language

Studies have shown that the words you use are least important, how you say something is number two, and your body language is the most important factor in determining the impression you leave someone with.

For example, if you say the words "I love you" in a barely audible tone while staring at the floor, they will have a far different meaning than if you were to say them with feeling and passion while looking lovingly into someone's eyes. Now say "I love you" with a Mickey Mouse voice. Now scream it.

You get the point. In order to project the right message, your words, voice, and body language must be consistent. Nail down the right words and make sure your words, how you say them, and your body language are all congruent.

Use Proper Grammar

People are a little more forgiving of language errors when they are delivered verbally. We don't expect people to be perfect. As long as the content of the presentation and the delivery are strong, you can make a couple of verbal mistakes. Notice we said a couple. If you make too many it *will* negatively impact your presentation.

People are far less tolerant of mistakes in the written word because it's much easier to check the written word before it is presented. Most people will allow at least one or two mistakes in writing, unless they involved the customer's name or something that relates to them. If there are numerous written mistakes, it looks as if you don't care, are incompetent, or both. Review your written words carefully, and then have someone who is *very* good with grammar and spelling check them too.

Mistakes People Make during Presentations

Be aware of the most common mistakes that salespeople make during presentations and do your best to avoid them.

1) They're not prepared.

They arrive with no meeting agenda, are disorganized, or are way off the mark about their prospects' needs and objectives.

Here's a quick example from our experiences. We went into a meeting to discuss service concerns with a customer and our service manager opened the meeting with, "Gee, I really didn't have a chance to look at these service records before the meeting."

This was our largest account! Not a good thing to say to a customer who was not happy with our service and our attention to service.

2) They have poor presentation skills.

Poor presentation skills include, but are not limited to:

- Butchering the English language.
- Butchering names.
- Poor delivery.

- Too many *ahs*, *ums*, *ya knows*, and other similar unnecessary fillers.
- Giving a presentation that is unclear and/or confusing.
- Bad content.

3) They don't know their product or material.

This is someone who does not stay current with what is happening in the industry and is not able to answer a good number of the prospect's questions. This is also someone who "wings" the presentation. If you are brand new, it is understandable that you won't know everything. If that is the case, you should not be on the sales call alone.

4) They show up late.

Being late makes you look unprofessional and disorganized.

5) They fight among themselves at a customer meeting.

This seems obvious, right? You'd be surprised. We have heard people call co-workers to task in front of the customer. Bad idea. It shows that you have problems internally and it is *extremely* unprofessional. If you undermine a colleague in front of a customer, not only will it look bad to the customer, but you may even permanently destroy your relationship with that colleague.

6) They argue with the customer.

You may need to make a strong point and even defend yourself or your company in a meeting. However, you need to be very careful about how you do it. Obviously, you should never get into a verbal confrontation with the prospect.

7) They don't have an action plan.

These salespeople don't outline objectives, fail to tie everything together at the end of the meeting, fail to debrief with co-workers later, and don't follow up in an appropriate or timely manner.

8) They sell features instead of benefits.

They inundate the prospect with all sorts of information about color, shape, size, and technical data that has nothing to do with what the product will actually do for the prospect. While features can be important, they should be used only to lead to the benefits of the product.

9) They don't close or take the next step in the process.

This one is self-explanatory. You need to either close the sale or take the next step in the selling process.

Some Notes on Group Presentations

Group presentations can differ greatly from one-on-one presentations. Here are some ideas to keep in mind:

1) Become informed about the group before you meet.

Knowing the group's history will help you talk about items that are of interest to each member. You also want to include information that lets them know you have researched and studied them. This shows that you are a professional and you care.

2) Arrive early and meet people.

Take time before the meeting to get to know people in the group and build rapport with them. Remember their names and refer to each of them by name during the meeting.

3) Find out who is the important person.

You want to play to the power in the room, or to the person or people with the most influence and authority. This person or people are the key to getting a decision to go your way and, as a result, can completely make or break your presentation.

Note: If you find yourself in a meeting where you want to learn who the power person is, ask an off-the-wall question such as, "What if the solution you choose to implement doesn't work?" Everyone will look at the key person to see his or her reaction. They may only look for a second, but this always works.

4) Be professional, honest, and mix in some good, clean humor.

Being a consummate professional who is honest and has integrity can carry you a long way in sales and in life. It is particularly important to emphasize these traits in group sales, where so many people are watching and judging you. Use good, clean humor to create the right environment and draw your audience closer to you, but use it sparingly. You want the audience to perceive you as a businesslike professional who is down to earth, not a clown who is only occasionally serious.

5) Address everyone's concerns.

You are likely to have several different personality types in the room. Make sure you can answer all technical questions and other curve balls that may be thrown at you. If there are questions you can't answer, have other people with you who can.

6) To keep their attention, keep the audience involved.

Here are some ways to do that:

- Ask questions and have the audience participate during the presentation. For example: "A quick show of hands. How many people here are small business owners?"
- Have people do something physical at some point in the presentation. "Okay, we've been sitting for a while. Everyone stand up for a moment and greet the person to the right of you. Now greet the person to the left of you. If you already know those people and they're boring, try the person in front of you and the person behind you." Notice we used a little humor there too.
- Have your audience practice some of the techniques you talk about. You may say to a group of salespeople: "Okay, now I want you all to stand up, turn to the person directly to your right and give him or her your best sales line in the most confident, enthusiastic manner that you can muster."
- Hand things to your prospects, or let them test your product right there during the presentation.

7) Follow up and move toward the close.

As with any other type of sales call, you need to have a system in place to follow up and move toward the close. In addition, try to send a note or e-mail to every member of the group, thanking them for their attendance and participation. Use handouts if appropriate during the later stages of your presentation.

Chapter 17

A Sample Presentation

Now that we've looked at putting together your presentation, preparing to deliver your presentation, and actually delivering your presentation, let's take a look at a sample presentation from start to finish.

Introduce Other Team Members

After you've greeted the prospect(s) and engaged in some small talk and rapport building, the first step is to introduce any other people in attendance from your company and let the prospect know what that person's role will be. They may have an active part in the presentation, or they may be there for technical support, or they may simply be observing. Give the person's name, what they do for your company, and explain their presence at your meeting. For example, "This is Dennis Bradshaw. He's a software engineer, and he's here today for technical support."

Have the Prospects Introduce Themselves

You may know every person in the room; still, it is a good idea to go around the room and have people give their name and position within their company.

Note: If you have twenty or more people, you'll want to avoid this step just because it will take too long. You also don't want to do this if you are sitting with four or five upper-level executives. In that case, you should know in advance who everyone is and what they do, and you should brief everyone from your company before you enter the meeting. In that situation, another good idea is to introduce everyone to each other before the meeting begins.

The Beginning of Your Presentation

Once you have said hello, you've had some general discussion on non-business items (rapport building), and everyone has been introduced, you will then set the agenda for the meeting, clarify the objective, and confirm this with the customer(s). Here is an example:

"Thank you for being here today and taking time out of your busy schedules. The objective today is to take a look at XYZ Manufacturing's needs, desires, and requirements with regard to machine parts and to see how our solution fulfills those needs. Overall, we want to show you how to maximize your savings, your profits, and employee and customer satisfaction.

"We'll start with a quick PowerPoint presentation, which I promise will not put you to sleep. We will then look at some of your machine parts and talk about what we can do specifically for XYZ Manufacturing.

"If you like what you see, the next step would be to set up a meeting at the plant with your technicians to look at your machine parts and determine exactly what you need. We would also set up a plan for parts exchange and for the business relationship going forward.

"Does that sound like a good agenda and some good objectives for the meeting today?"

Note 1: Notice the benefit statement in the opening, "The objective today is to take a look at XYZ Manufacturing's needs, desires, and requirements with regard to machine parts and to see how our solution fulfills those needs. Overall, we want to show you how to maximize your savings, your profits, and employee and customer satisfaction." As mentioned, you need to catch the attention of your audience immediately and then keep it throughout the presentation.

Note 2: If you are presenting to an individual, it is best to sit next to him or her during the presentation. You can either go over your presentation right on your computer or you can project it onto the wall. It is always better to sit alongside the prospect than stand while the prospect is sitting.

If you are presenting to a group, stand up as you transition into the business conversation and continue standing throughout the presentation. Also, you want to have your presentation projected onto the wall when you present to a group.

Note 3: It's a good idea to throw in a little humor in immediately following your introductory statement. As we mentioned in the Cold Calling section, you can refer to Darren LaCroix's website at www.humor411.com for help with humor. Use a joke of the day, or something from a joke book that you can relate to sales, meetings, or anything else you may be talking about. We have also seen some salespeople work funny video clips into their presentation. Another idea is to refer to humor without telling a joke at all. The following is an example.

"You know, they say the best way to start a presentation is by telling a joke. But since I can't think of any right off the bat, I'll save everyone the pain and agony." (Take a brief pause for effect.) "So, this guy walks into a bar and there's a gorilla sitting behind the bar…okay, just kidding. But seriously…" (Now you will bridge into the opening of your presentation.)

"Thanks for being here. We'll now go through the PowerPoint presentation and again, I promise I'll go through this quickly and not put anyone to sleep. Before I begin, though, is there any particular direction you'd like me to take this, or any area you'd like me to focus on? Okay, great. Let's get started."

At this point you will bring up your first slide. Know your slides by heart. You don't want to be looking at them and reading them word for word. Quickly look up to ensure the proper slide is showing, and then immediately focus on your audience, speaking directly to them. Your slides will make up the body, or main part of your presentation.

The Body of the Presentation

In the body of the presentation, show how your product or service meets and exceeds the needs and desires of the prospect.

Here is an example of some presentation slides along with what you might say under each one:

Slide 1:

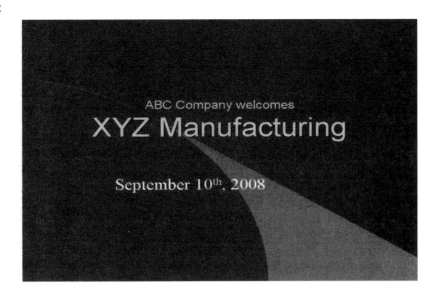

You: "There you are in lights again! (assuming you had their name up on a board as they came in the front door), and we really appreciate you being here today."

Slide 2:

You: "Briefly, here's an overall history of our company and how we've developed into the type of company that can really help you today. Established in 1970, ABC began welding plastic injection molds. We've done work for companies such as Ford, General Motors, Pfizer, and IBM, among many others.

"In 1975, we started welding small, intricate parts found in the helmets that astronauts wear. We actually use wire that is about the thickness of a human hair. Very high-tech, critical stuff. (Pass a sample piece of wire around.)

"In the 1980s, we began welding small machine parts, some of which we'll be talking about today. In that area we are saving people roughly 60 percent on parts, and our parts are actually lasting longer than an original part. (Pass around a "before" and "after" part.)

"In 1991, we started manufacturing parts at a substantial cost savings. We'll talk more about that soon. In 1998, we began working on obsolete parts. In a moment, we'll also cover this more in depth.

"In 2002, we began customizing parts based upon specific needs within specific industries. We also introduced our 100 percent satisfaction guarantee. If you're not happy with a part for any reason, you don't pay for it. In other words, we put our money where our mouth is. Are there any questions at this point?"

Note: In this example, we mentioned passing parts around. Passing the samples around is a good idea as it allows the prospect(s) to become more involved. Also, welding wire that is the thickness of a human hair is impressive to prospects in this particular industry. Pass only a few items around. You want the prospect(s) involved, but not overwhelmed to the point where they miss what you are saying.

Slide 3:

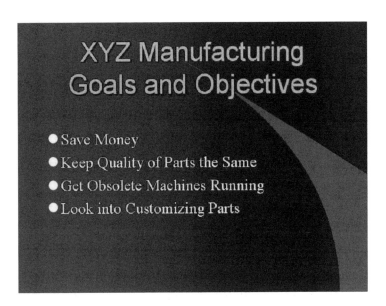

You: "Now, here on Slide 3 we have your goals and objectives, as we understand them from our previous discussions with you. Obviously, you'd like to save some money; at the same time, your mechanics have said they need new parts to make sure the high quality remains. Correct?

"Okay, so saving money and preserving the high quality of your equipment are two of your top priorities." (Wait for affirmative response.)

"Also, you have some old machines that are obsolete simply because you have broken parts that can't be replaced, right? Okay. And then you'd like to look into customizing some parts, right? (Wait for an answer.)

"Now, it's my understanding that you'd like to get some longer points on the hooks because of the manufacturing you're doing, but you're not quite sure how long, is that right? (Wait for answer.)

"Okay. We've got some ideas, but generally, do you have any idea as to how much longer? (Answer.) Okay, we'll look at that in a moment."

Slide 4:

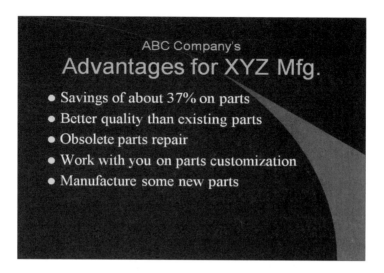

You: "Slide 4 shows the advantages of your company working with our company to reach your goals and objectives. First off, in our earlier discussions, you mentioned that you're spending $50,000 on parts every six months, for a total of $100,000 per year, correct?

"Okay, let's bring up the next slide and see what your cost looks like under your current system and how it will look if you're refurbishing parts with us."

Slide 5:

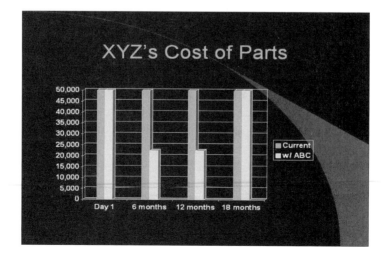

You: "Now, under the current system, you'll buy your first batch of parts for $50,000. Because we're starting from square one here and there are no parts for us to refurbish yet, working with us will not impact your cost, so I've got us at $50,000 also.

"Now, let's go six months out. At that time, the first $50,000 worth of parts will be worn out so you'll need to buy $50,000 more worth of new parts. Correct?

"Okay. Now, if you were working with us, you would send us the first batch of worn parts and we would refurbish the parts for a price of $22,500—or a savings of 55 percent. Going out another six months, instead of spending $50,000 again, you're going to invest only $22,500 once again refurbishing the same parts, so you'll save 55 percent on parts.

"Our process allows us to refurbish the parts twice, so by the third time you'll need to go out and spend another $50,000 on new parts.

"Okay. So here's the current scenario as far as cost of parts":

Slide 6:

	Day 1	6 Months	12 Months	Totals
	$50,000 = 100%	$50,000 = 100%	$50,000 = 100%	$150,000 = 3 x 100% or 300%
	$50,000 = 100%	$22,500 = 45%	$22,500 = 45%	$95,000 = 100% + 2 x 45% = 190%

XYZ's Cost of Parts

You: "So you'll spend the full $50,000 or 100 percent in either scenario. After six months, however, you'll spend only $22,500 with us, or just 45 percent of what you would have spent on new parts.

"Another six months out, you'll spend another $22,500 or, again, 45 percent of what you would have spent had you bought new parts. So with *all* new parts you'll spend the $50,000 three times or 100 percent three times for 300 percent cost. A total of $150,000 dollars.

"With us, you'll spend 100 percent up front on the new parts and then only 45 percent twice for a total of 190 percent versus 300 percent. Correct? When we do the math, that equals a savings of…"

Slide 7:

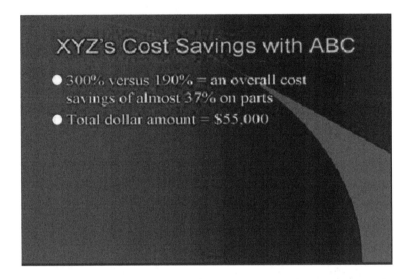

You: "Thirty-six and two-thirds percent, or nearly 37 percent on parts. A total dollar amount of $55,000. Are there any questions on that so far?

"So would you agree that you will definitely save a good amount of money on parts working with ABC Company?

"Now let's look at some of the other advantages of working with ABC Company."

(Bring up Slide 4 again.)

Note: As opposed to going back to Slide 4, you want to have Slide 4 in the presentation again as Slide 8. That way, you don't have to jump back and forth in your presentation.

Slide 8 (the previous Slide 4):

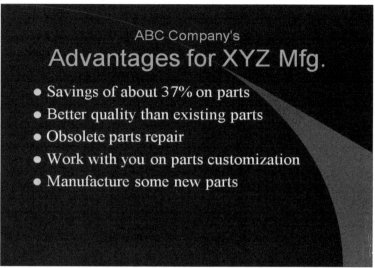

You: "Let's look at advantage number 2, *better* quality than existing parts. Clearly, that's a pretty bold statement to make for parts we are refurbishing. Two factors lead to this statement.

"First, we use a more wear-resistant steel than what is on the original part. That means your parts will last longer than an average part, and you'll need to buy parts less often. This will actually help you to save even more than 37 percent.

"Second, we can customize the parts. More on this in just a second. We also have very high-tech gauges to measure parts and make sure they are up to standard. The gauges, for which we have a patent pending, are unlike any others in the industry.

"Other companies typically have only one person who inspects parts before they go out. We have three inspectors. Our quality control is second to none. You won't spend time, money, and people-power removing parts you just put on, replacing others, or sending the parts back.

"And, we put our money where our mouth is. We have a 100 percent satisfaction guarantee. If you are not happy with any of our refurbished parts for any reason, you don't pay for them. We simply can't afford to turn out anything less than the highest-quality parts.

"Do those factors make you feel good about our quality?" (Wait and acknowledge response.)

"Next, let's look at obsolete parts repair. You have some older machines that are fine, except for the fact that they have some broken parts that you can't replace, correct? The good news is that we both repair and manufacture obsolete parts.

"Now, while it isn't always cost-efficient to manufacture one or two parts, often we can repair the parts if they are simply cracked or broken. We will visit your plant, take a look at these parts, and let you know what we can do. You'll be happy to know that in 90 percent of the cases we're able to help people out and save them money.

"How much does a new machine cost these days? Well, think of the additional cost-savings to you if we are working together and getting those older machines up and running. That could save you quite a bit of additional money, right?

"Now the next item—parts customization. Again, you mentioned you had some parts you wanted us to look at and see what we could do about putting longer points on them, correct? Okay, we can definitely do that. That's something we'll cover on a trip to your plant.

"Now, you already have a general idea of what you're looking for, right? Good. It will be important to sit down with you and some of your mechanics to go over exactly how long, in what direction you want the points to go, and so forth. We can then customize a part, let you try it out, and tell us what you think.

"Another thing we can do, if you can't specifically nail down a length and angle, is make a few different parts to different specs and get your feedback. We can then customize them further until we produce exactly what you want. Does that sound like a good plan?

"That's another advantage we have over the major parts manufacturers. When they make parts, they make them the same for everyone and mass produce them. We can actually tailor them to your specific needs, maximizing your efficiency and saving you time. I'm sure that's a benefit you'd appreciate, right?

"Let's look at the next item on the list—manufacturing new parts. We noticed that manufacturers in the necktie industry are going through a lot of two particular parts, board guides and board wheels. (Hold up samples of these two parts.)

"In our business, we deal with many metal fabricators, so we talked with them about making these parts. We found that we could save the necktie manufacturers about 50 percent on new parts, and they were working just as well. We had a similar situation with several jeans manufacturers.

"On the trip to the plant, let's take a look at the parts you wear out quickly. Let's see if this might be an area where we can help you out and save you some substantial money."

The Close of the Presentation

""Okay, so let's recap. You'll get 37 percent cost savings on parts, plus the additional savings with our more wear-resistant steel that will give your parts longer life.

"You'll get better-quality parts, backed up by our 100 percent satisfaction guarantee.

"You'll get obsolete parts repair, which will save you thousands because you won't have to go out and buy new machines.

"You'll get customized parts, which will lead to a better end product for your customers and more customer satisfaction.

"Then, potentially, you may be able to get some new parts manufactured, which will save you even more money.

"Would you agree that there are some great advantages to doing business with ABC Company?

"Great! The next step..."

Slide 9:

"...is to set up a time to meet at the plant. What do your schedules look like next week and the following week?" (Come up with a time that works for everyone.)

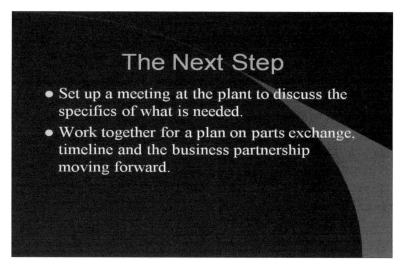

"Thank you very much for your time today. We are looking forward to a long relationship with you and XYZ Manufacturing, and we look forward to saving you substantial money as well as getting you parts that actually improve the quality and efficiency of your manufacturing process."

* * *

That's an example of a specific presentation. You can add all kinds of animation and other appealing and eye-catching elements to your presentation, but our sample here should give you a good base on which to build.

You should also be working on your benefit statements and ways to involve the prospect in the presentation. Remember to speak in terms of what each benefit means to the prospect in terms of saving money, achieving higher quality, and/or looking good to their customers.

At this point (after your first close) you may get some questions and/or objections. When you get a question, answer it, confirm the answer, and then close once again. When you get an objection, answer it, confirm the answer, give another compelling reason to buy, and then close one more time. We will address this in more detail in the objection section.

Chapter 18

More Presentations Points to Consider

Appointments That Cancel or Are Absent When You Arrive

If you encounter either of the above scenarios, either your communication is not clear when you set the appointment, people aren't taking you seriously, or you don't have solid prospects.

First, you want to ensure your communication is clear when you set the appointment. Be specific about the day and time you will be there. Use a statement such as, "I'll see you *at* three o'clock *on* Tuesday the fourth," rather than, "I'll be there *around* three."

Have the person you're meeting with verify the time and day. You might say, "Okay, so I'll see you at three o'clock on Tuesday the fourth, right?" You can also say, "Okay, so we're meeting at three o'clock on…let's see…" and let the prospect jump in and give you the day.

Let people know your time is valuable. If you are professional and treat your time as valuable, prospects will tend to do the same. Set your appointments in a friendly but businesslike tone, and let people know you have a tight schedule.

Before you get off the phone, you might say something like, "Okay, great, so I'll see you at three o'clock on Tuesday the fourth. I have a lot of people to see that day and my schedule is tight, so I'm happy I could squeeze you in. I look forward to meeting you then."

Call ahead of time. Some salespeople don't want to call ahead of time because they are afraid the prospect will cancel. Trust us, you'll save far more appointments by calling ahead than you'll lose. Call an hour or two before your appointment and say something like, "Hi, this is (your name) from (your company), and I wanted to let you know that I'm on schedule so I'll see you at three o'clock today." Of course, if you're running late, you'll let the person know that along with when you'll arrive.

Give the prospect a second chance, but not a third. If you've been very clear twice about when you were meeting and the prospect did not have a legitimate excuse for not being there, move on. There are better places to spend your time.

How to Introduce Tough Subjects

Sometimes you have to talk about tough subjects, and you have to make people uncomfortable in order to educate them and move them out of denial.

Obviously, some subjects—such as nursing home care or death (when talking about life insurance)—can be a challenge. For example, one of us sold long-term care insurance, otherwise known as nursing home insurance. If you think people enjoy talking about getting sick and going into a nursing home, you're wrong. Many people refuse to face reality.

In a situation such as this, build some rapport and make your prospect comfortable before proceeding. Next, put the prospect in the right frame of mind. Let him know up front that some of the things you will be talking about are not pleasant.

Open the prospect's mind to the conversation by complimenting his or her ability to talk about these issues. Open with a statement like this:

"Mr. Smith, we're going to be talking about some things today that most people don't like to spend much time thinking about. Obviously, no one likes to ponder what will happen if they become sick or have to go into a nursing home for any reason.

"At the same time, unless someone is living in a complete state of denial, they realize that this risk is very real and one that requires serious consideration. Wouldn't you agree? (Wait for agreement.)

"That being said, I want to compliment you on having the foresight to look into what you can intelligently do to protect yourself, your assets, and your loved ones."

Now bridge into your presentation.

Once you have opened with this or a similar statement, the prospect will realize that if he tells you he isn't interested, doesn't believe this will ever happen to him, or believes he can afford to wait, that's the equivalent of saying, "Look, I'm in a state of complete denial, so don't bother me."

You'll still get these objections from time to time, but you can dramatically reduce them by addressing this issue up front.

How Location Affects Your Presentation

You will be holding your presentation in one of three places, either at your place of business, at the prospect's place of business, or at a neutral location such as a hotel or conference center. Where you hold the presentation will affect your preparation. Here are some ideas for all three scenarios.

Your Location

If the prospect is coming to your place of business, be sure you have all your presentation materials set up and working well before the prospect's scheduled arrival time. If your meeting is in the morning, have coffee, bagels, and Danishes available. If it's around the lunch hour, have lunch scheduled to arrive at the appropriate time. For the afternoon, coffee, bagels, or similar snacks are appropriate. Have items on hand that you can give to your prospect such as pens with your company logo, golf balls, calculators, or other small promotional items.

Have your full business attire on before the prospect arrives. You also want your place of business to be clean.

If possible, have a display case by the door for the prospect's company name. It should say something like: (Your company name) welcomes (the prospect's company name).

Make sure all the appropriate people know your prospect is coming, and have all the key people there to welcome her. Ensure everyone is on their best behavior. We once had a situation where company employees were yelling at one another as a prospect arrived. Not good.

When the prospect arrives, greet her and exchange some small talk. This involves many of the factors we've already discussed: a firm handshake, good eye contact, mirroring, and demonstrating to the prospect that you have a sincere interest in her.

Point out her company name on the greeting board and say something like: "We have you up in lights." You can also ask how the directions were (if you gave her directions) and travel in general. You will then lead the prospect to the location where you are holding your meeting. You also want to ask the receptionist or office manager to inform the other people in your company who will be involved in the meeting that your prospect has arrived and the meeting is starting.

Get the prospect seated comfortably and ask if she would like anything to drink or eat. Continue with some small talk and rapport building. Look for things the prospect is wearing that you might positively comment on. You should also notice what kind of car she is driving as this might be a topic of conversation.

The Prospect's Location

If you are meeting at the prospect's location for the presentation, arrive well in advance to set up any presentation technology or other items.

Bring coffee, bagels, donuts, etc., or lunch if the meeting is scheduled around the noon hour. If the meeting is scheduled immediately before or after lunchtime, you should also offer in advance to take the prospect to lunch either before or after the meeting, whichever is appropriate. Bring small promotional gifts to give to the prospect.

Note: Before you bring any edibles to your meetings, ask people if they have any preferences or allergies.

Once you arrive at your prospect's place of business, introduce yourself to the receptionist, present your card, and let her know that the prospect is expecting you. It's also important to have a smile on your face and be pleasant to everyone at the facility.

At this point, observe your surroundings to find things you can talk about or use to build rapport. In the main facility, this may include photos, letters, or awards on display and other interesting items. In the prospect's office, if for some reason you didn't have a chance on the cold call, look for diplomas, trophies, plaques, keepsakes, and anything else that will give you an idea of her interests, hobbies, and family life.

If you need time to set up, let the prospect know in advance how long this will take. If you've brought food or other items, ask her where she would like you to put those. And of course, engage her in small talk and build some rapport before you begin the presentation.

If you are calling on a prospect at his house, the same rules apply as if you were showing up at his place of business. Again, take note of your surroundings both outside and inside the house to see what interests the prospect might have. Are there birdhouses out in the yard or a nice garden? How about a dog, cat, or pictures of family?

A Neutral Location

If you are meeting the prospect at a neutral location such as a hotel conference room, act as though the prospect is coming to your place of business.

It is your job to direct the prospect to the proper meeting location, have coffee and other refreshments available, and ensure all things are in the proper working order for the prospect's visit. Call the facility a couple of days in advance to find out what items are available at the facility in order for you to give your presentation.

Show up well in advance of the presentation in order to check cleanliness, lighting, temperature, the sound system, and so on. Make sure the food and other items arrive on time.

Finally, know the name of the facility's contact person if something goes wrong or needs to be changed. Meet the person in advance, discuss your needs, and make sure you can reach him immediately if something goes wrong.

A Summary of Ideas on Presentations

- A good presentation—in fact all selling—starts with a belief that you are selling the very best product or service and that the prospect will be *much* better off as a result of the transaction.

- Your presentation needs to capture and keep your prospect's attention by being interesting and to the point.

- Make sure you've done your homework on the company and individuals to whom you are presenting.

- Create an agenda for the meeting.

- Deliver your presentation with energy and enthusiasm.

- Use humor.

- Involve the prospect in the presentation.

- Involve as many of the senses as possible.

- Use logic and emotion.

- Make people feel the appropriate emotions that move them to action. The emotions may be fear, desire, peace of mind, security, insecurity, or a host of other feelings.

- Create a big picture or overall strategy, and tie everything back to the big picture as you go through your presentation.

- Make the presentation relevant to your prospect and his or her needs.

- Focus on what's unique and great about your company, you, and your product.

- Make your points easy to understand and personal.

- Keep it simple but not below the intelligence level of your audience.

- Use examples of how you've helped people in similar situations.

- Name-drop.

- Keep your objective in mind, which is to solve the prospect's problem.

- Many times your job as a salesperson will come down to changing the prospect's perspective by educating him or her.

- Sell the relationship in addition to the product or service.

- Have fun, simply have conversations with people, and relax—it's not life or death.

- Remember, the prospect does not only want to be educated, he also wants to be enlightened and entertained.

- Be up front and honest. If you're new and you don't know the answer to a question, let people know you don't know but that you'll find out. The next time, know the answer.

- Build urgency, excitement, and value into your presentation. Your presentation needs to provide both compelling reasons to buy *and* compelling reasons to buy *now*.

- Be persistent, straightforward, and firm in your approach.

- And when you've concluded your presentation, *close!*

- Last but not least, work on your speaking ability. Earlier we discussed Toastmasters and other organizations you can join to overcome your fear of public speaking. Organizations such as Toastmasters, The National Speakers' Association, and other professional speaking groups are great places to hone your speaking skills and practice and perfect your presentations. Find them at www.toastmasters.org and www.nsaspeaker.org.

SECTION IV

COMPETITION

Introduction

Competition challenges us to thoroughly and realistically assess our product or service. Competition can be very helpful when putting together sales presentations, answers to objections, and in preparing to sell.

Think of the competition as opposing counsel in a trial. They'll try to paint the strengths of your argument as weaknesses and will put a huge spotlight on your true weaknesses. For every solution you have for the prospect, they'll come up with a counterpoint and a reason why your solution won't work or isn't the best one. They will then present their solution and try to make a case for why the prospect should see things their way rather than your way. At the end of the day, they're hoping that the "judge," or prospect, will find in their favor due to a preponderance of evidence on their side.

Note: Use this section along with Section III on presentations to focus on strengths, weaknesses, and compelling reasons why someone should get excited about owning your product or service.

Let's begin by looking at opposing counsel.

Chapter 19

Gathering Competitive Intelligence

When it comes to the competition, you have to thoroughly know their strengths, weaknesses, and overall approach—everything about them. You need to learn:

- Every detail about their product or service.
- Their primary strengths and weaknesses.
- On which points do they directly compete against you?
- How can they beat you, and how can you beat them?
- What is their approach?
- What are their prices?
- What are their typical features and functions?
- What are their presentation techniques?
- Who are they calling on?
- Who are their largest accounts?
- Who they are doing business with?

Where to Get Competitive Intelligence Your Company

People within your company are a good place to begin gathering competitive intelligence. Start by asking other salespeople and your manager for competitive information. Most companies also have specific resources assigned to competitive intelligence. Seek out these sources within your company. Other salespeople, your manager, and the resources on competitive intelligence will likely give you all the ammunition you'll need on those occasions when you're facing the competition.

People who used to work for the competition and now work for you will be one of your best sources. They can give you "inside" information such as detailed facts on weaknesses, strengths, and how the competition competes with you. These people may be salespeople, technicians, or management.

The Internet, Industry Publications, Public Information, Trade Shows, and Other Industry Events

Go to the competitor's website for competitive information. Websites generally don't carry detailed military secrets; however, they will give you an overview of most of the products, background on the company, a mission statement, and a list of the key personnel.

Occasionally, you'll find you've "struck gold" with information you can profit greatly from. For example, we once looked on a competitor's website and found a listing of jobs they were working on but hadn't yet secured. Granted, they had been doing a good deal of work for the three they listed, yet we managed to draw one of the three to our company.

In addition to the competitor's website, you also want to get all the public information you can such as annual reports, letters to shareholders, SEC filings, advertising, and the like.

Next, look for newspaper, magazine, and trade publication articles on the company, and any other information you can unearth. The Internet is a good place to search for this information. Use the different search engines and type in keywords related to the industry or specific products. The library is another great place to gather information on companies.

Attend trade shows, business functions, and other industry events. At these events you'll find literature, brochures, and other product information and samples. Many companies put on informative demonstrations of current equipment and unveil new equipment. You can also speak with the competition at industry events and garner valuable information. We'll discuss speaking to the competition a little later in this section.

Buy from the Competition

That's right, buy the competition's product. For example, let's say you sell computers. Who is your chief competitor? Perhaps you have several. Go out and buy their products and dissect them. What does the competition have and how does it work? What are its products' advantages and disadvantages?

In addition to the product itself, you want to get all the information that goes along with it. Information would include users' manuals, brochures, and any other literature you can get hold of. In addition to dissecting the product, dissect the information that goes along with it. What promises does the literature make? What is the competition touting as its major advantages?

You may have to lay out a lot of cash to make this happen, but the returns will be worth it. In addition to gaining intimate competitive information, there are other advantages to purchasing the competition's product. Once you have it, you may be able to train your technicians on the competitive product and begin offering service on the competitor's units. Of course, you would need to have a source for parts, and there may be other complicating factors, but this is just one of the possibilities.

Get as many heads involved in this process as possible and brainstorm together.

Your Customers and Prospects

Your customers and sometimes even your prospects are another excellent source for competitive intelligence. They may have the competitor's proposals, brochures, and other literature. Some of your best customers will happily give you this information if you simply ask. Others will take some prodding. If you have a source that needs some prodding, be careful how you do it. You don't want to push people into revealing something they don't wish to reveal, or that they feel might be unethical. Following are some ways to get competitive information from prospects and customers.

First, let's look at a situation in which you're trying to obtain a competitor's proposal. You can use the following technique in person or over the phone with anyone from a good customer to a buyer at a competitive account that you don't know well. Use this during the bidding process when you know you are competing.

"Joe, just to make sure we're comparing apples to apples here, can I get a copy of what the competition is proposing?" If he balks at this, respond with, "You can block out the prices and make a copy of it if you'd like. I just want to see the features and functions they're listing because there are always some differences."

If he says something like, "Bob, I've looked them over and they look the same to me" or "Bob, I'm really not comfortable sharing this information you," respond with, "Joe, you're right, I understand that. I compete against these guys weekly and there are always a few subtle differences. For example…"

Give an example of a competitive situation in which the proposals appeared to be the same but were quite different in price, features, and function. Then give examples of areas where you and the competition usually vary that may not be obvious to someone who doesn't know your product inside and out.

A conversation one of us had with a customer went like this:

"Chuck, I compete against these guys at least every other week. I had a situation over at my largest account, ABC Bank, where I was quoting on ten machines with all the equipment ABC typically puts on their machines. Our competitor came in at about $25,000 per machine; I was at roughly $35,000 per machine. ABC Bank was very upset with me. They thought I had been taking advantage of them all these years. Once I assured my key contact, Chere, that there had to be some distinct differences in equipment, we set up an appointment to sit down and investigate. By the time I stripped down my machines to match what the competition was quoting, we were $300.00 per machine less expensive than the competition.

"My competitors get their foot in the door with price. They're a good company and they make a good product. Yet every time I compete with them they come in far below me dollar-wise and there are some distinct differences in the machines.

"For example, our machines have surge protectors as standard equipment; their machines come with none. It's a $250 option for them. Also, you get diagnostic software with our machines and not with theirs. It's a $1,000 option with them. These are not obvious parts of the proposal, yet they're real dollars that add up quickly.

"If I could have a look at their features and functions, I could definitely point out some differences—probably some major ones."

It's pretty tough for a prospect to argue with that logic. If he does, our guess is that you have little chance of doing business with him anyway.

Here is the information you want to get from the competitor's proposal:

- What does the competition list as its specifications?
- Which features and functions does it list as standard?
- Which ones does it list as options?
- Which ones does it leave completely off the list?
- Are you quoting the same features and functions?

When trying to get a competitor's proposal from your best customers, simply say, "Barb, can I get a look at what the competition quoted?" Once she shows you the quote, ask if it would be possible to obtain a copy of it.

Once you have your copy, ask, "Did they send any literature with this?" Usually the response to this question will be, "Yes, I've got it right here," and then they'll hand it to you.

At that point you ask, "Will you be needing this?" Nine times out of ten the answer will be, "No, you can have it if you'd like." Although many will willingly give you the information, others may be reluctant. If they are, *don't push too hard.*

If asked, often your best customers will fill you in on your competitor's approach. While it's great to have a proposal and literature, it is often just as valuable to learn *how* it was presented. Ask:

- Was it mailed to the customer or did the competition drop it off in person?
- Did they simply hand it to the customer, go over it briefly, and leave?
- Did they have a PowerPoint presentation to go along with it?
- Did they have anything else to present such as samples, testimonials, and a competitive comparison?

If they did a presentation, ask what was it like:

- Were they animated, upbeat, and interesting, or were they dull and boring?
- What were they focusing on?
- Were they pushing their sleek, new sunlight viewable, color screens versus boring monochrome?
- How long and how impressive was their presentation overall?
- Did they have any interesting anecdotes to go along with the presentation?

Your best customers can give you plenty of information that will give you a true portrayal of your competition. In most cases, all you have to do is ask.

A prospect who has just signed with the competition is an excellent source for competitive information. They can educate you on your competition's strengths and their approach far better than anyone else. Certainly, they must have been impressed by the competition's offer because they closed the deal. In order to get the information, however, you must react properly to the news that you just lost the account. The key is to be both humble and professional. And be genuine.

Here's an example of what you might say: "I knew this was going to be tough so I worked hard at putting our best offer on the table. But obviously I missed something somewhere. Hopefully, I at least forced the competition to sharpen their pencils and sweeten the offer they put on the table."

Be professional, genuinely thank the prospect, and mention some benefits of the competitive exercise. It will strengthen your position with the customer and also leave him with a good impression of you as a person. Acting in this manner may ensure you are considered for the next project.

Next, you want to narrow down exactly in which area you fell short. Say the following: "While I sure wanted our proposal to look good, obviously the key is what you thought of it. I thought we looked all right on the hardware, so I'm thinking perhaps it was price?"

Note 1: If your product or service has several different components, your proposal and the competitor's proposal must be broken down item by item. Mention this to the prospect before they get pricing from anyone. Where you have some components that are superior though more costly than the competitor's, a proposal that breaks down all the key elements is important. While many prospects focus on the total proposal cost, a breakdown will detail the key price variations.

In addition to key price variations, you want to go over the major advantages of your higher-priced components and why they are worth the added cost. For example, your tires may have an 80,000-mile guarantee, whereas your competitors' tires have only a 40,000-mile guarantee.

Note 2: If you get a copy of the competitive proposal and the prospect has blanked out the numbers, you can fill those in later. If you lose the business, find out what your competitor's price was by using a technique that we will soon discuss. If you win the business, you'll still want to find out where the competition stood.

How complete is the competitor's offering? Are they pricing according to the specifications and detail the prospect is seeking? If their proposal does not meet certain criteria, their prices may look better than yours. You need to go through the details of the competition's proposal to make sure you both are quoting the same equipment.

Because you are now intimately familiar with your product and your competitor's product, you will be aware of aspects of your product that may be significantly more or less expensive than your competitor's. In the example above, the tires with the 80,000-mile guarantee may be 35 percent more than the competitor with the 40,000-mile guarantee.

If the tires are broken out in your proposal it becomes much easier for the prospect to focus on the individual items as opposed to just your final *big* bottom-line number. Priced individually, the price difference of the tires will likely catch the prospect's attention. Whether he does or does not notice, you need to discuss this difference.

Exactly Where Is the Competition on Price?

Let's assume the prospect tells you the major differentiator in his decision was price. If you do have individual items broken out in your proposal, say the following:

> "Certainly the bottom-line number is a factor, but generally I find that key items always carry a higher price than our competition's.
> "For example, our tires are under warranty for twice as long as the competition's because of our higher-quality rubber. This means they are typically about 35 percent higher in price, but I tried to squeeze my price as much as possible. I should be reasonably close to them with the total proposal price. Was I somewhat close or not close at all?"

After you ask the question, it's important to be quiet and wait for the prospect to respond. If the prospect comes back with, "You were somewhat close," continue with, "Was I off by $1,000 to $1,500?" If the prospect comes back with, "Not close at all," you continue with, "Was I off by $3,000?"

The total price of your product will dictate what number you use when responding to the statement that you were somewhat close. For example, for the "somewhat close" response we used $1,000 to $1,500 to represent a product that might sell in the range of $30,000 to $45,000. If your product sells for $500,000 and the prospect tells you you're somewhat close, that might mean anywhere between $5,000 to $30,000. Everything is relative. Use the lines we're giving you and plug in numbers that make sense for your product or service.

Once you've asked if you were off by a certain number, the prospect will either respond with a yes or no. If he says no, ask, "Was I was closer than that or further away?" Whatever he says, throw out a number that corresponds with the answer. For example, if he says closer on the $1,000 to $1,500 figure, say, "Was it only $500?" If he says further away, you would say, "Was it $2,500?"

Continue in this fashion until you nail down the competition's price. If the prospect gets tired of answering questions, at least get an affirmative answer to one of your ballpark numbers. By getting a yes, you will at least have a general idea of where the competition stands on price.

Note: With this technique your approach is very important. You need to be very relaxed both in body posture and the tone of your voice. It also helps if you project an image of being defeated as you ask these questions. If you are too direct and forward with this line of questioning, it may seem like an interrogation.

Where the Competition Stands on Everything Else

Use the same approach we used to determine pricing to find any other areas where you may have differed from the competition. Start with the same question that you did when trying to determine price: "I thought we looked all right on the hardware, so I'm thinking maybe it was price?"

If the prospect responds with, "No, you were close on price," ask, "Hmm, where did we miss the boat?"

Once you get an answer such as, "Well, they threw in a service contract for nothing," you can then begin to ask questions such as, "That's pretty nice. How long is their service contract for?" and other questions to quantify what the competition included that you did not.

The important thing is to ask questions to determine *exactly* what the competition included that ultimately won them the deal. Once you know exactly what you're up against, you can have an answer prepared when you encounter it again.

Get Competitive Information When You Win Too!

Even if you win the business, you still want to know where the competition was at and how close it was to your bid. To determine this, ask the following: "So how close was the competition on this one?"

From there you will ask more questions to get the specifics, as we did in the examples above.

Note: Be careful here. Certainly the last thing you want to do is badger someone who just gave you some business. If this is an established customer, you can ask these probing questions when you meet to sign the contracts. Just be sure you wait until *after* the contracts are signed. If this is a customer whom you are doing business with for the first time, use a follow-up meeting to get the competitive information a few days after all contracts are signed, sealed, and delivered.

Chapter 20

The Competitive Comparison

The competitive comparison is a comprehensive analysis of your company and your product versus your competition's. Your comparison will consist of a competitive matrix along with supporting information. The comparison will spell out all the differences and similarities between your product and the competition's. It may include comparisons with your company and only one company or with several companies.

Typically, you will use your competitive comparison with competitive accounts you are trying to break into. However, you can also use this tool with accounts where the competition is making a run at the business. In that case, you need to give clear, precise reasons why you are the best choice for your customer and demonstrate how you are better than the competition.

IMPORTANT: *You must protect the information in your competitive analysis.* If you leave this information behind, there is a good chance the information will find its way into your competition's hands and the competition will work to counter your comparison. As well, they will now know what your approach is.

Do not leave any copies with anyone. When you present your comparison, simply hand the information to your prospect and go through it step by step. When you are finished, tell them that you would like to leave a copy of the information, but your company prohibits it. It will be helpful if you can refer to a copyright on the material, even if it is something you have developed yourself.

When going up against the competition, begin with your strengths and weaknesses. You need to know which strengths are the best to hang your hat on, and you need to compile strong feature/benefit statements for each. By knowing your weaknesses, you will know where you are most likely to be attacked by the competition and where objections might arise.

The first step is to put together a competitive matrix. It will simply list the features of your product and your competitor's product. What follows is an example of a competitive matrix for a random product that we've invented. The product is not important; the features, benefits, and comparison are.

Figure 1: Competitive Matrix

ABC Company	XYZ Company
Band pick technology	Air pick technology
Single-sheet paper divert	No single-sheet divert – batch divert – must divert whole stack
6 high paper cassettes	6 high paper cassettes
Totally upgradeable	Very limited upgradeability
Print size decreases for smaller paper	Print size does not decrease
Based in Boston, MA	Based in Hong Kong
Pentium 4 – 2.0 GHz processor	Pentium 4 – 2.0 GHz processor
Bin capacity = 1,000 sheets of paper	Bin capacity = 500 sheets of paper
Printer speed = 15 lines per second	Printer speed = 20 lines per second
Processor in protected chest	Processor not in chest
Maximum dispense capability = 80 copies at one time	Maximum dispense capability = 20 copies at one time
Smallest keyboard in the industry	Larger, spread-out keyboard
Imaging – can accept paper inserted in any direction	Imaging – can only accept paper entered in one direction
Dot matrix or thermal printer	Thermal printer
Braille on operation keys Keys more user-friendly for customers using Braille	Braille on operation keys – an option
100 percent guarantee	No guarantee
Delivery – 30-40 days	Delivery – 100 days
Dispense speed – 10 notes per second	7 notes per second
Individual keys can be replaced on keypad	Whole membrane screen underneath must be replaced
Intelligent module 20 percent higher acceptance rate than XYZ	More than one step to verify quality of paper
Alarm location in protected chest	Alarm outside protected chest
Cassette capacity = 4,000 pieces of paper	Cassette capacity = 3,000 pieces of paper
Cassette size = 374 mm, 15 percent more capacity than XYZ	Cassette size = 325 mm
Document printer capacity = 2,000 forms	1,000 forms
Paper dispenser self-contained within unit	Paper dispenser attached to side of machine
Locked or open cassettes	Open cassettes or bins – tamper indicator optional
15" & 17" screens	8", 13", 15" & 17" screens
Manual or motorized paper supply	Motorized supply only
Dot matrix or thermal receipt printer – thermal has the ability to retract receipts	Thermal *only* receipt printer – does not have the ability to retract receipts

Focus on the features that make your product look good; at the same time, be thorough and cover *all* aspects of the product. When you go over the competitive matrix with a prospect, go through it feature by feature and discuss the benefits of each feature.

The Competitive Comparison: Supporting Information

Now let's take a look at an example of the pages following your feature comparison. The next figure, ABC's Advantages over XYZ, shown below, goes into more detail about the features found on this competitive matrix. It also spells out the benefits of each feature, which we have highlighted in bold typeface. You need to drive home the benefits of each feature. Remember, the benefits are the key, not the features.

Figure 2: ABC's Advantages over XYZ

⇒ ABC band pick vs. XYZ air pick dispenser
- ABC band pick is more reliable, faster
- fewer moving parts – 50 vs. 150
- can dispense lower-grade paper
- **less downtime with ABC, fewer parts to break down**

⇒ ABC has single-sheet paper divert
- ABC diverts only bad sheets of paper, singles them out, doesn't fill up divert bin
- XYZ batch divert doesn't single out bad sheets; can't tell which sheets in divert bin are bad
- **ABC has less maintenance, lower cost**

⇒ ABC can dispense 80 sheets per transaction; XYZ, only 20

⇒ ABC 10 sheets of paper per second; XYZ, 7 per second
- **less time with ABC**

⇒ ABC cassettes can hold 4,000 new sheets of paper; XYZ, 3,000
- **less replenishment with ABC, lower service cost**

⇒ ABC depository capacity twice that of XYZ (1,000 sheets of paper vs. 500); XYZ has only motorized envelope supply
- **more flexibility, options with ABC**

⇒ ABC printer speed 15 lines per second; new XYZ machine 20 lines per second

⇒ ABC machines totally upgradeable

- **ABC provides investment dollar protection**

⇒ ABC printer decreases size of print for discrepancies in paper size

⇒ ABC based in the U.S., also U.S. made and manufactured

- **ABC provides faster delivery**

⇒ ABC processor is secure in chest, XYZ processor outside of chest

- **ABC provides better security, safety for employees**

⇒ ABC paper dispenser is contained within the unit; XYZ's is attached to side

- **adds to the footprint of the XYZ machine and installation cost**
- **much greater cost if added later because the wall that contains the unit has to be altered.**

⇒ ABC's document printer capacity is double that of XYZ's (2,000 forms vs. 1,000)

⇒ ABC 100 percent guarantee; XYZ no guarantee

- **ABC provides peace of mind**

⇒ XYZ has no on-board, step-by-step maintenance system

- **ABC is easier to use**

⇒ XYZ does not have locked cassettes

- **ABC is more secure**

⇒ XYZ does not have a manual paper supply

- **ABC has more options**

⇒ XYZ has only a thermal receipt printer, expensive paper is needed, print life five years

- **less cost with ABC, greater record retention and customer information security**

⇒ ABC Braille is located on keys and is easily read without creating false entries

⇒ XYZ had to uninstall 200 machines and redesign due to design flaws

- **ABC – no headaches, less cost, time, and money**

⇒ XYZ drive-up machine is difficult to reach from one's car

⇒ XYZ doesn't do shared liability contracts on maintenance

- **ABC – much less risk to customer**

Next, you will list other information you want to convey that was not included in your competitive matrix.

What XYZ typically quotes/doesn't quote:

⇒ They may not include shipping and handling charges – **add $1,000 to price**
⇒ May not include technical support in the price – **add $1,500.00**
⇒ May not include the PC software – **add $900.00**
⇒ Often may not include paper supply, can only offer motorized paper supply, no manual
⇒ Often may not include special duress alarm in price – **add $300.00**
⇒ XYZ's processor is not in a secure area (outside of chest)
⇒ No surge protectors – **add $480.00**
⇒ No heater in drive-up unit – **add $250.00**
⇒ Needs two floppies; only includes one – **additional floppy $125.00**
⇒ Braille on keys an option with XYZ – **add $225.00**

Other ABC advantages:

⇒ Most frequently purchased and recognized machine in U.S. – **provides comfort in familiarity.**
⇒ ABC's original equipment manufacturer – completely responsible for our product, most XYZ products are sold by third-party vendors – **less risk with ABC**
⇒ Largest and most reliable service organization in the industry – **more uptime**
⇒ Can provide solutions for *all* your needs – **easier, one-stop shopping**
⇒ Industry leader from 1801 inception to present day – **over two centuries of experience**
⇒ Most variety in number of machines and options – **freedom and choice**
⇒ ABC has all the major accounts in United States – **they must be doing something right!**
    (list your major accounts here)

The above matrix and supporting information will comprise the customer's version of your competitive comparison. You will create a separate one for yourself that includes additional information. Your version will have even more descriptive notes and extra information that you want to go over but don't necessarily want the prospect to see, such as information that will help you answer questions about the competitor's product. For example, you may list the competition's machine types.

XYZ's machine types:

2675 – similar to our 3095, 2 paper cassettes, Pentium 4 Windows software.

1660 – similar to our 3084, PC based, Pentium 3, color screens

2660 – latest model of the 1660, similar to our 3084, PC based, Pentium 3

2665 – similar to our 3054, 1 paper cassette, PC based, Pentium 3, not upgradeable

1064, 1664, 2664 – through-the-wall machines – like our 3015

1061 – Similar to our 3098

You may also have competitive product or service pricing on your sheet.

XYZ service pricing:

2675 – $2,400 per year

1660 – $2,100 per year

2660 – $2,000 per year

2665 – $1,800 per year

1064, 1664, 2664, 1061 – $1,600 per year

You may also want to list more detailed information on specific features.

Intelligent data module:

ABC – perforated paper can be inserted in any direction – **ease of use**

XYZ – only one direction

ABC – copy of either handwritten number or whole document on receipt

XYZ – only copy of whole document – **ABC easier to use**

You can also have information about specific machines and specific situations.

Areas to pay attention to when competing against the XYZ 2675:

- The amount of paper that can fit in the depository is very small. It has about half the capacity of our depository.
- Customers have to bend down deeply to get to it.
- It is two-handed operation as opposed to ours, which is one-handed operation.

- Security is also an issue. XYZ machines are more prone to vandalism/theft.

In today's world, with security issues and the fact that this machine doesn't meet the requirements of the Americans with Disabilities Act, this machine doesn't quite deliver.

Following are even more points that are advisable to have on *your* competitive comparison.

Points to stress regarding XYZ:

- The cost is about the same when you add in all the items they leave off.
- Lack of upgradeability. Since 1990, you would have had to buy 3 new XYZs if you wanted to add each new machine feature as it came out.
- Severed relationship with DEF Corporation.

Questions to ask/statements to make:

- Obviously this is a fairly substantial investment. Is protection of your investment important to you?
- A machine bought from ABC in 1990 is totally upgradeable to today's version.
- With XYZ, you would have had to buy three machines to stay current.
- The competition focuses on us as the industry leader, whereas we focus on the customer.
- XYZ's new dispenser copied ours. The problem was the new dispenser didn't fit into their current machine. If you wanted it you had to buy a new machine.
- Both the DRE Corporation and Garvin Industries tested our machines against XYZ. You can still see the machines in the Eid Operation Center in Boston. Both companies tested the machines for one year and ABC won hands down.
- Stress XYZ's lack of commitment to the industry. XYZ has their hands in everything else from A to Z. Give some examples of their other products. Have little commitment to the New England market.

Finally, sell yourself and what you bring to the table.

Sources of competitive information: Dave Eid (Boston), Jim Smith (Boston), Joe Johnson (Seattle).

So That's Your Competitive Comparison

It includes the competitive matrix, more detailed information of feature differences and the benefits of those differences, other advantages you have, some specific information on the competition, key questions and statements to stress in competitive situations, reminders of other areas you want to cover, and anything else that you need to remember. We have also seen some competitive comparisons where the salesperson includes the entire sales script in his or her copy. Although they don't usually use it, they feel more secure knowing it is there, just in case.

Occasionally, a prospect might ask why you have five or six pages and he has only two. If this happens, simply show him your copy and explain that you have some extra notes because you want to make sure you cover all the bases. For this reason, make sure your copy doesn't contain anything that you would not want the prospect to see such as negative or derogatory comments.

Remember: Be *very* careful with this information. You don't want to leave it with someone who might give it to your competitor(s).

One last note: Use language that is easy to understand. Do not use internal company lingo, abbreviations, or acronyms to describe features and functions. When you are referring to an acronym, use the full wording.

Critique the Above Competitive Comparison

A critical part of competing is analyzing your product and your competition's product in depth in order to make the strongest case possible for your product while defending yourself against the competition. To prepare for that, let's take a closer look at the competitive comparison we've just outlined. If you were defending the competition (XYZ Company), where would you start? Obviously, because you do not know their product intimately, you must take the information at face value.

Begin with these questions:

- In what areas does XYZ appear to be equal to ABC?

- In what areas does XYZ have an advantage, according to ABC?
- Are there any possible weaknesses in ABC's product?
- What is ABC listing as its strengths, and how much of an advantage are these strengths, if at all?

Here's what we came up with:

1) Evaluate areas in which both companies are equal.

ABC Company may say the two companies are equal in certain areas, but are they? Or does XYZ have an advantage? Again, taking the information at face value, what are some questions you could ask on the items in which both companies appear to be equal? Take, for example, one factor where both companies are equal: 6 high paper cassettes.

- Are the cassettes the same size, or does one company have larger cassettes? If so, how much larger?
- Are there any other factors that make one company's cassettes better or worse than the other? These factors might include:
  - ➢ easier loading.
  - ➢ greater longevity.
  - ➢ improved dispensing.
  - ➢ higher cost of replacement.
  - ➢ greater maintenance or cleaning requirements.

The answers to these questions can have a dramatic effect on cost, efficiency, and ease of use. So although ABC Company simply says "6 high," you need to go deeper to find out who has the "real" advantage in this area.

The second item where both companies appear to be equal is the Pentium 4 – 2.0 GHz processor. Again, dig a little deeper. First, is that information accurate? Second, what else affects that equation? What is the size of the hard drive, and what software is being run on the two machines?

Typically, one company has an advantage over the other, even if slight. You need to obtain more information to decide if both companies are in fact equal or if one really does have the advantage.

The only other area where the two companies seem to be somewhat similar is in regard to screen size – both have the option of either a 15" and 17" screen. XYZ also has an 8" and a 13". Most of us are conditioned to believe that bigger screen size is better, but is it in *all* cases? Consider privacy. In some locations you may want a smaller screen so the operator can see it but no one can peer over her shoulder. Suddenly this becomes an advantage to XYZ Company.

Let's look at other aspects of the screen. Is the screen a tube or flat panel display? Is the screen LCD or VGA? Is it digital or analog? How much of the screen is actually visible to the user? These are just a few of the questions you can ask to determine who has the true advantage. As a vendor, these are factors you want to consider with regard to your product versus your competitor's.

If you have areas of your product that seem to be equal to the competition's, ask the kinds of questions we've asked above. Look for strengths in your product that set it apart. Think in terms of speed, capacity, efficiency, and cost savings.

2) List as strengths any areas where ABC gives XYZ an advantage.

In most of your competitive matrixes, you will not list too many of the competition's advantages. The above matrix lists only two—XYZ's option of smaller screen sizes, and faster printer speed.

The key reason for listing some competitor advantages is credibility. The prospect knows that one product cannot be superior to another product in *every* respect. When you point out your competition's advantages, it makes your competitive comparison more believable and makes you more credible.

That being said, let's look at one area where ABC Company lists an advantage for XYZ—printer speed twenty lines per second versus fifteen lines per second. If you're XYZ Company, how can you make the most of this advantage?

What does that speed difference really mean? How many lines have to be printed? If you are printing 200 or 300 lines, the printer speed is significant, but if you are printing only five lines, the difference is not as significant. Does the XYZ printer have fewer moving parts and thus less of a chance of breaking down; does it use a different technology—thermal versus dot matrix, for example?

Again, look at factors related to speed, capacity, efficiency, and cost savings to come up with the overall benefits. Make your strengths significant.

3) Go to work on what ABC is referring to as its strengths.

Now, many of these will actually be strengths that ABC hangs its hat on. When this is the case, you will need to come up with an answer that will appear to lessen ABC's strengths and make them less significant.

For example, ABC boasts that their deposit bin capacity is 1,000 sheets versus XYZ's 500. If only 100 to 200 sheets are typically deposited, then obviously this is not an important factor. If it's more than 500, perhaps XYZ has an answer for this. If not, this could be a legitimate ABC strength. As an XYZ sales rep, you either need to have an answer or acknowledge ABC's strength—just be sure to do it in an understated fashion.

In another example, ABC says their processor comes in a protected chest whereas XYZ's does not. This may actually be an XYZ advantage. Since the processor is outside the protected chest, it may be easier to service since the service person is not required to go into the secure area. Of course, ABC will counter that it's more difficult for someone to tamper with the processor in the protected chest. Suddenly, this could be argued as an advantage for either side.

ABC also boasts about their 100 percent guarantee. However, if XYZ arrives at a service call in one hour and ABC gets there in three, you can shift focus from their guarantee to this XYZ advantage.

We won't go through all the items here. The purpose of this exercise is to get you used to analyzing both your product or service as well as the competitor's. And this leads to another important point.

Critique Your Product or Service

In order to completely prepare yourself to sell, you need to critique your product and your competitive comparison. Once you have studied the competition thoroughly and compared yourself favorably to them, it's time to turn a critical eye to your own product or service and see how you really stack up.

When you are looking for "weaknesses" in your product, start with what the competition is saying about your product. Here's an example from our experience.

For years, as representatives of a particular ATM manufacturer, we stressed the advantages of our keypad, among other items. The polymer keys could be individually replaced, thus the *entire* keypad rarely needed replacing, which made servicing much easier. Also, the keys did not easily depress, allowing the blind to feel the Braille on the keys without accidentally pressing the wrong button.

We learned that the competition was pointing out that the Braille on the polymer (a fancy word for plastic) keys wore down quickly, whereas their metal keys were much more durable.

We thought that was a weak response until one of us went to an ATM to withdraw money. And guess what? *They were right!* The Braille had worn significantly. While we still spoke of the strengths of the polymer keypad, we formulated an answer to the worn keypad objection, should it have arisen.

Sometimes we are brainwashed by our company. Play the devil's advocate. Put yourself in your competition's shoes. How would you attack your product? Listen to what the competition is saying with an open mind, logically evaluate it, and then come up with some truthful and creative responses.

Next, we'll look at more examples of comparing your product with the competition's by examining the process of building value. We will also look at the importance of you and your company in the competitive equation.

Note: If you're lucky enough to obtain a copy of the competition's presentation or competitive comparison, get together with other salespeople, current employees that used to work for the competition, customers who have compared your product with the competition's, and your company's competition department and/or research and development department (if there is one), and brainstorm some answers to their comparison.

Chapter 21

More Elements of Competition

Price and Value

As soon as they hear the word *competition*, most salespeople begin to look for areas where they can cut price or make other concessions. When competition enters the selling conversation, you need to build value and focus on your solution instead of looking for ways to give more for less money. If you know your competition well, you'll know where you have to be with pricing and what added value you bring to the table that they don't.

Important: If you can get the customer to focus on a highly desirable benefit exclusive to your product, or on a problem your product solves that the competition's doesn't, you will quickly remove the prospect's focus from the price issue.

When comparing your product with the competition's, your company is in one of two positions. You're either the highest-quality, highest-priced alternative, or you're a lower-quality, lower-priced alternative. If you have the best quality and you can be price competitive, you've got it made—almost. If you have the best price and can be competitive from a quality standpoint, once again you've got it made—almost.

Your job from either position is to show the prospect that you are the best solution for the price you are asking. If you are the lower-priced option, you have price covered. You need to focus on providing adequate value for the low price. If you are the higher-priced option, you need to focus on why your superior quality and value are worth paying more for. In either case, value must be equal to or greater than the asking price in the prospect's view. At the same time, the value-to-price ratio must be greater than the competition's. The prospect must recognize more value compared to the price you're asking than he does when comparing the value and price of your competition.

If you are the lower-priced provider, use low price as an up-front benefit. If you are the higher-priced provider, use added value as the up-front benefit.

Note: Often, if your prices are higher up front, you will have a lower long-term cost. For example, the most expensive clothing tends to last the longest. One good shirt may cost twice as much as a cheaper one, but will often last four or five times as long. If you are the more expensive product up front, you may be able to show that the long-term price of your product or service—amortized over time—is actually less when compared with the competition's.

Areas to Look at When Building Value

Product Efficiency

Where is your product or service better, faster, stronger, or more reliable than the competition's? Does your machine turn out ten widgets per minute as opposed to the competition's eight widgets? Does your machine have a faster printer or processor? Is there *anything* that your product produces more quickly than the competition's product?

Does your product have better uptime? Is it more reliable? Again, these can't be vague items; you need to be able to quantify them. For example, if yours has more uptime, what are the actual percentages and how can you document those? What do the percentages mean in bottom-line dollars to the customer? Do your machines average 99.6 percent uptime versus the competition's 97.2 percent and what are the time and dollar results of that? Are there any areas where your product or service is more reliable than the competition's?

Is your laundry service faster? Do you turn around dry cleaning in two days as opposed to three or four? Does your service show results more quickly than other methods available? Can your business deliver pizza in twenty minutes as opposed to thirty-five? If you're a personal trainer, can you get people the results they're looking for in six months as opposed to a year? Can you respond quicker and get people going faster?

Is your product, or any of its parts, stronger or more wear-resistant than the competition's? Do you use stronger, more wear-resistant steel or other alloy? Can your product handle one million flexes versus the competition's 750,000? Do you have 1 terabyte of memory versus 500 megabytes? Is the signal on your communications lines stronger? Is *anything* about your product or service more powerful than the competition's?

The bottom line: Where is your product or service better, faster, stronger, and/or more reliable?

Your Company's Efficiency

In what areas is your company more efficient than the competition? Do you fix equipment right the first time versus making two or three trips? Is your response time faster? Do you have a faster repair time? Are your repair people more experienced and better trained? Do you have more support? Are your technicians more customer-friendly? Test the bottom line again: Where is your company faster, better, or more efficient than your competition?

Your Product or Service's Longevity

Does your product, or anything associated with it, last longer than the competition's? If so, how much longer? Do your machines last, on average, 33 percent longer than the competition's machines? Does the motor inside your product last twice as long as the competition's motor? Do your machine gears last longer? How about your warranty?

Does your service, or anything associated with it, last longer than the competition's? Is there any aspect of your cleaning, refurbishing, preparing, or repairing process that outlasts the competition? Do the items you clean stay cleaner longer due to your special process? Do the effects of your restoration process last longer?

Cost

What aspects of your product or service are less expensive than your competition's? Is the up-front cost of your product or service lower or is the long-term cost lower? Use the advantage you have. If you have both, exploit the heck out of them.

In what areas is your service saving money for the end user? Does your service replace workers? Are costs such as maintenance, licensing fees, and other expenditures associated with your product or service less than the competition's? For example, is your annual service contract less expensive?

How about operating costs? Are less time and maintenance required with your product? Does it take employees less time to complete certain tasks with your machine? Does it take less time to shut down your machine at the end of the day? Does the toner cartridge get changed half as much as with the competition's product? Do other supplies last longer in your machine and thus require less time and maintenance? Come up with the average amount of time it saves and then assign a dollar value to it based upon the hourly wage of the employee completing the task.

Is your product or service easier for customers and/or employees to use? Where does this save the customer money and/or headaches? Here you'll present the tangibles (time and money) and the intangibles (stress, worry, anxiety, etc.).

If these associated costs are lower than the competition's, present them to the prospect to consider in addition to the up-front cost of the product or service.

Note: If your product costs more in any of these areas, why is that the case and can you sell that as a benefit? Do you have the largest service organization in the industry? Do you have a guaranteed response time? If you cost more, there is a reason. Find it and sell it as added value.

Other Ways in Which Your Product or Service Is Superior

Does it have more bells and whistles, more options, or more flexibility? Is protection of investment somehow built in? In other words, is your product upgradable, or do you have a trade-in program that allows the present technology to be applied to future technology? In what other ways is your product or service "better" than the competition's?

What problems are you helping your customers solve and how are you doing it better than everyone else? Ask your customers this question. Why are they using your product and what do they like best about doing business with you and your company? If you have customers that used the competition, ask what they like better about you.

What else do you have going for you that the competition does not? Do you have the most experienced, comprehensive support team in the industry? Do you have a 100 percent satisfaction guarantee? Are you the largest company in the industry? Is your company more financially stable than any of your competitors? Do you have the most familiar name in the industry?

Here are some additional product and service questions to spark more value-building ideas in your imagination:

- Does your product have fewer moving parts, resulting in fewer things that can go wrong?
- Does your product or service operate differently, making it more efficient, more cost effective, etc.?
- Does your product have features that make it more secure and less prone to theft or security breaches such as attacks by hackers?
- Does your product or service have extra safety features that protect the consumer?
- Does your product or service exceed industry standards?
- Is your product or service endorsed by any prominent organizations?
- Are there any well-known individuals or companies that use your product? Name them, with their permission, of course. As well, use a testimonial and have them on your reference and user lists.
- Has your product or service received any positive press or won any awards?
- Does your product or service have more flexibility than the competition's? For example, do you have two types of calling plans while the competition only offers one? Do you offer free additional lines? Can you operate in several different environments with several different frequencies?
- Is your product easier for physically, visually, auditory, or mentally impaired individuals to use?
- What individual features on your product or service stand out from the competition's? Do you have a particular feature that is twice as reliable as the competition's?
- Do you use a different technology from the competition, and how is that technology superior?
- Do you offer more choice? Do you have a more diverse product line or does your product as a whole offer more options? Do you adapt your product to the consumer's needs or does the consumer have to adapt his or her needs to your product because of a lack of options?

Remember: Your overall objective is to build value and do everything you can to avoid dropping your price. Occasionally you may have to budge a bit on price to get the deal done, but do it *only* as a last resort.

Proving Your Point

Next, how can you *prove* your advantages to the prospect? Proof will be in the form of testimonials, newspaper, magazine, and trade publication articles, independent market research, and studies that are easily verifiable by the prospect. Back up your information with hard numbers wherever possible. Quantify your claims.

Once you've proven your point, use this information in one of two ways. For example, let's say your product lasts 33 percent longer than the competition's. You can present a "per year" price or you can have the prospect multiply the competition's price by 1.33 in order to fairly compare products. If you don't prove your 33 percent longer life, the prospect will not take this request seriously. You must present solid proof and leave absolutely *no doubt*.

Positioning You and Your Company against the Competition

During your presentation, you will spend the majority of your time talking about your product or service. This is because your prospect has to live with your product or service every day, but they don't live with you or your company every day. At the same time, both you and your company are key differentiators that separate you from the competition, and you should spend some time discussing these differentiators during your presentation.

Following is an extensive list of strengths and weaknesses applied to both you and your company. Examine these two areas from your own standpoint and that of your competition's. Brainstorm with your manager and other salespeople and come up with further strengths and weaknesses.

You

1) Are you a local representative or are you from out of town?

Clearly, being local can help you with selling a prospect. The fact that you are only ten or fifteen minutes away can be a powerful selling point. You can emphasize the personal attention that you, as a local representative, can offer. Not only are you in a better position to discuss local issues, but you'll likely have more in common with the prospect such as where you grew up, went to school, what groups you belong to, and who you mutually know.

If you are not local and your competitor is, is there any advantage to being where you are? Are you closer to the manufacturing plant, suppliers, or other resources that make you more effective when servicing the customer? Do you have any kind of local presence that you can talk about? Do you have a local office or do you have company people who are very close? Do you have any other customers in the area? Are you, or some employees from your company, originally from the area? Are you in the area often?

Look at your proximity to the prospect and see what you can take advantage of and what your competition can use against you. From there, capitalize on your strengths and prepare answers for your weaknesses should the prospect bring them up.

2) Do you have a great deal of experience or very little?

Having a lot of experience can obviously be an advantage. If you're an investment broker with thirty years' experience, you can hang your hat on that immediately. That fact alone is usually enough to give you some credibility. After all, with thirty years in up and down markets, you can spot the trends quickly and you know what is going on.

Are you the top salesperson in the office? Have you been the top salesperson for the past eight, ten, or fifteen years? What is unique about your experience that you can leverage?

On the other hand, what if you have very little experience? Does your education help you out? Did you go to college for finance? Do you have an MBA? Did you do an internship with a major company? What experience—both real world and educational—do you have that you may be able to use?

Let people know you make up for a lack of experience with hard work, dedication, and education. Let them know they will always be able to get hold of you. You will treat them as a VIP. You are not on the verge of retirement—working half days, taking long lunches, and spending too much time at the club with all your rich friends. You are motivated and driven. You will work late hours, study the market diligently, absorb insight from those who have been around awhile, and give the prospect 100 percent of your attention. You will do what you need to do to stay on the cutting edge.

Note: If you are brand new, you needn't volunteer that information up front; however, if you are asked, you can then highlight the advantages of being new. And often people want to help someone who is just starting out. We have all had someone along the way who believed in us when we were just getting started. If you run into someone who is unsure about you because of your lack of experience, say, "Mr. Prospect, has there ever been a time in your life, perhaps when you were just starting out, when someone simply gave you a chance?" Most people will answer yes to this, to which you will respond: "That's what I'm asking of you right now." And then be completely quiet. Don't speak until the other person does.

3) Are you young or older?

This can be effectively argued either way. If you are older you can use the same argument as the experienced person above. Even if you are new at a job or you're in a new industry, you'll typically command more respect if you are older. As someone who's been around for a while, you can fall back on your overall life experience and the wisdom you've gained over the years. You can tout your dedication, your loyalty, your superior decision-making ability, and your commitment to get things done and see them through to the end.

If you're young you can emphasize your enthusiasm, energy, and your ability to adapt and learn new things. What you lack in experience you make up for with hard work and determination. You are willing to get up early, stay up late, and do whatever it takes to get the job done. You are eager to make your mark and get ahead.

4) What else makes you unique?

Outside of age, experience, and your proximity to the prospect, what sets you from the crowd? What makes you different and puts you in the best position to serve your prospect?

Take a personal inventory. Do you speak a foreign language? Are you good with numbers? Are you a CPA, did you go to law school, or do you have any other degrees that make you unique? What experience, real world or otherwise, puts you in a better position in your job? Have you been with the same company for twenty-five years? What seems to come naturally to you that others have trouble with?

Next, put those strengths into a feature/benefit format that you can express to your prospect in the rapport-building stage. Also, be wary of what can be used against you, be it your physical location, age, experience, or anything else, and be prepared for that "objection."

Here's an example of what you might say regarding yourself:

"Joe, I've been in the investment business for thirty years and in that time I've seen it all a thousand times or more. What that means is I have the experience to guide you in good times, bad times, and everywhere in between.

"Obviously, I'm no spring chicken. But you may be assured I'll work hard to make sure your money works hard for you. Having been with ABC Company for the past twenty-one years, I have the knowledge and experience to maximize your profit potential while minimizing any downside.

"Joe, in a nutshell, with my experience and resources, and as someone who's thrived in this industry for the past thirty years, I think you'll agree I have what it takes to put your money to work for you and achieve the results you're looking for. Am I right?"

Here's another example:

"Kathy, my office is in our manufacturing plant in St. Louis. Because of this I can stay on top of orders you place and get you faster delivery. If you ever have a need for an emergency delivery, I can walk into the plant and personally make sure it gets taken care of. Locally, we have six service people within a fifteen-mile radius of your facility and a parts depot seven miles away. As a result, we can get to you fast and take care of all your service issues quickly.

"Also, you have my business, cellular, and home phone numbers so you can get in touch with me at any time. Considering those factors, along with the experience of the three references I gave you, are you confident you'll get the service from me and my company that you deserve?"

One more:

"Cindy, I understand your concern with my age and, on the surface, my lack of experience. First off, I assure you that I passed all the rigorous state and federal exams necessary to put me in the position I'm in now. In addition, I was a finance major at the University of Wisconsin. I have belonged to an investors' club for three years, and my father has been an investment advisor for twenty-nine years.

"I like to think that, in addition to my experience and my dad's tutelage, I have the brains, the enthusiasm, and the determination to work long, hard hours to make sure I do right by you. Although you may find someone with more experience, I doubt you'll find a person with lots of experience who's willing to work for you as hard as I am and who will also treat you as one of their most important clients.

"I'm sure there was a time in your life when someone believed in you and gave you an opportunity. I'm not looking for you to give me all your investment dollars right away; I'm just looking for you to give me a chance. Is that fair enough?"

Your Company

There are many considerations to take into account when you examine your company and the factors that can work for or against you. Some of these will overlap with the "you" category. For example, does your company have a local presence or are they based out of town? On a larger scale, is your company headquartered in the United States or a foreign country? Essentially, your company and its characteristics can be broken down into three areas: physical, historical, and financial.

1) Physical

The physical aspect of your company concerns its location. Factors to consider are: where your company is based, where the branch offices are located, and where other physical resources are located such as people, parts, manufacturing plants, and the like.

Are you a regional, national, or international company? Where are your various offices located including your headquarters, branch offices, parts depots, etc.? How many employees do you have and where are they located? Do you have more than one manufacturing facility and if so, where are they located?

If you are a U.S.-based company doing business in the U.S., you probably have an advantage over a company from England doing business in the United States. If you are a Massachusetts-based company doing business in Massachusetts, you probably have an advantage over a company based in Alabama doing business in Massachusetts. You get the point. The closer your primary resources are to your target market, the more of a psychological advantage you usually have up front.

If you're the local company, emphasize the local, hands-on approach:

> "Joe, as a company five miles down the street, we will be able to give you the personal service you deserve. If you have a problem we are literally less than ten minutes away by car. We can be here in no time to service you and get you up and running again. If you need something from us we can get it to you quickly. There's also the fact that we belong to the same community and can help each other grow together. I'm sure you'd appreciate the benefits of working with a local company. Am I right, Joe?"

If your company is located out of town, you may have some work to do. Are there any advantages to being from out of town? Are you closer to a source of a material that is important for the prospect to have and, as a result, you can obtain it personally and quickly, and respond better than your competitor? Do you have any local presence at all? If you are from out of town, you will ask some of the same questions that you asked in the "you" section. What puts you in a position to service the customer better than anyone else? Are you the largest company in the industry and thus have more resources? If your competition is a local company and you are not, be prepared for this objection.

In a nutshell, think about how your company's physical location may affect shipping, servicing, and overall responsiveness to the customer. Are there any physical factors that either put you in a better position or more difficult position to service your prospect?

Here's an example of a non-local company showing their advantages over a local company:

> "Joe, I realize that ABC Company is local and there's something to be said for that. At the same time, as the largest company in the industry, with massive resources, we actually have twice as many service people in your geographic area as they do. What that means is we can respond faster and more effectively when you need us to.
>
> "In addition, our technicians go through the most rigorous training program in the industry putting in more hours of training to keep them current

than technicians from any other company. What that means to you is they will get things done right the first time, and in the majority of cases, they are faster and more efficient. That leads to less machine downtime and more productivity for your company, resulting in more dollars straight to your bottom line. It also leads to happier customers and employees. So although we're not right next door, I think you can see how we are in a better position to service you. Am I right, Joe?"

Here's another example of an U.S.-based company showing its advantages over a foreign company:

"Kathy, our manufacturing plants are in the United States, whereas XYZ Company's plants are overseas in Japan. Not only is our product completely an American product, we can also get you better delivery because it is much easier to truck equipment seven hundred miles from North Carolina than to ship it from overseas. As a result, I can get you two-week delivery whereas with the competition, you're going to have to wait at least six.

"In addition, a lot more can go wrong shipping overseas than by truck in the U.S. I mention this because you said you were concerned with shipping and lead times. Do you see how dealing with our company would be a major advantage as far as shipping and lead times are concerned?"

Of course, if your company *is* based overseas, you might talk about how your lower prices are a great advantage—most products are cheaper to manufacture overseas.

2) Historical

Historical aspects of your company include how long the company has been in business, the size of the company within your industry, the overall history of your product or service, and your company's reputation throughout the industry.

The following are some questions regarding the historical aspects of your company:

- How long has your company been in business?
- Do you sell only one product or service?

- Do you specialize in a specific area within your field or have a certain market niche?
- Are you the leading company in the U.S., but not in the world, or in the world but not in the U.S.?
- Is your company ISO (International Standards) certified?
- Can you offer a total solution (one-stop shopping)?
- How large is your service organization?
- What kind of support do you offer? Do you have different levels of service or is it "one size fits all"? Is it twenty-four hours a day, seven days a week?
- Do you provide phone support and Internet support?
- Do you have a website and how easy is it for people to find it and use it?

Here's an example of a small regional company pointing out their historical advantages over a large international company:

"Cindy, that's a good point about XYZ Company being a Fortune 500 Company with twenty-three technicians in this area. At the same time, we have been selling and servicing this particular product for fifteen years, whereas they added this product to their line only five years ago. We also have twice the number of machines in New England as they have. What that means is we've had three times the experience and amount of time for research and development. As a result, we are able to bring you more experience and expertise, which means a smoother-running operation and more cost-efficient system for you.

"As well, very few of their twenty-three technicians are trained to service this type of equipment; most only work on the other products XYZ makes. So even though we have only twelve technicians in the area, they are all trained to repair this equipment. What that means is we can respond to you more quickly, and nineteen times out of twenty we can get you up and running faster, leading to more machine uptime, happier customers, and more money to your bottom line. I'm sure that's important to you, right?"

Here's another example in which a large international company shows their advantages over a smaller regional company using historical examples:

"Joe, it's true that ABC Company is coming in at a little better price than we are. They're a good company, regional, in about twenty states, roughly two hundred employees, and have been in business since 1987.

"On the other hand, we have been in business since 1882, we're an international, Fortune 500 company, we have about 7,000 employees total, and we have more employees in New England than ABC Company has total employees. We have thirty-four service technicians trained on this equipment, while they have six. We have three tiers of service: our regular technicians, our super technicians, and then we have experts at our home office. That way, if there's ever a problem our techs can't handle in the field, they can escalate it to the super techs, and those people, if need be, escalate the problem to our experts at the home office. We have not seen a problem yet that we can't handle.

"When you look at these numbers, you can see that we have a vast amount of resources with which to service you. That means faster service, more uptime, and ultimately more dollars to your bottom line.

"Also, this product accounts for about 52 percent of our annual revenues; because of this, it's a product we are *very* focused on. That means we need to keep you happy and we need to have you coming back to us for more business. Joe, in business, you either have a better product and better service, or you have better price. It's impossible to have all three. Would you agree with me that you get what you pay for?"

Note: Some of the features in the two examples above could be categorized under either physical, historical, or even financial, which we'll look at next. Often only a fine line separates these three categories. In any case, we hope you get the idea of how you can use different company characteristics to form a compelling argument for your company, be it big or small.

3) Financial

Financial aspects of your company include anything related to money—your stock price, your amount of debt, your expenses, your revenues, and your earnings.

The following are some questions concerning the financial aspects of your company:

- Is your financial base growing or shrinking? Are you cash rich or cash poor?

- Are you in a position to make acquisitions, and if so, are you planning to make some?
- Do you have cash on hand to make them, or do you need to finance them?
- Are revenues increasing or decreasing?
- Are profits increasing or decreasing?
- Is your stock price at an all-time high, all-time low, or somewhere in between?
- What are the insiders (executives) doing with regard to stock? Are they buying, selling, or exercising options?
- Who else is showing an interest in your stock? Institutional investors, certain brokerage houses, corporate raiders?
- What percentages of your resources are allocated to research and development, training of employees, or a particular product line?

Here's an example of financial differences between a small regional company versus a large international company:

"Kathy, while it's true that XYZ Company is a huge international conglomerate with seemingly endless resources, they just showed their first quarterly loss in ten years. For the past six months they've had a hiring freeze and now, according to an article in the *Wall Street Journal* on July 15, are scheduled to lay off 5 percent of their workforce over the next six months.

"On the other hand, we are profitable, debt free, and in a position where we are actually expanding our workforce by 6 percent over the next nine months. This includes hiring six more technicians in your area alone. In addition, we were written up in *Investors Business Daily* as one of the top one hundred up-and-coming companies to keep an eye on this year.

"While XYZ Company is cutting back resources for this particular product, we are increasing the money spent on research and development, as well as hiring and training new personnel. What this means to you, Kathy, is that we will be able to offer you more and pay more attention to you—not less, as is the case with XYZ. In addition, this particular product line makes up about 7 percent of XYZ's business whereas it makes up about 40 percent of ours. In other words, not only is XYZ cutting back, but history has shown that companies that cut back tend to do so in the areas in which they have the smallest stake.

"With 40 percent of our revenue coming from this product line, and as a growing company, we are going to be putting even more resources into this line—it is our bread-and-butter product. That means more service, more resources, and a better end product to you, adding more dollars to your bottom line. Do you see how the current financial picture puts us in the best position to serve you?"

Here's another example in which a large international company shows their financial advantages over a smaller company:

"Joe, while it's true that ABC Company is a good company and their stock price and growth is at an all-time high, we are still about *twenty-three times* their size. We were a very cash rich company and the time was right for us to grow by acquiring some good, solid companies. In fact, we just acquired a small regional video company for cash. The video company has been a solid player in the market and adds about sixty years of expertise to our already solid knowledge base. We already have seventeen technicians in the area and they'll add another five.

"What that means is you'll get serviced faster and better, which in turn will maximize your uptime. The acquisition will also add some new lines to our already extensive line and as a result you'll have more choice. As we take advantage of our strong cash position by acquiring more companies and product lines, you will be able to enjoy the benefits of even greater selection and more resources to rely on.

"Joe, the bottom line is that ABC is a good company with good service and at the same time, we can offer you far more choices, better service, and much more expertise. Do you see how we can offer you the most options and best service?"

Most of the focus will be on your product or service during your presentation, yet all factors are important. Make sure when you compete that you also sell yourself and your company, as those are the two factors that your competition lacks.

Some Final Thoughts on Comparison with the Competition

All products, services, companies, and salespeople have strengths and weaknesses. You need to be able to walk on both sides of the fence objectively. Ask all the questions, and see all the angles. Explore every nook and cranny for every little piece of information you can find. Completely analyze your product, your company, yourself, *and* the competition's offering to the point where you know your competition better than they know themselves. Your overall objective is to build on your strengths and minimize your weaknesses while you knock off the competition's strengths and exploit their weaknesses.

Examine your offering and the competition's offering in these critical areas:

1) The cost of your product or service.

Are you the highest-priced solution on the market, the lowest-priced, or somewhere in the middle? What are the short-term and long-term costs associated with your product and other items such as service contracts, maintenance, etc.?

2) Features and functions.

What features and functions do you have that the competition does not and vice versa?

Again, focus on speed, capacity, efficiency, and cost when looking at each feature.

3) Ease of use.

How easy is your product or service to use versus the competition's? How can you save your prospect time, money, labor, headaches, etc.?

4) Familiarity.

Is your company a household name? How about your competitor? Do you have more units out in the field or does your competitor? Does your company enjoy a certain amount of "good will" in your community or have a good reputation that you can use in your favor?

5) You and your company.

What unique aspects do you bring to the table in these two areas?

Now that you have completely and thoroughly studied both your offering and your competitor's, use what you've learned thus far in this section and in the *Presentation* section to formulate a strong presentation.

Chapter 22

Competitive Accounts

Be Number One

When you are doing *most* but *not all* of the business in a particular account, we call that being number one in a competitive account. This usually means that there really is no number one, there are just two or more number twos. So even though you have most of the business, you still need to treat this as a competitive account.

You can't always be all things to all people. You may have to settle for part of the business now. For example, in the banking business we did not always get the ATMs, but sometimes we still got the hardware: safes, vaults, and other items. Stick your foot in the door anywhere you can and then make sure you stay there. Once you're in the door, you will be compared with the competition from a standpoint of customer service, product reliability, etc.

Make sure that your product, your company, and you shine in all areas possible. If you do a great job in one area, you earn the right to ask if you can at least quote the other business. At that point, build as much value as possible, sharpen your pencil, and take your best shot at impressing the customer. Ask to quote but don't push. Just continue to do a good job with what you've got, nurture the relationship, and keep asking to quote on the other equipment every time a new project arises. Eventually either the competition will mess up or the customer will say yes.

In the banking business, when someone called us for a vault, alarm and video, or other equipment, it was a safe bet that they were also looking for equipment such as ATMs. If we were asked to bid on all the equipment except the ATMs, we would take that opportunity to ask if we could provide a competitive quote.

Here's how to phrase your question to ask for the other business: "Joe may I assume you're also going to have at least one ATM at this location?"

After the customer answers in the affirmative, you say, "I know we're not your ATM vendor currently. Why don't we simply give you a quote just to keep the others guys honest and to make sure you're getting the best deal?" Most people won't argue with you on that.

If you do get the opportunity to quote, get aggressive. By this we mean build value, get your best price, pull out all the stops, and really dazzle the prospect.

Important: Make sure you're quoting on the same thing as the competition. If you're comparing apples to oranges, either the prices will be far off the mark or the customer won't be getting what they expect. Either way, it won't be a fair comparison.

If you don't get the opportunity to quote, use some humor: "Joe, I'll tell you what. You tell me what price and what features and functions you want, and I'll put them in print on a proposal so you can use it to get a better price from XYZ. Of course, I'll have you sign a letter that says there's no way you're holding us to that price."

Hopefully this will elicit a smile or laugh from your prospect. After that, just pause for a moment and let the prospect speak first. Most likely he'll stick to his original answer, but at least you've given it another shot. From this point forward, just keep asking whenever the opportunity arises in the future.

The bottom line: in accounts where you are one of several suppliers, ask to quote on the other equipment and put yourself in a position to eventually be the sole supplier.

Be Number Two

If you can't be number one, you'd better be sure you're number two!

Obviously, our goal as salespeople is to be number one. We want to be the first person that our customers/clients call and buy from. However, if you can't be number one, be the backup—be number two. By being number two, you're ensuring that if your prospect has a problem with number one, you'll get the call. Then the door is wide open. If you're number three or four, you're a long way from any business from that prospect. If you're number two, you're one late delivery, one botched install, or one of any other mistakes away from some potential business.

You don't need to spend the same amount of time and effort with these number two prospects as you do with number one customers. After all, they are number two and that's where they lie on your priority list. However, you need to do enough so that when they have a problem with number one, you're the first one they think of. You need to make sure they don't have to jump through hoops to either contact you or remember how to contact you, and most important, you need to respond quickly when they do call. If you don't, they'll move on to number three.

278

If you're in face-to-face sales, at a minimum, you'll want to mail to them monthly and stop in quarterly; if you're in telephone sales, mail monthly and call on the phone quarterly. Do what you need to do to be fresh in the prospect's mind when number one eventually trips up.

Providing a Competitive Account with a "Token" Quote

You're all fired up. You've just received a phone message from a prospect who has never done business with you or your company, and she needs a quote from you. You call her back to set up an appointment and somewhere in the conversation she says, "We actually need three quotes to fulfill the requirements of our bidding process."

It's clear that she's using you simply to "fulfill the requirements of the bidding process" and probably to make the current vendor look good to the board of directors. What should you do? You're going to be professional and help her do her job. At the same time, you're going to raise her level of respect for you, cement yourself as the number two vendor, and completely set yourself apart from all other salespeople.

Prepare for and begin the meeting just as you would any other by building rapport and talking about current events or points of interest. When the conversation turns to business open up with:

"Well, I have to say, when you called me for a quote I became very excited. Of course, we haven't done much with you over the years." (Say, "haven't done much" even if you haven't done anything. You don't want to emphasize a negative or get the prospect thinking, "Wow, we've *never* done any business with him? Why did I even bother calling him this time?")

"And then you mentioned the point about having to get three quotes to meet your bidding requirements. Let me ask you, you've been dealing with our competitor ABC Company for quite some time now, right?"

After you get her answer, follow with, "How are things going with that relationship?"

You want to find out if something has changed or if your suspicion that you were simply called for a "token" quote is right. If she tells you they are unhappy, have had recent problems, or something else has changed with the current vendor, you may have a legitimate shot at the business. However, if she tells you that things have been going great, your "token" quote suspicion is probably correct.

For this example, let's assume she told you everything is going fine with the present vendor. At that point, respond with, "Bobbi-Jo, frankly, I'd love to tell you about all the exciting developments with our company and our product line." Next, give her your top three "hit 'em between the eyes" attention grabbers about your product:

"For example, our recently released machine with twenty-two exclusive features helped our customers' profits to shoot through the roof as never before. I'd also love to give you more details about why the largest company in the world decided they had to do business with us because it was costing them too much not to, and I'd love to tell you how our product has advanced to the point that it will make your job and your life much easier. I'd love to tell you all that, but that's not my objective today."

Pause here and look at her for effect. "My objective today is to help you reach your objective."

You need to say this next part with as much empathy and understanding as possible:

"With all due respect, and at the risk of being direct, if your objective is to keep ABC Company on their toes and use my quote to get them to make some concessions or cut their price, I'd be happy to help you do that. If you'd like me to give you a quote with a ridiculously low number in order to achieve that result, I'll give you a quote with a ridiculously low number. Of course, I'll have to have you sign something that says there's no way you're holding me to that quote.

"On the other hand, if your goal is to use my quote to make ABC Company look good to your board of directors, I'll be happy to give you a quote to achieve that end. Now I'm also going to tell you exactly why I'm willing to do that. I know that if I work with you and help you achieve your objective, if ABC Company ever makes a major mistake I'll be the first person you'll think of, and you'll call me and give me a shot at the business. Is that fair enough?"

After she answers affirmatively, follow with, "So Bobbi-Jo, how can I help you reach your objective and look good to everyone involved?" If that doesn't give the prospect a positive impression of you, nothing will.

By throwing out your top three "hit 'em between the eyes" attention-grabbers, you are hoping to pique her interest. Your objective is to get her interested to the point where you are no longer there for a "token" quote but are now in a position where you actually have a shot at the business. If she asks about any of your three attention-grabbers, the door is at least slightly open.

In the above real-life example, the prospect asked why the largest company in the world was doing business with us. If this happens to you, don't give her something for nothing. She's interested and she wants an answer from you, but before you give her the answer she needs to give you something. She has to agree to give you the time to tell your whole story.

Start with a teaser to build even more interest. "Actually, they did some analysis showing that by working with us they could significantly increase their profit margin, whereas by dealing with our competitor they were actually cutting into their profit margin. I'm sure if you did the analysis you'd reach the same conclusion."

Notice that we didn't give any specific numbers in our example. We simply said, "significantly increase their profit margin." If we used a number the prospect might decide the number is not that substantial, or she may not believe the number and lose interest.

Next, ask her for a commitment. "Bobbi-Jo, are you telling me that if I can show you some significant benefits of our product, I'll have a shot at your business?"

If she answers yes, find out where you stand with her in terms of getting the business. Can she make the decision or do others need to be involved? Is she ready to move now or is she waiting for something? So your next step is to ask some questions. "Bobbi-Jo, who else will be involved in the decision-making process?" If she says she is the only decision-maker, ask, "If I can show you unequivocally that we have the best product to suit your needs, is this a decision you're prepared to make right now?"

If she is the only decision-maker and she answers yes to the second question, bridge into your presentation. Start with, "Bobbi-Jo, in order to fully answer your question about why the number one company in the world is doing business with us, I'm going to need to go into some detail." Pause slightly after this comment and then launch into your standard presentation.

Treat the presentation as you would any other and then ask for the business. Of course, if you've handled the "talk it over with someone" and "I'm not prepared to make a decision now" objections up front, it will be awkward for her to give you those at the end. If she does, call her on it.

If there are other people involved in the decision-making process, ask her when you can explain the details to everyone involved in the decision. When you do sit down with all the decision-makers, give them the benefits, let them know their colleague was interested in hearing more details, make sure they are open to your company as an option, and then go into your presentation.

Following up after a Meeting with a Competitive Account

After you've met with a competitive account, send a note out immediately. In the note you want to thank the person(s) for their time and summarize what you covered. Make sure it's personalized and doesn't come off as a boiler-plate letter. Cover some specifics of the points you discussed. Also, highlight some key areas or your "hit 'em between the eyes" attention-getters. Make the note friendly, yet professional and concise. Ensure that your contact information is included.

The objectives of the letter are to set you apart from the other salespeople and to define yourself as a true professional. How many times do you think the prospect's current vendor sends a letter out after a meeting? Rarely if ever. You want the prospect to think, "Wow, this is different. I never get a letter from my present salesperson." Very few salespeople send out *any* letters thanking prospects and customers for their time or business and even fewer send them after a presentation or simply a meeting. Letters will get you noticed.

It's advisable to get into the habit of sending out letters to *all* your accounts. With established accounts you can either do it every time or occasionally. Make sure you do it at least occasionally to stand out from all the other salespeople.

Important: Send the letter as soon as possible after the meeting. On the next page, you'll find an example of a thank-you letter.

In addition to sending a letter and being a consummate professional in the process, make sure you do what you say you'll do when you say you'll do it. Following this rule is the one sure way to build credibility quickly. Breaking it is a sure way to lose credibility and every chance you have to get business from the account. Also, remember to under-promise and over-deliver. If you know you can get the prospect something by Wednesday, promise it by Friday and get it there on Wednesday or Thursday. The spotlight is on you in these very early stages, so be sure you shine.

Figure 3: Thank-you for Meeting Letter

Complete Selling, Inc.
27 Curtis Street
Auburn, MA 01501

Mr. Bruce Weisberg   August 28, 2008
Senior Vice President
XYZ Bank and Trust Company
1 N. Main Street
Auburn, MA 01501

Dear Mr. Weisberg,

It was very nice meeting you today. Thank you for your time.

Clearly, you appreciate the latest ATM technology and how it will make your life, your employees' lives, and your customers' lives easier.

As we discussed, you can expect to see an average increase in ATM uptime of between 7 and 11 percent with our latest line of ATMs. This will increase customer happiness and loyalty while saving you and your employees time and headaches. Also, our twenty-two exclusive features will give you the individual branding that is so important to you. Finally, you will find that ABC Company offers you the most choices and flexibility in the industry. This will give you the peace of mind in knowing the new machines will fit seamlessly into your network, thus saving you time and money.

I hope to work with you on this project. As discussed, I'll follow up with you in about a week. If you have any questions or comments in the meantime, please give me a call. Thanks again, Bruce.

Sincerely,

Signature goes here

Robert J. Chapin
Phone: 508-555-6444
Cell phone: 508-555-7464

Chapter 23

Interacting with the Competition

Occasionally, you will run into the competition in your travels. It may be indirectly while competing for a prospect's business or it may be face-to-face at a prospect's location, a trade show, or another industry event. In this Chapter we will talk about both indirect and direct interaction with the competition and what you should and shouldn't do.

Never Bad-Mouth the Competition

Bad-mouthing the competition is never a good idea for several reasons. First, when you belittle the competition, you come across as unprofessional. Second, if you make a habit of bad-mouthing the competition, word will get around the industry and your reputation will suffer there as well. It's difficult to respect someone who undermines others. As well, you never know who in your industry you'll end up working with in the future. As a result, you want to keep your reputation intact.

Third, there has never been a perfect product or service in the history of mankind. When you start to bad-mouth the competition, you lower the perceived product value from your company as well as the competitor's. It's akin to saying, "They're terrible. Obviously we're not perfect either because no one can be, yet we're not as bad as they are." Bad-mouthing the competition lowers the bar for everyone in the industry including your company.

Keep in mind the saying, "What comes around, goes around." If you habitually sling the mud, it's entirely possible that your competition will feel they need to get some shots in themselves. You see this in political campaigns all the time. Candidate A vows to run a clean campaign no matter what the other candidate does, then as soon as Candidate B begins negative campaigning, Candidate A almost always follows suit.

On the other hand, if you speak of your competition in a professional manner, chances are the word will get back to them and they will usually give you the same professional courtesy. This won't always happen, but it tends to be the rule and not the exception.

If the prospect is already using the competition's product or service, you have another reason to refrain from bad-mouthing them. By criticizing the competition, you are bad-mouthing the prospect's decision to purchase the competitor's product and perhaps even insulting his intelligence. It's okay for your prospect to bad-mouth your competition's product and/or his decision to buy it, but don't get caught up in it yourself. Even if your prospect or customer criticizes the competition, while you certainly don't want to defend them, do your best not to jump on the bashing bandwagon.

Finally, treating others with courtesy and respect is simply the right thing to do. You may fight tooth-and-nail with your competition over business, and that's fine. At the same time, *keep things professional*.

Note: Talking about the competition's weaknesses, which we did in the competitive comparison, is necessary and is not the same thing as bad-mouthing the competition.

Talking to the Competition versus Not Talking to the Competition

All things considered, it *is* a good idea to talk to the competition. First, you may speak with someone who is an incessant talker and will give you all sorts of good intelligence. Second, it is politically correct.

By politically correct, we mean several things. If your competitors think you're a good person, most of them will have trouble saying anything negative about you. In fact, once they know they are up against you, they may say something like, "Oh yeah, I know Bob, he's a great guy." If you are pleasant to the competition they'll have less ammunition with which to snuff you out of business.

Also, as we mentioned, it's a small world and you never know who will be working with whom in the future. If one of your major competitor's top salespeople becomes disenchanted with her current position, you'd like to have her come see you or your company for a job. Similarly, if you find yourself out of a job, it's important to have built some positive bridges in advance.

We must all understand that business is business, and it's often necessary to fight hard to beat the competition and expand our market. But by showing your competitor respect and common courtesy, you add an exclamation mark to your high level of professionalism.

Let your competitors know who you are. You don't need to sneak around and keep your identity a secret at trade shows and other industry events. Ask a few pertinent questions and be a good listener. You'll be surprised at how some of your competitors will sing like canaries when given the opportunity.

We once had a customer come to us with a printing job for which they required one-time stick plastic adhesive to attach a plastic membership card to a postcard. We looked everywhere for a supplier, using the usual channels, but were unable to find any company that could produce exactly what we needed. A few months later, while at a trade show where other printers were present, we noticed a sample at one booth that was exactly what our customer was looking for. We simply asked who did the adhesive work for them. They gave us the company name, phone number, address, and contact person. They raved about what great work the company did and gave us the pricing they had received, including quantity breakdowns. We could now help our own customer while we added another facet to what we were able to do as printers. Eventually, we also negotiated a better price than our competitor was getting.

Rules to Follow
When Talking to the Competition

1) Keep the conversation friendly.

Your objective is to leave the competition with a good feeling about you as a person. Smile and keep the conversation cordial. Many competitors will be pleasant and talk to you. You may run into some who become defensive and use both verbal and body language to let you know you are the enemy and they have no interest in talking to you. In this case, give them a valid compliment or two about their product and their effectiveness in the marketplace. If this does not breakdown their defensive stance, simply end the visit with something like, "Well, best of luck. Have a nice day." Above all, remain pleasant and smile.

2) Talk on a personal level and keep business talk to a minimum.

Keeping the conversation on a personal level isn't the easiest thing to do the first time you meet a competitor. In the first meeting you'll need to talk about things you have in common—namely, business. You can ask some general questions such as, "How is business?" and discuss common industry trends. You don't want to give out any details about what's happening within your company, or any industry knowledge where you feel you have an edge. You can ask some questions about their company or product and see if they'll open up, but if they don't, don't push. Your goal is to leave them with a positive impression of you personally, not to leave them thinking the only reason you were there was to get inside information about their product and their company.

After talking a little business, you can start with a few personal questions such as where they live, where they went to school, what they do for fun, and the like. You should probe for common interests just as you would with anyone else you meet. Once you get some personal information, it will be easier to talk on a personal level, and the next time you see them you can open by asking how the kids are instead of how business is.

If they want to talk business and tell you everything they and their company are up to, that's fine—let them talk. Two points to remember: Do not be deceitful in trying to extract information, and don't beat them up.

3) Keep the conversation brief.

For the most part, you do not want to spend a great deal of time talking to the competition. Most of your meetings will occur either at business events, where you will have other more important business priorities, or they will happen unexpectedly and you do not want to spend too much time throwing off either their schedule or yours. Keep the conversations anywhere from two to ten minutes. There may be some exceptional circumstances in which you will bend this rule, but, in general, try to keep the meetings brief.

When Not to Talk to the Competition

Occasionally, you will want to avoid talking to the competition. Avoid engaging the competition in conversation when there is a major issue pending. This may include a court case where one company is suing the other or negotiations for one company to buy the other. In such circumstances it may be illegal for you to talk with each other.

Your company may have something in your employee contract that prohibits conversation with the competition. This may be the case if you are in a high-security industry such as the defense industry.

You may also want to avoid the competition if you have previously tried to approach them, but they made it clear that they want absolutely nothing to do with you. Similarly, there may have been a personality conflict in the past.

Outside of the above examples, it makes sense to talk to the competition. Again, when you do, make sure you do so in a relaxed and friendly tone, treat them as you would anyone else you're getting to know, and stay pleasant and professional no matter what. Always take the high road.

A Final Word on Interacting with the Competition

When talking to the competition, remain friendly and professional, but remember that business is business. No matter how friendly your competitors are or how much business you believe there is for both of you, they would love nothing more than to see you go out of business. Some people may argue this point but ultimately it's true everywhere. Keep the competitive conversation friendly, but *do not* be generous with information.

Chapter 24

Other Ideas Related to the Competition

Make Sure the Competition Does
What They Say They Will Do

The best way to describe the technique of making sure the competition does what they say they'll do is through an example. We once had a situation in which we lost a competitive deal because of price. We were very surprised at the competition's low price for the equipment they quoted. We figured we'd better do a little investigating.

Now, this was a customer with whom we had a good relationship. We let him know that the competitor's price shocked us, and we asked if we could be present when the equipment was installed. He agreed to let us be there. When the equipment was installed, we discovered it was in fact the cheaper version of the competitor's equipment and not what they had quoted in the proposal. When we brought this to the customer's attention, he called our competitor, telling them to rip out what they had installed and put in what they had quoted instead. Not only did this cost the competitor some money, it also cost them the chance to ever do business with this organization again. Ultimately, it put us in a solid position in the account.

The other advantage to watching the competition install their equipment is that very few salespeople watch the equipment installation process, even their own. Most of them are completely unfamiliar with the process. This goes back to knowing more about your competitor's equipment than they do. You can learn a great deal by watching the competitor's installations. You will see:

- How efficient they are at installing equipment.
- If they have any problems.
- How friendly their installers are.
- If they use their own installers or subcontract the work.
- If they deliver on vehicles bearing the company name.
- If they clean up and leave the area looking neat after the installation.

If possible, you should try to observe some of the competition's installations. You should also be watching some of your own. You don't have to go to every single one. However, if the installers know you might show up to check on them at any time, they will likely be a little more mindful of their work. Also, because few salespeople go to installs, you'll impress the customer.

Have the Competition Put Misrepresentations in Writing

If you've been in sales long enough, you've more than likely run into a situation where the competition has made a statement to a prospect that you knew was, at best, less than the truth, and at worst, a flat-out lie. When the competition has made a promise, guarantee, or some other representation of their product that is completely false, or they make a misstatement about your product and you're lucky enough to hear about it from the prospect, simply tell him that the information the competition is giving him is incorrect. Then ask the prospect to have the competition put it in writing.

Here's an example of a conversation we once had with a prospect:

Prospect: You know what XYZ Company told me? They promised they will install their machine and if we're not happy with it after one year, they'll put in one of yours.

Us: Matt, did they promise you one of our new machines?

Prospect: Yes. If we're not happy for any reason, they'll rip theirs out and put in a new one of yours.

Us: And did they actually put that in writing?

Prospect: No, they haven't given it to us in writing, but they told us they would do it.

Us: So if after a year you don't like the machine and they have to make good on that promise, where are they going to get one of our new machines from?

Prospect: Well, I don't know. But it won't be my problem; it will be theirs.

Us: Matt, we hear what you're saying. But what will happen if you call them after a year and tell them to remove their machine and replace it with one of ours? Well, they know you'll never do business with them again, and they know they can't get a new one from us, and you don't have anything in writing… (At this point we raised our eyebrows and gazed at him. We didn't have to go any further.)

Prospect: Okay, I see what you're saying. Fine, I'll have them put it in writing.

We returned two days later to get the order signed because the competition couldn't or wouldn't put their promise in writing.

In the above example, we knew that the competition was selling our company's refurbished machines. We knew, too, that it was not legally possible for them to get their hands on a brand-new one, which was what the prospect had been led to believe he would receive. In reality, the competition knew that if they installed their own machine, the odds were slim to none that the prospect would ever have them make good on the offer of ours.

At the same time, the prospect figured that if someone was willing to go out on that kind of limb, they must really be confident in their product. The prospect also felt he now had a safety net. If things didn't work out, he'd get the other machine and everyone would live happily ever after.

When you tell the prospect to get it in writing, you're casting doubt on the validity of the "promise" and letting the prospect know that he potentially has something big to lose. You're also telling him, as an expert in the industry, that the information is incorrect, and all he needs to do to validate it—at the same time as covering his bases—is to simply get it in writing. It's a very powerful argument and it's coupled with the fact that people become very uneasy about putting anything in writing—even true statements, never mind statements that are in the gray area or completely untrue.

Note: We have never seen the following scenario happen however, if the competition does put the lie in writing, stick to your guns, present your proof to the contrary, and have the prospect verify the information with a higher authority within the competition's organization.

The Other Side of the Coin: Watch What *You* Say

Keep in mind that the above tactic can be used against you too, so don't get caught on the opposite side of the scenario. You don't want to find yourself in a position where the prospect has to ask you for something in writing because you've exaggerated just a little, and the prospect has decided to call you on it.

As salespeople, our mouths may occasionally be tempted to "write checks" that we, our company, or our product can't quite cash. This may happen for two reasons. First, most salespeople inherently don't like to say no to a customer or prospect, and second, as salespeople we want the sale. We know that telling the customer or prospect anything other than exactly what they want to hear may cost us a sale. Still, you must fight the urge to bend the truth.

Before you commit yourself, your product, or your company to doing something, make sure it is absolutely true and that you'll be happy to put it in writing if need be. Keep in mind what's at stake: if a customer or prospect catches you telling less than the truth, it will kill your credibility with that person—and possibly others—for good.

In addition to embellishing the truth to make a sale, some salespeople occasionally guess at an answer to a question because they don't want to look unintelligent or uninformed. If you don't know the answer to a prospect's question, say so. Simply say, "I don't know the answer to that, but I will get an answer for you." Avoid falling into the habit of using phrases such as, "I think," "I'm not sure, but," "I believe," or "I'm pretty sure." Speak with certainty and be sure that what you tell the customer or prospect is absolutely true.

The Domino Effect: The Importance of Beating the Competition

We once cold-called a prospect who said to us, "The new island ATM that XYZ Bank has outside their main office is really neat. Is that one of yours?"

That's a closed-ended question, the answer of which will make you or break you in a New York minute. Fortunately, we were able to smile and say, "Yes, it is." The person asking the question bought an identical one from us about a month later.

We cringed later when we thought about how close we had come to losing the first ATM. That was the one we just mentioned in the previous section where the competition had offered to install one of our machines after a year if the customer was not happy with theirs. Other machines followed until there were five or six of those machines in that area. If the competition had gotten their machine in the first location, it very easily could have gone the other way.

That's the domino effect; another word for it could be *momentum*. It's similar to the snowball effect or the saying, "success breeds success."

Realize what's at stake on each call and on each transaction. Every one makes you more successful or less successful, gives you more momentum or less momentum, is another reference for you, or one for the competition. You don't need to live and die with each sale, because all salespeople lose their share of sales. Just keep in mind the power of momentum when you're wondering whether to make that one final push for the business you think you've lost, or when you're wondering whether to take that one little extra step that could put you over the top. Make sure you do everything you can reasonably do. Don't leave anything on the table or any stone unturned.

Chapter 25

Other Ideas Related to Competing

Do You Sound Just Like the Competition?

You have probably been trained to do things just like everyone else in your industry. Consequently, your presentation may sound almost exactly like your competitor's. It's important to do things differently, ask different questions, give a different presentation, and have a different proposal and approach. The best way to do this is to focus on each customer's *specific* needs, wants, and desires. Tell stories about other companies with a similar need, want, or desire, and how your product filled that need. You also want to relate one or two nightmares that can happen if people select the wrong product or service. Ultimately, you want the prospect to see you as unique and a better solution than the competition. Do this by showing a strong concern and understanding of the issues the prospect faces. Connect pain to your competitor's solution and pleasure to yours.

How to Differentiate Yourself When Selling the Same Product as the Competition

When you are selling a similar product (such as the same kind of car), you have to examine the other factors that differentiate you from the other person selling the same thing. As with any selling situation, *you* are the unique factor. You need to get the prospect excited about doing business with *you*. Often the salesperson is the biggest reason why a prospect does or doesn't choose to buy. This means that part of your job is to set yourself apart in every way you can. Show your dedication, your commitment, your professional integrity, and most important, show how much you care about the prospect.

The second differentiator is the company you work for:

- How good is your service department and what are the people in it like?

- Are your back office or finance people easy to work with?
- How close is your place of business to the customer versus the competition?
- Do you have the largest service organization in the business?
- Are you the original equipment manufacturer?

Third, what can you do as far as pricing or features go?

- Can you actually sell the same product at a better value or for a lower price?
- Can you throw in an option or two that the competitor does not? Does your product have a variety of colors or other features that the competition lacks?
- Is your overall cost lower, thereby putting you in a position to make as much money as a competitor while giving the customer a better price? For example:
  - ➢ Do you buy the equipment outright before you sell it?
  - ➢ Are you mortgage free?
  - ➢ Do you have lower overhead, rent, personnel costs, office costs, etc.?
  - ➢ What other factors such as these make your overall cost lower?
- Can you arrange better financing?
- Can you give an extended warranty?

You have to concentrate on the little things when you are selling the same product or service as someone else. Where can you give more value, more options, or a better price?

In conclusion, if your product and your competitor's product are the same, the decision comes down to you, your company, and your price. In these three areas there are many potential differences you can accentuate. Review Chapter 21, in which we discussed selling you and your company. Once you've covered what you and your company bring to the table, look for ways to make the product you are selling better than what the competition is selling. Look at every aspect of the product and see what you can add to make your product better than the competition's.

Phantom Competition and Misrepresenting the Competition

You may have a prospect, or even a customer, create what we call "phantom competition." By this we mean competition that doesn't exit. The prospect will tell you there are several other companies competing for their business in the hopes of getting some leverage with you on pricing and other concessions.

In addition to creating phantom competition, your prospects or customers may also misrepresent the competition. In other words, they may tell you that the competition is offering a lower price or "extras" when this is actually not the case.

Your best defense against both misrepresentations and phantom competition is to know your competition thoroughly and know how far you're able and willing to bend. If your prospect tells you she's been offered something out of the ordinary, you'll be able to sense whether she is shooting you straight or trying to get you to come up with more for less.

Occasionally, the competition does change strategies, and you need to be aware of that. However, changes are usually gradual and not massive or sweeping. The only time you might see a major shift is if there has been a change in ownership or upper-level management, or the company is in trouble. Of course, knowing your competition, you would be aware of these changes.

If you hear something about the competition's offering that seems out of the ordinary, ask for proof. Say something like, "Wow! That sounds very out of the ordinary for them. Can I see a copy of the proposal?" If the prospect won't let you see the proposal, you are probably dealing with a misrepresentation or phantom competition. In this case say the following: "Hmm, again, that does seem out of the ordinary and I compete with these guys all the time. I've come to you with a great price and great value. What will it take to get the deal done?"

Based upon your experience with the competition and how the prospect presents this "competitive situation," you will probably get a gut feeling as to whether the prospect is shooting you straight. Use your best judgment and either stick to your guns or give a reasonable concession to get the deal done.

Chapter 26

Other "Competitive" Items in This Book

The following ideas are found in other sections, but relate to competing.

Name-dropping in Competitive Situations

In both the *Cold Call* and *Presentation* sections, we talked about how important name-dropping can be. In competitive situations, you want to be dropping the names of companies or people you do business with. If you are doing business with most of the top companies in town, that can help the prospect become comfortable with you more quickly. Testimonials, references, user lists, and concept books are all great ways to drop names.

The Competitive Advantage Close

The competitive advantage close highlights your advantages over the competition and is an effective way to sum everything up and close. Please refer to *The Competitive Advantage Close*, which begins on page 474, for more information.

Objections Created by the Competition

Occasionally, your competition will paint some of your features as weaknesses even though they may not actually be weaknesses. Please refer to *Objections Created by the Competition* on page 408.

Going Over Someone's Head

If all else fails when you're competing and you're about to lose the business, one possibility is to go over the person's head. You have to be careful with this technique, which is discussed on pages 500 through 504.

Also, make sure you have several contacts within any organization. This will make it more difficult for a single decision-maker to snuff you out. Refer to the section titled *After the Close*, where we discuss going over someone's head.

A Summary of Ideas on Competing

Keep these ideas in mind with regard to competition and competing:

- Know your competition and their product or service as well as you know your own company and product or service. Look at your product or service through the competitor's eyes with objectivity.

- Concentrate on building value when competing.

- Leave some wiggle room on price, but not much. Come in with your best price right up front, and only cut price as a last resort.

- Always find out why you lost or won and what the key differentiators were.

- Learn to build on your product's strengths and minimize its weaknesses.

- Build value that is greater than the asking price of your product or service.

- Emphasize the things that make you, your company, and your product unique. How are these three better than what the competition has? Also, emphasize the qualities of the one thing your competition does not have: *you!*

- If you can't be number one in an account, be number two.

- When you get an opportunity at a competitive account, treat it like gold. Make the purchaser's life as easy as possible and give him more than he asked for. Put your best foot forward, be professional, send thank-you notes, and follow up promptly.

- Don't bad-mouth the competition. Always be professional and treat them with respect. Be sociable but don't give away any trade secrets.

- Have the competition put misrepresentations in writing.

- Visit sites where the competition is installing equipment; see what they are installing and how they install it.

- Finally, do everything you can from a fair, legal, and ethical standpoint to win when you're competing. You need to go to bed at night feeling good about yourself, knowing you gave it your best shot possible, and you did everything you could do to win fair and square.

SECTION V

SELLING TO EXECUTIVES
and
BUILDING A BUSINESS CASE

Note: If you sell business to business solutions in the technology marketplace, and need to call higher and wider in your accounts and build a compelling business case that advocates how your solution creates value for your customer, then this section is for you.

By solutions we mean any combination of hardware, software, services, and outsourcing—that is aimed at solving specific business problems. In this realm, the approval process typically involves multiple buyers and a strong business case. Selling in this environment presents a variety of challenges, not the least of which is getting to the real decision-makers.

Chapter 27

Selling to Executives

Has your boss has been insisting that you sell higher in your prospects' organizations? Is she saying that you are positioned too low and wasting your time with the "seymours"? You know, the people who never make a decision but just want to keep "seeing more." More of you, more of what you sell, more free lunches, more gifts, more of everything. They want to see more but they don't want to buy more! In fact, they don't really want to buy, and perhaps they don't even have the authority to buy.

The above scenario is a problem many salespeople face today. They waste time and lose other sales opportunities. One of us remembers the days when he thought he was actually accomplishing something by trying to sell to the "seymours." Of course, he didn't really know they were "seymours." He thought he was doing well, since he was building relationships with people in the prospect company. But he was building the wrong relationships, and lost more than one sale because of it. He sometimes even lost sales that he thought were almost closed. He was half right—they were closed with the competition! Higher-level relationships had won the sale for the competition.

Why is this situation so common? As sales professionals, are we to blame when this happens? Well, yes and no. Yes, because we should know better, and no because of many factors beyond our control. First, look at many of our backgrounds. Where did we come from? Often we came right from the industry we're selling into—perhaps we were in operations, marketing, or service in that same industry. Perhaps we were technically savvy and parlayed that into a sales career. Perhaps we were a technician and are now selling the same technology to those who once were our peers. This creates a comfort level at the wrong level, the level where buying decisions can be influenced but where the final decision is rarely made. The budget certainly doesn't reside there.

Then there's the area of "sales training." What do most companies refer to as sales training? Too often, it's product training. We go through countless hours of it, learning all about the features and benefits. While it's true that we need to be well versed in our products and services, we also need to understand what our products and services do for our customers, and how they produce benefits they can measure.

That said, to whom should we sell? You will hear the word *executive* mentioned often. In this Chapter, it will be used as a catch-all for selling to the highest appropriate level. What does that mean? You would not be selling pencils to the CEO. On the other hand, you are not selling an enterprise-wide customer relationship management (CRM) solution to a technology manager when the budget and true business plan for that solution resides two levels higher. So the highest appropriate level means just that. And often there is more than one "executive," but only one person who writes the check.

What about selling to committees? In that situation, we need all the relationships we can get; at the same time, we need to realize that the team decision is really an individual decision with consensus. Every buying committee has one dominant person who will influence the others to his or her way of thinking. That's your true buyer.

Regardless of whom we are selling to, we need to focus on our prospect, not ourselves. We need to work collaboratively with the prospect to uncover their business problems and/or opportunities, then determine and prove the business benefits our proposed solution will provide. The benefits of that solution need to be defined in a business case and framed according to the prospect's executive decision-making criteria. In other words, what is the business problem the solution is solving, how it is being solved, and what is the business value that is created for the executive?

What Executives Value in Salespeople

If we are going to sell to executives, it would certainly help us to understand what they want from us. Many salespeople believe that their prospect wants to know everything there is to know about their products and services. And since much of their sales training covers that, there seems to be a perfect match. Unfortunately, this match is far from perfect. There are people in your buyer's organization who do want to know about what you are selling. Despite that being true, buyers who fulfill that role are often not the decision-makers, but decision influencers. And they don't have budget authority to actually make the purchase. The final decision is made higher up the corporate ladder. Does that mean we should ignore the influencers? Of course not. But we need to target the decision-makers in our sales process while also satisfying the needs of the influencers. And the conversations are quite different.

So what do executives value in us? They value different things than the influencers. While many influencers value those with good product knowledge, executives value salespeople who have good business knowledge. They value salespeople who have done the research to understand their business and those who ask relevant questions to get their particular insights on business problems and solutions. They appreciate those who don't jump to conclusions but instead listen well and think before proposing, while also considering alternatives. Salespeople who understand how their solutions solve business problems and keep the executive meetings focused on business are highly valued.

What Prevents Salespeople from Calling High?

If the above is true, why don't we just do it? All salespeople have been told that they need to call higher, but they are rarely given the necessary tools. Consequently, many fail. Not only that, many never make that first attempt. Why? Many are afraid and intimidated. What will they talk about? What are the business issues the executive wants to address? They don't know the executive language. They may feel they are not important enough to associate with the executive. Perhaps they can't get past the gatekeeper or don't otherwise know how to start the process of gaining access. Whatever the reason, many salespeople just can't seem to get access to the executive.

And there are great reasons to call high. Here are a few:

- Executives make the decisions.
- They have the budget and the authority to buy.
- They have a broader and deeper understanding of the organization.
- They see the broader enterprise reach of your proposed solutions.
- They can provide their unique perspectives on problems and solutions.
- They have a deft understanding of the politics of the organization.
- They can open doors among their peers and beneath them.
- Of the many "versions of the truth," theirs is probably most accurate.

Once you have called at that level, you can always go back without risk of alienation from below. Executive networks are extensive, and top people may provide other opportunities inside and outside of their company.

There are also risks to calling high. For one thing, it's likely that you'll only get one shot, and if it goes poorly, there is a good chance that you will not get back in for a long time—perhaps never. If your current relationships are lower, and those individuals don't want you to go higher, you risk alienating them. But remember, our job is to sell, and if calling higher is required to do our jobs, that's what we must do.

And what about calling low? One of the biggest advantages is that calling lower is probably right for your comfort zone. And if you have a bad meeting there, others exist with whom you can meet. They can also provide information on the details of their specific department, and answer the technology questions that are imperative to ensure what you are selling is a technological fit.

On the other hand, the view at this level is limited to their specific area; thus the solutions you can propose will be limited as well. It is clear that the disadvantages of calling low far outweigh the advantages. It is far better to start high and work your way down than the other way around.

Why Use Value Assessment?

Selling higher and broader doesn't just happen. You need a methodology for doing so. Next, we will discuss in detail the five phases of value assessment, which culminate in the presentation of a business case that advocates your solution based on the business benefits to gained by your prospective executive customer.

To begin the value assessment discussion, it will be useful to understand the impetus behind value assessment in the first place. Technology is no longer bought for technology's sake, but to improve the business. Period.

Technology planning now takes place concurrently with business planning with the hopes of keeping the two aligned. Business managers have set higher expectations for justification of their purchases. Technology innovations are measured against how they create positive change. Executives now make the decisions.

Now let's look at executive decision-making criteria. It is obvious that executives are interested in the financial return, but in reality they consider a number of factors when making investment decisions. We divide these into five specific areas. They are: financial return, strategic alignment, risk assessment and mitigation, political effects, and intuition. As solution providers, we have a distinct impact on the first three, and we indirectly impact the others.

The first criterion is **financial return** and is somewhat self-explanatory. This can include both revenue increases and cost savings. It is important to note that there is a big difference between a proposal that shows a $1 million cost savings and one that touts a $1 million revenue increase. Two areas merit examination here. First, it is much easier to quantify and almost guarantee a certain degree of cost savings. An example could be an outsourcing solution that eliminates fifty jobs. As long as the buyer eliminates those fifty jobs, that cost-savings benefit is virtually guaranteed. The second point is that cost savings goes right to the bottom line, the profit number; therefore, a $1 million benefit is truly a $1 million benefit.

Let's look at the other benefit—revenue. Again we will look at the same two areas. First, if we talk about a benefit to revenue of $1 million, the buyer has to generate enough new business to create that new revenue. So even if the solution typically creates that sort of benefit, there is always risk since it is never guaranteed that the buyer can generate that much additional revenue. The second area to look at is the true cash benefit. Generating $1 million in revenue doesn't mean that $1 million flows to the bottom line. There is a cost of doing business, and those expenses must be deducted to get the true benefit. So only a percentage of that revenue number flows to the bottom line. Simply put, it costs money to make money.

The next executive decision-making criterion is **strategic alignment**. Depending on the company, this may be the most important. In order to achieve a sense of strategic alignment with your solution, you need to understand the company's strategy and the top business initiatives that drive that strategy. If you and the prospect together determine that your solution either aligns with or enables their strategy, or even better, helps them define a new strategy, then your solution provides strategic benefit.

Next on the plate is **risk assessment and mitigation**. It is no secret that executives, and all buyers for that matter, consider risk in any investment decision. They look at risks of your solution, risks of your company in general, risks of moving forward with another provider, and the risk of the "do nothing" alternative. Many salespeople are afraid to confront the subject of risk, but these discussions should happen early and often in your sales process. In this way, you will uncover perceived risks you didn't know existed and have the opportunity, in a safe setting, to show how you will mitigate those risks. You will also appear consultative because you can raise risks that other customers felt before buying from you, and then explain how those risks were overcome. The prospect will appreciate this in the end and feel confident that all risk issues were covered and dealt with. If you leave risk discussions to the end of the sales process, you risk having to backpedal and being caught in traps laid by your competition, and risk losing the deal altogether.

The fourth decision-making criterion is **political effects**. Each investment decision carries with it those constituents who favor another course of action. No matter how popular your solution, there will always be opponents. Understanding and having an appreciation for those internal politics and building the right alliances accordingly will go a long way to alleviating political issues.

Finally, there is **intuition**. Executives get paid to make tough decisions, and with each decision, gut instinct always plays a part. If the other four criteria are in your favor, then chances are that the executive's gut feeling will also favor your solution. And sometimes, when it is too hard to build the business case and quantify benefits, and the gut decision can carry the day.

In the following Chapter, we will discuss building a compelling business case, which will be necessary when selling to executives.

A Summary of Ideas on Selling to Executives

- If you want to have a good chance at winning, you must call higher and broader because:

  - Executives make the decisions.
  - They have the budget and the authority to buy.
  - They have a broader and deeper understanding of the organization.
  - They see the broader enterprise reach of your proposed solutions.
  - They can provide their unique perspectives on problems and solutions.
  - They have a deft understanding of the politics of the organization.
  - They can open doors among their peers and below.
  - Of the many versions of "the truth," theirs is probably most accurate.

- Executives value salespeople who have good business knowledge, who have done the research to understand their business, and who ask good questions to get their particular insights on business problems and solutions. They appreciate those who listen well and think before proposing, while also considering alternatives. Salespeople who understand how their solutions solve business problems and keep the executive meetings focused on business are highly valued.

- Too many salespeople fall into the trap of thinking the executive wants to know the minutiae of the products and services they offer. While executives may want to know a little, they are much more interested in how those products and services will solve their business problems. Focus on those *benefits* to dramatically increase your chances of success.

- Finally, decision-making. Although many personal and business factors influence decision-making, don't forget these five critical decision-making criteria: financial return, strategic alignment, risk assessment and mitigation, political effects, and intuition.

Chapter 28

Building a Business Case

When we consider the expansive and complex nature of technology solutions today—enterprise in scope, extensive professional and support services, integrated systems of various types and manufacturers—the justification process is difficult and often based on uncertainty. As sellers, we must approach our sales process in the same way our buyer approaches their buying process. We must work together with them to build the business case. It must be a collaborative effort.

If you are going to build a business case, you must know what it is and is not. A business case is a document that advocates a solution based on its ability to improve the prospect's business, and is framed according to the executive decision-making criteria. You may give a business case presentation in PowerPoint or other media, and at the same time have a written business case document. The presentation is just that, a presentation of your business case. The written business case, by definition, will be much more comprehensive.

This section describes the key elements of a written business case. The business case will take the form required by its use: a preliminary business case, a final business case, a written report, or a presentation. You will make decisions about the quantity and types of information included each time you prepare a business case.

The Major Elements of the Written Business Case

1 Introduction
2 Executive Summary
3 Assumptions
4 Tangible Business Benefits
5 Financial Analysis
6 Intangible Business Benefits
7 Mitigating Risk
8 Conclusions
9 Appendix

1) Introduction

The purpose of the introduction is fundamental. It simply contains appropriate information such as:

Name – Self-explanatory.

Date – Dating documents is standard practice but is especially important for a business case since the contents are based on information as understood at a single point in time. This must be clear when the business case is referenced in the future.

Purpose – The purpose should be stated briefly. Typically this would include whether it is either a:

a) *Preliminary Business Case* designed by you and the prospect to assess if solution consideration should move forward, or a

b) *Final Business Case* prepared by you and the prospect to fully support the final decision to move forward with your solution and to award the engagement to you.

2) Executive Summary

The executive summary sets the stage for the business case by "telling the audience what you are going to tell them." It should be provocative and brief and highlight only the most important business impacts of the proposed solution. Most of all, it must get their interest and attention.

❑ **Summary of findings** – Include a brief summary of the findings including the most compelling discoveries. These include the prospect's business issues to be addressed, how your proposed solution addresses these issues, and any copelling return on investment that results.

❑ **Scope of engagement** – This includes a definition of the "reach" of the project: geographical implications, areas of the organization that will be impacted, and the planning horizon used.

❑ **Scope of supply** – This includes a brief statement of your proposed solution. This is not a substitute for the detailed scope offered in a proposal, so do not make it so. Describe only the basics and be sure to include any part of the scope that differentiates you from the competition or that produces significant benefits.

3) Assumptions

Assumptions are a critical part of a business case. Without them none of the financial or non-financial effects of the solution can be estimated. When creating the business case, you and your prospect will develop many assumptions, all of which should be carefully documented and included in the appendix of the business case. This section is for emphasizing the assumptions that are overarching or have greatest impact on the conclusions. Important: Be sure to indicate the source and date of the information, and use assumptions whenever you cannot conclude that someone else will automatically use the same.

- **Business assumptions** – These are assumptions made about the prospect's business that are material to the case. For example: growth plans, divestitures, product launches, labor union status, etc.
- **Data assumptions** – These are assumptions that are required to calculate benefits. Since there are many data assumptions, be careful to emphasize only key ones that weigh heavily on the calculations or are likely to be points of contention when presenting your business case. You can include the remaining assumptions in an appendix.

4) Tangible Business Benefits

In this section you'll outline quantified benefits. All quantified benefits should be included but prioritized. (Note: When presenting the business case with stand-up presentation media, you may want to include a partial list in the body of the presentation and a full list in the report. Use your judgment.)

Give the most significant benefits the best visibility. Take the opportunity to emphasize *how* your solution produces the benefits. Do not allow the prospect to conclude that alternative solutions will produce the same benefits. This is a good place to differentiate your solution over a competitor's by showing benefits that only your solution can produce. If you can, include benefits that impact all levels of the organization.

Key Performance Indicators

Defining and explaining your value is far more meaningful if you do so using the language of your prospect. Managers at all levels manage their business to certain performance measures. We call them *key performance indicators* or KPIs.

Include here the key performance indicators that were considered. You should describe them in two ways when possible. Describe the change in the KPIs or its new value, and describe the measurable financial impact of the change. For example:

KPI	Impact	Financial Benefit
Inventory turns	Increase of 35 percent (3.1 from 2.3)	$235,000

5) Financial Analysis

In this section, summarize the financial impacts of the investment. Again, emphasize the measures that are most important to the prospect and the ones that reflect most favorably on your solution. For example, the prospect may be very focused on payback, but you may want to also emphasize net present value if your solution has significant long-term benefits.

Return-on-investment summary

Describe here the investment analysis measurements. Excel can do any of these calculations for you. Show alternative financial data if appropriate. For example, use two discount rates or a variation in the scope of your solution. Portray financial information graphically whenever possible. Explain the results and point out characteristics that may appeal to the prospect such as minimal upfront investment, short payback period, predictable cash flow, long-term benefits, and more.

Financial Measure	Value
Payback (months)	13.7
ROI (percent)	198 percent
Internal Rate of Return (17 percent discount rate)	142 percent
Net Present Value: 17 percent discount rate	$5.3 million

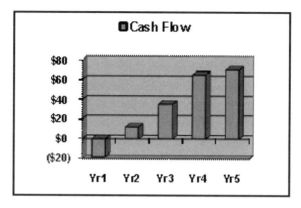

Net Present Value: 12 percent discount rate	$6.8 million

Financial statement impacts

If they have been determined, describe the impacts on the balance sheet, income statement, or key ratios.

6) Intangible Business Benefits

Depending on the prospect's decision-making criteria, the non-financial benefits often weigh in as some of the most important. Include in this section those benefits of your solution that have not been quantified. It may be useful to describe why they were not quantified—unreasonable assumptions, measurements not in place, too many assumed variables, etc. Always emphasize that it is the joint conclusion of you and the prospect that these benefits are realistic. Intangible benefits that can be tied to achieving the prospect's strategy often have the highest appeal.

7) Mitigating Risk

Risk analysis in a business case can take many forms from basic to sophisticated. Your risk assessment work should produce two pieces for your business case:

- **Risk assessment** – Include here the risks that are either the most important to the prospect or the ones that illustrate your strengths. Identify the risk and clearly state how your solution mitigates it. Also discuss the risk of the "do nothing" alternative.

- **Key dependencies** – Dependencies are the events, actions, or assumptions that success of the solution (and the ability to realize the potential outlined in the business case) are predicated upon. Outline here the ones with the highest impact on results. Use this section to assign accountability for the key dependencies.

8) Conclusions

As with the *Introduction* section, the *Conclusions* section is a summary.

- **Summary of findings** – Tell them what you told them. Repeat, in bulleted format, the major findings and emphasize those benefits that are most significant to the prospect based on their decision-making criteria.
- **Recommendations** – Your recommendation may be considered a given— to buy! However, if you have the opportunity to recommend alternative solutions for special circumstances or to position the implementation of the solution in a special way so as to help address special prospect concerns, then do so here. This will always increase your credibility.

9) Appendix

Include complete editions of key documents referenced in the business case, including:

- Investment analysis documents
- Key assumptions

Value Assessment Methodology

In order to work collaboratively with your prospects and build a business case with all the details discussed above, you must have a methodology to follow.

Value assessment is the consultative process of identifying the business impact of an investment according to the buyers' decision-making criteria, and assembling the business case that explains it. Value assessment is essential because of the shift in decision-making to the business buyer.

Value assessment is much more than using the word *value* or constructing a value proposition statement. The methodology teaches sales professionals to work consultatively with prospects to understand the financial and non-financial effects of their solution. Key prospect executives are involved early in the sales process to enable effective discovery and joint validation of value.

The Value Assessment Methodology

Implementing value assessment gives you a competitive advantage in a world of product-focused salespeople. Value assessment provides you with confidence and credibility when selling to business management and executives.

Value assessment requires certain selling behaviors that may be new or challenging for sales professionals. Among them are:

- Alignment of the sales and buying processes (not beginning your sales process late in their buying process, like with the issuance of an RFP [request for proposal], for example).
- Selling to executives (or the highest appropriate buyers for your solution); gaining access and executing high-impact meetings.
- Understanding the language of business (and each customer's business, specifically).
- Improved and focused account profiling methods.
- Developing collaborative efforts with the prospect to define the business impact.
- Being far more proactive in the sales process.
- Developing and presenting a business-based reason to buy. This is called a *business case*.

The Five Phases of Value Assessment

Before taking a deeper dive, let's take a quick look at the five phases of value assessment.

1) Profiling

Selling based on how your solutions impact your prospects' business requires solid, fundamental knowledge about their business issues. Profiling for value assessment goes beyond traditional profiling and must include those business areas that will prepare you for later phases. It should go without saying that profiling goes on throughout the entire sales process.

2) Executive Introduction

To make value assessment most effective, an executive mentor should be engaged early in the sales process, hence the name for this phase. In this phase, you aim to conduct the *first meeting*, where you will begin the executive-level relationship. Solid profiling will help make this meeting successful. Your goals for this meeting are to gain credibility and instill interest in your company as one that can provide value to the executive. There are two commitments you want from this meeting. First, you want permission to do the discovery work that will enable you to explore business issues and how your solutions might impact them. Once you've acquired this permission, you want assistance in knowing whom to meet with, and you want help setting up meetings with them. Second, you want to secure commitment for another meeting, the *executive feedback session*, where you will discuss the findings of your work with this executive.

3) Discovery

You got to this phase because the executive(s) believes there is an opportunity to create value, and you want to validate that. In this phase, you will work with key stakeholders in the prospect's organization to explore and validate all areas of value creation at each level of the organization, formulate and agree on assumptions, quantify the tangible benefits, agree on the intangible benefits, tackle issues of risk, and analyze the return on investment. The outcome of this phase is a jointly produced preliminary business case that explains the value that a solution you propose could create.

4) Executive Feedback Session

This is perhaps the most critical step in your value assessment. It is your opportunity to present the preliminary business case to the key executive(s). This is a "roll up your sleeves" type of meeting where, with the preliminary business case as a discussion document, you validate the findings of your discovery work and get agreement from the executive that the proposed solution (or an alternative) will produce value, and is worth considering more seriously. The ultimate objective is get their commitment for a final business case presentation to the buying team.

5) Business Case Proposal

It all comes down to this. Your business case has been modified and improved as a result of the executive feedback session. This is your opportunity, hopefully with your executive as a mentor, to present your final business case to the executive buying team in an attempt to win the business based on the business merits of your proposed solution.

With the overview of value assessment behind us, and using that as a frame of reference, we can discuss the importance of sales and buying process alignment. A fundamental requirement of value assessment is the alignment of the buying and selling activities.

What does that mean? It means that we need to put ourselves in a position to have access to the right people at the right time. If the two processes are not aligned, this can't happen. We might be trying to get in touch with the right people but at the wrong time, or be stuck with the wrong people at a time when they are in control. Here are some examples that show the advantages of proper sales and buying process alignment.

Let's first consider the dreaded request for proposal (RFP). When a salesperson engages a prospect in response to an RFP, this creates a reactive sales process whereby the prospect is in control. Why? Because the people we really wanted to meet were involved long before the RFP was issued, and now a different set of people are carrying on with the buying process. Unfortunately, the executives are no longer involved and have moved on to other activities. The buying process is now on a strict timeline, with deadlines for RFP responses and vendor selection. This part of the buying process is carried out by people who are below our prime targets. We are not in control, and in fact must react to them, and unfortunately our sales process becomes transactional in nature. Unless we can slow down their buying process by getting some high-level meetings, it will be tough if not impossible to win.

On the other hand, if the salesperson—the solutions provider—can engage the prospect earlier in their buying process, the required selling behaviors become much easier to accomplish. Why? Because we engage the prospect when they are not really buying; there is no pressure to buy or sell. We can actually get to know them and their issues and build the rapport and relationships that will be so important.

Moreover, we have easier access to executives because they have not pushed the latter phases of the buying process onto those who will execute it. We can be consultative. Perhaps they are still determining their strategy on the business and IT side, or looking at some internal ROI for technologies they may consider. Perhaps we have new knowledge or technologies that can provide business value the prospect was not aware of. In these cases, there may be an opportunity for us to help shape the characteristics of the process, or participate in writing the RFP, if there is one. Access to executives is imperative for value assessment, and it is important to note that one study shows executives are most often involved (80 percent of the time) in the early stages of the buying process. The earlier we can gain access the more success we will have. The lesson here is to align the earliest phases of our sales process with the earliest phases of our prospect's buying process.

A Detailed Look at the Value Assessment Methodology

Value Assessment Phase One: Profiling

Profiling is the beginning of value assessment. It is the research and information-gathering activities that prepare you for the sales process. Quality information is the *foundation* for value assessment and provides insights that enable more effective decision-making.

The objective of the profiling phase is to understand the prospect's business in order to prepare you for an executive-level relationship and to begin the value assessment process. Your opportunity for success in the next phase, the executive introduction, is greatly improved if you have a solid profiling foundation. Your credibility is improved. The questions you ask are more insightful. You differentiate yourself. You set the tone of the sales effort as *consultative* and focused on business improvement.

The profiling phase of value assessment should focus on current business conditions that influence current decision-making. This focus is critical because your objective is to influence their decision-making about an investment in your solution. Even though you are focusing on a decision in the near term, profiling data is both short and long term. Not only do you need to know what today's business pressures are, but you also need to align with long-term plans. Executives make decisions in the present that support or enable their long-range plans.

The key to profiling is simplicity, simplicity, and simplicity! Profiling documents have a tendency to become very complex and include far too much information. The process breaks down when too many people ask you to gather information that is important for *them*. Keep your profiling objectives focused. When considering whether a piece of information should be included in your profiling, use this question as a litmus test: Will it help me make better selling decisions? If the answer is yes, then include it. Always revisit your profiling practices to ensure a streamlined approach.

Most profiling tools we see are jammed with questions that have very little to do with the prospect's business. In fact, most are focused on the people and technologies in place, and not much else. Because of this shortcoming, we have developed the *Eight Critical Information Areas*, the *CI8*, that belong in every profiling tool.

1) Understand their current business strategy.

What is their business strategy and their top three to five business initiatives that will have to take place to fulfill that strategy?

2) Know their current financial status and trends.

Are they flush with cash? Profitable? Do they carry a lot of debt? What are their key financial metrics and how they compare to their competitors'?

3) Who are their key customers?

How long have they been with them, how do they help them, why do they stay with them (relationship, quality, satisfaction, cutting edge, etc.), and are any at risk of leaving?

4) Understand their key performance indicators.

Which KPIs are most closely tracked? How do they trend? How do they compare to industry averages or other targets? How can you help improve them?

5) Know the industry trends, threats, challenges, and opportunities.

What trends affect the prospect? Identify gaps with respect to the trends. How are they responding to them?

6) Know how the prospect competes.

What are their value propositions, their highest margin products and services? How do they position their products and services vis-à-vis the competition? Highest quality, lowest price, total solutions, regional, global, etc.

7) What are their plans for growth?

What is driving growth (acquisition, market share, new products?) How can you help direct resources to the Drivers?

8) Know how they would apply additional resources.

If they had more people, time, or money, where and how would they apply them?

Remember, profiling is an ongoing activity and solid work here will pay off enormously as you progress through the sales process.

Value Assessment Phase Two: Executive Introduction

Business executives drive investments and the sales professional must learn how to interact with them. While salespeople are conversant in all aspects of their solution, business executives typically are not. They speak a different language. A technology discussion will not produce a favorable result. A business discussion is a must.

The executive introduction phase includes all activities necessary to launch a high-level relationship in the account. The objective of this phase is to establish *credibility* for you and your company, to plant the seed of *viability* of your solutions, and as a consequence assert *control* over the sales process by involving the executive in your process.

Interaction with executives requires you to use their language. You must appeal to the framework of the business mind in areas such as:

- Strategic alignment.
- Management value.
- Dealing with risk.
- The financial dimension of investments.

To prepare for this phase, you need to build a foundation of profiling information that is focused on business knowledge. When you have gathered enough profiling information (remember, profiling is continuous throughout the sales process), it is time to schedule a meeting with one or more key executives. The best result of this meeting is approval to move to the next phase, discovery, where you will validate that you can produce value.

This meeting is called the *first meeting*, regardless of whether it is the first time you have met with this person. It is the first meeting in relation to the current opportunity. The commitment you want is the executive's support for a collaborative effort between you and his company to explore how value could be created by your solutions. Do not overreach! At this stage you are not seeking endorsement for your solution or, worse yet, an order.

First, you need to get yourself in the right mindset for this meeting. This means discussing the kinds of information that will enable you to have a more effective business conversation, ask educated business questions, and gain credibility with the executive. It is critical *not* to have an in-depth discussion of the solutions you offer in this meeting. Be cautious if the executive attempts to steer the conversation that way. But you can talk about the kinds of benefits your solutions have been known to create in other organizations. Just be sure to stay away from the technical details that will make their eyes glaze over.

That said, there may be a time when you would consider an in-depth discussion about your solutions; that is, when the customer has made some progress through his buying process and has already done some preliminary evaluation, and he has decided on a type of solution and called you in specifically to discuss that. If, through your research, you believe that he is going down the right path, then feel free to have that conversation, being careful to keep it at a level that is appropriate for the executive. But it is important to remember that the customer may not know how to best solve the problem and may not have evaluated all of the right solutions. Therefore, you should still ask intelligent questions to determine if he is on the right path, and if you believe he is not, be ready to act consultatively and make alternative suggestions.

To start down that road to understanding how your solutions create higher-level benefits, we will cover two topic areas: strategic and management value and risk mitigation. In conjunction with that, we will discuss the steps to conducting a first meeting that will achieve the desired impact. This knowledge will change the way you think about approaching such a meeting, and make you more business focused. Once you get to the discovery phase of value assessment, it will be incumbent upon you to discover and validate value you can produce at all levels of the prospect organization.

Let's get right into these topics to ensure you can make the most of your first meeting and beyond.

Strategic and Management Value

Strategic value is the value your prospect realizes due to your solution's ability to support or enable her business strategy. Supporting a business strategy has become a requirement. Enabling a business strategy is far less common but, if accurate, will be the single most powerful part of your business case.

Since business strategy is long range, strategic value will be realized over the long term. Business strategy is typically externally focused; examples are plans to deal with market share, competition, shareholders, the economy, and more.

Strategic value is recognized when there is alignment of your solution with the prospect's strategy. This means that the business impact of your solution is consistent with and drives her top priorities, contributing to the fulfillment of her strategy. For example, let's assume you are selling to a bank whose strategy is to capture market share as quickly as possible in a new geographical territory. Your solution is location-based intelligence that uses extensive data to show the locations in which to place new branches and/or ATM locations that will most quickly and profitably capture this additional market share. In this case, your solution not only aligns strategically, but also is a key component of helping banking executives to achieve their strategy.

It is likely that most or all proposed investments that make it to the executive's desk are good investments. So she will need to find the *best* investments. Clearly, investments that are tightly meshed with the top priorities of the company and also produce a compelling return on investment will be viewed most favorably. Having a solid understanding of how you have helped other customers in a strategic fashion will be very valuable here.

Management value is the value executives realize due to your solution's ability to improve how they manage their business. Management's work is internally focused and emphasizes the medium-range time frame. Management deals with financial results, organizational efficiencies, human resource matters (labor issues, employee satisfaction), and more.

An example could be a CRM (customer relationship management) solution for marketing that provides precise and detailed data to optimize marketing campaigns, enabling the VP of marketing make better decisions regarding upcoming campaigns. Because of the data available, the VP can target campaigns more effectively, optimize the money spent on each campaign, and get a better take rate, all while making those decisions more quickly and with less risk than before.

Accordingly, if your solution helps them make better and faster decisions with less risk, gives them more time to think strategically, enables them to make their budget go further, or helps them get more done in less time, those could all be categorized as benefits to management.

Risk Mitigation

Senior managers deal with risk in many aspects of their work. The life of an executive has few absolutes, so an important priority is to eliminate uncertainty and surprises.

It is true that effective managers are risk takers, but that is out of necessity. That said, there isn't a manager alive who doesn't welcome the opportunity to mitigate risk: the ability to make tough decisions with more certainty, to have predictable spending, to eliminate the stress caused by worrying.

When it comes to making investment decisions, risk is an evaluation criterion. More specifically, an executive is looking to minimize it. If risk is high, so must be the reward. Therefore, your ability to mitigate risk is a direct contribution to value. A sales plan designed to bring a measure of certainty to the prospect's uncertain world will be viewed favorably.

In this section, we will examine two categories of risk that will be important to your sales efforts: solution risk and business risk.

Solution Risk

Solution risks are all risks associated with the investment being evaluated. They can be risks of your proposed solution, a competitor's proposed solution, and even the risk of the "do nothing" alternative. These risks are generally internal and are to a certain extent controllable. Often the buyer can take steps to minimize them. Examples include:

- The solution itself, for example:
o Is the technology proven?
o Is the application proven?
o Integration issues.
o Information security.

- The project:
  - Possibilities for business disruption.
  - Timeliness.
  - Budget overruns.

- The solution provider:
  - Financial health.
  - Experience.
  - Project management skills.
  - Vertical market expertise.

Business Risk

Business risks are those risks associated with running the business; they are unassociated with your company or solution. They can be internal (labor issues) or external (the economy), and management may or may not be able to control them. Regardless, management seeks effective ways to deal with them, and they often figure into company strategy.

You may think it unusual for a solutions provider to have a significant impact on business risk. However, never overlook the possibility. In fact, some solutions are designed specifically around them. If you can logically link your company or solution to mitigation of a business risk, it will be a very powerful piece of your business case.

Business risks can be generic or very specific to the prospect's vertical industry. Examples include:

- Labor issues.
- The economy.
- Currency exchange rates.
- Weather conditions.
- Disgruntled employees.
- Fluctuations in consumer demand.
- Changes in supply chain models.
- Changes in government regulations.

Following is an example of a business risk that can be mitigated by a solution. Suppose you are the CIO of a major credit card company and your ability to quickly approve card purchases is key to your business. In fact, it is your business. It goes without saying that immediate access to your data and the ability to process requests is at the heart of that approval process. Any number of risks can jeopardize that data and temporarily shut down the business process of card approval. Examples include the actions of a disgruntled employee, flood, fire, power surges, weather, and more. A disaster recovery solution that ensures that data is mirrored on other servers, perhaps hundreds of miles away, can keep the business up and running in the event of disaster in the primary data center. So it is possible that you may sell solutions that mitigate business risk.

It is important to understand that risk is both a *business matter* and *personal perception*. Certain risks may be commonly believed or they may be conceived in one prospect's mind. Whether they are real or misconceptions, the bottom line is that they are real to your prospect.

Do not risk ignoring risk! Perception of risk must be addressed early and often in your sales process. If you address it early, you are in control and have the opportunity to address it in a positive manner. If you wait too long and have the prospect bring it up, you risk being put on the defensive. This is never to your advantage.

Here is an example of how you might address a potential risk early, and in a positive fashion. Perhaps you have reason to believe that your prospect feels risk in your solution because he is unfamiliar with the track record in the marketplace, or perhaps a competitor put a negative hint in his mind. You might say something like, "Mr. Prospect, you might be wondering about the track record of our solution since you have not seen it before. I'd like to share with you two specific successes, with substantiated and verifiable ROI, from two companies that had similar challenges to yours. I'd also like to bring in our VP of operations, who will share our proven seven-step project management methodology with you. As well, I will provide references who will share their experiences and insights." Addressing risk in this manner shows the prospect that you have been there before, helps cement the consultative nature of your sales process, and helps to instill trust in you, your solution, and your company. Also, if a competitor later tries to instill doubt about your project management methodology to your prospect, he will have already heard it addressed in positive manner by you, and will be much less likely to believe the competitor's story.

Risk is a central part of executive decision-making, and it should be leveraged to your advantage in the sales process and in your business case.

Gaining Access

We have talked enough about calling high that by now you should understand its importance. But you may be wondering how you actually get access to that level.

All research we have seen on this topic—and experience bears it out—says that the best way to gain access is to get an internal recommendation. In absence of that, having a recommendation from a well-known and respected colleague outside the prospect's organization is another great way to gain access. After that, we are back to the old methods of cold calling, sending letters, befriending the gatekeepers, voice mails and e-mails.

Having the ability to sell at the executive level is useless if you can't get in the door. Thus, mastering access skills is critical. Since we've covered this in other areas of this book, we won't discuss it here.

As you do your research on the prospect, look for technical and business issues that your solutions can address. Find out how far along the company may be in evaluating these issues and how to solve them. This will help you determine if they have begun a buying process, and if so, how far along they are. Armed with that knowledge, you can make a solid guess as to whether the company's executives are currently involved, and perhaps willing to see you.

Executives typically get involved early in the buying process to:

- Understand current business issues.
- Establish project objectives.
- Set the overall project strategy.

They typically move on to other, more pressing issues while their buying team examines alternative solutions, explores options, and evaluates vendors in order to make a decision.

After the decision has been made, executives typically re-engage:

- At the end of the buying process or later, and are usually part of the final approval.
- In planning and implementation of the project.
- To supervise the measurement of results.

As you can see, by the time many sellers come into the picture at the RFP phase, the executives have moved on to other matters while their buying team engages the vendors. Extraordinary circumstances notwithstanding, as the executives re-emerge late in the buying process, they are hesitant to overturn the decision or recommendation already made by an internal buying group.

The bottom line: if you want to build executive-level relationships, you must become involved early in the buying process. You must be perceived as someone who can help executives achieve their business objectives, otherwise you are just another vendor relegated to the RFP process. And in that situation your chances for success are dramatically reduced.

Before you continue, you need to ask yourself a very important question. "Just who are the executives important to my sales process?" Why is this important? First of all, you may not be familiar with who exactly gets involved in the decision. Often you are selling at a level in the organization that is too low, perhaps one to three levels too low. So you need to move up. But where? Depending upon a number of factors, your executives will be different. Some of those factors are:

- What are you selling?
- What is the required investment?
- How large is the company?
- What areas of the business does your solution impact?
- Where does your value message resonate most clearly?
- Is your solution strategic to the company and/or business unit?
- Where is your competition positioned?
- Who actually controls the budget and/or writes the check?
- Who are the stakeholders that benefit (or don't benefit) from the decision?
- Who has your own marketing department told you to call and why would the prospect be interested in talking with you?
- Where have others in your company had success?

If you are selling technology solutions and services, your "executives" will not always be only the "C" level types (CEO, CFO, COO, CTO, CMO, CIO, and others). Yours could be lower and/or broader. Most of the time, business unit executives have a big hand in buying what you sell. You need to answer the above questions and develop a plan to meet with the appropriate people.

Executives are busy and need a valid business reason to meet with you. Possible reasons for granting such a meeting are:

- Existing relationships.
- Your company's reputation.
- Product or service viability.
- An internal referral.
- You are a strategic partner.
- Quantified success in a similar organization.
- New technology that could shape their strategy or help them compete.

Along with the valid business reasons, you need to have a strong **initial value message** to get an executive's attention, and you need to provide a reason to listen. If you can educate him on market trends and best practices, that further strengthens your value to them. You may think of the initial value message as the thirty-second elevator pitch.

Initial Value Message

In value assessment you will use two value messages: the initial value message (IVM) and the specific value message (SVM).

The initial value message is a general yet compelling statement of the value you create for clients. It is not always prospect specific but must be specific to their market. And it must differentiate you enough that you won't sound like every other vendor trying to get in the door. So work hard to make your IVM as strong as possible.

An effective initial value message will:

- Generate interest and command attention.
- Offer a reason to listen further.
- Demonstrate credibility.
- Represent the rationale for exploring a business relationship.

The initial value message is used early in the sales process for generating:

- Demand for creation scenarios.
- Access to vehicles such as letters and phone calls.
- Business networking encounters.

The components of the IVM are:

- Your company's expertise in a particular product or service.
- Your experience with similar businesses.
- Business problem(s) you solve.
- High-level value that results from your product or service.

Here's an example of an initial value message:

Based on our expertise in	medical imaging technology
and validated through our work with	83 percent of East Coast hospitals and 72 percent nationwide,
we have proven our ability to	increase radiology staff productivity and diagnostic efficiency,
resulting in	a reduction in staff required to serve patients and an increase in accurate first diagnoses.

Tips and recommendations:

- Do not sound scripted when you deliver your IVM.
- Make it sound natural.
- Change the base wording to ensure it flows; for example:

"Based on our experience in medical imaging—which now covers 72 percent of hospitals nationwide and 83 percent here on the East Coast—we routinely increase radiology staff productivity and diagnostic efficiency. This results in serious improvements in staff-to-patient ratios, along with a significantly higher percentage of first-diagnosis accuracy."

Practice delivering the IVM out loud. Leverage your profiling data, especially regarding:

- Industry trends and threats.
- Known points of pain for this prospect.
- Verifiable success with similar organizations.

Remember, the IVM is only the beginning, by getting attention and providing a reason to listen. You must also be ready to discuss specific successes, preferably ones that are documented and verifiable.

That said, your competitors likely have good initial value messages and success stories as well. What will truly set you apart from your competition and build credibility is your knowledge of your prospect's industry and business, and the questions you ask. And the more sincere your delivery and the more you make an executive think, the more credibility you will build. Your best questions, and the way executives answer them, will expand their understanding (and yours) of the problem and solution.

Starting at the top can lead to more business and shorten the sales process. But you must be prepared because calling at the top can be risky. Once you get in, you must quickly establish credibility, ask insightful questions, and keep the conversation at a business level. Your goal is to get commitment from that executive for further discovery and have them be a sponsor/mentor and coach.

First Meeting

The first meeting is the ultimate goal of the executive introduction phase of value assessment. It is the opportunity to establish an executive relationship for the entire sales process and for the entire account relationship.

As we have stated, the first meeting can come about for a variety of reasons, but regardless of that reason, the purpose is always the same: to explore new ways to create value for them.

Your objectives for this meeting are to:

- Establish credibility for you and your company.
- Establish viability for investing in solutions such as yours.
- Continue to learn as much as possible about the CI8.

You are also seeking a commitment from them, which is this: You want the executive(s) to agree that a) you should work with his/her organization to discover *if* and *how* your solutions could create value for them, and that b) they will hold another meeting with you to review your findings.

The first part of this commitment is the *discovery* phase of value assessment, and the review meeting is the *executive feedback session*.

The due diligence work you have done in profiling and your evaluation of value and risk mitigation now begins to pay off. The insights you gained will help make the first meeting successful. If the meeting results in the commitment you seek, then your first meeting was a success and you have gotten off to a good start. If you can't gain any commitment from the executive following the first meeting, then you have likely not generated enough interest in working with you.

During your meeting planning process, it is always good idea to e-mail a proposed meeting agenda a day or two in advance to allow the executive to prepare effectively and have an understanding of expectations. If the executive has an assistant or secretary, you may wish to e-mail that person a copy of the agenda as well. That said, once you get into the executive's office, there is a four-step process for conducting this meeting.

1. Confirm the objective.
2. Feedback.
3. Body of the meeting.
4. Commitment.

Step 1: Confirm the Objective

From the outset you want to establish rapport. For this meeting, however, small talk is not suitable. Get to business quickly so as not to waste time (yours or theirs.) You will establish rapport by being consummately professional and respectful of their time and position. Therefore, from the outset, state the objective of the meeting and confirm it with everyone present.

A meeting objective should have these characteristics: *clear, measurable, achievable.* Also, your objective must be, by definition, linked to the commitment you seek.

A good example of an objective could be: To understand your specific issues relating to the performance of your sales resources along with the decision-making process for sales improvement solutions.

Step 2: Feedback

Always ask for feedback before proceeding. You planned this meeting based on a known set of circumstances and may not have had much dialogue with the executive(s). You need to learn about any previously unknown perspectives, or if anything has changed recently that would change the emphasis, direction, or even the objective of this meeting.

The previously e-mailed agenda will help in this process, and often there will be nothing extra to discuss. But when there is, it is essential to factor it into your meeting plan. You may need to quickly change the meeting strategy to meet your objectives. You may even need to revise your objectives or the commitment you seek.

Step 3: Body of the Meeting

This is bulk of the meeting and what you have prepared for. The structure of the meeting body will change depending on the type and objective of the meeting: it is a persuasive meeting if you are trying to close; it is informational and discovery oriented if you are probing for business issues and educating the executive.

As we discussed earlier, your objective is to establish credibility while working toward a commitment for discovery and an executive feedback session. So, for this meeting, there are three key elements to be prepared for:

- Deliver the initial value message.
- Tell a credibility story.
- Ask appropriate questions.

You can deliver an IVM, tell a credibility story, or both depending on the length and time you have. The reason for starting this way (after steps 1 and 2, of course) is to earn the right to ask questions. Imagine walking in, introducing yourself, sitting down, asking if they thought the agenda was okay, and then asking, "Could you please share with me the top three business priorities that are essential to achieving your strategy?" You will not earn the right to ask questions with that approach. But if you can show them that you have "been there" by sharing a little of what is going on in their industry and how you have helped other companies overcome challenges those industry trends present, or how you have helped them leverage those trends for business gain, you will get them thinking about whether you might be able to the same for them.

At that point you have earned the right to ask questions. It is never a bad idea to ask permission before asking questions. But don't think this meeting is all about you firing off a bunch of questions from your list. This meeting is very much a dialogue, not an interview, and your initial questions will start that dialogue. Don't be too adamant about getting through your list of questions in this meeting. Instead, be sure to listen to the executive's answers and ask questions based on his responses. He will appreciate that and feel that you were truly listening and probing for his business issues.

Step 4: Commitment

Every meeting must end with a commitment. Know your desired commitment in advance and organize your entire meeting accordingly. Your ultimate objective is for their support for discovery work, access to the right people to conduct that discovery work, and a meeting to review the findings.

You may not earn that commitment so it is important to plan for alternatives. Further, understand what is the minimum level of commitment (or lack thereof) that you are willing to accept in order to continue investing in the prospective customer.

Should you get that commitment, you need to make the most of the upcoming discovery phase. You should:

- Identify the key stakeholders you need access to.
- Ask for the executive's assistance in arranging meetings with them.
- Gain permission to keep the executive in the loop.
- Agree on the date for the executive feedback session.
- Establish the criteria for the success of that meeting.

If you don't quite get the commitment you want, you need to know why. In some cases, there is some interest but you are relegated to working with someone lower in the organization. In that case, it is important to ask, "Can you share with me why you feel that would be the best person to work with?" The answer will tell you a lot. In any case, try to get permission to keep the executive in the loop.

And what if the meeting is completely unsuccessful? At that point you need to re-evaluate the circumstances. Did you do a poor job, meet with the wrong person, not have a compelling value proposition, or fail to uncover or create a current need in the company? Any of these and more could be factors for an unsuccessful meeting. In any case, take a look at the reasons and decide if you still want to pursue an opportunity in that organization. Look at things like strategic importance to your company, other relationships, etc.

It is important to note that the first meeting is a phase of value assessment, and the term should not be taken literally. You will likely have more than one first meeting, especially in circumstances where a proposed solution would have multiple decision-makers or deliver benefits that cross different lines of business.

A Last Note on the First Meeting

What is the first thing you do when walking into a prospect's office? If you are like us, you look him in the eye, introduce yourself, shake his hand, and take a seat when you are directed. At some point, you steal a quick look around the office to quietly assess the person's interests and style. *Don't* ask questions about those interests before starting the meeting! That is waste of the prospect's time, and the closer you are to the executive level, the more that holds true. What about building rapport? Again, that rapport is built by being the consummate professional, and getting down to business and conducting the meeting as expected. There is time for nothing else. If you want to ask a personal question, save it for the walk to the door. For example, on the way out, you might say, "Joe, I really enjoyed our meeting and appreciate your insights. I couldn't help but notice that you went to Ohio State. My eldest son is considering that. Perhaps someday you could share some of your perspectives with me." That keeps the meeting all business, ends it at the right time, and shows respect for the time commitments of a busy executive. You never know— perhaps he or she will have some time and keep you at the door engaged in conversation for another fifteen minutes.

Value Assessment Phase Three: Discovery

The discovery phase of value assessment includes all the activities required to build your preliminary business case. Depending on what you sell, these activities will vary widely. Certainly you will need to meet with a number of people to uncover needs/opportunities and discuss possible courses of action to address them. The objective is to validate that you can create positive business impact, and collaboratively build the preliminary business case that explains it.

Following the discovery phase, you will be conducting another meeting (executive feedback session). This is a consultative meeting that will be a discussion of your findings—*not* a persuasive presentation of a business case and a solution. The most effective approach is to have a team consisting of you, key people from your company, and key people you met with from the prospect's organization. With this team in place, you will present your findings.

With this in mind, discovery work must be a *collaboration* between you and the prospect where you examine all possible ways to improve the business. Discovery work is all about *exploration* and *evaluation* of areas of improvement and *agreeing* on the expected areas of return.

Much of the work that you began with—profiling and the executive introduction—will be refined and reinforced in the discovery phase. Strategic and management benefits you thought you might be able to create should be validated, logically linked, and cross-referenced with others. Risk mitigation, a key subject at the executive level, is also an important subject to explore at all levels of the organization. Additionally, you will explore the operational benefits of your solution—how a proposed solution can positively impact the operational areas of the organization, and what KPIs are affected and how. This top-to-bottom assessment of value allows you to develop your solution value profile that highlights value created through:

- Strategic benefits.
- Management benefits.
- Operational benefits.
- Risk mitigation.

Discovery blends with many traditional selling activities and aligns with what are commonly called the *need creation* and *solution development* phases of many sales processes. Some of your sales process activities may include:

- Questioning to identify problem areas, uncovering pain, and aligning your solutions to provide relief.
- Identifying all decision-makers and developing positioning plans for each.
- Formulating the scope of your solution according to the expressed needs.
- Driving a gap between you and your competition.
- Validating your solutions via product demonstrations or references.
- Accommodating technical requirements by providing specifications, discussing service level agreements, defining terms and conditions, performing demos, and more.

In discovery, you will validate strategic and management value and how you mitigate risk, at the same time probing to discover and highlight the operational benefits a proposed solution could produce. Then, in collaboration with the prospect, you will quantify all benefits he should expect. With that in mind, the discovery discussion will include:

- Operational benefits.
- Quantifying benefits.
- Finance for salespeople.

Operational Value

Most solutions have direct impact on the operational level of a business—the business processes. Your products and services may improve throughput, save raw material, reduce overtime, shorten cycle times, create more sales, lower operational costs, reduce full-time equivalents (FTEs), etc.

Most technology solution salespeople are good at understanding how their solution produces benefits at the operational level. In fact, many of them had technical positions in similar companies before making the jump to sales, so they are in their comfort zone when talking technology.

Linked Processes

Most solutions are targeted at a specific operational process, area, or function; however, it is quite common that benefits in other areas of the business will happen automatically, and many salespeople don't consider this in their selling. We call these secondary process benefits *linked processes*. For example, a solution may be targeted at improving a function in marketing such as direct mail campaigns, but may bring benefits in sales, accounts receivable, and other areas. The best way to determine if this holds true is to ensure you meet with people of influence in other business areas of your prospect's organization and learn their business processes. Then you can confidently point to areas where your solution can add improvement. Since most benefits at the operational level are quantified in money, failure to identify all these benefits lowers the ROI projection and lessens the perceived value of the solution, not to mention making price a bigger issue than it has to be. So be sure to closely examine, through questioning, exactly how your prospect sees the solution impacting the operational areas of his business.

Understanding the concept of linked processes helps you in many ways as a salesperson, increasing the ROI of your solution, since you will identify broader-reaching benefits, and be able to include those in your business case.

- Providing greater access opportunities since you now understand the broader reach of benefits. If you don't gain access where you first target, you can create a business conversation that will appeal to other executives.
- Having the opportunity to develop more business-based relationships on any one account. The more people you know, the more successful you will be. And as people leave for other jobs, your network grows into other companies.
- Talking business with a broad-reaching executive base raises their perception of you as an asset and consultant.

Key Performance Indicators

As we've mentioned, you will have far greater success if you define and explain your value using the business language of your prospects. You will be more effective in articulating value if you are able to demonstrate your solution's impact on KPIs because they are inherently important to the prospect. You need only to seek agreement that your solution has a positive impact on the prospect.

Every manager is measured either on profitability directly, or on how well her operations perform when compared to certain measures (and compared to her budget.) For example, a production manager is measured on meeting production targets (widgets per day) or a quality target (percent of product within specs). A sales manager is measured on total sales, sales per salesperson, average margin, etc. An accounts receivable manager may be measured on days-sales-outstanding or a productivity measure such as invoices per employee.

If you can demonstrate that you will impact KPIs in a favorable way, you are speaking the language of the prospect and you are proving a very solid set of operational benefits.

Benefits Analysis and Quantification

Once you have looked into the benefit areas your solution can address, it is time to learn how to quantify those benefits that can be quantified. All return on investment measures compare two things: benefits and costs. *Cost* represents what the prospect pays you (and other cash outlays required to implement your solution), and that isn't too difficult to derive. ROI in any of its various forms—simple ROI, payback, NPV, IRR (see definitions below)—isn't hard to figure either with the aid of a calculator or spreadsheet. This leaves *benefits*, the numerator of the equation.

When it comes to benefits quantification, there are only two types of benefits: *tangible benefits* are quantified in money, and *intangible benefits* are not. Who decides if a benefit is tangible or not? The safest rule is to let your prospect decide. The prospect must measure the benefit and then have a means to convert the results to money. For example, assume that increased employee satisfaction is a benefit your customer recognizes from your solution. Does the prospect measure employee satisfaction? If so, can they convert a change in employee satisfaction to money?

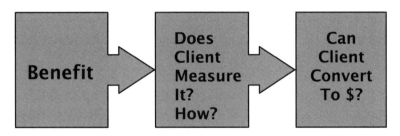

Assumptions

Assumptions are a critical part of a business case. Without them, none of the financial or non-financial effects of the solution can be estimated. In development of the business case, you and your prospect will develop many assumptions, all of which should be carefully documented and included in the appendix of the business case.

Assumptions come in two fundamental types: business assumptions and data assumptions. Business assumptions are those made about the prospect's business that are material to the business case. For example: growth plans, divestitures, product launches, labor union status, their part in implementation, etc. Data assumptions are those that are required to calculate benefits. Since there are many data assumptions, be careful in your presentation to include only key ones that weigh heavily on the calculations or are likely to be points of contention when presenting your business case. The remainder can be placed in your appendix.

Typically, when it comes to quantifying benefits, operational benefits are the easiest. As benefits become more strategic, they become more difficult to quantify. The foundation of all benefits analysis is the ability to make assumptions. Together, you and your prospect are trying to reasonably predict the future. For that reason, all benefits analysis efforts are based on making assumptions about the factors and figures involved.

Data assumptions are made for simplification and prediction. Here are examples of each. When calculating savings from overtime reduction, it may be too cumbersome to research the exact amount of overtime for each person and their associated wages. You may want to use approximate figures to derive an average. This is simplification. Similarly, it may be necessary to estimate the number of employees in a department over the next three years. In this case your prediction is your assumption.

In the absence of good assumptions, you may wish to use industry averages if they are available. They may be used as long as the prospect is fully aware and in agreement. To maintain your credibility, it is vital to have the prospect supply or agree on the assumptions. This is one more reason that collaboration is key in the discovery phase of value assessment.

Finance for Salespeople

Once assumptions are agreed upon and the benefits are quantified, it is time to look at the cash flow benefits. To sell effectively in today's business environment, it is imperative that salespeople have the knowledge and resources to show these benefits. They must communicate with senior executives in a language they understand—the language of business. That language is financial! Further, managers at all levels are being asked to look at investments with a financial eye, which makes financial knowledge essential.

Cash Flow Analysis

Measuring an *investment return* requires knowing the impact on cash flows. Return analysis is a comparison of benefits (positive cash flow) and costs (negative cash flow).

The following four measures may be the most common:

1. Simple return on investment 3. NPV – Net present value
2. Payback   4. IRR – Internal rate of return

While learning about financial concepts is important, it is equally important not to attempt to over-educate yourself. Your job as a sales professional is to be able to articulate the financial effects, in basic terms, of buying your solution. A CFO does not expect you to be as well versed financially as she is, so don't try to be. In fact, efforts to go too far can easily backfire if you allow yourself to wander into a discussion you are not equipped to have.

Make certain that you know the fundamentals: the measures, how and when they are used, and an understanding of discounted cash flows. Then progress to being able to recommend certain measures based on their advantages or disadvantages. Eventually you'll learn various forms of the investment analysis measures you're likely to encounter. And if you're working with someone in the prospect's organization who is not as well versed on cash flow analysis as you are, you may have the opportunity to educate that person and help her sell the financial benefits of a proposed solution to her boss.

You must *balance* your role as a sales professional and your role as an investment analyst. Always be prepared for a financial discussion, but never be afraid to say that you'll enlist the support of more knowledgeable colleagues. Now let's discuss the most common cash flow measures.

1) Simple ROI (SROI)

Definition:
Net benefit [benefits – costs] ÷ cost of the investment = [expressed as a percentage]

Formula:
ROI [percent] = net benefit ÷ costs x 100

Example:

	Benefits	Costs	*Net Benefit*
Initial		7,500	(7,500)
Year 1	3,200	0	3,200
Year 2	4,200	0	4,200
Year 3	4,800	0	4,800
Year 4	5,500	0	5,500
Year 5	5,500	0	5,500
	$23,200	$7,500	
		Simple ROI=	209%

The chart to the left depicts the ROI over a five-year period.

Notice the columns displayed in the chart—benefits, costs, and net benefit.

Net benefit is simply benefits minus costs.

So, remember, our formula for simple ROI is:

ROI [percent] = [benefits – costs] ÷ costs x 100
= $23,200 – $7500 ÷ ($7,500) x 100 = 209 percent

For a desirable investment, ROI must obviously be greater than zero, although the prospect "hurdle rate" (the required ROI) will be higher. (Hurdle rate is the rate that the prospect considers as the minimum allowed.)

SROI doesn't take into account the time value of money (to be discussed later), and the calculated ROI percentage is independent of the timing of the cash flows over the years. Thus, looking at the above example, no matter what years in which the $23,200 benefits occur, the simple ROI will be the same.

2) Payback

Definition:
The amount of time it takes for the initial investment to be recovered.

Formula:
Payback (in time) is calculated by summing the net benefits and determining when they equal zero. The result is expressed in units of time.

Example:

	Benefits	Costs	Net Benefit	Cumm Net Benefit
Initial		7,500	(7,500)	(7,500)
Year 1	3,200	0	3,200	(4,300)
Year 2	4,200	0	4,200	(100)
Year 3	4,800	0	4,800	4,700
Year 4	5,500	0	5,500	10,200
Year 5	5,500	0	5,500	15,700
	$23,200	$7,500		
	Payback=	24.3 Months		

Notice the cash flow of the benefits after the initial investment of $7,500. By the end of year two we have almost recouped the initial investment. So in this case, based on the incoming cash flows, we have a payback of 24.3 months.

Payback is often used as an initial hurdle for an investment, meaning that if it passes the payback test, it may be further evaluated.

When using payback, conventional wisdom says sooner is better. How soon is dependent upon the investment and defined by the prospect.

Payback doesn't take into account inflation or the time value of money. Also, the cash flows beyond the payback period are ignored; the benefits that occur after the payback has been achieved don't figure into the payback calculation.

Time Value of Money

Before we continue with the next investment analysis measures, let's talk about the time value of money.net present value and internal rate of return require an understanding of this concept.

$1 today is worth more than $1 tomorrow, right? Therefore, $1 tomorrow is worth less than $1 today. How do you calculate *how much less* the $1 is worth? By *discounting*. This involves using a *discount rate*. The discount rate is used to discount future sums in the same way an interest rate is used to compound present sums. In this way, a future stream of benefits (incoming cash flows) is "discounted" to determine what it would be worth today.

Discount rates are determined by such things as inflation, the prospect's cost of capital and various risk factors for that type of investment. The best way to find the actual number is simply to ask your prospect what value she would use for the investment.

3) Net Present Value (NPV)

Definition:
The value, in today's dollars, of a stream of net benefits received over time.

Formula:
Sum of discounted net benefits, value expressed in dollars.

Example:

	Benefits	Costs	Net Benefit	Discount Factor	Discounted Net Benefits
Initial		7,500	(7,500)	1	(7,500)
Year 1	3,200	0	3,200	0.893	2,858
Year 2	4,200	0	4,200	0.797	3,347
Year 3	4,800	0	4,800	0.712	3,418
Year 4	5,500	0	5,500	0.636	3,498
Year 5	5,500	0	5,500	0.567	3,119
	$23,200	$7,500		NPV= $	8,739
Discount rate = 12%					

The table at left shows the same cash flows again discounted at 12 percent. By summing the discounted net benefits including the *initial investment*, we get a total NPV of $8,739. When the NPV is greater than zero, that indicates a positive investment, so in theory the investment is acceptable.

NPV considers the time value of money, takes into account the entire life of the investment, considers cash flow timing, and shows the total net cash flow of the investment.

4) Internal Rate of Return (IRR)

Definition:
Assumes that NPV = 0; in other words, the rate of interest that would cause the discounted net benefits to be equal to the initial investment.

Formula:
It is the discount rate that makes NPV = $0. It is found by selecting discount rates, using them in the NPV calculation, and iterating until the result is NPV = $0.

Example:

In order to gain an understanding of how IRR is determined, let's calculate one manually. Since we need to find the discount rate that makes NPV = $0, we must begin by experimenting. Using the same cash flows from previous examples, let's find the NPV using a discount rate of 60 percent. As the chart below shows, the NPV = ($1,323). Using a discount rate of 50 percent, the NPV = ($265). NPV is still negative but getting closer to zero. Using a discount rate of 40 percent, the NPV = $1,127. We now know that the discount rate must be between 40 percent and 50 percent, much closer to 50 percent. By interpolation, the discount rate that sets NPV = $0 is 48 percent. Therefore, the IRR is 48 percent.

Never fear, however. IRR can be calculated easily with a financial calculator or spreadsheet application.

	Net Benefits	Disc Rate = 60%		Disc Rate = 50%		Disc Rate = 40%	
		Discount Factor	Discounted Benefits	Discount Factor	Discounted Benefits	Discount Factor	Discounted Benefits
Initial	(7,500)	1	(7,500)	1	(7,500)	1	(7,500)
Year 1	3,200	0.625	2,000	0.667	2,134	0.714	2,285
Year 2	4,200	0.391	1,642	0.444	1,865	0.510	2,142
Year 3	4,800	0.244	1,171	0.296	1,421	0.364	1,747
Year 4	5,500	0.153	842	0.198	1,089	0.260	1,430
Year 5	5,500	0.095	523	0.132	726	0.186	1,023
		NPV=	$ (1,323)	NPV=	$ (265)	NPV=	$ 1,127

IRR is approximately= _____ 48%

Your prospect will likely have an IRR hurdle rate that must be overcome. If this is the case, the IRR of your solution must be greater than this value in order to be considered.

IRR is effective in comparing investments of different amounts and lifetimes, given that you are comparing buy versus buy, or lease versus lease since it yields a percentage return.

Value Assessment Phase Four: Executive Feedback Session

The executive feedback session is perhaps the most critical stage of value assessment. It requires the most preparation and is the first opportunity to *validate* that a solution you are evaluating can actually produce the desired business result.

The objective of the executive feedback session is to gain commitment from the executive to sponsor or mentor you moving forward with a business case presentation to the executive decision-making audience.

This is not a persuasive meeting, but rather a discussion of the findings you uncovered as you worked with the executive and her team during the discovery phase. You should use the preliminary business case as a framework to discuss your solution and its impact on her business. The better your preparation and the more collaborative you were in the discovery process, the better your credibility and subsequent outcome will be.

This meeting should be well thought out and planned, and you should use the four-step meeting process. Here is a brief outline of the four steps for this meeting:

1) **Objective** – to share the results of the team's work that show how value could be created with a solution, and if warranted, take the steps necessary to prepare for the final business case.

2) **Feedback** – Don't forget to ask for input before proceeding! What has changed or transpired? What feedback has the executive(s) received from his own people about the discovery work?

3) **Meeting body** – a consultative sharing of information during which you are always seeking validation on each point, using the preliminary business case as a discussion document.

4) **Commitment** – You will need to decide how high to shoot. If you have a strong team and strong preliminary business case, perhaps you can press for submitting a proposal and final business case.

    During this open dialogue discussion, there are many items to cover. They include:

- The presentation of your preliminary findings.
- Validation of your solution and its impact on the prospect's business.
- Validation of your assumptions and financial calculations.
- Ensure the solution tackles the agreed upon business challenges and/or technology issues.
- Gaining agreement on the preliminary business case or major parts of it.

Since the desired outcome of this meeting is executive sponsorship and a commitment to move forward, keep the following in mind to help with the meeting:

- Use the team (you and the prospect).
- Prepare to defend your assumptions and prepare to get eaten alive (the executive *will* challenge you—he is putting his credibility on the line if you move forward).
- Be ready to tackle any objections that arise.
- Work together to retool your assumptions and other numbers if required (this may be very repetitive and you may spend extra time here).
- Tie in the eight critical information areas (CI8) from your first meeting and link your solution to those.
- Have your feedback session criteria in mind and be sure to meet them before leaving.
- Make specific recommendations for moving forward.
- Be ready to close if the meeting leads you there.

Specific Value Message

One of the outcomes of the discovery phase is the ability to construct and articulate an SVM (specific value message). The SVM is customer focused and is a specific statement of value based on prospect business information. It is a summary of the business case, and therefore the SVM is a great way to quickly summarize the value your solution will produce. It is also an effective way to open up the presentation portion of a meeting, including an executive feedback session.

An effective SVM will:

- Help establish the rationale for investing with you.
- Communicate that important problems are solved.
- Include financial results.

The SVM is used late in the sales process for:

- Quickly summarizing the value your solution provides.
- Converting interest to confidence.
- Competitive differentiation.
- Establishing the basis for buying.

It differs from the initial value message in that it must be specific to the company and your solution, it includes a stated ROI, and it is backed by solid discovery work and agreement on assumptions for business improvement.

The components of the SVM are:

- The team members.
- Problems solved or opportunities created.
- Measurable business improvement.
- Financial impact.

Here's an example of a specific value message:

Based on our findings working with	our industry consultants and your team, including the radiology chief of staff and clinical staff,
we are confident that we can	relieve the diagnostic bottlenecks without adding staff.
This would impact your business in the following ways:	a 13 percent increase in procedures that should prevent the requirement for additional staff for two years.
This would result in	a 79 percent ROI over two years with a seven-month payback.

Tips and recommendations:

- Like the IVM, do not sound scripted when you deliver your SVM.
- To help make it sound natural, change the base wording to ensure it flows, for example:

"We assembled a team of our industry consultants to work with various people in your hospital—the radiology chief of staff and clinical staff—and together we are confident that we can relieve the diagnostic bottlenecks that have frustrated doctors and patients and cost the hospital referrals. It is very realistic to achieve a 13 percent increase in procedures, which would allow you to maintain staffing levels for at least two years.

You could expect the investment to pay back in about seven months and have 79 percent return over two years."

- Practice delivering it out loud.
- Leverage your profiling data, especially industry trends and threats and known points of pain for this prospect.

Consider for a moment the reworded example above and visualize the tone of the meeting. The executives are receiving a briefing from their own staff, so when you use the word "we," it takes on a collaborative meaning. The facts, figures, and results have immediate credibility because of this approach.

There is an opportunity to make a powerful difference in this meeting as compared to the first meeting. In the first meeting you may have asked, "If you had the luxury of 5 percent more staff, what would you have them do?" Or, after discussing the industry challenges the prospect faces, perhaps you asked, "If you applied money or people, how would you address those problems?"

In your notes you have valuable nuggets. Your proposed solution avoided hiring for two years. You can now point out that the executive now has either money or people available to deal with those priorities. Citing the problems specifically is very powerful and demonstrates your problem-solving intention.

What's Next?

Obviously, the desired outcome of the executive feedback session is to move forward to the final business case presentation. In that case, your executive sponsor should assist in finalizing the business case and setting up the meeting with the executive buying team.

Unfortunately, the outcome is not always what you want. If you have to go back in the process, consider your options. All may not be lost. Some level-headed analysis of how good the potential opportunity is (big $, high margin, strategic customer, etc.) and if you still have executive sponsorship will help you decide whether to go backward and how much additional time to invest. Sometimes it is best to cut your losses and wait for another opportunity as market conditions and people change.

On the other hand, if you still have executive sponsorship after being asked to go back for more discovery, that is a good sign to continue. You just have to decide based on your criteria. If you stay in the game, decide with your sponsor and team what needs to be accomplished before the business case presentation. Then ask for another executive feedback session.

In the long run, if you did your homework, planned well for the meeting, and have a fairly compelling solution that will look great with some additional tweaking, your chances for success are quite good. But only you can determine how much additional time to invest.

Value Assessment Phase Five: Business Case Presentation

The business case presentation is the *culmination* of a successful sales process; you are finally ready to secure the business. The better the executive feedback session and resultant *coaching* from your executive sponsor, and the more *compelling* your business case is, the better your chances are for moving to the next phase— *closing!*

The objective of the business case presentation is obviously to win the business.

This is a persuasive meeting, and you have done a lot of work to get here. So be sure to treat it with the importance it deserves. There is no "winging it" at this point. You have to be perfect. Here are few keys:

- Get pre-meeting coaching from your sponsor and brief him or her on what to expect from you.
- Position the solution as dealing with key business issues.
- Fully understand the roles of each person who will be present.

Just like the executive feedback session, this meeting should be well thought out and planned, and you should use the four-step meeting process. In this meeting, the body will consist primarily of a final business case presentation with questions and answers. Along with that, here are a few other tips for success:

- Play to the power in the room.
- Have a compelling opening and closing.
- Make sure your assumptions are documented and defendable.
- Consider all possible objections and be ready for them.
- Link your solution to the eight critical information areas (CI8).

- Barring unforeseeable circumstances, make recommendations to move forward.

If you win the business—congratulations! When the decision to move forward is made, solidify the next steps to get the deal inked and on the path to implementation and delivery.

If there are no strong buying signals, try to determine what it is about the solution or business case that did not resonate effectively. If that can be overcome, perhaps you can still move forward without too much additional work.

What if you fail? That can happen. The best thing is to debrief with your sponsor and decide on a suitable course of action. Perhaps you go back to discovery, wait until conditions and people change, get others involved, or redefine your solution.

The good news is that if you sailed through the process and had strong executive sponsorship along with a compelling solution that addresses the company's key business issues, you will more than likely be successful.

Value Assessment Summary

Value assessment may be a departure from the way you are used to selling, but if you use it, you will get results. We have countless success stories to verify that. Imagine getting to a whole new level in your prospect organizations, having the knowledge to speak their language, being viewed as a trusted resource, and having the ability to build a business case with them—ultimately, advocating a solution that will improve their business.

Compare that with selling in a transactional environment where your contacts are low and you have no control over the sales process, trying to snag deals on price because you can't differentiate any other way. Which position would your rather be in? We thought so.

For more information please visit: **www.pretiumpartners.com**

A Summary of Ideas on Building a Business Case

- Value assessment is the consultative process of identifying the business impact of an investment, according the buyers' decision-making criteria, and assembling a business case that explains it.

- Perhaps the most important aspect of a successful business case is that it is built collaboratively with the customer. Too many buyers discount sellers' business cases as biased and invalid. But when you build it collaboratively with them it becomes "their" business case, and therefore becomes credible and believable.

- It is much easier to build a business case in a proactive environment, such as when you get high-level buy into the idea early in your sales process. Conversely, doing business case work in a reactive environment, such as in response to an RFP, is very difficult.

- Getting high-level buy into the idea of discovery and business-case work makes the process smoother because the executive can pave the way by arranging meetings with and providing insights into the critical stakeholders.

- The executive feedback session is a time when you can validate your findings and make adjustments to the preliminary business case so that it will be ready for a final business-case presentation with the decision-making team. This is not a persuasive meeting but rather a consultation-oriented one.

- There is a difference between a written business case and a business-case presentation. The latter is just what it implies, a presentation of your business case. Present the most critical elements but have the written business case or other supporting documentation on hand.

- Be sure to align your business case with the customer's strategy whenever possible, and differentiate from your competition by showing business improvements not otherwise achieved without you and your solution.

- Your high-level relationships are critical. When everything else is similar and differentiation between solutions becomes more difficult, your relationships and the credibility you have with the customer will usually tip the scales in your favor.

SECTION VI

OBJECTIONS

Chapter 29

Preparing for Objections

Many salespeople consider objections a bad thing, but they are actually a good sign. You *want* objections. An objection tells you the person is with you—they've been listening, they've been paying attention, they are considering your offer, but there is something in the way that may prevent them from taking action. View the objection as someone saying, "I'd like to buy your product, but you need to show me how or why I really need to buy it." They've given you an objection and now are waiting for your response.

While it's true that some people really aren't interested and will waste your time because they simply can't say no, you want to assume that if the prospect hasn't said, "I'm really not interested", asked you to leave or hung up the phone, you simply need to help them past the objection so they can buy.

So how do you get to the point where you look forward to objections? First, realize that only truly interested prospects will give you objections; and second, realize that objections actually move you closer to the sale.

When you become experienced at handling objections, you'll actually enjoy getting them. A prospect will give you an objection, and you'll practically laugh out loud and think, "I can't believe they think *that* one will slow me down." There's nothing like going into the sales call completely confident and prepared to answer any objections.

Ten Reasons You Get Objections

Here's our top ten list of "real" reasons people give objections and/or don't buy:

1) The prospect has no need or simply is not interested.

Example: The Eskimo looks around and sees nothing but ice, and there you are with ice to sell. "What would I ever need more ice for? Get outta here."

In a case where a person is truly not interested, he or she may simply say no and walk away without even giving you one objection. Again, if someone is listening to you and hanging around to give you an objection, it usually means he or she is at least considering your offer, but there is a hurdle in the way. You need to help the prospect find a way over the hurdle.

2) The prospect doesn't see the urgency.

Example: A tightrope walker with eight kids and a wife knows he should probably buy life insurance, but he just doesn't think he needs it *right now*. Another example: A twenty-seven-year-old musician with a wife and one child on the way has thought about life insurance, but it's not really a priority.

3) The prospect doesn't have any money.

Example: No money. Okay, another example: She may think she has to pay 100 percent up front and she's not able to do that.

4) The prospect can't make the decision by himself.

Example: His wife will kill him if he makes the decision without her. Another example: A person only has authorization to sign orders under $20,000 and this order is for $30,000.

5) The prospect doesn't like you, your product, your company, or a combination of the three.

Example: You played football for Michigan, the prospect is from The Ohio State University. Another example: He used your product a year ago and was thoroughly disgusted with it.

6) The prospect is satisfied with the current vendor.

Example: She gets what she wants, when she wants it, and it operates the way she thinks it should. Why ruin a good thing?

7) The prospect has a friend or family member in the business.

Example: His father is his supplier and they're best friends too. Good luck.

8) The prospect simply doesn't want to change.

Example: Similar to being happy with the present vendor but a little more laid back. "Hey, things are cool. Why change?"

9) The prospect believes his situation is about to change.

Example: A professional juggler just lost his hand while feeding the sharks at SeaWorld. Another example: A mid-level manager hears that substantial layoffs are just around the corner.

10) The prospect thinks she can do it herself. In other words, she doesn't need you.

Example: The guy down the street just bought the entire set of "do-it-yourself home repair" books, and now he's ready to build a skyscraper from scratch that will dwarf the Sears Tower. Yet another example: In 1999 and for the better part of 2000, everyone with a computer who was online trading was a stock market genius.

Those are the "real" reasons why people won't buy and why they'll give you objections. However, people may not give you their true objections. Instead of saying they can't afford it, they'll tell you they want to think about it. Instead of telling you "I don't like you," they'll tell you they're happy with their present vendor. Any objection a prospect gives may be true, but, more often than not the objection is simply a way to put you off without being rude. Most people don't like to say no. They would rather be polite by giving you an "excuse."

Often potential buyers are also affected by their egos. Prospects don't want to admit they can't afford it or can't make the decision on their own. Consequently, they give you an answer they think you'll buy and then they stick to it as long as you let them. It is your job, through questioning and listening, to find the true objection.

Becoming Great at Answering Objections

Here are the steps to becoming great at answering objections:

1) Write down all the possible objections you may encounter.

Every product and service has certain objections that come up over and over again. Ask other salespeople, especially the top salespeople, what objections they've had. They'll probably come up with quite a few. You should end up with at least ten or so depending upon what you're selling.

2) Come up with answers to each objection.

Once you have determined all the possible objections, ask the top salespeople for their answers to these objections. Record their answers. Don't ask mediocre or poor salespeople for their answers, even though they will likely be the most willing to help. You want "top" results, not mediocre or poor. Mediocre and poor salespeople can share their objections—these should be universal. But beyond discovering what the real objections are, stick with the top people for the answers.

Start with your first objection. Let's say it is "I have no money." Ask the top salespeople this question: "When you get the 'I have no money' objection, what do you say?" Record their response, if possible. You want to get the entire response from start to completion. Although each top salesperson will typically have a favorite response, you want to get more than one. Ask them what they say the second time they get the objection, the third, and the fourth. Take as many answers as they will give you.

As we mentioned earlier in this book, you want to ask these questions during non-selling hours. Also, ask the top salespeople if you can have some time with them to go over objections. Obviously, you don't want to run up to them, stick a recording device in their face, and start firing questions. Let them know it will probably take fifteen minutes or so and ask if the present time works for them. If not, ask them when they might give you a few minutes.

3) Write or type out your responses to the objections.

Play back the recording and write down all the responses to the different objections. With each new objection, start with a new sheet of paper.

You can change some *minor* words to make the responses feel more comfortable. However, *be very careful nor to change the meaning!* Keep the wording as close as possible to what you originally received in the recording. The top salespeople are getting the top results because of what they are saying and doing. If you change what they are saying, you will get different results. It's best if you don't change the wording at all.

4) Get all supporting information together.

By supporting information, we mean testimonials, newspaper or magazine articles, industry studies, and any other proof that helps support your response to someone's objection.

For example, let's say one of the objections on your list is, "I think our company is just too small for this program to be of any benefit." If this is a standard objection, your company probably already has some testimonials from companies similar in size to the one you're calling on. Here is an example of a testimonial to support your answer to this objection:

> "Before we began this program, we thought our company was simply too small to see any benefits, yet after the first three months we saw a 27 percent increase in production, a 16 percent reduction in cost, and a 21 percent reduction in turnover that led to a savings of nearly $34,000."

If you or your company don't have testimonials such as this one, get some immediately! For instance, you may also have an article from a respected industry publication that shows how companies similar in size are benefiting from a product such as yours.

Listen to the objection, hear the prospect out *completely*, answer the objection and use your supporting evidence to back up your answer to the objection.

5) Put all the pieces together.

Now that you have all the pieces, put them together. First read through the answers to the objections and see how they flow. Do you need to make some changes, or are the answers flowing fairly well? Add the supporting pieces and then practice the entire process. Next, get together with the top salespeople and your manager. Go over what you have and make any necessary changes.

6) Practice, drill, and rehearse.

Once you have a final version for each objection, practice, drill, and rehearse until you know each one like the back of your hand. You want to get to the point where you can answer objections in your sleep.

7) Practice on prospects and customers.

After you've practiced your objection responses, go out and answer some objections in the real world and see how it goes. As we've already said, don't call on your largest prospect first. Make your mistakes on the small guys.

After a few days of calling on people, evaluate your progress. Did your answers go as well as you expected, not as well as you expected, or better than you expected? Are there any changes you should make? Talk to the top salespeople and your manager again and see if they have any feedback for you. Make any final changes if necessary, and then go back out into the world with confidence! Continue to revise your answers and come up with better approaches as time goes on.

There you have it: the seven steps to preparing for objections. Remember, anytime you get an objection, welcome it as a sign the prospect is interested and listening. If you get one you haven't encountered before, get some answers from the top salespeople, practice, drill, and rehearse the answers. Then hit the streets confident that the next time you hear the objection, you'll roll right over it.

Rules for Handling *All* Objections

Here are the rules to follow when answering objections:

1) Listen well and hear the prospect out.

Listen well during an objection, maintain eye contact, and give the prospect visual cues that you are listening, such as leaning in and nodding occasionally. People need to know you are paying *very* close attention to what they are saying. If the prospect is not being straightforward with you, he will usually become uncomfortable and have a difficult time continuing to mislead you when he knows you are listening intently. If he is being straight with you, he will also lean in, look you in the eye, and convey his thoughts more thoroughly. In addition, he will get the sense that you care about him and his problem because you are paying such close attention.

Once the prospect has finished talking, sit in silence and slightly nod your head for five seconds before you begin to speak (count to five by 1-1,000, 2-1,000, etc.). Often, the prospect will be uncomfortable with the silence and will begin to expand on what he has just said. Occasionally, he will even attempt to explain away the objection himself before you get a chance to open your mouth. Even if he doesn't expand on his ideas any further, the pregnant pause gives the prospect the impression you are listening to him very well, and it gives you additional time to think about what the prospect has just said and how you're going to respond.

There are two other good reasons to pause after you "think" someone is finished speaking. First, she may not be done speaking and people hate to be interrupted. Second, often the prospect will give you key information after the pause.

2) Question the objection.

Your goal in questioning the objection is to get the prospect to expand and give you a better understanding of where he is coming from. A secondary benefit is that by expanding on the objection, he may talk it away all by himself. Sometimes, the more people talk about something and the more they think about it, the more they start to question their own reasons for the objection.

Here are a few different ways to question the objection:

a) State the objection back to the prospect as a question.

If he says it costs too much, say, "Hmm, it costs too much?" And don't say another word until he speaks. At that point, he will usually expand on the objection.

b) Ask the prospect what he means, how he means it, or if he can elaborate further on what he means.

You can say, "Could you expand on that a little for me?" "It costs too much" all by itself doesn't give you much to go on. He may mean he can't pay 100 percent of the cost up front, he may not know there are different pricing options, or there may be other reasons why he believes he can't afford it. In order to answer the objection, you need to know exactly what he means.

c) Ask a quick probing question that gives you more information.

After "It costs too much" you could follow with, "How much too much?" You could also follow with, "So, if we could resolve the issue of price, you'd be ready to go ahead?"

These questions allow the prospect to expand on the objection, and his answers will give you more information about the objection. Is it the only objection? How serious is the objection? Is this a true objection?

3) Isolate the objection.

In the last example, we isolated the objection with the question: "So if we could resolve the issue of price, you'd be ready to go ahead?" You want to ask this question to find out if price is the only objection or if there are others. If you get a yes to this question, you know you have only that one objection to overcome. You can then get on with handling it. If you get a no to this question, you need to ask what else is stopping him from moving forward.

For example, "Mr. Prospect, what else is preventing you from moving ahead today?" Get *all* the objections before you start answering them.

4) Handle the objection(s).

Once you've heard the prospect out, discovered all of his objections, and found out as much as you can about each one, it's now time to respond to the objection(s).

Although you will probably end up with a favorite answer to each objection, it's important to have several in your arsenal. When you answer an objection:

- Cushion your response.
- Handle the objection.
- Get an affirmative answer.
- Give three powerful features/benefits.
- Tie the prospect down to those benefits.
- Close.

Here's an example. Let's say you're selling dental equipment and a prospect tells you she has no money for a new machine that will streamline her tooth restoration business. You will:

a) Cushion your response.
"Jane, I definitely understand that, but let me ask you a question."

b) Handle the objection.
"If I could guarantee you that this new machine would pay for itself in the first year and then save you an additional $25,000 per year would you be able to come up with $25,000?"

c) Get an affirmative answer.

d) Give three powerful features/benefits and tie the prospect down to them.
"Jane, $25,000 is pretty much the minimum amount that most dentists are saving with this machine, we've seen some as high as $47,000 per year.

"Second, with this new machine you'll be able to do restorations on the same day, during the same visit creating additional cost savings and saving time for both you and your clients in that you won't need to schedule a second appointment.

"Third, you and your clients will see a positive difference in the quality of the restoration and the restoration will last longer. At the same time, you'll be able to charge more due to the added quality and convenience. Based upon this evidence, do you see how this machine will both make you and save you thousands of dollars?"

e) Get an affirmative answer to your tie-down question above and *close*.

You want to make your proof for moving ahead so powerful that she cannot help but answer your tie-down question with an affirmative *"Yes!"* Once she's answered in the affirmative, close:

"Jane, would you like to purchase this outright or would you like to see our payment plans?" Look her directly in the eye and be completely quiet until she answers you.

Those are the rules for answering all objections. Now let's look at when to deal with objections.

When to Deal with Objections

There are three times to deal with objections:

1) Up Front in the Qualifying Stage.

In the qualifying stage you aren't really handling objections; instead, you're making sure you don't have any. As you "qualify" the prospect for money, decision-making ability, and urgency, you effectively eliminate, "I have no money," "I need to talk to someone else," and "I think I'll hold off right now."

Here are some examples of qualifying to eliminate objections:

- "Joe, if I call you with an idea that you agree is a great investment opportunity, would you have fifty thousand dollars liquid and available with which to take advantage of such an opportunity?"
- "Cindy, who else will be involved in the decision-making process?"

- "Jim, when are you looking to make a buying decision on this equipment?"

The qualifying stage will vary based upon your product and how you encountered the prospect. For example, if you're a business insurance salesperson cold-calling business owners on the telephone, you generally will have to do a lot more qualifying than if you are selling cars and someone comes into your showroom. In certain circumstances you can make assumptions or it may be more or less important to qualify people. If Donald Trump walks in to buy a Mercedes, you can pretty much be assured he has the means to pay for it. Or if you're selling shoes that almost everyone can afford, obviously qualifying for money is not number one on your priority list. However, if you're selling houses, you need to know something about the buyer's financial means in addition to need and desire.

Some salespeople who have an objection that continually arises during the presentation will also handle that one before the presentation. We'll give examples of this soon when we look at handling each individual objection.

2) Hit it head-on during the presentation stage.

The second-best time to handle an objection is during the presentation stage. With this approach, you isolate the objection and get agreement from the prospect to move ahead once the objection is eliminated. You then take on the objection, make it go away, and close.

3) Never. With this approach you essentially ignore the objection.

This approach is probably the least used and is our least recommended way of handling an objection. You will simply hear the prospect out, give a strong benefit of your product or service that the prospect hasn't heard yet, and then close again.

Chapter 30

The Price Objection

We're dedicating an entire Chapter to the price objection because this is the one most salespeople run into most often. This objection can come at you from a number of angles. It can relate to not having enough money, not seeing the value in exchanging it for your product, or being able to purchase a competitive product for less than what you are charging.

Money is the one factor that causes more objections than anything else. Let's face it—if you were giving your product or service away, and people recognized any value at all to it, everyone would want it. What would make them pause and think? The amount of money required to pay for it. That being said, let's take a closer look at the price objection.

First, here are the "real" reasons you get the price objection:

- The prospect really can't afford it.
- The prospect doesn't want to get it from you or your company.
- The prospect is definitely not interested in buying and any excuse is as good as any other.
- You haven't built enough value and/or urgency.
- You're dealing with a cheapskate.
- A combination of the above.

Occasionally, you'll truly have a price objection as in the first point above. In other words, the prospect *really* can't afford your product, or thinks she can't. That's why it's important to qualify the prospect properly in the qualifying stage. That way you'll know whether you have a "true" price objection or if the price objection is simply a stall.

Preventing the Price Objection during the Qualifying Stage

The type of product or service you are selling and how you acquired the prospect will determine how you handle the price objection in the qualifying stage. Here are the factors to look at:

363

1) Is the prospect pre-qualified?

Have you, or someone else, cold called and qualified the prospect for money? Did the prospect respond to an advertisement that specifically spelled out the qualifications of those who should respond? Did someone who already has given you insight into the financial qualifications of this individual refer the prospect?

Even if the prospect comes to you pre-qualified, verify the information yourself. You don't have to use questions that are quite as direct as those you would ask on a cold call. However, you want to know that the assumptions you have are correct.

Let's say the person has responded to an ad that states: "Only people who have $50,000 liquid and available for a lucrative franchise opportunity should respond to this ad." You can qualify the prospect financially simply by saying something like, "And you have $50,000 available if this sounds like the kind of opportunity you're looking for?"

If someone has prc-qualified the lead for you, again, verify the information. The person who qualified the lead may have a certain lead quota or may be a little too enthusiastic to put the lead in without having qualified the lead as best as he could have.

Note: Most of us were taught when we were children not to ask people how much money they make, have, or anything even closely resembling the subject. We are here to tell you that this belief can literally kill your sales business. If you do not get over this, depending upon your product or service, you will spend hours upon hours trying to sell your product to people who are not financially qualified to buy. You will get all the way to the end of a long presentation and find out that the person is on government assistance or can not qualify for a loan on a Snickers bar. Not only is this a waste of time, it can also be very discouraging when you put in an enormous effort for absolutely nothing.

2) Are there certain assumptions you can make about the prospect's qualifications?

Do you have some background information on the prospect that qualifies him or her? For example, do you know if she is a member of a country club that requires a certain net worth? Is she a well-known public figure in the community who is recognized as someone extremely wealthy?

Note: Be careful not to make assumptions in this area. For example, don't assume that because the person who referred you is wealthy, the referral must be too. If you have reliable information, great. Otherwise, verify what you have before moving ahead.

3) How affordable is your product to the general public?

If you are selling a product that almost anyone can afford, qualifying for money becomes much less important. For discussion purposes, we are going to assume that your prospects require some type of financial qualification.

4) Did the prospect approach you or did you approach the prospect?

Did you cold call the prospect or did the prospect walk in off the street? If the prospect approached you, he or she probably has a pretty good idea of what your product generally costs. Simply ask how you can help.

5) Is your product or service something that everyone needs, or is it something that someone can either have or do without?

Are you selling something like insurance, or are you selling Lear jets? If you are selling something that everyone needs, it becomes a question of how much they can afford as opposed to whether they can afford it. After discovering needs and desires, present the plan you feel is best and be ready with alternative plans—one more comprehensive and one less comprehensive.

6) Whom are you selling to?

If you are selling to individuals or small companies, you need to qualify for money. If you are selling to major corporations, the government, schools, or banks, you need to find out what the budget is, but you also need to focus on "when" they plan on making a decision or which fiscal budget the money is in.

7) Does your product or service vary widely in price depending upon which model is chosen, options are chosen, or which additional services are chosen?

Some examples would be cars or technology items such as computers, cameras, stereos, etc. Ask questions to determine needs and desires.

8) Is the prospect currently getting your product somewhere else, and what is she paying for it?

If the prospect is already buying your product or service from someone else, she is already qualified and already has a budget set aside. If you don't know whether she is currently getting the product, ask. If she is getting it, find out what she is paying for it. Here are a couple of questions to ask to determine this:

- "What are you paying for this right now?"
- "Would you like to keep your payments in the same range they're in now?"

Here are some industry-specific examples of qualifying the prospect for money:

Real estate:
- "What price range are you looking in?"
- "Do you plan on financing some, most, or all of the purchase price?"
- "Do you already have a mortgage company or bank you're dealing with?"
- "Have they pre-approved you for a certain dollar amount?"

Brokerage / financial services:
- "If we find an investment that sounds and looks good to you, would you have fifty thousand dollars liquid and available for such an idea?"
- "When you see a company you'd like to own some shares of, how much do you typically invest?" After the prospect answers, say, "And if we come across an idea you really like, is that amount liquid and available now?"

Automobile industry:
- "Do you typically buy or lease your vehicles?"
- "Will you be financing the purchase?"
- "What amount of monthly payment are you looking for?"

Selling products to a large company or major institution:

- "How much have you set aside in the budget for this project?"
- "Will you be spreading the cost of this over more than one fiscal year?"
- "Are you looking to purchase or lease the equipment?"

The answers to the above questions will help you get a handle on where the prospect is financially before you spend an inordinate amount of time with him or her. Occasionally, however, you will still run into the price objection during your presentation.

Handling the Price Objection during Your Presentation

Building value and showing the prospect how she can own your product should be an intricate part of your presentation and, if done right, will eliminate the price objection all together. If there are other objections, or you *don't* do a good job of building value and showing the prospect how she can own your product, you'll then have to deal with price in the form of an objection during your presentation.

Think of the price objection as a set of weight scales with two sides. On one side is value and on the other side is price. What is your product or service worth? What does your prospect believe your product or service is worth? The second question is the most important and the one that will determine whether the prospect ultimately buys.

In order for the prospect to buy, the "value" side of the scale must be more heavily weighted than the "price" side, to a degree. If value outweighs price, the odds of making the sale are very good. If value is completely overwhelming, you may run into the "too good to be true" syndrome. This isn't good either. Your objectives are to ask a fair price and build value that is better than that price.

You build value by building "evidence" that your product or service is worth the money. Again, your objective when building value during the presentation is to prevent the price objection altogether.

What follows are some answers to the price objection when it does occur during the presentation.

Some Answers to the Price Objection

As we mentioned in the last Chapter, with any objection you first want to isolate it to find out if that is the only one or if there are others. When you get the price objection, simply say, "Kathy, outside of price, what other concerns do you have?"

If she has other concerns, you want to know about it. You don't want to overcome the price objection only to find there are five more objections behind it. At this point, the prospect will either give you some other objections or tell you that price is the only concern. For this discussion, let's assume that price is the only objection.

As we also mentioned in the last Chapter, you want to question the objection to determine exactly what the prospect means. When someone tells you she can't afford it, press her for more information about it. "When you say you can't pay for it, do you mean you can't pay cash up front for it or…" then look at her and wait for her to elaborate. If she says that it *is* the fact that she can't afford the whole cost up front, you can then offer her other methods of payment. Do you have a financing plan, a lease plan, or do you accept credit cards? Do you have no money down, same as cash, no interest for ninety days, or any other specials that make your product easier to own?

Give her all the options that are available and then break the number down to the daily cost. "Kathy, instead of paying the whole amount up front, you can take advantage of our financing plan and low interest rate. That way, the price breaks down to $2.37 a day over the life of the loan. How does that sound?" We will soon discuss more about breaking the price down to the lowest dollar amount. So your first answer to the price objection is to offer an option the prospect *can* afford.

Another approach to "it costs too much" is simply to ask, "How much is too much?" Let's say you're selling a car with a price of $20,000. If the prospect says it costs too much ask, "How much too much?" If she says, "Well, gee, the highest I could go is $19,000," you simply need to figure out how you can get into that price range.

Could you take off some options and get close to $19,000? For example, "Cindy, frankly the special alloy, 17-inch wheels aren't something that a lot of people are going to notice. It will take virtually nothing away from the car if we go with the 16-inch standard wheels and you'll save $400, which will get you down to $19,600. How does that sound?" You haven't taken her all the way down to the $19,000, but you've lessened the amount. Also, by removing some items from the product, you've found another way to get it into the prospect's range without cutting price, which should be your last resort.

Another approach is to spread the financing over a longer period and reduce the monthly payment to something more comfortable. The bottom line: if you ask, "How much is too much?" and the prospect gives you an answer, nineteen times out of twenty if you can hit the number, or come close, you'll have yourself a sale. Get creative.

At other times you may find that you are not that far apart. If you're at $20,000 and the prospect only planned on spending $19,500 and you know you can meet that price, simply offer to meet the prospect in the middle at $19,750, or you can go all the way and say, "Okay, I'm willing to do $19,500. When would you like to take delivery?"

Break price down to the lowest dollar amount. This is the Smallest Price Possible Close, which is also covered in the section on closing. With this approach, you'll break your total price down to yearly, monthly, weekly, and finally, daily cost.

Let's say the cost of your product is $10,000. Take the average life of your product—let's say it's ten years—and divide that number into the total cost. The cost of your product is $1,000 per year, or, divided by 365, the daily cost of your product is $2.74 per day. State the lowest number to your prospect as an investment, not cost, of $2.74 per day: "Joe, that's an investment of just $2.74 per day. Surely you can find that in your daily budget to enjoy all the great benefits we discussed. Am I right?"

Another variation of this approach is to break down the *difference* in price between you and your competitor to the lowest dollar amount. Let's say your price is $10,000, and the competition's price is $9,000. Take the difference, or $1,000, and break it down just as you did in the first example. Divide $1,000 by ten years (or the typical life of your product), and then divide the yearly number by 365 days to come up with a daily cost difference between you and the competition. Once you've done this, give the prospect your three strongest benefits versus the competition and ask if the additional daily investment is worth it. You might say something like this:

"Joe, with our product you will get protection of your investment with the ability to upgrade to any future features we come out with. You will also get a machine that will last, on average, 33 percent longer than the competitor's unit, which will keep more money in your pocket longer and save you additional money. Also, your uptime will be an average of 8 percent better than with the competition's machine, making for a higher profit margin for you and happier customers and employees.

"Now Joe, if we break down the price difference of $1,000 between us and the competitor over the average life of an ATM, or ten years, that difference comes out to 27 cents a day. Joe, let me ask you a question. Is protection of your investment, 33 percent longer life, 8 percent better uptime, and happier customers and employees—all of which will save you much more money in the long term—worth an additional 27 cents a day up front?"

Here's a third variation of the "lowest dollar amount" technique. Let's say your product has an average life of ten years and your competition's product has an average life of eight years. When you present the price for your product to the prospect, give her a per-year price as opposed to a total price. Once you've done this, urge her to break down the competition's price based upon the average life of their product. Now, instead of presenting a proposal to the prospect with an investment of $10,000, you present a proposal with a price of "$1,000 per year*" and put an asterisk after it. You then bring her attention to the note next to the asterisk on the bottom of the page that reads: Based upon an average life of ten years." Next, present your proof to the prospect showing that the average life of your product is ten years versus the competition's average product life of eight years. Again, tell the prospect to take the competition's price and divide it by eight to get the annual cost of the product. Now you're at $10,000 with an annual price of $1,000 per year, and the competition is at $9,000 with an average price of $1,125 per year.

There's a saying that statistics can be used to argue any side of an issue. This last variation of the "lowest dollar amount" technique is an example of this.

Note: You have to have some very strong evidence to use this third variation of the "lowest dollar amount" technique. The best evidence or proof is a study, or studies, done by a highly respected, independent researcher(s). Similar "proof" would be articles found in accepted industry publications by well-known and respected independent reporters. Next would be strong testimonials backed by thorough, objective research that could be presented to the prospect.

Remember that once you lower your product or service to the level where you're competing solely on price, you've now become a commodity and the prospect will see you as exactly the same as everybody else. Every time you go back for more business, you will be competing solely on price. You will not develop any loyalty with this customer. Price is a good case to build on, but don't leave it all by itself.

Build on value and the other unique advantages that you, your company, and your product bring to the table.

Following are more answers to the price objection:

1) "Joe, there are three components involved here. They are: low price, high quality, and the best service. And obviously you can't get all three. I'd think you'd agree that you get what you pay for, right? The question is, what do you want to leave on the table? Do you want low price, or do you want the highest-quality product and the best service?"

2) "Joe, every company has a decision to make when they go into business. Are they going to make a cheap, low-quality product that the masses will buy, or are they going to make a quality product that will deliver fewer headaches and less aggravation, yet cost a little more? Would you rather have the cheap price up front, with more headaches, more aggravation, and a shorter overall product life, or, would you rather pay a little more up front and enjoy the benefits of a quality product over a longer period of time?"

3) "Joe, if I were selling what you knew beyond a shadow of a doubt were genuine $10 bills for one dollar each, would you buy as many as you could get your hands on? (Wait for the answer.) How about if I was selling genuine fifty-cent pieces for a dollar, you probably wouldn't buy those, would you? (Again, wait for the answer.) So if my product costs $10,000, but over the long term it will return you $20,000 in value, while my competitor's product at $9,000 will return you $8,000 worth of value over the long term, which would you buy?"

From here you need to present proof that your product lasts longer than the competition's and delivers more value—then get agreement and close.

4) "Cindy, if I come in with a better price, can I have the order?"

This is direct, although not as direct as "What price do I have to be at?" If the prospect is in bed with the competition he or she will procrastinate or use hesitant language such as "Um...well...I guess so." That's not what you're looking for. You're looking for a *definite* answer. If she is unsure or doesn't give you a satisfactory answer, wake her up with:

"Cindy, I can go through the exercise of pricing up my product, putting together a proposal, and delivering it to you. Yet if I'm just here to go through the exercise and you have absolutely no intention of buying from me…"

At that point, just stop and look her squarely in the eye. If she fidgets, stammers, doesn't make eye contact, and tells you, "Oh no, um, you have a chance—really," then you have *no* chance. If she gives you a definite yes and tells you that you do have a chance, then put something together. When you make the statement point blank and look the prospect in the eye, you'll know from the reaction whether you have a shot.

Here's one more quick response to the price objection. Simply ask the prospect:

5) "If the price were right, would you buy it right now?"

This is another way to make sure that price is the only objection. If the prospect says yes, you've got a pretty good shot. If the prospect says "probably," "I think so," "maybe," or worse, a flat-out no, obviously you've got some more work to do.

If you get a yes, ask, "So price is the only thing holding you back right now?" If she says anything other than yes, ask, "Outside of price, what are your other concerns?" Don't take "probably" or "I think so" as an indication that you only have a price objection. If the answer is anything other than a definite yes to a price objection, assume there are others.

To summarize, be certain she's divulged all her objections before you answer any single one. As the prospect gives you objections, write each one down along with any other information given.

Other Answers to Specific Money Objections

Here we'll look at answers to three more specific money objections:

- "I have no money."
- "I'm waiting until after April 15."
- "Your price is too high."

I Have No Money

Before using any of the responses below, ask the question: How much is no money? Again, you may get an answer you can work with, and if you do, move forward and close. If you get the more typical response, "No, really. I have no money," use one of these three answers:

- "Mr. Prospect, I can definitely understand that, but let me ask you a question. If I could guarantee you (put one of your major benefits here, let's say it's:) a 15 percent return on your investment over the next six months, would you be able to find (whatever dollar amount is appropriate here)?" Wait for an answer, then say, "Mr. Prospect, there are no guarantees but death and taxes, yet at the same time, considering (your three major benefits), I think you can see how the stock will most likely make a pretty good move up, am I right?"
- "Mr. Prospect, a man like you has no money? We've already reached the conclusion that you're a successful individual. Successful individuals usually have some capital available when an exceptional opportunity comes along. Perhaps right now you don't have (whatever dollar amount you were originally talking about) but let me ask you, how close could you come?"
- "Mr. Prospect, I have to smile a little when a man like you tells me he doesn't have any money. Frankly, I'm sure that like you, if I'm absolutely convinced of the opportunity I can always get my hands on (whatever dollar amount is appropriate). If I had done my job of convincing you, you'd probably be in the same boat, right?"

Again, you should be qualifying people up front to the point that when you get the "I have no money" objection, you can simply say, "Mr. Prospect, when we spoke last week you said you had (whatever dollar amount it was) liquid and available. Are you telling me that suddenly that has changed, or are you telling me I need to convince you further?"

I'm Waiting until after April 15

This one is usually has the same meaning as "I have no money" and should be treated the same. With this one you can also agree to extend payment terms that revolve around how much money the prospect will be receiving from the government. You can also have the prospect start with a smaller amount up front or put the purchase on some type of payment plan. The payment plan may include setting up payment terms such that no money is due until sometime after April 15.

Your Price Is Too High

Start with the question: Too high by how much? Treat the answer the same way you treated the "I have no money" objection. If the prospect gives you an answer you can work with, great. The standard response to this question is typically, "Look, it's just too high." This objection can be handled by building value or by breaking the cost down into smaller chunks as you would with financing.

You also want to find out what you are being compared with. For example, if the prospect says "Your price is too high" say, "When compared with what?" The objective behind asking this question is to find out if you are competing with someone else for the business or if there has perhaps been a misunderstanding. You might hear, "Well, XYZ Company is a lot lower than you guys." At this point, you know you are in a competitive situation and can handle it that way. You may also run into a misunderstanding. For example, you might be quoting an *annual* price and hear, "I can't afford to pay that much per *month*."

Anytime you get a price objection, ask questions and get some specifics about why the prospect feels the way he or she does. Once you have specifics you can respond appropriately to the objection(s).

Ignoring the Price Objection

The least advisable way to handle the price objection is simply to ignore it. If you decide to go this route, ignore the price objection by hearing the prospect out, cushioning your response, delivering your response, giving a strong benefit of your product, and finally closing again.

In this case you might say, "Joe, I definitely understand what you're saying. At the same time, if we're only half right on our conservative numbers, you'll recognize an annualized return of 18 percent on your investment. Would 1,000 shares be enough or would 1,500 be better if I could get a block at fifty cents better?"

Listen, give a benefit, and then close. You will not address the objection at all other than to hear it.

How to Determine if Price Really *Is* the Sole Reason the Prospect Is Not Moving Ahead

If someone really is buying solely on price and yours is higher than the competition's, he will never buy from you. After you have built value, eliminated other objections, and used every other idea you can think of, here's a good way to determine if the sole factor really is price and price only.

Ask the prospect at what price you need to be in order to earn the business and get a specific answer. If he gives you a general answer, keep asking until you get a specific number. As soon as you get the specific number, pull out your order form and start writing up the order. Even if you can't sell your product at that price, start writing it up anyway. Your objective here is to see whether he will let you write it up or stop you. If he doesn't stop you and he's willing to sign, you have a *true* price objection. If he does stop you, then you've got a different objection on your hands. A conversation we had with a prospect went like this:

Us: Jim, what price do I need to be at to get the business?
Prospect: Well, you'd probably have to be in the mid-20K range.
Us: Um, 24K, 25K, 26K?
Prospect: I don't know, probably somewhere between 25 and 26.
Us: 25,500?
Prospect: Yes, that would be about right.
Us: Great.

At this point one of us pulled out the contract and began writing. The prospect sat for a few moments, then started to fidget and became noticeably nervous. He finally blurted out, "What are you doing?" We simply continued writing and said, "Writing up the contract for $25,500." He fidgeted a bit more and finally sputtered, "You're too late!" At that point we stopped, stared at him, and remained completely quiet. After no more than two seconds he began to sing like a canary and give us all the information he'd been holding back.

When you use this technique, it's important *not* to look at the prospect when he asks what you're doing. Just keep looking at the contract and keep writing as you answer, "Writing up the contract for $25,500." If price is the only issue and the price the prospect gave you is really what he'll buy your product for, he'll let you continue writing up the contract. If there is another objection, he'll say it once he starts singing like a canary. It may be the real one or it may not be; in any case, the price objection will go away. The other objections you'll hear at this point will run the gamut.

Once the prospect has given you the new objection, here's how to handle the situation: Let's say the prospect tells you he needs to talk to someone else before he can move ahead. First isolate the objection. Say, "Joe, outside of having to talk to someone else, what other concerns do you have?" Again, you're looking for other objections first. If he tells you there are no other objections and you eliminate the one he just gave you, he can't throw another one at you. Well, he can, but if he does, respond with, "Joe, first we were looking at price. Next, you needed to talk to someone. Joe, I'm just curious—what's the real reason for not moving ahead today?"

Part of selling is being direct with people. Remember, many people can't say no—it's simply too final. You need to cut through the red tape and make sure you're engaging with people who are ready, willing, and able to buy your product or service. Your life as a salesperson depends upon it.

Note 1: Make sure the price they give you is reasonable. If the prospect gives you a price of $1 for a $20,000 item, he's not taking the discussion seriously. If you get a ridiculous dollar amount, say, "Joe—for real—where do I have to be?" If you can't get a straight answer, thank the prospect and leave.

Note 2: If the prospect allows you to write up the order, but you know you can't sell it at the price the prospect gives you, or there is some question (this is assuming it's a reasonable number, not like the $1 example above), write up the order anyway and take it to your manager.

How to Deal with the "Price" Shopper

Regardless of how well you build value, you will eventually run into an individual who buys solely on price. This is the individual who believes Box A is the same as Box B, and Box C is the same as Box B, etc. This person does not care how much longer you say it will last, how much easier you say it is to use, or how much value you say they'll receive versus the competition. They are looking for one thing and one thing only: *What's the bottom-line dollar amount right now?*

One of three factors is at work here:

- The prospect doesn't believe what you're telling him as far as the value of your product is concerned; thus, the only difference he sees between you and the competition is price.

- He believes he will look good to his boss by saving money up front and showing how frugal he is, so his only concern is the up-front price.
- The prospect does not intend on buying from you and price seems like a good excuse.

If the reason is number three, you're sunk. Assuming it's one or two, you still have the same result: you are being compared with the competition based solely on price.

Your objective now is to build value, of course. Use the advantages of yourself, your product or service, and your company. If none of this seems to be registering with your prospect (which is common with the "cheapos"), give the following technique a try.

My Cost to You? One Cent

Completely strip down your product or service to get your proposal to the lowest possible price. If you can get it down to one penny, that's great—the lower the better. For example, if you ordinarily offer a service, in your proposal offer absolutely no service and do it for one cent. Put the proposal together and hand it to your prospect. He'll glance at it and then toss you a look that says something along the lines of, "What are you, a bad comedian?"

Follow with, "Joe, you told me you're buying strictly on price, right?" Again, you'll receive a less than amused glare. Continue with, "Let me give you a scenario, Joe. Let's say you buy a homeowners' insurance policy and subsequently your house burns down. If the insurance company doesn't make good on your policy either because they can't or they simply won't pay up, even if you only paid one cent for that policy, did you get your money's worth?"

He should start to get the picture at this point. Next say, "Joe, I can give you less product, less service, and a lower price—we both know that. At the same time, it is impossible for me to give you the highest-quality product, the highest-quality service and the lowest price, we both know that also. So of the two, a high-quality product with high-quality service, or low price, which one are you going to leave on the table today?"

In this case, you can also pull out long-term lower cost and other weapons in your arsenal. If you can't get the person to budge after hitting the objection with all of these answers, you're probably dealing with item three above, and

- The prospect does not like you or your company;
- The prospect has a very strong relationship with your competitor;
- The prospect really isn't interested but is having trouble telling you no; or
- A combination of the three.

Next, you need to find out exactly what the competition is quoting and make sure you're quoting apples for apples. If you know the competition well, you should be able to give an educated guess at what they are quoting. Other than that, how can you discover what the competition is quoting? Ask the prospect. If the prospect is not willing to share with you the features and functions that the competitor is quoting, you are probably better off spending your time with another prospect.

Are You *Cheap?*

Another way to approach this is to ask about the business your prospect is in and then compare it to your own. For example, let's say your prospect is in the mortgage business. Ask him if he has the "cheapest" mortgages around. Make sure you use the word *cheapest*.

Most prospects will be taken aback by the question and they'll respond with something like, "Well, of course not!" No one likes to be associated with something that's "cheap." Follow the prospect's response with, "Well then, why would anyone possibly want to do business with you if you're not the cheapest?"

Hopefully by now he'll understand your point. Ask what sets his company apart from the others and why someone should pay more. He'll now begin to make a case for why someone should buy a more expensive product. Once he's done, say, "Mr. Prospect, I couldn't agree with you more. Like you…" then draw the comparisons between you, your company, and product and the prospect, his company, and his product. Finish with, "Mr. Prospect, do you agree that you get what you pay for?" Wait for an affirmative response and close.

Will the *Real* Cheapo Please Stand Up?

Here's one more technique for the price shopper. The technique is a close we will cover in detail on page 463 in the *Closing* section. It's called the "They're Exactly the Same" close.

Use this when you have a prospect who believes that your product is exactly the same as the competitor's product and it really just comes down to price. In other words, your product is simply a commodity.

Other Things to Consider in the Price War
The Psychology of the Purchase Agent

If you are dealing with purchasing agents, you have to understand how they work. The purchasing agent is trying to get the best price on whatever product she's looking for. If she's using your competitor, and it is her intention to stay with your competitor, her goal in obtaining competitive pricing is to get her present vendor to lower his price. She'll go to him with your pricing in hand and say something like: "Charlie, Bob Chapin from ABC Company is proposing a machine that will do what your machine will do, plus it will do these additional things, and look at the price he's giving me. Is there anything else you can do?" If she is truly shopping price, she will play you off each other, going back and forth, beating the two of you down as low as she can. Either way, keep the purchaser's objective in mind. It is simply to get his or her company what it needs for the least amount of money.

In this case, you can attempt to build value with the purchase agent, but as purchasing agents have trouble understanding value, you'll need to deal with someone higher than this person, the higher the better. You need to talk with someone who understands value, because typically the purchase agent only understands price. Please refer to "Go over the Prospect's Head" on page 500.

Are You the Lowest Price in the Market, the Highest Price, or Somewhere in Between?

As we've already discussed in the *Presentation* and *Competition* sections, if yours is the lowest price, and you thus have a price advantage, you sell your "up-front" price. You can also ask a question such as "Mr. Prospect, are you determined to pay top dollar or are you looking for the best value for your money?"

If you are the higher-priced product or service, sell the added value for the additional money, such as a lower, long-term price, and the other advantages of you, your product, and your company. If you are in the middle, sell a combination of the two.

Build Value and Avoid Cutting Price

And now a final word on the price objection. As we discussed in the *Competition* section, building value is the best way to counter the price objection, and cutting price is the worst. With value you come from a position of strength, whereas with price you come from a position of weakness. When you drop your price, you become nothing but a commodity. Once you drop your price, you'll find yourself in a price war every time you present to that prospect. In addition, the prospect may get the notion that you were padding your price to begin with and trying to take advantage of her. The news of a low price also has a way of getting around the grapevine. If you give someone a "great" deal, and someone else a "not so great" deal, and those two talk, or one company buys another out and gets a look at the books, you'll have a problem.

Chapter 31

More Objections

Now that we've beaten the price objection into the ground, let's take a look at some other objections you may encounter. You'll find that you get most of these objections either before the presentation or during the presentation. In this section, we'll simply state the objection and then present the ways to handle it.

I Want to Think about It

Handling the objection before the presentation:

"Joe, occasionally we find that after we've gone through all the information we'll present today, we get to the end and some people tell us they'd like to think it over. What studies have shown, and we've found to be true, is that people forget about 80 percent of what they've heard over a twenty-four- to forty-eight-hour period. As a result, after this short period has elapsed they know much less than when we went over everything in the meeting.

"Moreover, right now you have an expert in front of you who can answer all your questions and give you all the information you need. Joe, does it make sense to you that you should make a decision when you have the most information available to you, or after you've forgotten most of it? (Wait for the obvious answer. By the way, if someone doesn't give you the obvious affirmative answer to this response, there might be better places for you to spend your time.) That's why our objective today is to get you the information you need and then to answer any questions so you can make the most informed decision as to what's best for you. Does that make sense?"

Handling the objection as it occurs:

1) **Isolate the objection.** "Joe, besides needing to think it over, is there anything else that's stopping you from moving ahead today?"

2) **Answer the objection.** "Joe, I can appreciate that and I definitely understand your wanting to think it over. That makes sense. At the same time, experts say we

forget about 80 percent of what we've heard over a twenty-four- to forty-eight-hour period. While you're armed with this knowledge and while you have an expert here to answer any questions, now is the best time to make the most informed decision. Let me ask you, Joe, what questions do you have right now?"

Another answer: "Kathy, do you really need to think it over or do I just need to give you some better reasons as to why *now* is the right time to move?

Leave Me Some Information

Note: When telemarketing, this objection will come in the form of "*Send* me some information." We will cover that one in detail in the *Telemarketing* section.

Handling the objection before the presentation:

"Cindy, occasionally we find that after we've gone through all the information we'll present today, we get to the end and some people tell us they'd like us to leave them some information. First and foremost, please realize that we are going to be very thorough with the information we give you today. We are going to cover all the information in our literature and much more.

"Right now, you have an expert in front of you who will answer all your questions and cover all the information you need. Cindy, I think you'd agree with me that it makes more sense to make a decision when you have all the information fresh in your mind, than it does to make a decision later, when you have nothing but a brochure and a fraction of the information in front of you. Am I right? That's why our objective today is to get you all the information you need so you can make the most informed decision as to what's best for you. Does that make sense?"

Handling the objection as it occurs:

1) **Isolate the objection.** "Cindy, besides needing to review the information, is there anything else that's stopping you from moving ahead today?"

2) **Answer the objection.** "Cindy, I can appreciate that and I definitely understand your wanting to study some information later. At the same time, you do realize that not only did I cover all the information I could leave with you, I actually covered more? While the information is fresh in your mind, and while you have an

expert here to answer all your questions, what specifically do you need more information on?"

Here's another answer: "Cindy, what specifically are you looking for in the information?"

If she is able to give you a specific answer, isolate the answer. For example, if she says she'd like to review the different plans and decide which one is right for her, say, "Okay, is that all the information you're looking for or is there something else?"

If she says there is something else, ask what it is and then qualify her answer by again asking if that's all the information she needs. Once you get her to the point where she has covered all the areas she needs information on, address her need for information and try to eliminate it right then and there.

Let's say she only needed to review the different plans. In this case, apologize for not addressing this area adequately and ask the questions that will help determine which plan she needs. For example you might say, "Cindy, I'm sorry I didn't cover the necessary details to make that decision clear. Let me ask you, will you need access on the weekends? How about at night? Will most of your calls be local, long distance but in state, or long distance and out of state?"

When you get an answer, again, proceed to give the information necessary. "Okay, based upon that information, here's what I would recommend…" Ask if that answers her question, and close.

Keep following this line of questioning until she gives you another objection or until you've answered all her questions regarding the information. If she comes back with, "Look I just want to review the information," be persistent in letting her know that you have time to review the information with her and answer her questions.

If she persists, the information objection is probably a stall. At that point, say, "Cindy, I kind of get the feeling that you're just trying to be nice by not directly telling me no. Is that the case, or do you really want to review the information?"

You could also say: "Cindy, do you really want to review the information or are you just asking why now is the best time for you to make a move?"

If she says she really wants to review the information, you can leave it with her and set a follow-up time to go over it with her. Say, "Okay, Cindy, I'll be happy to leave the information with you. Is Thursday morning or afternoon better for you to get together again?"

If the information objection is just a way of putting you off—which it probably is—she won't want to see you again. Remain persistent about when you can stop by to review her findings.

Note 1: If she is looking for information you don't have with you, ask her what she is looking for, then proceed to answer those questions.

Note 2: She may persist with the "*Send* me the information" objection. In this case, you'll want to handle things differently because this is typically a telemarketing objection. Please refer to pages 621 to 624 for more details.

Note 3: If she wants to see information because there is a question you can't answer, review our tips about what to do when you get a question you can't answer, and related ideas, which are on pages 440 through 444.

I Want to Check Other Places First

Handling the objection before the presentation:

"Joe, occasionally we reach the end of our presentation and someone says they want to check with a couple of our competitors before they go ahead and buy. Because of that, we've gone out and done a thorough comparison between our competitors and us. That way you don't have to waste your time chasing all that information. The other reason we've done the competitive comparison, besides saving you some time, is because in a head-to-head comparison we know we are going to come out on top. If that's one of your concerns, we can go over the comparison right now. If not, I'll get started with all the great benefits of our offer. Which would you prefer?"

Handling the objection as it occurs:

1) Isolate the objection. "Joe, besides needing to check around at a couple of other places, is there anything else that's stopping you from moving ahead today?"

"Okay, so what you're saying is, once you check the other locations, if we have the better deal, you're going to buy from me, right?"

2) Answer the objection. "Joe, I can definitely understand that and it makes sense. Let me ask, what particular areas do you want to compare?"

Make sure he has given you all the areas he wants to compare. For example, if he says, "I just want to compare price," ask, "Is price all you want to compare?" Once you get a yes, pull out your comparison. "Joe, with regard to price, here is a detailed comparison between our competition and us."

Note: Clearly, if the prospect tells you price is his key concern and you have the lowest price, you will simply show him you are the lowest in that area. If you are higher than a competitor on price, you need to shift the focus to what the prospect will get for his money and show that your product is the better overall value, even at the higher price. Your objective with the comparison sheet is to show the prospect that you are the best overall decision he can make.

If you don't have a comparison sheet, it's important to put one together as soon as possible. Refer to the *Competition* section to see how to put the comparison together. In the meantime, if you encounter this objection before you have prepared a comparison sheet, simply offer to go out and do the comparison for the prospect. Say, "Joe, I'll tell you what. I'll be happy to go out and do the comparison for you. Then we'll sit down together and see who comes out on top. Is that fair enough?"

If the prospect balks at this, continue to persist. Say, "Joe, not only will doing this comparison help me to earn your business, it will be great for me as a salesperson in that I'm bound to learn something in the process." If the prospect persists in saying he will do the comparison himself, respond with, "Joe, with due respect, what's the real reason for not moving ahead today?"

Call the competition for the prospect. This works *extremely* well in diffusing the "I want to check a couple of other places" objection. When the prospect tells you he wants to check a couple of other places, simply say, "I agree. I'll tell you what, I'll call them for you. Then you can tell them what you're looking for and ask what price they'll sell it to you for, okay?" Then pick up the phone and call.

Note 1: Make sure you're comparable to the competition or can explain your pricing if for some reason you are not comparable.

Post the competition's prices. You may have seen this at some car dealerships. Often they will list their price for an oil change or other car services, and they'll also list the prices that competitors in the area charge. If you have pricing you can post that compares you favorably with the competition, do it.

Note 2: In both of the above cases, you don't necessarily have to have the lowest price, but you either have to be close or you have to be able to explain the price difference in value terms.

I Want to Watch It

This objection usually refers to an investment or mortgage rates. The investment advisor calls the prospect, goes through his presentation, then hears, "So what is the symbol on the stock?" followed by "And what exchange does it trade on?" and finally "And how do you think it will perform over the next nine months?"

As soon as you answer all those questions—and close after each one—the prospect says, "Great. I'm going to watch this one for the next nine months. Call me on the next one." Or a mortgage broker tries to close a deal and the prospect says, "Hmm, I think interest rates are going lower. I'm just going to see what the Fed does during their next meeting."

In the two examples above, you have two reasons for the same objection, assuming it is a true objection. Regarding the investment advisor, the prospect wants to see how good the advisor and her recommendations are. In the second case with the mortgage broker, the prospect is waiting for the right time. In other words, the prospect is trying to get in at the bottom with the lowest possible rate and the least possible risk. Consequently, you handle both of these situations differently.

The first step with both examples is to get their attention with a "no-brainer" question. If you're the investment advisor above, you might ask, "Joe, if you knew this stock was going to increase 50 percent in the next nine months, would you buy it right now?" If you're the mortgage broker, ask, "Cindy, if you knew this was rock-bottom for interest rates, would you go ahead and refinance now?"

In addition to a "no-brainer" question (one which you'd better get a "yes" to), you are also isolating the objection.

When the investment prospect replies with, "Well, of course, but you can't guarantee that," try this:

"Joe, you're right, but let me ask you a question. What if you watch the stock and it doubles?" Wait a few seconds for an answer and then proceed: "I'll call you on the next one and you'll watch that one too. The point being that my first five stocks you watch could double, but that doesn't mean the sixth stock is going to go up. Or the first five stocks could tank and the six one could double. Joe, no one has a crystal ball and there will be absolutely no economic benefit to you if you just watch the stock. Our first step is the most important. I'm not looking for you to go head over heels on our first trade. Pick up 1,000 shares and allow me to show you what I can do for you. Okay, Joe?" Say nothing more and wait for an answer.

When the mortgage prospect responds with, "Well, of course, but you can't guarantee that this is rock-bottom for rates," try this:

"Cindy you're right, but let me ask you a question. What are the odds that you're going to get in at the absolute bottom?" Wait a few seconds for an answer and then proceed: "Cindy, leading indicators are showing that rates may go higher, not lower. If we move now, we can lock in this low rate today. If by chance the rates do go lower, which the industry does not expect, we can then lock in at the lower rate by…" (Explain how you would do this.)

"The bottom line is you have absolutely nothing to lose by acting now. But by not acting, you can miss out on the low rates now. For every quarter point that rates move up, you'll pay $9,000 more over the life of the loan. Surely you'd like to save as much money as possible, right?" Wait for an affirmative answer and then close. "Great. All I need is a little information."

I Need to Talk to Someone Else

Note: This is *not* the same as "I need someone else's approval," which we'll cover a little later.

Handling the objection before the presentation:

"Kathy, occasionally we get to the end of our presentation and someone tells us they need to talk it over with someone else. Obviously, we don't want to waste any of your time today. Our presentation will take about twenty-five minutes, give or take depending on the number of questions you have. Before we get started, is there anyone else you'll need to talk to about this?"

If you get a yes to this question, do *not* do your presentation until you have that person present. Ask the prospect when you can all get together. If she says something like, "That's okay, just give me the presentation and I'll pass it on," be nice but firm and ask for to meet with everyone involved.

Come back with, "Kathy, thank you for thinking of me and my time—I appreciate it. It's really no bother. Why don't we get them on the phone right now and we'll compare schedules?" If she remains persistent, suggest, "Kathy, I'd like nothing more than to give you the presentation, but my company requires that I present to all involved parties." If it's true, add, "I am legally required to discuss this with all parties that will have input into the decision." Conclude with, "Again, thank you for being so considerate of my time. When can we all get together?"

Handling the objection as it occurs:

1) **Isolate the objection.** "Kathy, besides needing to talk to someone else about this, is there any other reason for not moving ahead today?"
2) **Answer the objection.** "Kathy, most times when you talk to someone else about a purchase, they will tell you not to do it. The first reason is because they don't know all the particulars. The second reason, and the more important one, is because they have a lot more to lose if they tell you to go ahead than if they tell you to forget about it. What I mean is if the stock drops significantly and you lose all your money, they know you'll probably place some of the blame on them, and perhaps all of it. Obviously, there could be some major relationship implications there.

"On the other hand, if they tell you not to do it and the stock goes up a few points, you're a lot less likely to be upset with them, and even if you were, it likely would be minor. You can probably put yourself in that person's shoes and see how they'd feel, right? With that in mind, I can guarantee you that if you call someone immediately after we speak and ask for their opinion, one hundred out of one hundred times they'll tell you not to invest. Let me ask you, as the expert on the stock, what questions do you have for me?"

I Need to Talk to My Wife, Husband, Significant Other

Handling the objection before the presentation:

You will handle this one exactly the way you handled the above objection: "I have to talk to someone else." The same opening question will cover this subject:

"Kathy, occasionally we get to the end of our presentation and someone tells us they need to talk it over with someone else. Obviously we don't want to waste any of your time today. Our presentation will take about twenty-five minutes, give or take depending upon the number of questions you have. Before we get started, is there anyone else who you'll need to talk to about this?"

Note: Both this objection and the one above should be handled in the *Qualifying* stage. However, if you wait until the presentation and she answers "yes" to your question, don't do the presentation until you gather all interested parties together.

Handling the objection as it occurs:

   1) **Isolate the objection.** "Kathy, besides needing to talk to your husband about this, is there any other reason for not moving ahead today?"
   2) **Answer the objection.** "Kathy, I can definitely understand that. At the same time, if you make a good decision for your family (or for the two of you), he's probably going to go along with it. Am I right?"

Another answer: "Kathy, I don't have one client whose husband jumps up and down about her buying (your product), and I definitely don't want to start a domestic squabble. At the same time, considering (your three major benefits), I think you'd agree with me that this will be a good move for you, correct?"

Another: "Kathy, I understand that. At the same time, let me ask you a question. How will your husband react if you go home and say, 'Honey, I was looking at (product) today and I'm thinking about spending (dollar amount) on it. What do you think?' (Wait for an answer.) If you make a good, reasonable decision, he's probably going to go along with it, right?"

As a last resort if you can't get around the objection:

"Kathy, I definitely understand that and it's obvious you need to talk to your husband about this. Let me ask you, could you give me a firm yes or no by tomorrow at, say, ten in the morning? (Wait for an affirmative answer.) Okay, I'll tell you what. Why don't we get all the paperwork out of the way now just in case your answer is yes and then I'll be able to get you in at the best possible price (reserve the color you'd like, make sure we reserve one for you, or any other "timing" benefit you can come up with). If you did move ahead, that would be important to you, right?"

If you are facing a true "talk to my wife, husband, significant other" objection, the prospect will agree to let you do this.

I Need Approval from My Boss, the Accounting Department, Purchasing, etc.

Handling the objection during the qualifying stage:

"Kathy, who else will be involved in the decision-making process?" If she says she's the only decision-maker, she can't give you this objection later on. If she does, simply say, "Kathy, when we first spoke, you told me you were the only decision-maker." Say nothing further; simply look her in the eye, and let her respond to the statement. If you missed this question during the qualifying stage, ask it before you do your presentation.

Handling the objection during the presentation:

If for some reason you didn't ask or forgot to ask the question in the qualifying stage or before the presentation, and the objection arises in the presentation, you'll handle it just as you handle other objections that arise during the presentation.

1) Isolate the objection. "Besides having to get approval from (whomever), is there any other reason for not moving ahead today?" Wait for the reply, and then suggest, "So, in other words, if you had (whomever's) approval, you'd buy today, right?"

2) Answer the objection. First, find out why she needs approval from someone else. Is the order too large for her to sign? Does it involve other departments over which she does not have jurisdiction? You can ask a quick question and get to the bottom of this fairly quickly. "Do you need approval because of the dollar amount of the order, or does it cross department lines?"

After this question, simply stop, look, and listen. Typically, the prospect will give you all the reasons why she needs someone else to approve it. You may get responses such as, "I have to have all orders signed," or "I can't sign anything over $20,000."

If you find yourself in the second scenario, you may be able to structure the deal so you can do part of it now and part of it in a month or two, or you may be able to spread out your billing. Remember to keep your mind open and look for creative ideas. There just may be a way you can structure your order so she can sign it herself.

If that approach doesn't get you anywhere, proceed as follows: "Kathy, I understand you need (whomever's) approval. Let me ask you a question. If it were up to you, would you be buying from me today?"

Usually, your prospect will agree to this. If you get a no, it means you have some other objections to overcome. Assuming she says yes, ask, "Are you going to recommend my solution to (whomever)?"

An affirmative answer puts you in good position. If you get a negative response for either of the above two questions, suggest, "What else would prevent you from buying from me today?" or "Why would you not recommend my solution?" You need to probe into what the other objections are, isolate them, and determine if those are the only objections.

If you get a yes to the above two questions, continue with, "Can we visit that person right now?" or "Why don't we give that person a call right now?"

The point of this question is to catch the prospect off guard and watch his or her reaction. Chances are, as with most objections, she's bluffing.

Once you've asked the question, treat it the same way you would a closing question: be completely quiet, look the prospect squarely in the eye, and wait for her to talk. When she does stop talking, unless it's positive, remain quiet and continue to look her in the eye for at least a count of five seconds. Your goal is to have her eventually talk her way out of the objection or give you a complete, solid answer as to why she can't do that. If her final answer is no, she can't call, continue with, "Kathy, when will you be meeting with (whomever)?"

Whatever answer she gives, ask, "Can I be there to go over all the particulars and answer any questions they might have?" If she balks at this, ask, "Can I contact the other person involved in the decision?"

Note: It's wonderful if the person will wholeheartedly endorse your product. But don't let that person do your presentation, "hoping" to sell the other person. Be pleasant, but be persistent. Many times you'll find this objection will disappear and another will pop up. This happens because the present objection has stopped working and the prospect now needs another one to put you off.

I Need to Talk to My Accountant/Attorney

This one is fairly similar to the earlier objection in which the prospect needed to talk it over with someone except that you need to make your responses specific to the accountant, the attorney, or both. Also, take a more direct approach when overcoming this objection.

Handling the objection before the presentation:

Don't bring this objection up before the presentation. It is rare that this one will come up and by bringing it up yourself, you'll actually create more objections than you'll head off.

Handling the objection as it occurs:

1) Isolate the objection. "Joe, besides needing to talk it over with your accountant or attorney, is there any other reason for not moving ahead today?"

2) Answer the objection. "Joe let me ask you, is your accountant or attorney a certified financial planner? If he's not, it's actually illegal for him to give you any kind of investment advice. His expertise is in other areas, whereas my expertise is in this area, especially on this particular stock. I know more about this stock than virtually anyone. What questions are bouncing around in your mind at this point, Joe?"

Here's another answer: "Cindy, I understand that you want to talk to your accountant or attorney. However, 99 percent of the time, they'll give you two reasons not to invest. First, they don't have all the information. Second, their job is to save money, not invest it. Our job, on the other hand, is to uncover great investment opportunities. What other questions do you have about this investment, Cindy?"

And one more: "Kathy, I can definitely understand that. At the same time, let me tell you what happens when you call your accountant or attorney. You catch him off guard on a company that, in many cases, he's never heard of, never mind having studied inside and out. He's put on the spot with your question, doesn't have much information at his disposal and he's faced with a tough decision. He can either tell you, 'Yes, go ahead,' in which case you put up real dollars and risk the loss. Or he can tell you, 'No, don't do it,' whereby you put up no dollars and even if the stock doubles, you missed a profit but at least you didn't lose money, which would irritate you much more. The bottom line is, I can guarantee you that if you call him on twenty-five different stocks, he'll say no to every single one.

"I'm really the expert on this stock, Kathy. And I'd like to address any further questions you may have for me." (Wait for a reply and address the prospect's concerns.)

Annual Budget Spent/Not in Budget

This is also a money objection and you can treat it the same way. With this objection, one idea is to find a creative way to set up the deal so you can use next year's budget.

Handling the objection before the presentation:

"Joe, occasionally we get to the end of our presentation and someone tells us it's not in the budget or the budget's already been spent. Obviously, we don't want to waste any of your time today. Our presentation will take about twenty-five minutes, give or take depending upon the number of questions you have. Before we get started, if you see overwhelming evidence that this makes sense for you and you decide you really want it, is there money in the budget?"

Handling the objection as it occurs:

1) Isolate the objection. "Outside of your budget being completely spent for this year, is there any other reason for not moving ahead right now?" Wait for the answer, then ask, "In other words, if you had the money in the budget you'd be buying today?"

2) Answer the objection. The quickest way to make the budget objection go away is to set up payment terms so the prospect will owe nothing until the following year. This isn't always possible. However, if your company will allow the prospect to defer payment until next year's budget kicks in, you've eliminated the objection. If you can defer the payment terms after isolating the objection, simply say, "Great, Joe. I can set up the payment terms so you won't owe anything until next year. Will you be financing this or paying cash?"

If the prospect balks at this, you have issues other than the budget. In addition to pushing *all* the payments out until next year, it's possible there is a little room in this year's budget, just not enough to cover the entire transaction. Ask the question, "Joe, on occasion when there's a budget issue, we've learned that it's usually possible to squeeze something into this year and then push the remainder into next year's budget. Is your entire budget spent, or is there a small portion we could squeeze into this year and then leave the rest for next year?"

Occasionally, once you've eliminated the "this year's budget" objection, you'll get an additional objection: "Well, I'm really not sure we'll have room for it in next year's budget."

At this point you need to ask, "Joe, if you were completely convinced that my product would solve your problem, would you find room in the budget?" Again, just as you would with a closing question, look him squarely in the eye and say absolutely nothing until he answers. If you get anything other than a yes, ask, "Joe, the issue isn't entirely the budget, is it?" Stop, stare, and remain quiet until you get an answer.

Another answer to the budget objection: "I can definitely understand and appreciate that, Joe. At the same time, we know a budget is, of course, meant to be a guideline to keep things from getting out of hand as opposed to a tightly constricting hindrance to your company's progress. Let me ask you a question. If you were entirely convinced that this product would save you much more money in the long run than it will cost, would your budget be flexible?"

Other alternatives: "Joe, who might be in a position to find some extra money in the budget?" In other words, you know that if the President of the company decided he was going to find the money to invest in your program, he would find it. This question is a nice way of letting the prospect know you realize that the budget can be "expanded" if need be.

You can also ask, "Joe, is there another department that might have some additional money in their budget?" Or, "Joe, is there another area where the budget is not spent and we might be able to squeeze this in?"

In addition to questioning the objection, the above questions also help the prospect to think of other alternative ways to solve the problem.

If the prospect is successful at holding you off until the next budget period, aim for two things:

- Get into the budget meeting so you can present your proposal in person.
- Ensure the prospect is committed to your product or service.

This can be as simple as asking if she is willing to push your product or service in the budget meeting. You might say, "Cindy, are you willing to recommend and endorse my proposal at the budget meeting?"

If she does allow you to present at the budget meeting, find out who the key players are and learn a little about each one. You also want your presentation to be in the proper format. Ask:

- if there are certain criteria or if there's a certain format you need to follow when presenting your product;
- what has been successful in the past or if the prospect has any advice about anything that might help; and
- if you can contact the key individuals before the meeting.

If you know the key players and they know you, this will often help your cause.

I'm Happy with My Current Vendor

You will handle this objection a little differently from how you handle most others. First, the prospect is likely to give you this one during the cold call. Second, when you hear this one it is usually *not* a stall, like most other objections. This doesn't mean that you can't handle this objection, it just means you have to be creative in handling it.

1) Isolate the objection. You can still isolate the objection as you do others. Say, "Shelly, if you were not happy with your present vendor, would we be doing business today?"

If she says "no" you obviously have some other issues to work on. You need to ask what other factors are preventing her from doing business with you. Usually, she will agree; at that point, you move to eliminate the objection.

2) Answer the objection. "Shelly, I can definitely understand that, and I appreciate the relationship you've had with XYZ Company over the years. Let me ask you a question. What do you like most about your present vendor?"

She will now tell you why she does business with her present vendor. Her answer will shape how you handle the objection. Write it down, and then qualify it. "Shelly, is that the only reason you do business with XYZ Company, or are there some other reasons too?"

Get all the reasons she does business with her present vendor and write them down. Once you've done that, ask another question. "Shelly, if you could improve upon XYZ Company in any way, how would you improve their service to you?"

If she answers, "There is nothing I would change," you'll have to work with what she likes about her present vendor. If she gives you a couple of areas in which she would change her present vendor, you've got a little more ammunition to work with.

The two areas you will now go after are what she likes about XYZ Company and what she would change about it.

For example, let's imagine your prospect likes the price of XYZ Company's product, they have good quality, and they always deliver the product quickly. You now know the areas in which you have to shine or outperform XYZ Company. If she wishes XYZ Company had a little more variety and could respond to service calls a little faster, show that you have more variety and that you have a faster service call response time (if in fact you do).

At this point, you can draw upon your competitive comparison and go to town, if it shows you in a favorable light in those areas you need to be favorable in. You may not be favorable in all areas, but you may be favorable in enough of them.

For example, you may not have a lower price than XYZ Company; however, you may have better quality and more variety. On the other hand, you may not have more variety or better quality, but you may have lower prices and be able to respond to service calls more quickly.

You need to be able to think on your feet and adapt. You need to be prepared for the prospect to throw a multitude of different scenarios at you, yet you're ready to pull out your competitive comparison and know exactly where you need to concentrate.

Note: Refrain from making negative comments about the current vendor. This is especially important when you're doing a point-by-point comparison. The person to whom you're trying to sell may have been the one who decided to use the current vendor. By making the current vendor look bad, you may be making his decision to use that vendor look bad. This can alienate you quickly.

Instead of showing how bad the other company is or how much better your company has always been, focus on how much better your company, service, or product is *right now*. Focus on recent developments that have made your company stand out. "Joe, about six months ago we unveiled our latest line of machines, which have seventeen exclusive features that no one else in the industry has." Or, "Joe, in the past twelve months we've added six service technicians in your area, and it's cut our average response rate from three hours to two hours."

If your prospect has used your company at one point or unfavorably compared you with the competition in the past, you'll need to show how your company has changed since then. Let the prospect know about everything that has changed in your company from the last time she compared you to the competition. Cover all aspects related to your product, service, and personnel. In addition, sell what *you* bring to the table. This will be especially applicable if you were not with the company the last time the prospect did a comparison.

On your cold call, when you hear that your prospect is happy with his present vendor, respond with, "Joe, I definitely understand that. But let me ask you, do you believe in keeping your present vendor honest?"

If he asks what you mean by that, follow up with, "What I mean, Joe, is if you're getting some competitive quotes, your present vendor is much more likely to sharpen his pencil, or at least make sure his pricing is in line. Does that make sense?"

Invariably, you will get a positive response. In that case, say, "Great! All I'd like to do is supply you with some competitive pricing. Is that fair enough?"

What you're doing here is simply asking for a chance to show the prospect what your company can do for her. Sell the idea from the viewpoint of helping your prospect achieve some perspective. "Shelly, it's simple. I can talk to you all day long about how our machines last twenty years versus the competition's lasting fourteen. I can talk about how our machines are much easier for your employees and customers to use, and how you'll have much more uptime, more profitability, and many fewer headaches. At the same time, if you never try one of my machines, you'll never appreciate that perspective.

"Right now your people assume they have to buy a new machine every fourteen years. They assume the machine will be up 90 percent of the time and down 10 percent of the time. Their machine may be much more difficult to load than ours, but your people know only the competition's way. They don't know there's an easier way. They don't yet have the perspective to realize how much better things can be because they have nothing with which to compare XYZ Company's machine.

Your argument is: "Shelly, obviously I can't afford to live off selling you one machine. It's critical that I get that machine in, after which you'll notice a dramatic difference between it and XYZ Company's. Perhaps then you may buy more machines from me. That's really the only way I can survive. Give me the opportunity with one machine. If you're not completely satisfied, I'll never bother you again. Is that fair enough?"

With this scenario, you simply want to get your foot in the door. Ask for a small order or suggest they use you for a trial period—perhaps a month or two.

I'm Waiting to See What Happens with the Election

This objection usually occurs where stock investments and real estate are concerned. Bear in mind that ninety-nine times out of one hundred, any objection is simply a stall. And this is a great example of a stall.

When you're faced with this objection, your goal is to separate what happens with the election from what happens in your industry or with your product. If you can help the prospect understand that the election will have no affect on your product, you will have eliminated the objection.

1) Isolate the objection. "Cindy, besides the outcome of the election, is there anything else holding you back from moving ahead today?" Or, "In other words, if you knew the election was going to turn out a certain way, you would still consider investing with me today. Is that correct?"

2) Answer the objection. "Cindy, who are you looking for to win the election?"

Let's imagine she says the Republican candidate. "Now if Mr. Republican wins the election, how do you feel that will affect the stock market?" Wait for an answer. "Okay, and how do you feel that will affect this particular stock?"

Often you will throw her off with these questions because she won't have a great answer. If she says: "I believe the market will go up," ask, "Why do you believe that?"

The bottom line is that unless this is a true objection, she won't be able to answer you with anything that makes sense and she'll realize she's not making sense. At that point, she'll either give you the true objection or find a way to remove herself from the conversation. In the event that she sticks with the objection and doesn't leave, you will now proceed to educate her.

"Cindy, as you know, when we study the market we look for trends. We use history as a guide when studying those trends. That makes sense, right? It's essentially the same as saying, 'Okay, now in the past, every time we have added one and one, we've gotten two, so it's a pretty safe bet that if we add one and one we'll get two again.' Cindy, let me ask you, do you know how past elections have affected the stock market?"

She'll likely answer no unless she really knows her stuff. You will then give her the history showing that elections affect the market very little. You must then persuade her to agree with you. "Cindy, you and I have already agreed that trends are the best indicator as to what will happen with the market in the future. Right?" Wait for the affirmative answer, then say, "Great! So we can see from the past trends that the outcome of the election will affect the market very little. After all, that's what the trends show, correct?" As soon as you get agreement, *close!*

However, if she somehow suddenly changes her mind and says no, be up front and call her on it. "Cindy, you agreed with me that trends are the best indicator as to what will happen with the market in the future. But now you're telling me you don't agree with that. Cindy, let me ask you, what's the real reason for not moving ahead today?"

Now she'll likely give you another objection, remove herself from the conversation, or stubbornly stick to her objection. If she does stick to her objection, you can tell her you'll call her after the election, depending upon what happens. You can then either throw the lead away or make one more call if her candidate wins.

We know of one investment advisor who had three piles of leads—one pile to call if the Democrat candidate won the election, one if the Republican won, and one if the Independent won. After the election in which a Republican won, he called everyone in the Republican pile. Guess what happened? All those people now had some other excuse. Sometimes there's an exception to the rule. Just remember, when you get this objection, it's probably just a way to get rid of you.

I'm Waiting until Next Year

This is either a "no money" objection, an "I'm waiting to see what happens" objection, or a nice way of saying no. With this objection, you need to learn what will be different next year. To do that, simply ask the question, "What will be different next year?" This will allow you to determine which objection you need to handle. If she says: "I'll have more money next year," you have a "no money" objection. If she says she's waiting to see what happens with the election, you then have that objection to deal with. You're always talking about the bottom line. Right now, you need to find out your prospect's bottom line and what circumstances are preventing her from going ahead now. Then you need to overcome the "real" objection.

Another Answer for *All* "Wait and See" Objections

Another way to handle "wait and see" objections is with the Contrarian View Close.

Use the Contrarian View Close when you get an objection about the economy, the presidential election, the level that the stock market is at, or any other reason someone is sitting back and waiting for in the outside world to happen. Please refer to page 475 for complete information on this close.

Call Me Back at Some Point in the Future

You need to be direct with this objection and ask some pointed questions.

Let's say the prospect tells you to call him back in three months. Be direct and ask him, "What will happen in three months that will put you in a position to buy then?" Based upon his answer, you may be able to structure the deal so he can do it now.

For example, if he says he has no money now but he will have it three months from now, you now have a "no money" objection. You can then set up special financing, no money for ninety days, or any number of other creative deals. Whether it's money—"I might be moving," "I might be changing jobs in a month,"—or some other factor, you need to learn why the prospect is waiting. Once you know the differentiators, you have objections you can work with.

You need to be aware that this may also be a stall to get rid of you. If it's a money issue and you come up with a creative way for your prospect to buy now, yet he still doesn't buy, it's clearly a stall. You now need to ask more questions to discover the true underlying objection.

Another way to handle the "Call me back at some point in the future" objection is to offer incentives to move now. You can let the prospect know that the price will be going up in the near future (if it will), or, once again, use the Contrarian View Close, which we will discuss in the section on closing.

You can also imply that your product may not be available to the prospect in the future. In other words, let your prospect know if there is a good chance this item will be out of stock by the time he gets around to buying. You can also offer the him a special deal since the new models will be coming out soon. "These are brand new, but because the new models are coming out in a few months, you can get a substantial discount on these now."

I Want to Wait until the New Models Come Out

You saw this one coming, right? You might hear this one straight up, or you might hear it after you've informed the prospect about the great deal on the current models because the new ones are coming out in a few months.

If you get this objection, you need to nip it in the bud immediately. Your first response should be, "Great! We are taking orders for the new models now."

Next, ask a question you need answered in order to move the buying process along or to fill out the order form. "What color would you like it in?"

Questions will quickly determine if this objection is real or not. If it is a real objection, the prospect should have no problem "reserving" a unit. However, if the objection is a stall, it will quickly disappear once you ask these questions.

I Do It Myself or I Use the Internet

This objection is becoming increasingly popular these days with the advancement of technology and the Internet. In 1999 and 2000, any investor could throw a dart at a list of stocks and find a sure winner almost every time. Investors became quite confident in their own ability and didn't see the need to pay a broker when they could trade online for a fraction of the cost and do just as well. We have also seen an explosion of "how-to" books on just about every subject under the sun. Finally, the massive amount of information available today gives all of us the opportunity to take a crack at something we never would have considered a few short years ago. So how do you handle this objection?

First, get some details. If you're in investments, say something like, "Oh, great. So what have you been investing in recently?" Follow that with, "And what kind of returns have you been seeing?"

This will give you some ideas about whether this is a true objection and also give you some ideas as to where you may be able to help.

Next, find out how qualified the prospect is to do what he's doing. For example, if someone tells you he does all his investing online you could say, "Oh, that's great! Do you have your Series 7?"

If he says yes, you can further qualify him. You may ask, "So you were a broker?"

You can continue this line of questioning, which can both build rapport and give you an idea of where he may be lacking in knowledge. You may also discover other areas where you can help. On the other hand, if he asks, "What's a Series 7?" or answers no, which are more likely answers, you have a solid opening to stick your foot in the door and sell your experience.

Note: You need to be careful with your line of questioning. You don't want to belittle or insult your prospect—much is dependent on your tone of voice. If you use a sincere tone to ask whether he has his Series 7, it will come off just fine. If you say it with some sarcasm or attitude, you're going to have a problem. Make sure you take a genuine interest and don't allow your ego to get involved in an attempt to show him how much you know and how little he knows.

Your overall goal when answering this objection is to sell your expertise on the subject at hand—without boasting. In other words, sell the value you bring to the table and show why that value is worth paying a little extra for.

If you're an experienced brain surgeon you're going to have a leg up on someone who has just read a book and thinks he has it down. What you're selling is value. Yes, you cost more, but if he wants his brain in proper working order, it's best to spend the money on quality than save it on a botched job that will ultimately cost him much more.

That's an extreme example to make a point, but the same holds true for any product or service in any industry. The general contractor who has been in business for thirty years can do a much better job than someone who is following instructions in a "how-to" book. The investment advisor who has been in the market for twenty years will probably have better luck than someone reading the *Wall Street Journal* for the past six weeks.

Some people enjoy dabbling on their own and are just doing it as a hobby. Whether it is building, investing, working on their car, or anything else, you will probably have a tough time convincing these people to have you do it for them. You probably also won't change the minds of people who *are* experts, or *believe* they are. Typically, the only way these people will let you help is if you somehow convince them that they are not experts and that you are. This can be an uphill battle you may not want to take on.

The other people you will have difficulty with are those that don't care much about quality and/or are extremely cheap. Again, build value and minimize the impact of cost as much as possible. Find a way to make the scales tip towards paying a little more for high-quality results.

The people you have a shot with are those who have the primary objective of saving money by doing it on their own. At this point "I do it myself" becomes a price objection. In other words, low cost, low quality versus higher cost, high quality. This is where you want to sell value and what you bring to the table as an expert in the industry.

An online investor may like the fact that he can make a trade for a fee of $9.99 versus $70 with a broker. And yet, if he makes $200 on his trade and $2,000 on the trade with the broker, the extra $60.01 is worth it. In this situation sell yourself, your company, your product, and overall, the high quality of work you do. Also, give some of the downside of low quality.

Here is an example of what you might say: "Joe, we've shown our clients an average of 22 percent per year on the kind of investments you've been dabbling in. What I'd simply like to do is share some powerful investment ideas with you from time to time. Is that fair enough?"

I Just Lost My Job, My Cat Just Died, My House Just Burned Down

Life changes can be tough objections to deal with. Your odds of overcoming these types of objections will come down to the severity of the situation, the cost of your product or service, and the perceived value of your product or service. Oh, and whether or not the objection is true to begin with. Believe it or not, people will make up some pretty awful personal stories simply to throw you off.

Let's start with the severity of the situation. If someone gets laid off but she has a substantial stash of cash put away, you stand a much better chance of selling your product than if she is living paycheck to paycheck. It's also possible to run into someone at a time when the company she works for is considering sending her to Brazil for a year.

The second factor to consider is the price of your product or service. If you are selling a small-dollar item, her life situation becomes less of an issue.

The third factor to consider is the perceived value of your product or service. If you're selling calling plans and someone has just lost his job, you may be able to structure a plan that will lower his overall monthly bill. You may ask if he will be working out of the house more now, or if he will need to access the Internet in order to look for a new job. If so, you may be able to set up cable service that will allow him faster and easier access the Internet. You may also be able to tie it in with his regular phone plan and lower his cost.

The point: Don't let the objection catch you off guard and don't make assumptions before you have all the facts. Most salespeople are stopped dead in their tracks when they call on someone who has just lost his job. Most will remove themselves from the situation as quickly as possible without asking questions such as:

- Is there a way around this?
- Is there a way this person could still own my product?
- Is there a way in which this person may actually benefit from my product more?

You have to think outside the box and be ready for unusual situations. Inquire as to the severity of the situation and then look for creative ways around the objection.

I Only Deal Locally

We've already talked about this a bit in the *Competition* section. You will typically hear this one on the cold call; it tends to be a knee-jerk reaction that most people have to someone calling from across the state or country. When you're on a cold call and you get an objection, take a quick shot at it and see how strong it is. You might try something like this: "Joe, if I could guarantee you better service and a better product would you be slightly interested?" If you get a flat-out no to this, don't waste your time.

The key to answering this objection is to show the prospect that you can offer more value or a better price from wherever your location is, at the same time demonstrating that he will not suffer any ill effects from the fact that you're not "local." In other words, show the prospect you are just as capable of servicing him from a distance as well as bringing more to the table than the current vendor.

Another quick response to the "I only deal locally" objection is, "I am local." Everything is relative, right? Let's say you have customers in Sri Lanka and the prospect you're calling is simply in the next state. You might follow "I am local" with "I have customers in Sri Lanka (or wherever in the world they are). On the other hand, you're only in the next state." If you get a laugh at this line, continue with the line we used above: "If I could guarantee you better service (or a better price, or whatever it is), would you be slightly interested?"

I Only Buy… (Stocks, Real Estate, etc.)

This is another objection you will typically hear on the cold call. This objection is usually legitimate, but you still want to take a quick crack at it before you move on.

Let's say you're an investment advisor and someone tells you he only buys real estate. In this case say, "Let me ask you a question. If I could guarantee you a 25 percent annual return on your investment, would you be interested?"

If you get any response other than no, follow with, "The nice thing about the stock market is liquidity. If you sell your stock, you can get a check in seven days or less. A piece of property is obviously less liquid, right?"

At the same time, if you find people who don't invest in real estate, you can stress the benefits of real estate, namely: it is a good hedge against inflation and usually not as volatile as the stock market.

In either situation you would also talk about the benefits of diversifying investment dollars as opposed to being dependent upon one type of investment.

I Don't Like You

Okay, this one usually doesn't come in those exact words and it usually comes after you've been calling on a prospect or customer for a while. If you get the idea that she really doesn't like you, or if she does in fact tell you something to that effect, your only real options are to let her go or offer to give her another sales representative from your company. You should at least take a shot at offering another sales rep. This way, your company still has a chance at the business, although it may be remote. Simply say, "Ms. Prospect, I'm sorry if I've done anything to offend you in any way. That surely was not my intention. Let me ask you, is there any way you'd consider speaking with another sales representative from my company?"

That's it—short and simple. The prospect may say no and hang up or kick you out of her office, but at least you took a stab at the objection before you let her go.

I Had a Bad Experience with…or
I Don't Like Your Company or Product

If the prospect has a problem with your company or your product, you may not have a great shot at the business. But it's better than the prospect not liking *you*.

First, you need to find out the reason(s) the prospect feels the way she does.

- Did the prospect try you in the past and have a bad experience?
- Has the prospect simply heard some bad things about your company or product?
- Is there anything else that has led the prospect to feel the way she does about your company or product?

Begin with this question: "Can I ask why you feel that way?" If you get a rude no to this question, you may want to move on. After all, do you really want a customer with this kind of attitude?

If you want to test it, simply look at the prospect and say nothing, as if you are waiting for her to expand on her answer. People don't like silence, and if you can remain silent for long enough, she'll usually say a little more and perhaps open the door for you to respond.

That being said, in most cases the prospect *will* give you some feedback when you ask why she feels the way she does. For example, you might hear, "We used to use you and your service was terrible." Although this may not be great news, you at least have begun a dialogue and you know of one area you need to address if you're going to have a shot at the business.

After the prospect's initial answer, drill down and get some more information. After a comment such as "poor service," say, "Okay, I can understand that. Let me ask you, what in particular was the problem with our service?"

Now you will hear reasons such as:

- Your response time was terrible.
- The attitude of the technicians was bad.
- It always took five trips for you to solve the problem.
- An assortment of other complaints.

Next, isolate the "problem(s)." If the prospect tells you that she was unhappy with your service due to slow response time, you should ask, "Okay, so in addition to our response time, was there anything else you were unhappy with?"

If she says no, further qualify her answer by asking, "So in other words, if we had good response time, you would have continued to do business with us?" If you get a yes, you now know the one objection you need to address. If she tells you she would not have continued to do business, you need to ask, "So what else, other than response time, contributed to our demise?" Be sure you have *all* the objections before you begin to address any of them.

Let's say in this case that the only reason your company lost the business was due to slow response time. You will now ask, "Cindy, if I could show you all the improvements we've made to our service department, and specifically in the area of response time, and prove to you that this would no longer be an issue if you were to do business with my company, would you be open-minded to doing business with us again?"

If you get a no, you've got other issues and you need to learn what they are. If you get a yes, proceed toward "proving" your case and getting back in the door. After all, it is entirely possible that your company had some issues previously that have since been resolved. If this is the case, you can say, "Yes, that used to be an issue because of (give the reasons why), (explain what's been done to resolve it), and assuming this is now resolved, is there any way we can earn your business back?"

Comebacks to *Any* Objection

Following are some quick response comebacks you can use with almost any objection.

- "Cindy, is it really (whatever the objection is) or are you simply asking me why you should be investing in (your product) at this point?"
- "Kathy, I called you today so we could move quickly and I could show you results. It is a major disadvantage not to capitalize on timing. You do agree that timing is important, don't you? (Wait for an affirmative answer.) We must be precise and to be precise we must move now. If you work with me, Kathy, this will be a good move for you, okay?"
- Ignore the objection and simply give another reason to buy. We have referred to this method under the heading, "When to Deal with Objections." We've also mentioned this method under the heading, "Ignoring the Price Objection." However, it can be applied to *all* objections. With this approach, you will cushion your response, respond, and close. "Joe I definitely understand where you are coming from. At the same time, with (mention a feature) I think you can see (mention the benefit). Am I right?" *Close!*

As a Last Resort
If You Are Unable to Find the Objection

When you simply cannot find the real objection and are ready to give up, give the Doorknob Close a try. Please refer to this close on page 476.

Objections during the Cold Call

As we mentioned in the *Cold Call* section, if a prospect gives you objection after objection during the cold call, there may be better places you can spend your time than arguing with him. When you get an objection during the cold call, take a quick swing or two at it, then move on. Simply ask the prospect if he would be interested in your major benefit. If the answer is no, move on. If the answer is anything other than no, continue with your cold call.

Objections Created by the Competition

Another form of objection you'll get, different from the others we've discussed, is one created by weaknesses, or perceived weaknesses, in your product or service. As you know, every product or service has "real" weaknesses from which objections will arise. The other objections you need to look out for are those that your competition will paint as weaknesses, even though they may not actually be weaknesses. Treat these areas as possible objections and work hard on your responses to these "weakness objections." Here is a common example:

Prospect: "Well, I like the fact that your price is low, but I realize that you get what you pay for. How do you respond to your competition's contention that your service organization is half the size of theirs, so your response time is four hours instead of two?"

You: "Kathy, I definitely understand your concern, and on the surface, that would seem to make sense. What my competition probably didn't mention is that they have the five major accounts in this area and those major accounts are going to be more of a priority than you and your company.

"In addition, our competition is also in a position where their resources are more spread out and could be severely strained by the sheer number of accounts they have, thus significantly affecting the service you get from them.

"On the other hand, you would be one of our largest accounts and, as a result, you would get priority service and our utmost attention meaning that, more than likely, you will get the best overall response time. So considering you will be a priority and we will have more resources dedicated to you and your company, do you see how we will be in a better position to service you than the competition?"

Now let's look at the same issue from the other side.

Prospect: "I realize you're the largest company in the industry and probably have, overall, the best product out there. At the same time, there is quite a difference in price between you and your competitor. Is your service really that much better?"

You: "Kathy, the answer to your question is 'Yes, it is.' As the original equipment manufacturer we will be using genuine parts and we are also the most familiar with our product. What that means is you will only get the highest quality of service along with increased machine uptime, which will add to your overall profitability.

"Also, we are the only company that has a 100 percent satisfaction guarantee on our service. If you're not happy, for any reason, we will refund a portion of your service contract. For you that means we have to perform and we have to fix it right the first time. Again, higher-quality service, more uptime of your machines, happier customers, and more profitability.

"We also have the largest, best-trained service organization in the industry so we will be able to respond to you better and faster than anyone else will. As the original equipment manufacturer providing you with more uptime, guaranteed service, more and better-trained technicians, and overall much better service, do you see how you really *do* get what you pay for?"

Both the competition and your potential customers will do their best to seek out your weaknesses and use them against you to leverage their position. As we discussed in the *Competition* section, know your weaknesses, or the potential weaknesses your competition will try to exploit, and design strong answers to address each one.

Do You Work on Commission?

This may not look like an objection, but when you hear this question it's important to realize what the prospect is really asking. That is: Are you potentially trying to sell me something just to make money for yourself? And are you charging me too much? Either of those scenarios is the same as an objection.

The first thing to do is answer the main question. Your answer will be one of the following:

- "Yes, I do." Use this if you're on straight commission.
- "Yes and no. I have a base salary, but they also pay me commission on whatever I sell."
- "No, I work on salary only."

Once you've given your initial response, expand on it. In the case where you *do* receive commission, be it on commission-only basis, or salary and commission, follow up your answer with the following question: "I'm curious. Why do you ask?"

The response you get will usually be something like, "Well, for all I know, you're just trying to make a sale so you can make some money." People who are a little more laid back will say something like, "Just curious." Trust us, they're all thinking the same thing when they ask this question. Reply with this: "Mr. Prospect, I think I understand where you're coming from and let me assure you, if I was selling you something you didn't need, or at the wrong price, I wouldn't be around long and that wouldn't be a great career move either. Would you agree?"

You can then use any money back or other guarantees you have to further reduce the prospect's fear. For example, "We have a thirty-day, money-back guarantee. If you're not happy for any reason, simply return it, and we'll give you your money back, no questions asked. Is that fair enough?"

Many companies also have a price guarantee. If that is the case with your company, that would be another benefit you could talk about.

In the case where you are strictly on salary, follow your answer with, "The company did not want us potentially motivated to sell something that someone may not need. That makes sense, right?" Once they agree, either close or continue with your presentation depending upon where you are in the selling process.

What If You Keep Getting the Same Objection?

Have you ever noticed that the objection we fear most tends to pop up repeatedly? You can do three things if you have an objection that keeps coming up.

1) **Analyze your presentation and see if there is anything you are saying or doing that is creating the objection.**

In addition to studying your presentation yourself, have your manager and others listen to it. Record a live presentation, if possible. If this is not possible, do a presentation for your manager just as you would for a real prospect.

As salespeople, we're sometimes so afraid of getting an objection that we end up saying something that leads to the objection. Are you asking a certain question or making a certain statement that is planting the objection in the prospect's mind? After listening to your presentation and having others listen to it, you'll discover whether there is something in it that needs to be changed.

2) **Thoroughly prepare yourself to answer the objection.**

Begin by writing out all the possible responses to the objection. Once you have them, practice them by yourself. After you've done that, practice them with others and get feedback. Next, make a final version of the responses. Finally, go out and practice them on prospects and customers.

3) **Answer the objection in advance.**

If you find you are getting the same objection almost every time, answer the objection before you get it. What do we mean by that? Let's say that during each presentation the prospect invariably brings up the objection that, while you make your software program look easy to use, it will be too difficult for him or her to use. In this situation you might try the following in your presentation:

"Now at some point in my presentation, someone usually says that I make working with this software program look easy, but they will never be able to work it as easily as I do. This maybe somewhat true—after all, I work with this software day in and day out and know every feature and function.

"Having said that, I want you to be assured that we will thoroughly train you on the system until you're satisfied that you know all there is to know. You will have access to our toll-free support line, which is available 8 a.m. to 8 p.m., seven days a week. We will also leave you with this very thorough, easy-to-use guide that will answer *all* your questions, and you will have my office and cell phone numbers so you can get in touch with me at any time to help you out.

"I think you'd agree with me that service after the sale is extremely important—am I right? (Wait for a response.) Those whom we've trained and given these resources have found they've become very adept at using this software quickly and have found our support second to none. And I'm sure you will too. Do you feel comfortable that you'll get the support necessary to use the software at the level you need to in order to get the most out of it?"

This is an example of answering the objection at the beginning of the presentation in order to prevent it from surfacing later.

The Best Way to Avoid and Defuse *All* Objections

Build urgency and excitement, and make sure the prospect sees the value in what you're offering. With urgency, excitement, and perceived value, half of the objections will not arise. Even in cases in which you are dealing with a true objection, building urgency, excitement, and value will make the objection either disappear or, at the very least, make it much easier to overcome.

A Summary of Ideas on Objections

- Objections are a good thing. They are part of the selling process. When you hear an objection, hear it as, "I'm interested, I'm listening, and I would like to buy your product but I need you to help me with this obstacle."

- Most objections are simply stalls. The prospect can't yet give you a definite yes, and at the same time doesn't want to write you off with a no.

- The above being said, treat each objection as a real one and handle it with respect and empathy.

- Anytime you get an objection, you need to ask questions and learn specifically why the prospect feels the way she does. Once you have specifics, you can respond appropriately to the objection.

- Your goal when overcoming objections is to change the prospect's opinion or perspective. For example, if a prospect tells you your product costs too much, your goal is to show him how it is actually costing him more *not* to have your product than it costs to own it.

- When you get an objection, isolate it, answer it, confirm the answer, give another compelling reason to buy, and then close once again.

- Be persistent. Stay firm in your approach but don't push. Answer objections in an assertive way as opposed to an aggressive way.

- If a prospect succeeds in putting you off with an objection, make sure you have a commitment for follow up. When you do follow up, set an appointment and get to the prospect in person. This will give you the maximum amount of leverage.

- The best way to avoid objections is to have a great presentation that is delivered with enthusiasm and builds lots of value and urgency.

SECTION VII

CLOSING

Introduction

Without closing nothing happens, products aren't manufactured, trucks don't move, people don't work, and money doesn't change hands. If there is no closing there will be no business. Until you close, you have nothing.

Clearly, then, closing is important. Is it the most important part of the sale? Arguably, yes. However, if you have a great presentation and you give it to a prospect who is not qualified to buy your product, the best closing skills in the universe won't bail you out.

For the sake of clarity in this Chapter, we're going to assume the only thing you have left to do is close. In other words, you're speaking the same language as the qualified prospect, you have a good presentation, and essentially have everything else it takes to complete the sale. Now the only thing left to do is close the sale.

Depending upon how you do your job at selling, closing will either be the easiest or the most difficult part of the selling process. If you've done everything else right, closing will simply be a technicality. It will be a smooth transition from the end of the presentation to the close, to the handshake after the sale is completed. If you sell incorrectly up to the close, the only ways to close will be by hammering or coercion. If you do hammer or coerce, and by some miracle you close the sale, you probably won't have it for very long. And if the person does go through with the sale, you'll likely never sell to that person again.

Closing and its importance are definitely affected by the size of the sale. A higher number of closing attempts in one sitting is more likely to be effective when a small-dollar item is involved. With a smaller-dollar item, you don't have to do quite as good a job before the close. You can rely on the closing portion of the sales call to uncover objections, needs, and other aspects that are normally covered prior to the close. This isn't to suggest you should cut corners and get to the close more quickly; it simply means you have a little more room for error with small-dollar sales.

Furthermore, the salesperson himself is not as important in the small-dollar sale as in the large-dollar sale. It's easier for a prospect to overlook an obnoxious or unlikeable salesperson when the sale is small and short-term in nature. The prospect thinks he or she won't have any further dealings with the salesperson once the sale is complete, and hopefully it will all be over in a few minutes. In any case, to improve your chances, even when selling small-dollar items, you want to take all the proper steps during the presentation and close, and you want to be as likeable as possible.

The most important part of closing is to *do it*. Closing doesn't always mean getting a sale, it may mean closing on the follow-up appointment, or whatever the next step in the process may be. It's amazing how many salespeople do not actually close. A typical situation usually goes something like this:

The salesperson goes through the entire presentation, arrives at the end, and says something like, "So, what do you think?" which of course is not a closing question.

The prospect responds, "Well, it looks pretty good. Why don't you call me in about a week and I'll tell you what I think."

The salesperson says, "Okay," packs up his materials, says goodbye, and leaves.

The prospect was the only one in the above example who closed; she closed the salesperson on buying her excuse for not moving forward and thus she was only one who made a sale.

Remember: A sale is always made, someone is always closed on. Either the salesperson closes the prospect on buying or the prospect closes the salesperson on waiting until later. Thus it's critical that you close during all sales calls. Whether it's closing on the sale, closing on the appointment, or closing on the next time you'll phone or meet in person, you have to close on every call.

Chapter 32

Preparing to Close

Closing Rules

As with almost every aspect of sales, there are rules to follow when closing. They are:

1) *Do it.*

We've just mentioned this one, but it's worth stating again. You must be closing either on the sale or the next part of the sales process, whichever your objective is. If you don't close, most prospects will be happy to simply exchange pleasantries with you and not buy today, even though they may have been perfectly willing to.

2) Work hard on your closing techniques.

Practice, drill, and rehearse your closes and your closing techniques. Know them in your sleep. Most important, practice and perfect your closing out in the field.

3) Always be prepared to close.

Make sure you're mentally prepared, have all materials with you, and that your materials are presentable, operational, and ready to go. Have calculators, pens, contracts, and everything else necessary to consummate the sale. Add the numbers *before* you show up. Know how far you can go with your discount and other concessions. Know what all the terms and conditions of your contract are and what they mean.

4) Once a decision has been made, close the sale as soon as possible.

When a prospect is ready to buy, *close the sale.* If you are on the phone setting up an in-person appointment with a prospect who has just decided to buy, *get over there as soon as possible.* Let as little time as possible pass between the point when a decision is made and when the signature goes on the contract.

5) After you close, remain silent.

After you close, keep your mouth shut. The first one to talk buys. Either the prospect buys your product or service, or you buy the prospect's excuse for not moving ahead.

6) Make the closing process as smooth, relaxed, and as simple as possible.

Try to limit paperwork, the time it takes, and the level of work that goes into it. Do as much of the paperwork as you can *before* you get there, such as filling in the prospect's basic information. One of the worst things you can do is close the prospect then spend ten minutes filling out paperwork before getting the contract signed.

7) Keep yourself busy, avert your eyes, and stay quiet while the prospect is signing.

You don't want the prospect to feel as if he or she is under a spotlight. Look at your calendar, Daytimer, or anything else you have with you.

8) Smile and thank the customer for his or her business.

Make sure you cover all necessary details including what will happen next in the process. We will cover this in detail in Section VIII: *After the Close.*

9) Follow up after you close.

Follow up promptly after the close and make sure the sale is *solid*. You want to prevent buyer's remorse and anything else that could "unclose" the sale after it's been closed.

The Right Attitude

Before you close anyone else, you must first close yourself. The top producers in any industry go into a sales call confident they will make the sale. They *know* they will eventually find a way to do business with even the most difficult prospect.

Top salespeople *know* they will have to take some rejection. They also *know* they will eventually win the prospect over in time. That confidence is important when closing. If you know the sale is simply a technicality, you will persist, deal with the barrage of objections, and you'll hang in there and give it your best shot, regardless of what happens.

Moreover, if a top salesperson gets hammered on a particular call, he or she will go on to the next call as though nothing had happened. In fact, as an observer, you would not be able to tell if the salesperson had just made a record sale at the last call or had the most horrendous sales call to date. No call is taken personally and no call is a matter of life or death.

Get in Front of the Prospect to Influence a Decision in Your Favor

You have the most influence over a decision when you are face to face with the prospect.

We once found ourselves in a highly competitive battle at a bank that was buying its first ATM. At our monthly sales meeting, the competition was discussed extensively and we determined we had some great, new, "enlightening" information that we thought might finally put us over the top. We called the CEO.

Us: Matt, we just got out of a meeting and we have some *major* information you need to see before you make a decision on the ATM. Is your schedule better tomorrow morning or tomorrow afternoon?

CEO: Hmm, I'm pretty busy. Why don't you just fax it to me?

Us: Matt, in order to effectively convey this we need to see you in person. It won't take long. How about Wednesday, morning or afternoon?

CEO: How long will it take?

Us: Not long, Matt. 10 a.m. or 2 p.m. Wednesday?

CEO: Umm, ten is probably better.

Us: Great! See you then.

We made that sale on Wednesday. Unsurprisingly, in the meeting the CEO told us he had been planning to go with the competition before he saw the new information. That was probably why he'd wanted us to fax it—because it would have been much easier to get rid of us at that point.

In this situation, had we faxed the information as asked, we probably would have lost the sale. When you are fighting for business, keep yourself in front of the prospect.

Sometimes a scenario like the one above will begin with a comment from the prospect that goes something like this: "Bob, I have to be honest—I think I'm going to go with Brand F on this one."

Again, at this point you need to get in front of the prospect *as soon as possible*. Use any excuse you can, but make sure you get an in-person meeting with him.

The prospect will most likely try to brush you off. He is starting to see the light at the end of the tunnel in the long decision-making process and he just wants the work and the agony to end. He wants to be at the finish line and doesn't want to turn around and revisit things when he is so close. Be professional and be polite, but be persistent. You've got nothing to lose and everything to gain.

Note: You always want to be truthful in your communications, yet you may occasionally have to walk a fine line in order to get in front of the prospect. In reality, it took us about forty-five minutes to convey the information. We had told him that "It wouldn't take long." Now, he did have some questions and comments that helped stretch it to forty-five minutes, and he could have cut us short anywhere along the way. "Not long" is a relative term. Not long compared to what? In any case, you need to get face to face with the prospect in order to put yourself in a strong position to close.

Create the Right Closing Environment

As we've noted, you want the prospect as relaxed as possible during the closing process. If you close at your place of business, make the environment conducive to closing. You want the area to be pleasing to the senses and comfortable for the prospect. Make sure it smells good. You can even play some soft, soothing background music. Make sure the prospect is sitting when you are closing and make sure he or she is in a comfortable chair. And finally, have water, coffee, and other beverages available for your prospects. Subtleties count. You want to have as many things going in your favor as possible.

Chapter 33

Closing the Prospect

Adapt to the Personality of the Person You're Closing

As with every other part of the sale, you need to be able to adapt to the person you're closing. Some people appreciate a direct approach; others may find a direct approach pushy. For prospects with whom you have no problem getting down to business, use a direct approach. These people will tend to be Drivers and Partiers.

With the people who want to talk about everything but business and who keep trying to take you off on tangents, you'll need to use a softer approach. These people tend to be "Yes" People and Thinkers.

In either case, be persistent and keep your objective in mind—closing the sale or closing on the next step in the selling process. As with all other aspects of selling, only *practice* with prospects will give you the necessary experience to determine *how* you need to close.

Here are the approaches to use with the different personality types:

Driver: Use a direct approach. You can build some rapport—and you should—and yet Drivers like to get down to business quickly. Use options and alternatives when selling to a Driver. Give them a Plan A and Plan B and then close with, "Do you believe Plan A or Plan B will work better for you?"

Thinker: Build personal rapport. Be specific with any information. Know your "technical" stuff or have someone with you who does. Use advantages and disadvantages when selling to a Thinker. "How many disadvantages can you come up with in regard to buying our product?" "Now let's look at the advantages."

The Advantage, Disadvantage Close, which we will discuss on page 464, is a good one to use with this personality type.

"Yes" Person: Concentrate on building strong personal rapport with this person. The "Yes" Person *needs to know you care* about him or her personally.

Tell positive stories about how your product worked well for someone. Also, let the prospect know that the relationship is very important to you and ensure him or her that you will continue to be there after the sale.

Partier: Build some rapport, but be direct. Get down to business fairly quickly. Use stories, both good and bad, about where your product helped, and where someone was affected negatively by not having your product.

For more information on personality types, please refer to our more detailed descriptions of them in the *Cold Call* section.

Speak the Same Language as the Person You're Closing

In both the *Cold Call* and the *Presentation* sections, we spoke about the importance of speaking the same language as the prospect. Remember to continue that into the close. Match the volume, pitch, speed, and other aspects of your prospect's speech. Also, use the prospect's words and phrases in the close, along with words that relate to his or her preferred sense be it visual, auditory, or kinesthetic.

Timing is Important When Closing

Just like a good joke, the timing of your close is important. Your prospect must be ready before you close the sale. Just as you don't step onto second base before you step on first, you don't close until you've built the necessary need and desire in the prospect for your product or service.

While it's possible to close too early, it is also possible to close too late. You may have heard the saying, "Don't buy it back once you've sold it." This saying refers to talking too much and over-selling after the prospect is ready to buy.

Think of closing as an arc or even as a storyline. You start at ground zero and begin to build your case. You continue to build your case and your story line rises toward the top of the arc. When you are at the top of the arc, or the climax of the story, you have built maximum interest, need, and desire and the prospect is ready to buy. It is time to close.

If you don't close at the top of the arc, the line starts to go back down. Negative thoughts may begin to run through the prospect's mind. "Hmm, this is starting to sound too good to be true" or "Obviously, he can tell by my responses that I'm ready to buy. Why is he still selling? Is there something he's worried about or I should be worried about?"

You'll also run into people without a lot of patience who will simply start to tune you out after a certain point. They may be interested enough to buy but then they begin to focus more on the time and all the other things they've got to get done today. In any case, your chances of closing start to decline. So how do you know when it's time to close?

Look for Indicators That It's Time to Close

When do you close? The answer is: you close when the prospect is ready to be closed. You can tell when he's ready by his actions, his body language, what he says, and how he says it.

What kind of feedback is the prospect giving you?

- What is his facial expression telling you? Is he smiling, frowning, or poker-faced?
- What about his body language? Is he leaning in or leaning back?
- Is he nodding his head yes, or shaking his head no?
- Is his posture open or closed?
- What do his eyes tell you? Are they wide open with interest or does he look like he's daydreaming or struggling to keep his eyes open?
- Is he giving you any verbal feedback, and what is his tone? Are his words and tone positive, negative, sincere, skeptical, or sarcastic?
- Is he asking questions or providing valuable information?
- Is he making any sounds at all, and what is the tone of the sounds, positive or negative?
- Is he completely silent?

If you appear to be receiving positive feedback and all seems to be going well, you want to close sooner rather than later. If someone is truly interested and you close before she is ready to buy, she will answer your closing question with a question about the information she needs before she buys.

For example, let's say you close with, "Would you like a half dozen, or would a dozen work better for you?" If she isn't ready to buy yet, but she's interested, she'll respond with something like, "Would I be able to get all of them in black?" At that point you would of course answer her question, and if it's an affirmative answer, close immediately.

For example: "Yes, you can get them all in black. I just need a little information. Will we be shipping to your home address or business?" She might then respond with, "How soon can I get them?" If you have flexibility with delivery, you would say, "When do you need them by?" After she answers, say, "Great, we'll have them to you for (whenever she needs them). Will we be shipping to your home or office?"

Simply continue this technique of answering each question and closing until the prospect has finished asking all her questions.

What if you are dealing with a prospect who seems completely bored and uninterested? Should you still close? Before you close, you'll want to find out how your presentation is actually going. To gauge where you are, you'll need to ask some questions.

Ask tie-down and trial closing questions. For example, you might say, "Jane, do you see how this product could significantly increase your profit margin?"

The answer to this question, along with the prospect's tone of voice and body language, will let you know where you stand. If you get an affirmative response, you're in good shape. If you get a less than positive yes, you need to go back and build the foundation once again. You either have not created the need or have not found the problem, or possibly both.

Here are some other examples of trial closing questions:

- "When do you need delivery?"
- "What color are you looking for?"
- "Does it look like we have the solution that meets your needs?"
- "Have I adequately shown you how this is the best investment for you?"

These questions require the prospect to give you a commitment. When a prospect gets a question like one of these, she knows she is being pinned down. If she likes your idea, you have no problem, but if she doesn't, she might start to sweat because she knows her answer will commit her one way or the other. If she's ready to buy, she'll answer your question and you can continue to complete the order. If she isn't ready to buy, she'll either flat-out tell you and/or ask a question she needs answered before moving ahead. If you find that she is not ready to be closed, continue with your presentation and search for the prospect's hot buttons and issues that stand between you and the close.

In this case, ask questions to make sure you have identified the needs, desires, and/or problems. Simply say, "Ms. Prospect, as I understand it, you are looking for (fill in the prospect's needs, desires, and problems to be solved here). Is that correct?"

If you have not identified the proper information, ask the prospect to define things for you. Once you have the proper information, accentuate those needs, desires, and/or problems and then build the value of your product and service and show how it is the prospect's best solution.

In the end, you are better off closing too soon and too often as opposed to too late and not enough. Sure, closing too often can annoy some people, but closing too often isn't a problem most salespeople have. Not closing enough is.

Here are the five categories of buying signals along with some specific examples of each:

1) The prospect is asking buying or ownership questions. These include:

- "How soon can I get it?"
- "What colors does it come in?"
- "Can I finance this?" (And other questions about methods of payment.)
- "Do you have any specials?"
- "What kind of guarantee or warranty does this come with?"
- "What kind of service plans do you offer?" (Or other questions about customer service or support.)
- "Can I get the plasma screen along with a thermal printer?" (And other questions about the product or services features and functions.)
- "Do you have some references I can talk to?"
- "Would I be able to add that feature a year from now?"
- "What was that you mentioned earlier about your trade-in program?"

These questions tell you the prospect wants your product or service and is trying to figure out a way to get it. Or she may be picturing herself owning it and wants to know what situations might arise in the future.

2) Positive statements or questions about you, your company, or your product or service. These include statements and questions such as:

- "Wow, that's a great feature."
- "Yes, that's what people say they really like about your company."
- "That would be much easier to use than what we have currently."
- "Would you also be able to provide me with all the supplies?"
- "What would you recommend?"

These statements and questions tell you that you are making a positive impression on the prospect and that he or she is listening, interested, and following along with you.

3) Negative statements about the prospect's current vendor, equipment, or situation in general. These would include statements such as:

- "The machines we have right now are a nightmare."
- "Our machines never get fixed right the first time."
- "When I call the company for support, I always get the runaround."

These statements tell you the prospect is dissatisfied and looking to make a change. Statements like these are *very* important because they tell you what the prospect's hot buttons are and what areas you need to concentrate on to make the sale.

For example, if the prospect tells you the machines never get fixed right the first time, you want to focus on your company's stellar record of fixing the machine the first time, if that is actually the case. Also, in a case such as this, it is also a good idea to emphasize some of the reasons for your company's stellar record, or let the prospect know how you will make sure this area of concern is covered. You might assure the prospect that you will monitor the installation and servicing of the machines by staying in touch with the installation and service managers and the technicians in the field just to have that extra level of visibility and attention to detail.

In order to discover and better understand a prospect's hot buttons, get as much information as possible. For example, in the first statement when the prospect said the current machines are a nightmare, you want to know exactly *how* they are a nightmare. Ask, "In what way are they a nightmare?" Continue to ask questions and get the prospect to expand on the "nightmare" until you have a clear and complete picture of what the problem is. Then talk about the strengths of your product and how your product will solve the "nightmare."

4) Statements about conditions of ownership. These statements include:

- "Hmm, I really need a machine in the next two weeks."
- "I really want my new machine in red, white, and blue."

These statements tell you that the prospect has already mentally bought the machine and is picturing his "ideal" new machine at his home or business. At this point you will assume the close and ask a closing question based on his comment.

5) Body language and other positive signs.

In addition to the questions and statements we discussed in items 1 through 4, look for body language and other cues that it may be time to close.

For example, is the prospect nodding and smiling along with you during your presentation or at a particular time in your presentation? Perhaps immediately after you mentioned a new feature or function, the prospect's eyes lit up and he began nodding his head. If this happens, treat that just as you would one of the above questions or comments. In other words, acknowledge the prospect's response and make a statement and/or ask a question. You might say, "You like that feature, do you? What in particular do you like about it?"

This will give you an opportunity to uncover some hot buttons. Once the prospect has answered your question, you can follow up with, "So that's a feature you'd like on your machine?" Then use that to move toward the close.

Once you get questions, comments, or other positive signs that fall into one or more of the five categories above, respond to them and close. Some you'll close on immediately and others you'll use to lead to the close later in the presentation. For example, if you are in the first minute of a thirty-minute presentation and the prospect says, "Wow, that's a neat feature!" that's not quite as strong as "Can I get it in red?" asked twenty-five minutes into the presentation.

If you get "Wow, that's a neat feature" in the beginning, answer, "Yes, it is, isn't it? Is that a feature you'd like on your machine?" When the prospect answers yes, say: "Great—I'll make a note of that." As you come to the end of the presentation, you can return to that point to close. Say, "Earlier you mentioned you'd like to see this feature on your machine, correct?" Then continue to ask the necessary questions to complete the order and close the sale.

When you get a buying signal toward the end of your presentation, close on it immediately. For example, when the prospect asks, "Can I get it in red?" respond with, "Yes, you can. So we should order it in red?" Then ask all the other questions necessary to take the order.

Specific Answers to the Closing Indicators Above

Here are some specific answers for some of the above questions, comments, and other closing indicators.

Section 1) Buying or ownership questions:

Prospect: "How soon can I get it?"
You: "How soon do you need it?"

Prospect: "Can I get this in green?"
You: "Yes, you can. So green is the color you'd like?"

Prospect: "Can I finance this?"
You: "Yes, you can. We have finance terms for twelve, twenty-four, or thirty-six months. Did you have a certain time frame in mind, or should we simply run the numbers and see what payments you'd be looking at on the different plans?"

Prospect: "What kind of warranty does this come with?'
You: "This comes with a one-year warranty that covers all parts and labor. It's the most comprehensive in the industry. As you may know, our warranty covers *everything* from A to Z. I think you'll appreciate having the most comprehensive coverage in the industry and not getting any surprises. Am I right?"

Prospect: "What kind of service plans do you offer?"
You: "We can offer you flexible terms. Ninety-five percent of our customers go with parts and labor 8 a.m. to 8 p.m. seven days a week. Does that sound good to you or did you have other hours in mind?"

Prospect: "Can I get the plasma screen along with a thermal printer?"
You: "Yes. So you want the thermal printer as opposed to the dot matrix?"

Prospect: "Do you have some references I can speak with?"
You: "Absolutely. I'll get you a list of references. Assuming you like what they have to say, when would you be looking for delivery?"

Prospect: "Would I be able to add that feature a year from now?"
You: "Yes, absolutely. Of course, it will cost a little extra to upgrade later as we will have to do it out in the field. We could add it now or would you rather wait?"

Prospect: "What was that you mentioned earlier about your trade-in program?"
You: "We currently have a trade-in program in which we will give you $5,000 for your old machine toward the purchase of a new one. With that in mind, will you be trading in your old machine when you purchase this one?"

Section 2) Positive statements or questions:

Prospect: "Yes, we've heard people really like that feature about your company."
You: "Yes, with the largest, best-trained service organization in the industry, we're able to get to you quickly and minimize your downtime. We're also able to fix your machine right the first time. This means maximum profitability and less stress and frustration on your end. Does that sound like the kind of service you're looking for?"

Prospect: "That would be much easier to use than what we have currently."
You: "Yes, we've heard this from other people who used to use the same product as you are now. Specifically, what do *you* see as some of the advantages here?" (Wait for response.) "Yes, I'm sure you'll appreciate all the time and effort you're going to save with our machine, right?"

Prospect: "What would you recommend?"
You: "Based upon everything you've told me, this plan here would suit your needs best. How does that sound to you?" (Once you get an affirmative

answer, simply start asking the questions you need answered to complete the order.)

Section 3) Negative statements about current situation:

Prospect: "The machines we have right now are a nightmare."

You: "A nightmare in what way?" (Wait for the prospect's response.) "Yes, we've heard the same kind of stories from other customers who've used brand X. What most of them appreciate about our machines is the fact that they (express a feature of your product that dissolves the nightmare the prospect is currently facing), which in turn (express the benefit of that feature). I'm sure you'll appreciate that benefit as well. Am I right?"

Prospect: "Our machines never get fixed right the first time."

You: "I think you'll appreciate the fact that our company leads the industry by a wide margin in fixing equipment right the first time. In addition, our machines experience the greatest amount of uptime across the industry, which will lead to maximum profitability for you. I'm sure you'll appreciate that, right?"

Prospect: "When I call the company I'm dealing with now for support, I always get the runaround."

You: "Yes, we've heard that complaint about our competitor, and that's why you will talk to a live person whenever you call, twenty-four hours a day, seven days a week. Each person is highly trained and can answer all your questions. You won't get caught up in a voice-mail loop or be put on hold because someone doesn't know the answer to your question. We pride ourselves on having the best support in the industry. I'm sure you'll appreciate that, right?"

Section 4) Statements about condition of ownership:

Prospect: "Hmm, I really need a machine in the next two weeks."

You: "How about if I have it delivered at the end of next week?"

Prospect: "I really want my new machine in red, white, and blue."

You: "We can do that. Let me make a note of that. And when would you like it delivered?"

Section 5) Positive Signs and Body Language:

Respond to each positive sign you get from a prospect. If you are getting many positive signs, as you will with a "Yes" Person, simply respond with similar gestures. For example, if the prospect is smiling and nodding his head during the whole presentation, then do lots of smiling and nodding.

Most other buyer types will give you only occasional positive signs. These occasional signs will be truer than the constant ones you're getting from the "Yes" Person. As a result, you want to nail them down and investigate further. If the prospect smiles and nods her head, stop, acknowledge the positive sign, ask about it, and then use it to close now, or make a note and use it as a tool to close later in the presentation. Here's an example:

You: "We put Windows software on our machines because it works much better than OS2 when it comes to advanced functionality." (As you are making this statement, you notice the prospect starts to nod his head.)

You: "That's a subject that interests you?"

Prospect: "Very much so."

You: "In what way?"

Prospect: "Your competitor is actually recommending OS2 and steering us away from Windows because they feel Windows is too advanced and too unpredictable."

You: "How do you feel about Windows versus OS2?"

Prospect: "Windows is definitely the way to go."

You: "So I'm guessing you probably weren't too happy to hear their opinion that you should go with OS2, am I right?"

Prospect: "You're absolutely right."

You: "It sounds as if we're the company with the solution you're looking for?"

Prospect: "Yes, I guess it pretty much looks that way."

You: "So when will you need delivery of these units?"

The above story sounds a little too perfect, but that's exactly how it happened on one of our calls. React to the positive signs you get from prospects and customers, investigate them, expand on them, and turn them into closing opportunities.

Paint Pictures When Closing

In the *Presentation* section we talked about helping the prospect paint mental pictures. After you've painted those pictures, bring them to the close. You paint pictures in the presentation by asking questions. For example, you might ask, "Will you mostly be driving this car around town and to work, or will you be taking some long trips in it?" In order to answer that question, the prospect must go into her mind and picture what it will be like to own and enjoy the car, driving around town and to work, or taking special trips.

Once you have an answer, you will refer to this picture during the close. For example, when closing you might say, "Ms. Prospect, would you rather have the neighbors see you driving around in the black Cadillac or the white one?" At this point, she'll go in her mind and picture herself waving to the neighbors as she drives past in her new (whatever color she prefers) Cadillac as they turn green with envy. You need to paint the picture during the presentation, and repaint it during the close.

After you have painted a picture of driving past the neighbors in the above example, you could then paint a picture of pulling into the parking lot at work, or you could paint a picture of driving down the road in luxury and safety, if those items are important to the prospect. Once you've asked the question about color and filled that information in on the order form, you might then say, "And as you see yourself cruising down the highway in luxury, are you enjoying the lumbar seats as well?"

As we discussed in the *Presentation* section, you can paint more than one picture. However, don't overuse this technique—you can aggravate people by using it too much. One or two good pictures should be sufficient.

Bring the Other Senses into the Close

In the *Presentation* section, we talked about including as many of the senses as possible. You also want to involve as many senses as possible during the close.

In the *Presentation* section, we used an example of selling a boat. Here is a slight variation. During the presentation, after asking about enjoying the boat on either a special occasion or the weekends, you might say, "Yes, around this time of year I can't help but start thinking about summer parties, picnics, swimming at the lake, and everything else, especially watermelon (or whatever your favorite summer food or activity happens to be)."

At that point the prospect will say something like, "Oh yes. I love (some particular type of food or other 'summer' element)." You will then tie that information into your close. Your close might sound like this: "When you see your brother from Chicago enjoying the boat this summer while he eats watermelon with the smell of sunscreen in the air, do you see him enjoying the red boat or the white one?"

Notice that we added not only the sense of taste but also the sense of smell with the inclusion of the sunscreen.

Bring the Prospect's Family Members and Dreams into the Close

In the *Presentation* section, we mentioned that subjects such as a child's future, taking care of parents in their later years, and the death of a loved one can all be highly emotional topics, and ones that your product or service may help the prospect to handle.

Topics revolving around loved ones can also be positive, such as a college education, buying a dream home, or securing the financial future of one's family.

After you paint pictures with regard to these life situations in your presentation, bring those pictures to the close. For example, if you are selling life insurance and painted pictures of college educations and weddings during the presentation, you might close with, "Mr. Prospect, in conclusion, we've agreed that this life insurance will give you the piece of mind in knowing college educations and weddings will be paid for should something unexpected ever happen to you. Would you prefer to make the insurance investments monthly or quarterly?"

Hard Sell versus Soft Sell

When we talk about hard sell, we're not talking about hammering someone into doing something that isn't right for him. We're talking about being direct and getting the prospect involved in what he needs, cutting through fear, denial, and other roadblocks that can stop a sale.

By soft sell, we're not talking about using touchy-feely language and letting the prospect completely control the process. Rather, we're talking about listening with empathy and truly understanding your prospect and his needs, putting yourself in his shoes, and sympathizing with him and his situation.

Keeping those definitions in mind, a fine line exists between soft sell and hard sell, and you have to learn when to cross it. The problem with most salespeople is that they are either hard sell or soft sell, not both. To be the best salesperson you can be, you need to be able to use both approaches and you need to know *when* to use each one.

As a general rule, you want to be soft in the beginning of the relationship. When you are just getting to know the prospect and you're building rapport, you want to be soft, slow, and listen a lot. Once you have a full understanding of what the prospect needs, it is then time to be direct and make sure he gets what he needs. At this point you need to cut through everything else and get to the bottom line: the sale.

The type of person with whom you are dealing will also dictate whether you are hard sell or soft sell and *when* to cross that line. With a hard-nosed, straightforward, no-fluff individual, you will go from soft sell to hard sell faster than you will with someone who is more laid-back, easygoing, and slower in his approach.

In some cases, you may feel as though you never need to cross the line between soft sell and hard sell. You will have a great connection with certain people. They will see the opportunity, they will know what they have to do, you will be able to lead them directly down the path toward the sale, and it will seem as natural as taking a walk on the beach.

In other cases, you will feel as though you need to be more forceful. You may have someone who truly needs your product or service. She knows she needs it, and yet fear is holding her back from doing what she knows she needs to do. At that point, you'll need to skillfully push a little.

Develop both the hard and soft side of your selling approach. As with every other area in selling, you need to be able to adapt your approach to the person to whom you are selling. Only by practicing will you get good at using both approaches and knowing when to use which one.

Be Prepared to Hear "No" a Few Times

Obviously, when closing, you can expect to get a no from time to time. The first rule about getting a no is: *Don't take it personally.* If you're going to take no personally, you're in the wrong business. The second rule about getting a no is: Don't see it as the final answer or a done deal. *Many* sales are completed after hearing no two, three, four, or even more times. You must persist, yet not hammer the prospect.

So how do you continue to ask for the order without hammering? You overcome an objection, present new information, and help the prospect better understand; in short, you change the perception of the prospect, and then, based upon her new perspective, you ask her to buy again.

For example, let's say the prospect tells you, "It costs too much." You proceed by dealing with the objection, showing the prospect how to afford your product, and then closing again. Now the prospect says, "Hmm, okay, I see what you're saying, but I really want to think about it." Now you deal with that objection, show the prospect why now is the best time to go ahead with the purchase, and then close again.

The first time you got a no, you changed the prospect's perception by showing her she could afford your product. Then, based upon the prospect's *new* perception, you once again asked her to buy. It's only hammering when you continually ask the prospect to buy when nothing has changed in the conversation. If she said it cost too much and you responded with, "Oh, come on, I know you can afford it. Just buy it" and asked for the order in this manner several times, you'd be hammering the prospect.

It's entirely possible to hear no in more than one sitting. You may get a no on your first sales call, a no on your second call, two no's on your third call, and a maybe and finally a yes on your fourth call. The key is to return each time with new, enlightening information that educates and changes the perspective of the prospect.

Your goal is to eventually change the prospect's mindset to the point where he decides that your offer makes sense for him. Thus, whether you close seven times in one sitting or only once, the key is to get the necessary number of no's to determine whether you've got a prospect who will eventually buy.

While you are in the process of receiving several no's that hopefully will lead to a yes, keep several rules in mind:

- *Always* be professional, kind, and courteous.
- *Always* show empathy and understanding for the prospect's situation.
- *Always* be straightforward with the prospect.
- *Always* try to get some insight into why the prospect feels the way she does. Why does she feel she can't afford it, or why does she feel she needs to think it over? Once you have that information, use the fifth rule, which is:
- *Always* present new, enlightening, and interesting information that further educates the prospect before attempting another close.

The bottom line is not to quit after one or even a few no's. *Be persistent*. Seek to understand, seek a solution, seek to educate the prospect and change her perspective, and then close on the solution based upon the prospect's new understanding.

Also, remember to *always* be conversational, and break up the conversation occasionally with humor.

How Many Times Should You Hear "No" before You Give Up?

First, the tone, and intensity of the no's are key factors that will determine when you should give up on a prospect. Second, the prospect's situation or reason for rejecting you will determine how long to pursue the prospect. Third, the law of diminishing returns will determine how many times you should take no from the prospect.

Let's take a look at the first factor: the tone, intensity, and condition of the no. Clearly if someone is vulgar, rude, or threatens you with bodily harm, it's probably a good idea to move on. If you are selling over the phone and someone hangs up on you, in some cases you *may* want to call back once. However, if she hangs up on you again, you are probably best off calling another prospect.

These are extreme examples to make a point. You want to pay very close attention to *how* your prospect says something, not just to *what* she says.

- How does the prospect's tone of voice sound?
- Does the person sound certain about the no, or is there some doubt in her voice?
- How about her body language and facial expression?

Second, the prospect's situation or reason for rejecting you will determine how long you will endure it. If she tells you, "I have no money, I'm heavily in debt, I'm filing for bankruptcy, and I'm unemployed," you can give up on selling that Rolls Royce over the phone.

This is an extreme example to make a point. If a prospect has a condition or conditions that make owning your product nothing but a pipe dream, let it go and move on. If someone comes in to look at a Corvette and he is fresh out of college with years of student loans to pay off, is making $20,000 a year, and is the sole source of money for this transaction, once you've qualified him—or unqualified him—move on. Again, a little extreme, but you get the point. You won't get blood from a stone, so recognize it as a stone and move on.

The third and most difficult reason to understand for moving on is the law of diminishing returns. Essentially, what this means is if you have to spend three days with someone in order to make a sale, you might have been better off calling on fifty other people and making five sales.

How much is one person and one sale really worth? You need to know that information and you need to determine how much time you should spend on someone before you move on. Occasionally, you will encounter people who can't give you a final no, yet they won't commit to a yes either. You will reach a point where you need to cut your losses and move on. This can be tough because it's like a carrot dangled just out of reach. You think that maybe, just maybe, if you try a little harder, reach a little further, or spend a little more time, you might make it. Next thing you know, you've wasted three hours and you still have no sale.

Use your best judgment, and remember judgment comes with experience. The more calls you make, the more experienced you'll be, and the better you'll become at recognizing when to hang on and when to let go.

Close…close…close, and be persistent! But remember, once you've given it your best effort, *move on*.

What If a Prospect Asks You a Question More than Once?

If a prospect asks you a question more than once, he or she either didn't understand your answer the first time, or is testing your honesty and conviction. A question asked more than twice is usually also the key to the prospect either buying or not buying. If you answer the question correctly, you will more than likely close the sale.

If the prospect did not understand your answer the first time, she will typically have a quizzical or confused look and appear to be paying close attention to your answer. In this case, answer the question again and finish with, "Does that clarify things?"

Listen closely to the answer. You want to make absolutely sure the prospect understands. If you get a weak yes, or there is a question mark in the prospect's response, she clearly doesn't understand. Go back to the beginning and take her pulse several times during the explanation.

For example, if your answer has three parts, make sure your prospect is clear on the first part before you proceed to the second part, then make sure parts one and two are clear before you proceed to part three. This will help you determine which part of the explanation is a problem; you can then focus on clarifying it.

If the prospect is testing your honesty or conviction, she will have either a slight smirk or a completely serious facial expression. In this case, she wants to make sure you answer the question in the same way you did previously. Simplqy answer the question as you did before and then finish again with, "Does that clarify things?"

If you get the same question a third time, this is the *key reason* for either buying or not buying. If you answer this "objection" correctly, you've likely got a sale. In this situation the prospect is trying to find a way around this obstacle. This time, you need to answer the question in a different way than you did the first two times. You want to answer the question in parts, as we've just described, but you need to add something.

Again, let's assume your answer has three parts. After the first part say, "Are you with me so far?" Once you get an answer to that question (assuming it's affirmative), ask, "And are you okay with my answer so far?"

Your goal is to find out what part of the answer the prospect is trying to work around. Once you find the part of the answer she has a problem with, help the prospect find a way around that issue and then close. Say, "Okay, now that we've found a solution to that issue, are you ready to go ahead with the investment?"

Note: *Do not ever say*, "As I said earlier" before you answer again. "As I said earlier" is the equivalent of saying, "Look, pay attention this time."

Don't Let *Not* Having an Answer to a Question Stop the Close

Here's the scenario: you're getting close to the sale, there are just a few more details to clarify, and suddenly the prospect asks you a question you can't answer. What do you do? You could guess at the answer, but if you give incorrect information you're setting yourself up for problems, either immediately or down the road. You could tell the truth and say you don't know, but that probably will halt the selling process. If you get a question you can't answer, use the following approach.

First, begin with the truth: "I don't know the answer to that question." Next, qualify the importance of the question to the selling process. You want to learn if the answer to this question will be a crucial factor in determining whether the prospect moves ahead with the purchase, or if the answer really doesn't make much difference either way. However, if it is a crucial, determining factor, you'll have to come up with an answer before the sale can take place. If the prospect simply asked the question out of curiosity, then you can proceed with the selling process. Let's look at an example.

Prospect: "If I'm using the collating and stapling features and the machine is running low on staples, will it somehow let me know?"

You: "Hmm, that's a good question and one I don't have an answer for. I'll write that down and be sure to get an answer for you as soon as possible. Let me ask you, is the answer to that question critical to whether you purchase this machine?"

Prospect: "No, not really—it just crossed my mind as we were talking about this feature. Obviously it would be nice if it did, but in the big picture I guess it's really not that important."

You: "That's good. I'll make sure I get back to you with that answer." (Then pick up where you left off in your presentation, close, etc.)

Now let's take the same example, but this time assume the answer to the question would affect his decision to buy.

Prospect: "If I'm using the collating and stapling features and the machine is running low on staples, will it somehow let me know?"

You: "Hmm, that's a good question and one I don't have an answer for. I'll write that down and be sure to get an answer for you as soon as possible. Let me ask you, is the answer to that question critical to whether you purchase this machine?"

Prospect: "Yes. With the number of copies we make, the machine could be running for quite a while and produce hundreds of copies before we realize it is out of staples. At that point we'd need to staple them by hand. Our current machine doesn't show when it's close to running out of staples, and that usually leads to a lot of extra work."

You: "Okay, let me try to get someone on the phone and get an answer to your question."

Think of someone who may have an answer to the question and use your cell phone to call that person. You can talk to the expert you're calling one on one; sometimes, however, in certain situations it's better to put that person on speakerphone. Let him know you're with the prospect, and then ask the question.

People you would call for help might include your manager, other salespeople, the office manager, technicians, installation and/or implementation personnel, billing or accounts receivable people, or anyone else who might have access to the answer(s) you're seeking. Once you get that person on the phone and he has answered the question, keep him on the phone while you make sure the question has been answered satisfactorily and ask the prospect if he has any other questions. This way you won't have to keep calling the expert back for further answers.

If the prospect asks a question that neither you nor your company contact on the phone can answer, let that person go and call someone else. Continue with this process for as long as the prospect has questions that you can't answer.

Note: You only want to put the expert on speakerphone if he or she is very well spoken and is good at customer situations. If the person you're calling does not generally have a lot of contact with customers, you probably want to talk to that person one on one rather than on speakerphone. But if he is giving you some good, detailed answers that you would like the prospect to hear, by all means go the speakerphone route and have the person talk directly to you and your prospect.

If you are unable to get anyone on the phone to get the question answered, be straightforward and let the prospect know. Then say, "So I've written it down and I'll be sure to get you an answer as soon as possible."

After making that statement, continue with your presentation, go all the way through it, and close. Do not refer back to the question you could not answer. Let the prospect bring it up again. If he does, or if you are at the end of your presentation and are closing when the question first comes up, ask if there are any more questions in addition to that one for which you don't have an answer. If there are no other questions, ask the following: "Mr. Prospect, if the machine does have a feature that lets you know it's running low on staples, are you ready to go ahead with the purchase of the machine?"

That question will help you determine if there are any other roadblocks to the sale, and it will nail down the prospect to a commitment.

If you get a yes to that question, ask for a further commitment. Say, "Mr. Prospect, since that's the only thing holding you back at this point, assuming the answer to your question on the stapling feature is satisfactory, what I'd like to do is get all the paperwork taken care of now so we can simply move ahead once you have your answer. Would that be okay?"

To summarize, the three keys here are:

- Determine how important the question is.
- If it is important, try to find someone to answer it.
- Finally, if you are unable to find someone to answer the question, get the commitment that the prospect will be ready to move ahead if you do get the answer he's looking for.

Don't Let the Wrong Answer to the Prospect's Question Stop You

If you come back with an answer other than the one the prospect was hoping to hear, don't let that stop the selling process. For example, in the above situation, let's assume your machine does not allow the customer to know when it's running low on staples. Considering the prospect has told you this is an important factor in the buying process, what do you do now? It'simple—come up with some alternative answers to the problem.

For example, examine how your current customers are handling that potential problem. Perhaps they check the staples each morning, or before they do a major job. Whatever the case may be, find out how current users are handling that issue and present solutions to the prospect.

Once you've proposed some solutions to the problem, highlight areas where you outperform the competition. Who are you up against and what are your major advantages over them? For example, let's say the toner cartridge on your copier is 30 percent larger than the competitor's unit. Your complete answer to the prospect's question may then sound something like the following:

"Mr. Prospect, our machine does not let you know when the staples are running low. In speaking with several customers, I discovered there are several ways they make sure the machine doesn't run out of staples during a print job.

"Some customers check the staple supply each morning, while others check the supply before they do a major job. Still others refill the staple supply at the end of each day. Considering it only takes twenty seconds to get to the staple supply to check it and roughly another forty-five seconds to fill it, they find this requires minimal time and ensures they do not spend lots of extra time hand-stapling copies that the machine may have missed.

"You said you were comparing our machine to the XYZ machine, correct? (Wait for the prospect to answer in the affirmative.) I also spoke with several customers who compared our machine with theirs or who used to use theirs and now use our machine. They prefer our machine over the XYZ machine, because our machine's toner cartridge is 30 percent larger than XYZ's. While it was easy for our customers to remedy the issue with the staples, they found it was much more difficult to handle the toner issue.

"First, because our toner cartridge is much larger, our customers need to change it less often. Second, our customers have found that the feature that lets you know the toner is running low is much more accurate on our machine the competition's. With the XYZ unit, when the machine said it needed toner, users found that the cartridge might still be half full, while at other times it would run out without any warning. The low toner indicator was completely inaccurate. Consequently, they found themselves guessing how many more copies they could run and many times they were wrong.

"Imagine doing a large job and you come back to the copier to find that 70 percent of the copies didn't turn out. That, obviously, could be much more cumbersome than having to staple some copies if the staples run out. Can you see why, although we have no staple counter, our customers prefer working with our machine?"

The point is that you have advantages over the competition. If you cannot beat them in one area that the prospect says is critical, you're not out of the game. Focus on the solution and how your other customers are handling this issue. And then shift the focus to the other areas where you are superior to the competition.

The Words You Use When Closing

Use the right words when closing. For example, instead of "cost" or "payment," use the word "investment." When you are talking about less money with regard to your product, say that it's "less expensive" instead of "cheaper." Also, don't use slang terms when talking about money. For example, if something is $20,000, express it as "twenty thousand dollars," not "twenty grand." These are small, subtle items, but you want to have as many things as possible going for you in the selling process. Use words that demonstrate you are a professional.

Note: The only time you want to use the word "cheaper" is when you are referring to the competition's product costing less money.

How Far Can You Go?

As a salesperson you have to know what leeway you have before you go into a sales call.

- What are the terms of the agreement and which terms can you change?
- How much can you change them?
- How flexible can you be on pricing?
- What other concessions can you make?

You don't want to give things away; at the same time, there will be situations where you can entice someone with a little extra. You may have a prospect barter with you, saying something such as, "If you can come down another $100, I can do it." Know where you can and can't go to get the deal done.

Presenting the Contract

Most products and services involve some sort of contract that must be signed. For the most part, people don't like to sign things. We've all been repeatedly reminded to read the fine print or to have our lawyers and accountants look over the contract first. Then there is that fear of closure once we sign, knowing that this is it and there is no turning back. Because of these factors, you must be careful when presenting the contract. Here are the rules to follow:

1) Instead of asking for a signature, ask for someone's John Doe, Jane Doe, their okay, or better yet, ask for their autograph.

Try to avoid asking for a *signature* because of the negative connotations of finality we discussed above. It may be subtle, yet when you are getting orders signed, you want *everything* to be going positively for you.

The autograph approach works well for a few reasons. First, it puts a little humor into the situation. Again, whenever and wherever you can interject humor in a potentially stressful situation, do it. The other reason the autograph approach works well is that *very* few salespeople use it. It sets you apart, and for most customers it is a refreshing change. Also, the word "autograph" has a positive connotation.

2) Present the contract and a pen, and stay silent.

Turn the contract around to the customer, slide it over in front of him, present the pen, point to the area for him to sign, ask for his autograph, and then find something else on which to settle your eyes and keep quiet.

If you have to fill out the contract or write some things on it before you present it, it's okay to talk at this time. However, make sure the talk is light in nature—the weather, vacation plans, family, and other subjects. Try to stay away from talking about business unless you need your customer's input to fill out certain parts of the contract. You want to occasionally look up at the customer while the two of you are talking. However, your primary goal is to get the paperwork filled out as quickly as possible and get it in front of the customer to sign.

One consideration to take into account is *when* to fill out the paperwork. Some salespeople like to have the paperwork filled out before the sales call; others like to work on it while they are there. Some prefer to have the paperwork typed, others prefer to write it out. Yet others prefer to fill in the paperwork while they're in the sales call to use it as part of their closing technique (as with "The Order Form Close," which we'll discuss in the next Chapter). Some salespeople want to have it all filled out so they can get it in front of the customer as soon as possible.

As a rule, it is best to have the paperwork filled out before you arrive. If you can't fill it all out, do much as you can in advance of the meeting. Get together with the top salespeople and find out their approach with regard to paperwork.

Once you've presented the paperwork and indicated where the person is to sign, be quiet. Presenting the paperwork for a signature is the same as asking a closing question. Keep quiet so you don't distract the person as he is signing. When you present the contract, he is focused on it and signing it—you don't want his mind wandering at this point. Once he's signed it and handed it to you, you can then speak freely and thank him for the business, which is the final step in getting the contract signed.

Note 1: Always make some sort of mark next to the area where the person must sign. For example, most people use an X, which is appropriate. When you present the contract, place your index finger just above the mark you've made and say, "I just need your autograph right here."

Note 2: Where you look while the customer is signing is also important. Never look directly at the customer, the contract, or even in that general vicinity while the customer is signing. If you do stare, your new customer will feel your eyes burning a hole right through him. This creates a feeling of being under the spotlight. People don't want to be under the spotlight while they are signing a contract.

Instead of staring at him, look off to your left or right at something on the wall, or pull out your planning book and start to do some work in it. When the prospect sees you with his peripheral vision, you want him to notice that you are not paying attention to what he is doing. This will make the signing process much more relaxing.

Note 3: As we stated earlier, make sure you have a decent black or blue pen to present the customer with and make sure it works. You don't have to have the most expensive pen in the world; just make sure it is consistent with your professional image. Also, have a backup pen of equal quality should the first pen fail for some reason.

3) Thank the customer for his or her business.

Here we are referring to the thank you done at the signing of the contract, not the thank you that you'll do as part of the follow up to the sale.

Thanking the customer for his business is a *very important step* when getting a contract signed. It doesn't have to be anything lengthy and what you say will depend upon what product you are selling. For example, if you are in financial services, you may say something like, "Kathy, thank you very much for your business. This is a great first step for us and I look forward to a long and profitable relationship."

Obviously, the word *profitable* could be used with regard to many other products and services, but it definitely applies when talking about financial services. Here are some other examples:

- "Joe, thank you very much for your business. We really appreciate the opportunity."
- "Kathy, thank you for the confidence you've shown in me. I am looking forward to working with you on this project."

You may be selling a product or service that requires a somewhat more detailed thank you. For example, you may need to give the customer some information on what will happen next. Here's an example:

"Joe, first, thank you very much for the business. Jim Smith from our installation department will be calling you back sometime today to set up a time to stop by and go over the details of the window installation. Do you have any other questions for me at this point? Great. Once again, we appreciate the business and Jim will be in touch shortly."

The most important thing is to work a sincere thank you into your final comments after you've received an order.

In addition to what you say, how you say it is also important. Look the person in the eye, smile, and nod your head up and down slightly as you speak your words of thanks. Put emphasis on your words and give them some emotion. Don't go overboard, just be sincere.

The type of sale will also dictate the intensity and extent of your thank you. If you have just received a $1 million order from a company, the level and intensity of the thank you will clearly be different than if you were to receive a $500 order.

Your thank you will vary on factors such as order size, the length of the sales process, what kind of competition you faced, if any, and how much business the customer has done with you previously.

In the section titled *After the Close*, we'll talk about the different ways to thank a customer for business as part of your follow up.

Chapter 34

Various Closes

Now we're going to discuss some different closes you can use. Some of these closes have been out there awhile and still work well today, while others are a bit newer.

The Puppy Dog Close

This close was developed in pet stores and involved letting a potential customer take a dog home for a few days to "try it out." Picture the following scenario: A family walks into a pet store to simply look at some dogs. The children are crazed with enthusiasm while the parents are less than enthusiastic. The pet store salesperson says to the parents: "Look, I'll tell you what. We'll let you take the dog home for the weekend and if you're not happy with it for any reason you can bring it back—no questions asked. How does that sound?"

By the time the weekend is over the entire family has become attached to the dog. How could they take the dog back after it has been part of the family for two days?

In short, the "puppy dog" close is a try and buy close. Car dealers have used this kind of close for years, when they let you take a car home and test-drive it for the weekend. They are counting on the fact that after you've enjoyed it for two days, received all sorts of compliments, and your spouse continually tells you how much better this car performs than the current piece of junk you own, you won't be able to give the car back on Monday.

This close works very well with the right product. If you have a high-quality product or service that performs well and thus sells itself, use this close. People are usually reluctant to give back or have things taken away from them. Let the prospect "borrow" all the benefits of ownership for a couple days and let your strong product or service sell itself.

As with any other sales technique, evaluate your success rate. If 98 percent of the people that try actually buy, that's pretty good. If only 50 percent of the people buy and your product is coming back damaged or worn, that's not good and you may want to stop using this close.

The Assumptive Close

This isn't so much a close as it is a state of mind. With this close, you "assume" the sale will be made. All your actions and what you say revolve around the premise that the sale is a foregone conclusion; you're simply getting the details worked out. Assuming they're going to buy, you just ask the questions to which you need answers to get the order underway.

- "What color do you want it in?"
- "When would you like it installed?"
- "Will you be paying with cash or credit card?"

All the questions you ask during the assumptive close could be seen as trial closing questions. Obviously, if someone answers you with what color they want along with when they want it installed and how they want to pay, they've made the purchase.

Try the Assumptive Close the next time you call on a prospect. After your presentation, simply *assume* she is going to buy and begin asking the questions you need answers to if that were the case. Many prospects will assume you are doing business as usual and they'll let you go all the way through the entire order process without stopping you.

Note: Another close that is similar to this one is the Order Form Close. The Order Form Close is the Assumptive Close used with an order form. If you have an order form that needs to be filled out, pull it out at the beginning of the conversation and fill the details in as the prospect answers your questions. Assume the sale and use the order form as a guide for your questions.

The Alternative Choice Close

The Alternative Choice Close involves giving the prospect two options, both of which are buying decisions. For example, "Would you like your monthly investment to be due on the first or fifteenth of the month?" Whether the prospect says the first or the fifteenth, she has agreed to your product. The answer to the question is a yes-yes as opposed to a yes-no. Instead of "Do you want it or don't you," you're assuming they want it you're simply asking how they want it: "Do you want it this way, or that way?"

Try rephrasing some of your typical closing questions as "either/or" questions. For example, instead of saying, "I'm looking at 1,000 shares at $49.50 per share. How does that sound to you?" Try: "Would 1,000 shares at $49.50 be comfortable? Or would 2,000 be better?"

The Take Away Close

The Take Away Close is based on the premise that people want what they think they can't have or what might be difficult to obtain. This close works well if someone needs to qualify for your product or service or if your inventory varies.

Qualifying refers to financial, health, or some other qualification standard. Inventory varies in almost every business, such as car, retail, and even the housing industries. Thus you can use the Take Away Close in industries where people need to qualify and where inventories fluctuate.

Use this close when you have someone who you believe wants your product or service, but is on the fence. Psychologically, when someone is unsure of whether to buy your product and you take it away or remove it, that will be enough to convince the prospect that she simply *must* have your product. Let's look at an example.

Let's say a person is shopping for a new house. She finds a house she's pretty certain she likes, but then again, she might be making a mistake. During her meeting with the realtor it becomes evident that the potential buyer is playing mental ping-pong: "Yes, I want it. No, I don't. Yes, I do. No, I don't." The realtor is not 100 percent sure that no one else has made an offer on this property and as a result says, "Ms. Prospect, I'm not sure this property is still available. It is entirely possible that someone else has already made an offer and it has been accepted. Would you like to make an offer just in case it is still available?"

Other examples of Take Away Closes in various industries:

Insurance: "Mr. and Mrs. Jones, this isn't something I can sell to you today even if you wanted to buy it. This insurance requires that you qualify from a health standpoint before we can do anything. Lately, it's been real hit or miss. I recently had a person who looked to be in fine health and whom I had absolutely no reservations about. Then, much to our surprise, she got rejected. I know at this point you're not even certain you want insurance. Before we waste any more of your time even looking at it, why don't we just go through some health questions so I will have a better idea of where you stand?"

Auto: "I'm really not sure we have the model you're looking for with all the features you want in the color you want. I'll have to run a check to see if we can find one somewhere in the area. I know you haven't decided yet, but if you were to buy, would you be financing or paying cash? While I run a check to see if there's one anywhere out there, why don't we simply make sure we can get you qualified for the financing? Obviously, we don't want you to get too excited about the car only to find out we can't finance it for you."

Any product or service where the prospect needs to qualify financially: "For some reason, we've recently had problems getting people qualified for our product. Not long ago, I had someone whose credit and income looked great, yet he didn't qualify. Now, I know at this point, you're not even sure you want this product. So before we spend any more of your time even considering it, why don't we first find out whether or not you'll qualify? Then we'll know if we should even consider it any further."

In all of the above examples, you want to get the paperwork completely filled out. In other words, you're not only going to ask the questions you need to get the prospect financially or health qualified, you're going to start at the top and go all the way through the application.

Once you've finished, spend some time personally reviewing it. Take out a separate piece of paper, look at the application, and take some notes. After a few minutes, if it looks as though they'll qualify, say, "Well, based upon everything I see here, it looks as though you should qualify." Mark an X where the prospect is to sign, turn the form toward him, hand him the pen and say, "I just need your autograph right here."

Note: The Take Away Close can also be referred to as The Qualification Close when based solely on financial, health, and other qualification standards.

The Feel, Felt, Found Close

The Feel, Felt, Found Close is a fairly straightforward close. Use this close to answer certain objections and bridge from the objection to a close.

Let's say a prospect tells you she'd really like to invest in the company you're recommending. However, she's been burned in the stock market before. You would say,

"Joanne, I definitely understand how you *feel*. In fact I have a client now who *felt* exactly the same way when I was recommending a similar company. However, what he *found* was that his one bad experience was actually preventing him from taking advantage of some other tremendous opportunities. After talking with me, he *found* he needed to invest in the market if his money was ever going to really work for him, so he decided to invest a comfortable amount of money in a company I felt very strong about, as I do with this one.

"Joanne, you never get a second chance to make a first impression, and this recommendation is my first impression. Let's get you started with 1,000 shares at $10 per share and I'm sure you'll *find* this is one of the best steps you've ever taken toward financial independence. How does that sound to you?"

This close starts with empathy: "I definitely understand how you *feel*." It continues with an example of someone else previously in the prospect's shoes: "I know someone who *felt* exactly the same way you do." It follows with that person *finding* that your product was the solution to his or her problem: "What he *found* was that my product allowed him to…" and ends with a closing question.

The Similar Situation Close

This close is similar to the Feel, Felt, Found Close, but it is more detailed and specific.

With this close, as with the close above, you will use a previous example of someone in the same situation as your present prospect. For example, let's say the prospect is concerned about the cost of training new employees due to the high turnover rate. With this close, you want to recall a similar situation with a current customer and tell the prospect how your product helped your current customer solve the same problem. The close goes like this (this is the salesperson's side of the conversation only):

"Joe, I definitely understand what you're saying and it's interesting because Waters Company was in exactly the same shoes that you find yourself in and they used our product to solve their problem.

"As we've discussed, and as you already know, handling cash is by far the most stressful part of the bank teller's job, which results in high stress and high turnover. Also, as we talked about, you spend a lot of time and money training these new tellers. I'm correct on both those points, right?

"What Waters Company found was that our Teller Cash Machine completely eliminated the teller cash counting errors because the machine was counting the cash. If there was a mistake, it was the machine's fault, not the teller's. They found that teller stress level went from about an eight on a scale of one to ten down to about a two. They also found that they had roughly 75 percent less teller turnover in the two branches in which they'd installed our machines. The tellers were happier, which led to less stress, and ultimately to fewer turnovers. They then added a machine in a third branch and after about six months noticed the same trend—75 percent less turnover.

"If we start with one machine in the branch with the highest turnover, I'm confident you'll see almost exactly the same results that Waters Company saw. How does that sound to you?"

Again, think of a similar situation you had with another company and how your product solved their problem, then describe the situation, tie in some benefits, get agreement, and close.

The Follow-up Close

Use the Follow-up Close on a return call after the prospect has successfully held you off on your previous visit in which you attempted to close. It doesn't matter what the reason was—you are now following up and once again attempting to get the order.

After your previous call, take these steps:

First, send out a letter thanking the prospect for his time and highlighting the benefits of your product or service. Inform the prospect that you will follow up on the day agreed upon.

Second, review the previous call.

- What are the prospect's hot buttons?
- What exactly is the prospect looking for?
- What have you established?
- What do you have to build your case on thus far?

Third, speak with other salespeople and your manager and get some more ammunition together. You need to go into the second call with new, fresh, exciting information; your objective is to greatly impress your prospect and influence a positive buying decision. You need new benefits, new answers to the prospect's objection, new features—anything that you may have forgotten in the original presentation.

Often after we leave a call, we think of something else we could have or should have said, or we think of some critical information we left out that might have made a major difference. The key is to follow up with something new. If you don't add anything to what you've already given the prospect,

- you will not be doing anything to alter the prospect's view of your product,
- you will not be giving him a new perspective, and
- you will not be giving him a good reason to get off the fence and buy your product.

When you make your follow-up call, the prospect will have cooled off somewhat since your last call. Open with, "Joe, I have some new, critical, and exciting news to share with you today. And I'll get to that information in a second. When we met last time…"

Now briefly summarize the main points of the last meeting, go over your product's key "hot button" features and benefits that you discussed in the last meeting, and then hit him with the new information. Here is an example (this is the salesperson's side of the conversation only):

"When we last met, you expressed that two of your primary problems are teller turnover and morale, correct? You also mentioned that you'd like to get the cars through the drive-up lane quicker on Saturday morning to avoid the traffic problems, right? Were there any other concerns in addition to those?

"Now, from the standpoint of our product, we talked about how it takes the responsibility of counting cash from the tellers and places it on the cash machine. Because counting cash is the most stressful part of the teller's job, we agreed this would significantly reduce the stress level of the tellers. This would make them much more content, thus leading to much less turnover, correct? In fact, in the example with Waters Company, we discussed their results in which they reduced teller turnover by 75 percent. Joe, this is not an extreme. It is pretty much the norm in the industry.

"We also showed how you will be able to move four cars through the drive-up lane in the time it used to take you to move only two or three cars. And we agreed this would significantly cut down on drive-up traffic problems, right?

"In addition to training fewer people because you have less turnover, we also discussed our feature that cuts training time in half. That would obviously be valuable, correct?

"Joe, here's the additional information I have for you that I'm sure you'll appreciate. It seems as though the purchasing decision comes down to the cost of the machine versus your return on investment, is that correct? Here I have a Return on Investment model. (Have supporting information such as charts, graphs, and other similar materials on good paper and in full color.) This chart shows your return using the lowest numbers possible, the highest numbers possible, and the industry average numbers."

Present the new information, get confirmation from the prospect that this adequately addresses his concern, and then close.

In this case, you would present the Return on Investment (ROI) model showing how much time it would take for the machine to pay for itself with the highest numbers, lowest numbers, and then the industry average numbers. You would then use the lowest numbers possible, which would, of course, take the longest time for the prospect to see the payback, and ask if that time frame was acceptable. If the prospect answers yes, you've just made the sale. If the prospect answers no, then you need to talk about the time saved in training, turnover, and other areas both tangible and intangible.

Wherever possible, you want to put a specific number on these items, thus making them tangible, as you did with the ROI model. Calculate the effects of 75 percent less turnover. Ask the prospect how much it costs to train a new employee and find out what other costs and factors are associated. What about mistakes a new employee makes? Has the prospect calculated those costs? You can also do a ROI model specifically for the prospect's company, in which you plug in their specific numbers.

Continue to build your case until you've tipped the scales in your favor. The key point here is that when you get your second shot, make sure you go in with *everything* you have. You may not have to use it all to make the sale, but be prepared to. Everything you have includes the good stuff you've already mentioned, the good stuff you forgot to mention, and the good stuff that you got from the other salespeople and your manager.

Leave no stone unturned! If you don't get the sale, you want to know that you gave it the best possible shot you could.

The Summary Close

This close is similar to the way in which an attorney presents closing arguments. It also resembles what many of us were taught with regard to giving speeches. The rule is to have an introduction, a body, and a conclusion. Use the introduction to tell them what you're going to tell them, the body to tell them, and the conclusion to tell them what you told them.

It is the conclusion that this close focuses on. With this close you will outline the prospect's problems, needs, and/or desires, show how your product fills those needs and desires, get confirmation on each one, and then close.

The following is an example. "Joe, let's summarize what we have discussed. 1) You are not happy with the lifespan of your current machines. 2) You are not happy with the response time of your current vendor. 3) You would like to be able to take advantage of the latest technology. And 4) You want to make sure that there are no hidden charges or surprises with regard to the delivery and installation, training, and the service contract. Did I miss anything or does that pretty much cover it?"

Now make your case on each of the above items, get confirmation that the prospect is happy with each of the answers, and then close the sale. For example, number one would go something like this: "Joe, let's take number one, the lifespan of your current machines. I believe you mentioned that currently your machines are lasting about ten years. Is that correct? I've shown you the records of my customers, and the average life of their machines has been fifteen years. Is that more in line with what you're looking for as far as lifespan on your machines?"

Get a yes on this one and then move to the next issue. Issue two is response time. Through questioning you will know what his current response time is. Have your documentation showing your superior response time, confirm that it's acceptable, and then move to issue three, the desire to take advantage of the latest technology, and finally issue four.

Incidentally, if you get a no on any of the confirmation questions, you need to dig further and at least get confirmation that you are the best game in town. For example, if you ask the prospect if fifteen years is acceptable for the lifespan of a machine and he says no, you need to find out what is acceptable and what he'll live with. After you've received a no, the conversation would go like this:

You: "Joe, what would you consider acceptable?"

Joe: "Hmm, I think about twenty years."

You: "And based upon what you've seen in the industry, do you think that's attainable?"

Joe: "I don't know. Currently, I'm getting ten. Your company's machines do fifteen. I think Brand X does about twelve. So, all things considered, that might be asking a little too much."

You: "Joe, would you agree that we're much better than your current vendor is as far as longevity goes?"

If the facts are indeed accurate, you'll get a yes to this question. You can either ask one more question that will commit him further or move on to the next issue. If you do ask another question, it would be: "Joe, would you agree that we're your best solution as far as longevity goes?" Now you're not just talking about his current vendor, you're talking about *all* of the other vendors.

Once you have made your case on each point and obtained confirmation on each one, you will then summarize how your product meets all the prospect's needs and desires, and then close. For example, in this case you would begin with, "Based upon the lifespan of fifteen years for our current machines, our average response time of forty-three minutes…"

Continue to summarize until you've covered all the points. Your close would then be: "Joe, based upon what we've just discussed, would you agree that we are the best solution for you?"

If you get a no, you need to ask directly where you are missing the boat. Say, "Joe, we agreed those were all your issues and we also agreed that my product adequately addresses all your concerns. Where am I missing the boat?" Take the new information the prospect gives you, show how your product or service addresses this concern, get confirmation, and close once again.

The Shortened Summary Close

This close is similar to the above close but it's shorter—that's probably obvious. A Shortened Summary Close of the above situation would go as follows: "Joe, based upon the fact that our machines have the longest lifespan of any in the industry, our response time is second to none and is guaranteed, we have the most advanced technology and support team, and I've covered all your concerns about hidden charges and surprises, it seems clear that the only thing left to do is to get the order written up." Then smile, look the prospect in the eye and be completely quiet until he speaks.

That's all there is to the Shortened Summary Close. This close is more direct than most others. If you have a prospect who requires a softer close, instead of saying, "It seems clear that the only thing left to do is to get the order written up," use "It seems to me as though we are the perfect solution for you. Do you feel the same way?" And say it in a relaxed and easy tone. After you've said it, however, you still need to smile and be quiet.

The Largest Amount Possible Close

Use the Largest Amount Possible Close to show the prospect how much something will cost *not to have* your product or service. With this close, you want to maximize the prospect's pain. Pain in this case is equivalent to the amount of money she will lose by not owning your product or service.

Let's take an example from the *Presentation* section, where we talked about trying to sell a $100 water filter. The prospect thinks the price of $100 for a water filter is a little high. Currently she is buying bottled water. She buys seven gallons a week at $1.00 per gallon.

Start by asking her how many years she's been buying bottled water. Let's say she says five years. You will then take $1 per day, which equals $365 per year times five years, which equals $1,825 over five years. You don't need to add a leap year.

Next, ask how much longer she plans on buying bottled water. She'll say something like, "Well, I don't know, forever or until they come out with another alternative, I guess."

You: "So you'll continue to buy it indefinitely?"
Prospect: "Um, yeah, I guess so."
You: "So, in another five years you will have paid another $1,825. Or you could buy this water filter, have it paid for in about fifteen weeks with what you're currently spending on water, and you can pocket $1,725 over the next five years. How does that sound?"
Prospect: "That sounds pretty good."
You: "Well then, will that be cash, check, or charge?"

You could also take this to more of an extreme and figure out how much she'd pay in ten, twenty, thirty, or even more years.

This close is even more effective if you write it out on paper. On one side of the paper show the implications of buying your product, and on the other show the implications of not buying your product. Your sheet of paper would look like this:

Continue to Buy Bottled Water	Purchase Water Filter
Cash position after purchase of water filter:	minus $100.00
Cash position after 20 weeks: minus $140.00	plus $40.00
Cash position after 1 year: minus $365.00	plus $265.00
Cash position after 5 years: minus $1,825.00	plus $1,725.00

You can also chart mortgage/refinancing and other items in the same way. Writing things in a linear fashion like this simply adds one more dimension to your presentation—it gets the prospect visually involved. You can also have the prospect help you do the math or work the calculator. Get her involved in the presentation as much as you possibly can.

Whatever product or service you're selling, find a way to equate use or non-use to dollars and then start from the lowest common denominator—daily cost—and multiply out to the largest number possible.

In another example, if you are trying to convince your prospect that refinancing a fifteen-year mortgage is a good idea, you want to show how much money he will save over the remaining life of the loan if he refinances with you.

Your particular product or service may not have as obvious a "cost factor" as in the examples of the water filter or mortgage, yet virtually every product has some cost that can be equated as we have done here. Get creative! Create cost leverage.

The Smallest Amount Possible Close

Use the Smallest Amount Possible Close to show the prospect how much something will cost to *have* your product. Your objective here is the opposite of what it was with the Largest Amount Possible Close. With the Largest Amount Possible Close, you maximized the prospect's pain, which could be equated to the amount of money she was losing by *not* owning your product. With the Smallest Amount Possible Close, you want to minimize the prospect's pain, which in this case can be equated to how much money the prospect is parting with to own your product. Here is an example.

Let's say you're selling a car for $20,000. Let's further assume that the monthly loan payment will be $500, for a total cost of $6,000 per year. With the Smallest Amount Possible Close, you will reduce the number to the smallest amount possible. In this case, break the yearly amount down to the daily number—$6,000—divided by 365, or $16.44 per day. While $20,000 may seem overwhelming, $16.44 a day is much easier to grasp. You might say, "Jane, this car will run you about $16.44 per day."

Another way to use this close is with a dollar difference. For example, let's say the person buying the car only wanted to spend $17,000 rather than $20,000. In a case like this, break down the difference to the daily number. In this example, you would take the balance of $3,000, calculate the effect on the loan—say it's $75 per month—and say, "Jane, for an extra $2.50 per day, you can own this car."

You can use this close with virtually any product or service.

Note: *Anytime* you are presenting "cost" or "payment" numbers you want to use the lowest numbers possible. And when presenting "savings" or "payback" numbers, you want to use the largest numbers possible.

For example, the "cost" of a car at $16.44 per day sounds much better than a cost of $20,000. On the other hand, a "payback" number of $3,000 in interest over three years for a certificate of deposit sounds much better than a "payback" of $2.78 per day.

The Price Is Going Up Close

This one's been out there awhile and some people see it as a gimmick. At the same time, many people also realize there is some validity to it, as prices do increase occasionally. In any case, use this sparingly and *only* when it is actually the truth.

Look at the Price Is Going Up Close this way. If you're meeting with a prospect on December 24th, but he wants to wait until the new year and you know prices will increase January 1st, you are simply being up front and giving full disclosure when you tell him the price will be higher after December 31st.

This close is most effective at the end of the year because prices usually go up at the beginning of a year. It is also effective when a certain model year is being closed out. For example, if a car dealership still has some 2007 model vehicles in the showroom in June of 2007, they need to move those before the 2008s come in. As a result, the salespeople will be able to talk about the deep discounts *now* and the higher prices for the 2008s that are right around the corner.

Here is an example of this close. Let's say a prospect is looking at watches in late December. She's 95 percent sure she wants to buy but is still hesitant. She finally says: "You know what? I'm going to go home and think about it. I'll be back." Be polite, show empathy and understanding, and then use the Price Is Going Up Close: "Yes, Ms. Prospect, I completely understand that you want to think about it and that makes sense. Just keep in mind that we will have a price increase the first of the year, so making a decision now could save you money."

That is your close. Simply make the statement and then wait for questions such as, "How much will it increase?" and others like it.

Answer the questions and close.

The You Get What You Pay For Close

Use the You Get What You Pay For Close when price is an issue and you have the higher-priced product. This close utilizes the logical belief that, for the most part, you usually get what you pay for. If you want the Cadillac, it will cost you more than the Yugo. The Rolex will cost more than the Seiko. Here's an example of the close:

Prospect: "Boy! That's more expensive than the other guy is!"
You: "You're right, Mr. Prospect, we are more expensive. As you know, you can't get the lowest price along with the best product and the best service. In other words, you get what you pay for, right? So you can either have the best product that is the easiest to use, will last the longest, give you the least headaches, and make your job much easier—not to mention the best service, or you can have the cheapest price and the cheapest product. Which of those would you prefer?"

If the prospect responds with, "I want the cheapest price and cheapest product," come back with "You're kidding, right?" If the prospect says, "No, I'm serious," say, "Thank you for your time"…and move on!

With the You Get What You Pay For Close, things can unfold in two ways. 1) The prospect answers the question your way, and you, in turn, pull out your order form and start filling it out. Or 2) the prospect says, "I'm not too bright, so I want the cheap product." In that case, you stop wasting your time and go spend your time with a more promising prospect.

The They're Exactly the Same Close

We touched on this one earlier in the *Objection* section. Use the They're Exactly the Same Close when you encounter a prospect who believes your product is exactly the same as your competitor's product, and it really just comes down to price. In other words, your product is simply a commodity. The close goes like this:

Prospect: "You know what? At the end of the day your product is exactly the same as XYZ Company's product. It all comes down to price."
You: "You're right, Mr. Prospect. There are some similarities. Let me ask you a question. Have you ever seen a real diamond right alongside a cubic

zirconium?" Whatever his answer, continue with "The amazing thing is, to the untrained eye, or 99.9 percent of the population, there is no way to tell the difference between a real diamond and a cubic zirconium. At the same time, I think you'd agree that one is still much more valuable than the other, am I right?"

Prospect: "Well, yes."

You: "Let me ask you another question. If you were going to buy an engagement ring for the most important person in your world, and you knew the ring had to be special, would be scrutinized by many people, and would make a loud statement about you as a person one way or another, would you ever dare buy a cubic zirconium instead of the real thing?"

If the prospect says yes to buying the cubic zirconium, follow with, "You're kidding, right?" If the prospect isn't kidding, apologize and move on. If, on the other hand, the prospect answers the way you want him to with "No way!" continue with, "I know our products look similar, but there are some very distinct differences." Then proceed to do a feature and function comparison, explaining the benefits of each.

Finally close with, "Mr. Prospect, you do want the highest-quality product and service at the best price, right?" Once again, *yes* equals write up the order, and *no* equals move on.

The Advantage, Disadvantage Close

The Advantage, Disadvantage Close is basically the Ben Franklin Close that you may already be familiar with. With this one, however, you don't have to go into the old, worn-out story about how Ben Franklin used to make decisions, which is the premise for the Ben Franklin Close. The Advantage, Disadvantage Close goes like this: "Mr. Prospect, we've come up with some reasons for going ahead with this and some reasons for not going ahead. One decision-making process that seems to work well for people is simply to weigh the advantages against the disadvantages. Let's take a sheet of paper and simply list what we have so far."

Pull out a sheet of paper and pen and draw a line down the middle. One side of the paper is for the advantages; the other side is for the disadvantages. "Now, as you see it, what are the disadvantages for moving ahead today?"

Let the prospect come up with the disadvantages on his own. *Do not help.* As the prospect comes up with his own disadvantages, write them on one side of the sheet.

Once the prospect has come up with all the disadvantages he can think of, say, "Now let's look at the advantages."

You will now write down the advantages on the other side of the paper. You will help with the advantages not only because it's in your best interest to do so, but because you truly believe the advantages outweigh the disadvantages, hopefully significantly.

When you finish, simply total up the advantages and disadvantages, then give the results and close. For example, if you had six reasons for and three against, you would say, "Well, let's see. We have six reasons for and three reasons against, so I guess the answer is fairly self-evident. Would you like this delivered on the first or the fifteenth?"

The He Said, She Said Close

The He Said, She Said Close is a variation of the Advantage, Disadvantage Close. You will use this close when you have two decision-makers going back and forth, each looking for the other to make a decision. For some reason, this "You decide— no, you decide" ping-pong match usually only happens between spouses. The intimate relationship between a married couple often brings this duality out during stressful times of decision-making.

Typically, it happens because neither party wants to be held responsible if something doesn't work out. Yet neither party wants to take the blame if they *don't* buy and, in hindsight, see that it would have been the best decision.

Here's a quick example. The wife decides against buying a new house. Property values continue to skyrocket and the next thing you know, the same house costs 25 percent more than it did one year earlier. The husband says, "See, I told you we should have bought that house."

How do you handle this situation? First, you need to interrupt the verbal volleying because they will go back and forth until one of them says, "Well, obviously, we can't decide, so we'll need to go home and think about it."

Your second objective is to get both of them to agree to the purchase—that way there will be no fear of blame. Here's how the general conversation will proceed:

Mrs. Prospect: "Hmm, I don't know, honey. What do you think?"
Mr. Prospect: "Well, I don't know. You'll be using it more than I will."
Mrs. Prospect: "Well, maybe, but if you're not going to be happy with it…"

Mr. Prospect: "Look, you decide. It's up to you."

Mrs. Prospect: "Hmm, I'm just not sure. What do you think?"

You: "Mr. and Mrs. Prospect, if I may intercede for just a moment. Let's take a logical look at this. First, you both agree that you need it, correct?" (Get an affirmative answer.) "And you both agree that you like it, right?" (Once again, wait for an answer.)

You will then present all the other reasons why 1) *they* determined it would be a good idea to go ahead, and 2) *you* have other "good" reasons of your own why they should move ahead. Just as you did with the Advantage, Disadvantage Close, state all reasons, both theirs and yours.

As you're covering all the positive reasons for going ahead, keep a count of them with your fingers. Once you've covered all the positive reasons for going ahead, hold out your fingers and say, "So, that's seven (or whatever number it is) reasons for going ahead, correct?"

Once you get an answer, follow with, "Now, let's look at the reasons *not* to move forward. What reasons can you think of?"

Let them work on this one on their own. As they come up with reasons, count them on your fingers. They probably won't be able to come up with more than two or three. Once they come up with all the reasons "not" to go ahead, proceed with, "Okay, so we've got seven reasons for and three against. I guess the logical decision is obvious. Would you like to take this with you or have us deliver it?"

That's all there is to it. With this close, you use your fingers to keep track of advantages and disadvantages as opposed to a sheet of paper with a line down the middle as you did with the Advantage, Disadvantage Close. If, however, you still feel like using the pad of paper with the two columns with this close, by all means, feel free to do so.

The Can You Do Me a Favor Close

The Can You Do Me a Favor Close is one that you will use with your friends when you need to hit your quota at the end of the year, win that sales trip, or anytime you need some business *immediately*. When we say "friends," we are referring to customers who have become close, trusted friends and business partners over the years. These people truly care about you on a personal level, not simply a business level. Consequently, they will help you when you need business.

Of course, you also want to do something special in return. You can give them special payment terms, a gift certificate to a restaurant, or some other similar "bonus" for helping you out. The bottom line is that when you need business, you know you can give these people a call and ask for some. After your opening greeting, you will have some small talk as you would with a friend. Once you've caught up a little, you can let your customer know what the situation is and ask for some business.

"Joe, I'm wondering if you could possibly help me out with something. Of course, it's getting toward the end of the year and I'm having a pretty good year, but I could use a little more business. I'm in a position to give you some special payment terms and work with you in some other ways. Let me ask you, is there anything we could possibly squeeze into this year and bill next year?"

This close is meant to be very conversational and low key because you're talking with a friend whom you shouldn't need to hammer over the head. With this close, you simply need to have a reason you're asking for the business, state to your "friendly" customer what that reason is, and then close.

Finally, if your customer says that he really can't help you, just thank him, finish up with a little more small talk, and move on. Don't push or jeopardize the relationship in any way.

The Guinea Pig Close

The Guinea Pig Close is another close to use with your clients who have also become friends. However, you need to be a little more prepared for this one. You will use this close only when you have 1) something new on the market and you want to be the first one to sell it, or 2) you want to get the new product in your territory so you'll have a local reference and can learn more about how the product operates in the real world.

With this close, you *need* to give your client/friend some concessions because being a guinea pig on a new product involves some risk. Cover the downside of the risk with incentives and perks. Usually companies will make a guarantee such as, "If for some reason this product doesn't live up to expectations, we will remove it and reinstall your previous unit at no cost to you."

In addition, the first unit to go live in the field is usually at a good discount to "encourage" the customer to try it out and further cover any downside.

In the final analysis, if your customer truly is the first one to try this product, your company should be willing to make certain concessions. If she's not the first customer to use the product, but the first in a certain area, your company should still be willing to make some concessions. If the company is not willing to make concessions in these cases, you want to get as much backup information as possible before you go to your customer with what you have. That backup information should include some feedback from the first *real* customer.

Friends are good prospects in this situation because if *you* believe in the new product, your friends will too. They trust you so they are usually willing to try the product.

The following is an example of the Guinea Pig Close. After your opening greeting, you will have some small talk as you would with a friend. Once you've caught up, you can let your customer know what the situation is and ask for some business. "Joe, we've just come out with a great new product, and I'm in a position to get it to you at a great price."

Give him some detail about the new product and what it can do. You want to be enthusiastic and sell the benefits of the new product. Once you've done this, continue with,

"Joe, because there aren't any of these new items out there currently, you would be the first. Of course there are some advantages to that; at the same time, you're a bit of a guinea pig too. As a result, we'll get you a great price in return for some feedback on your experience with it.

"Also, if you aren't happy with it for any reason, we will of course remove it and reinstall the previous unit. Joe, I think it's a great opportunity for you to be the first one on the block to have one of these and offer your customers something that no one else can. Also, I believe strongly in this product and feel it would be great for you to be on the cutting edge *and* get a fabulous price. How does that idea sound to you?"

The Best Solution for the Prospect Close

Your first objective as a salesperson is to help your prospects solve their problems. If the prospect comes to you looking for a specific item that you don't have but your competition does, it is your job to tell the prospect where he or she can find that item, namely, at your competitor's.

Now, bear in mind that if you have a similar solution and you believe it is actually better, then your job is to educate the prospect as to why he or she should be using your solution above all the others.

For example, let's say you sell cars. Someone comes in looking for a particular make of used car because they have heard that the cars are very safe. You don't have any of these cars but you do have some used Volvos, which are arguably the safest cars around. You would begin by saying, "No, we don't have any of those used cars, however…" and then proceed to ask about the importance of the safety issue.

If the primary objective is safety, you can show some research reports on the Volvo and ask if they are of interest. If the prospect says, "No, I'm specifically looking for an X car," either tell him where to find one or figure out where you can get your hands on one.

Note 1: If you don't have what the prospect is looking for but you can get your hands on it, say, "No, I don't have any in stock. However, I can get you one." Then proceed to get all the information you need to secure the order.

Note 2: Don't use the bait and switch. Many of us have run into a scenario where we went into a store looking for something, and because they were out of that product, or something else had a better commission, the salesperson was adamant about selling us something else. It soon becomes crystal clear that the salesperson is more interested in making a sale than in giving you what you really want.

People want honesty. If you don't have what they want, say so. If you can get it, let the prospect know that. If you *don't* have it and you *can't* get it, let the prospect know where he can get it and then probe to find out why he wants that particular item. Then investigate whether you have a solution that is just as good or better. If you do, educate the prospect and close.

People also don't like to hear, "No, sorry, goodbye." People want you make an effort to help, even if you are not able to solve the problem yourself. Make a few phone calls, ask a few people, give the best possible lead or idea you can come up with, and show a sincere effort. People simply want to know that you sincerely care about them and their problem.

The best-case scenario is to help the prospect solve a problem and be monetarily involved in the equation. The next-best scenario is to help the prospect solve a problem even though you are not benefiting financially.

You want to be part of the solution even if it is only helping the prospect to discover where to go to find what he *really* wants and *truly* needs.

What comes around does go around, and when you help people they'll remember you and either come back or send others to you. Will it always happen? No. And yet if you don't help or don't attempt to help, the odds of that person ever coming back are virtually zero.

The Something to Live up To Close

The Something to Live up To Close is most effective when you have a buyer who is on the fence, or when you have two buyers and one is sold while the other is not. This close involves making a statement that gives the buyer a reputation to live up to. Here are two examples of the Something to Live up To Close.

In the first example, a man is inspecting a new car at a neighborhood dealership. The salesperson has qualified him, uncovered all his needs and desires, presented the features and benefits, effectively handled his objections, and has seemingly done everything else right. Then she hears, "Hmm, you know what? I'm just really not sure."

The salesperson follows with, "Okay, what exactly are you unsure about?" The prospect responds with, "Hmm, I don't know, I'm just not sure."

At this point, the salesperson should respond with, "Mr. Prospect, I definitely understand how you feel. At the same time, we both agree you want the car. Is that correct?"

Also, the salesperson should mention a few of the other reasons her prospect should consider when buying the car. For example, "And we both agree the car will save you from all the money you're putting into your current automobile, right? In addition, we agree that this car will give you the peace of mind, knowing that it won't break down and leave you stranded out in the middle of nowhere. Is that right?"

Next, she should give the prospect *something to live up to*, and then close. "You know, Mr. Prospect, you're one of the lucky ones. Many people who look at this car simply don't have the resources to pay for it. Because of that, they either hesitate or decide not to buy altogether. I'm envious of the position you're in. Do you feel you'd really *need* to finance this car, or would you rather buy it outright?"

By stating the fact that she's aware the prospect has the resources and then asking if he feels he'll need to finance it, she's put him in a position of "living up to" the image that he can afford it without financing it.

Now, keep in mind that she's qualified the prospect and knows he can afford it. The salesperson also believes deep down that the prospect needs her product to solve his current problem—in this case an unreliable car that might leave him stranded in the middle of nowhere.

When she says, "You know, Mr. Prospect, you're one of the lucky ones. Many people who look at this car simply don't have the resources to pay for it," she is simply making a statement of truth. She knows he can afford it and she also knows many other people cannot afford it.

Now let's put you, as the salesperson, in the same scenario except this time a husband and wife are deciding on a new car. In this situation, the wife needs a new car to replace her old clunker. You have gone through all the qualifying, presenting, and all other steps, and have closed. After you ask the closing question, the husband turns to his wife and says, "Well honey, what do you think?" She retorts with, "Hmm, I think it's too expensive."

At this point, you need to jump in immediately. If you let that thought just sit out there, the wife will start to justify why she feels it's too expensive. You need to come back with, "Mr. and Ms. Prospect, I definitely understand that. At the same time, we all agree you need the car to replace your old unreliable one. Correct?"

Next, mention a few of the other reasons why they are interested in buying the car. For example, say, "And we both agree the car will save you all the money you're putting into your current automobile, right? In addition (looking at the wife), you obviously don't want to break down and be stranded in the middle of nowhere (now look at the husband), and you don't want her to break down out in the middle of nowhere. And you know with your current car that's a very real possibility. Right?"

Next, handle her price objection. "Ms. Prospect, I think you'd agree with me that you get what you pay for, is that right? This car has received the highest rating for both reliability and safety." Show copies of articles and other proof you have at this point. "Of course, it's important to both of you that you can rely on the car and that you're safe in case of an accident, correct?"

Cast your eyes equally between husband and wife as you make this statement. Now finish answering the price objection. "In addition, this car has a history of lasting 50 percent longer than other similar cars in its class, yet it only costs 20 percent more. That means that if this car lasts seven and a half years as opposed to only five, but you're only paying 20 percent more. In the long run you're actually saving 30 percent. So you can see how you're actually saving money in the long term. Am I correct?"

Wait for an affirmative answer, then give the husband "something to live up to" and close. "You know, Ms. Prospect, you're very lucky. While many husbands have a desire to protect their wives with a car as safe and reliable as this one, very few have the resources to do it. Would you like to take a look at our financing options? Or do you think you will you be buying the car outright?"

With this close, your compliment both gives the prospect something to live up to and issues a challenge. When you say, "Very few have the resources to do it," one of two thoughts cross the prospect's mind. 1) "Is this salesperson wondering whether I can afford this?" or 2) "That's right, I am in a financial position to do something that most other people can't." Both ideas will tend to get the prospect focused on either demonstrating to you that he can afford it or on living up to the reputation you've given him. Either way, this usually leads to a sale.

In some situations the prospect may think you are challenging him, and call you on it. If this happens, simply apologize and reassure the prospect that you realize he does have the financial resources, and you are simply pointing out how lucky he is to be in that position. If you do this with sincerity, your prospect will feel he has been genuinely complimented.

The Price Sheet Close

The Price Sheet Close is a great way to gain the confidence of new prospects. It's also a successful technique you can use to express confidence in the positive relationship you have with existing customers. With prospects or customers whom you don't know very well, use this close when there is a question about your price or discount level. With your best customers, use this close to solidify the relationship even further. In other words, use this close on the two extremes of your account base, but use it differently with each group.

Here's an example of when you might use the close with prospects or new customers:

Prospect: "Is this the best you can do in terms of price?"
You: "Yes, Mr. Prospect, it is. We've discussed all the value you're getting from this product, and from a price standpoint we should be very competitive. I've discounted the product 20 percent to show you how much we want your business and we promise to continue to give you the best value at the best price. That's what you're looking for, right?"

If you get any answer other than a definite yes to this question, follow with, "Mr. Prospect, let me show you my price sheets. Obviously this isn't something my company likes me to do. At the same time I want you to know you are getting the best I can offer."

Show the price sheet(s) you've used to calculate the price in this particular situation and then continue with, "Mr. Prospect, does this give you confidence that I am doing the best I possibly can on price?" Once you get an affirmative answer to this question, close. "Great, would you like standard delivery or overnight service?"

With an existing "great" customer you use this close a little differently. The following is an example of how the close would go in this case:

Prospect: "Okay, I need A, B, C, and D. What's the best price can you give me?"

You: "Mr. Customer, here's my price sheet. Just take 20 percent off anything on there."

It should be clear that this close used with a great customer is much different than one used with a prospect.

Note 1: *Very important!* Be very careful with your price sheets, especially with prospects and new customers. These people pose the greatest risk for getting your price sheets into the hands of your competitor. *Never, ever leave price sheets with prospects or new customers*; only show them the pricing. If they ask to keep a copy, tell them you would like to give them one, but it is strictly against company policy. State that you could lose your job, which is probably the truth in any case.

Note 2: Clearly, it is helpful to have your pricing sheets ready before you use this close. If you don't have them ready, but you have them on your computer, and if it's a short, basic quote, you can work through them from the computer screen with your prospect or customer.

Note 3: It appears more "official" if you have the price sheets stored on a computer file or if you retrieve them from an online source. Paper copies still work, but price sheets stored electronically that a prospect or customer watches you download have more credibility than those simply printed on paper.

Note 4: Your company probably does have some kind of policy regarding showing price sheets to prospects and customers, and they may not want you doing it at all. Use your best judgment here. This is a gray area that you want to be careful with.

The Competitive Advantage Close

We referred to this close in the *Competition* section. Use the Competitive Advantage Close to highlight your advantages versus the competition's and to paint a picture of your product as being so far ahead of the competition's that the prospect will be at a severe disadvantage without it.

We're going to give you the close as we used it in the banking industry. With a little work, you can adapt it to your own product or service. Here's the example:

"Mr. Prospect, today the banking industry is faced with the issues of Triple DES, Voice Guidance, Check 21, the death of OS2, and the challenges of Windows. Additionally, there is the goal of making your ATMs more profitable rather than simply being a service for the customer. Does that sound about right?

"Okay. Now, you also realize this is a large opportunity to get a leg up on the competition. At the same time, you know that some banks and credit unions will handle all these issues better than others will. As a result they have a distinct competitive advantage in the marketplace, right?

"With that in mind, here is your scenario.

"Both we and X Company have Triple DES covered. Regarding Voice Guidance, that's still down the road. Yet, through our experience with the largest bank in the world, we know that we're capable of giving you the proper amount of memory and processor power, whereas X Company cannot. That means a future upgrade to the X Company's machine.

"Regarding Check 21, we've also discussed our advantages there. Our machines have superior software and hardware along with the large paper acceptor, which X Company does not have.

"One of the most blatant differences is in the OS2 and Windows arena. We will put Windows software on the machines because that gives you the most advantages and flexibility. X Company will put OS2 on the machines because they don't have a Windows solution yet. The death of OS2 is imminent, and this means another upgrade to your X Company machines.

"Finally, the best way to make your machines profitable is through marketing to your customers via the ATM, correct? We've already talked about the huge advantages of Windows over OS2 in this area. Also, our machines give you twenty-two industry exclusives, of which eleven are directly related to using your ATM as a marketing tool. Again, X Company cannot give you these features. The features are exclusive to our machines.

"So on one side, you have our company, which, in addition to all the advantages I've just mentioned, is the original equipment manufacturer, has the largest service and support staff in the industry, and is the leader in the world, or a third party, regional distributor selling the X Company machine. All that considered, who do you think will give you a competitive edge in the marketplace?"

That's the close. Simply plug in the issues facing your industry and your competitive advantages and adapt the close to fit your selling situation.

The Contrarian View Close

We referred to this one in the *Objections* section because it's an answer to an objection in addition to a close. Use the Contrarian View Close when you get an objection about the state of the economy, the presidential election, stock market fluctuations, the price of gasoline, or any other reason someone is sitting back and waiting for something in the outside world to happen. The close goes like this:

"Joe, I definitely understand how you feel, and that's exactly why the time to move is *now*. Let me ask you a question. Would you rather buy a stock after everyone else has bought, when it's as high as it will go, or before everyone buys when it is low and poised for explosive growth? (Wait for an answer.)

"Would you rather get into the housing market before everyone else, when prices are low and ready to take off, or afterward, when the house has already doubled in value? (Wait for an answer.)

"Joe, it's a fact that, per capita, more millionaires were made in this country during the Depression than at any other time in history. Would you rather have been one of those millionaires or one of the people in the soup lines? (Wait for an answer.)

"It's also a fact that the richest people in the world have a contrarian view. In other words, they are buying when everyone else is selling and they are selling when everyone else is buying. When other people are saying no, those rich people are saying yes, and vice versa.

"Joe, the question today isn't really whether you want to buy, it's whether you want to be one of the elite few or one of the crowd. Joe, what else do you need to know so you can take advantage of the current (marketplace, economy, or whatever excuse he gave you)?"

Note: When you get an objection such as the economy, the impending presidential election, the stock market, and other similar "state of something" objections, these are typically smokescreens. Unless the market crashed yesterday or civil war is imminent, the "wait and see what happens" objections are simply the best excuse the prospect can come up with off the top of his head. Answer the objection the way we did above and then be prepared to get a completely different objection.

The Doorknob Close

We also referred to this close in the *Objections* section because it is appropriate when you are not able to overcome the current objection or find the real one. Use this close as a last resort when you have tried everything you can, closed many times, but for some reason you just can't sell this individual. Here's how it goes.

Begin this close by giving the prospect the impression that you are leaving. Pack up all your things, thank the prospect for his time, exchange goodbyes, and get up to leave. Walk toward the door and as you place your hand on the doorknob, turn to the prospect and say, "Mr. Prospect, let me ask you, what's the *real* reason you didn't buy from me today?"

Believe it or not, often the prospect will actually give you the real objection at this point. When he does, you say, "I can't believe I missed that. It's crystal clear now. If I were you, I wouldn't have bought either."

You now walk back toward where you were sitting and say, "Mr. Prospect, I have some great information to share regarding that." Now handle the objection, get verification that you've handled it, and close.

The theory behind this technique is that, psychologically, the prospect drops his defenses as soon as you are exiting the situation. When the prospect's guard is down and you strike with a question, the prospect will usually respond because he is now in a more relaxed, defenseless state.

Note 1: Go after the objection once or twice, but don't overstay your welcome at this point. This is a final effort and one you simply want to bat at a couple of times to see if you can overcome it and break through. If not, thank the prospect once again for his time, turn the doorknob completely this time, and keep walking.

Note 2: You can use a variation of this technique, which also works well. The variation involves asking for the prospect's help. When you put your hand on the doorknob, instead of saying, "Mr. Prospect, let me ask you, what's the *real* reason you didn't buy from me today?" say, "Mr. Prospect, I'm wondering if you could help me out a little. I'm always trying to learn and improve as a salesperson. I thought I did everything right today, but obviously I didn't get the sale. Is there any advice you have for me on how I might have done better or what I could have done differently today?"

You're looking for the reason or objection for why the prospect didn't buy. When the prospect gives you the real objection, use the same "I can't believe I missed that" approach and take one more shot.

Also, you don't want to come across as a silver-tongued salesperson. You want to give the exact opposite impression. To do this, drop your head, shoulders, and voice tone a little and come across as someone who is somewhat defeated. This will generally help the prospect to open up to you.

Note 3: You don't actually need a doorknob. If there's no door you can simply take four or five steps and then turn around and ask the question.

The Why or Why Not Close

The Why or Why Not Close is as short, sweet, and simple as closes get and it can be surprisingly effective. Here's an example of this close.

You: "So would you like to finance this or will you be paying cash?"
Prospect: "Hmm, I don't know. I really want to sleep on it."
You: "Why?" (or why not, if that's the appropriate question)

Once you ask why or why not, you must follow it up with complete silence. Don't say anything until the prospect gives you an answer.

"Why?" and "Why not?" are very simple questions, but they're very effective because people don't expect them. Because they catch the prospect off guard, she is more likely to answer your question. Once the question is answered, you have your objection and can go to work on it.

The What Would You Tell Your Salespeople to Do in This Situation Close

This is an effective close you can use on sales managers and other people who have salespeople working for them. Outside of other good salespeople, sales managers and others involved with overseeing salespeople will be your easiest people to deal with. Why? Because they appreciate a good salesperson who is professional and persistent. If you find yourself in a tough situation when dealing with these people, you can usually gain the upper hand by asking them what they would have their own salespeople to do in a similar situation. Let's look at an example.

In reviewing the sales call, you believe you've done everything right. You built sufficient rapport, you uncovered the prospect's needs and desires, you showed how your product more than satisfies the prospect's needs and desires, you've overcome several objections, and you've asked for the order several times. Yet, for some reason, *you aren't getting anywhere.* At this point say,

"Mr. Prospect, I'm wondering if you could help me out a little. You have salespeople who work for you, correct? I believe I've covered all the bases. I built what I felt was sufficient rapport. I believe I uncovered your needs and desires, and showed how my product more than satisfies your needs and desires. I've overcome several objections and I've asked for the order several times. Yet, for some reason, I'm not getting anywhere. Can you tell me, if I was one of your salespeople in a similar situation, what advice would you give me?"

If your prospect is a sales manager or upper level executive with any sort of decency, she will take you under her wing at this point and help you to "become a better salesperson." At the same time, she will help you close the sale. For example, you might hear, "Well, I would probably direct my salesperson to make sure he or she uncovered the true objection."

Or you might hear, "Well, I would tell the salesperson to make sure he or she uncovered the primary need for the product." Whatever the prospect says at this point is where you want to direct your attention.

Once the prospect has set you in the right direction, step back and discuss what you've learned about that area. Don't hesitate to ask the prospect to help you through. It's important to note that you do have to do some work here. The prospect will not do all the work for you and simply give you the order on a silver platter—in fact, they usually won't. They want you to learn something at this point, but they also want to know you are at least trying.

Note 1: When you call on sales managers and other people who have salespeople working for them, do the things they wish their salespeople would do. In other words, call early in the morning and after five o'clock, call on weekends, call on lunch breaks, or when you have some down time. Be the consummate professional, send thank you notes, be persistent, and do what you say you'll do when you say you'll do it. Don't forget one of the most important items, *ask for the order.* You will score major points if you work hard and go the extra mile because these people appreciate good salespeople.

Note 2: Because these people are in top-level sales positions, ask them for their advice. Ask them what books they read, what audio programs they listen to, and what other similar insights they may have.

The Friend, Family Member, Neighbor, Colleague, Significant Other Close

This isn't so much a close as it is a way to obtain more business from the relationships you're creating with customers. This close requires that you build strong rapport with your customers, and it requires you to keep an open mind to opportunity. Here are some examples of this close.

Let's assume you are selling a product or service to companies as opposed to individuals. Once one company buys, you would be wise to call on any adjacent or neighboring companies. Obviously, it would be best if you could get the customer who has just bought your product to give you a referral to the other business.

Perhaps you have a product you can demonstrate to neighboring companies. Do you sell landscaping, remodeling for the outside of the building, signs, paving, or anything else that the neighboring companies could see?

Ask if a company for whom you've just done work will allow you to put a sign out front. You could even give them a discount or some other incentive to let you put the advertising out front.

Did you just sell something to an office manager? Could she refer you to other office managers? Perhaps she could refer you to the office manager at the company next door, or perhaps her sister or best friend is an office manager across town. In any event, you can still go to the company next door or across the street and say, "Hi, I was just speaking with the office manager next door and she bought one of our new units. Is it okay if I take a brief moment of your time to demonstrate it?"

If the office manager at an adjacent business has recently bought, but doesn't know the other office manager(s) personally, use this line *after you've cleared it with the office manager you just sold to:* "Hi. I was speaking with the office manager next door who bought my product and although she doesn't know you personally, she said that if she did she would have called you and highly recommended my product. Can I show you something I believe you'll find very interesting?"

How about other people in the office? Did you just sell an insurance policy to the boss? What about the employees? If the boss bought, that can have a strong influence on the employees.

Your goal: Target people who are friends, family members, colleagues, significant others, and those people otherwise in proximity (such as neighbors of the person who just bought), and ask them to buy also.

The keys to this close are a solid sale and *solid* delivery. If you've just done some outstanding landscaping for a company, other companies in the area will notice. If you just delivered excellent service to someone, it's easier to approach the neighbor and be enthusiastic about it. You want to make sure the sale is *solid* because occasionally the neighbor won't buy your product and she will tell your customer he or she wasn't too bright for doing so. However, if you sell your product in the right way, your new prospect will be immune to the criticism.

The See How Great My Product Is Close

You may have heard of a recent marketing trend that has gained much attention and much success. Although it's technically a marketing idea, it can also be classified as a closing technique because it does create sales. This closing technique involves using your product in public and letting others try it out.

Many companies that use this technique have been hiring salespeople to venture out in public and use their product simply to create consumer interest. Your goal is to have people approach the salesperson who is using the product and inquire about it. Going one step further, some of the salespeople hired by the company will actually approach people and ask if they'd like to try the product. Obviously, it is helpful to have a unique product that will sell itself. However, with the right technique, you can adapt this method to many different products.

Consider these factors:

• Do you use the product you sell?

- Is there a way you could use the product you sell in public?
- How about carrying or reading information about your product in public?

With this close, your objective is to look for ways to advertise what you sell in a non-verbal way. Once people ask about your product or information, you can then give your inspirational, short, "hit 'em between the eyes" power statement about your product.

This close is more passive than most of the others. Let people gravitate toward you and show an interest. If possible, allow them to test the product themselves. When they do express an interest, don't pounce on them—simply give them the strongest features and benefits and keep their interest sparked. You should still be determined to close; however, your close will be more like a trial close rather than an "up front, straightforward" request for the order. Suggest something like, "If you were to get one of these, would you prefer one with our optional feature or one without?"

Once you have an answer to that question, you can follow with, "Actually I have a few (with or without the option, however the prospect wants it) right here. Would you want only one, or can you think of someone else who might want one as well?"

The key with this close is to get your product or service out there in the spotlight. Use the product or read literature in public and allow people to approach you. Once they do and have expressed an interest, begin a conversation that leads to the close.

The Prospect Close

The Prospect Close is the easiest close and the one you'll run into the least. This is a close whereby you don't close at all; instead, the prospect closes himself or herself. Obviously, this doesn't happen too often, but it does occasionally occur, so when it does, you need to be prepared.

The Prospect Close occurs when you are in the middle of a presentation and the prospect enthusiastically agrees, saying something like, "Wow! That sounds great! How do I get started?" At that reaction, simply smile and say, "All I need is a little information." Don't hesitate. Pull out your order sheet and begin asking the questions necessary to complete the order.

A friend of ours had an experience with the Prospect Close where he was on the buying end. He had visited a gym to research the possibility of joining. The salesperson began by walking our friend around and showing him the entire facility.

Next, he brought our friend into his office to explain all the features of the gym. After the salesperson had given our friend a few of the best features, our friend pulled out his American Express card, handed it to the salesperson, and said, "Do you take American Express?"

The salesperson reached out his hand, pushed the card away, and said, "Wait, I have much more to tell you." Our friend responded with, "Look, I understand, but I'm a little short on time and I really want to join, so here's my card. Do you take American Express?"

The salesperson responded with, "Yes, we do, but we have a couple other neat things I'd really like to tell you about." Our friend replied with, "Okay, I don't mean to be rude. But please, I only have a few minutes, so can you make it brief?"

Our friend had to close himself three times before the salesperson finally took his credit card. *After* the sale is made, close it. Too many negative things can happen between the time the prospect is ready to buy and the time you're ready to close him. You need to be aware of these situations.

The K.I.S.S. Close

We know of one investment advisor who is a major advocate of the KISS (keep it simple, stupid) method of selling. On his second call to the prospect, which is his closing call, he briefly says hello and works on building some more rapport, he then bridges into his sales call. "John, I have a very exciting opportunity that fits your goal of (long-term growth, short-term growth, or whatever the prospect had told him he was looking for) perfectly. What else do you need to know?"

In this case, the theory and the ideal is that the prospect will receive *only* the information he needs to make a decision—nothing more, nothing less. This example of selling may sound ridiculous to some people, and it does take a good deal of practice to get good at it, and yet this salesperson is highly effective with it.

The main idea behind KISS is that you don't want to use a fire-hose approach that leaves your prospect totally overwhelmed. Second, you don't want to be talking well after the prospect has already decided to buy.

Listen to what the prospect is asking for, give *only* the information necessary, and clarify that the prospect has understood what you've just said. Once you have agreement, *close*.

Chapter 35

Other Thoughts Regarding Closing

Offer Incentives to Make the Sale *Now*

Following are some incentives that can influence people to purchase your product or service.

1) Include something for free.

Including something for free is a good way to increase response and interest. We're certain you've seen advertisements where, with the purchase of the product, you get a free gift. Perhaps you can include some free supplies such as paper, some ink cartridges, or some spare parts that may not be expensive but can still help to sweeten the pot.

2) Offer a special price.

If you are giving a seminar and have products with you, you may offer the products at a discount if attendees buy that day. You may also have a "one-day-only sale" or other similar event.

3) Have a money-back guarantee.

Money-back guarantees are a great way to reduce risk and make the prospect feel as if she has nothing to lose.

Note: Many money-back guarantees run for a year or more. We have even seen some that run over the lifetime of the product.

4) Have a deadline on your offer.

"We are offering this model only until August 31st, 2008" is a good example of an offer with a deadline. Given the opportunity to procrastinate, most people will. You want give people enough time to respond, but not too much time. A good rule of thumb is thirty days from the date they are in front of you, receive the letter, see the ad, etc.

5) Have a free trial period.

Offer a free trial period that allows people to review their purchase for a certain number of days before they have to pay for it. A typical trial period is thirty to sixty days.

6) Guarantee your product.

Most products come with some sort of guarantee. Product guarantees are another way to reduce the prospect's risk. In this case, you guarantee a product will last for a certain amount of time, one year, two years, or even the life of the product. This is somewhat similar to a new car warranty. If you know the car is covered, bumper to bumper, for three years or 36,000 miles, this gives you assurance and a comfort factor that it will last for a while, and the company is standing behind its product.

7) Offer an extended warranty.

Extended warranties can also serve to give a prospect peace of mind. For example, you could give the prospect a six-month warranty on the product as opposed to the standard three-month warranty. If you do this, be sure you attach a dollar value to the warranty so you can show the prospect how much money this will save him.

We once saw a car dealership advertising "Free Tires for Life!" When you break it down, the dollar amount is probably the same as or less than some of the factory rebates and other promotions car dealerships usually run. Also, there are certainly some restrictions. At the same time, the dealership got people's attention with a great eye-grabber.

8) Budge on the price of something besides the product itself.

If you need to budge somewhat on price, you may be able to do it on one of the associated costs instead of the product or service itself. For example, maybe you cut your annual service contract price from $1,000 to $900, telling the prospect that you've done all you can with the price of the product; however, you can show him some additional savings on the service contract end.

9) Cut the price of the product.

Cutting price should be your last resort.

Watch out for legal issues with any of the above offers.

If you make a guarantee, offer something for free, warranty a product, or include anything else in your offer, you have to honor it.

An Important Ingredient behind Your Incentives

Keep in mind that guarantees and other offers are only as good as the company backing them. The incentive to act will have no effect if the prospect feels the company or the salesperson making the offer lack credibility. For the most part, people will be comfortable and will not question the validity of the source of the incentives. Here are some rules to follow to ensure your offer and incentives aren't questioned:

1) Build rapport with the prospect and sell yourself and your company.

This will help eliminate any credibility issues and will help ensure that the prospect is comfortable with the person, the company behind the offer, and any incentives.

2) Save any talk of guarantees and incentives until the end of your presentation or when covering the final details after the close.

Don't throw out an incentive in the beginning stages of the conversation. That's almost as bad as dropping your price right away. When you start throwing out incentives in the beginning of the selling process you're operating from a position of weakness.

3) Watch what you say when you verbalize the terms of your guarantee or other incentives.

You don't want to give the prospect the wrong idea. For example, let's say you have a guarantee that covers everything contained within your product but does not cover items outside your product such as phone lines, customer or employee error, or acts of God such as the weather. In this case you *don't* want to say something like, "We have a 100 percent service satisfaction guarantee. If you're not happy with our service for *any* reason we'll refund your service contract."

The primary problem here relates to the words "any reason" and "we'll refund your service contract." A prospect could interpret "any reason" to be anything under the sun, including someone crashing their car into the machine, or a bolt of lightning frying the electronics. When you say, "we'll refund your service contract," the prospect may interpret that to mean the *entire* contract as opposed to just a portion of the contract. In this case, say this instead: "We have a 100 percent service satisfaction guarantee. I'll go over that with you when we get everything finalized, and then of course I'll leave a copy of the guarantee with you." You want to ensure your guarantee spells out the exceptions and other conditions and that you *do* cover them when you give your explanation.

4) Be thoroughly familiar with the terms of your guarantees and incentives.

If you work for a large company, or one that has some good legal resources, chances are good that someone spent a good deal of time coming up with the proper legal wording on your guarantees and incentives. Read through the wording carefully, and if you have any questions, get them answered by the proper authorities at your company. You should be able to clearly explain the terms of guarantees and incentives and understand all the small print and details.

If asked a question, answer it thoroughly. If you don't know the answer, find out. Don't guess at an answer if you don't know. Phrases such as "I think" and "I'm pretty sure" are usually missed by the prospect in conversation.

You don't need to go into great detail initially. If the prospect asks a question about your guarantee, or another incentive, be short and to the point, make sure he is comfortable with the answer, and then move on. For example, when asked a question about how to invoke the guarantee, you might say something like, "This is a ninety-day, no-questions-asked guarantee. You simply need to give me a call and I'll take it from there. Sounds pretty simply, huh?"

Once you get an affirmative answer, say, "Once we wrap things up, I will go over the guarantee and leave information that covers what we go over. Is that fair enough?"

5) If you are a small company, are in business for yourself, don't have a crew of lawyers at your disposal, and/or are developing your own guarantee and other incentives, make sure the wording for each is straightforward and clear.

Also, make sure it protects you and your customers. Vague language can open the door to potential problems, including legal issues. Guarantees and incentives that are not thorough can leave you open to unwanted, sometimes overwhelming liability or leave your customers' rights unprotected. It is a good idea to run the wording of your guarantee and other incentives past a lawyer just to be safe. You can go to your local Small Business Association for a referral to a lawyer who specializes in this area.

Finally, if you have written your own guarantee and incentives, revisit them from time to time and look for ways to improve them. Can you change the wording to remove any areas of doubt? Can you make it easier for the prospect to understand? What do your customers think of the guarantee? Survey the customers who have used the guarantee and find out how they feel about the process. Also, gauge their level of satisfaction.

Other Ways to Consummate the Sale *Now*

It's the last business day of the month, maybe even the last business day of the year, and you're trying to get in as much business in as possible. You're speaking with a customer about a recent proposal and she gives you the okay to go ahead. You know there is no way you will be able to get over there to get a contract signed. What do you do?

1) What constitutes an order?

Is there anything besides a signed order that will suffice as an order? Can you take a verbal order, can you have the customer sign the proposal and fax it to you, or will a purchase order work? If you have any of these options open to you, take advantage of them. In addition to helping you out at the end of the month, these other methods of getting an order signed may save you some travel time.

2) Enter the order now and get it signed later.

Just make sure you know your customer *very* well, and make sure this technique won't get you in any trouble with your company.

3) Talk to someone at a higher level at your company about what can be done.

If you work for a smaller company, it is usually easier to work around the issue of not being able to get a contract signed immediately. If you don't have any of the contingencies in place that were mentioned above, your best bet is to go to someone with some influence and authority, let him or her know what the situation is and see what can be done.

Some Great Times to Close

The December Holidays and the Fourth of July are great opportunities to get business and impress a customer, or a prospect you've been trying to land as a customer. At these times of year there are several factors at work. First, the people you are calling on are generally in a better mood, and second, they will be impressed that you are working when most salespeople are leaving work to start the holidays early. Here's an approach that works well.

As the last work before the holidays approaches, make a list of all companies you're still waiting for a buying decision from. Many times the companies you are calling on have parties around these times of year. If you show up around noon and there is a party, you will usually be invited to participate.

When you join the party, keep business discussion to a minimum. Concentrate instead on building rapport with everyone but particularly the decision-maker(s). If the key-decision maker is the purchasing agent, your objective is to eventually work your way around to her and partake in small talk and rapport building. When you finally get to her, say hello and exchange pleasantries. Ask what her plans are for the holidays. Find areas of commonality, or if you already know a bit about each other, build on your mutual areas of interest and look for more things you have in common.

After you've built some rapport for ten minutes or so, go for the close. As you wind down the rapport-building conversation, if you are in a competitive situation, say, "Sue, I know you're still in the process of making a decision on that printing job (or whatever your business is). I promise I'll make it a priority, get it done the way you want, on time, and you'll be more than happy with the end result. Why don't you let me take care of it for you?" Then be silent.

If you are in a non-competitive situation, say, "Sue, concerning that printing job we've been discussing—as usual, I'll make it a priority, get it done on time, and make sure it's done to your satisfaction. Is there any way we can get that wrapped up?"

You'll be surprised how well this works. The prospect has her defenses down, she's having good thoughts about the holiday, she sees you involved in the festivities, working when most others are out playing. In short, you are seriously stacking the odds in your favor. When you get the order, make sure you *do* make it a priority, get it done the way she wants, on time, and make sure she's more than happy with the end result.

To find out who's having holiday parties, call each company the morning of the last working day before the holiday and tell the receptionist you're thinking about stopping by. Ask if it's a normal business day, a shortened day due to the holiday, or if there are any events going on. If they are having a party, she will say something like, "We're having a party at noon and leaving at 1:00. So make sure you stop by before that time." Bingo! Get ready to show up at noon.

If they're not having a party, a pre-holiday call is still a good idea.

This close works best with the December holidays and the Fourth of July but the day before any holiday is a great time to stop by and follow up on unfinished business. Again, people will usually be in a better mood, have their guard down, and be impressed that you are working.

Fridays are another great day to do business as people are generally in better moods on Friday than on any other day of the week. Simply make your list of customers with pending business decisions and go out and start calling on them. As in the other examples, after some rapport building, close using either the competitive or non-competitive close in the previous examples, whichever is appropriate.

What If You Are Leery about Your Prospect?

Occasionally your instinct will tell you something just isn't right about the person whom you're about to sell to. In cases such as this, it is often a good idea to listen to your instinct. If you are in this situation and you decide to make the sale anyway, just make sure all your bases are covered.

Have everything in writing and make sure all is understood. Define time frames and what constitutes success versus failure. Make sure deadlines are spelled out. Also, have contingencies covered. What happens if something does go wrong? Have terms in the agreement that address any conflict that may arise and the terms and conditions under which it will be settled.

Check the person or business out through credit reports, the Attorney-General's office, or the Better Business Bureau.

Finally, if there is no way to cover yourself in a satisfactory manner, you're better off passing on the deal.

Each Sale Must Be Win-Win

You don't want to get the sale if it costs too much. Each situation should be a win-win. Although most sales are slightly weighted in one direction or the other, if the sale is significantly in one party's favor and at the cost of the other, doing the deal is bad business. Let it go.

Remember that bad prospects usually become bad customers. If you have a prospect who seems as if he is going to take an inordinate amount of your time or effort for very little return, let your competitor have the headache.

Keep Track of Your Closing Percentage

How many presentations are you converting to sales? Are you at, above, or below the average for your industry? The answers to these questions will give you a good idea of how you're doing.

You also want to find out *why* you aren't closing the ones you miss. This will give you an idea of where your problems are.

You always want to be reviewing both your successes and your failures with your manager and other salespeople. You especially want to be doing this if you are below the industry average for closing percentage.

A Summary of Ideas on Closing

Keep these ideas in mind with regard to closing:

- You must be convinced that your product is a great product before you close the prospect on it being a great product.

- Close on every call.

- Close different people differently.

- Look and listen for indications that it's time to close.

- Get in front of the prospect to put the odds in your favor.

- Bring as many senses as possible into the close.

- Be prepared to hear "no" from time to time.

- Know how far you can go to get the deal done.

- Do what you can to get the deal done *now*.

- Trust your gut. If the deal doesn't seem like a good one for some reason, let it go. Sometimes it's better *not* to close business.

- Keep track of your closing success rate.

- Take advantage of holidays and Fridays when closing. Both tend to find people in better moods and with their defenses down.

- And last but not least, you will be most effective when closing, and selling in general, if you are enthusiastic, motivated, ethical, and completely believe in your product or service. If you are motivated and have a strong belief in your product, you'll ask people to buy and you'll fully believe they are better off with your product than without it. You'll also have conviction when selling. If you are ethical, you'll always do the right thing for your prospects and customers.

SECTION VIII

AFTER THE CLOSE

Chapter 36

What If You Don't Get the Business?

Here's what to do, and what not to do, if you *don't* close the sale.

1) Don't get upset or tell the prospect off. Don't burn any bridges.

The first thing you *do not* want to do is become upset with the prospect if your proposal gets rejected. This sounds obvious, yet you'd be amazed at how many salespeople do not keep their cool when they learn they did not get the order.

We know of cases where salespeople have flat-out told the prospect off, and in the process, they've burned a bridge not only for themselves, but also for the company they represent.

If you are tempted to blow up, you *must* bite your lip and keep quiet. If you blow up, you'll close the door to the prospect for good. If you are professional and courteous, you will most likely be around to quote again.

Also, people talk. If you make a bad impression on one prospect by losing your cool, chances are the prospect will tell several other people. Do your best to remain professional and treat the prospect nicely, even when you lose the business. Little impresses people more than graciousness.

2) Find out if it's a done deal.

When you learn you've just lost the business, you need to find out whether it's a done deal. You'd be surprised how often the door is still open a crack when it looks as though it's completely closed.

Begin with, "Have you already bought from (the competitor's name)?" If the answer is no, no matter how remote, you still have a shot at getting the business. You need to find out why the prospect chose the competition, and then go to work on that objection.

For example, let's say the prospect says, "XYZ Company came in $1,000 less than you." In that case, you have a price objection to overcome. The objection may be a little stronger because of the fact that the prospect has "made a decision"; however, still treat the response as simply an objection.

Watch out for false objections in these situations. It may not be price, it may be something else; however, the prospect feels that the price objection is the best way to get rid of you. Just as with any other objection, you need to isolate it first. "So, Ms. Prospect, you're telling me that if we were lower in price we would have gotten the business?" If she answers yes, and you don't already know the number, ask, "How much lower?"

You need to find out what the price difference is because you need to know if it's a number you can work with. Please refer to the *Objection* section for a more detailed discussion on overcoming this kind of objection.

Next, nail the prospect down. "Ms. Prospect, if we had been the same price and everything else remained the same, would you have gone with us?"

If she says yes, you're halfway home. Now you have to consider what you can change to make your offer $1,000 lower. Will you have to increase your discount or remove a feature? Once you've figured out how you can drop the price by $1,000, continue with, "So what you're telling me is, if I can figure out a way to get my product to you for $1,000 less, we're your decision?"

She's just told you that you would be, so she can't back down. If she says no, ask what would be standing in the way at that point.

What are the keys to closing in this situation?

- In most cases you must catch the prospect before she has actually signed a contract or bought from the competition.
- You must have the correct objection and fully understand it.
- You must effectively handle the objection.
- You need to get in front of the person as soon as possible.
- You need to have some very compelling reasons for the prospect to change her mind.

In a scenario such as this, you may only turn the prospect around one out of twenty times, but that's better than zero. And you never know what positive ripple effect that one sale will have.

The bottom line: don't jump to conclusions and assume the sale is dead. See if the door is even slightly still open. And if it is, take your best shot at getting the business.

3) Thank the prospect for the opportunity to quote and for her response.

The third step after losing the business is to sincerely thank the prospect for the opportunity to present your proposal and for her answer. Not everyone will let you submit a proposal, and of those who do, not everyone will give you an answer. Occasionally, people will simply not return your calls or want to see you again. This may not happen often, but from time to time you can expect it.

4) Find out why you didn't get the business.

When you lose business, you need to get the specifics of why. Many salespeople do not take steps to find out why they lost a sale, yet this is a very important step. Finding out why you lost will give you a better idea of how to approach this prospect in the future.

- Was it price?
- Was it the relationship the competition has with the prospect?
- Was it perceived product quality?
- Was it something else altogether?

If it was price, what was the price difference? If it was product, what features set the competition apart? You need to nail down the specifics so you know where to tweak future proposals.

Open the conversation with the following sentence: "Well, Joe, once again, thank you for the opportunity to quote on this project. I really appreciate it."

Follow that phrase with one of the following questions: 1) "What was the key differentiating factor in your decision?" 2) "Gee, I should have been very competitive with regard to price. Was I?" 3) "I'm pretty sure we were quoting the same features and functions. Was there anything different with their equipment?" 4) "I'm sure my references were solid." Now stop and listen. Simply wait for a response from the prospect.

The first question is the best to ask—if you can get a straight answer to it. If you ask what the key difference is and the answer comes back "price," you're off and running.

If, on the other hand, the prospect is somewhat elusive with the answer to this question, start asking "area-specific" questions such as: "Was I close on price?"

Cover all areas, price, service, quality, etc., until you find the area where the competition beat you.

From there, ask more questions and find out more specifics. For example, if the prospect says, "We liked the features on the competitor's machine better," you need to ask which features and which aspects of those features he liked better.

Also, if possible, you want to get a look at the competitor's proposal.

5) Ask for a chance to quote the next job.

Ask that the door remain open for future opportunities. It can be as simple as saying, "Cindy, once again, I very much appreciate the opportunity to submit a bid for this project. Although I wish the outcome had been different this time, I would be very grateful for the opportunity to quote on your next job." Then stay silent, look her in the eye, and wait for an affirmative response.

6) Don't lose the lesson.

A lost sale is an opportunity to learn about your product, the competition's product, pricing, customer opinions, and where you stand in the market. Look for the lesson in each lost sale and then refine your approach based upon what you've learned. Look at what you did wrong, what you did right, and see where you can make improvements. Talk to your manager and other salespeople about what may have gone wrong. If you had other team members involved, get their opinions.

7) Keep the lines of communication open.

Continue to stay in touch and update the prospect just as you would one of your customers. Continue to develop the relationship.

8) Don't let the lost sale ruin your day.

Hopefully, you will win much more often than you will lose, yet you have to be prepared for that occasional defeat. Let it register, learn what you can, and then move on.

9) Send a thank-you note.

Send a note that reiterates much of what you said verbally. Thank the prospect for her time, the opportunity to bid, her response to your proposal, and the information she gave as to why you lost. Write that you look forward to bidding on future projects and let her know that you will do your best to present her with a winning proposal the next time.

Also let her know you will be staying in touch and keeping her up to date on the latest industry trends. Finally, ask her to call with any questions or concerns, or if you can help her in any way. A thank-you note like that will get you noticed and it will put you well ahead of the rest of the pack.

In Person versus Over the Phone

You will have a much greater impact in person than you will over the phone when finding out why you lost the sale. Many salespeople let a phone call suffice for what should be an in-person visit. We realize it isn't always possible to follow up in-person due to physical distance or time limitations. But, if it is possible, *do it!* An in-person visit will yield the most information and have the greatest impact.

You're Never Completely Down and Out

In step 1 above we talked about remaining as gracious and professional as possible once you find out you've lost the business. One great reason to do this is because you may not be completely out of the running even after the prospect has signed a contract and has officially given the business to someone else.

We once had a situation where we followed all of the steps above including making sure it was a done deal, which it appeared to be. Two days later we received a call from the prospect asking us how quickly we could get the equipment once we took an order. After we told her six weeks, she asked if we *really* meant six weeks from when she signed an order or six weeks from when we got approved drawings. We assured her that we could guarantee six weeks from the date of a signed order. She then asked if we could stop by the next day to get an order signed.

It seemed the salesman for the competing company had lied about how quickly he could get the equipment. He told the customer six weeks from the day of the order, but it was actually six weeks after the order was entered in the system and was approved by everyone concerned. This usually takes an additional two weeks.

Incidentally, there were three bidders on that particular job. It's possible she also called the other one to ask what his lead time was, but our guess is that she called us because we were completely professional and gracious in defeat.

Go Over the Prospect's Head

After losing a sale, there is only one situation in which you can go over a prospect's head and have any chance of getting the business while not burning any bridges. That situation is one in which the prospect pins the decision on her boss. Many buyers use this excuse because it is a very convenient one. It usually sounds something like, "If it were up to me, we would definitely be buying from you, but my boss chose XYZ Company."

If this happens to you, say, "So, Ms. Prospect, what you're telling me is that if it were up to you, you'd be buying from me?" Once you get an affirmative response to this question, nail her down. Find out why the boss decided on the competition, then ask the prospect for an audience with her and the boss.

For example, let's say the prospect told you her boss had decided on the competition because of price. In this case, simply say, "Ms. Prospect, I have some major cost factors that I'm sure would convince your boss we are the right company to do business with. Since you see the value here and are in our corner, why don't we sit down with Ms. Boss and I can give her this very pertinent and critical information? Do you think later today or tomorrow morning would be better?"

At this point, you'll get an idea of whether it is actually the boss or if that is just an excuse. If the prospect seems determined to keep you from speaking with the boss, you most likely have a "prospect" rather than a "boss" objection. If this occurs, or you are not able to get an audience with the boss for any reason, try this: "Ms. Prospect, I'm curious, what's the real reason for not going with us?" As with a closing question, be completely quiet after you ask this question. If you still can't get anywhere, use one of the following techniques to go over the prospect's head.

Except for the above scenario, in which the prospect blamed her boss, your best bet is to focus on the next selling opportunity with this company and work on establishing some higher-level contacts so you're in a better position the next time around. You especially want to do this if you find yourself in a situation where you've given the prospect several proposals, tried every possible angle to get the business, but are simply unable to get anywhere with the prospect. This usually happens when the competition has a very strong foothold in the account. Often the only reason you are there is because the purchaser needs more than one quote. If you find yourself in this situation, and it is clear that you are never going to get anywhere dealing with this person, it's time to step above him or her.

Going over a prospect's head can be a tricky situation and has to be done in a particular way. Here are some effective ways to go over someone's head:

1) Start over the person's head to begin with.

The best way to go over someone's head is to start there. Calling on the President, the CEO, or the Chairman of the Board is a great place to start. Granted, you may get bounced down to the next level or further; however, you can still use this in your favor. Once they tell you to call on Mr. Lower Level, call him and say, "Hi, Mr. Lower Level, this is (your name with your company) and Mr. Top Executive told me to give you a call." At this point Mr. Lower Level is listening.

2) Ask to go over the prospect's head.

Ask if you can attend the board meeting where the buying decision will be made or some similar function where the top executives will be. You can also ask your contact to go golfing and ask if she'll bring the top executive along. Your objective is to get in and around the upper-level people in the organization.

3) Have your manager or boss take you to the next level.

Tell your prospect you will be bringing your boss or manager to the meeting and ask that he have his boss or manager there also. In the meeting, you will get a chance to put you and your company's best foot forward, and of course your boss will help in that effort. From that point, your boss can stay in touch with your prospect's boss and effectively make sure your prospect's boss is involved in the next buying decision.

4) Get yourself to the next level by rubbing elbows with the top people at golf tournaments, social events, and other functions.

This is somewhat similar to asking the prospect if you can attend the board meeting or having the prospect invite her boss golfing, but in this situation you leave the prospect out and look for other out-of-the-office occasions in which to rub elbows with upper-level management. Discover what organizations the top executives belong to and join or participate in events. What charities are they active in? What causes do they give their time and/or money to? What golf tournaments are they involved in? Get active in those charities and organizations. Find creative ways to meet and get to know the top executives.

5) Find similar interests and things you have in common with upper level people.

Do some research on the upper-level management. Are they in Who's Who? Learn where they went to school and where they're from originally. If it turns out you went to the same school, you can use that as an excuse to meet the top executive and discuss the similarity. You might say something to your lower-level prospect like, "Gee, I was speaking with someone and found out that Mr. Top Executive went to the same high school I did. I'd like to talk to him about that. Do you think I could meet him?"

Look for other areas of interest. Do they collect baseball cards, stamps, or antiques? Find similar interests and use those interests as a point of discussion and a way in the top executive's door. Send them articles and books on these subjects.

6) Give perks such as holiday gifts, baseball tickets, gift certificates, and other tokens of appreciation to the upper-level person in addition to the person(s) you're dealing with on the lower levels.

By sending a gift basket to the top executive *and* your contact below them, you are subtly building a relationship with the top executive. Send holiday cards, birthday cards, and the like to the top executive also. Develop the relationship behind the scenes for a while and then eventually ask to meet the top executive.

7) Have someone else go over the prospect's head.

This could be someone at a higher level than you or someone in a different department in your company. For example, you can have someone from your service department, installation department, telemarketing department, or almost any other department within your organization make a phone call to an individual higher up the ladder than the prospect. Here's an example:

Let's take a situation where ABC Company is looking for five new copiers. The same purchaser you've been dealing with at the company for two years, the one who goes golfing, fishing, and camping with your chief competitor has once again called you on the phone and said, "Sandy, come on down. I need a quote for five copiers for five of our branch offices. I need you to quote product and annual service costs for the five machines. I need the quote tomorrow. By the way, Sandy, are you listening really hard? Sharpen your pencil." Just as with every other time, even though you've done everything to build value and even persuaded the prospect to agree that your product will last longer, run more efficiently and give him more bang for his buck, you'll get the old, "Oh, Sandy, I'm so sorry you missed it by fifty cents. Thanks for the quick response, though." If you've been in sales for any length of time, you've had a few people just like this and you know the line about fifty cents is only a slight exaggeration.

The first thing you want to do in a situation like this is to stall for time. If the prospect is really asking for your proposal tomorrow, try to push him off for at least a couple of days. Use any excuse you want, meetings, vacation days, anything—just buy some time.

Next, bring in someone from another department. Let's say for example that you've decided to use someone in the telemarketing department. Have that person call the key decision-maker above the purchaser you're dealing with and make him an offer he can't refuse. An example of a call made by someone from our telemarketing department went like this:

"Hi, Mr. Top Executive, this is Jill Smith with the XYZ Company telemarketing department. We have been saving companies an average of 18 percent on the cost of copiers when compared to our closest competitor. I'm calling to let you know about a special we are running right now in which we will match any competitor's documented price and on top of that give you an additional three free months on your warranty.

"Considering the life of our copiers is, on average 30 percent longer than that of our competitors and the uptime of our copiers is 7 percent higher than our closest competitor, in the long run we will save you a great deal of money on the highest-quality, longest-lasting copiers in the industry. Any way you look at it, we will be, by far, your least costly, highest-quality solution.

"Mr. Top Executive, I could go on about having the largest, fastest-responding, and most efficient service organization in the industry and give many other advantages of our company. At the same time, I don't want to fill up your voice mail. If you have any questions or comments, please call me at (her number) and I'll be happy to fill you in or I can contact your local sales rep and have him give you a call."

This was the voice mail message. If she had reached Mr. Top Executive live, she would have said something very similar.

In a way, the call above worked. Mr. Top Executive called back within twenty minutes to ask questions. He then met with the person below him, the purchaser, but discovered that person had already signed a contract with a competitor. He called back to say it was too late. The person in telemarketing did get the okay, however, to call him back when any other specials came up. Thus, someone in the company is now over the purchaser's head. Now the telemarketing department can get the upper-level executive on their mailing list. The next time there is an opportunity, the telemarketing person can now introduce you to the top executive.

If your contact, the purchaser, calls you and asks why you went over his head, say something like, "Occasionally, when we are running specials, the telemarketing department is instructed to call all the local accounts. They usually pick the Top Executive and make what they call a 'courtesy call.' I'm sure it was completely coincidental." They may believe you and they may not. Just remember, you were at ground zero before you involved the telemarketing department, so if you used your usual approach you weren't getting anywhere in any event.

Note 1: We knew ahead of time that we could match the competition and give an additional three months on the warranty. You need to know how far you can go to get the deal done, and you need to know your competitor very well.

Note 2: The purchaser asking for the proposal had already signed a contract and was simply looking for another proposal. This happens often with competitive accounts.

Please refer to Chapter 30, beginning on page 363, for some other ideas on handling people who are supposedly only shopping on price.

8) Go over the prospect's head when you know she isn't there.

Use this technique when you have given the prospect a proposal and you're waiting for an answer.

Stop by your prospect's office when you know she isn't around but the top executive is. When you arrive, ask to speak with the prospect, and when you are informed she isn't in, ask to speak with the top executive. If the prospect later asks why you went over her head, simply tell her you had dropped by but she wasn't in, and because you knew the decision was imminent you simply went to the other person to find out if there was anything else that you needed to provide.

So how do you arrange to show up when the prospect isn't there? First, if you know the prospect is on vacation, or won't be in at a particular time or on a particular day, make your visit then. You can also call ahead and ask to speak with the prospect. If you learn that she isn't in, ask if the top executive is in—even though you don't need to speak with him immediately. If the top executive is in, make the call in person. By the way, if your contact is in, you can simply tell the receptionist you don't need to speak with her, you were simply thinking about stopping by but wanted to make sure she was there.

Note: There are many advantages to dealing at higher levels. In addition to talking to the people who are the true decision-makers, deals get done faster at higher levels, your message will not get lost in translation, and you'll be taken more seriously.

For more information on calling on executives, please refer to Chapter 27, which begins on page 301.

Go Under the Prospect's Head

Important note: You will only use this technique as a last resort after you have tried everything else, have been *completely* shut out of an account by the top person in the organization, and have *almost zero* chance of ever getting any business.

What do we mean by going "under" someone's head? Let's assume you've spoken with the Chairman of the Board and he flat-out shot you down. Obviously it's a little difficult to go any higher in the organization than that. So what should you do? Go to the people under the Chairman of the Board. Believe it or not, the Chairman of the Board answers to someone. If the company is publicly traded he answers to the share holders, his employees, and other Board members. If the company is not publicly held, the Chairman answers to those below him even though he answers indirectly. Although the Chairman in any organization pulls a lot of weight, he or she must still have the support of those below including other members of the board.

If you can gain the support of the other board members and the employees, including the President, CEO, COO, CFO, and other upper-level people, you still stand a chance of breaking this one. Granted, your chances may not be stellar, yet we have seen this work. Besides, it's better than disappearing from the company forever.

It should go without saying that you need to be careful how you go under someone just as you need to be careful how you go over someone. If the Chairman of the Board gets the idea you're up to no good—let's just say that's no good.

To go under the Chairman of the Board you need to build relationships with other high ranking people in the organization. Sometimes the Chairman is also the President and CEO. If this is the case you're going to have to go to the next level. The next level may be CFO and COO. From there you're usually looking at Executive and/or Senior Vice Presidents.

If you don't already know, do a little research and find out who's who at the organization. In addition to discovering who's who, find out as much about the company as you can. The more information you have on the company, the better your odds will be at getting in and talking about issues that interest the people you talk to.

Once you've gathered all your information, go to work on the other people within the organization. This will involve getting them on your mailing list, stopping in to see them, having someone introduce you to them, or finding other angles by which to meet them. Continue to build and work these relationships until you are in a solid position with as many of these high-level individuals as possible.

Earn the right to bid on the next project and then ask to bid. If you have worked hard at building relationships within the organization, have stayed in touch, and have kept them abreast of what's going on in the industry, you have earned the right to ask for an opportunity to bid the next time a project is in the works.

If you can get enough people on your side and pulling in your direction, even the Chairman of the Board won't be able to stop you. When your goal is to bypass the most powerful person in the organization, you need strength in titles and in numbers. An Assistant Vice President will not be enough ammunition to put you over the top if the Chairman said no. However, the President, COO, and CFO have some leverage.

Here's an example in which going under someone worked:

We had been trying to get some business from a particular bank for quite some time. The Chairman of the Board was not only extremely tight with the competition, we believed he was actually getting a kickback on the business the competition received. We had about as much chance of getting into that account as a wooly mammoth had of getting into a Volkswagen Beetle.

Nevertheless, we began building relationships with other individuals at the bank, in particular the President and COO, and put ourselves in a position to bid on the next project. We made several suggestions for the bidding process that would give us an advantage. One suggestion involved a very detailed specification of what was to be priced out. The detailed specification ensured we would have an advantage as our product was used as the "baseline" product and as a result the bid specs favored our features and functions. Another suggestion involved having sealed bids opened publicly at a specific time and read aloud in front of the entire board, several executives, the vendors bidding, and several other interested parties. This meant no one was able to see our bid ahead of time, so the competition could not get a heads-up from anyone on our pricing. The numbers, when read aloud, would speak for themselves. If we looked like the best choice, it would be difficult for the Chairman to argue for the competition in the "public" forum.

We had two more things going for us. First, we had gone to our manager and received some very good pricing. Second, the competition either wasn't aware of the sealed bid format, or they overlooked it. They assumed they were going to get the business as usual and as a result they came in with inflated numbers.

We had suggested this bidding format because we knew it was the best way to keep the competition, and everyone else, honest. We were able to pull it off because the President and COO were in charge of the bidding process. The Chairman of the Board was unaware of the change until he arrived at the meeting the day the bids were to be opened. He believed he was simply meeting with the President and COO to go over the bids as had happened in the past.

At the scheduled time, the meeting began. The President opened the first bid, which happened to be that of the competition, and read it aloud. "Company X comes in with a bid of $116,560." He then opened our bid and read, "Company A comes in with a bid of—wait, is this right?" He looked at us for an indication. We nodded our heads in the affirmative and smiled. He continued, "Company A comes in with a bid of $98,954." The Chairman of the Board exclaimed, "What? That can't be right! There's no way they can come in at that price!" The President looked to us again, along with everyone else, and we assured them that we had bid on exactly what was specified and we could deliver for that price. The competition could have chimed it at that point but for one fact—they weren't there. We had gone from the size of wooly mammoths trying to get into the Volkswagen to the size of the common house fly. We were in.

Our bid was accepted and we had successfully gone under the Chairman of the Board. Let us assure you that he did not invite us out for coffee afterward; in fact, he was quite unhappy with us. But we did manage to get the majority of business from that point forward.

The moral of the story is: don't give up, look for a creative way to get over, under, or through obstacles. Think outside, inside, around, and under the box. No, we did not make friends with the Chairman of the Board but we hadn't been friends with him before that deal either. Remember, everyone has someone he or she answers to, someone who can put the pressure on. You need to find out who those people are, then build relationships with them and get them on your side.

Why Bother Going Over and Under?

Why bother going over and under when the odds against you are so great and when this can consume so much time? The answer depends upon what your account base looks like.

If you *do not* have an assigned territory with assigned accounts and thus are free to call on anyone and everyone, you would most likely pass on giving such a large amount of time and effort to one organization—unless you are going after an account in which the eventual payoff is *enormous*.

On the other hand, if you have a limited market, you want to take a good, solid crack at everyone in your territory. For example, if you have a territory with one hundred accounts in it and the competition has a solid foothold in one of those one hundred accounts, you are now down to ninety-nine unless you can figure out a way to break in. In this scenario, if the account is tiny, you probably want to limit the amount of time you spend. If the account is one of the largest, you may want to invest plenty of blood, sweat, and tears as the payoff could be tremendous.

Bottom line: Do some cost/benefit analysis to determine whether the potential payoff is worth the time and effort involved. Look at two factors: one, the amount of potential business from that account, and two, the amount of potential business from other accounts. In other words, is the account large or small, and are your opportunities limited or unlimited?

Chapter 37

What If You *Do* Get the Business?

Closing Is Not the End of the Road

Now let's take a look at what to do if you *do* get the business. Closing the sale is great, but it's only the beginning. After you've made the sale you must make sure the product stays sold. In other words, fend off "buyer's remorse" and cancellations. You must also deliver what you have promised and solidify the customer relationship. What follows are the steps to ensure all of the above.

1) Thank the customer for her business.

The first step after the sale is to verbally thank the customer for her business.

2) Get competitive information.

If this is a fairly solid account for you, but you found yourself up against the competition, you need to find out *why* you won and how close it was. After you have thanked the customer for her business, simply say, "Jill, let me ask you a question. I get the feeling the competition was close in terms of price. Were they?"

Accept the customer's response and continue to question, as we showed under the heading, Exactly Where is the Competition on Price? which begins on page 245.

If this is a new account or an account that isn't solid, skip this step now and use it during your follow-up call.

3) Review expectations and what will happen next.

For this example, let's say the customer has just bought some computer equipment. Review the proposed installation date, the action items that you will be following up on, and any action items you're expecting your customer to follow up on. From there, review what will happen next.

The next step might be to enter the order, get a delivery commitment from the factory, and have the installation coordinator follow up with the customer to verify the install date. Whatever your particular steps are, go over these steps with the customer and let her know how and when she will be kept up to date.

4) Ask the customer if she has any final questions, thank her once again for her business, and reiterate when she will next hear from you or someone from your company.

Your conversation with the customer covering steps 1, 3, and 4 would sound something like the following: "Jill, thank you very much for the business and for the opportunity to work with you. I look forward to a long and happy relationship.

"As we discussed, we will be targeting an installation date of February 12th with training to begin on the 15th continuing through the 20th.

"Shortly after I enter the order, manufacturing will confirm the delivery date of February 12th. At that point the installation coordinator will follow up with you to verify that everything is also a go on your end for the 12th. You will hear from the installation coordinator in about seven days.

"I will be following up with you to get your network information along with the software emulation and protocol. When do you think you'll have that information ready?

"I will check with my software engineers to find out which one will be able to do the training on the 15th. I should know who that person will be in the next two days. As soon as I find that out, I'll give you a call. Do you have any other questions for me at this point?

"Jill, once again, thank you for the business and the opportunity. You will be hearing from me in the next day or two and the installation coordinator in about a week. In the meantime, if you have any questions, please give me a call."

5) Get another sale.

The best time to make a sale is right after you've just made one. Are there any supplies that go along with your product such as paper rolls, ink cartridges, or other items? Is there something you can add to your product or service? How about a service contract? If adding items to the sale is not common practice for you, you should look for some add-ons that enhance or are natural additions to the product you're selling.

You can also set up automatic orders on repeat items. For example, if someone calls in to order a thirty-day supply of a product, ask if you can set up a shipping schedule to ship more product to her every thirty days.

Note: You have to be careful with this technique. One or two "add-ons" is good; more than that typically is not. Limit your add-ons to one or two items.

6) Ask for referrals.

We will devote the next Chapter entirely to asking for and getting referrals.

7) Send a thank-you note.

Send a thank-you note out as soon as possible, preferably the same day. This note should be concise and succinct. It will consist of a thank you, a brief description of what will happen, and your contact information. A sample thank-you note is included on the next page.

7a) Thank customers for an order in other ways too.

Depending upon the size and significance of an order, it may be appropriate to thank a customer with more than a note. Here are some various ways to do that:

- Small gifts: golf balls, beanie babies, pens, pencils, cups.
- Gift certificates to restaurants, stores.
- Tickets to sporting events, shows, dinner events.
- Gift baskets.
- Books and other items associated with the customer's hobbies, interests, or industry.
- A gift to one of his favorite charities.
- A small investment in her business or something else she is involved in.
- Vacations or trips to trade shows and other industry events.

Again, the extent of the "thank you" will depend upon the extent of the order. If you get a $500 order you're not going to send them on a vacation to the Bahamas, but an order for $10 million or more might warrant such a gift.

Give gifts intermittently. You don't need to give a gift every time you get an order. If an existing customer enjoys baseball, instead of giving him baseball tickets for every order, you might give him tickets once or twice a season. It's the same with the other gifts. Typically, you won't reward someone for every order, but you'll do it once in a while.

Sample Thank-you for Your Business Note:

Mr. George Joseph   June 12, 2008
Senior Vice President
ABC Bank
675 Main St.
Newbury, MA 01444

Dear Mr. Joseph,

Thank you very much for your recent order.
The purpose of this letter is to review the installation schedule for the following equipment:

- Order No.: 123-01590-00
- Equipment Type: Vault, ATM, Undercounter, Pneumatic Tube, Drive-up Window and Drawer, Fire-insulated Door, Alarm, etc.

We have scheduled the above equipment to be delivered and installed on 08/15/08. Your ABC Company Installation Supervisor, John Henry, who can be contacted at (508) 555-6428, will be managing your project. We will be calling you shortly to verify the above installation date. In the meantime, if you have any questions, please contact us immediately. The Installation Coordinator will be discussing the following items with you:

- Is contractor/site ready according to drawings?
- Is all electrical wiring pulled and ready?
- Are communications lines installed and ready?

NOTE 1: Installations are typically scheduled 30 days in advance.

NOTE 2: If you are unable to keep the original schedule, let us know and we will reschedule your installation.

If you have any questions or comments, please give me a call at (508) 555-6403.

Sincerely,

Robert J. Chapin

cc: Kim Gross

8) Follow up and deliver what you say you'll deliver.

Follow-through after the sale is one of the most important aspects of selling. Follow-through means doing what you say you'll do, when you say you'll do it. If you say you'll have your product there Tuesday, have it there Tuesday and make sure it is everything or more than the customer expects. If you say you'll call Wednesday, call Wednesday. To take things one step further, if you say the installation manager will call on Friday, make sure the installation manager calls on Friday.

In some cases you may deliver sooner than expected, assuming the customer can take it sooner than expected. Go above and beyond and deliver more than you say you will. At a minimum you *must* deliver *what* you say you will, *when* you say you will.

You need to take ownership and full responsibility in order to follow through effectively. This includes owning items you will be following up on as well as items you pass off to others. If you ask someone to do something, you cannot automatically assume he will do it. Follow up and make sure it got done.

It takes too much time to micromanage follow-up items; instead, you need to be able to rely on those whom you work with. At the same time, you do need an effective system to stay on top of things. One of the best ways to follow up with others is via e-mail. By sending an e-mail, you have the information documented and you can send an e-mail any time of the day. An e-mail leaves a trail to follow if something goes wrong and accountability needs to be tracked. If for some reason you can't follow by e-mail, make a quick phone call.

If you pass something off to someone, follow up with that person a few days later to make sure all went well. In other words, you're checking up on her without offending her. Say something like, "Julie I just wanted to follow up on the issue with ABC Company. Do you need anything else from me or are we all set?"

The above statement is unassuming and non-confrontational; it's just a simple follow-up and/or reminder.

Once you've followed up with your people and know the job has been done, follow up with your customer and make sure he is satisfied. Also, while the job is in progress, give your customer updates from time to time to let him know how things are progressing and to keep him in the loop. Communication is very important.

9) Continue to stay in touch with your customers.

Whether the nature of your relationship with your customers is constant and hands on with lots of interaction and potential for repeat business, as with a financial planner or office supply salesperson, or it is occasional, such as a realtor or car salesperson, you want to be in touch with your customers from time to time.

Even if you can't get immediate follow-up business, you can probably either get some more business down the road or some referrals. As a result, keeping your name in front of your customers and keeping the lines of communication open is essential. The nature of your relationship will dictate how you communicate and how often. The following are two ways to do that.

a) **Thank your customers for business year-round.**

In addition to thanking customers for business right after a sale, let them know they are appreciated throughout the year.

Around the holidays in December is probably the most obvious time to send gifts to customers. In addition to sending out holiday cards, you should be sending gift baskets and the like to your best customers. Bottles of wine, champagne, and other spirits are a good idea, but make sure you know your customer well. It may be a problem if you give a bottle of scotch to an alcoholic. Stay away from any cheesy gifts such as fruitcakes.

In addition to the December holidays, pick other random times during the year to appreciate customers. Drop by occasionally with baseball tickets and some of the other gift ideas we mentioned earlier. You can also take customers to lunch and dinner, sporting events, shows, or out to play golf or some other activity. You want your customers to know they are important not only when they give you an order, but *all* the time.

Note: Some customers' companies have rules about what they can and can't receive from a vendor. There may be a certain dollar amount that the gift cannot exceed. As a guideline, if you do not know whether an organization has such rules, assume they don't and give accordingly. If there are rules, leave it up to the customer to tell you. Once you've presented her with a $100 bottle of champagne, let her give her regrets due to the rule and return it to you. That way, you still get credit and you still have a bottle to give to someone else. Of course, if this happens, ask what the rules are and then return with another appropriate gift or sign of your appreciation.

b) Reach out and touch your customers in other ways.

Sales is all about relationships. You not only want to stay close to your customers, you want to get closer. In addition, you want to have your name in front of your customers as much as possible.

Gift giving is a great way to show customer appreciation, keep your name in front of your customers, and let them know you're thinking about them. In addition to gift giving, here are some other key ways to keep your name in front of your customers and stay in touch with them:

- Stop by occasionally to say hello.
- Send birthday cards.
- Send cards for promotions.
- Send Get Well cards.
- Visit customers in the hospital.
- Send items pertaining to their interests and hobbies.
- Act on personal information about your customers' family members and send out notes to acknowledge birthdays, anniversaries, graduations, etc.
- Get your customers on the mailing list for company publications.
- Develop your own newsletter and send it out to your customers.
- Attend events sponsored by customers.
- Send copies of industry articles.
- Send information out on new products.
- Send promotional items.
- Send out company news releases.
- Donate money to their favorite charities or events they sponsor.

Get involved in the lives of your customers and let them know you're thinking about them throughout the year. Brainstorm with your manager and other salespeople and see what other ideas you can come up with. We know of several salespeople who find an occasion to send cards out to customers and prospects every month.

Faxes and e-mails are also great tools to stay in touch, but you have to be careful not to overdo it. Be sure both are welcomed and appropriate.

Chapter 38

Referrals

When and How to Ask for Referrals

In step 6 of the last Chapter we spoke about referrals. Let's look at this step in detail.

The first rule of referrals is to always be asking for them. Even the person who just said no to you on a cold call is a candidate for referrals, albeit not the best. Your greatest referrals will come from satisfied customers. The best referrals they'll give you are close friends or family members who trust their opinion.

Ask for referrals:

- **Right after you've made a sale.**
- **When you're making a follow-up call after a sale.**
- **After you've helped a customer solve a problem or have had some other positive interaction with him or her.**
- **Anytime.** After a cold call (successful or unsuccessful), at a social event when careers become a topic, at a business event, and almost any other time you can think of. Asking for referrals should be automatic and it should be done often.

When getting referrals, follow these steps:

1) Ask for referrals and help the customer come up with names.

Asking for referrals is the most important step; however, how you ask for referrals will determine your success. Most salespeople have a generic question they like to ask such as, "Who else do you know that might be interested in my product?"

Asking for referrals with this type of question will ensure you'll fail to get referrals more often than you'll succeed. When you ask for referrals, you need to help people think of names. In order to do that, try this: "Mr. Customer, thank you very much for your business. Let me ask you a question. Do you belong to any (groups associated with your industry) or organizations?"

If he answers yes, ask, "Whom in the group have you spoken with concerning the decision-making process for purchasing (your product) or whom might you tell of this decision today?"

That question will narrow down the number of people the customer has to think of. If you just ask, "Whom do you know?" psychologically, the person starts running through everyone he knows from Aunt Martha to his next-door neighbor. If you're selling an industry-specific product such as backhoes, he may narrow it down a little; however, you want to guide the prospect. Allow him to focus on a small group and then expand from there.

If you're selling appliances you may ask the same question about professional organizations. After your prospect has answered that question, expand it a little further. For example, you might ask her if she participates in any league sports or is involved in any other groups. If she tells you she's in a golf league, say, "Is there anyone in your golf league you've spoken with about your need for a washer and dryer who may also be looking for one?"

If she says no, ask if there is anyone in her neighborhood whom she feels may have a need for one, or any of your other appliances. From there, you can ask about close friends and family members.

Into which groups you break it down will depend upon your product. Cars, real estate, and insurance are easier because almost everyone needs these at some point in their lives. Phone networks, Lear jets, and heavy construction machinery can be more of a challenge. Yet there will still be people your customers associate with who are potential leads.

2) Qualify the referral and get some personal information.

Ask your customer some questions in order to get background information and to qualify the referral a bit further.

Again, the questions will depend upon your product, but for the most part you will start with a question such as, "Joe, has Bob mentioned he's looking for a new boat or is there another reason why you feel he might looking?"

Continue with more qualifying questions:

- "Does Bob have a boat right now?"
- "What size and type is it?"
- "What does he mostly use it for?"

- "Is he happy with the size or do you feel he's looking for something a little bigger, smaller?"
- "Is there anything else you know of that Bob is looking for in his boat?"

Once you get the background information on the prospect's current product, get some personal background information. For example, you might ask:

- "Is Bob married?"
- "Does he have any children?" If so, how many and ages.
- "Does he have any hobbies or outside interests outside of fishing and boating?"

Important: If you're asking for referrals from a new customer, you want to wait until a follow-up meeting. Make sure their business is solid first. Also, regardless of who you're asking these questions of, you need to be very low-key, almost subdued. If you rapid-fire these questions at someone, you can come across as confrontational. Thus, your tone and manner are extremely important. You don't have to ask all these questions, yet you want to get enough background information to use to build rapport when you call the referral.

3) Get contact information for the referral such as a telephone number.

Once you get the person's name and some background information, at a minimum you want to get his or her phone number. Ask for both the home and work number. Going a step beyond the phone information, it's a good idea to get a business name and location and find out where the prospect lives. Finally, you may also want to get the prospect's position at the company if that is a factor associated with your product.

Note: If your customer says he doesn't have a phone number, ask if it is something he can look up or otherwise get for you.

Once you get the phone numbers, ask where the referral works. From there get the location. Finally ask where the prospect lives. Say something like:

- "And Joe, tell me, does Bob work with you or where does he work?"
- "Where are they located?"

- "And what is Bob's position there?"
- "What town does Bob live in?"
- "Do you two play golf together?"

If at any point your customer asks why you need this information and he sounds a little uncomfortable giving it to you, just tell him you like to get a little background information on people before you call them out of the blue. Don't push your customer to obtain any of the information. The key is that you have a phone number so you can contact the prospect. If your customer is uneasy about giving you a phone number, assure him that that you will simply contact the person to see if there is any interest. You promise to be professional and to not be a nuisance.

4) Ask your customer to call the referral for you.

Ask your customer if he would be so kind as to call the referral and give him a heads-up that you'll be calling. After you ask him to call, tell your customer you will follow up with him tomorrow to make sure he got through to the referral. Once he's contacted the referral and you have verification that the referral is awaiting your call, go ahead and call.

Sometimes the customer will be hesitant to call the referral. Whether he feels he doesn't know him that well or whatever the case may be, do not push. If he's uncomfortable calling, simply ask if it's okay for you to use his name when you call.

Note: Here are two more approaches you can take. One is to set up a conference call where all three of you get together on the phone. Another approach—if all three of you will be attending a trade show, business function, or social gathering—is to have the customer set up a time when the three of you can meet.

These two approaches will simply serve as introductions. In both cases, set up another time when you and the referral can talk about his particular situation. It's possible that the referral doesn't want the person who referred you to be privy to certain business details.

Whichever approach you ultimately take, you want to follow up as soon as possible. If there is a trade show next month, that's too late. You can still arrange for the three of you to get together at the trade show, but you want to call, make contact, and start the sales process immediately.

Here is a sample conversation asking for referrals:

You: "John, as usual, thank you very much for your business. Let me ask you, are you a member of any banking groups or organizations?"

Customer: "Yes, I belong to XYZ Banking Group. Why do you ask?"

You: "Well, I'm curious if there's anyone in that group that is currently looking for some new ATMs or other banking equipment."

Customer: "Actually, there are two: Joe Brown and Jim Smith."

You: "Okay. Are they looking for ATMs or some other type of equipment?"

Customer: "Well, Joe Brown is looking for ATMs and Jim Smith needs some new drive-up equipment."

You: "Does Joe currently have some ATMs?"

Customer: "Yes, he has about five, I think."

You: "And what kind of ATMs are his current ones?"

Customer: "They're Brand X."

You: "Is he happy with his current ATMs and service on them?"

Customer: "I think so, but we haven't talked about it all that much."

You: "So he hasn't given you any idea of what he's looking for in the new ones in the way of features and functions?"

Customer: "Well, he did mention that he wants to cover all the new regulatory issues. And with Joe, price is always a factor."

You: "Okay, how about Jim? Has he said what drive-up equipment he needs?"

Customer: "Yes, he's doing a whole setup. He needs the drive-up window and drawer, pneumatic tube system, and some teller equipment."

You: "Is this his first drive-up location or does he have others?"

Customer: "This is his first. They're adding a drive-up to a current branch."

You: "Do you know what type of equipment he's using currently?"

Customer: "I think he has a mix."

You: "Has he given you any idea of what he's looking for in the equipment?"

Customer: "Not really, but Jim tends to be a "top of the line" type of guy. I'm not saying price doesn't matter, but he definitely focuses more on value."

You: "That's good. Do you know how much research either of them has done to this point or how close they are to purchasing equipment?"

Customer: "I think they're both in the preliminary stages."

You: "Okay, that's great. Do you happen to have their phone numbers handy?"

Customer: "Yes, Joe's number is 555-1234 and Jim's is 555-4321."

You: "And are those work numbers?"

Customer: "Yes, they are."

You: "What banks are they at?"

Customer: "Joe is at DEF Bank and Jim is at GHI Bank."

You: "Those are both in Springfield, right?"

Prospect: "Yes, they are."

You: "What are their positions there?"

Customer: "Joe is CFO and Jim is Senior Vice President of Retail Banking."

You: "Do they live in the area?"

Customer: "Yes, Joe is over in Springfield and Jim is in Westfield."

You: "Do you golf with them too, or do they have other interests?"

Customer: Joe is more of a fisherman, but Jim and I golf every Wednesday."

You: "Really, that's great. Let me ask you, could you do me a favor and give them a quick call and let them know I'll be contacting them?"

Customer: "Sure, no problem."

You: "Do you think you'll be able to catch them today?"

Customer: "Probably. I'll give them a try."

You: "Great. I'll give you a ring tomorrow, say late morning, just to make sure you've reached to them, and then I'll give them a call."

Customer: "Okay, that sounds good."

You: "Oh, one more thing. When I call a referral I like to mention that you've just invested in some equipment with me. That wouldn't be a problem, right?"

Customer: "That's fine."

You: "John, thanks once again for the business and I'll talk to you soon."

Potential Roadblocks to Getting Referrals

Occasionally, you may run into the following problems when getting referrals:

1) Your customer can't think of anyone.

This will happen from time to time. All you can do in this case is come up with as many groups of people as possible for your customer to refer to. For example, if he's in banking, after asking about banking groups or organizations, you can ask if he belongs to any other clubs or interest groups. Obviously he has friends in the banking business somewhere. Ask which of his friends in banking are looking for equipment. If he still can't come up with anyone, tell him you'll give him a call in a week or two and see if anyone has come to mind.

2) Your customer doesn't want to call the person.

In this case, just ask if you have permission to use your customer's name. Don't push your customer to call.

3) Your customer doesn't want you to mention her name.

This can be a problem. In this case, begin by agreeing with her and telling her that you will be professional and won't push the referral. Then ask something like, "If I promise to be on my very best behavior and say you just happened to mention their name in passing…" Pause and wait for a reaction. She'll let you know if she still doesn't want you to use her name, or she'll reluctantly agree. "Well…I guess it would be okay."

Whatever direction the conversation takes, err on the side of *not* pushing. If ultimately you can't use the customer's name, simply call the referral, tell him who you are, and give your cold call opening.

Creative Ways to Get Referrals

Giving rewards is a great way to get referrals. You can give sports tickets, gift certificates, or cash, such as $50 or $100. When you offer rewards, you'll find that people who couldn't think of anyone suddenly have all sorts of names for you.

You need to have some rules for the rewards and you need to stick to them. For example, if you promise $50 for each referral who becomes a client, pay promptly when a referral becomes a client. Don't hesitate, even slightly. If the client has to call you and ask for the money, you will lose some trust and credibility.

It is best to pay cash rewards with a new $50 or $100 bill. For some reason, this tends to have more impact than five $20 bills that you withdrew from an ATM. Depending upon your business, you may decide that more or less money is appropriate. Too much is better than not enough. You don't want to look cheap.

Another approach is to send out referral sheets. Mail out a form that allows the client to fill in names and other pertinent referral information along with a space to identify him or herself. Tell the client, on the same form or a letter you send along with the referral sheet, what you are offering for referrals who become clients. Follow up with a phone call to each client within a week or so.

Calling the Referral

Now that you have the referral, all the background information you need, and the customer has called and prepped the referral, it's time for you to call. Here are some general rules for calling the referral:

1) Immediately mention the customer who referred you, identify yourself, and build some interest.

The beginning of your call might go like this: "Hello, Joe? John Johnson asked me to give you a call. This is Bob Chapin from XYZ Company. We've been helping him save about 37 percent annually on office supplies for each of the past seven years." Mentioning the person who referred you will immediately cause the referral to drop his or her defenses.

2) Build some rapport before getting down to business.

You might say something like, "So John said you two are on the same banking committee?" This allows the referral to open up about an area of common interest and helps them become comfortable with you and the conversation. After some light conversation, bridge the conversation to business with, "John just invested in some ATMs with me and he said you may be looking for some as well."

3) Qualify the referral.

Your client may have qualified the prospect to a certain degree for you, but make sure you have someone who needs your product and is capable of owning it. See "Qualifying the Prospect" in the *Cold Call* section on page 90.

4) Close on the next step.

Either set up an appointment or close the sale, whichever is appropriate.

5) Send a personal note to the referral and thank-you note to your customer soon after you speak with the referral.

Note: When calling a referral, you should not have to worry about getting through the receptionist. If the receptionist asks why you are calling or what the call is about, simply say, "Yes, this is (your name) with (your company). (The name of your customer) asked me to give (the name of the prospect) a call."

The bottom line is to immediately let the referral know who told you to call, catch the person's attention with a benefit of your product, build some rapport and finally, close on the next step in the process.

Chapter 39

Servicing Your Customers

How Often Should You Contact Customers?

Under step 9 of "What to Do If You Get the Business" we looked at the different ways to reach out and touch your customers. Now we'll look at *when* to reach out and touch your customers.

How and when you reach out to your customers will depend upon their personal preferences and the closeness of your relationship. Some customers will require more of a hands-on approach, while others seem to be happy if they hardly hear from you at all. Some you'll need to talk to once a week, some once a month, and others once a quarter.

Usually Drivers and Partiers only need to talk to you once a quarter or whenever they need something. A typical reaction from these personality types if you "just stop by to say hello" is, "Do we have an appointment?" These two groups tend to have tight schedules. If you stop in too often just for a visit, you'll irritate them.

Thinkers and "Yes" People, on the other hand, usually require more visits and phone calls. When a project is in progress, you want to talk to them once a week. Even when nothing is going on, it's a good idea to stop in and say hello about once a month. "Yes" People, in particular, are usually always happy to see people and chat a little.

If you're unsure how often you should call on someone, ask. "Ms. Prospect, I know you have a busy schedule. Assuming we are not working on any projects or installations, how often would you like to hear from me? Once a month, once a week?"

As a rule, it's better to touch base too often rather than not enough. Yet you don't want to be a pest. If you don't have any current projects that require you to stay in touch on a regular basis, a good guideline to follow is a mailing once a month and an in-person visit once a quarter to each customer.

If you are in car sales, real estate, or similar markets where a lot of time can pass between sales, the best bet is to simply send birthday cards, holiday cards, and articles and other items related to the customer's interests.

Information You Want to Have on Each Customer

The steps you took after the sale helped solidify your relationship with your customer. From there you want to build upon those steps even more.

The more information you have about a customer and the better you know them, the better your relationship will most likely be. You want to know everything you can about the people you are dealing with. Specifically, you want to know about their family, their hobbies and interests, and their history.

Here is an outline of the information you're looking for on each customer:

1) Name:

2) Title:

3) Company:

4) Address:

5) Phone number:

6) Fax number:

7) Cell phone number:

8) Home phone number:

9) E-mail address:

10) Birth date: (month and day)

11) Where they live now:

12) Where they grew up:

13) Where they went to school (high school, college, other):

    a) What degrees they have:

    b) If college, what was their major:

14) Activities they were involved in growing up (sports, clubs, student government, fraternities, sororities, etc.):

15) Military service, and at what level:

16) What, if anything, do you know about their political or religious beliefs:

17) What subjects do they like to talk about and what, if any, subjects should you avoid:

18) Where they were employed previously:

19) What activities are they involved in now (sports, clubs, trade associations, travel, hobbies):

19a) What is their level of involvement and proficiency (are they on a board of directors, are they an instructor, scratch golfer, etc.):

20) Are they related or connected to anyone else you know (someone's sister, cousin, close friend, etc.):

21) What do they consider their most significant accomplishment(s):

22) Do they plan on retiring some day, and what would they like to do:

23) Where they would like to vacation:

24) Married, single, divorced:
   a) If married now, how long:
   b) Anniversary date:
   c) Wife's/husband's name and birthday:
   d) Wife's/husband's occupation:
   e) Wife's/husband's interests:

25) Children:
   a) Names, ages, and birthdays:
   b) Are they involved in any activities, and what are they:

26) Other information you've gathered on the customer. Examples:
   - Have they had knee surgery?
   - Do they have diabetes?
   - Did they go to an Aerosmith concert last year?
   - Have they climbed Mt. Fuji?
   - Have they run the Boston Marathon?
   - Do they have a famous uncle, aunt, cousin, etc.?
   - Is their son the wrestling champion in the state of Iowa?

27) Did they give you some information on family members that doesn't fall into the categories listed above?

28) What other personal information will help you understand and relate better with your customer?

Now, you're probably thinking, "How the heck do I get all that information?" Obviously, the first pieces of information—name, company address, and the like—are fairly easy to obtain. Once you get past those, however, you'll have to do a little more work. So how should you start? Simple: look, ask, and listen.

Let's return to the section on building rapport for a moment (page 94). In that section, we talked about looking around the prospect's office for awards, plaques, trophies, degrees, and other evidence that will enlighten you about someone's background. This is also the place to begin when filling out your Customer Information Sheet. Ask about the evidence you see, and then sit back and listen. This will help you to fill in those areas on the information sheet.

From there, you continue to ask questions. Remember, your Customer Information Sheet doesn't have to be filled up in a day. Some of these will be pieces of information you'll pick up later. For now, let's give an example of how a conversation might go.

You (looking at the degree on the wall): "So, I see you went to Yale."
Prospect: "Yes, I did. That was a few years ago."
You: "That's a great school. What was your major?"
Prospect (laughing): "Well, my degree says business administration, but I had a lot of fun too."
You: "Yes, fun was one of the better parts of college. So were you involved in any activities? Sports, fraternities?"
Prospect: "Actually, I played on the golf team for three years. That was about it."
You: "Wow! So you must have been pretty good."
Prospect: "Yeah, I was okay."
You: "Did you play in high school also?"
Prospect: "Yes, four years varsity."
You: "So you were probably an okay golfer, then. Did you go to high school around here?"

That's a small portion of the conversation you could have using the degree on the wall as an opening. You can see how all the items above are closely related. You can start in one area, expand to others, and by the time it's over you'll have quite a bit of information. You could also start with family pictures and expand, as in the following example:

You (looking at a picture of three children on the desk): "Are those your children?"

Prospect: "Yes, they are."

You: "Wow, what a great-looking bunch of kids. How old are they?"

Prospect: "Kathy here is ten; this is Gail, eight; and this is Jim, who's six."

You: "All close together in age. So by my math that would put them in, hmm, probably fifth, third, and first grade. Is that right?"

Prospect: "That's right. Do you have any?"

You: "Yes, three also. Two are in high school and one in college. So are yours involved in any sports?"

Prospect: "Yes, the youngest two are in soccer and the other one plays baseball."

You (noting ring on fourth finger): "So how long have you been married?"

Prospect: "Twelve years, and you?"

From there you could ask some questions about the prospect's spouse. Then you could ask if he lives in the area, which would lead to where he went to school and so on.

Some prospects and customers will obviously be more talkative than others. If you have someone who likes to talk, take the opportunity to gather lots of information. If you have someone who doesn't seem to be comfortable sharing information, take it slow and stick to one subject per visit. Occasionally, you'll hit a conversational hot button with someone and they'll really open up. At that point, run with it and get as much information as you can.

Don't pry or force information out of those who don't want to speak. Take it slow. Offer personal information of your own and see if they respond to anything you offer.

For example, you may tell them briefly about the trip you just took to the Bahamas and see if you can get them to talk about any trips they've taken. If this subject gets absolutely nothing out of them, try bringing up family the next time. Each time you go in ask a few questions and give up a little of your personal information. Eventually, you're likely to hit a subject they'll talk to you about.

Use the twenty-eight items we've listed as a guideline. Your objective is to get as much personal information on the prospect or customer as you can. The more you have the better your relationship will likely be. Maximum information, coupled with the use of that information, is what you're after.

What to Do with All That Customer Information

You're now going to take the customer information you have gathered and use it to build a solid relationship with your customer, one that your competition will be unable to penetrate. Here are some ideas on how to utilize your customer information. Some of these ideas will overlap with the ideas related to thanking your customer for business and keeping your name in front of the customer.

1) Send a birthday card.

You don't have to do anything extravagant here—simple is just fine. Watch out for joke cards unless you know your customer very well.

2) Send an anniversary card.

You can send a congratulations card in which you write something to the effect of, "Congratulations on your seventh anniversary." If you include the number, you'll get extra points. Send these cards early to your male customers as they are more likely to forget an anniversary. They will *very much* appreciate the reminder.

3) Add customers to your e-mail list.

We are not referring to your company e-mail list here, which should list customers and prospects in order to share quality business information; rather, we are referring to the e-mail list to which you send out quality personal e-mails.

You need to be careful with this one. First, notice we wrote *quality*. Stay away from junk and chain letter e-mails. Before you send any jokes, editorials, or the like, you need to know your customer extremely well. If you send non-business-related e-mails, make sure they are in good taste and are generally positive and/or very informative. If you have any question in your mind, *don't send it!* Also, some companies have rules against personal e-mails. Be sensitive to this.

Your objective is to send positive, wholesome e-mails that will brighten someone's day and that they'll appreciate.

4) Study their areas of interest.

If your customer is interested in Van Gogh, learn something about Van Gogh. If he likes hunting or fishing, learn a little about those. The more you learn about the subjects your customer is interested in, the more intelligent conversations you'll be able to have in the areas that are most important to him. Your customers will notice that you are taking a sincere interest in them and what they care about.

You can also study subjects that your customers' spouses or children are interested in. You will score points when you are able to give them information they can pass on to the other important people in their lives.

5) Give them books, articles, and other items related to their areas of interest.

Look for books, articles, and anything else you can find on your customers' areas of interest and pass them on. They may have mentioned what they'd like to do when they retire, or when they have more time on their hands. They may also mention something they've always wanted to do, but have never found the time for. Keep these items in mind and pass on information related to these subjects as well. Also, as we mentioned above, this relates to their families' areas of interest too.

In addition to books and articles, give your customers small gifts that are related to their areas of interest. Look for T-shirts, coffee mugs, and similar items. If you have a customer who is a bird watcher, you could get her a T-shirt with birds on the front of it. Each time she wears it, she will think of you.

6) Pass on articles and other information about your customers' high school, college, and hometown.

If your customer's college is featured on the cover of *Sports Illustrated*, pick him up a copy. If his high school just won the state championship, pass on your copy of the article. If you have a customer who went to school or lived in another state, you can impress that customer with articles related to her high school or hometown. Find the hometown paper online and look for interesting articles to pass on.

If your customer is mentioned positively in an article, get a few copies for her. If you know your customer's son plays tennis for a local high school, keep an eye out for any favorable articles during tennis season. Of course, if there is an article relating to his tragic defeat, you may want to forget you even saw the item.

7) Unearth articles and other stories written about your customers' companies and industries, and occasionally discuss some of this information with them.

Stay on top of all information on your customers' companies and their industries. You want to know exactly what's going on within each company and each industry because it may effect the business you are doing with them.

Depending upon the size of the company, you can find information on them in several different sources. If they are a very large company, they may appear regularly in *The Wall Street Journal*, *The New York Times*, and similar papers. Also, the local paper for the city in which they are based will be a good source of information.

Obviously, if you see stories that relate to business changes, procedure changes, etc., within your client's company or industry, you want to study these in depth and be prepared for discussions with her. You may talk to her about how your product or service can help her company adapt to the new atmosphere they are trying to create. Mention the article you read, give your understanding, and let your her know you've been thinking about how your product could help them. Get her take on the article to make sure your understanding is correct. Approach whatever subject you're discussing with your customer in a positive fashion.

In general, it is a good idea to bring up articles and information you've read about your customers' individual companies or industries. This lets them know you are a professional who is interested. However, there are certain areas you need to be careful with.

For example, if there is an article about a potential hostile takeover situation, you need to be very careful about how you approach this subject. Unless you know the customer extremely well and have a very solid relationship, you probably want to steer clear of any negative articles unless your product or service is a direct solution to the problem. If you have a solution and you don't know the customer very well, talk about the solution without mentioning you've read anything about their problem. If you do know them well, mention what you heard, get their take, and then discuss your solution.

Note: Your goal is *not* to show the customer how much you know compared with him or her, or to test the customer's knowledge. It's also not to discuss information about the company that isn't public.

Bear in mind that people generally don't like "know-it-alls." You also stand a good chance of annoying or angering someone when you talk about sensitive, "non-public" issues. Your job is to inform the customer about your product or service and how it can help her while letting her know that you are taking a sincere interest in her company and her industry.

Keep your customer conversations positive. Concentrate on what you can learn from your customers or what helpful information you can provide them with. Respect your customers' intelligence and privacy, and take a sincere interest in them and the position they're in.

8) Remember your customers when you are on vacation.

This doesn't really relate to the twenty-eight pieces of customer information you've acquired, yet it is worth mentioning. Send your customers postcards and/or pick up little trinkets for them when you go away.

Caution: You don't want your customers thinking you take too many vacations. You also have to be aware of those customers who may be jealous of a certain trip you're taking. Although this is often the exception to the rule, you may have a customer who has been dreaming of a trip to Hawaii for years. When they get your "Greetings from Hawaii" postcard, they naturally become envious. Know your customer well and realize that an extravagant or top-shelf vacation may cause some negative feelings. Moreover, if a customer receives a postcard from you from a different location every six weeks, you're sure to raise some questions about your work ethic, among other things.

Here are a couple of examples related to this idea. If you have a customer who loves dolphins and you go to Sea World in Orlando, pick her up something with dolphins on it. If you have a customer who collects shot glasses from around the world, pick him up a shot glass. Be creative and come up with items of interest to your prospects and customers.

9) Pass on items of religious and political interest to your customers.

Obviously, these are topics of conversation where you should know your customer *extremely well*. You may have heard the saying, "When you first meet someone, avoid discussions of religion and politics." People usually have very strong feelings about both, so these areas can be landmines. The odds of saying something wrong are simply too great.

On the other hand, once you know a customer extremely well and know her political and religious beliefs, you can use this information to strengthen the relationship.

The first rule here is to make sure your gifts, cards, etc., are appropriate. For example, if your customer is Jewish or Roman Catholic, the appropriate cards and/or holiday greetings will differ. If atheist, steer clear of any cards or other material discussing religious holidays. If you aren't sure, send generic cards that read Happy Holidays instead of Merry Christmas or Happy Chanukah.

Be equally sensitive with regard to politics. If you have a customer who is a big fan of a particular politician and that politician comes out with a book, buy one and give it to her. If she already has a copy, you'll get points anyway and you'll still have a copy to either keep or give to someone else. You can also send out appropriate articles.

10) **Review and use the items listed in the section titled Closing Is Not the End of the Road, beginning on page 509.** As we discussed in that section, you want your customer to be thinking of you as much as possible.

11) **Get creative and come up with other great ideas to turn customers and prospects into loyal customers and great friends.**

Think of other questions you can add to your customer profile. What other information would be helpful in developing strong relationships with your customers?

To summarize, the point of the Customer Information Sheet is to gather important information about your customers so you can use that information to create strong, long-term relationships with them. You always want to be focused on getting all the people in your pipeline to the next level. You want your prospects to become customers, your customers to become happy and loyal customers, your happy and loyal customers to become friends, and finally, your friends to become close friends.

Gather the information we've suggested and more if you can, and then *use that information!* The more you get into the lives of your customers the more business you'll do and the more joy you'll have in your life.

Give Your Customers Such Great Service That They Sell for You

If a customer is absolutely ecstatic about your product or service, she will tell her friends about it and also be willing to give you testimonials, referrals, reference letters, and all other sorts of ammunition you can use to go out and sell more of your product. So how do you get a customer so fired up about your product that she will speak with enthusiasm to all her friends? Simple: Deliver more than you promise, faster than you promise, and do it in a way that makes the customer feel not only important, but special.

Show Great Appreciation for Gifts Received from Customers

We have a friend who recently received a tie as a gift from a customer during a visit. His reaction? He jumped up enthusiastically, removed his tie, and put on the one the customer had just given him.

When a customer or prospect presents you with a gift, always show great enthusiasm and appreciation. If the gift giver is even slightly unsure of whether you like the gift, she is unlikely to repeat the gesture in the future and will probably be a little disappointed and even annoyed. Make certain the gift giver knows you are very appreciative.

Always send a thank-you note when you receive a gift from someone. Short and sweet is fine. All you need to send is something like the following: "Joe, thank you very much for (whatever you received). I very much appreciate the fine gesture. Thank you again, (your name)."

Reciprocate at some point, if not immediately. If you receive a $50 gift from a customer for the December holidays, order a gift certificate from a local restaurant and have it sent over to the customer. Another idea is to purchase some tickets to the theatre or a sporting event. Going forward, put that person on your list for the following December holidays.

Take Anything a Prospect or Customer Hands You

It's okay to say, "No, thank you" to extreme items such as large sums of money, expensive gifts, illicit drugs, or pet cockroaches, but for the most part you want to accept anything a prospect or customer offers you, and do so with enthusiasm.

Accepting things that someone offers to you is polite and builds rapport. When you decline something offered, unless it is a borderline item such as those mentioned above, there is always a feeling of rejection, no matter how slight. Even if you circular file it once you get back to the office, accept the item offered to you with grace and gratitude.

Respond to Mailings and Other Information You Receive from Customers and Prospects

Depending upon the kind of business you're in, you may occasionally receive mail from customers and prospects. When we were in the banking business it was common for banks to send us credit card, loan, and other account applications and information.

When possible and appropriate, respond positively to these mailings. If you think the marketing department did a terrible job with a particular piece, or you see any other flaws in the mailings, keep the negative comments to yourself. The only time you want to give some feedback is either if you are in that business or if you are asked.

If you are in the business, approach it from an angle of, "I think we can improve on what you're doing" as opposed to "Your marketing piece is awful and you need our help." If you are not in the business and they ask your opinion, you can be honest, but not blatant. Instead of "It's terrible," go with, "Well, have you perhaps considered (whatever your better idea is) instead?"

Be Your Customer's Customer

As salespeople selling to banks and credit unions, it was easy for us to be our customer's customers. We used our best customers for car loans, home loans, and any other banking needs we had. All of our checking and savings accounts were also kept with a local financial institution that also happened to be a great customer of ours.

If you can, become a customer of your customer's and make sure *you're a good customer*. Always be polite, pay on time, and compliment the individuals working at the business whenever possible.

Give out Your Home Phone Number

You want to make sure you are the primary contact for your customer. While it's true that you are part of a team and want customers to be able to contact the other important people in your organization, you need to make sure you're the first person your customers think of when they need something immediately or have a pressing issue.

Also, your customers need to be able to reach you *anytime*. While most people have your office phone and fax number, and may even have your cell phone number, make sure your customers also have your home number. There aren't many salespeople who give out their home number and doing so will definitely catch people's attention. You will build instant rapport and credibility and show the customer that you truly care.

There are a couple of rules to follow when giving out your home number. They are:

1) Check your messages on your home number during the day.

You don't have to check messages on your home phone with the frequency of your business phone. Once before noon and once around 4:30 p.m. is fine if your typical day is from 8 a.m. to 5 p.m. While most customers know to call your home number only during off-business hours or on weekends, some will call your home number during normal business hours, leaving a message and expecting you to get back to them promptly. We know that some of what we have just said about people calling you on weekends and off-hours might scare you, but rest assured, most of your customers will only bother you when they really need to, which leads us to rule number 2.

2) If you have a customer who is a pest, don't give him your home number.

Chances are the "pest" customer will see nothing wrong with calling you at home at the worst possible times. If you still want to give out your number to this person, that's fine; just don't complain when you get a call in the middle of Thanksgiving dinner.

3) If you aren't willing to be called at home, don't give out your home number.

Giving out your home number will definitely set you apart from most other salespeople; at the same time, you need to be willing to take the calls, sometimes at inconvenient times.

4) Make sure your home message is presentable.

It's okay to have a "home" message on your home answering machine; after all, people will not expect your home message to sound businesslike. However, the message should not be so relaxed that it's obnoxious. The following message is an example of a good home message that is also suitable for business callers: "Hello. You've reached the Chapin residence. We're not available to take your call right now. Please leave a message and have a great day. Thanks."

Your Business Voice Mail and Related Information

Here are some guidelines to follow with regard to voice mail etiquette:

1) Have voice mail.

We occasionally call a number that does not have voice mail. The voice mail system available through the phone company is very good—there is no mechanical device to break down and it is very easy to pick up voice mail from anywhere in the world.

2) Have the basics.

The message you leave on your voice mail should be professional, lively, and to the point. Your name, followed by a nice, professional message works well. Here is an example: "Hello. You've reached the voice mail for Bob Chapin. I'm not available right now. Please leave your name, number, and the time you called, and I'll get back to you as soon as possible. Thanks for calling and have a great day."

3) Make sure it's *your* voice on your voice mail message.

Do not have your secretary, significant other, or a five-year-old child record the message for you. It's okay to delegate some tasks, but your voice mail message isn't one of them.

A voice mail message with someone else's voice suggests that not only are you too busy to take people's calls, you're also too busy to record a message. Other poor impressions it may leave are that you like to have other people do everything for you, or you just don't care.

4) If possible, update your voice mail daily.

By updating your voice mail daily, you let people know whether you're in the office, in meetings, on the road, out sick, or any other particulars about your schedule for that specific day. Make sure you mention the date on your voice mail.

5) Always have a "vacation" message when you're on vacation.

Catch the caller's attention immediately and let him know when you'll be back and who to call if it's an emergency. Here is a good vacation message: "Please listen carefully to the following message. You've reached the voice mail for Bob Chapin. I will be away Monday the 4th through Sunday the 10th, and returning to the office on Monday the 11th. If this is an emergency, please contact Doris Smith at 508-555-6401. If this is not urgent, you can leave me a message and I will call you when I return. Thanks for calling and have a great day."

A note on points 4 and 5: After you leave your voice mail message, be sure to review it. This is especially important when you leave a vacation or extended absence greeting. The last thing you want is to come back from a week's vacation to find a bunch of irate customer messages because, for some reason, your new "vacation" message didn't replace the old "I'm in the office all day" one.

The other reason to listen to your message is to determine how it sounds to the person calling. You may hear your message and think, "Wow, I sound dead and monotone in that message." It's better for you to find out the message sounds terrible before the people calling you do.

6) Make sure people can reach you immediately in an emergency.

If callers typically go to your voice mail, there needs to be a way people can get in touch with you in case of an emergency. It may be by pager, cell phone, or an option you have on your voice mail system. For example, at the end of your voice mail message you may say, "If this is an emergency, please dial zero and ask for Doris Smith."

Note: If a customer or prospect needs help urgently and she can't get in touch with you, there's a chance she will call your competitor.

7) Don't have endless loop voice mail.

Avoid using voice mail with endless menus and choices. Having more than four choices before you go to a sub-menu, and eight or nine choices followed by eight or nine more can be a real annoyance. If possible, stay away from voice mail altogether and have a live operator.

8) Sell on your voice mail.

Give out your website address, a short advertisement, or even your weekly specials on voice mail. Keep it short, however; you don't want to go more than a minute or so.

9) Have more than one point of contact.

The best case scenario is to have a work number, cell phone or pager number, e-mail, and home phone number by which people can reach you if they need to. In some businesses it is more important to be accessible at a moment's notice. Recognize what the case is and treat it accordingly. Finally, you will impress someone immensely if you give her all the above points of contact, particularly the home number.

Note: Over the years, we've had some important customers who took priority over everyone or everything else. The receptionist was instructed that if one of these "special" customers called, we were to be interrupted regardless of we were on another call or in a meeting. There is only one way to treat a VIP customer—like a VIP.

Chapter 40

Account Management

Maximize the Business You Do with Customers

Your best source for business is current customers. Your current customers are already sold on you and your product so they naturally take less work to sell to again. Once you have a customer, you want to ensure you are maximizing the potential of that relationship. In other words, you want to make sure you are selling them *everything* they need. Here are the steps to ensuring that happens:

1) Treat your customers right.

Take the necessary steps after the sale, and do your best to build the relationship. Also, avoid the mistakes we'll discuss a little later.

2a) Make sure your customers are aware of every service and product you provide.

Inform your customers about all your products and capabilities. No matter how well you are known in the industry or how long you've been doing business with a particular customer, it is possible that you can help your customer in ways he is unaware of.

In the banking industry, we represented the number one security vendor in the world. Over the years we were amazed at the number of customers who thought we sold *only* automated teller machines. Some had no idea we sold alarm and video equipment, safes, vaults, teller equipment, and a wide variety of other products. We made it a habit to discuss the different product lines we offered and to inform people of new products when they came out. We also sent newsletters, new product ads, and other information to inform people about the breadth of our equipment lines. Educating and reminding customers and prospects of all you offer is a continual process.

2b) Add-ons.

Add-ons are related to 2a. We discussed add-ons in step 5 in Chapter 37 (pg 510). That step refers to supplies, service contracts, and other items you can add to your product or service. Selling the product is one thing, but selling the service contract and all the supplies along with it can significantly increase the total dollar amount of your sale.

Limit your add-ons to two or three items, and make sure they complement your product or service. More than two or three add-on items tends to irritate people.

3) Become a business partner.

Analyze your customer's business and get creative. You have to go beyond the role of vendor to the role of business partner if you want to maximize the amount of business you do with a customer. In order to do this you need to thoroughly understand your customer's business along with the overall goals and objectives. You must also thoroughly understand your product and how it can best be utilized to help the customer's business. From there, you want to set up a brainstorming meeting with the customer to discover how you might be of assistance in as many ways as possible.

After that meeting, put all your supporting documentation together, such as ROI models, profit projections, and the like, and then sit down with the customer once again to propose a "complete" solution.

4) Never assume "business as usual."

As salespeople, we often assume that if a customer has done things the same way for any length of time, he or she probably won't be changing anytime soon. You'd be amazed how positively customers and prospects will respond if you simply keep an open mind and present new ideas.

We had a customer who had been using the same video company for over forty years! Well, we got the video business. How? We simply asked if we could provide a competitive bid for video. The competition had been significantly inflating the numbers.

What do you have to lose by asking? The worst the customer or prospect can say is no. If you ask and you do get a no, simply go back to the drawing board and come up with a better way to ask the next time.

Challenge your own assumptions about customers. Don't assume they won't want to do something new, try something new, or change something just because it would be new for them.

5) Stay in touch with customers and keep them updated.

This one should go without saying. You don't want to be a pest, but you do want to have a schedule with which you regularly contact customers. Use this contact to let them know about current trends in the industry and how they may be affected. Often they will be aware of changes, but they will appreciate the fact that you have thought about them. Personal visits are very important; however, you also want to be reaching out to your customers in other ways. Use e-mail, faxes, webinars (web seminars), phone calls, mailings, and other mediums to stay in touch and keep customers updated. Do these in addition to the items listed on page 530 under the heading, What to Do with All That Customer Information.

Establish Relationships throughout the Organization

You want to have good relationships with as many people as possible in the organizations you are calling on. There are several reasons for establishing lots of relationships within the companies you deal with.

1) You never know who will be leaving and where he or she will be going.

If someone with whom you have a good relationship leaves one company and joins another you already have a relationship with, that's good—that relationship is further solidified. If the person moves to a company you don't have a relationship with, that's also good. You can now get your foot in the door and build from there. Clearly, if the person you know is a decision-maker, that's an immediate help. If not, wait until he establishes some relationships and then have him introduce you to people. Stop by occasionally for lunch and begin to visit the new company from time to time. You'll eventually meet other people and start to build some new relationships.

2) You don't want to be "left out in the cold" if your key contact leaves.

If you know all or most of the key people in an organization, the competition won't have an opportunity to break in just because *one* key contact left. The people you know who are still there will introduce you to the person who replaced your previous contact and help ensure your first impression is a good one. From there, you can start to build a strong relationship with the new person.

3) You never know who will be moving up the corporate ladder and have future say in decisions.

The head teller at a bank may be the future CEO. The employee just starting out may be the future President. You just can't know. Obviously, you need to be nice to everyone you run into, from the secretary and janitor to the President and Chairman of the Board. One of the companies we worked for employed a salesperson who would snub anyone except the person he was there to call on. One of the people he snubbed was the security officer. You have probably already guessed, but that security officer became an Executive Vice President in charge of purchasing all new equipment. Guess who ended up selling all the equipment to that account? Right, the competition.

The more people you know and have a good relationship with inside an organization, the more influence you will have and the stronger your position will be. Obviously, if you know and have a good relationship with the CEO, COO, CFO, and Controller, you'll be in a better position than if you have a relationship only with the CEO. Although the CEO may ultimately make all the decisions, the others most likely have some influence in the matter. If they all know and like you, the odds of the competition gaining an edge with any one of them is remote. Also, if the CEO leaves, retires, or dies, you're still solidly connected with the person who will most likely take over the reins.

4) The more people you know within one organization, the greater your potential to get to know other people at their level in other organizations.

In other words, birds of a feather flock together. This works well in the area of referrals and testimonials. As you get to know individuals well, you can begin to ask who else they know in the industry. What groups and organizations do they belong to? From there, you can ask to be referred or introduced to other individuals. You can also join the groups and organizations to meet these other people, while also getting to know your customer better.

Introducing the Rest of the Sales Team

There are very few sales positions, if any, that are truly one-person efforts. You most likely rely on other people to help you get the job done. From receptionists to managers and installation coordinators to the people who make the product, a team effort is usually necessary to ensure your overall success.

Because your customers may need to interact with some of your support people from time to time, it is important to make your customers aware of these other people within your organization. This will serve several purposes:

- Your customers will recognize the person's name when one of them calls.
- These staff members can take some weight off your shoulders.
- When you are out of town or otherwise unreachable, your customers will have someone they can contact.

There are several ways to introduce your co-workers to your customers:

1) Mention the names of your support people in everyday conversations with your customers.

Talk about your support people in a positive way that will allow them to be locked into your customer's mind. In particular, your manager can get involved in a number of ways that will benefit the customer. You should be using those situations to "verbally introduce" your manager to your customer. If the customer is looking for something special, such as rush delivery or unusual payment terms, and your manager helped out, make mention of that.

Your manager is the key person to introduce to your customers. It is very important that your customers feel comfortable getting in touch with your manager if you are not available for some reason.

The office manager and/or manager's secretary can also be a key person for your customers to be familiar with. Introduce this person in the same verbal fashion that you used to introduce your manager. Let your customers know this person is available if an emergency arises and they are unable to reach you. Give your customers her name and phone number and also mention the importance of her job and the commitment she has to doing it well.

Occasionally, you'll want to set up a phone introduction between one of your customers and the office manager. For example, let's say you're headed off for vacation and an important customer project is scheduled for the same week you'll be gone. In this case, let the office manager know the situation and tell her this customer may be calling in with some issues while you are away.

As well, tell her you would like to put her on the phone with the customer so she can introduce herself personally and let the customer know she will be available while you are away. This will give the customer a feeling of comfort knowing that he will be taken care of during your absence. The conversation you and your office manager have with your customer might sound something like this:

You: "Hi, Mr. Customer. This is Bob Chapin over at ABC Company. How are you?

"In the past I have talked about our office manager, Cindy Smith, right? As you know, I will be out of the office next week while your project is underway." (Hopefully, if it's an important project, your customer will know well in advance that you will be away.)

"I will be checking in with the office from time to time (say this only if you will be), but if something comes up and you need immediate attention, I want you to call Cindy directly, okay?

"I actually have Cindy here right now and I'd like to put you on the phone with her so she can personally introduce herself, okay?"

Cindy: "Hi, Mr. Customer, this is Cindy Smith. How are you? As Bob mentioned, if any issues arise next week when Bob's gone, please give me a call and I'll be more than happy to help you out.

"One other thing—you may already have it, but let me give you my direct phone number. If for some reason you get my voice mail, press zero, and then have the operator page me, okay?

"Great, very nice talking to you, Mr. Customer. Again, please call me if you need anything. Have a nice day."

With this done, another "business family member" has been introduced. The two family members we've mentioned so far, the manager and office manager, are the key business family members with whom you want to make sure your customers are familiar. Other key people whom your customers should be familiar with might be your service manager and your installation manager.

2) Bring key people into your accounts.

This point is fairly self-explanatory. You should be setting up meetings with your customers to introduce key personnel.

In addition to an initial introductory meeting, bring your staff members with you on sales calls from time to time. You want your customers to become very familiar with them so that when you have to pass something off or there is a problem, they are comfortable talking with them.

3) Send out a listing of all key personnel to your customers.

Once you have verbally and physically introduced the key people in your organization to your customers, you'll want to put a list of these key individuals in print and mail it to all your customers. On the following two pages is an example of a package we put together.

Remember, your key people can be backup for you and they can also pick up the slack when you need them to. Eventually you want to be able to delegate issues to other department heads, but before you do that, your customers must be comfortable with them.

How to Handle Difficulty in Getting Two People Together

Sometimes it's impossible to get two people physically in the same place at the same time. They appear to be on completely opposite schedules. If you find yourself in a situation where you need to get two people together and it is proving to be a monumental effort, set up a conference call. Simply find out when both of them are available for a phone call and let them know that you will arrange it.

Sample Letter

Mr. Jim Smith   December 5, 2008
Executive Vice President
XYZ Bank
123 Main Street
Wakefield, MA 01880

Dear Mr. Smith,

XYZ Bank is a very good customer of ABC Company. We appreciate that and thank you very much for your loyalty and business through the years.

We want to assist you and make your day-to-day dealings with ABC Company as pleasant and easy as possible. As a result, we have attached a listing of ABC Company personnel assigned to serve XYZ Bank. On a daily basis, these people cover product sales, product service and installation, and professional services, items of key importance to financial institutions such as yours.

Of course, as sales representatives, we are your first contacts. But in the event that you can't reach us immediately regarding an urgent matter, please feel free to call the appropriate individual based upon the kind of issue you have, be it related to sales, service, or installation. When in doubt give Doris Smith, our office manager, a call.

As always, we look forward to your questions and comments and continue to look for better ways to serve you.

Thank you again,

Bob and John Chapin
508-555-6400

ABC COMPANY PERSONNEL – ASSIGNED AND AVAILABLE
AUBURN REGIONAL OFFICE – (508) 555-2600

SALES
Bob and John Chapin – Sales Representatives, Auburn (508) 555-2644
Home Office (508) 555-6429
Cell phones: Bob (508) 555-5832; John (508) 555-5831
Joe Brown – Regional Sales Manager, Auburn (508) 555-2641
Doris Smith – Office Manager, Auburn (508) 555-2607

SERVICE
Joe Harvey – Service Manager, Auburn (508) 555-2670
Backup Service Manager, John Anderson, Auburn (508) 555-2677

INSTALLATION
Coordinators: Cindy Harrah, Auburn (508) 555-2634
Charley Johnson, Auburn (508) 555-2683
Project Advisors: Paul Smith, Auburn (508) 555-2628
Wayne Anderson, Auburn (508) 555-2632
Installation and Project Managers: Paul Cain, Auburn (508) 555-2616
Jim Jones, Auburn (508) 555- 2631

TECHNICAL SUPPORT
Software Engineers: Steve Henry, Concord, NH (603) 555- 6902
Dennis Murphy, Auburn (508) 555-2669
Paul Harvey, Auburn (508) 555-2920
David Eid – ATM Tech Specialist, RI (401) 555-4315

ADDRESSES
ABC Company Sales and Service
538 Albacore Street – Building G
Auburn, MA 01501
Phone: (508) 555-2600 Fax: (508) 555-2699
ABC Company Eastern Division Office
7 Creative Street
Concord, NH 03103
Phone: (603) 555-6900 Fax: (603) 555-6999

The Correct Way to Pass a Customer to Someone Else in Your Company

Follow these rules when you put a customer in touch with another person in your company:

- Let the customer know why you are passing him off to someone else and who that person is. Tell the customer you will have the person call him.
- Call the person with whom you're putting the customer in touch and let her know what the situation is and why you are putting the customer in touch with her.
- Make sure she calls the customer instead of the other way around.
- Better yet, call the person from your company, explain the situation to her, then call the customer and set up a conference call.
- Follow up to make sure everything was resolved to everyone's satisfaction.

Note: Make sure you take responsibility for the follow-up even though you are passing the customer off, and always call the customer afterward to make sure everything was taken care of to their satisfaction.

Chapter 41

Customer Challenges

Set a Positive Tone for Challenging Customer Meetings

If you've been in sales for any length of time, you've undoubtedly had a customer or two who were a challenge to manage. When you are preparing an introductory meeting between one of these customers and one of your colleagues, you want to do your best to set a positive tone before the meeting.

The best way to do this is to tell your associate what a nice person the customer is prior to the meeting. You don't need to overdo it, just put a generally positive spin on the situation, then sit back and see how things unfold. In our business, interestingly enough, about 50 percent of the time, the meeting would go well and our associate would say something like, "Wow, you were right. That person was really nice."

When you set people's expectations ahead of time, often those expectations will become reality. When the person in your organization is expecting to meet someone nice, he or she will go into the meeting with a positive attitude and energy, and often that will be enough to turn the "tough" customer around.

However, this won't always work. The other 50 percent of the time your co-worker will say, "Gee, I thought you said that person was nice!" Still, 50 percent positive is much better than 100 percent negative. If you took the opposite approach in a similar situation, you would *greatly* increase your odds of having a negative experience.

We've also used this technique when one of our associates was calling on a difficult customer by himself. We've had situations where a service or installation manager had to call on a customer either in-person or on the phone. In speaking with the manager ahead of time, we always made sure to say something to the effect of, "Oh yes, Jim's a very nice guy." Again, 100 percent of the time the manager went in with positive expectations, approaching the customer with a positive demeanor, and at least 50 percent of the time, if not more, the manager returned with a story of a positive experience.

It's also entirely possible that there is simply a personality conflict between you and the customer. Your associate may be better suited to deal with this person and, as a result, the two of them may get along well. If it *is* the case that you have a personality conflict, you definitely want to consider trading this account with another salesperson. If, on the other hand, no one else gets along with this person either, you can hang on to the account, trade it, or give up on it altogether.

When you are speaking with prospects or customers, avoid discussions about negative events from the past that may still be fresh. For example, we once had a prospect at a competitive account who absolutely refused to do business with us.

Then one day the phone rang, and it was the prospect. His bank had been bought out and he was now working for one of our very good accounts. The potential problem for us was that one of our key contacts at our good account had left the company, and the prospect had moved into his influential position. Fortunately, we knew plenty of other people at the account so we were fairly confident we'd be in good shape. Yet we were on pins and needles fearing that he might want to bring in the competition.

Our first and second meetings with him went exceedingly well. Our third meeting with the customer was at our office and one of our new salespeople was going to be attending the meeting.

As it turned out, this new salesperson had also had the most recent contact with the prospect when he was still at the previous bank. Upon arrival at our demonstration hall, this salesperson said, "Oh yes, I'm sure you remember me. We spoke a couple of times when you were at (the previous bank)."

The point here is this: The few conversations they'd had were negative ones that had occurred long ago, so it was entirely possible that the prospect would not have even remembered the exchanges. You never want to remind the prospect about a bad experience with your company. Also, if you do remind him, and he remembers most of what he said, he may feel as though his integrity is on the line.

What should you do instead? Do what we did when we first met with him at the new bank—be very pleasant, be very professional, and say nothing that remotely refers to any past negative encounters. Act as though this is the first time you've heard his name and be a little nicer than usual.

Keep things positive and avoid unnecessary negatives when dealing with prospects and customers. We say *unnecessary* because there will be times when you need to discuss negative business with clients. The unnecessary negatives we are referring to are past conversations or situations that can have nothing but a negative influence on present or future business.

Dealing with Unhappy Customers

Occasionally, you will run into an upset or even irate customer. Here are the steps for dealing with unhappy customers and customer complaints in general.

1) Listen.

Hear them out completely. Do not interrupt. Make sure they have said all they want or need to say.

2) Empathize with your customers.

Sincerely apologize for what they have gone through. Let them know you understand their frustration and agree with them where you can.

3) Never argue, debate or get upset with them.

4) Ask questions to make sure you have all the facts straight and thoroughly understand the problem and how it happened.

5) Take notes about the problem and confirm that they agree with the information you have written down.

6) If the solution is obvious, propose one.

If it is a little more ambiguous, ask what it will take to satisfy them and make them happy. Agree upon a solution. If at all possible, give the customer several choices.

7) If you cannot approve what they are asking for, immediately contact someone who can.

8) Take personal responsibility, even if you need to pass it off to someone else in the company. Follow the process every step along the way.

9) Respond immediately.

Start the process of resolving the problem right away.

10) Let the customer know what you plan to do and then do it.

Also, let them know when they can expect to have their problem solved. Make sure that they agree with your plan of action and your timeline for resolution.

11) Before ending the conversation, emphasize to the customer again that you apologize for the error, and that you will do your best to see that the error is corrected and is not repeated in the future. As well, thank them for calling you and making you aware of the problem, and thank them for their patience and understanding.

12) Make a follow-up call after the situation has been resolved to confirm that the customer is satisfied.

13) Ask yourself how this type of problem can be prevented in the future and what you've learned from the situation. Is there something you can do better? Is there a process or procedure that needs to be changed?

Here are the most salient points:

- Empathize with the customer and let her know that you genuinely care.
- Tell her that you will go to work on the problem immediately.
- Take personal responsibility in making sure that the problem is resolved quickly and effectively.
- Ensure that once the problem is solved, the customer is completely happy with the resolution.

Don't Add Fuel to a Customer's Fire

When a customer is upset and venting his anger, the last thing you want to do is add fuel to the fire. This is best illustrated by an example.

We once had a situation in which we were going along with a new salesperson to call on an unhappy customer. We were planning to review what went wrong, why it went wrong, and what we could do to make amends.

The meeting started off well, but soon afterward the customer began to become emotional as he recounted the details of his unpleasant experience. He then became even more emotional as he projected possible future ramifications of the mistakes that had been made and how they might affect his business. He brought up the possibility that if the local news media got hold of some of the details they might run some very damaging press. He even came up with some ugly stories that one of the local talk radio stations might come up with.

The new salesperson chimed in, saying, "Oh yes, that station's terrible! If they get wind of this they'll crucify you, but you know who's worse than that station? Station X. If they send a couple of their reporters after this, you'll be cooked."

The last thing you want to do is help the customer paint negative pictures. This customer was referring to events that hadn't yet happened, and worse, he was turning this situation into a worst-case scenario. The new salesperson had raised the bar and made the situation far worse. The direct result was that the customer became even more worried, agitated, and upset. This is the opposite direction that you want to take the customer.

Your goal in this situation is to hear the customer out, allowing him to release his anger and get the bad experience off his chest, and then decide how you can make amends. Let him know this is not life or death, there is a solution to his pain, and you are committed to making that solution happen.

When you study the comments of the new salesperson closely, his mentality is not difficult to discern. By taking the customer's thoughts and expanding upon them, he was showing that he understood how the customer was thinking and agreed with what he was saying. He was attempting to show empathy for the customer.

His intentions were good. The only problem was the method used. Instead of expanding on the customer's ideas, the new salesperson should have listened intently, looked the customer in the eye, nodding and otherwise showing signs of agreement, all the while taking notes.

Here are some steps that should have taken place before the meeting:

- All the salespeople involved should have had a conversation before going into the meeting. Typically, the experienced salesperson leads the meeting and the new salesperson is there simply to observe.
- The salesperson leading the meeting needs to know from someone in authority—perhaps the sales manager—what concessions he can make and how far he can go in the negotiating process.
- As discussed above, the goal is to hear the customer out, let him vent and get the bad experience off his chest, and decide how to rectify the

problem. You want to appease the customer, and you certainly don't want to help him embellish the bad experience.

Taking Attitude from Customers

If you have a chip on your shoulder, generally don't like people, prefer solitude rather than interaction with others during your work, or can't take criticism or rejection, don't get into sales. If you're already in sales, you're in the wrong business. Salespeople need to be consummate professionals and they need to have long fuses.

If you are in sales for any length of time, you're going to be faced with bad customers and/or bad attitudes. If you encounter a bad customer, that is probably a permanent problem from which you want to separate yourself as soon as possible. On the other hand, if you encounter a bad attitude, it may very well be just a temporary situation that you'll need to deal with.

While it's true you're not a punching bag, and there may be occasions when you need to draw the line, for the most part you'll need to become experienced at remaining calm on the other end of a customer's wrath. Occasionally, a customer may become extremely upset and you may need to take some verbal abuse and let him vent his anger.

Usually when a customer loses his cool, he is simply letting off some steam. Most likely, the person simply lost control for a moment and allowed his temper get the better of him. After you let him vent or call him back if he left an angry message, you will usually find him in a better state of mind. Often you will even get an apology.

Do your best to stay professional, keep your head, and take the high road when a customer goes off.

How to Handle Problem Accounts

In addition to examples such as the one above, you may occasionally run into an account who is simply difficult to deal with. If this is the case, this may be a customer you want to fire. We'll discuss that soon. Assuming this is a customer you've decided to hang onto for the time being, let's look at how to handle these difficult accounts.

1) **Go out of your way to be pleasant and accommodating.**

2) **Let the customer know you are doing your best to meet her needs, and do what you can to make her feel important.**

3) **Remain calm and professional.**

This can be difficult at times, yet you must do your best to keep from losing your temper.

4) **Cover all your bases throughout the sales process and follow up after the sale.**

Make sure the customer is satisfied and nip potential problems in the bud immediately.

5) **Ask questions to determine what your customer is looking for or what the problem might be.**

6) **Find out if something has changed in the customer's situation that is causing her to act in this way.**

7) **Change the terms of your agreement.**

If you have a customer who already owes you money, require payment for the new product in advance. If you have a customer who constantly contradicts what she has said, make sure you have everything agreed to in writing. Look for solutions to the problems you've been having with the account and then make adjustments.

Our greatest challenges can actually provide the greatest opportunities for growth, and problem accounts are no exception. They can be a very valuable learning tool. Is it possible that the problem is with you or your company, and not the account? Often what we see as problem accounts are simply those willing to give us some feedback, while others silently fume or are dissatisfied but say nothing. Look at your side of the equation first, and if the problem is with you or your company, do your best to fix it.

Firing Your Customers

As a last resort, you can fire a problem account. From time to time you will find a customer much too costly—financially, emotionally, or otherwise—to continue to deal with. If you have done everything you can to accommodate the customer and the situation still is not resolving itself, it may be best to part ways. Here's how to fire a customer.

1) Be honest and straightforward.

"Ms. Customer, frankly, we've tried very hard to please you, but I don't think we're going to be able to make you happy. I very much appreciate the opportunity to do business with you, but I'm afraid we're going to have to part ways."

"Mr. Customer, we've continued to extend your line of credit again and again, and I'm afraid we can no longer do so."

You don't want to be long-winded. Simply state the facts.

2) Offer some solutions that don't involve you and your company.

"Mr. Customer, there is another company that does (whatever you do) that I think might be a better fit for you."

"Ms. Customer, have you considered having these done (another way or by someone else)?"

Once again, short and sweet—just get it out there.

3) Simply bow out of future jobs.

If the customer brings a job to you, say, "I'm sorry, Ms. Prospect, we're going to have to bow out on this one."

The customer should get the idea fairly quickly.

4) Stop calling on the account.

If you are getting your business from a particular account because you are calling on them, stop calling on them. Perhaps they will never take the initiative to call you.

5) Give the competition a lead.

This works best if the competition is somehow better suited to handle a customer. For example, the customer may be too small for you to deal with, but a smaller company and/or one just starting out may appreciate the business.

Note: Never be rude. We once heard a business owner rudely tell a customer, "Get out of our store. We no longer wish to do business with you!" She then turned to us, smiled, and very nicely said, "Hi, can I help you?" We said, "I guess we're all set. Thanks." And left. We never knew what the situation was, but it was a lesson. You need to smile and keep your head, even in bad situations.

How to Annoy or Anger Customers

The following are customer mistakes to avoid:

1) Dishonesty.

Dishonesty is the fastest way to lose a customer. Always be straightforward and honest.

2) Indifference.

Indifference is the second fastest way to lose a customer. If a customer feels you don't care, they won't care to do business with you. Unlike dishonesty, you may get a second chance if a customer suspects indifference, but you've got to turn the tables quickly and immediately begin treating this customer like a VIP.

3) Incompetence.

Incorrect bills, incomplete proposals, botched installations, and other miscues all fall into this category. Problems in this area either stem from indifference, a lack of knowledge and training, or both. Obviously, it's important to have competent people who care. Customers understand that everyone makes a mistake from time to time, and they'll usually allow a few. It's when things start to become more the rule than the exception that customers will fire you.

4) Not delivering.

If you don't deliver what you promise to deliver, customers will be rightly upset. The severity of the situation will be affected by two factors: how much you miss by and how long this customer has been with you. If you miss by a large margin and this is a new customer, you're finished. If you miss by only a little or you've had a good track record with this customer up until this point, you'll probably have a chance to make things right. Strive to under-promise and over-deliver.

5) Not following through.

This is a close relative of not delivering. Not following through is one of the fastest ways to anger someone and at the same time lose credibility. For example, you say you'll call Tuesday, and instead you call Thursday, or you promise the proposal on Friday and it shows up the following Tuesday. You simply must do what you say you'll do when you say you'll do it.

6) Lack of communication.

Phone calls that aren't returned, e-mails that aren't returned, and a lack of follow-up in general all fall into this category. Try to return all phone calls within a few hours and all e-mails within twenty-four hours. If you are on vacation, have a backup plan that allows people to be properly serviced while you're away. Above all, keep your customers in the loop. If something is happening that your customer needs to know about, you must stay in touch.

Two More Ways to Annoy Customers

Here are two more ways to tick off customers. These are a little more indirect than the ones we just looked at.

1) Hound them.

Calling, visiting, e-mailing, and otherwise communicating with prospects or customers more than they want to be communicated with will only serve to irritate them. One of us recalls a situation in the first few months of his selling career in which a customer called him an eyesore. This was because he called this customer incessantly asking for business.

When you're new in selling and you have only a few customers, it's sometimes easy to overdo your calls or visits. This is because it's easier to call on existing customers than to do the more difficult tasks such as cold calling. If you find yourself in this situation, you *must* avoid the temptation of overwhelming your current customers with requests for more business. Not only will you start to frustrate your current customers, thus reducing your chances of getting more business from them, you will also give them the impression that you're not very busy and don't have many customers to call on. Finally, by wasting too much time with your current customers, you are also taking time away from the tasks necessary to grow your business.

We had a situation in which we had asked Bill, a new sales rep, to drop off some information to a customer. When Bill dropped off the information on a Wednesday the customer was not available to see him, so he simply left the information with the customer's secretary. Because he had not seen the customer, we asked Bill to follow up with a phone call to see if the customer had any questions.

On Friday afternoon we received a call from the customer. "How much does Bill charge to haunt a house?" he asked. His tone was half-serious.

It turned out that Bill had called the customer five times in two days. He'd left messages all five times along with his phone number for the customer to call him back. The information he had dropped off was very basic with a low level of urgency. In that case, you don't need to hound a customer by calling with that kind of frequency.

2) "Sorry, they're all in a meeting."

This could fall under indifference and perhaps even incompetence. How many times does a customer take a back seat to a company meeting or other corporate concoction? A customer should *never* be told, "I'm sorry, no one's available" because of a meeting, conference call, or other inter-company event during regular business hours.

Remember: The customer always comes first. Don't let anything stand in the way of that fundamental principle of sales.

What If You Truly Anger a Customer?

If you seriously anger a customer to the point where the relationship seems damaged beyond repair, you should first do everything in your power to rectify the situation. Second, you should offer to find the customer another sales rep. Certainly, you may have lost the customer personally, but perhaps there's still hope for your company to keep the account.

Stop Customer Complaints before They Begin

How do you stop customer complaints before they begin? Simple: Ask your customers if they are happy with your product or service, what they would change, and how they think you could improve upon your product or service.

You might be surprised at how many people will say nothing when they are dissatisfied. They will simply go away and no longer do business with you.

Here are some questions that work well:

- Joe, on a scale of one to ten, how happy are you with our product and the service you receive from us?
- If there was anything you could change about our product or the service you receive, what would it be?
- What do you like most about our product or the way we service your account?
- What do you like least about our product or the way we service your account?
- How do you feel we could improve our product or service?
- Do you feel you will continue to do business with us as long as we continue to service your account the way we are currently?
- Why or why not?

Note: If you are told, "No, we will not continue to do business with you," ask the following question: "Is there anything we can do to save you as a customer?" At this point, you also want to get your manager(s) involved. Let your manager know about the situation. Even if the customer told you that you are finished and can do nothing to salvage the business, your manager may have some ideas to repair the damage, or perhaps she can go to a person above your contact and attempt to resolve the situation.

Ask mostly open-ended questions in which the person has to give you more than a simple yes or no answer. If you simply ask someone if she is happy with your product or service, a simple yes or no would rob you of valuable information about *why* she is or isn't happy. When you do ask a close-ended question, make sure it is a probing one that provides you with the necessary details behind the yes or no.

The objective here is to find out where you stand with the customer and why. Discovering *where* you stand is good, but finding out *why* will really give you something tangible to work with.

Preventing Problems with Good Customer Notes

Many problems can be avoided by keeping good customer notes with regard to account activity and what was said during business transactions.

The securities industry serves as a great example here. In this industry most conversations are, or should be, recorded in print. This is because when a dispute arises about the purchase or sale of a security, memories can get foggy after the fact. Solicited versus unsolicited transactions, margin calls, the clients desire to invest in a particular type of security, and similar types of information need to be noted as all of these can become future landmines if not documented properly.

It is also a good idea to put some things in writing to a customer. We know of one instance in the banking business where a security officer did not take the advice of the security equipment salesperson. When that bank was later broken into, what cleared the salesperson was a letter both he and the security officer signed that stated that the salesperson had recommended a certain security feature and the security officer declined. The signed letter was the best evidence for the salesperson. If the salesperson had not written the letter, the next best thing would have been specific, detailed, dated notes.

When a customer wants to do something that is in direct conflict with your recommendation, have it documented and make sure you have solid details.

Here are some examples of when to document customer communications.

1) Any and all current business transactions.

When a customer calls to buy or sell something.

2) Any potential future transactions.

When a customer calls and gives you "when" or "if" instructions. Example: "When the stock hits $46 sell it, even if you can't get a hold of me."

Note: In this case it is also a *very* good idea to get this in writing. In fact, the law may require it. Make sure you know the rules.

3) Any change in the customer's situation that effects, or may effect, business.

Example: Your customer just lost HIS biggest customer and you are concerned this may effect his cash flow.

4) Any communication that, for any reason, raises a red flag.

You may not be able to put your finger on it, but for some reason you have a strange feeling something is up or the customer is not acting right. Document it with as many details as possible.

5) All communication.

It is a good idea to have a record of all communications, even if you simply called to touch base. Better too much information than not enough.

Note 1: Use the "five Ws and one H" rule when documenting: who, what, where, why, when, and how.

Note 2: Detail is important and putting things in writing is always a good idea. There are essentially five ways of recording information, they are: by preprinted form, by hand written form, via voice recorder, via video recorder, and via computer or e-mail. Use the method which is appropriate.

Another Potential Hot Potato—Employee Turnover

Informing a customer that an individual they have worked with is no longer with your company can be a tricky situation. It's easy if the individual was causing LOTS of problems and wasn't getting along with anyone—co-workers and customers alike. However, if the employee was well liked by co-workers and customers, your job of explaining will be a bit more difficult.

The terms under which the employee left will also affect the ease of breaking the news. If the employee left on good terms you can usually pave a fairly smooth road for transition. If the employee left on bad terms, you may need to do some damage control.

Let's take the best situation first. The best scenario is one in which the employee is able to give you plenty of notice and is also concerned about any fallout that may be a direct result of him or her leaving. For example, let's say an employee is leaving the company, yet he is able to give you three months notice and wants to help in the transition process.

The first thing you should do in this situation is to decide where your business will be effected as well as who will be effected. Let's say the service manager is leaving. In this case you would want to get together with him and visit your accounts to inform them of what is taking place. If your company has found a replacement for him, visit the customers with the service manager, as well as his replacement to make the transition as smooth as possible.

In addition, you want to bring the replacement up to speed on the accounts he will be responsible for. If he was not available to call on customers when you visited with his predecessor, bring him to your accounts as soon as possible.

Help him in his new position any way you can. You might help him get educated on the different types of equipment, features, functions, etc. You may also talk to him about certain policies that will effect your relationship with him, for example, service pricing discounts. You don't want to overwhelm or take up too much of his time. You simply want to give an overview of some basic items and let him know you are available should he have any questions.

The worst-case scenario happens when an employee is either abruptly terminated or quits without warning. As we mentioned earlier, if the employee was a major problem, explaining the situation to a customer is usually fairly easy. On the other hand, if the employee was good and/or liked by most everyone, your job of explaining will be more difficult.

As a salesperson what should you do in the worst-case scenario? The first thing you have to do is evaluate the situation. In order to do that you'll need to ask the following questions:

- Did the person quit or was he fired, and why?
- Do we have a permanent or temporary replacement for this person?
- Was he a problem and/or generally disliked, or was he a good employee and/or generally liked?
- Will he be competing against you?
- What is your relationship with this person like?
- Can you call him on the phone and ask him what happened?
- Will the person's boss tell you what happened?
- What will the fallout be, what is the worst-case scenario?
- What can you do to make sure you limit any possible damage?

Once you've assessed the situation, you are now ready to put a plan of attack together regarding how to handle it.

1) If the person was well liked.

Break the news, give as few details as possible on why the person left, and then focus on solutions. In this case, a conversation with a customer might sound like the following:

> "Hi. Joe, Bob Chapin over at ABC Company, how are you?
>
> "I wanted to give you a quick call and inform you of a recent development within our company. Joe Smith is no longer with us. I'm not sure of all of the details or exactly what happened, however, Dan Jones will be filling in until we can find a permanent replacement.
>
> "Now let me stress that your service will not be effected. I just wanted to let you know what was going on because I know you had a relationship with Joe Smith."

2) If the person was NOT well liked.

Break the news, and then focus on solutions. In this case, a conversation with a customer might sound like the following:

> "Hi Joe, Bob Chapin over at ABC Company, how are you?
>
> "I wanted to give you a quick call and let you know that Joe Smith, the service manager, is no longer with us. Dan Jones will be filling in until we can find a permanent replacement. In the short term your service will not be effected. However, over the long term I think you'll see quite an improvement."

In both cases the customer may have some comments one way or the other. Hear the customer out, acknowledge what he or she has said, and then focus again on the solution and how service either won't be affected or will eventually be improved.

Note: If service will be negatively affected, you don't want to say service won't be effected or will be improved. In this case, focus on the contingency plan and let the customer know your company will be doing all that it can to address the situation.

Another Place to Be Careful

A bank security officer recently asked a new vendor to make some recommendations on the alarm system at one of his branches. As the vendor walked in and started to look around, instead of focusing on what he was there for—the alarm system—he started checking out the camera system, and noticed some potential issues.

He proceeded to tell the security officer all the flaws in how the video system was set up. What the vendor did not realize was that the security officer prided himself on his expertise of video. As the vendor continued with his critique of the video system, he continued to lose any opportunity to do the alarm work, or any work for that matter.

If you have an opinion on something, unless you're there to make recommendations on that specifically, or someone's life is in eminent danger, *remain silent*.

In the case of the video system, it really came down to preference. The security officer preferred it one way and the security consultant felt it would look better another way. In any case, it was not even close to life and death.

In another similar scenario, you may find yourself in a vendor meeting where one of your areas of expertise is being discussed, yet you are not the vendor for that particular equipment.

Using the above example, let's assume you are at the meeting to discuss the alarm system and the video system is being discussed. During the part of the meeting where video is mentioned, just sit back and observe. Incidentally, this is a good opportunity to see how your competition works and that should be your only objective, so sit back, listen, and learn. Again, only jump in if there is a life at stake.

There is one other time in the above scenario when you want to say something. It is okay for you to speak up if the customer asks for your opinion or your input. If this happens, and the video vendor seems to be on the mark, simply say, "Yes, I agree with the proposed solution."

If the customer asks for your input and you are not in total agreement with what the video vendor is recommending, but it's close or adequate, say, "I think the proposed solution is one that could work."

If you notice some major flaws in the other vendor's solution, the best way to handle it is to say something like, "Hmm, that looks like it might possibly work…" then get in touch with your customer contact after the meeting and bring your concerns to her attention.

It is best *not* to bring up the concerns during the meeting. You do not want to make the other vendor look bad in front of everyone else.

Note: Here is an example of a major flaw that could put an individual, or individuals, in grave danger. Let's say you're in a vendor meeting and you notice that the floor probably won't support the weight of a certain piece of equipment. In this case, address the issue if you are asked about it directly. If you are not asked, and it looks as though someone overlooked it, pull your customer aside after the meeting and address the issue. Again, if it doesn't make a difference one way or the other, let it go.

Don't ever go out of your way to nit-pick the other vendor's proposal simply to make him look bad. You may think it's an opportunity for you to grab some more business and get the other guy out of the picture, but you're more likely to do yourself more harm than good. A better approach to going after the business is to wait until the next job comes up and then ask for the opportunity to bid on that portion of the project.

One More Landmine

Let's say you beat your customer in golf by two shots and you really rub it in. After all, you've always harassed your buddies when you win, and they you. With your regular golfing buddies this joking around brings you closer. This guy seems just like you and you two are friends so you assume it's no big deal and that this "razzing" may also bring you two closer.

What you don't know is that your customer eats, drinks and sleeps golf. In a nutshell, golf is *huge* to him. He goes home and says to his wife, "You know what? Bob beat me by two shots today and he really gave me a hard time about it. He was actually taunting me while I was putting on 18 and he exploded with jubilation when he won." Monday morning, goodbye you…hello competition.

That's an extreme example, and yet, we *guarantee* you it's happened. Until you know your customer extremely well, don't take chances. It's fine to go golfing, go out to dinner, and engage in other social activities with your customers, in fact, we recommend it. Just err on the side of politeness and stay away from discussions concerning politics, religion, and other heartfelt causes that people are usually passionate about until you know where your customer stands on these issues.

Oh, and one other thing, when playing competitive games you're always better off losing than winning. But on the occasion that you do win, make sure it's awfully close, and don't say a word!

A Summary of Ideas for after the Close

Keep these ideas in mind with regard to winning or losing the business:

- Find out *why* you won or lost.

- If you don't get the business, remain professional and make sure you stay in the door to quote on the next job.

- If you do get the business, treat the customer right, exceed expectations, under-promise, over-deliver, and do more than can be reasonably expected of you.

- Keep your word. We can't reiterate this enough: Do what you say you will do, when you say will do it.

- Reinforce the decision after the sale to fend off buyer's remorse.

- *Never* forget a customer. Continue to stay in touch with customers. Send cards and other correspondence—but not so frequently as to annoy them. Keep your name in front of them. Even though they may not buy anything again in the near future, they undoubtedly know other people who might.

- Always ask for referrals.

- Know your customer well and use that information to strengthen the relationship.

- Appreciate your customers and become *their* customers too when you can.

- Develop accounts by getting to know many people within each organization.

- Make sure your customers know many people within your organization.

- When dealing with customer complaints, stay calm and professional. Hear the customer out and do everything you can to make things right.

- Challenge your paradigms and your beliefs regarding your customers. Continue to ask pertinent questions, and continue to introduce new products, new ideas, and new uses for your primary product or service. Keep educating your customer, keep educating yourself about your customers, keep asking for orders, keep an open mind, and never assume anything.

SECTION IX

TELEPHONE SELLING

Introduction

In this section, we will focus on the intricacies of selling over the telephone. If you do all your selling by phone, you'll still want to review the other sections of this book, as they will round out and add significantly to what we talk about here.

Telemarketing offers some unique advantages when compared with other types of selling. They are:

1) You can reach a lot of people quickly.

2) It's easier to overcome your fears.

In telephone sales, you can hide behind the phone. The other person cannot see you and would never recognize you if you passed him on the street.

3) You can project the image you'd like.

Whether you're young or old, tall or short, fat or thin, or you're calling from a large office building or your bedroom, no one on the other end of the phone will know. You can sell in your pajamas or workout gear.

4) Time is on your side.

In seconds you can jump from one continent to another.

5) You can expand your sphere of business.

You can call the most isolated location on earth as long as there is telephone service.

6) Telemarketing is cost effective.

There are no car or other travel expenses, only the phone bill. As well, it won't be necessary for you to spend a fortune on business attire or a new wardrobe.

7) If necessary, you can quickly remove yourself from a delicate situation.

You can end a phone conversation politely and quickly.

8) It is much easier to control the conversation and selling process.

With judiciousness, you can use the hold button, "I have another call," and other tricks we'll discuss later.

9) You don't have to worry about "No Soliciting" signs.

Chapter 42

Preparing to Get on the Phone

Do as the Top Telephone Salespeople Do

Please refer to page 13 of the *Introduction* section for information on this subject. If you take the same actions as the top salespeople, you'll get the same results.

On page 14 of the *Introduction* section, we talk about having a binder that contains all the information you get from the top salespeople. Here is some information on how to specifically use your binder when selling over the phone:

1) Always have your binder with you and open to the appropriate section.

Even though you should know exactly what you want to say, have your binder in front of you to stay on track and focused. The key is to know the information like the back of your hand, so you do not have to read it. The binder should be there simply as a guide in case you forget something or get off course. When you already know *what* you want to say, you can concentrate on *how* you say it.

2) Buy yourself some time to flip through your binder to find an appropriate answer to an objection.

Say the following: "Mr. Prospect, I can appreciate that and I definitely understand where you're coming from. At the same time…"

That phrase should buy you enough time to find the appropriate tab for the objection.

Note: You can pick up some good phone techniques by simply watching and listening to top salespeople while they're on the phone. However, don't spend too much of your day sitting and listening. Your most important daily goal is to make as many phone calls as possible.

Mental Preparation

There's no getting around it—in telephone sales you will encounter a lot of rejections. As we've mentioned earlier in the book, begin your day early and on a positive note by reading something positive and informative that will improve your telemarketing skills. You need to have a healthy mental diet of reading material that will get you psyched up for the day.

Have a plan. You'll feel much more confident if you know what your focus will be during the day. Your plan will consist of:

- Your goals and objectives for the day, including your "to do" list.
- Any possible appointments to make return calls.
- The number of calls you need to make—do you have a daily quota?
- The number of leads you need to get.
- The number of accounts you need to open.
- The number of sales you need to make.

Part of your mental preparation may include facing your fear of calling people. If you are a little hesitant, refer to the heading "Getting Mentally Prepared to Cold Call" on page 57.

After you've mentally prepared by making a plan, take time to reflect upon one of phone sales' most positive features—and one that is unique to telephone selling:

The phone is a great place to hide. No matter how bad you sound, or how large a mistake you make, the person you've just called wouldn't know you even if you walked right past them thirty seconds later. One technique used by great telephone salespeople is to picture the lead card (or call list) as the actual prospect. They actually "talk" to the card while they talk to the prospect. This mind game helps to minimize the intimidation felt by calling a real person. After all, who's afraid of a 3" x 5" index card?

Great salespeople attack the phone, focus on the rewards of their efforts, and make call after call after call—nothing gets in their way. They see themselves as an unstoppable force, and they are determined to be extremely successful despite rejections or any other obstacles.

Now that you've mentally prepared to get on the phone, you need to prepare everything else.

Phone Attire

Despite the fact that we've suggested you can wear whatever makes you feel most comfortable, it is nevertheless true that your "phone" attire and physical appearance can have an impact on your attitude and when to make your overall telephone success. If you're dressed for success and feel good about the way you look, you'll be more confident, and the person on the other end of the phone will hear it in your voice. Dress well and make sure you're neat and clean. One way to approach this is imagining the impression you would make if your prospect suddenly dropped in on you for an in-person visit.

Your Surroundings

The right surroundings will have a positive impact on your phone selling. Surround yourself with an upbeat atmosphere. Soft, soothing, low-volume music is a good way to create a positive atmosphere. In front of you, have pictures of your goals, family, vacation destinations, and all the things you are working toward. Also, keep your work area clean, organized, and smelling good.

Phone Etiquette

Phone etiquette is straightforward and encompasses many of the basic principles we've discussed in other areas of this book. Here are the general rules:

1) **Be professional, pleasant, friendly, honest, straightforward and persistent, but never pushy.**

2) **Keep your mouth empty when you're on the phone.**

Don't eat food, chew gum, smoke, or do any other "mouth" activities while on the phone. People at the other end of the line can often hear these things. Also, they distract you from focusing 100 percent on your prospect.

3) Don't breathe directly into the mouthpiece while listening.

Hold the mouthpiece down below your chin. When you do speak, make sure you *do* hold the mouthpiece to your mouth so people can understand you.

4) Make sure you are in an environment that is conducive to communication.

Stay away from loud music and other distractions. As we mentioned, make the selling atmosphere as pleasant as possible.

5) Focus on the conversation.

Don't let your mind drift to last night's baseball game or what you're doing this weekend. *Listen hard* to the other person and really *hear* what he or she is saying.

6) Use the speaker phone as little as possible. More about this later.

Phone Physiology

People on the other end of the phone will receive a good impression of your physiology simply by hearing you speak. The next time you talk to someone on the phone, try to picture what her posture might be. You may be surprised at how often you'll be able to pick up on various aspects of physiology such as whether the person is sitting or standing and what expression is on her face. On the other end of the phone, you will hear energy, or a lack thereof, and other subtle indicators of willingness to buy. Your own physiology is equally important.

What are the keys to having good phone physiology?

1) Sit up straight or stand.

2) Keep your shoulders back, not slumped.

3) Breathe.

That's right, breathe. Many of us take short shallow breaths. This robs your body of oxygen and causes you to feel fatigued.

4) Smile!

People can hear you smiling on the other end of the phone. Place a small mirror on your desk where you can see yourself, and put a sticky note with the word *Smile* on it. While you are on the phone, look into the mirror as though you are looking at the person to whom you are speaking.

Make Your Phone Work Easier

Following are a few ideas that will make your phone work easier and more efficient:

1) Become familiar with your phone.

Where is the hold button, the flash button, the intercom button and other buttons you will need to use? Learn how to quickly dial local and long distance numbers, put a call on hold, set up a conference call, program phone numbers into your phone, forward calls, and so on.

This should be a quick review. In the beginning, just knowing how to dial local and long distance numbers and how to put someone on hold should be enough to get you started. Your primary objective is to get on the phone as soon as possible and start banging out numbers. Do not spend half your day figuring out all the intricacies of the phone. Learn phone techniques one at a time.

2) Decide whether the regular handset or headphones are best for you.

People who use headphones rather than a regular handset notice the following advantages:

- Your hands are free.
- You are able to move more freely, stand up, walk, and possibly multitask while you're talking. Those who favor the use of headphones believe they can have a more natural conversation.

If you are going to use a headset, you need to consider whether you should use a wired or wireless headset. Clearly, a wireless headset will give you much greater freedom to move around and even walk over to other people or other departments while you're on the phone. If someone calls your extension, and you're on the other side of the building with a wireless headset, you can still receive the call.

On the other hand, people who use the handset give the following advantages:

- They feel more involved in the conversation. They actually feel as though they are physically "holding on" to the conversation and thus have more control.
- Similarly, they feel closer and more connected to the person with whom they're talking.
- Many of us have been conditioned to use the handset; thus it feels more natural.

If you do use a handset, here are some gadgets that can maximize your effectiveness:

- A cushion on the earpiece to make it more comfortable.
- A device that makes it easier to rest the receiver on your shoulder, minimizing strain on the shoulder and neck muscles.
- A larger earpiece that covers the ear more fully and cuts down on background noise.
- A very long telephone cord can give you a lot of mobility. The long cord allows you to stand up and walk around while talking on the phone.

When using a handset, the way in which you hold the phone to your ear can affect your voice, your stress level, and your overall effectiveness on the phone. For best results hold the phone using one hand and press the phone lightly to your ear.

Using your shoulder to hold the phone to your ear can cause stress on your shoulder and neck muscles. Squeezing the phone or holding it too tightly against your ear can also become uncomfortable. If you cannot train yourself to relax your grip, try headphones.

Put some thought into the "headset versus handset" issue. Any extra small degree of comfort or convenience will go a very long way when you're making numerous phone calls throughout the day.

3) **Use a paperweight or another similar device in the phone cradle to hang up the phone after each phone call.**

Rather than placing the handset down after each call, you simply move the paperweight up and down in the cradle to hang up the phone or make the next call.

4) **Use the flash button to hang up the phone quickly before dialing the next number.**

5) **Another reminder: Place a mirror on your desk with the word *Smile* on it.**

Other Ways to Be at Your Best on the Phone

Following are some other ways to be more effective when selling over the phone;

1) **Keep your energy level high while on the phone.**

When you spend all day on the phone, you need to be able to stay alert and create energy at a moment's notice. So how do you stay energized?

a) **Maintain your health.**

Eating right, exercising, getting the proper amount of sleep, and taking care of your mental and emotional health are the keys to staying fit. If you keep your mind and body healthy, you'll have plenty of energy to carry you through your day.

b) **Move your body in ways that create energy.**

If you move as if you have energy, your mind and body will follow. When you need some quick energy, try the following:

- **Stand up and stretch.** Simply standing up will snap your body to attention. Use your standing position to stretch and flex.
- **Do some deep breathing.** Take ten deep breaths.
- **Make some quick movements.** Pump your fist, jump up and down, or come up with some of your own creative quick moves to wake yourself.

- **Make a fist, stretch, or flex any muscle group in your body.** All of these will get your blood flowing and your adrenaline pumping. A good five- or ten-minute walk will also work wonders for your energy. If you go for a walk, use the time to also recharge yourself psychologically. Repeat positive affirmations such as, *I feel great, I am the best*, or *I am doing the very best I can do today.* Create new affirmations of your own.

c) **Some other ideas for increasing energy quickly:**
- **Drink water.** Drinking water is a great way to revive yourself and get some quick energy.
- **Pick up the volume and pace of your speech.** Increasing speech volume and speed can greatly affect your energy level.

2) Have everything you need at your fingertips.

This includes contracts and all other paperwork, a calculator, a pen, something to write on, and anything else you can think of. You don't want to become distracted while you are busy searching for something—or worse, you have to put the prospect on hold.

3) Keep your desk clean and stay organized.

You don't want to be fumbling through things on your desk or flipping through paperwork while you're on the phone. Make sure your desk is organized *before you get on the phone*, and clean it up and reorganize it *before you quit* for the day.

4) Use your time wisely.

Being on the phone and talking with prospects and customers is the most productive thing you can do during business hours. Several times during the day, ask yourself: Is this the best use of my time right now? If not, move on to what *is* the best use of your time.

Here are some do's and don'ts of prime phone time:
- **Do** spend time on the phone talking with prospects and customers.
- **Don't** spend too much time on one call.

- **Do** take clear, concise, legible notes while talking to people on the phone. You need to learn how to take good notes at the same time as you are listening intently.
- **Don't** spend too much time making notes between phone calls.
- **Do** say what the top producers say on the phone.
- **Don't** take too much time out of your day simply listening to what they say and not making calls.
- **Don't** say what mediocre and poor salespeople say.
- **Do** keep the momentum going by making new calls immediately after you get a sale or lead.
- **Don't** take a break or get coffee after getting a sale or lead. You'll lose your momentum and energy.
- **Do** start work early. Try to get on the phone before everyone else.
- **Do** try to get a lead or some new business early in order to start off on the right foot.
- **Do** make phone calls after everyone else is done for the day.
- **Do** be a self-starter, and **don't** rely on others to get you motivated.
- **Don't** wait until after the morning meeting to get on the phone.
- **Do** stay focused throughout the day and stick to your plan.
- **Don't** "wing it" or ad lib throughout the day, trying to figure out what to do as you go.
- **Do** make your toughest call the first thing you do in the morning. Get it out of the way! This will help motivate you and charge you up for the rest of the day's calls.
- **Don't** put off the call you dread most until the end of the day.
- **Do** be persistent, **do** ask for the order, and **do** what it takes to get the leads and sales you need to be successful.
- **Do** be enthusiastic. **Do** have a burning desire and a passion to meet and exceed your goals and dreams.
- **Don't** be pushy and/or obnoxious; conversely, **don't** be meek and/or timid. Try to strike a middle ground no matter what is happening on the other end of your call.
- **Do** push yourself.
- **Do** one more thing, or make one more call, before leaving for the day.
- **Don't** procrastinate and put off today's tasks until tomorrow.

- **Do** take short five- to ten-minute breaks every two hours and **do** spend as much time as possible at your desk. This includes lunch and dinner breaks.
- **Don't** take fifteen-minute breaks every hour and don't take hour-long lunches.
- **Do** eat light, healthy snacks and small, healthy meals.
- **Don't** go for lunch or dinner at "all you can eat" establishments and stuff yourself to the point where you need a nap. Your goal is to remain alert, positive, and healthy throughout your selling day.
- Finally, **do** believe in yourself, your company, and your product.

Here are a few other timesaving ideas:

- Put frequently called numbers on speed dial.
- Let the phone ring a maximum of four times before you hang up.
- If cold calling, only hold a maximum of thirty to forty seconds when calling a work number and one minute when calling a home number.

Please refer to Chapter 3 letter d under #9 the heading, "Use Your Time Effectively" beginning on page 22 for more ideas on time management.

When to Make Phone Calls

As a general rule, the best time to call businesses is from 7:00 a.m. to 5:00 p.m. The best time to call residences is from 6:00 p.m. to 9:00 p.m.

These are general rules. If you're cold calling business owners, try them before and after the receptionist is there, which translates to before 8:00 a.m. and after 5:00 p.m. If you're calling on retirees, before 10:00 a.m., or 4:00 p.m. to 7:00 p.m. seem to work best.

Do not call residential lists during the day unless you are calling retirees. We know this sounds basic, but you'd be surprised how many people do this.

Be careful of the assumptions you make. Do not assume that all people take lunch from noon to 1:00 p.m. We've seen new salespeople take an hour for lunch because they believe no one is at their desk from noon to 1:00 p.m. Because of this erroneous thinking, they begin dreaming about lunch at 11:30 and don't get back into the swing of things until 1:30. So, in fact, they spend *two hours* eating lunch and shuffling papers. In this situation, the most important point to consider is that in some cases the only time prospects are at their desks is when they're eating lunch.

We have also known salespeople who assume prospects and customers don't want to hear from them first thing in the morning, especially on Mondays, or right at the end of the day, particularly on Fridays. Some people have lots of energy with which to pay attention on Monday mornings; others are looking forward to the weekend, are in a great mood, and thus are much more receptive on a Friday afternoon than at any other time of the week.

It's all right to take a break for lunch or dinner. But you still want to be on the phone during prime contact hours.

The only rule you really want to stick with is to refrain from calling residences after 9:00 p.m. (their time) unless the prospect or customer specifically asks you to call then.

Take Advantage of Different Time Zones

One of the advantages of telephone selling is the ability to call anywhere in the world. If your product or service offers you the ability to call across time zones, take advantage of this to maximize your sales.

Let's say you are marketing your product across the country. You now have access to every time zone from the New York to Hawaii. When it is 5:00 p.m. in New York, it's 11:00 a.m. in Hawaii. Here's a quick review. (Keep in mind that these zones are based on Standard Time. Adjust for Daylight Savings Time.)

- 5:00 p.m. CST is 6:00 p.m. EST
- 5:00 p.m. MST is 7:00 p.m. EST
- 5:00 p.m. PST is 8:00 p.m. EST
- 5:00 p.m. in parts of Alaska is 9:00 p.m. EST
- 5:00 p.m. in Hawaii is 11:00 p.m. EST

You could also call nighttime lists, or residences, across the country until 9:00 p.m. Hawaii time or 3:00 a.m. EST.

Adjust the above according to the time zone in which you work. If you're in Hawaii and you're calling businesses, you can start calling businesses in Eastern Time on the east coast starting at 7:00 a.m. EST or 1:00 a.m. Hawaii time.

Granted, this would add up to a long day. However, the point is to be aware of the advantages of working the different time zones and to take advantage of them whenever possible.

What to Do When You're Unsure of
How a Name Is Pronounced

If your goal is to reach as many people as possible because you are marketing a product that could apply to anyone, such as insurance, say either the first name or the last name, whichever you know how to pronounce. For example: if the name is John Schemmerhaumershmiten (slight exaggeration to make our point), simply say "Hi, is John there?" If the name is Theusaissenth Smith, say: "Hi, I was looking for Mr. Smith."

If you have a specific product for a specific target audience, you will handle names you don't know how to pronounce a little differently. In this case, use the approach we talked about under the heading "Name Pronunciation" on page 65. Have your cold call ready to go just in case they ask whether you would like to be connected. If they don't ask, and if you would like to be connected, simply call back later in the day and ask for the person using the correct name pronunciation.

How to Discover the Name of the Person
You Need to Cold Call

For this information, please refer to this same heading beginning on page 66 in the *Cold Call* Section.

What If You Don't Know the Name or the Title of the
Person with Whom You Should Talk?

For this information, please refer to this same heading beginning on page 68 the *Cold Call* Section.

Sources of Names and Calling Lists

For this information, please refer to this same heading beginning on page 69 in the *Cold Call* Section.

Chapter 43

Calling Prospects

Getting through the Receptionist

The receptionist can be one of your biggest stumbling blocks when cold calling. If the receptionist decides not to let you through, there'll be no cold call, no lead, and no sale. Here, we provide some suggestions to get past the receptionist.

1) **Avoid the receptionist.**

   a) **Call when the receptionist isn't there.**

   Call before the receptionist arrives at work or after she has left. Most receptionists start at 8:00 or 9:00 a.m. and work until 5:00 p.m. Thus, if you call before 8:00 or 9:00 and after 5:00 p.m., often you won't have to deal with the receptionist at all. The problem is most people work the same hours as the receptionist. This "call early, call late" technique works best with owners and other high-level executives who often work early and stay late. Other employees may be difficult to reach with this method, but it's worth a try.

   b) **Ask for a salesperson.**

   As a general rule, most salespeople like to help other salespeople. When the receptionist answers the phone, ask to speak with a salesperson. When you get the salesperson on the phone, use a brief description to tell her who you are and what company you're with. Then ask whom you should be talking with about your product.

   c) **Dial direct extensions.**

   Many companies now have voice mail systems that allow you to dial direct extensions by number or by dialing in the letters of person's last name. Typically, upper-level executives and owners still have their own receptionists who answer their extension. The nice thing is that they are usually the people who work off-hours when the receptionist is not there.

In general, the best way to reach executives without being screened is by calling off-hours. The best way to reach everyone else is by calling the direct extension during regular business hours.

Note: If you call during off-hours when the receptionist isn't there, you will get the voice mail system and will likely be able to get individual extensions.

d) Ask for the "wrong" extension.

Another approach to getting around the receptionist is to ask for a random extension. Then, once you've been transferred, have the person at the "wrong" extension transfer you to the right one.

For example, let's imagine you're trying to get to Sue Smith, the COO. Call the main number and ask for extension 222. When the person at extension 222 answers say, "Oh, I'm sorry. I had asked to be transferred to Sue Smith."

That person will either transfer you or give you Sue's extension. And if you give the receptionist an extension such as 222 and she says there's no such extension, say, "Hmm, I'm having a little trouble reading the writing here. In any case, I'm trying to reach Sue Smith."

At that point, the receptionist will be much more focused on the extension than the person you are asking for and will usually transfer you without screening the call.

e) Change a company phone number slightly to get people's direct extensions.

If the main switchboard number ends in 5600, try 5601, 02, 03, and so on. Often, upper-level executives have extensions that are one or two digits away from the main number.

As well, the phone extension of the top executive's secretary is often one or two numbers from the executive's. If you find out her extension, change it by one or two numbers to get the top executive's extension. To find out her extension, do the following:

Call the main number and ask for the top executive. When the secretary answers, use the usual tactics to try to get beyond her to her boss. If that doesn't work, say you would like to send some information to "Mr. Prospect." Once she gives the okay, ask for the correct mailing address.

Next, suggest that you would like to send it to her attention and that you hope she'll get it to him. Most secretaries will agree to this because they are doing their job of running interference between you and the top executive. Finally, ask her for her direct extension. You'll likely need it in the future.

If she will not give you her direct extension, try this approach. For this example, let's say her name is Mary Jane Smith. Call back later in the day and say, "Hi, I was trying to get Mary Jane Smith. I had her extension here somewhere but I seem to have misplaced it. Can you give it to me, please?"

If the person says she'll transfer you, say, "Thank you. That's great and for future reference, can I get her extension?"

That should work. And if she does transfer you and Mary Jane answers the phone, just tell her who you are again, mention that you'd called earlier, then ask for some information about the top executive such as his official title. The call might go something like this: "Hi Mary Jane. This is Bob Jones again with ABC Company. For the letter I'm addressing to Joe Executive, I was just wondering, is Joe's title CEO or President and CEO?"

Once you have the receptionist's extension, call before or after business hours and dial one number above or below her extension to see if you can get the top executive's direct line.

Note: In this case, you want to send something to the top executive, but make sure it is only basic information. By sending information, you are doing what you told the receptionist you would do, thus not "losing face" with her. By sending the receptionist only basic information, you will not give the top executive enough information to make a decision about your offer before you call back. Of course, you won't be mentioning the information when you call him back anyway. We'll discuss this later.

Changing a company phone number by a number or two also works well if you have someone's extension and you are trying to reach another person in their department or someone of similar rank.

For example, if you can't get to Rob in the IT Department, you may want to try his counterpart, Jill. The problem is the switchboard isn't open yet, or you're in endless loop voice mail and can't get her direct extension. If Rob's number ends with 5632, try 5633 or 5631. Even if you don't get Jill, often you will get someone who can get her or give you her direct extension.

Another technique to get the prospect's extension is to call the switchboard and say, "Hi, this is (your name) with (your company). I'm calling because I forgot Mr. Top Executive's extension." Typically, they will either give it to you or transfer you to the prospect or the prospect's secretary.

2) Follow proper rules when talking to the receptionist.

a) Be pleasant and professional, and have a smile on your face when you speak to the receptionist.

Be businesslike, but not to the point of sounding stern, harsh, or rude. Never speak to the receptionist as if she is a nuisance that you'd rather avoid altogether. You also don't need to take it to the other extreme where you're being overly friendly and nice. Use your judgment and maintain a pleasant, professional approach.

b) Be direct, succinct, and conversational.

You want to be on the phone with the receptionist for the shortest amount of time possible. The first words out of your mouth should be a simple request to be sent through to the prospect. For example, ask, "Hi, Jim Smith, please."

That's it. Don't try to befriend the receptionist or win her over. Also, don't make any comments about the weather or anything else non-business related. Very few people can ask such questions and not sound phony. Be pleasant, professional, have a smile on your face, and speak in a friendly tone. Stick to business.

c) If you are asked a question, give the receptionist just enough information, but not too much.

After you ask for the prospect, you may get some questions from the receptionist. Answer any questions in a very matter-of-fact tone. Here are a few sample situations.

First situation: The prospect does not know you at all and is probably not familiar with the name of your company either.

Receptionist: "And may I ask who's calling?"
You: "Yes, it's (your first and last name)."
Receptionist: "And does he know you?"
You: Well, I'm with (the name of your company).
     You didn't actually answer her question. However, psychologically, what she's likely to hear in that response is, "The prospect has a relationship with my company and I'm calling on the company's behalf."
Receptionist: "And can I ask what this is about?"
You: "Yes, I'm just calling to briefly touch base. Is he in?"
     This comment makes it sound as though you are calling to update the prospect on something in particular that you might be working on for him.

In the next two situations, the only part that will change is your response to the question: "And does he know you?"

Second situation: The prospect does not know you; however, he is most likely familiar your company. For example, your company might be a large supplier to the industry that everyone is familiar with, or your company might be a household name such as IBM.

Receptionist: "And can I ask who's calling?"
You: "Yes, it's (your first and last name)."
Receptionist: "And does he know you?"
You: "Well, he knows my company (the name of your company)."

Third situation: You have met the prospect before and there is a very good chance he remembers you.

Receptionist: "And may I ask who's calling?"
You: "Yes, it's (your first and last name)."
Receptionist: "And does he know you?"

You: "Yes, he does."

If you get through and the prospect says, "I don't know you. Why did you tell my receptionist that?" Simply remind him where and when you met.

Note: Most sales books will tell you that if you get a question from the receptionist, you are to give a quick response and then come back with another question of your own. Here is an example of what we're talking about:

> **You:** "Hi, Mr. Smith, please."
> **Receptionist:** "Can I ask who's calling?"
> **You:** "Yes, Bob Chapin. May I speak with him please?"

We *do not* recommend this approach. Not only is it confrontational, it is also a red flag that you are a salesperson. If the receptionist doesn't like you, thinks you're a salesperson, or both, your odds of getting through to the prospect are remote. Your overall objective is *to get past the receptionist*. The best way to do this is by being pleasant and low key, and by flying under the radar. If you don't sound like a typical salesperson, you won't be treated like one.

You can and should ask a question after you answer the third question from the receptionist. The question we recommend is: "Is (he or she) in?"

After answering three questions, the receptionist should expect any normal human being to come back with a question. Here is an example we used earlier:

> **You:** Hi, Jim Smith, please.
> **Receptionist:** And can I ask who's calling?
> **You:** Yes, it's (your first and last name).
> **Receptionist:** And does he know you?
> **You:** Well, I'm with (the name of your company).
> **Receptionist:** And can I ask what this is about?
> **You:** Yes, I'm just calling to briefly touch base. Is he in?

Occasionally you will run across a secretary who says something like, "Look, if you're selling something, Ms. Johnson isn't interested."

This probably blows 90-plus percent of the salespeople off the phone. You need to be different at this point and take at least one shot at this. When you get a line like that say, "I'm not calling to sell (prospect's name) anything; I'm simply calling to introduce myself. If she could extend me the courtesy of a few minutes of her time, I'd really appreciate it."

d) Do not misrepresent yourself.

We know a salesperson who got the mayor of a major city on the phone by saying he was with another major city's mayoral office. Creative, but not a good idea. The mayor got on the phone, realized she'd been lied to, obtained the salesperson's name and whom he worked with, and called his boss and boss's boss. The outcome was that the salesperson got into trouble and gave his company as well as its salespeople a bad name. Never say you're someone you're not or use any other misrepresentation to get through to someone.

3) Use the "amateur" approach to get through the receptionist.

This approach requires you to sound like the very opposite of what a silver-tongued salesperson would sound like. Of course, you don't want to sound like a silver-tongued salesperson to begin with, but if you do, the amateur approach would sound quite the opposite.

The approach is similar to the one you use when calling associations for directories. Here is an example: "Yes…hi…um…I'm looking for someone who handles your printing supplies? Um, would you be able to help me with that?"

The last thing you want to sound like is a salesperson cold calling someone. Granted, the approach doesn't work too well if you're calling CEOs, COOs, Senior Vice Presidents, and other people in similar positions. You want to use this approach when you are calling mid-level people and you don't have a specific name. For example, "Hi…um…I was looking for someone in accounts receivable? Could you help me with that?"

When you ask for mid-level titles you will probably get screened, but not as harshly as if you're calling on upper level executives. If you are asking for mid-level titles and you throw the receptionist off with a different approach such as the one we're suggesting here, there's a better chance that you *won't* get screened.

4) Send a letter and let the prospect know you will be calling.

You can also send a letter requesting an appointment. Please refer to page 143 for ideas on this and a sample letter.

5) Do something unique that sets you apart from other salespeople.

You can get the prospect's attention by sending gifts, packages, and by coming up with other creative ideas to get your foot in the door. For more ideas please refer to the following headings in the *Cold Call* section:

- Creative ideas to crack that account when all else fails—page 129.
- Become involved in businesses to which you'd like to sell—page 131.

Always Start at the Top

Please refer to item 2 on page 64, Always start at the top.

Ask for the Prospect Using His First Name When Calling Residences

By far the most effective way to get to the prospect on the phone is by asking for the person by his or her first name.

Many people believe that in order to show respect you need to ask for Mr., Mrs., or Ms. (last name). The problem is that when you call and ask for someone by his or her last name, you have immediately tipped the person off that you are a telemarketer. Even if the person you're seeking answers the phone, the most likely response will be: "I'm sorry, but he's not here right now. May I take a message?"

Here are some *incorrect* ways to ask for someone on a cold call followed by the right way when you're calling residences.

- "Hi, is Mr. Smith in?"
- "Hi, is Mr. Smith in? This is Joe Harvey with ABC Company."

Or if you think the person you're looking for has answered the phone:

- "Hello, Mr. Smith?"

In these examples, asking for the person by their last name, as well as any other additional information you add, is incorrect.

Here is the correct way to ask for the prospect if you are calling a residence:

- "Hello, is Joe there?"

Here's the correct way if you are calling a residence and you think the prospect may be the one who's just answered the phone:

- "Hi, Joe?"

If you have been asking for people by their last names and you switch to using their first names, we *guarantee* your contact rate will rise significantly. We have seen people double, triple, or even quadruple their contact rate using this method.

Note: Occasionally you'll run into a first name that may vary. For example, people with the first name James may go by either Jim or James. In a case such as this, play the odds. Since most people with the name James go by "Jim," ask for Jim. Yes, you may anger a "James" or two. But asking for Mr. Last Name will almost definitely get you nowhere.

Similar names are Michael, David, John, and Richard. While occasionally you may actually get a Michael, David, or Jack, go with the odds—Mike, Dave, and John. Richard can be a little more difficult as you can get Rich, Rick, or Dick. In this case ask for Rich.

When you're calling prospects at home, you want your voice to be friendly and upbeat, yet laid back. When asking for the person, pretend you're asking for a friend. How do you call and ask for friends? Usually something like, "Hi, is (first name) there?" in a friendly, upbeat tone.

Ask for the Prospect Using His First and Last Name
When Calling Businesses

Here are the correct ways to ask for a prospect if you are calling a business:

- "Hi, is Joe Smith there?"
- "Hi, Joe Smith, please."

All the other rules above apply. Pretend you are asking for a friend and play the odds with regard to the names people go by.

Leaving Effective Messages on Cold Calls

Leaving Effective Messages with the Receptionist

There are three rules to follow when leaving a message with the receptionist. They are:

- Be professional.
- Speak with confidence.
- Catch the prospect's attention with the message you leave.

You must set yourself apart from other salespeople and present yourself as someone important enough to warrant a return call. Here is an example of a message: "Can you please tell her that Bob Chapin from ABC Company called? My number is 555-555-1234. We've been doing business with both XYZ and PQR in the area and I wanted to talk to her about something I think she'll find very interesting."

With this message, we dropped names of companies in the area that the prospect would be familiar with, as well as using a teaser: "I wanted to talk to her about something I think she'll find very interesting."

Use any leverage you have, such as companies you're doing business with, endorsements you've received, or other benefits.

Leaving Effective Messages on Voice Mail

If you're going to leave a voice mail message for someone with whom you've never spoken before, you'd better give that person a good reason to call you back. In other words, you need to catch the prospect's attention and create enough interest.

When leaving a voice mail message, give a benefit and build some credibility. For example, if you work for an office supply company, you might say something like, "Hello, Mr. Prospect. This is Joe Smith from ABC Company. We work with XYZ and DEF companies in your area and are saving them over 35 percent on office products. I believe we can also save you a significant amount of money. My number is 555-555-1234. Thanks for giving me a call."

Clearly, it would be best to get a referral from one or more of the companies in your area. However, this should give you a general idea. Also, if you are endorsed by someone in the industry, you could mention that. Look at opening lines under Cold Calls in this section and in the *Cold Call* section earlier in the book.

One other note: In the above example, we simply asked the person to call back and left a number. Some sales books will tell you to leave a specific time to return your call in order to give the impression that you're busy. That's fine, especially if you know you won't be in all day. If that is the case, and you believe the person may get your voice mail, you could request that the person call you back at a certain time and then say, "In the event that you do get my voice mail, please let me know the best time to reach you and I will try you back then."

Your overall objective on the voice message is to be brief, build interest, build credibility, and then ask the person to call you back.

Here are some other ideas for voice mail messages:

1) Use humor.

Humor in your voice mail message can work with the right people. Driver and Partier personality types are usually good with humor. Thinkers tend to find humor obnoxious and "Yes" People can be uneasy with it. If you know the personality type of the prospect, and they are a Driver or Partier, use some humor.

It is a good idea to use humor on a second or third call when the person hasn't called you back. You could say, "Hello, Mr. Prospect. This is Jim Jones over at ABC Company again. And again, we save companies an average of 35 percent on office supplies. Of course, you already know that from my previous messages. The reason I'm calling again is that my boss won't let me leave until I talk to you live. Please call me at 555-555-1234. My dog misses me."

You can come up with all sorts of ideas from "I'm going on a hunger strike" to "I'm going to hold my breath." You can finish with, "By the way, if you don't call back today, please make a donation to your favorite charity in lieu of flowers to the funeral home."

You can also get a joke book and let the prospect know you want to give him the joke of the day or, give the first half of the joke and tell him when he calls you back he'll get the second half. Again, still include your name, company name, phone number, and number one benefit.

2) Leave an abbreviated message.

Here is an example: "Hi Joe, this is Bob Chapin. My number is 508-555-4321. I wanted to talk to you about" then hang up. The person, believing you got disconnected, may call you back. Another approach is to leave your name and number, mention your primary benefit, and then hang up. Example: "Hi Joe, this is Bob Chapin. My number is 508-555-4321. In your area we've been saving customers over 35 percent on…" Then hang up. Some people think this is deceptive, so use your best judgment.

3) Offer an incentive to call you back.

Baseball tickets, golf, and similar incentives can be a great way to get someone to call you back. Granted, those may be a little high priced to throw at a cold call, but if it's an important enough cold call and an account you've been trying to get into for a while, you might want to give it a try.

4) Use urgency.

This point is best illustrated by an example. We know of one stockbroker who built up a sizable stock position in a particular company. One day he had some questions so he called the President and left a message with his secretary. He basically said, "I'm a broker with (the company he was with) and I'd like to ask Mr. Henry some questions."

After not receiving a phone call all day, he called the following day and left pretty much the same message. After another day passed without a call, he called back, left his name and number again and then said the following to the receptionist: "My clients and I own over ten million shares of your stock. Tell Mr. Henry that if he doesn't call me back today, I'm selling all of it."

Guess what? Mr. Henry called back about a minute later. What happened? Well, for one thing, the broker gained some credibility. For another, he finally gave Mr. Henry a "good reason" to call him back. By the way, they became very good friends.

Note: If you're going to say something like that, make sure it's the truth.

Other Important Points on *All* Voice Mail Messages

These points relate to *all* voice mail messages, not just ones you leave while cold calling.

1) When leaving a voice mail message, talk at your normal pace until you get to important information.

When you give your phone number or other critical information, slow down and make sure you are speaking very clearly. We're sure you've received voice mail messages where you only caught eight or nine of the necessary ten digits in the person's phone number. Don't let that happen with your phone number or other important information you leave on a message. Also, always say the phone number twice just in case a piece of it got cut off the first time.

2) Get to the point quickly.

We're sure you've also received some messages in which the person took forever to get to the point. Make your phone messages short and give only necessary details.

3) Give your name and phone number at the beginning of the message.

Start with, "Hi Cindy, Bob Chapin at ABC Company. My number is (555) 555-5555" and then go into your message. This way, if you happen to get disconnected while leaving the message, the person knows how to get in touch with you.

An Example of a Good Message

Here's a message that a woman from a dating agency leaves every six months or so on one of our voice mails: "Hi John, Judy Shea. I figured I'd give you a call. I don't know whether that relationship worked out for you. My number is 555-567-8765. Thanks for giving me a call."

The message is to the point, delivered in a sincere manner, and the last line: "Thanks for giving me call," which we also used at the end of our earlier message, is the best way we've ever heard of to politely ask someone to call you back.

Incidentally, Judy has been calling since 1996. I've bought four cars in that time frame. If the first car salesperson had stayed in touch, not only would he have made the subsequent sales, he probably would have made some to friends and family too.

What If You Can't Get Someone to Return Your Call?

If you've left several messages and can't get someone to call you back, you may want to spend your time elsewhere. However, if you've decided this person is still worth chasing, give these ideas a try.

1) Find out when the prospect will be in the office.

It's possible that you're getting voice mail because the person is never in the office. Get to the receptionist and ask when the prospect will be in, then call at that time.

2) Call the prospect every hour.

Please refer to the heading, "Getting in Touch with the Hard-to-Reach *Hot* Prospect" beginning on page 129.

3) Call before normal business hours, at lunch, or after business hours.

It's possible that these are the only times the prospect is at his or her desk.

4) Show up in person.

If you continue to try to get to someone and he or she won't return your calls, show up in person if it is feasible to do so.

5) Send a letter.

This was discussed when we talked about getting through the receptionist. The idea here is to send a letter to pique the prospect's interest and then follow it up with a phone call. This is similar to the letter on page 147.

6) Send a creative fax.

Fax half of a joke of the day with the promise to give the other half when they call you back. (If someone other than the prospect calls back for the joke, say you've taken a blood oath to give it only to the prospect.) You can also fax testimonials or a reference letter. Another idea is to fax your schedule and let the person mark off a good appointment time and fax it back. Make sure to include all your contact information on your faxes.

7) Call from a plane or foreign country.

Granted, you don't want to be making dozens of calls via this method because it can get expensive. At the same time, if you're trying to reach a prospect with great potential and you're looking to impress him, it is a great way to get noticed. If you get voice mail again, leave a message complete with where you're calling from and let the person know either how they can reach you or that you'll call back.

8) Try some of our creative cold call techniques discussed under the heading, "Creative Ideas to Crack That Big Account When All Else Fails," beginning on page 129.

When *Not* to Leave a Voice Mail Message

If you have an unlimited market, which is usually the case with industries such as securities and insurance, and you are cold calling and trying to maximize the number of people you reach, do not leave voice mail messages.

First, very few people will return unsolicited phone calls for these "mass market" type of products, and second, to have people returning your calls when you are attempting to make as many outbound calls as possible is both confusing and counterproductive.

Always Get the Receptionist's Name at the End of the First Unsuccessful Call

If you have made one attempt to get to the prospect on the phone and plan on making another, always get the name of the receptionist at the end of the first call. Simply say to the receptionist, "Thank you for your help. Oh, and I'm sorry, what's your name?" When you call back, use her name.

Calling the Prospect the Second Time

If the prospect does not return your call, by all means, call again. This time, after getting the receptionist's name on the first call, open up with her name and ask for the prospect. "Hi, Cindy?" After she answers you, continue with, "This is Bob Chapin again from ABC Company. Is Jim Smith available?"

If she says he isn't, ask her what time you should call back but do it in such a way that it doesn't sound like you have nothing better to do with your time. "Hmm, let's see. I'm going to be in meetings and running around for most of the day. When do you think would be the best time to reach him?"

You want to give the impression that you are busy and important and command enough respect that she'll give you an answer. If she doesn't think you're all that important, she may just give you an answer like, "I really don't know. Mr. Smith is pretty busy all the time."

Note: If someone other than the receptionist you spoke to the first time answers the phone, simply ask to speak with the prospect.

Chapter 44

Talking to the Prospect

Your Cold Call

Once you've gotten through to the prospect, your real work begins. At this point you should have your binder open with your *Cold Call* script in front of you. Refer to the heading "Your Cold Call Script" on page 74 for more information. Also refer to Chapter 9 for ideas on talking to the prospect.

Note 1: Some of your lines will vary slightly from their face-to-face counterparts. For example, instead of: "Hi, Mr. Prospect. Bob Chapin with ABC Company. Very nice to meet you. We have been saving companies in your industry an average of 36 percent on office supplies," you will say, "Hi, Mr. Prospect. This is Bob Chapin with ABC Company. We have been saving companies in your industry an average of 36 percent on office supplies."

The difference in the second sentence is the addition of "this is" and the removal of "Very nice to meet you." These are small changes but ones that make your call sound better when on the phone.

You'll want to make the same changes to other similar lines mentioned in the *Cold Call* section.

Note 2: *Why* you are calling and your commitment question will also vary slightly from a face-to-face call. For example, instead of: "All I'd like to do today is set up a time when I could spend about fifteen minutes with you to determine if and how much we could help you. Could we take a look at your schedule right now?"

You would say something more along the lines of: "All I'd like to do today is get some information to you on our company and what we're all about. I think you'd find it very interesting. Would that be okay?"

Alternatively, you could say, "I'm going to be in your area next Tuesday and I'd like to show you specifically how much money we may be able to save you. Would the morning at ten or the afternoon at two be better?"

Once you put it all together, your entire opening would be similar to the following example: "Hi, Joe. This is Bob Chapin with ABC Company. Joe, we've been saving companies such as yours an average of 34 percent on information storage and backup. I'm going to be in your area next Tuesday and I'd like to show you specifically how much money we may be able to save you. Would the morning at ten or the afternoon at two be better?"

A Note on Qualifying over the Phone

Prospects may not be willing to give you much information over the phone, especially about their financial situation. They might say something like, "I don't give out that kind of information over the phone to someone I don't know."

While it's true that you don't want to come on too strong with someone who may be sensitive to discussing her financial information, you also don't want to back down completely. If you back down on the cold call, you'll call the person back in a week, only to hear, "Gee, that sounds great but I have no money."

In a situation where someone does not want to discuss finances, say the following: "Mr. Prospect, I appreciate that and I definitely don't need any personal or specific financial information at this point. My only real question is, is there some money around if I can show you (the primary benefit of your product)?"

In addition to money, some people are sensitive about discussing other things (for example, the state of their health) over the phone with people they know don't know well. If the discussion relates directly to information you must have to qualify someone, use a soft approach but stick to your guns as we did in the example above.

Another approach is to build some more rapport, send out some information about your company in order to build credibility, and then obtain the final pieces you need during a second or follow-up call. Again, make sure the prospect is qualified before you spend a lot of time doing your presentation.

Building Rapport with the Prospect

Building rapport with the prospect is one of the key objectives during your cold call. You build rapport by showing the prospect that you are like her, you can help her, you have her best interests in mind, and you can be trusted.

Keep in mind that when you are selling via the telephone, you will be judged by what you say and how you say it. If you talk extremely fast and the prospect talks very slowly, you will have a rapport problem no matter what other positive things you have going for you. If you have the greatest product in the world, you might be able to convince the prospect of that, but you'll need to break down the "voice" barrier first. Put another way, you have to speak the same language as the prospect.

For detailed information on building rapport, please refer to the following headings and pages in the *Cold Calling* section:

- Mirroring speech—page 97.
- Speech factors that alienate you from the prospect—page 98.
- Topics of discussion to avoid—page 101.

Find Similarities between You and the Prospect

After ensuring your voice and the overall tone of your language are agreeable with your prospect, the next step will be to search for similarities between you and the prospect.

This is not as easy over the phone as in person. When you call on someone in person you can look around the person's office and see pictures, awards, and various other items that will tip you off as to the prospect's hobbies, interests, education, family, and other similar facts. Over the phone you won't have these visual clues so you have to rely on the information you *do* have.

For example, let's say you happen to be calling someone in the town where you grew up. You could say, "I notice you're in Madison. I was actually born there. Are you from there originally, by any chance?"

From there you can learn where the prospect is from, where he or she went to school, and then bridge into interests and activities. After the opening question above, your side of the conversation might go as follows: "I actually went to school at the University of Wisconsin. Did you go to school in Wisconsin?" (Wait for a reply.) "Oh, you went to Minnesota. Great hockey team. Did you play any sports or were you involved in any other activities up there?"

These questions help to build the personal side of the relationship and help the prospect to feel comfortable with you. Here are more examples of rapport-building questions:

- "Where are you from originally?" (If someone is from somewhere other than this country, you can ask these follow-up questions.)
- "How long have you been here?"
- "Do you like it here?"

- "Do you think you will stay here?"
- "How large is your family?"
- "How old are your children?"

In addition to the example above in which we used the town you are calling, you may also know what company the prospect works at. Do you have *any* connection at all with the company that you can fall back on? You can also ask how long the prospect has been at that company and then ask what other companies he has been with. You may have some connections with the other companies if not the present one.

What about the person's name? Do you know anyone with the same last name? Even if the person you know is from another part of the country, you can ask if the prospect has relatives there. Also, listen for accents that may give you an idea of someone's background.

You can also ask about sports teams in the area in which you are calling the person. Local events are another good subject to hit.

Don't ask too many questions here but ask enough to get some good background information and build a personal connection. Listen to how someone is responding to you. If you have someone who is willing to talk, you can extend the conversation. On the other hand, if you have someone who is not too talkative, ask a couple of questions, get some information, and move on.

Write down the information you get in a place where you'll be able to refer to it on future calls.

These are some of the more common ideas. It truly is a small world, as you've surely discovered in some situations. Start probing with the above questions and see what turns up. When you do finally hit a common area of interest or knowledge the rapport will begin to build quickly, and that is your key objective here.

Note: For more information on rapport-building questions, refer to "What Is the Prospect *Really* Interested In?" on page 103.

A Quick Note on Questions

Asking the right questions during the cold call conveys an image of professionalism and caring. These are two of the most important factors in building rapport with a prospect. As the saying goes: "People don't care how much you know until they know how much you care." By asking the right questions and actively listening, you will convey the right message and people will both open up to you and want to do business with you.

If you already have great questions and great listening skills, terrific—keep working on these strengths. If your questioning and listening skills could use some work, do everything you can to improve both. These two skills will pay enormous dividends.

Please refer to "Asking Questions and Listening to the Prospect" on pages 107 through 111 of the *Cold Call* section for more key information on this subject.

Name-dropping in Your Opening

Please refer to page 106 of the *Cold Call* section for information on this.

Personality Types

Please refer to "Identifying the Personality Type of the Prospect" on pages 113 to 121 of the *Cold Call* section. While much of that section will cover visual cues to identifying personality types, there are some verbal cues discussed that you will be able to pick up over the phone.

Note: The key point to keep in mind with personality types is that some people prefer a more direct, business selling experience while others prefer a more indirect, rapport-building or personal style.

Also, refer to the sections titled: "I See, I Feel, I Hear" on page 123, "How Age Affects Your Prospect's Focus" on page 123.

The Conclusion of the Cold Call

Conclude your cold call by thanking the prospect for her time and letting her know how you will be following up. Your conclusion will be short and explain what will happen next.

Here is an example of a conclusion to a cold call: "It was great speaking with you today, Cindy. I'll get the information out to you today and I'll give you a call back in about a week or so to make sure you received it, okay?" (Wait for response.) "Great. Cindy, thanks for your time today, and you'll be glad we spoke."

Your Cold Call in a Nutshell

When all is said and done, your cold call should contain the following:

- Your name.
- Your company name.
- Your primary benefit.
- Why you're calling followed by a commitment question.
- Some discussion to determine interest.
- Qualifying.
- Rapport building.
- Closing on the next step.
- A strong final statement.

Your cold call should:

- Be brief.
- Spark some interest.
- Build rapport.
- Help you discover how ready, willing, and able the prospect is to purchase your product or service.
- Bridge to the next step in the selling process.

An Important Note

As we've mentioned several times throughout this section, please refer to the *Cold Call* Section for more information. Although some of the information is repeated here, we go into great detail on all subjects related to cold calling in that section.

What If You Cold Call Someone Who Already Has an Account with Your Company?

If you cold call someone who already has an account with you, turn the call into a service call. Here's an example of how your side of the conversation might go once the prospect tells you she has an account with you: "Oh, that's great. Who handles your account? How long have you been with us? Have you been happy with the service we've been providing?" Assuming you got a positive answer to this question, follow with, "Great. Well, Mr. Customer, thank you very much for using our company and I'll be sure to let (the name of their representative) know we spoke. Have a nice day."

Note 1: If you got a negative response to the question about being happy with the service, get some specific information and let the customer know that you will pass this on to the representative.

Note 2: Occasionally a prospect will say, "I already work with your company" just to get rid of you, and that's why it's a good idea to ask who they are working with from your company. It's also possible that someone may think they have an account with your company when they don't. That's another good reason to ask a question or two.

Make Sure They're with You on the Cold Call

There may be times when you'll wonder if the person on the other end of the phone is really interested and paying attention, or if she's simply trying to be nice and get you off the phone as soon as possible.

When you find yourself in this situation, you can test the waters by incorrectly reading back some information the prospect gave you. For example, let's say you're going to mail the prospect some information and she gave you an address of 123 Main St., Auburn, Massachusetts, 01501. You might read it back as 231 Main Street and see if the prospect catches it. If she does, she's paying attention and she's with you. If she doesn't, she's not listening to you and you either need to get her attention and interest quickly or resign yourself to the fact that you probably don't have a great lead.

Rather than waiting until the end of the cold call, when you're getting mailing information, you can also use this technique earlier in the conversation. If you ask for her best investment and she says, "Oh, I don't know. It was probably a stock I had about ten years ago. I think it was XYZ Company and it did pretty well." You can come back with, "What was that, ABC Company?" Again, as in the example above, if she corrects you at least she's listening to some degree; if she doesn't, you don't have her attention.

Note: Use this only once during a cold call. People will get tired of correcting you and they'll start to think either you're not too bright or you're not listening to them.

The Tough Prospect

Occasionally, you'll run into the extremely difficult, even rude prospect. Although you don't want to spend too much time with these prospects, you do want to at least test them and find out if you can break through their hard shell. You want to make an attempt because 99 percent of salespeople would give up *immediately* under similar circumstances. As a result, if you can get past the initial rudeness, you may actually find a decent customer.

When the prospect lashes out with "G!@#$ D!@##$!! You're the ninth salesperson that's called me today!" respond with, "Mr. Prospect, I couldn't agree more. I've actually got a ton of salespeople that call me, believe it or not, and it is a major pain in the butt. At the same time, I'll bet we have something in common."

If the prospect hasn't hung up by now and says, "What's that?" reply with, "I don't like making these calls anymore that you like getting them." Then continue with, "Let me ask you just one quick question," then ask if the prospect would be interested in one of your main benefits. For example, you might say, "If I could guarantee a savings of 40 percent or more on office supplies, would you be interested?"

You may get a yes, no, maybe, or the prospect may just hang up, but *you have to at least take a shot.* If you run into someone who gives you objection after objection on the cold call, you probably want to let that person go. On the other hand, if someone gives only you one or two objections, hang in there and take a shot at them.

Your Cold Call Follow-up Letter and Information

The follow-up letter and information you send out after your cold call should be short and succinct. The point of your follow-up information is not to sell anything, it is to:

- Pique interest.
- Add credibility to you and your company.
- Serve as a reminder of you and your phone call.
- Touch the prospect one more time through a different medium.
- Build the relationship a little further.

In most cases, your follow-up letter and information will be no more than a letter on 8.5″ x 11″ paper with a tri-fold brochure and your business card included. Your information should fit in a standard envelope. Obviously, what you send will depend upon what you're selling. If you're selling financial services, your information will probably be a bit different than if you're selling replacement windows. Overall, you want something that looks professional, is clean, crisp, clear, and builds interest but doesn't sell the product—that's your job.

If possible, send your follow-up letter and other information on the same day as your call. The latest it should go out is the next day. That being said, it's important that you don't take time out from prime phone time to put letters together and assemble your mailing package. If you have a secretary or someone else who can assemble the information for you, that's good. Otherwise, put the letters together in the evening after prime calling hours.

The letter and other information must arrive before your next contact, whether it is an in-person meeting or another phone call. If need be, fax the letter, drop it off personally, or send it by overnight or two-day courier, whichever is appropriate to get it there before your next contact.

Please refer to the next page for an example of a follow-up letter with related notes.

Sample Follow-up Letter

(Start with your company information.)

Complete Selling, Inc.
27 Curtis St., Auburn, MA 01501
(508) 555-7982
(**Note:** Stay away from P.O. boxes here. Use an actual street address. Also stay away from apartment numbers. If it's apartment 20, make it Suite 20.)

June 12, 2008

Mr. John Jartz (Always use Mr., Ms., Mrs., Dr., etc.)
XYZ Company (Alternatively, use the person's full name including middle initial.)
President (Obviously, skip company and title if sending to a residential prospect.)
1 N. Main St.
PO Box 68
Worcester, MA 01604

Dear Mr. Jartz,

It was a pleasure speaking with you today concerning office supplies.

As I mentioned, Complete Selling, Inc. has been saving companies an average of 38 percent. I look forward to sitting down with you next Tuesday at 10:00 a.m. to discuss how we may be able to help you and XYZ Company.

If you have any questions or comments before then, please give me a call.

Sincerely,

(Your signature. Make sure you sign your letters. Use blue ink.)

Robert J. Chapin
(508) 555-6403
(Include your direct line or cell phone number on the letter even though you also included your business card in the package.)

The above letter should be sent along with your company's brochure.

Chapter 45

The Second Call

Second Call Opening Lines

Your second call opening line needs to hit the prospect right between the eyes and wake him up, just as you did on the cold call. You also want to prevent the prospect from cutting you off and ending the phone call right at the beginning.

Begin your second call with your name and company, a quick reminder that you spoke last week, and finally, an attention-grabbing line. Here is an example: "Hi Joe. This is Bob Chapin over at ABC Company. I spoke to you last week about refinancing. After a little homework, I've discovered that we can save you over $57,600 dollars over the life of your loan."

Here is another example: "Hi Joe. This is Bob Chapin over at ABC Company. We spoke last week about some investments and I sent you out some information." Without pausing and waiting for a response, continue with, "I have a situation here that I *know* (say *know* with extra emphasis and conviction) you'll be very interested in. We're looking for a 25 percent return on this investment in the next twelve to fifteen months." (Once again, without pausing, begin your presentation.)

Note 1: You *don't* want to pause during the opening lines because this is where you have the greatest chance of being cut off by the prospect. After you've stated your first line or two, it will be obvious to the prospect that you are calling to sell something. This is typically when the defenses go up and the prospect wants to blurt out, "I'm not interested," "I don't have time right now," or several other similar stalls and objections.

Note 2: Any numbers you give the prospect, such as return on investment numbers in the above example, must be believable. For example, if the prospect has always had his money in a savings account and certificates of deposit, a number like "25 percent for twelve months" may be completely unbelievable to this person, and he will immediately tune you out. If the prospect does not believe those kind of returns are possible, you'll lose credibility.

On the other hand, you may have a prospect who has taken great risks and has seen returns much larger than 25 percent. In addition to overwhelming a prospect with a large number, you don't want to *under*-impress with too low a number.

Obviously, if these two prospects are looking for their usual type of investments, you'll be looking at two completely different situations and be talking about completely different numbers anyway. However, if the conservative investor said he wanted something with a higher return and the aggressive investor said he wanted something a little more conservative and safe, you would want to qualify your numbers to help each prospect "understand" the number better.

Let's say you were presenting a stock with a potential 25 percent annual return to the conservative investor. In this case, use a more conservative number, say 18 percent. Also, explain that these types of numbers might "sound high." You might say, "Joe, I realize that with your investment history, 18 percent may sound a little high and even unbelievable, but let me assure you that these types of returns are entirely possible and happen in the market all the time. Also, I believe that you know there are some investments with much better returns than what you're currently getting, and that's why you asked me to find you some with returns like this particular stock, correct?"

With your aggressive investor looking for a more conservative investment, keep the 25 percent projection and say, "Jane, I realize that with your investment history 25 percent may sound a little low and yet, I know you said you wanted some more conservative investments, correct?"

You could then briefly explain how this investment is much more conservative than what she has presently and then bridge into your presentation.

Two Questions to Ask about Your Second Call Opening

1) What statement can you make to hit the prospect between the eyes and catch her attention?

What is your greatest benefit and how can you work it into your opening line as we did in the two examples above? You may want to have several, interchangeable opening lines depending upon whom you are calling.

2) What objections or stalls are you likely to get after your opening line(s) and how will you respond to them?

We'll address the second call objections in a moment. First, let's look at some second call opening line *don'ts*.

Second Call Opening Lines *Don'ts*

1) Do not begin the second call by asking if the prospect got the information.

Ninety-nine percent of the time you will get one of two responses to this question: "No, I didn't receive it," or "Yes, I got it but I haven't had a chance to look it over yet." Either answer gets you off on the wrong foot.

2) Don't pretend you're not calling to sell anything if you really are.

Here is an example of such an opening: "Hi Joe. This is Bob Chapin over at ABC Company. I spoke to you last week about refinancing and got you out some information. I'm just calling today to touch base and give you an update on rates."

That's almost as bad as "Did you get the information?" Almost. Be upfront and straightforward with people.

Second Call Objections

Occasionally, the prospect will cut you off at the beginning of your second call with an objection. Usually you'll hear one of three objections:

- "I didn't get the information."
- "I've thought about it and I'm really not interested right now."
- "I don't have time right now."

Let's take them in order.

If the prospect says she didn't receive the information, say the following: "Ms. Prospect, that was just some very basic information and my business card. What I'm calling with today is an investment opportunity that we believe will (mention one of your benefits)." Then roll into your presentation.

If you hear, "I've thought about it and I'm really not interested right now," say, "Mr. Prospect, I can definitely understand that. After all, if you were interested you would have called me, right?" Then follow with, "Mr. Prospect, if I can show you (your number one benefit, perhaps a 33 percent savings on office equipment, for example), would you be interested?"

If he says, "I don't have the time right now," that might be legitimate. In this case, say, "Okay, would later today be better, or sometime tomorrow morning?"

If this is a legitimate objection, he'll give you a time; if it isn't, he'll come back with another objection such as, "You know, I've thought about it and I'm really not interested." The prospect may even come back with, "This whole month is crazy. Call me back in three months."

In the case of a stall like this, respond with the question we used above: "Mr. Prospect, if I can show you (your number one benefit, perhaps a 33 percent savings on office equipment, for example), would you be interested?"

The key is to open your second call with energy and enthusiasm and a good attention-grabbing line. If you do, most of these "reflex" defensive objections never even rear their ugly heads.

The Presentation

Note: The first thing to remember about your telephone presentation is that you must deliver it with enthusiasm, energy, and conviction.

The presentation portion is the key to the selling process. If you have a qualified prospect and do this portion correctly, you will end up with a sale.

As with your cold call, everything related to your presentation *must* be written out and well rehearsed. Remember that you must have your presentation down to the point that if someone were to wake you at 3:00 a.m., you'd be able to fire it off word for word. In fact, you shouldn't even need to have your presentation in front of you. However, do have it there as a guide to ensure you remember all the points you need to convey.

The Three Parts of Your Presentation

Your presentation will consist of three parts: an opening section, the main presentation section, and a closing section. The opening will be brief—a minute or two; the main presentation, about three to five minutes; and the closing can take anywhere from a couple of minutes to ten or more depending upon the type and number of objections and questions that arise.

Your Presentation Opening

Your presentation opening should be short, build some credibility, and catch the prospect's attention with what your product or service will do for him. You will also ask an involvement question or two to bring the prospect into the conversation.

Here is an example: "Joe, as one of the top brokers with over twenty years' experience working for the top company in this market niche, it is crucial that I bring you a winner up front and make a good first impression. I think you'd agree that you never get a second chance to make a first impression, right, Joe?

"Again, with the company we're looking at today, we expect to show a 50 percent return over the next twelve to fifteen months. We have started to see the buying volume shoot up and the stock is really beginning to make a move. As a result, timing here is critical. Joe, I think you'd agree with me that timing is a very important aspect when investing, am I right?

"Joe, the name of the company is D Detection. It currently trades on the NASDAQ. Joe, how familiar are you with in-home or over-the-counter test kits?"

In the first paragraph we used "one of the top brokers" and "the top company in this market niche" to build the image of the salesperson and the company he represents. We also tried to impress upon the prospect the fact that it's critical that the salesperson make a good first impression. Finally, we also asked three involvement questions to bring the prospect into the conversation.

Your Presentation Body

The main part of your presentation will focus on the three or four most compelling reasons to buy, and these will depend on your prospect's needs, wants, and desires as identified in the qualifying section of the cold call. You will talk about features, but more important, you will *stress the benefits or what the product will do for the prospect.*

Here is a continuation of the above presentation: "Some of the more popular kits over the years have been the pregnancy kits. This company, D Detection, has in-home test kits that allow the user to put saliva on the test card and check for such diseases as hepatitis A, B, and C.

"They are currently working on three more test kits for diabetes, anemia, and AIDs. These kits are presently in front of the Food and Drug Administration for approval. Joe, the company's FDA approval percentage is *72 percent*. I think you'd agree with me that with odds like that the chances are *very good* that one or more of these kits will pass. Am I right, Joe? The market for each of these kits is *huge* and approval of just one will likely have a *significant and positive* effect on the price of the stock."

Note: Say important words in your presentation with extra emphasis. We have put the important words here in italics. Emphasize important words that accurately describe your features and benefits.

"In addition, Joe, the company is projecting an *increase of 25 percent in revenues* over the next year in the United States alone. It has just gone into a partnership agreement with a Fortune 500 Company that is going to sell its product *internationally.* The sale of its current test kits internationally could *literally send revenues through the roof* over the next twelve to fifteen months, not to mention what the above three kits that are currently in front of the FDA could do to those revenues. Can you see the enormous potential here, Joe?

"Also, the analysts are projecting a stock price of $15 and the stock is currently trading at $10. With the test kits in front on the FDA, the huge international market potential, and the current stock price of $10 compared to what the analysts are looking for—which again is $15—I think you can see how your downside risk is minimal and your upside potential is *huge.* Am I right, Joe?"

Again, you should only give three or four compelling reasons to buy. People can typically only keep track of a few good points before becoming overwhelmed. When someone becomes overwhelmed, he or she will simply mentally shut off and stop listening. Too much information will lead to objections such as, "Send me some information," or "I need to think about it."

You will use *additional* compelling reasons to answer objections.

The Close

After the prospect gives you an affirmative response to the question about upside potential, close immediately. Your close might sound something like the following: "Great. Joe, at $10 per share, I'm looking at a block of 5,000 shares. If this stock does what the analysts are projecting, that will give you a return of $25,000 over the next twelve to fifteen months. Would you be happy with kind of return, Joe?" After an affirmative response, continue with, "Great. All I need is a little information. Joe, would you like the confirmations sent to your home or work address?"

Generally, the closing section of your presentation is where you will handle most of your objections and questions. When you get a question, answer it, confirm the answer, and then close once again. When you get an objection, answer it, confirm the answer, give another compelling reason to buy, and then close once again.

It's important that your presentation provides both compelling reasons to buy and compelling reasons to buy *now*. One without the other will most likely leave you without a sale.

Note: Please refer to the *Presentation* section for more information on presentations.

Objections

We've already talked about objections extensively in the *Objection* section so we won't repeat that information here. The objections we will cover here are the ones that most often occur with telephone selling, namely:

- "I don't do business over the phone."
- "I only do business locally."
- "I'm not sending money to someone on the other side of the country."
- "Send me some information."

Here are some answers to the above objections.

Prospect: "I don't do business over the phone" *or* "I only do business locally" *or* "I'm not sending money to someone on the other side of the country."

You: "Well, Mr. Prospect, I can definitely understand that; at the same time, let me ask you a question. Have you ever ordered anything over the phone before?" You should get a yes to this question. If for some reason you get a no, proceed with, "Have you ordered a pizza over the phone?" Wait for an affirmative answer, then continue with, "And did the pizza (or other product he ordered over the phone) ever show up?

"Well, my clients basically look at me in the same light. We do business over the phone and I deliver my services as promised. Mr. Prospect, I've got many clients in California, Illinois, Massachusetts (or whatever states you do business in), and many other areas throughout the U.S. Some are about as far away from me as you can get.

"The fact is, once they see my results they don't care if I'm calling from (whatever state you're in) or Pluto because I'm committed to providing *all* my customers with…" Mention whatever benefits you're delivering to your clients. In this case, we'll use an example of what a financial advisor might say: "…making them money, which of course is the name of the game in investing, otherwise you wouldn't be talking to me right now. Making money (or delivering whatever service you deliver) is the bottom line, right, Mr. Prospect?" Once you get an affirmative answer to your question, close.

Here's another answer for the above objections: "Mr. Prospect, I can definitely understand that; at the same time, before I was a financial advisor on this side of the phone I was an investor on your side of the phone. One day a financial advisor from out of town called me. The idea sounded good, I took advantage of it, and it turned out to be one of the best investments I've ever made. In hindsight, I'm glad I relied on my gut instinct and didn't have to meet that person face to face before investing.
"Mr. Prospect, deep down inside this idea either makes good business sense to you or it doesn't. Based upon the fact that…" Give your three major benefits here. In this case, it might sound like the following: "…the company is going international this year, they will see an increase of at least 28 percent in revenues, and analysts are looking for a stock price of $15, I think your gut would have to tell you this stock is most likely going to go up. Am I right, Joe?" Once you get an affirmative answer to your question, close. Adapt the above answers to your particular product or service.

Here's a quick and humorous comeback for, "I don't do business over the phone." After you use this one, and hopefully get a chuckle, you will give another feature and benefit and then close. "Mr. Prospect, I'm really too ugly to do business in person." Wait for the laugh and then continue with your feature/benefit. "Seriously, Mr. Prospect, this company is completely debt free and they are also looking for acquisitions. Just one acquisition in this industry could have a huge, positive effect on the price of the stock." (Then close.)

Here's one more for, "I don't do business over the phone." "Mr. Prospect, I can definitely understand that. Ninety-six percent of all transactions in the stock market are done over the phone. Even if your broker was right across the street, you'd probably still be doing business via the telephone. The only difference between me and the broker across the street is the caliber of broker you're dealing with." At this point sell *yourself* and what *you* bring to the table. After some talk about what sets you apart and why you are the best person for the prospect to be talking to, continue with, "Also, I have a toll-free number you can contact me at, which I'm sure you'll appreciate. Wouldn't you agree, Mr. Prospect, that it's important to deal with someone with a high level of expertise when it comes to investing?" After the prospect's affirmative answer, close.

In the example above, we again used an investment advisor. However, if you are selling over the phone, that's probably the way selling is done in your industry. As a result, you should be able to take the above example and simply plug in terms relative to your own industry where we've made reference to stocks and investing.

Here's one for, "Send me out some information." "Ms. Prospect, I can appreciate you wanting to see some information. At the same time, not only did I cover all the information I would be sending out, I actually covered more. While the information is fresh in your mind and while you have an expert here on the other end of the phone to answers all your questions, what specifically do you need more information on?"

Here's another one for, "Send me out some information." "Cindy, let me ask you, does it make more sense to make a decision based upon old, stale, dated information or on current, up-to-date information?" Obviously she'll say, "current, up-to-date information," to which you respond, "Great, you're talking to it. What information are you looking for?"

And another, "Cindy, I can definitely send you out some information, but what I have is about as thick as a Sears' catalog. In order for me to narrow it down a bit, what specific information are you looking for?

In each of the above responses, if the prospect is able to give you a specific answer, isolate the answer. For example, if she says she'd like more information on how long the company has been in business and what their revenues have been historically, say, "Okay, is that all the information you're looking for or is there something else as well?"

If she says there is something else, ask what it is and then qualify her answer by again asking if that's all she needs to know to make a decision. Once you get her to the point where she has covered all the areas she needs information on, proceed to answer her questions, attempting to eliminate the "information" objection right then and there.

Let's say the only information she needed was how long the company has been in business and its revenue history. You would then give her that information and confirm that the information you just gave her is what she is looking for. You might say something like the following: "Okay, on that note, here's a little background for you. The company has been in business since 1914, and their revenues have been increasing steadily for the last five years. In 2004, they did $717 million in revenues, in 2005, $803 million, and in 2006, they did a hair over $900 million. Does that answer your question?"

If you get a yes, close immediately. If you get a no or anything other than a yes, ask, "Okay, what other information with regard to revenue history do you need?"

When you get an answer, again, proceed to give the information necessary, ask if that answers her question, and then close. Keep following this line of questioning until she gives you another objection or you've answered all her questions concerning information on the company.

If she comes back with, "Look, I just want some information," be persistent in letting her know that you have piles of information and you really need to narrow it down. In addition, remind her you can also answer any questions she has. If she persists, the information objection is probably a stall. At that point say, "Cindy, I kind of get the feeling that you're just trying to be nice by not directly telling me no. Is that the case, or do you really want to see the information?"

Alternatively, you could say, "Cindy, do you really want more information or are you just asking why now is the best time for you to make a move?"

What If You Simply Can't Get around the "Send Me Some Information" Objection?

If you are not able to get past the objection, catch her in person with the information. We realize this may not be possible if your selling is done strictly via the phone and the person is six states away. However, if you can drop the information off, try this: "Okay, Cindy, I'll be happy to get the information to you. Is Thursday morning at 10:00 or in the afternoon at 2:00 better for you?"

If the information objection is just a way of putting you off, which it probably is, she won't want to see you in person. Stay persistent as to when you can stop by to share the information with her.

Note: Don't accept, "Sure, you can stop by and if I'm not here, you can just drop it off." If you get that answer, you can bet a lot of money the prospect won't be there when you get there. You need to have a firm appointment set up.

If for some reason you are not able to set up an in-person appointment, whether it is not feasible for you to travel to where she is, or if she simply continues to put you off, let her know you will send the information and then set up a firm time to follow up. This is *very important*. You want to nail her down on a specific time.

"Okay, Cindy, I'll send out some information to you. Is the address I already have the best address to send it to? Okay, it will go out today using next-day FedEx. (Use whatever mailing method is most appropriate here. You may not want to send every package out via FedEx.) Today's Monday, and that means you'll get it tomorrow before 10:30. Is 2:00 good or would 4:00 be better for me to call you back tomorrow? Great. Oh Cindy, one more quick question. Once you see the information and we discuss it, will you be prepared to give me a firm yes or no?"

If she says yes, respond with, "Great. I'll get this out and talk to you at…" (Use the time she decided on.)

If she says no or "I don't know" or she's wishy-washy, say, "Cindy, obviously I don't want to waste your time by sending out information you really don't want or need to see. Let me ask you, what's the real reason for not moving ahead today?"

If she says something like, "Look, just send the information," you should still do it, but you shouldn't spend a lot of money getting it there quickly, and you shouldn't kid yourself that you've got anything close to a hot prospect.

Note: You *must* ask the qualifying question, "Once you see the information and we discuss it, will you be able to give me a firm yes or no?" This way, if you send the information and the prospect tries to put you off again, you can remind her of the "yes" answer she gave to this question.

Again, you don't want to be rude or too aggressive; simply be assertive. You are a professional and you're busy. You don't have time for people who string you along and won't give you a firm yes or no answer.

What Do You Say When You Call the Person Back after You've Sent the Information?

Do not ask the prospect whether she received the information when you call back. When you open with that question, the prospect will either say, "No, I didn't get it," or "Yes, I got it but I haven't had a chance to look at it yet."

Instead of referring to the information, open your call by identifying yourself. Then, before the prospect can cut you off, immediately give her new information you haven't shared before. Be upbeat and enthusiastic with your delivery, ask a tie-down question, and then close. Here is an example:

"Cindy, This is Bob Chapin over at ABC Company." Don't pause here. "The stock we were talking about is up $.25 since yesterday and the trading volume is really starting to pick up. We can still get in at a decent price; however, we need to move quickly. You do want to get in at the right price, right Cindy?" Wait for an affirmative response. "Great, I'm looking at 5,000 shares or roughly $51,250. Does that sound like a good starting level or could you go stronger?"

At this point, if you don't close the sale, you'll get questions and/or objections. Handle them, confirm the answers, and then close.

Another Way to Answer Telemarketing Objections

Rather than directly answering objections, another approach is to ignore them altogether. With this approach you will come back with some urgency, offer another feature and benefit, or both. You will then use a tie-down question and close. The following is an example of using urgency and closing: "Joe, based upon the fact that (your three or four major points), we're looking for the stock to increase 50 percent over the next twelve to fifteen months. However, I think you'd agree with me that if all goes right we could see even higher returns. Joe, would you be happy with a return of 50 percent over the next twelve to fifteen months? Great! Would 5,000 shares be a good starting position for you or would 10,000 be better?"

Here's another example: "Joe, I can definitely understand that. At the same time, once the company gets FDA approval on one of these test kits, there's no telling how high the stock could go. Approval could happen today, next week, or next month, and once it happens it may be too late. Also, with the way the volume has been increasing, I want to make sure we're not at a higher price and thus in a position where we have to wait to take profits.

"You do believe that timing is important in the market, right Joe? Joe, I'm not looking for you to go head over heels here. Let me ask you a question. If I don't make you money on this investment, how much more money are you going to send me in the future?" Wait for the "none" answer then continue. "Right, Joe. So you see why I have to do well for you on our first trade. Why don't we start with a block of 1,000 shares to allow me to show you what I can do for you? How does that sound, Joe?"

Note: Each time you ask a question you will wait for the prospect's response. In the above examples we are showing only your side of the conversation.

Make sure you have some urgency factors and at least three or four more features and benefits to respond with. The more ammunition you have the better. Also, have plenty of closes to follow them up with.

In addition to the "send me information" and other telephone objections you'll also get some of the other objections that are common in face-to-face selling. These objections are:

- Your price is too high.
- I have no money.
- I need to talk to my wife, husband, significant other.
- I need to talk to my lawyer, accountant, dog, etc.
- I want to think about it.
- I want to check around at a couple of other places first.
- I'm happy with my present supplier.
- I'm waiting to see what happens with the election.
- I'm waiting until after April 15, or until I get my refund check.
- I'm waiting until next year.
- I want to watch it for a while and see what happens.
- I need approval from someone else or another department.
- Call me back at some point in the future.
- I handle all this stuff myself or I use the Internet. I don't need any help.
- I just lost my job, my cat just died, my house just burned down.
- We already spent our entire budget for the year, or it's not in the budget.
- I only buy… (stocks, real estate, whatever).
- I don't like you, your company, or your product.
- I had a bad experience with your product or company.

Please refer to the *Objection* section for answers to the above objections.

Other Things to Remember about Objections

In telemarketing, you will get most of your objections after your first close.

Most objections you will encounter are simply stalls. The prospect doesn't want to say yes; at the same time, he can't tell you no. The true objection may be due to distance or the fact that you're not in person, yet you might hear: "I want to think about it." Often there is no rhyme or reason to the objection; it is simply the best excuse the prospect can come up with at the moment. It is your job to isolate the objection, answer it, and eliminate it. Your best approach is to have many reasons to buy. The more reasons you give to buy, the more likely you are to hit the prospect's hot button.

Note: When answering objections stay firm in your approach, but *do not* become aggressive. Think of answering objections and closing in an *assertive* way as opposed to an *aggressive* way. With assertiveness you say what you need to say with confidence and in a conversational tone. When you begin raising your voice and jumping up and down you are becoming aggressive and pushy.

In addition to handling objections in the two ways we looked at here, you can also handle them up front in the qualifying stage before your presentation. Please refer to page 363, item number 1 under "Preventing the Price Objection during the Qualifying Stage" in the *Objection* section for more detail.

Questions during the Presentation

If you are asked any questions during your presentation, simply answer them, confirm the answer, and then either continue with your presentation or close, whichever is appropriate. If you get your question toward the end of your presentation, or it is a "buying question," you will close.

Here's an example of answering the question, confirming the answer, and then continuing with the presentation:

Prospect (in the beginning of the presentation): What does this new dispenser do again?

You (after your explanation): Does that clarify your question completely?

Prospect: Yes.
You: Okay, great. (Then continue with your presentation.)

Here's an example of closing after you answer the question and confirm it:

Prospect (toward the end of the presentation): Do you have a leasing option available?
You: Yes, we do. Would you rather lease than buy outright or is this just something you're considering at this point?
Prospect: Well, I usually lease.
You: Okay, great. Let's put the numbers together here and see what we come up with for you. (Then continue as if the prospect has decided to buy.)

Questions from the prospect will give you an idea as to likes, dislikes, potential hot buttons, and overall how he wants to be sold.

How Much Time Should You Spend with One Prospect?

Your prospects have to-do lists and most of them also have a boss who likes to make sure business hours are spent on business. Keep your presentations to fifteen minutes or so. Some may go twenty, however twenty should be the maximum length. Of course there are exceptions.

If you have an interested and qualified individual and that person is staying with you through all your closes and answers to objections, you may find yourself presenting a bit longer. Still, you need to be aware of how much time you're spending with one prospect. If you have someone who simply cannot make a decision, but can't let you go either, you have to decide to move on at some point and use your time on a better-quality prospect.

As with everything else in sales, developing a sense of when to hang in there and when to let someone go will come only with experience, and lots of it.

Follow up after an Enthusiastic Telephone Sale

We talked about the follow-up in the section titled *After the Close*; however, there is an important point to mention with regard to "enthusiastic" phone sales. After you make an enthusiastic sale, thorough follow-up is very important. Don't get us wrong—follow-up is always important. However, in the case of an enthusiastic phone sale, it becomes more important than ever.

We knew a stockbroker who had only opened two accounts in three months. One day there was some *big* news on the company he had been telemarketing to prospects. The news caused the stock to begin to rise in price. The broker hit the phones like a madman. He was utterly convinced that the stock was going to make people a lot of money and he simply would not take no for an answer. As a result, he opened three accounts in two hours. When we called his new customers back to verify the accounts, they were asking questions such as, "What's the name of the stock?" and "What's the name of the broker?" They had become so caught up in his enthusiasm, they'd bought purely on emotion.

Now picture yourself as one of these clients. After you hang up the phone your logic begins to catch up with your enthusiasm. Immediately you start to ask yourself questions such as:

- "What did I just buy?"
- "How much did I pay?"
- "What was the name of the person who just called me?"
- "What company did he represent?"

As the questions and the logic begin to roll in, the enthusiasm starts to wane. Thoughts such as, "Maybe I made a mistake" can begin almost immediately.

Now let's take it a step further. A colleague stops by your office at this point, you mention you've just bought a stock, and he asks the same questions you have just asked yourself. This person does not share your enthusiasm. His viewpoint is completely based upon facts, and *you don't have any*. Being completely objective, he thinks you've just lost your mind for making an investment you know nothing about with someone whose name you don't even know.

By now, we think you get the point. You'd better get this person back on the phone and solidify this sale—and fast. You need to add logic to the "good" decision the client has just made. You also need to build some rapport, stress the good decision, and build trust and credibility by letting the client know you are there to service and support him and that you are looking to build a long-term relationship.

Make the call as soon as possible after the sale has been made and make sure the client has all the facts. Here is a sample of what you might say, "Joe, This is Jim Harvey again with ABC Company. I wanted to call you back with your account number. Do you have a pen handy? Okay, it is 54321-234. Once again, Joe, I want to congratulate you on a great investment decision. Again, the name of the company is XYZ Company. We got the stock filled at $10 per share and it is already trading slightly higher than that at $10.25. Again, we're looking for the stock to go to $14 over the next 6 months. Certainly, that would be a nice return for you. You'll be receiving an official confirmation from ABC Headquarters in New York along with a self-addressed, stamped envelope for you to return your check in.

"Joe, I'd like to just add that this is our first step and it's critically important for me to make a good impression with this first trade. I want to make sure you have my direct number, which is (505) 555-6789. I am looking forward to a long and profitable relationship with you and I'm here to help in any way I can. Joe, do you have any other questions for me at this point?"

"Okay, I'll be giving you a call in a couple of days to make sure you've received the confirmation. In the meantime, if you have any other questions or comments, please pick up the phone and call me at my direct number, okay?

"Great, Joe. Once again, thank you for the opportunity and I'm looking forward to working with you. Have a nice day."

Note: You want to say the above in a relaxed, professional manner. Don't rush and don't be overly energetic.

Obviously, there can be quite a few variations based upon your product and other factors. The key points to keep in mind are:

- Stress the *benefits* of what your product will do for the client.
- Start to solidify your relationship by letting the client know you are there to serve him.
- Make sure he has all the facts: your name, company name, how he can reach you, the specifics on the product such as delivery, payment, etc.
- Congratulate him once again on a good decision and let him know you are available should he have any comments, concerns, or questions.
- Let him know what will be happening next and when you will be in touch next.
- Call within the next two days and focus on building rapport.

Chapter 46

Other Thoughts on Telephone Selling

How Long Should Your Calls Last?

We touched on this briefly when discussing the length of your presentation. In general, you always want to be aware of how much time you spend on each telephone call. Spending too much time on each one can seriously cut into your total number of calls and keep you from other potentially more productive calls. Not spending enough time on each call can lead to less qualified leads, less rapport, or less business.

Your call should last long enough to reach your objective and convey the information. This will depend upon what type of call it is. It could be a cold call, presentation call, follow-up after the sale call, a service call, or a call that came from the customer. As a general rule:

- Cold calls should last about three to five minutes.
- Service calls about three to five minutes.
- Follow-up calls anywhere from three to seven minutes.
- Presentation calls about fifteen to twenty minutes.

Two effective ways of keeping track of your time are using either a stopwatch or the second hand on your wristwatch. You can also use customer contact management software that will display a countdown timer on your computer screen as soon as you lift the phone's handset. You can set program this to begin at five minutes, and keep one eye on it as it counts down your call time.

In addition to the time you spend speaking, you also need to watch other aspects of your phone calls—places where you may be wasting much valuable time. Don't sit on hold too long waiting for someone to pick up the phone. If you're cold calling, hold for a maximum of thirty to forty-five seconds when calling a work number and one minute when calling a home number. Also, as a general rule, wait four rings for someone to answer the phone unless you're calling retirees. In that case, make it six.

Keep Track of Calls and Results

To see where things are going right and where they're going wrong, you must keep track of your phone calls and your overall success rate. Do this by starting with two sheets of paper. On one sheet, you'll keep track of your cold calls, and on the other you'll keep track of your presentations.

On your Cold Call sheet, you will have three columns:

- Calls
- Contacts
- Leads

Every time you make a phone call, put a hash mark under the heading Calls. Each time you make a contact, put a hash mark in that column and of course, put a hash mark under the Lead column for each lead you get. This will give you your calls-to-leads ratio.

For example, if you make twenty calls, ten contacts and get one lead, your calls-to-leads ratio is twenty to one. Thus, if your goal is ten leads, by the averages, you need to make about two hundred calls.

Next you will have your Presentation page. Under the Presentation heading, you will have four columns:

- Calls
- Contacts
- Presentations
- Appointments/sales (whichever your goal is)

You will then follow the same procedure explained above to calculate your presentations-to-closings ratio. You may find that you get one sale or appointment for every five presentations. In that case, your ratio is five to one. If your goal is two appointments or sales per day, you'll have to make ten presentations to reach your goal.

If the goal of your presentation is appointments that you will eventually be closing, you'll need a third sheet that shows your closing ratio.

From your cold call and presentation numbers, you can find out where you are doing well and where you may have some problems. Let's take a look at your cold calls.

How Many Calls Did You Make?

Your first goal should be to make a high number of phone calls. The number of calls you make is easy enough to handle; it simply comes down to making the phone calls. If you're a new salesperson, your objective should be to make more phone calls than anyone else in the office. This should be easy for two reasons.

- Most of your calls will be cold calls as opposed to presentation calls and customer follow-up calls.
- You won't be fielding calls from customers or dealing with other aspects, such as paperwork, of having a lot of business under your belt.

If your first column is low, you need to dial more numbers. To achieve this, work longer hours, find more efficient ways to make more calls, and motivate yourself to make as many cold calls as you possibly can.

How Many Contacts Did You Make?

If you are making a lot of calls and getting a lot of contacts, that's great. It means you're getting through to people and you're calling at the right time. On the other hand, if you are making a lot of cold calls and *not* getting many contacts, you need to look at the reasons behind it.

- Are you getting voice mail?
- Do you need to work on getting past the person screening your calls?
- Are the prospects out of the office when you call?
- Are you calling at the wrong time of day?
- Do you have a bad list?

If you're running into voice mail or people out of the office, you need to adjust your calling time. Try early in the day, late in the day, lunchtime, or before or after regular business hours. If you're calls are being screened that means the people are in, and you simply need to get good at either getting around or avoiding the receptionist. Please refer to "Getting through the Receptionist" beginning on page 587.

A bad list can consist of either wrong numbers or wrong contact information. If you are getting disconnected numbers, or you're asking for people who are no longer at that number, you need a new list. Please refer to Sources of Names and Calling Lists beginning on page 69 to learn how to get good, current lists.

We've also encountered salespeople calling home numbers during work hours. This is an example of calling at the wrong time of the day. It's fine to call home numbers if you're calling retirees, but unless this is the case, don't hope to call residential listings during the workday and have a high contact rate.

There is another instance in which you may have good phone numbers and good contact names and still have a low contact rate. Sometimes this will happen if you're calling a company directory and are getting voice mail. In this case, you can either come up with a creative voice mail message (refer to "Leaving Effective Messages on Voice Mail," which begins on page 596), or you can call at different hours—usually early morning, at lunch, or late in the day—or you may just decide to call another list altogether.

How Many Leads Did You Get?

If you have lots of contacts and few leads, either something is wrong with your call or you're talking to the wrong people and thus have the wrong list.

If the people qualify and are right for your product, or they are hanging up on you before you have a chance to find out whether they're the right people, there is something wrong with your call. In either case you're not building urgency, rapport, value in what you're offering, or a combination of all of these. You need to create a more interesting call and work on your selling skills.

If the people seem interested but don't qualify for your product, there is something wrong with your list and you need to get a new one with people who qualify. In this case, there may also be something wrong with your call, but you won't know that until you talk to qualified people.

Once you've broken down, analyzed, and hopefully corrected anything wrong with your cold calls, it's time to move on to your Presentation page.

How Many Presentations Are You Doing?

If you're making the contact and not making the presentation, something is wrong with your opening or, you didn't have a real lead to begin with. Most of your contacts in column two should lead to presentations in column three. If they are not, you need to look at why.

If you're reaching prospects and they're shutting you down before you can do your presentation, you either have not built enough interest in your product on the initial call and/or you're not grabbing the person's interest and attention when you call him back to do your presentation. While you will occasionally get someone who is late for a meeting or on another call, if most prospects are putting you off, you either have a weak opening or you never had a real lead.

You must create interest on your cold call and re-create it when you call the prospect back to make your presentation. If you don't, the prospect will get off the phone quickly with an excuse that he's on another call, late for a meeting, or otherwise busy and doesn't have time right now. You need to be able to catch his attention with one quick tidbit of information. Do this by stressing a benefit or a new and exciting piece of news, and use energy and enthusiasm in your delivery. Please refer to "Second Call Opening Lines" on page 613.

How Many Sales or Appointments Are You Making?

If your number of presentations looks good, the only column left to look at is sales. If you have good numbers in the fourth column, or sales column, that's great—which means you're doing something right.

If you don't have good sales or appointment numbers either there's something wrong with your presentation (you're not building enough interest and urgency) or you're talking to the wrong people (you're not qualifying your prospects properly on the cold call).

If you're not making sales, what roadblocks are you encountering?

- Is there a particular objection you keep getting that you're having trouble handling?
- Are you closing but your prospects aren't qualifying for financing?

Find out if the problem is with your presentation or with your qualifying and then tackle that problem.

If you are not getting sales, you are:

- Talking to the wrong people.
- Talking to people who are not qualified.
- Talking to the right people the wrong way.

If you are talking to the wrong people you need to go back to the qualifying section of your cold call and you may need to get a new list of qualified people to call. If you are talking to people the wrong way you need to work on your selling skills and presentation. Record your presentation, analyze it, and then have your manager and the top salespeople analyze it.

Here is what you want to determine from the information on your Cold Call and Presentation number sheets:

- Are you making enough calls?
- Are you calling the right list?
- Is your call good or does it need to be revised?
- What is your success ratio?

Go over the numbers and share them with your manager and the top salespeople. Once you've done this, make the necessary changes to your lists, your call, or your number of phone calls. If all seems well, move ahead with the current plan.

There's One More Number to Look At

If you're making the calls, getting the contacts, doing presentations, and making sales, you have a formula that works. However, there is one more statistic to keep track of. That is, how many sales do you lose after the sale? In other words, you make the sale, the buyer gets cold feet (buyer's remorse) and they back out of the sale, or the paperwork does not go through because the prospect does not qualify, or any other reason the sale falls through.

Typically, your numbers in the "sale fell through" category won't be too high, and if they are you need to investigate and discover why. If people are backing out of the sale, you probably did not build enough rapport, or you rushed them through the process and slam-dunked them into the sale. They either don't trust you or they feel like they were forced to do something they ultimately didn't want to do. If you have a large number of prospects who are not qualifying once you've filled out all the paperwork and passed it on to corporate, then your presentation is working but you didn't do the proper job of qualifying the prospect.

We know of one investment advisor who was opening a lot of new accounts only to have about half of them fall through. His problem was in his approach. All the accounts that were falling through were ones he opened on a cold call. Instead of following the standard routine of cold calling the prospect, sending out information and calling back with a recommendation, he was closing people the first time he spoke to them. He believed that the name of the firm he worked for carried so much credibility that he did not have to build any personal credibility with his prospects. Virtually all his answers to objections centered on the premise that this large firm was recommending the stock and that was all the prospect needed to know. The prospect did not need to know the advisor personally and did not need to have all the particulars; he just needed to put his faith in the company recommending the stock. In addition to not building personal rapport with his prospects, he was closing *hard*. He simply would not take no for an answer.

The answer to the above situation was simple. The broker needed to use a two-call approach at minimum. On the cold call, he would simply build personal and professional rapport with the prospect. He would begin to instill the prospect with confidence in himself as well as company. He would let the prospect see some information and then he would close on the second call. Though persistence and asking for the order are very important, he needed to tone down his approach and be a little softer.

Hopefully you won't have a problem such as the one in the above example; however, if you do, there is usually a fairly easy remedy. Consult your manager and the top salespeople for help.

Meeting Someone in Person

One of the best ways to bring an account up to a higher purchasing level is with an in-person meeting with a prospect you've thus far only known via phone conversations. This can add a new dimension to your relationship and can really cement things. When someone can put a face to your name and voice, and reach out and shake your hand, psychologically you become much more of a real person; you become more like her. You also have the added benefit of visual cues. You can read gestures, facial expressions, and see other things you miss on the phone.

Also, people tend to become much more comfortable once they have met you in person. Psychologically, there is a trust factor involved. Often people have their guard up when talking to someone over the phone. In most cases, when someone meets you, it will be much easier for her to trust you. Not only does the meeting make you more human, the customer also realizes you have taken time out of your day especially to see her.

We know of one stockbroker who had a client worth over thirty million dollars but the client had only about $30,000 invested with him. The broker continually tried to get larger orders but nothing seemed to be working. He finally bought a plane ticket and flew to the client's city to meet with him in person. He repeated this three times before the client trusted him enough to start taking some larger positions. The broker now has *all* of his client's investment dollars and that client has become his largest account.

The broker had invested some money, taken a chance, and the risk had turned out to be well worth the reward. The client had several small accounts and he consolidated all of them to the one broker because that broker had made an extraordinary effort that no one else had been willing to make to establish that personal connection.

We know of another investment advisor who had great "in-person" charisma. Her approach was to cold call local prospects then get out to meet them as soon as possible. She would use a standard cold call, but instead of sending introductory information out she would offer to drop it off in person. Most prospects agreed to this and she went on to make an outstanding impression when meeting them face to face.

Note 1: It is a good idea to meet people in person as quickly as possible after the phone relationship has begun. After about a minute of phone conversation people begin to develop a mental image of what they believe you look like. If a prospect or client has had many months, or even years, to establish that mental picture of you, the odds are great that their image will only remotely resemble you. If that image has only begun to form, it is still fairly fluid in the early stages. The more phone conversations and the longer you speak with someone over the phone, the more that image begins to solidify.

Note 2: Even a picture can add that extra dimension, although a picture clearly won't work as well as an in-person meeting. Overall, there seems to be an important psychological benefit when the visual aspect is added to the voice on the other end of the phone. While sending holiday cards with your picture can add credibility and a more personal connection to the relationship, you should be meeting customers in person whenever possible.

WARNING!!

Meeting someone in person can be a double-edged sword. Now that you know all the advantages of meeting someone in person, you need to be warned about the *bad* things that can happen. You must think of meeting someone in terms of risk versus reward.

The payoff of meeting someone in person can be tremendous, but if you are *not* what that person expected, the in-person meeting can backfire in a hurry. A negative result usually occurs when extremes are involved. If you are much older, much younger, much larger, or much smaller than the prospect imagined, you are at the greatest risk to surprise the person you are meeting and end up with a negative result. Rarely will extreme beauty be an issue, but it can be. If you are "average" to "above average" in most respects, as well as well groomed, you will usually be in good shape when meeting a phone contact in person.

Be honest with yourself when considering meeting a phone contact in person. Some people have outstanding phone voices, but their voice does not fit their actual physical image. One of the authors of this book became a stockbroker at age twenty-one. People typically want a stockbroker who is older and experienced, thus his age was a potential problem. The fact that his deep voice made him sound much older on the phone helped to negate this problem; however, when some clients met him inperson, he had issues. In many cases, once clients realized they were dealing with a twenty-one-year-old, they stopped doing business with him.

For some people, doing business over the phone can be a major advantage, while other people have an advantage in person. Use whatever works best for you. If most of your business is done over the phone, yet you have a good in-person presence, go out and meet as many customers and prospects as you can.

As a general rule it is usually best to meet your customers face to face because most of the time the meeting will serve to solidify the relationship. However, if for some reason you're better off hiding behind the phone, as in the example above, do it.

Note: By saying "hiding behind the phone" we are not suggesting that you should deceive anyone. The reality is that we live in a society in which you are judged by your appearance. You may have all the qualifications in the world, but if you're a twenty-one-year-old investment advisor out meeting people, you may find it extremely difficult to get prospects to take you seriously. If someone insists on meeting you, of course you should comply, but you need to keep in mind that there may be a difference between the phone image someone has of you and your actual physical image.

As we've mentioned, if you find yourself in these circumstances—you're young and someone doesn't want to give you a chance—remind the prospect of a time in his life when someone gave him a chance. Let him know you're simply looking for the same opportunity and you promise to work extremely hard for him.

Keeping the Listener's Attention

The average person's attention span is about fifteen seconds. Attention spans can be even shorter over the phone, which is why it is critical that you hit the prospect right between the eyes immediately and keep the momentum going from there.

Use a great opening line that builds interest and intrigue and then continue to build interest throughout the call.

In addition, use plenty of enthusiasm and energy and ask unique, thought-provoking questions. By unique, we mean questions that will make the prospect stop and think because they are completely different from the questions other salespeople are asking. It's also very important to use voice inflection and the proper volume while talking on the telephone.

Use varying tones to keep the listener's attention and keep him awake and tuned in. Vocal inflection is particularly important in phone sales because the voice—and the content of your message—is all the person has to go on. If you sound monotone, people will tune you out quickly.

The *best* way to keep someone's attention is by talking about things that interest her. Talk about the benefits of your product or service and relate those benefits to what the prospect is interested in.

Keeping Control of the Conversation

Clearly, keeping control of the conversation is important when you're doing any kind of selling. Here are some effective ways to stay in charge of the conversation.

1) Preparation.

You know what you're going to say and what direction you want the conversation to go in. As a result, you will be more prepared than the prospect. Use this preparation to keep you on track and focused. When the prospect tries to take you in another direction, acknowledge what has been said, then get back to the script.

2) Questions.

Use questions to direct the conversation where you want it to go. If the prospect tries to get you off track, respond to what has been said, then ask a question to bring the conversation back on track.

3) Use the Hold Button.

Use the hold button when you're losing control of the conversation and you need to get it back. If you are talking with a prospect who is off on a tangent and simply won't let you get a word in edgewise, use the hold button to break his rhythm.

Let's say for example, you've asked a qualifying question and now the conversational ball is in the prospect's court. The prospect answers your question and then expands on the idea, continues to expand it, and then jumps to another subject that the qualifying question reminded him of, which leads to yet another thought. Okay, you get the idea.

What you do want is the answer to your question along with an explanation. The explanation could contain valuable information you can use later. What you *don't* want are the peripheral subjects that arise that add no value to either the sales process or rapport building. Here's an example:

You: "Joe, can you tell me about the best investment you ever made in the market?"

Prospect: "Oh sure. That would have to be my investment in the company stock through our plan at work. Not only did the stock jump significantly, the company also matched our contributions dollar for dollar and gave us the right to purchase options on the stock. That afforded us the right to buy the stock well below what it was currently trading at. It worked out great. I remember Charlie Smith had close to a million dollars' worth of stock after only five years with the company. Of course, Charlie really knew how to invest. That was one of his hobbies in addition to fishing. Charlie used to go fishing twice a year in the Caribbean…"

If Joe had been talking about *himself* as a fisherman, that would be a different story. You want to find out about your prospects and what makes them tick. A conversation about Charlie Smith, on the other hand, serves no purpose and will be a complete waste of time. Thus, as soon as Joe gets into the Charlie Smith story, gently interrupt, saying, "Joe, I'm sorry, could you please hang on a second?"

Put him on hold, wait about seven seconds, and come back with, "Joe, sorry about that. Now, you said your best investment was the company stock plan. What in particular did you really enjoy about that investment?"

Then continue on with your line of questioning. If he starts to ramble again, repeat the "hold" process then come back with your follow-up question. Each time you do this, tell him how sorry you are for having to put him on hold, then continue with your questions.

4) Use the "I Have Another Call" Technique.

"I have another call" can be used as a variation of the "hold button technique," and it can also be used to end a conversation. Used as a hold technique, it would sound like, "Mr. Prospect, can you hold on one second? I have another call."

Used to end the conversation, it would sound like, "Mr. Prospect, I have another call coming in that I really need to take." You would then make a closing remark or two and end the conversation.

You can use this technique on a cold call to get someone off the phone who is not qualified for your product but wants to talk anyway. For example, a financial planner may run into someone who wants a free education on the stock market. You can also use this technique if you have a qualified lead, have all the information you need, yet the person wants to continue talking and talking and talking. In this case, say, "Ms. Prospect, I have another call I really need to take. I'll get the information out to you and follow up with you next week. It was great talking with you." Yet another use for this technique is for friends who call during prime calling hours to shoot the breeze for half an hour.

5) Breathe in the Middle of Sentences.

Breathing in the middle of sentences is an advanced technique for keeping control of the conversation. The easiest place to jump in during a conversation is *between* sentences when most people take a quick breath. By breathing in the middle of sentences, instead of at the end, you can combat these interruptions and keep control of the conversation. It takes some work, but with a little practice, you should be able to pick it up fairly quickly. Here's an example:

Standard conversation with breathing at the end of sentences: "Hi Joe. This is Bob Chapin from ABC Company (breathe). I'm calling to let you know about a great situation I think you'll be very interested in (breathe). The name of the company is…"

Especially during the first few sentences of the sales call, the prospect is likely to have a fear of being sold something and as a result may jump in when the salesperson takes a breath after a sentence, which creates a slight pause. But to throw the prospect off and confuse his natural defense mechanism, the "breathing between sentences" technique works well. Here is the same wording above but with the breathing in the middle of the sentences: "Hi Joe This is Bob Chapin from ABC Company I'm calling (breathe) to let you know about a great situation I think you'll be very interested in The name of the company (breathe) is…"

You'll notice we took the periods out at the end of the sentences. We did this for extra emphasis. The point of breathing in the middle of the sentence is to talk right through the end of the sentence. Don't hesitate at the end as you typically would. Any slight pause, even one without a breath, will open the door for the prospect to cut you off.

This technique will completely throw off the prospect's defense mechanism, which says, "Oh no, she's calling to sell me something. I've got to interrupt her and get off the phone now!"

Improve Your Voice with a Recording Device

Even if your voice is offensive, most people will not mention anything negative about it. As a result, you'll need to analyze your voice yourself. The best way to do this is to record yourself. Most people hate to hear themselves on a recorder, but that is exactly how they sound to everyone.

So what are you listening for in your recorded voice? You're listening for negative traits such as a weak voice, a nasally voice, a high-pitched voice, and other similar extremes.

We covered all these negative traits on page 98 under the heading Speech Factors That Alienate You from the Prospect. Please refer to that section for more details.

One other area you want to pay attention to in your recordings is voice inflection. You don't want to be monotone. Monotone equals boring. Raise and lower your voice appropriately.

In addition to extremes and obvious voice idiosyncrasies, look for small changes you can also make. Perhaps you want to speak a little faster, a little slower, drop or raise your voice a bit, or put more fluctuation in it. You may hear "ahs," "ums," or dropping of the *g* on words ending in *ing*.

Whether extreme or subtle, you will most likely hear some traits that you'll want to change once you hear your voice on tape. Your overall objective should be a strong, but not overpowering, clear, confident voice. Eliminate extremes, weaknesses, and any wavering in your voice.

Record yourself daily and concentrate on making the vocal changes you desire. After you've done this for about four weeks, you'll find that the changes start to become automatic. Working on your voice for about twenty minutes a day, every day should be enough. After the initial four-week period, tape yourself periodically, say once a month. This will ensure that you haven't slipped back into any old habits.

Record Yourself When You're in a Slump

It's also a good idea to record yourself when you're in a slump. It's often difficult to discern problems with your cold call or presentation unless you can sit back and listen to a recording of what you really sound like. Also, have your manager and top salespeople review your recording to see if they hear any problems.

Note: If you can record both sides of the conversation, that's great. Just make sure it's legal in your state.

Even Veterans Should Record Calls Occasionally

Even if you're a veteran salesperson, record your calls from time to time just to see if you can pick up on any problems or things you should be doing better.

Keep Some Recordings of Successful Calls

Keep recordings of successful calls to motivate you, get you in the groove, or even help get you out of a slump. Before you head into the office, listen to calls that went well.

Up, Down, and In-between Notes

How you end your sentences is very important in selling as well as in general conversation. As a rule, questions end on an up note, statements end on a down note, commands end on what we'll call an in-between note. That is, your pitch stays the same—it does not go up or down.

You can hear this easily if you ask a question or make a statement or command. As you ask, "Is Bob there?" your pitch rises on the word *there*. You say *there* at a higher pitch than *is Bob*. As you say, "My name is Bob Chapin," the word *Chapin* is spoken at a lower pitch than the rest of the statement. A command keeps the same pitch from beginning to end.

This distinction is important because many salespeople use up notes when they should be using down notes or in-between notes. For example, when the receptionist asks who's calling, many times a salesperson will state his or her name with an up note—this statement of fact is now really a question. Receptionist: "Can I ask who's calling?" Salesperson: "Yes, Bob Chapin?"

Of course, the answer above isn't meant to be a question, but that is often how it sounds. Psychologically, the salesperson is saying, "Bob Chapin. Is that enough to get me in?" It is a fear of rejection that causes the statement to be spoken like a question.

On the other end of the phone, the receptionist hears what she knows should be a statement spoken as a question and she thinks, "Jeez, why does this person sound uncertain?" This tips her off that you're no one she knows and she probably shouldn't let you through.

Be aware of how you end your sentences. If it's a question, end it on an up note; if a statement, end on a down note; if a command, end on an even note. You want your tone to match what you are trying to convey: confidence!

Using Humor on the Phone

Using humor during the selling process is very important. Humor lightens the mood and gives people a better feeling about the entire selling process. Using humor brings people closer to you, helps them let their guard down, and helps them to like you. You want to use humor at all points of the selling process, yet you *don't* want to overdo it. If you use too much humor, people won't take you seriously. The best place to begin using humor is with your first line during the cold call.

Here are some opening cold call lines you can use to lighten things up a little:

- "Hello. This is (your name) with (your company) and although I don't know a thing about you, I can guarantee you one thing. (Slight pause) You don't like receiving these calls any more than I like making them. Am I right?"
- "Hi, (prospect's name)? Congratulations, you're the next contestant on the (your full name) Show. You know, because I don't like cold calling and you don't like getting cold calls, I have to do something to lighten the mood, which is why I open up like this. My name is (your name) with (your company) and the reason I'm calling is…"

Look for other places to interject humor. Subscribe to a "joke of the day" service and give your joke of the day on each call. Obviously, you'll want to make sure the jokes are clean. Try using the joke in your opening line on a cold call. Here is an example:

- "Hi there. This is (your name) with (your company) and I'm calling with the joke of the day." (Pause slightly and then tell your joke).

Note: You can also use the joke of the day before presentations to customers.

Yes, some of these ideas are different and some take some guts, and yet the reward is well worth it. You will *definitely* set yourself apart from the rest of the selling crowd and find that many more people will listen to you and buy what you're selling.

Left Ear versus Right Ear

Most of us use our left ear to listen when we talk on the phone. For telephone salespeople, that's good. We tend to get more emotionally involved and things seem to make more sense when we listen with our left ear. This is because the left ear is controlled by the right brain and the right brain is our creative and emotional brain.

Occasionally you may run into someone who either can't seem to follow you or doesn't get emotionally involved, no matter what you try. This person may be completely uninterested or she may be listening with her right ear.

If you find yourself in this situation, try saying this: "Ms. Prospect, do you have the phone on your right ear right now?"

If she agrees, say, "I was going to suggest you switch ears. I just did because the ear I was using is getting a little tired."

Often the person will become more aware of the phone on her ear and switch ears. The bottom line: the prospect might switch ears or might not; in any case, your odds of selling the prospect are better if the phone is on their left ear.

Incidentally, if she says "no" and wants to know why you asked, simply say you're doing a side study on peoples' phone habits and that's a question you needed more responses to.

An Advanced Technique Using More Than One Phone

An advanced cold calling technique to maximize your phone time is to have two telephones going at the same time. To do this alone takes some practice. A more effective way of applying this technique is to use a second person to dial the numbers for you.

To work this technique alone, pick up the first phone and dial the number. As the phone call is going through, pick up the second phone and begin dialing the second number. If you contact someone on the first call, hang up the second phone and take the first call. If you don't contact someone on the first call, or someone answers the second call before the first, hang up the first phone and stay with the second call. Again, working this technique alone is difficult. You need to be able to listen to the two different calls at the same time and make split-second judgments.

When using a second person, you make the first call, she waits about ten seconds then makes the second call. Then follow the rules above. If someone answers your call, simply stay with that call while she drops the second call. If the second call goes through, grab the phone from her and she will in turn grab the first phone and prepare to dial the first phone while you're on phone number two. With a little practice you'll get the hang of this technique and use it to maximize your phone time.

Using the Speakerphone

Stay away from using the speakerphone; it is very impersonal. People are naturally very wary of being on speakerphone because they know that anyone within earshot can hear what they're saying.

There are only four instances when using the speakerphone is appropriate. They are:

1) **If you're on hold.**

This will give you two free hands to get some work done.

2) **While dialing the phone or waiting for someone to answer.**

As soon as someone answers, pick up the receiver and get off the speakerphone.

3) **You're on a conference call and there is more than one person on your end.**

In this case, make sure the person on the other end of the phone knows they are on speakerphone and ask if they're okay with that. After you've introduced who you have with you, you can simply say: "Bob, I've got you on speakerphone so we can hear you on this end, okay?"

4) **You are not physically able to pick up the phone.**

Outside of those four cases, don't use the speakerphone. Some salespeople feel they have more control, or can multitask using the speakerphone. However, if you do, you're simply more likely to irritate your prospect or place him on the defense.

Automatic Calling Machines

We emphatically do *not* recommend automatic cold calling machines that dial thousands of numbers, play a recorded response, and expect the person on the other end to interact with it. These devices irritate 99.9 percent of the people they reach and help to solidify a negative attitude toward telemarketing. In addition, the one person you do reach out of 1,000 or 10,000 isn't likely to be the highest-quality prospect. In fact, you're likely to find just the opposite.

Have an Assistant

Eventually, you want to have an assistant who does all your paperwork and other tedious tasks. You should also have an assistant make phone calls for you. Initially these can be the easy calls, such as getting back to a customer with the answer to a question and similar calls. You eventual goal is to have an assistant who can cold call for you and even open accounts.

Ask for Referrals

You should always be asking for referrals. For more information, please refer to Chapter 38, which begins on page 516.

Have Conversations

You want your telephone calls to be telephone *conversations*. Whether the objective of your sales call is an appointment, selling something, a service call, or any other reason for that matter, try to view the sales call as a conversation you are having with a close friend. If you keep your sales calls conversational, you'll find the person on the other end of the phone will be much more relaxed and will open up to you more easily.

Put Yourself in the Other Person's Shoes on All Calls

How do you like to be treated? Chances are most people feel much the same way you do. Think of the various telemarketers who have called you over the years.

Were there any that you liked? What did you like about them? They probably came across as friendly, honest, and straightforward. There were probably others you did not like. Why not? Were they pushy, obnoxious, mechanical, or rude?

Be straightforward, honest, and professional on the phone.

A Summary of Ideas on Telephone Sales

- Do as the top salespeople do and you'll get the same results.
- The best salespeople over the long haul always have a genuine interest in the people they serve.
- Each call gets you closer to your goals and dreams.
- Make more phone calls than anyone else.
- Get on the phone as soon as possible, don't wait for everyone else or some cue that it's time to start calling.
- Don't take a break immediately after a sale or getting a lead. Again, there is power in momentum that you'll lose if you take a break.
- Be prepared. Have everything you need in terms of a script written out in front of you; have any other tools you need while on the phone within arms' reach.
- Work on the sound of your voice and what you say; they are all you have in telephone selling.
- Meet as many customers as you can in person unless it will work against you.
- Listen well. The more you listen, the better your chances of making a sale.
- Be persistent.
- Sell your product, your company, and *always sell yourself.*
- Talk in terms of "you," not "I."
- Talk about *benefits* rather than features.

SECTION X

SELLING WITHIN
YOUR COMPANY

Introduction

Salespeople don't do their work alone. If you're like most salespeople, you have an installation department, service department, finance department, and accounts receivable in addition to several other departments. In a setup such as this, there is usually a good deal of interaction between the salespeople and the various other departments. In addition, many salespeople find themselves in a position where they report to a boss or sales manager. They may also report to other department heads from time to time. In this section we will look at the dynamics of working with various other people and departments within your company.

Chapter 47

Getting Along with Others at Work

Rules for Getting Along

The rules for getting along with others at work are essentially the same as the rules for getting along with people everywhere. They are:

- Be professional and courteous.
- Respect the other person.
- Be honest and straightforward.
- Put yourself in the other person's shoes.
- Align with the other person and try to make a friend.
- Give the other person the benefit of the doubt.
- Be flexible.

Here are some keys to working with people in other departments:

- Team up with the right people who can help you get things done.
- Give people the benefit of the doubt.
- Focus on what you can do for these people to make their job easier.
- Build strong relationships.
- Never back people into a corner, especially in front of others.
- In summary, treat all people with respect.

Keep Your Manager Happy

Your manager is your number one customer within your company. If your manager is happy with you, you are doing something right and you have job security. If your manager is unhappy with you, you're one small mistake from being shown the door. Thus, it's a good idea to keep your manager happy. Here are some ideas:

1) Make your manager's job as easy as possible.

Go to your manager and ask what you can do to support her and her efforts. Often, she'll tell you that just hitting your quota, or exceeding it, will be the biggest favor you can do for her. However, there may be other things you can do such as helping to train new salespeople, setting up for a trade show, or organizing a company event.

Also, keep in mind that managers and bosses like it when people can take initiative and handle issues on their own rather than involving them on every occasion. You do need to use management to support your efforts and keep them in the loop, but keep in mind that they are very busy and do not want or need to be involved in every tiny situation.

2) Keep your manager informed and involved in your business.

Support is one of the characteristics of a management team. You don't want to overwhelm your manager, but you do want to take him with you on calls from time to time. Also, ask your manager's opinion when you are faced with challenges.

Keep management informed as to what is going on in your territory. This would include how business is going in general, any opportunities they may be able to help with, and any potential problems.

3) Follow rules and regulations.

This should be self-explanatory.

4) Meet with your manager on a regular basis.

Make it a point to meet with your manager on a quarterly or bi-quarterly basis to discuss how things are going. Give your manager any other ideas on what she may be able to do to help you.

5) Ask your manager's opinion.

Your manager will typically have some helpful insight on how to handle various situations. He also has access to many resources and may be able to contact others in the company who may have helpful insight if he does not.

6) Contribute wherever possible and be a team player.

Contribute to the team and get along with your colleagues and other departments within the company. This makes your manager's job much easier and it creates a more positive and upbeat environment. People who do not get along with others can cause high levels of stress and anxiety in the workplace and make for a very unpleasant experience for management. Often management has to let someone go when people aren't getting along. Be kind, respectful, and professional to everyone.

Contributing includes giving good ideas as well as pointing out those that may not be so good. As long as constructive criticism is put forward properly it is generally taken in the right way. Also, if you've discovered a problem, try to have a solution or two.

7) Don't embarrass yourself, your manager, or your company.

Wherever you go, you represent your company. This includes all business and social gatherings. Ending up as the negative subject of morning gossip sessions, or worse, in the paper or in jail, will not reflect well on you or your company.

8) Be pleasant, positive, and supportive.

People like to be around and work with positive people. This includes management. If your manager asks for reports or business plans, support her by getting these done thoroughly and ahead of schedule. If there are any new company initiatives or directives, be positive and give the new policy your best effort.

9) Be honest with your manager.

No matter what you've done, you need to be honest with your manager. Management is there to support you. In most cases, they will do the best they can to help you out of a tough situation. Not being honest with management is a sure way to get fired. This is true particularly if they have gone to bat for you on false information you've given them.

Remember, management is there to support you. They are people just like the rest of us. Appreciate them and support them in their efforts, and you'll find the workplace a much more positive and inspiring place to be.

Finally, if you learn only one thing from this section, learn this: For the most part, managers are looking for lots of good, clean, honest, complaint-free, "happy customer" business that they do *not* need to micromanage.

Take Your Manager on Sales Calls

Occasionally you should be taking your manager along with you on sales calls. We mentioned this briefly under number 2 above. Here is a list of the times to take your manager along.

1) **When you find yourself in a *very* important meeting or situation.**

2) **When you're trying to get to the next level, or trying to go over someone's head.**

3) **When you're making scheduled calls to current customers.**

You want to introduce your manager to all your accounts at some point. Take your manager along when you have a full slate of scheduled calls with customers. You don't want to waste your manager's time by calling on people who aren't there.

Cover for Other Sales Reps

Covering for other sales reps, and having them cover for you during vacation and other similar times, is a good habit to form. Not only will you and the other sales reps take the pressure off one another, you may also be able to do some business for one another.

Go on Calls with Other Sales Reps

Go on sales calls with other sales reps from time to time. This exercise serves several purposes. First, it may give you ideas on better ways to do business; second, it helps build camaraderie; and third, it can be beneficial for a less experienced salesperson, be it you or someone else. Finally, if you've met the customers of other sales reps and they've met yours, this will be helpful when you cover for one another when one of you is on vacation or otherwise indisposed.

You don't have to go on a lot of these types of calls. You might pick one day a month. In addition to calling on customers, you can do some cold calls together.

Ask Other Sales Reps for Their Input and Opinion

Hopefully, you already have a forum at your company where you speak with other sales reps, discuss best practices, and bounce ideas off one another. If you don't, you should start doing this. Even if you do have a system in place whereby you discuss ideas during monthly meetings or in other venues, you should still be talking at other times—reviewing tough sales calls, objections, new information you've discovered that you think may be helpful to the group, and other items with which you either need help or feel you may be able to help.

Trade Accounts with Other Sales Reps

Occasionally, you may find you have an account that you're simply unable to get anywhere with. Your lack of success may be for one of several reasons. First, the competition may be firmly planted in the account; second, the account may simply not be that active; third, you or someone else at your company may have previously angered the customer; or fourth, there may be a personality conflict between you and one or more key people at the account. Once you've tried everything and gotten nowhere, it's a good idea to hand off the account to another sales rep and let her take a shot at it. The worst that can happen is that the new sales rep doesn't get any business either. Your company is starting from zero with the account so it can't get any worse. However, the new sales rep may use a different approach, or her personality type may be a better fit.

Of course, it's a good idea to talk to your manager before you trade or give an account to another rep. Your manager will usually be in agreement with your idea and be willing to have you give it a try. Approach one or more salespeople and ask if they'd like to swap some accounts with you. Be completely up front and honest with the sales rep you're trading accounts with. Tell her the entire history of the account and what, if any, honest potential you feel there might be.

Be a Good Sport

Finally, be a good sport around other salespeople. When you're doing well, don't toot your horn. Celebrate with your spouse or even good friends that truly are happy for your success, but stay low key at work. You can be confident, secure, and even quietly cocky, but the keyword here is "quietly." In addition, congratulate other salespeople who are doing a great job.

Watch Whom You Get Caught Up With

You want to fit in at work and be just another "one of the guys" or gals, yet you need to walk a fine line. It's all right to go out after work and socialize occasionally, but every night may be overdoing it. It's also all right to talk to the other salespeople from time to time, but missing valuable selling time is not good.

Do what you can to fit in but don't compromise your ethics or standards along the way. If all the salespeople where you work go out every night and that's what you enjoy, that's fine. If not, hopefully you can respect one another, or you may want to find other work somewhere where the salespeople more closely reflect your values and morals.

Of course, be very careful about embarking on romantic liaisons at work. While the workplace can be a great place to meet people, it can be a difficult place to keep a relationship going. One of you will likely eventually have to leave.

The best rule regarding whom and what you get caught up with at work is to use your best judgment. Follow your moral compass and do what's right for you. Again, it's important to fit in but not at the expense of your character, integrity, and self-image.

Rules for Effective Communication

Communication is important *everywhere* and the workplace is no exception. Here are some rules to follow when communicating in the workplace:

1) Have a clear objective for your communication.

The key in this first step is to stop and think about what message you're trying to convey and how you can maximize the results of your communication.

2) Decide what form of communication is most appropriate.

Is it more appropriate to communicate verbally or through written means? Should you send an e-mail, should you pick up the phone, or should you visit the individual in person?

3) Prepare for your communication.

Make sure you have all your facts straight and decide what you want to say. Prioritize the various points and put them in order from most to least important. In addition to preparing to present your communication, prepare for how your communication will be received. What are the possible reactions and how will you respond to those reactions?

4) Communicate positively.

Even if you are dealing with a bad situation, try to focus on the positive side. You don't want to don't sugar coat the situation as if there is no problem; however, if you can find some positives, start with those and then lead into the more serious situation at hand. Most important, remain professional.

5) Be direct and specific.

Your communication can't be wishy-washy and unclear. Don't dance around a subject. Say what you mean and mean what you say. Here is an example:

Non-direct: "Your report was good but needs work in a few areas."
Direct: "The overall idea and content of your report was very good. I did notice some spelling and grammatical errors that I've marked for you."

If you want something specific, you need to be clear instead of giving vague instructions that are open to misinterpretation. Here is an example:

Non-specific: "Could you please go to the store and get some apples?"
Specific: "Could you please go to XYZ Supermarket and get six McIntosh apples?"

6) Keep your communication simple.

Use as few words as possible while still giving all the detail necessary. Use language that is easy to understand. Don't use fancy words, abbreviations, acronyms, or industry jargon unless the person you are talking with will know what you are talking about.

7) Speak clearly and with confidence.

When you speak clearly while looking the other person in the eye, you exude an air of confidence and credibility. Don't mumble, cover your mouth, or drop your volume. Whatever you are saying, make sure that others both hear and understand you.

8) Always be truthful when you communicate.

Do not deny truths or give wrong or misleading information. Always be honest with people. In addition, if you're reacting to communication, always strive to know the truth and have your facts straight. If a story gets out, or the rumor mill starts up, you may have to do some investigative work to get to the bottom of things. If people are talking, you need to nip it in the bud. If you do not have all the facts, let everyone know you are aware of the situation, are working on it, and will get back to them as soon as you have the facts.

9) Whenever possible, communicate directly with the person or people you want to get your message out to.

"If you want a job done right, do it yourself" is true with communication. When you ask someone to give information to someone else, your message will not have the same meaning as if you deliver it yourself. The message may be only slightly different, but it *will* be different. In addition, you may give the recipient the impression that he is not important enough for you to take the time to deliver the message personally. Gauge the importance of the message. If the message is important, deliver it yourself, if it is not of major importance, you can delegate it— just make sure the person ultimately delivering the message is clear about the point you're trying to convey.

10) Communicate differently with different people.

Some people require a more direct, business-only delivery, while others respond better to a softer, more personalized approach. Know whom you're talking to and how best to communicate with that person.

11) When you want someone to do something, ask directly.

Ask him to do it, explain what the objective of the task is, and let him know why the task is important. When you ask in this way, you show consideration for the other person and make him feel important. As a result, the person will generally do a better job for you.

12) Make sure your timing is right.

A conversation on Monday morning will sound different from the same conversation on Friday afternoon. Pick the right time to communicate. You want to catch people when they will be in the best frame of mind to respond the way you want them to.

13) Document communication when appropriate.

Having the facts in black and white will make sure everyone has the same understanding and is on the same page. This will also help establish responsibility and a timeline.

14) Communicate often.

A lack of communication can lead to problems. When you don't communicate with someone, you begin to slowly grow apart from him.

15) Don't avoid communicating bad news.

One of the biggest customer complaints is a lack of communication. Letting bad news sit can only make the situation worse. People realize that things won't always go perfectly, and while they won't be happy to hear bad news, the majority will appreciate it.

16) Keep all appropriate people in the loop.

Make sure your boss and other interested parties are kept informed of what is going on. Nothing will annoy a manager more than being blindsided by a bad situation that he knew nothing about. Also, keeping colleagues with a vested interest in a situation up to date shows that you respect them.

17) If you are communicating about a problem or challenge, go into the conversation with some solutions.

If the situation puts you in a position where you need to compromise, know in advance what you are looking for, how far you are willing to bend, and what you are willing to accept.

18) Don't argue or find blame.

Try to take a team approach to the problem and put yourself on the same side of the table as those whom you are communicating with. Give the benefit of the doubt wherever possible.

19) Watch the emotions you include in your communication.

If emotion helps you convey your message in a positive way, use it. On the flip side, negative emotions rarely get you anywhere. Be careful of the emotional tone of your communication.

20) Take notes when communicating if appropriate.

If you are given a simple task you probably don't need to take notes; however, often communications can quickly become complex. Take good notes and read them back to make sure you understand them correctly.

21) Act on communication as soon as possible.

The facts are the clearest in your mind immediately after the communication has taken place. If you wait for several days to act, or even several hours, you may find that you have forgotten crucial pieces of the conversation.

22) Communication is a two-way street.

In addition to delivering your message, you need to *listen well*.

23) If appropriate, conclude your communication with a summary of what was discussed and determined, and what will take place next.

It can be as simple as stating what steps each person will take next, and when he or she will take them. If necessary, document the results of the communication in an e-mail or formal letter.

We realize these are a lot of steps to keep straight. However, not all steps will apply to *every* communication. Just keep this list handy and take a glance at it before you communicate something important.

Document Inter-company Projects and Communications

It is important to have a paper trail within companies to ensure everyone knows his and her job and responsibilities. As you're aware, there will be occasions when something gets missed and then it's a question of who said what to whom or who was ultimately responsible. Your documentation should include who, what, where, why, how, and under what conditions.

Probably the best way to document tasks and communications is via the computer and e-mail. Hopefully your company has e-mail so you can keep e-mail documentation. For example, if you had a fairly extensive phone conversation with someone, send a follow up e-mail to that person. You can start it with, "Kathy, as we discussed in our phone conversation today…" then give details: the five W's and one H. Yes, it's an extra step, but the aggravation the e-mail can save down the road can be immense.

After you've had a meeting you can send out an e-mail that outlines the details of the tasks to be completed, who is responsible for each task, and a timeline. Keep the notes clear and concise.

Note 1: If you don't have e-mail, draft a short letter and keep a copy in your records.

Note 2: Keep a paper copy of all e-mails and other computer documentation in a folder specifically labeled with a project name or other title to stay organized.

By documenting company projects and conversations and sharing them with the other people involved, you will ensure that everyone is clear about the task at hand and that credit is given where credit is due. You don't want to use this as a tool to point the finger when something goes wrong, but you want to make sure everyone is on the same page and understands his or her role. You also want to cover all your bases.

Some Other Notes on Company E-mail

1) **Keep interoffice e-mail messages short, but make sure you include all the necessary details.**

Your communication should cover all the questions that might arise and nothing more. What questions could someone ask? Again, who, what, where, when, how, and on what condition? Your message should be polite and not demanding. *Ask* instead of *tell*, and always use the words *please* and *thank you*.

2) Take advantage of two features that most interoffice e-mails systems have:
   a) Mark e-mails and other communications urgent *when prudent*.
   b) Copy yourself on e-mails and flag them with "reminder" follow-up dates if necessary. In addition to reminding others of your e-mail, this feature will also help remind you and keep the item off your to-do list.

3) Try not to use the tool that allows you to see if and when someone opened an e-mail and read your message.

This gives people the impression that you're checking up on them. There are definitely appropriate times to use this tool, so do so if necessary. However, most people overuse this tool. Use it very rarely if ever.

Save e-mails, save backup files with communications, and print and keep hard copies of important communications. It's better to keep too many records than not enough.

A Summary of Ideas on Selling within Your Company

- Be professional, have integrity, and treat all people with respect.

- Your manager is your number one customer within your company. Keep him or her happy.

- Develop strong relationships with people in other departments.

- Work closely with other salespeople.

- Communicate effectively and often. Always keep the lines of communication open.

- Take advantage of company e-mail to effectively communicate and document communications.

Conclusion

Keys to Remember

- Being great in sales really comes down to having a great attitude, a sincere interest in other people, and a burning desire to succeed. With those elements in place, everything else will follow.

- Complete job security in sales comes down to working hard, working smart, having integrity, being honest, and doing your best to understand, serve (help), and get along with other people.

- On that same note, honesty, integrity, sincerity, and empathy are four of the most important traits you can have as a salesperson and as a human being.

- Become a student of selling if you want to master it. You need to hunger for knowledge and absorb everything you can on the subject.

- Have conversations with people and focus on how you can help them.

- Do what's best for the customer and look forward to serving people.

- Do what you say you will do when you say will do it.

- Anticipate as many scenarios as you can and be prepared for each one.

- You can practice, drill, and rehearse for each scenario, and you need to, but you will get the experience you need and become great only by being out in the field selling to real, live prospects.

- The job of selling is not always easy and can sometimes be extremely difficult. Keep your chin up and persist. If you continue to work and push on, you will be successful.

- The bottom line in selling is that today we must be both salespeople and business people; a strong business and personal relationship backed by a solid business case and a product and service that delivers maximum value for the price paid is what it takes to get the job done in today's selling arena.

- Partner with your customers. Consider yourself one of their employees, deliver more than they expect, and go the extra mile. Understand your customers' businesses and what problems they have and are trying to solve. Know your customers' personal lives too. You want to become friends, hopefully very good friends, with your customers. Give your customers the peace of mind and assurance that together you can work out any problem, together you can weather any storm, that you are truly in this situation together, and their business is just as important to you as it is to them. Assure them that you have as much at stake as they do, that you are their trusted advisor and friend, and that you would never leave them.

The Rest Is up to You—You Control Your Destiny

We've laid out many ideas in this book that can assist in making you a great success in sales, but ultimately, only *you* will determine your level of success. You can be, do, and have anything you want in life—and in selling—if you pay the price that needs to be paid. If you pay the price and follow our directions, you will arrive at the destination of your choosing.

Good Luck!

Contact Us

Robert Chapin, John Chapin, and occasionally Keith Mooradian, and Jean Marie Reheuser, are available for both group and individual coaching and training or to come speak to your salespeople. We will design a highly-effective sales program specific to your needs.

You can also go to www.completeselling.com and sign up for a free monthly newsletter and weekly sales article. If you join our sales group, you get access to us and can get your questions answered via private messaging. In addition, you will have access to a ton of other sales information.

Please contact us at:

Complete Selling, Inc. • 27 Curtis Street • Auburn, MA 01501
T: 866-443-6778 • F: 508-757-2639
www.completeselling.com

Kyle Andrews and Bill Hall can design a customized program to address your specific selling challenges. With a focus primarily in the technology, services, and outsourcing marketplace, we will help you articulate and define the value your solutions bring to your customers.

Please contact us at:

Pretium Partners, Inc. • 1631 Northwest Professional Plaza
• Columbus, OH 43220
T: 614.457.1726 • F: 614.442.1786
www.PretiumPartners.com

Author Bios

Robert J. Chapin, President
Complete Selling, Inc.

Bob Chapin is currently the President of Complete Selling, Inc. He has over 45 years of selling experience, which include many sales records and industry firsts. While at Diebold, Inc., Bob sold the first ATM Machines in New England in 1975 beating out strong rivals NCR and IBM. While selling office equipment for IBM, Bob was the first salesperson in New England to receive a National "Best all-around Sales Performance" award. In addition to his many years of selling, he has had many years of experience in sales management and training.

While at IBM and Diebold, Bob Chapin was the #1 salesperson in New England for many years. After consistently achieving Diebold's highest annual sales award, Master's Circle, Bob was eventually asked to serve a term on its committee, the Master's Circle Advisory Group. Over the years Bob was also asked to do several sales presentations at National and International annual kickoff meetings.

Bob began his sales career in 1959 selling professional furniture to the Medical, Dental, and Drafting Industries. From 1959 to 1963 Bob expanded business in the New England Region by over 600% and in the New York Region by over 300%.

After being offered a management position, which would have meant moving his family out of New England, Bob accepted a sales position in 1963 with IBM. In his first year Bob achieved his annual quota in June; the earliest of anyone in the office.

From 1964 to 1968 Bob led the office each year in sales production. Each time he greatly exceeded his annual quota and generated monthly, quarterly, and annual sales awards. As a result of his success, Bob was asked to participate in office training and at the request of Senior Management he served as a guest instructor at IBM Headquarters in Armonk, NY.

Bob has a Bachelors degree in Psychology from the University of Wisconsin.

Contact Information:

Complete Selling, Inc. • 27 Curtis Street • Auburn, MA 01501
T: 866-443-6778 • F: 508-757-2639

www.completeselling.com

John J. Chapin, Vice President
Complete Selling, Inc.

John Chapin is currently the Vice President of Complete Selling, Inc. He has over 20 years of highly successful selling experience both in telephone and face-to-face selling. He has sold products and services locally, nationally, and internationally. He's dealt with individuals and major corporations in both emerging markets and established industries. John has spent the majority of his years in straight-commission sales.

John started his selling career as a stock broker. Within 2 ½ years John became the youngest branch manager for a National Brokerage Firm with over 50 offices Nationwide. While still maintaining his own clients, he managed the office from #46 out of 52 to #11.

After 6 successful years as a broker, John became the Marketing Manager for Micro Arc Welding Company. There he took a struggling branch of their existing business and made it profitable within 4 months. He expanded the business from 2 to 48 states and 5 continents around the world. He secured accounts with companies such as Levis, Lee Jeans, and Fruit of the Loom and showed them a new and better way of doing business. While with Micro Arc, John was responsible for all aspects of sales and marketing. Through expansion of this one branch, over a three-year period John doubled total company annual revenues.

At his next sales position with Diebold, Incorporated, John became the top salesperson in the New England Region his first full year (2000). At the request of upper level management, John spoke about his success selling against the competition at semi-annual and annual meetings for Diebold in 2000 and 2001.

John is also an award winning public speaker and holds a Bachelor of Arts degree from the University of Massachusetts, Amherst.

Contact Information:

Complete Selling, Inc. • 27 Curtis Street • Auburn, MA 01501
T: 866-443-6778 •   F: 508-757-2639
www.completeselling.com

Kyle J. Andrews, Vice President
Pretium Partners, Inc.

Kyle Andrews is Vice President and Partner of Pretium Partners, Inc., a firm dedicated to helping technology solutions companies improve sales effectiveness through application of Pretium's Value Assessment methodology.

After graduating from The Ohio State University, Kyle was a U.S. Marine Corps Officer, AV-8B Harrier pilot and flight instructor. As the Harrier analyst at the Naval Safety Center, he was responsible for highlighting aircraft and training deficiencies and spearheading changes required for accident rate reduction.

Kyle's sales expertise was forged in technology and services sales, and helping companies develop and institute business recovery plans. For the past 13 years he has been devoted to developing, selling and facilitating solution selling and return-on-investment workshops that have increased sales effectiveness broad array of technology and service companies in over a dozen countries.

Kyle is the co-chair of the Sales and Marketing Chapter of The International Association of Outsourcing Professionals (IOAP), and has spoken on the subject of selling at the IAOP Outsourcing World Summit, Association for Services Management International (AFSMI) World Conferences, The Outsourcing Institute's Vendor Summit, the Information Technology Council, Federal Sourcing Partnering and Privatization Conference and other events.

Pretium's clients include: NCR, Verizon Information Technologies, Teradata, Diebold, MapInfo, Logicalis, ABB, Sonosite, Xerox, Siemens, ADP, Alcatel-Lucent and Philips Medical Systems.

Kyle resides in Upper Arlington Ohio, is a volunteer high school lacrosse coach, serves on various charities, and enjoys cycling, skiing, backpacking, flying and golf.

Contact Information:

Pretium Partners, Inc. • 1631 Northwest Professional Plaza • Columbus, Ohio 43220
T: 614.457.1726 • F: 614.442.1786
www.PretiumPartners.com

Bill Hall, President
Pretium Partners, Inc.

Bill Hall is President and Partner of Pretium Partners, Inc., a firm dedicated to helping technology solutions companies improve sales effectiveness through application of Pretium's Value Assessment methodology.

After graduating from the University of Virginia, Bill has 25 years in sales and marketing. His expertise was developed in technology sales, worldwide services marketing and services management. For the past 15 years he focused on developing methodologies for improved sales performance.

He has authored several articles on the subject of value selling and "Value Assessment in Outsourcing, A Study of Outsourcing Justification Practices." The study was conducted by Pretium and The Fisher College of Business at The Ohio State University.

Bill chairs the Member Services Committee of The International Association of Outsourcing Professionals (IAOP). His speaking engagements include: The Ohio State University's *Building Professional Services* Executive Education Program, the Outsourcing World Summit, the Information Technology Council, The Outsourcing Institute's Vendor Summit, the International Association of Outsourcing Professionals, AFSM International World Conferences, North American Materials Handling Conference, Information Systems Security Association, and other events.

His training experience crosses a broad array of industries and companies in over a dozen countries. Clients are companies of all sizes who sell technology, software, support and professional services and outsourcing.

Pretium's clients include NCR, Verizon Information Technologies, Teradata, Diebold, MapInfo, Logicalis, ABB, Sonosite Xerox, Siemens, ADP, Alcatel-Lucent and Philips Medical Systems.

Bill resides in Upper Arlington Ohio, is married and has 3 very active sons, is Past President of the Swim & Racquet Club and volunteers with various charities in the community.

Contact Information:

Pretium Partners, Inc. • 1631 Northwest Professional Plaza • Columbus, Ohio 43220
T: 614.457.1726 • F: 614.442.1786
www.PretiumPartners.com

Keith Mooradian, Owner
Universal Business Forms

Keith Mooradian has a total of 31 years of successful selling experience. After college, Keith sold printing and printing supplies for Moore Business Forms for 17 years. While with Moore Business Forms, Keith was the top salesperson for the Eastern United States several times.

For the past 13 years he has sold printing as the President of Universal Business Forms, Inc. He has secured business with several major companies including Holiday Inn and Crown Plaza Hotels.

Keith also sold radio advertising and office products during his college years.

Keith holds a Bachelors Degree in Marketing from Southern New Hampshire University. While studying for his degree, he also took many courses in sales.

Jean Marie Reheuser, Sales Representative
Patterson Dental Supply, Inc.

If there ever was a natural born salesperson, Jean Marie is it. Customers describe her as an extremely dedicated and very hard working individual with a magnetic personality and a "heart the size of the world." Jean Marie Reheuser has spent 19 years in the Dental Industry. The past 9 years have been spent selling Dental Equipment for Patterson Dental, the largest dental supply company in the world.

Jean Marie can talk to and relate to anyone as she brings depth of knowledge from both the blue-collar and white-collar worlds.

Jean Marie holds a Bachelors Degree from Westfield State College.

INDEX

A

Ability to stand out, 5
After losing a sale, 500
Asking, 107, 110, 516, 606, 607
Attention, 140, 156, 196, 199, 208, 639
Attitude, 40, 181, 420, 556

B

Body Language, 112, 433
Brochures, 49
Building rapport, 94, 95, 604
Building rapport with the prospect, 94, 604
Building value, 367
Business cards, 72

C

Challenges, 551
Closing, 77, 145, 378, 417, 418, 419, 422, 423, 424, 430, 434, 444, 483, 490, 491, 509, 534, 608
    Questions, 107, 110, 197, 198, 254, 401, 606, 607, 614, 626, 627, 640
    Section, 415
Cold call, 57, 148, 630
Cold calling, 57, 148
    Sample, 214, 512, 548, 612
    Script, 74, 180, 603
    Section, 55
Communication, 513, 660
Company product and support, 8
Competition, 154, 166, 237, 240, 245, 246, 260, 265, 275, 284, 285, 286, 287, 288, 289, 290, 292, 294, 296, 297, 379, 380, 385, 404, 408, 410, 474, 509
    Interacting with, 284, 288
    Section, 235
Complaints, 561

Cost, 162, 163, 166, 262, 336, 377
Creativity, 31
Customer, 49, 52, 473, 516, 520, 521, 526, 528, 530, 534, 535, 536, 543, 546, 550, 551, 554, 558, 561, 563, 609
    Challenges, 551
    Complaints, 561
Customer's customers
    Put Prospect's customers first, 133

D

Dressing for Success, 44

E

Efficiency, 261, 262
    Product, 162, 200, 258, 261, 262, 263, 294, 327, 405, 480, 484
    Your company, 77, 229, 287, 327, 328, 458, 473, 608, 659
E-mail, 526, 665
Emotion, 157, 160
Empathy, 6
Endorsements, 189
Energy, 196
Etiquette, 48, 577
Eye Contact, 47, 96

F

Fear, 181
Follow up, 26, 85, 213, 420, 513, 523, 550, 627

G

Gifts, 535
Giving, 211, 522, 537
Goals, 18, 62
Going over someone's head

After losing a sale, 500

H

Handshake, 46, 96
Humor, 102, 597, 645

I

Incentives, 483, 485

K

Keep recordings of successful calls, 644

L

Letters, 143, 282
Listening, 107, 110, 607
Logic, 124, 157, 168

M

Manager, 549, 655, 658, 672
Meeting someone in person, 638
Mirroring, 96, 97, 101, 124, 605

N

Name
    Pronunciation, 65, 586
Name Dropping, 33

O

Objection, 363, 367, 368, 374, 407, 408, 411,
    463, 496, 619, 622, 626
Objections, 16, 127, 297, 353, 355, 358, 361,
    372, 381, 399, 407, 408, 412, 413, 475,
    476, 615, 619, 624, 626
    During the cold call, 103
    Phone, 283, 499, 517, 526, 536, 549, 560,
        575, 577, 578, 579, 581, 584, 604, 645,
        646

Section, 351
Open strong, 196
    Cold call, 57, 148, 630
    Presentations, 173, 210, 212, 227, 232, 631,
        634
Opening Statement, 139
Organization, 543
Other salespeople, 239
    Cover for, 658

P

Painting pictures, 167
Persistence, 21, 31
Personality type
    Identifying, 113, 334, 607
Phone, 283, 499, 517, 526, 536, 549, 560, 575,
    577, 578, 579, 581, 584, 604, 645, 646
    Attire, 577
    Building rapport with the prospect, 94, 604
    Cold calling, 57, 148
    Etiquette, 48, 577
    Meeting someone in person, 638
    Objections, 16, 127, 297, 353, 355, 358,
        361, 372, 381, 399, 407, 408, 412, 413,
        475, 476, 615, 619, 624, 626
    Physiology, 578
    Section, 571
Preparation, 4, 182, 198, 576, 640
Presentations, 173, 210, 212, 227, 232, 631,
    634
    Group, 63, 212, 520, 671
    Sample, 214, 512, 548, 612
    Section, 149
    Tools, 181, 183
Price, 154, 245, 260, 363, 367, 368, 369, 370,
    374, 375, 376, 379, 380, 407, 462, 472, 509
    Objection, 363, 367, 368, 374, 407, 408,
        411, 463, 496, 619, 622, 626
Product, 162, 200, 258, 261, 262, 263, 294,
    327, 405, 480, 484
Pronunciation
    Name, 65, 586

Proposals, 50

Q

Questions, 107, 110, 197, 198, 254, 401, 606, 607, 614, 626, 627, 640
    Asking, 107, 110, 516, 606, 607
    Rapport building, 77, 608

R

Rapport, 77, 94, 604, 608
    Building, 53, 94, 95, 124, 167, 190, 193, 261, 308, 350, 367, 549, 604, 674
Record
    Keep recordings of successful calls, 644
References, 192, 195
Referrals, 70, 516, 521, 522, 648
Relationship, 154, 200
    Building, 53, 94, 95, 124, 167, 190, 193, 261, 308, 350, 367, 549, 604, 674

S

Salespeople, other
    Cover for, 658
Script, 74, 180, 603
Selling to executives, 314
Selling within your company, 667
Set yourself apart, 53
Speakerphone, 647
Speech, 97, 98, 100, 605, 643
    Mirroring, 96, 97, 101, 124, 605
Success, 3, 44
    Dressing for, 44

T

Telemarketing, 89, 382, 573, 624
    Section, 571
Testimonials, 184, 186, 195, 297
Thank you letter
    Sample, 214, 512, 548, 612

Thank you note
    Sample, 214, 512, 548, 612
Time, 28, 126, 341, 425, 573, 584, 585, 601, 627

U

User Lists, 195
    Building, 53, 94, 95, 124, 167, 190, 193, 261, 308, 350, 367, 549, 604, 674

V

Value, 94, 260, 261, 302, 304, 311, 312, 313, 314, 315, 317, 319, 321, 327, 333, 335, 341, 342, 343, 345, 348, 349, 350, 380, 673, 674
    Building value, 367
Value assessment
    Why, 10, 32, 92, 109, 126, 134, 154, 177, 263, 277, 279, 301, 303, 304, 316, 317, 326, 354, 387, 389, 391, 398, 410, 418, 421, 425, 437, 477, 478, 488, 508, 520, 562, 592, 603, 608, 625, 649
Voice, 474, 538, 596, 599, 601, 633, 642
    Tone, 551
Voice mail
    Yours, 326

W

Words, 178, 205, 207, 208, 444
Work hard, 21, 26, 419
Work smart, 53

Y

Your company, 77, 229, 287, 327, 328, 458, 473, 608, 659
    Selling within, 667
Your product or service, 77
    Critique, 255, 258

I didn't see anything in this book on the new, cutting-edge ideas on sales, where I don't have to cold call and instead can take short cuts and make my life easier?

These days there are many anti-selling strategies being proposed by a plethora of salespeople and even marketing people claiming to know about selling. There's a good reason why these specific ideas aren't mentioned in this book. For a free report on "Why the New Sales Strategies Don't Work" please visit www. completeselling.com for all the details.

Got a sales question? Join us online!

Consider becoming a member of our online group. As a member you can ask unlimited sales questions. You will also find many valuable tools to become even better at sales. Some of these are also available to non-members. Visit www. completeselling.com for all the details.